Taro Kageyama and Wesley M. Jacobsen (Eds.)
Transitivity and Valency Alternations

Trends in Linguistics
Studies and Monographs

Editor
Volker Gast

Editorial Board
Walter Bisang
Jan Terje Faarlund
Hans Henrich Hock
Natalia Levshina
Heiko Narrog
Matthias Schlesewsky
Amir Zeldes
Niina Ning Zhang

Editor responsible for this volume
Volker Gast

Volume 297

Transitivity and Valency Alternations

Studies on Japanese and Beyond

Edited by
Taro Kageyama and Wesley M. Jacobsen

DE GRUYTER
MOUTON

ISBN 978-3-11-061069-7
e-ISBN (PDF) 978-3-11-047715-3
e-ISBN (EPUB) 978-3-11-047530-2
ISSN 1861-4302

Library of Congress Cataloging-in-Publication Data
A CIP catalog record for this book has been applied for at the Library of Congress.

Bibliographic information published by the Deutsche Nationalbibliothek
The Deutsche Nationalbibliothek lists this publication in the Deutsche Nationalbibliografie; detailed bibliographic data are available on the Internet at http://dnb.dnb.de.

© 2018 Walter de Gruyter GmbH, Berlin/Boston
This volume is text- and page-identical with the hardback published in 2016.
Typesetting: RoyalStandard, Hong Kong
Printing and binding: CPI books GmbH, Leck

♾ Printed on acid-free paper
Printed in Germany

www.degruyter.com

Table of contents

Taro Kageyama and Wesley M. Jacobsen
Introduction —— 1

I Standard Japanese

Wesley M. Jacobsen
1 The semantic basis of Japanese transitive-intransitive derivational patterns —— 21

Yo Matsumoto
2 Phonological and semantic subregularities in noncausative-causative verb pairs in Japanese —— 51

Taro Kageyama
3 Agents in anticausative and decausative compound verbs —— 89

Hideki Kishimoto
4 Valency and case alternations in Japanese —— 125

Natsuko Tsujimura
5 The role of lexical semantics in the reorganization of the resultative construction —— 155

II Dialects and Ryukyuan

Kan Sasaki
6 Anticausativization in the northern dialects of Japanese —— 183

Michinori Shimoji
7 Aspect and non-canonical object marking in the Irabu dialect of Ryukyuan —— 215

III History

Heiko Narrog
8 Japanese transitivity pairs through time – a historical and typological perspective —— 249

Bjarke Frellesvig and John Whitman
9 The historical source of the bigrade transitivity alternations in Japanese —— 289

IV Acquisition

Keiko Murasugi
10 Children's 'erroneous' intransitives, transitives, and causatives: Their implications for syntactic theory —— 313

Ayumi Matsuo, Sotaro Kita, Gary C. Wood, and Letitia Naigles
11 Children's use of morphosyntax and number of arguments to infer the meaning of novel transitive and intransitive verbs —— 341

Zoe Pei-sui Luk and Yasuhiro Shirai
12 The effect of a 'conceptualizable' agent on the use of transitive and intransitive constructions in L2 Japanese —— 357

V Beyond Japanese

Andrej L. Malchukov
13 "Ambivalent voice": Markedness effects in valency change —— 389

Søren Wichmann
14 Quantitative tests of implicational verb hierarchies —— 423

Masayoshi Shibatani
15 The role of morphology in valency alternation phenomena —— 445

Appendix A: List of core transitivity pairs in Japanese (by Yo Matsumoto, a revision of Jacobsen (1992)) —— 479

Appendix B: List of additional transitivity pairs in Japanese (by Yo Matsumoto, a revision of Jacobsen (1992)) —— 489

Subject index —— 497

Taro Kageyama and Wesley M. Jacobsen
Introduction

1 Transitivity and verb alternations

Understanding the way languages encode alternations in the transitivity of verbs is key to understanding numerous and wide-ranging phenomena in the syntactic, semantic, and morphological behavior of languages. Transitivity is fundamentally concerned with the valency of a verb – the number of arguments it takes, something which can be altered either by syntactic means such as passivization and causativization or by morphological devices for changing the lexical form of a verb that vary widely from language to language. English is a language that does not employ such morphological means to mark transitive alternations, as seen in the unchanged shape of the verb in transitive versus intransitive sentence pairs such as *The baby spilled the milk* and *The milk spilled*. In the absence of such form-meaning correspondences of a morphological kind, transitivity alternations in English have been treated in a wide spectrum of primarily non-morphological approaches, beginning with early generative grammar (e.g. Lakoff 1970; Guerssel et al. 1985) and extending to more recent lexicon-based analyses (e.g. Levin & Rappaport Hovav 1995; Everaert et al. [eds.] 2012) and typological approaches (e.g. Haspelmath 1993; Nichols et al. 2004). A different mechanism for marking transitivity alternations is seen in languages that employ reflexive pronouns or suffixes to convert transitive forms to intransitive forms (Geniušienė 1987; Schäfer 2008). Japanese may be seen to occupy a midway position between English-type languages that involve no overt marking and reflexive-type languages that use a single means to consistently mark transitivity alternations in the direction of transitive to intransitive. Japanese marks transitivity alternations by means of verb suffixes that pattern into various directional types, including transitive to intransitive, intransitive to transitive, or in neither direction. There is therefore no one-to-one correspondence in Japanese between transitive function and the morphological shape of transitivity-changing suffixes, presenting a complex picture of the relationship among transitive-intransitive pairs that is not quite like that found in any other language. In light of the fact that influential work in this area has so far been confined primarily to English

---

Taro Kageyama, National Institute for Japanese Language and Linguistics
Wesley M. Jacobsen, Harvard University

and other European languages, a detailed study of the unique properties of Japanese valency alternations thus has the potential to shed fresh light on the nature of valency change as a universal phenomenon of human language.

Growing out of an international conference on "Valency Classes and Alternations in Japanese" held on August 4th and 5th, 2012, at the National Institute for Japanese Language and Linguistics (NINJAL) in Tokyo, Japan, the present volume is the first in English dedicated to transitivity alternations in Japanese from a multidisciplinary perspective, representing the culmination of the progressively deepening interest this topic has attracted over a broader and broader range of fields in linguistics over the past quarter century. The fifteen chapters in the volume, thirteen of which originate in presentations given at the conference, include work by specialists in a diversity of fields ranging from the syntax, semantics, and morphology of contemporary standard Japanese to dialects of Japanese, earlier historical stages of the language, first and second language acquisition, and language typology.

This volume aims for adequacy of description and analysis rather than coherence of theoretical framework, so that the theoretical perspectives found in these chapters are varied. This approach is, we believe, the right one for a phenomenon so complex and multifaceted in character as transitivity alternations, one that cuts through the heart of the Japanese verbal system and leaves virtually no aspect of the language untouched. The contributions in this volume, we trust, fully bear this out, not only for the way they bring to light new data on myriads of properties particular to transitivity phenomena in Japanese, but in the deeper understanding they offer of the cross-linguistic dimensions of transitivity and valency alternations.

The current volume serves as a companion to the *Handbooks of Japanese Language and Linguistics* series (edited by Masayoshi Shibatani & Taro Kageyama and published by De Gruyter Mouton). Although the series is intended to provide a comprehensive coverage of the grammar, history, and use of the Japanese language, the topic of transitivity alternations was considered to exceed in its wide-ranging scope the ability to be fully treated in a single chapter in this series, and to merit treatment in a separate volume of its own such as this. This volume also serves as a complement to the online database entitled *The World Atlas of Transitivity Pairs* (NINJAL 2014), where transitive/intransitive alternation patterns involving 31 verb pairs listed in Haspelmath (1993) are collected from about 60 languages across a variety of language families and language groups and visually compared. This atlas may be accessed on the NINJAL website, where the raw data are also downloadable.

2 The basic phenomenon in Japanese

As noted above, Japanese manifests differences in transitivity (transitive vs. intransitive) by means of formal distinctions marked on the predicate. Specifically, the differences appear in the form of affixes that distinguish transitive vs. intransitive members of verb pairs, such as *nao-s-u* tr. 'fix' vs. *nao-r-u* intr. 'be fixed,' *ak-e-ru* tr. 'open' vs. *ak-u* intr. 'open,' *ue-ru* tr. 'plant' vs. *uw-ar-u* intr. 'be planted,' etc. Transitive-intransitive verb pairs typically fall into sentence patterns such as those in (1), associated with the syntactic and semantic properties listed in (2).

(1) a. *Zitensyaya   ga   panku   o   nao-si-ta.*
       bicycle.shop NOM punctured.tire ACC fix-TR-PST
       'The bike shop fixed the punctured tire.'

   b. *Panku   ga   nao-t-ta.* (< *nao-r-ta*)
       punctured.tire NOM fix-INTR-PST
       'The punctured tire was fixed.'

(2) a. The transitive verb requires one noun argument more than the intransitive verb.

   b. The noun arguments of the transitive and intransitive members are case marked as follows, so that the noun argument of the transitive member receiving accusative marking corresponds to the noun argument of the intransitive verb receiving nominative marking, represented here by NP2 (= *panku* 'punctured tire' in the earlier example (1)):

   NP1 *ga* (NOM) NP2 *o* (ACC) V_{tr} ↔ NP2 *ga* (NOM) V_{in}

   c. The transitive verb expresses an intentional action; the intransitive verb the result of that action.

Though the properties in (2) characterize typical transitive-intransitive verb pairs, many pairs that exhibit the formal morphological properties of such pairs nevertheless depart from (2) in some aspect of their syntactic behavior or meaning. Herein lies the complexity of transitivity phenomena in Japanese, as reflected in the first place by the sheer number of such verb pairs in the language.

At the end of this volume will be found two appendices containing the most comprehensive list compiled to date in an English publication of transitive-intransitive pairs occurring in Japanese. This list, an expansion and revision by

Yo Matsumoto of an earlier list appearing in Jacobsen (1992), contains a total of 460 verb pairs, divided into 306 core pairs in Appendix A exhibiting in the main the properties in (2), and an additional 169 pairs in Appendix B that depart in some significant respect from these properties, either in meaning, syntactic behavior, or frequency of usage. The formal distinctions fall into three patterns, depending on whether the transitive member can be seen as derived from the intransitive member, normally by exhibiting an affix that is absent from the intransitive member (markedness type I, e.g. *ak-e-ru* tr. 'open' vs. *ak-u* intr. 'open'), or the intransitive member from the transitive member (markedness type II, e.g. *war-u* tr. 'break' vs. *war-e-ru* intr. 'break'), or neither, with both the transitive and intransitive member exhibiting an affix not appearing on its partner (markedness type III, e.g. *nao-s-u* tr. 'fix' vs. *nao-r-u* intr. 'be fixed').

Verb pairs exhibiting a directionality of derivation, either intransitive to transitive (the "causativizing" pattern) or transitive to intransitive (the "anticausativizing" pattern), raise two basic questions: which pattern is dominant overall in Japanese, as compared to other languages, and why certain verbs exhibit one pattern over the other. In Japanese, the causative pattern is dominant over the anticausative pattern (see the chapters by Jacobsen and Matsumoto), consistent with the pattern more commonly seen among the world's languages in general, as demonstrated by the sample of 84 languages studied in Nichols et al. (2004), which shows the causative pattern to be dominant in twice as many languages as the anticausative pattern. Viewed in historical perspective, however, the predominance of the causative pattern has become less pronounced in modern Japanese than it was in premodern Japanese (see the chapter by Narrog).

One common approach to answering the second question – why certain verb pairs exhibit patterns of derivation in one direction versus the other – is to look for patterns in the meaning of the verbs in question. Three chapters in this volume (by Jacobsen, Matsumoto, and Shibatani) consider evidence for and against that approach as formalized in the semantic markedness hypothesis. According to this hypothesis, there exists a correlation between markedness of form, such as greater length or complexity, and markedness of meaning, that is, meaning that expresses situations that are less commonly encountered in human experience. One implication of this hypothesis is that less marked forms are expected to occur more frequently in naturally-occurring speech. Statistical evidence from modern Japanese cited in the chapter by Shibatani from internet searches provides mixed support for this, but raises questions as to how to best obtain data samples that are both representative and token-based, rather than type-based, and how to account for possible shifts in the meaning of linguistic forms that may occur over time, obscuring patterns of markedness that may have existed at earlier stages of the language. Some patterns of apparent formal markedness, furthermore, may better be explained by phonological patterning than by semantic markedness, as argued in the chapter by Matsumoto.

3 Past traditions of research on transitivity

There is a long tradition of interest in questions of transitivity in the native Japanese grammatical tradition of *Kokugogaku* ('native language study') that dates back to the 18th century, originating in some early anonymous treatises and developed in the work of scholars such as FUJITANI Nariakira, MOTO'ORI Nobunaga, and, most notably, MOTO'ORI Haruniwa. Early conceptions of transitivity centered on the distinction between *zi* 'self' and *ta* 'other,' understood roughly as the individual self as opposed to the world surrounding the individual. Beginning with the work of Haruniwa, this distinction began to be treated in specifically grammatical terms, as reflected in the detailed analysis of morphological forms found in his *Kotoba no kayoiji* (1828) and its six-way classification of verbs into categories corresponding roughly to intransitive, transitive, ditransitive, causative, spontaneous, and passive. The concern with morphology has been passed down through the history of the *Kokugogaku* tradition, virtually to the exclusion of attention to other dimensions of transitivity. This can be seen in more modern work in this tradition such as Shimada (1979), a study devoted solely to a taxonomy of transitive and intransitive affixes and their pairing that views the conception of transitivity defined by the presence of a direct object as a foreign notion borrowed from western grammar. With the advent of generative grammar in the 1960s, however, analyses of transitivity in Japanese appeared that depart from this tendency to view transitive morphological oppositions as a self-contained system, instead treating them as surface forms triggered by syntactic features such as accusative case marking or number of arguments, as seen in works such as Okutsu (1967) and Inoue (1976). More recent descriptive studies in this tradition within Japan are found in collections of papers such as Nitta ([ed.] 1991) and Suga & Hayatsu ([eds.] 1995).

Research on transitivity in the various western traditions of modern linguistics, by contrast, has been characterized by a marked lack of attention to the morphological dimensions of transitivity, with even the concept of transitivity itself playing at best a secondary role as an organizing principle of grammar. This lack of concern is a natural consequence of the virtual absence of a morphological dimension to transitivity in English, where most transitive vs. intransitive 'pairs' exhibit a 'labile' pattern involving no change in form of the verb, as illustrated by the English counterparts to the Japanese sentences in (3).

(3) a. *Ken ga   mado   o   ak-e-ta.*   ↔ *Mado   ga   ai-ta. (<ak-ta)*
     Ken NOM window ACC open-TR-PST   window NOM open-PST
     'Ken opened the window.'   'The window opened.'

  b. *Kokku ga   tamago o   wat-ta (< war-ta)* ↔ *Tamago ga   war-e-ta*
     cook NOM egg   ACC crack-PST   egg   NOM crack-INTR-PST
     'The cook cracked the egg.'   'The egg cracked.'

Grammatical constructions with a formal dimension in English such as the passive counterpart to the Japanese intransitive construction in the earlier (1b) and, to a lesser extent, causative and causative-like constructions such as the English counterpart to the Japanese transitive form in (4) have, by contrast, received extensive attention in western linguistic traditions, generative and otherwise.

(4) *Ryoosi   ga   ookina sakana o   nig-asi-ta.*   ↔
     fisherman NOM big   fish   ACC escape-TR-PST
     'The fisherman let a big fish escape.'

     Ookina sakana ga   nig-e-ta
     big   fish   NOM escape-INTR-PST
     'A big fish escaped.'

In the absence of a morphological dimension to transitivity in English, western-based treatments of transitivity have centered on its semantic dimensions. In the classic study by Hopper & Thompson (1980), transitivity is viewed as a bundle of features clustering around the effective carrying over of an activity from agent to patient, involving volitionality in the agent and total affectedness of the patient, and having aspectual and modal dimensions such as punctuality, telicity, and high realis status. Taken together, these features lead to a scalar conception of transitivity measured by the degree to which these features are present or absent in a clause and to what extent. For Hopper and Thompson, clauses exhibiting high transitivity are motivated in discourse terms by the need to impart prominence to an event or situation, foregrounding it against less prominent background information so that it serves to move a narrative or discourse sequentially forward in time. Of the many morphosyntactic features correlating with high transitivity in the broad range of languages present in Hopper & Thompson's study, though, morphological marking on the verb is notably absent.

In another influential account of transitivity, Levin & Rappaport Hovav (1995) propose a semantic analysis of English 'labile' verbs exhibiting transitive vs. intransitive alternation with no change in form, such as *break, open, close, begin, change, turn*, etc. Specifically, they propose that both the transitive and intransitive uses of such verbs, such as in (5) are derived from a common semantic structure represented in (6).

(5) a. The child broke the vase.
    b. The vase broke.

(6) [DO(x)] CAUSE [BECOME (*broken*(y))]

The transitive verb is realized when both *x* and *y* slots are filled by lexical forms as in (5a), whereas the intransitive verb is realized when *x* is bound by a process of 'argument binding' that does not allow it to appear on the surface, allowing only the *y* argument to surface, as in (5b). Both the transitive and intransitive uses of labile verbs in English thus have a common transitive origin, entailing that intransitive verbs represent events that uniformly express the result of an event of external causation.[1] In this framework as well, phenomena of morphological alternation make no significant contribution to the analysis proposed.

Jacobsen (1992) and Kageyama (1996) are two works that attempt to provide a corrective to approaches to transitivity that are either exclusively syntactic-semantic or exclusively morphological, and thereby to synthesize historical contributions to the study of transitivity from within both the native Japanese and western traditions. Both of these works assign inherent semantic value to the morphological affixes marking transitivity and intransitivity in Japanese, Jacobsen (1992) through an application of the semantic markedness hypothesis, and Kageyama (1996) through adoption of a lexical-semantic framework that contrasts the transitively-based system of English, much like that described in Levin & Rappaport Hovav (1995), with a system in Japanese that allows for unique surface expression of either transitive or intransitive meaning.

A western tradition constituting a prominent exception to prior trends in the west in its concern with the morphological dimensions of transitivity is typological linguistics, with its emphasis on generalizations based on data bases from large numbers of languages wide-ranging in both geographic area and genetic affinity. While this tradition traces back to earlier work such as Nedjalkov (1969), it has flourished in recent years as the cumulative fruits of decades of field work have made data available from a wide variety of languages in a form increasingly accurate and accessible, making possible studies that incorporate a truly representative sample of the world's languages, such as the 21 languages

---

[1] See the chapter by Jacobsen in this volume for difficulties posed for this view by patterns of morphological alternation observed in Japanese.

targeted in Haspelmath (1993) and the even larger sample of 84 languages targeted in Nichols et al. (2004). What has emerged is a picture of the centrality of morphology to the phenomenon of transitivity across the world's languages, a picture both diverse and yet exhibiting some common underlying patterns that make it possible to more accurately situate the transitive alternations characterizing Japanese in a global perspective. Two of the chapters in this volume, those by Wichman and Malchukov, are representative of the work being carried on in this tradition and illustrate well the challenges and possibilities of finding order in the diversity of morphological patterns exhibited by the world's languages.

4 Contributions of the current volume

The body of the current volume is divided into five parts, organized broadly under the following topics:

Part I: Standard Japanese (5 chapters)
Part II: Dialects and Ryukyuan (2 chapters)
Part III: History (2 chapters)
Part IV: Acquisition (3 chapters)
Part V: Beyond Japanese (3 chapters)

Following is a summary highlighting the principal contributions made by each of these chapters to the study of transitivity alternations in Japanese and other languages across the world.

Part I: Standard Japanese

Part I focuses primarily on topics of morphology, syntax, and semantics in standard Japanese. In the opening chapter, Wesley Jacobsen argues that the markedness patterns exhibited by transitivity pairs in modern Japanese, in particular the dominance of pairs with a formally less-marked intransitive member over pairs with a formally less-marked transitive member, call into question the uniquely privileged place given to prototypical transitive meaning in studies such as Levin & Rappaport Hovav (1995), who posit transitive meaning as underlying both the transitive and intransitive members of transitive alternations. The Japanese data instead point to the existence of an intransitive prototype that plays a role at least as fundamental, and perhaps more so, as the transitive prototype in transitive alternations. He distinguishes three fundamental types of intransitive meaning in Japanese, a passive-like type where the agent role is present but left unfilled on the surface, a reflexive type where both agent and patient roles are identified with a single entity, and a spontaneous type where no agent role is present at all. The third of these he identifies with the intransitive prototype, typified by the occurrence of a change in state, or coming into existence, of an entity apart from the influence of any force, internal or external. This intransitive prototype is maximally differentiated from the transitive prototype championed by Hopper & Thompson (1980) in making reference to a purely singular semantic role. Evidence from first-language acquisition (Ito 1990) suggests that this intransitive prototype is more cognitively "basic" in being acquired earlier than the transitive prototype, at least for Japanese. Jacobsen argues that this is accounted for by situating the cognitive origin of this prototype in a primal experience of an entity impinging on the senses, an epistemological form of coming into existence that is more directly experienced than, and a prerequisite to an understanding of, causal connections between agent and patient that are embodied in the transitive prototype.

In Chapter 2, Yo Matsumoto considers various difficulties posed by Japanese noncausative-causative (intransitive-transitive) alternations for morphological analysis and the interface between form and meaning. As noted earlier in this introduction, these alternations exhibit three different directions of morphological derivation, the 'noncausativizing' (intransitivizing) and 'causativizing' (transitivizing) patterns and a third, neutral, pattern where neither the transitive or intransitive form can be seen as being derived from the other, each of these alternations involving multiple affix types. Matsumoto undertakes a close semantic and phonological examination of all existing noncausative-causative verb pairs in Japanese in search of semantic and phonological regularities that might account for the directionality of derivation and choice of affix types in each of these three patterns. Through statistical analysis, he confirms a correlation between derivational directionality and semantics, with certain classes of alternating verbs, such as verbs expressing natural phenomena, predominantly exhibiting the causativizing pattern, and other classes, such as verbs of disintegration, predominantly exhibiting the anticausativizing pattern. These semantic correlations are, however, constrained by phonological restrictions on suffixation. Matsumoto proposes an analysis within the framework of construction morphology (Booij 2010) to capture the regularities observed among the various alternation patterns at both the semantic and phonological levels, formulated at differing levels of generality.

The chapter by Taro Kageyama considers the behavior of transitive-intransitive verb alternations in Verb-Verb compounds in Japanese, providing fresh evidence for a distinction between two forms of intransitivization in Japanese: anticausativization, in which agents are completely erased from lexical semantic structure, and decausativization, where agents are present in lexical semantic structure but are invisible on the surface (Kageyama 1996). Previous studies on transitivity alternations in Japanese have been focused primarily on alternations between simplex verbs, with little or no attention paid to the abundant data source available in V-V compound verbs in the language. Although compound verbs do not participate in transitivity alternations as regularly as simplex verbs, certain compound verbs do exhibit transitivity alternations with some regularity, such as transitive *ami-ageru* lit. knit-raise = 'knit up, finish knitting' vs. intransitive *ami-agaru* lit. knit-go.up = 'be knit up' and transitive *tate-kaeru* lit. build-change (tr.) = 'rebuild' vs. intransitive *tate-kawaru* lit. build-change (intr.) = 'be rebuilt'. Drawing on a novel classification of lexical V-V compounds into thematic compound verbs (compound verbs that consist of two lexical verbs that have their own thematic relations) and aspectual compound verbs (compound verbs whose second member has lost its original lexical meaning and acquired auxiliary status exhibiting a variety of Aktionsart (aspectual) meanings), Kageyama shows that aspectual compound verbs exhibit decausativization fairly systematically, characteristically coded by the suffix -*ar*, whereas thematic compound verbs exhibit only sporadic instances of what appear to be anticausativization by analogy. This disparity strongly suggests that anticausativization, found in many languages, is motivated by semantic factors whereas decausativization, characteristically observed in Japanese, is triggered by particular morphology.

In Chapter 4, Hideki Kishimoto takes up a syntactic dimension of transitivity, that of variations seen in the case marking of verbs and other predicates related to the valency of those predicates (the number of their noun arguments). It is commonly accepted that Japanese sentences must have at least one argument marked with the nominative case, a constraint often referred to as the "nominative-case constraint." While many valency-related alternations in Japanese are governed by the nominative-case constraint (e.g. the dative-nominative alternation for transitive stative predicates, the nominative-accusative alternation for predicates of (dis)liking, the genitive-nominative alternation involved in the possessor-raising pattern), there are some alternations exempt from the nominative case constraint where the nominative case on a subject is replaced with an oblique marker (e.g. source-subject and plural-agent alternations). On the basis of this fact, Kishimoto argues that whether or not an alternation is subject to this constraint is due to the property of tense (T): the nominative-case constraint is imposed on clauses in which T carries case features (nominative or dative) to license arguments, but is voided in cases where T is rendered inactive by the replacement of nominative case with an oblique case on an argument.

The fifth and final chapter in Part I by Natsuko Tsujimura describes a phenomenon of language change in contemporary Japanese that is integrally bound up with its system of transitivity. Resultative constructions in *-te aru* and *-te iru* have traditionally been analyzed in terms of the transitive characteristics of the predicates to which they attach. The *-te aru* construction, in particular, has been treated as a valency-reducing operation when conveying a resultative meaning: under this interpretation, *-te aru* must be attached to a transitive verb and is otherwise ill-formed. In this chapter, Tsujimura examines an apparent violation of this restriction, a non-standard pattern where intransitive verbs appear with *-te aru*. Citing numerous examples of this non-standard pattern from the literary work of the author Mieko Kawakami, Tsujimura argues that intransitive verbs appearing in this variant *-te aru* construction form a coherent class definable on the basis of their lexical semantic properties, namely that they express either spatial configuration or contiguous location. Through a close examination of three types of resultative constructions (the standard *-te aru* construction, the non-standard *-te aru* construction, and the *-te iru* construction) in Kawakami's writing, Tsujimura shows that strategies for expressing resultant states may reflect a new organizational principle, one based on lexical semantic features of the verbs appearing in each construction type rather than their transitivity.

Part II: Japanese dialects and Ryukyuan

Part II of this volume is devoted to transitive phenomena in languages and dialects in the Japonic family other than standard Japanese. In the first of these two chapters, Ken Sasaki describes a prominent feature of Japanese dialects spoken in the northern areas of Tohoku and Hokkaido, the existence of a productive anticausative morphological form. Specifically, these northern dialects employ a spontaneous suffix /-*rasar*/ (or /-*rar*/) to impose a meaning corresponding to that of the anticausative (intransitive) member in transitive-intransitive lexical alternation pairs in the standard language. These dialects share in this respect an areal feature present in genetically unrelated languages in the vicinity of Hokkaido such as Ainu and Nivkh, but lacking in southern dialects of Japan or Ryukyuan. The range of predicates over which anticausativization is observed in the northern dialects is wider compared not only to other Japanese dialects where anticausativization is lexical, but also to other languages where anticausativation is manifested in the form of the reflexive construction. The anticausative construction is similar to the passive construction in involving promotion of the internal argument (object) and demotion of the external argument, but differs from it in that the demoted external argument cannot appear overtly in surface structure. Sasaki considers various grammatical features of the anticausative construction, such as its non-occurrence with intentional adverbs, its achievement-like aspectual character, and its co-occurrence with verbs specifying agent-related features, concluding from these that the anticausative pattern preserves an external (agentive) argument in its semantic structure that is existentially bound, and thus prevented from appearing overtly, in a way similar to the decaisativization pattern described by Taro Kageyama in Chapter 3 of Part I.

Turning from the northern-most dialects to the southern-most varieties of Japanese, Michinori Shimoji in the second chapter of Part II considers a syntactic feature of transitivity in the Irabu dialect of Ryukyuan: the presence of two distinct accusative (object) markers. One of these is a non-canonical object marker that marks low transitivity in clauses in which it appears. Shimoji describes a restriction on the distribution of this object marker whereby it is primarily limited to occurrence in dependent, chained clauses that encode non-sequential events or states. This connection between low transitivity and clause chaining provides empirical support for the Transitivity Hypothesis of Hopper & Thompson (1980), which posits that high versus low transitive morphosyntax has the effect of disambiguating between temporally sequential events (perfective aspect) and temporally non-sequential states (imperfective aspect).

Part III: History

The two chapters of Part III are devoted to treatments of transitivity phenomena in Japanese from a historical perspective. In the first of these chapters, Heiko Narrog considers Japanese in light of the claim made in Comrie (2006) that languages with transitive verb alternations are diachronically stable in their preference for one of the four patterns posited in the typological framework of Haspelmath (1993) and Nichols et al. (2004), namely transitivization, detransitivization, neutral derivation, and indeterminacy. On the basis of a comprehensive list of attested verb forms in pre-modern Japanese, Narrog shows that the verb inventory of Japanese has exhibited a preference for the transitivizing pattern throughout its history, that is, that the verb repertory of Japanese is based primarily on intransitive verbs. Japanese conforms in this respect to an areal pattern observed across Northeast Asia. He shows, however, that in recent times there has been a slight shift in favor of neutral derivation (equipollent) or indeterminate (labile) patterns in transitive-intransitive verb pairs, and suggests several factors that might account for this.

In their chapter, Bjarke Frellesvig and John Whitman examine the historical development of transitivity alternations between vowel (modern monograde, Old Japanese bigrade) and consonant (Old Japanese quadrigrade) stems, where the valency of the stem is not predictable by its shape. In some pairs a transitive vowel stem such as *tate-* 'stand (it) up' is paired with an intransitive consonant stem such as *tat-* 'stand up,' whereas in others an intransitive vowel stem such as *sake-* 'split' is paired with a transitive consonant stem such as *sak-* 'split (it).' In each case the vowel stem appears derived, but which stem is transitive and which is intransitive is unpredictable. These alternations are mastered only at later stages of first language acquisition (see Murasugi this volume), but they are consistently observed with minor variation across Japanese languages and dialects. Frellesvig and Whitman reconstruct in this chapter a diachronic source for these stem-shape-based transitivity alternations, positing an older layer of verbal derivation in Japanese involving Verb-Verb patterns where V2 was attached directly to the basic stem (root) of V1, unlike later stages of the language where verbal derivation requires a derived stem (primarily the infinitive) of V1. They argue that the consonant-stem/vowel-stem alternation derives from the attachment of the verb **e-* 'get' to the underived basic stem (root) of V1, a combination that results in certain subregularities observed to this day, namely transitive accomplishment verbs originating from the combination of 'get' with intransitive achievements, and anticausative intransitives originating from the combination of 'get' with semantically causative transitives. They also discuss the relationship of the 'get' derivation to other Vstem1 + V2 combinations at the proto-Japanese level, such as the combination of Vstem1 + **ar-* (which they suggest is cognate with the verb *ar-* 'exist') to derive stative intransitives and the combination of Vstem1 + **s-* (possibly cognate with **sE-* 'do') to derive causative transitives.

PartT IV: Acquisition

Part IV presents research on the acquisition of transitivity alternations in Japanese, both as a first language and as a second language. The first chapter by Ayumi Matsuo, Sotaro Kita, Gary C. Wood, and Letitia Naigles (hereafter Matsuo et al.) reviews experimental studies testing the idea that children infer the meanings of verbs based on the structure of the sentences they appear in. In particular, the studies tested the hypothesis that children use morphosyntax and argument structure to infer whether a verb denotes an event with a causal agent and a patient (expressed, for example, by a transitive sentence with nominative and accusative marking) or an event with one participant (for example, an intransitive sentence with nominative marking). Based on a review of typologically different languages (English, Turkish, Chinese and Japanese), Matsuo et al. note that structural cues to verb meanings in input by adults to children differ considerably across these languages. Case marking, for example, while pervasive in Turkish and also often present in Japanese, is mostly absent in English and completely absent in Chinese. Argument dropping, by contrast, is common in Turkish, Japanese and Chinese, but not in English. Argument order is very flexible in Turkish and Japanese, but not in Chinese and English. The studies found that American English and Chinese children make use of argument structure to infer the causal vs. non-causal meanings of verbs and that Japanese and Turkish children make use of the morphosyntax to infer such verb meanings. Thus, children acquiring a variety of languages all use the structural cues available in those various languages to infer the meaning of verbs.

The chapter by Keiko Murasugi examines so-called errors produced by children in the morphosyntax of transitive expressions, such as the use of the intransitive form where transitive or causative forms are expected (e.g. *Daddy, I will feel you better* instead of *Daddy, I will make you feel better* in English or *Huusen hukuran-de* [balloon inflate$_{in}$-GER] for *Huusen hukuram-asete* [balloon inflate$_{in}$-CAUS-GER] with intended meaning 'Please blow up the balloon for me' in Japanese). These "errors" are presumably not a response to the children's environment, nor can they be easily explained by the limited processing ability of children. Based on an analysis of errors commonly observed in the speech of Japanese-speaking children in the previous literature, longitudinal studies by Murasigi with two Japanese-speaking children, and data bases collected by the National Institute for Japanese Language and Linguistics (NINJAL) and the Child Language Data Exchange System (CHILDES), Murasugi presents in this chapter a uniform account of errors observed in the production by children of Japanese verbs and complex predicates, adopting the v-VP frame, or VP-shell, hypothesis of Larson (1988). Specifically, Murasugi proposes that the predicate-argument structures of large V's (verbs that are pronounced) and small v's (such as [±cause], indicating either causativization or non-causativization) are acquired early, but errors in producing these are due to the assumption made by children that [±cause] is phonetically null, much like labile verbs in English that are unmarked for transitivity (e.g. *open, crack,* etc., illustrated in (3) in Section 1 of this introduction). What requires time, according to this analysis, is the acquisition of the lexical form of each V and the overt form taken by small v's expressing [±cause]. Murasugi argues that innate linguistic principles define a range of possible human language and possible linguistic variation. Linguistic errors by children arise because, at an intermediate stage of language acquisition, they are experimenting with possible features of adult languages that may be overt in other human languages, even if not overt in the language they are acquiring. The 'errors' they produce are therefore errors only from the standpoint of the language they are acquiring, but never violate the principles of possible grammar.

In the final chapter of Part II, Zoe Luk and Yasuhiro Shirai examine the acquisition of transitivity alternations by learners of Japanese as a second language. Specifically, they consider how the presence of a perceivable agent (a 'conceptualizable' external cause in the framework of Ju (2000)), in combination with factors such as the affirmative versus negative form of the verb, affect choices among transitive, intransitive, passive, and potential forms in Japanese produced by native Chinese learners of Japanese. In a comparative study of Japanese speech produced by native Japanese speakers and Chinese learners of Japanese, they report that the Chinese learners tended to use more transitive and passive forms than native speakers did in affirmative sentences expressing an externally-caused event, and more potential forms in negative sentences expressing an externally-caused event, under conditions where native speakers uniformly showed a preference for the use of intransitive forms. Luk and Shirai argue that the difficulty in choosing among these different verb forms in Japanese can best be explained in terms of event conceptualization, an account consistent with Ju's (2000) account of the overuse of passive forms by learners of English as a second language.

Part V: Beyond Japanese

The final Part V of the volume presents three studies on transitivity alternations and related grammatical phenomena from a cross-linguistic typological perspective. The chapter by Andrej Malchukov deals with the phenomenon of 'voice ambivalence', that is, with the fact that certain markers of voice or valency perform different functions when applied to different classes of verbs (e.g. transitives vs. intransitives). While such polysemies have been noted in typological studies of individual voice categories (e.g. Shibatani 1985 on passives), this chapter provides a more general cross-linguistic overview of ambivalent voice categories, including (a) categories that are both valency increasing and valency decreasing (e.g. polysemy between causative and passive and between antipassive and applicative), (b) categories that are both valency-increasing and valency-preserving (e.g. a single stem alternation in Arabic that produces either causative or intensive function), (c) categories that are both valency-decreasing and valency-preserving (e.g. passives of intransitives), (d) categories that are valency increasing, but yield different effects when applied to different valency classes (e.g. causative-applicative polysemy), and (e) categories that are valency decreasing, but yield different effects when applied to different valency classes (e.g. polysemy between passive/anticausative and antipassive). Focusing on categories (a), (c), and (d), Malchukov suggests that an explanation of voice polysemies may partly reside in shared syntactic features, which he summarizes in the form of a semantic map.

In Chapter 2 of Part V, Søren Wichmann investigates the question of whether there are implicational hierarchies constraining which verbs undergo different alternations across languages. He asks whether it can be predicted, for instance, that if a language can apply an antipassive to a verb meaning FEAR then it can also apply an antipassive to a verb meaning EAT. Hierarchies intended to account for such implications have been proposed in the past, such as one proposed in Tsunoda (1985) among verbs expressing Direct Effect > Perception > Pursuit > Knowledge > Feeling > Relationship > Ability. In order to test this hierarchy, as well as to look for implicational hierarchies in general, Wichmann applies the technique of Guttman scaling, a scaling technique from psychology, to a large corpus of linguistic data obtained from the Leipzig Valency Classes Project (ValPal). In addition, he uses a more recent phylogenetic visualization technique called NeighborNets to investigate to what degree there is a unidimensional behavior in the way that verbs cluster across languages, again with respect to their liability to undergo different alternations. Neither Tsunoda's semantic categories nor the general structure of the hierarchy he proposed turn out to be well supported by the data and the methods utilized by Wichmann. Nevertheless, he shows that there do exist implicational hierarchies across languages that are able to account for the tendency to undergo alternations of the following kind: antipassive, passive, reciprocal, reflexive, and causative, although the hierarchies differ in some ways from those of Tsunoda.

In the final chapter of the volume, Masayoshi Shibatani considers the role of morphology in valency alternations, calling into question the sometimes uncritical reliance on morphology in analyses of applicative and transitivity alternations. He notes that these phenomena, which overlap to some extent, provide good test cases because there is such a wide array of morphological patterns associated with them, ranging from those involving highly productive morphology to no morphology at all, with many intermediate types involving morphology of various degrees of productivity. In the first half of the chapter, Shibatani takes up the case of Balinese applicatives, which he argues pose a challenge to a number of assumptions made in the study of valency-changing phenomena including (a) that verbs have a basic valency value characterizing them as intransitive, transitive, or ditransitive in their basic form, (b) that valency alternation is to be characterized in terms of increase or decrease in valency, and (c) that productive valency alternations are syntactic processes. He goes on to compare Balinese and English, discussing the role of morphology in indicating direction of derivation in alternating applicative constructions. In the second half of the chapter he turns his attention to transitivity alternations, in particular the Japanese transitive-intransitive pairs forming the focus of this volume, many of which exhibit different morphological marking patterns suggestive of direction of derivation. He examines in particular the semantic markedness hypothesis posited in the earlier chapters by Jacobsen and Matsumoto, noting difficulties for that hypothesis posed by data on frequency of occurrence of the marked versus unmarked members of such morphological pairs. In the final section of the chapter, Shibatani proposes a Principle of Functional Transparency, which pays critical attention to the productivity of morphology and is intended to capture a functional motivation for morphology.

Acknowledgments

The editors wish to thank all those who participated in the NINJAL international conference on "Valency Classes and Alternations in Japanese" (2012), organized in cooperation with the Linguistics Department of the Max Planck Institute for Evolutionary Anthropology. We are also grateful to the anonymous reviewers of the chapters in this volume, to Volker Gast, chief editor of the *Trends in Linguistics* Series, for his valuable suggestions on the content and editorial style of the manuscript, and to Uri Tadmor and his colleagues at De Gruyter Mouton for their assistance in the editing and preparation of the manuscript of this volume for publication.

References

Booij, Geert. 2010. *Construction morphology*. Oxford: Oxford University Press.
Comrie, Bernard. 2006. Transitivity pairs, markedness, and diachronic stability. *Linguistics* 44 (2). 303–318.
Everaert, Martin, Marijana Marelj & Tal Siloni (eds.). 2012. *The theta system: Argument structure at the interface*, 20–51. Oxford: Oxford University Press.
Geniušienė, Emma. 1987. *The typology of reflexives*. Berlin & New York: Mouton de Gruyter.
Guerssel, Mohamed, Ken Hale, Mary Laughren, Beth Levin & Josie W. Eagle. 1985. A cross-linguistic study of transitivity alternations. *Papers from the Parasession on Causatives and Agentivity, CLS 21, Part 2*. 48–63.

Haspelmath, Martin. 1993. More on the typology of inchoative/causative verb alternations. In Bernard Comrie & Maria Polinsky (eds.), *Causatives and transitivity*, 87–111. Amsterdam & Philadelphia: John Benjamins.

Hopper, Paul J. & Sandra Thompson. 1980. Transitivity in grammar and discourse. *Language* 56 (2). 251–299.

Inoue, Kazuko. 1976. *Henkei-bunpō to nihongo* [Transformational grammar and Japanese], Vol. 2. Tokyo: Taishukan Shoten.

Ito, Katsutoshi. 1990. *Kodomo no kotoba: shūtoku to sōzō* [Children's speech: acquisition and creation]. Tokyo: Keiso Shobo.

Jacobsen, Wesley M. 1992. *The transitive structure of events in Japanese*. Tokyo: Kurosio Publishers.

Ju, Min Kyong. 2000. Overpassivization errors by second language learners: The effect of conceptualizable agents in discourse. *Studies in Second Language Acquisition* 22 (1). 85–111.

Kageyama, Taro. 1996. *Dōshi imiron: Gengo to ninchi no setten* [Verb semantics: The interface of language and cognition]. Tokyo: Kurosio Publishers.

Lakoff, George. 1970. *Irregularity in syntax*. New York: Holt, Rinehart & Winston.

Larson, Richard. 1988. On the double object construction. *Linguistic Inquiry* 19. 335–391.

Levin, Beth & Malka Rappaport Hovav. 1995. *Unaccusativity: At the syntax – lexical semantics interface*. Cambridge, MA: MIT Press.

Moto'ori, Haruniwa. 1828. *Kotoba no kayoiji* [Pathways of words]. Reprinted in Suga & Hayatsu (eds.), *Dōshi no jita* [Intransitive/transitive distinction in verbs]. Tokyo: Hituzi Syobo, 1995.

Nedjalkov, Vladimir P. 1969. Nekotorye verojatnostnye universalii v glagol'nom slovoobrazovanii. In I.F. Vardul' (ed.), *Jazykovye universalii I lingvističeskaja tipologija*, 106–114. Moscow: Nauka.

Nichols, Johanna, David A. Peterson & Jonathan Barnes. 2004. Transitivizing and detransitivizing languages. *Linguistic Typology* 8. 149–211.

NINJAL. 2014. *The world atlas of transitivity pairs*. http://watp.ninjal.ac.jp/en/ Tokyo: National Institute for Japanese Language and Linguistics.

Nitta, Yoshio (ed.). 1991. *Nihongo no voisu to tadōsei* [Voice and transitivity in Japanese]. Tokyo: Kurosio Publishers.

Okutsu, Keiichiro. 1976. Jidōshika, tadōshika oyobi ryōkyokuka-tenkei [Transitivization, intransitivization and bipolarization of Japanese verbs]. *Kokugogaku* 70. 46–66.

Schäfer, Florian. 2008. *The syntax of (anti-)causatives: External arguments in change-of-state contexts*. Amsterdam & Philadelphia: John Benjamins.

Shibatani, Masayoshi. 1985. Passives and related constructions. *Language* 61(4). 821–848.

Shibatani, Masayoshi & Taro Kageyama (eds.). 2015–. *Handbooks of Japanese language and linguistics*. Berlin & Boston: De Gruyter Mouton.

Suga, Kazuyoshi & Emiko Hayatsu (eds.). 1995. *Dōshi no jita* [The intransitive/transitive verbal distinction]. Tokyo: Hituzi Syobo.

Tsunoda, Tasaku. 1985. Remarks on transitivity. *Journal of Linguistics* 21. 385–396.

I Standard Japanese

Wesley M. Jacobsen
1 The semantic basis of Japanese transitive-intransitive derivational patterns

1 Introduction

This chapter revisits the hypothesis originally proposed in Jacobsen (1985) and discussed widely in the literature that patterns of morphological marking in Japanese transitive-intransitive verb pairs correlate to a significant extent with the meaning of such verbs, specifically as to whether the event expressed by a verb pair is more commonly seen in human experience to occur under the influence of an external force or apart from the influence of such a force. It will attempt to clarify what this hypothesis does and does not claim with a view to improving its usefulness as a tool for future research.

Secondly, the chapter considers the challenge posed by Japanese to what may be seen as a pervasive "transitive bias" in linguistic theory, one that tends to view transitive occurrence as having a more central place in human experience and linguistic meaning than intransitive occurrence. Intransitive meanings of three types are distinguished: those where the occurrence of an event is attributed to the effect of a force internal to the event, a force external to the event, or to no force at all. Evidence will be considered from the morphological patterning of Japanese transitive-intransitive verb pairs and from adverb occurrence that the third of these three modes of intransitive occurrence, one that involves no force at all, internal or external, is more basic to some categories of verb meaning than transitive occurrence, and that such meaning constitutes a prototype of intransitive meaning that is in fact more cognitively fundamental to human experience than the commonly recognized transitive prototype.

2 The morphology of transitivity alternations in Japanese

With few exceptions, transitive-intransitive verb pairs in Japanese exhibit a morphological stem common to both the transitive and intransitive member of the pair. As illustrated in (1), these pairs can be categorized into three broad

Wesley M. Jacobsen, Harvard University

groups depending on whether this stem is augmented in the transitive verb (the "causative" pattern of Class A), the intransitive verb (the "anticausative" pattern of Class B), or in both (the "equipollent" pattern of Class C). In each example pair in (1), and hereafter throughout this chapter, the intransitive form is the one on the left.

(1) A. Transitive marked   (Causative pattern)
        ak(u)/ak-e(ru)   'open$_{in}$/open$_{tr}$'
        sizum(u)/sizum-e(ru)   'sink$_{in}$/sink$_{tr}$'
        sodat(u)/sodat-e(ru)   'grow/raise'
        tuk(u)/tuk-e(ru)   'become attached/attach'
        ukab(u)/ukab-e(ru)   'float$_{in}$/float$_{tr}$'

    B. Intransitive marked   (Anticausative pattern)
        kir-e(ru)/kir(u)   'become cut/cut'
        kudak-e(ru)/kudak(u)   'become smashed/smash'
        nuk-e(ru)/nuk(u)   'come out/pull out'
        war-e(ru)/war(u)   'break$_{in}$, split$_{in}$/break$_{tr}$, split$_{tr}$'
        yak-e(ru)/yak(u)   'burn$_{in}$/burn$_{tr}$'

    C. Equipollent   (Transitive and intransitive equally marked)
        ag-ar(u)/ag-e(ru)   'rise/raise'
        kaw-ar(u)/ka[w]-e(ru)   'change$_{in}$/change$_{tr}$'
        mag-ar(u)/mag-e(ru)   'bend$_{in}$/bend$_{tr}$'
        sag-ar(u)/sag-e(ru)   'become lower/lower'
        tom-ar(u)/tom-e(ru)   'stop$_{in}$/stop$_{tr}$'

Classes A and B may be seen to represent differing patterns of markedness: the longer form in each case is "marked" with morphological material that is absent in the shorter form. The notion of markedness here is understood purely in terms of the relative presence or absence of morphological material, apart from the particular status that extra material may have as a derivational affix. Since marked linguistic forms that are longer or more complex in this way than their corresponding unmarked form require more linguistic effort to produce, the question arises as to why such extra linguistic effort is justified in some cases in the transitive form, in other cases in the intransitive form, and in yet other cases equally in both forms.

The example pairs chosen in (1) all involve the suffix *-e(ru)*, a suffix that marks sometimes transitive, sometimes intransitive forms. The markedness patterns in Classes A and B may also be viewed as a relationship of derivation:

in Class A, the transitive member of the pair is derived from the intransitive member by attachment of the -e(ru) suffix, and vice versa in Class B. In the case of Class C, the equal level of markedness would suggest that neither member is derived from the other, but there are differing views on this. Matsumoto (2000, this volume), for example, considers the transitive -e(ru) forms in Class C to be basic, and the intransitive -ar(u) forms derived from them. In line with this, Narrog (this volume) shows that the transitive -e(ru) forms in this class historically predate the intransitive -ar(u) forms. Assuming that the pattern in Class C is a case of transitive to intransitive derivation in modern Japanese requires that the -e(ru) form be treated as derived for certain transitivity pairs and non-derived for others. To avoid complications such as this, I will restrict my attention here to a stricter notion of *synchronic* derivation, whereby the derived form is created by the addition of morphological material lacking in the basic form, without the loss of any material present in the basic form, so that the derived form is always longer than the basic form.

The pairs listed in (1) are a small subset of the larger group of 306 'core' transitive-intransitive Japanese verb pairs listed in Appendix A of this volume. This list is a revision by Matsumoto (this volume) of the list of transitive-intransitive verbs in Jacobsen (1992), which originally included over 350 pairs categorized into 15 different patterns according to the differing patterns of suffixes used to mark the opposition. Matsumoto's 'core' list adds a number of pairs missing in the original list (indicated as "not in J" in the Appendix), but excludes even more, including numerous compound and deadjectival verb pairs appearing in the original list. There is therefore an overall reduction in the total number of verb pairs listed in the category of 'core' oppositions, though 169 additional pairs are listed in Appendix B that depart from the standard formal and semantic character of the 'core' oppositions, bringing the total in the two lists to 474 (see Matsumoto this volume).

A type count of all transitivity verb pairs in Japanese in the original Jacobsen (1992) list yields the result that of the three patterns in (1), Class C, the equipollent pattern, is the most dominant, accounting for 58.3% of the total, as opposed to 28.2% for the causative pattern of Class A and 13.5% for the anticausative pattern of Class B. Following Matsumoto's revised list in the Appendix, where the pattern in Class C is viewed not as equipollent, but as a case of anticausativization, the corresponding percentages are 14.5% for the equipollent pattern, 47.5% for the causative pattern, and 38% for the anticausative pattern. In his historical study, Narrog (this volume) arrives at results similar to those of Matsumoto: 15% (equipollent), 42% (causative), 29% (anticausative), and 14% (indeterminate) for modern Japanese, as compared to 16% (equipollent), 51% (causative), 24% (anticausative), and 9% (indeterminate) for premodern Japanese. All of these results are based on a type count, which is less reflective of actual usage than a token count based on a large corpus of actual data would be. Still, the differences in frequency here are wide enough to allow us to predict with confidence that a token count would yield similar results, at least in terms of relative prominence of the three patterns.

In this way, the causative pattern, involving a marked, derived transitive form, emerges as dominant over the anticausative pattern, involving a marked, derived intransitive form, in all the counts above, and in the counts by Matsumoto and Narrog, emerges as the dominant pattern among all three verb pair types. As Narrog shows, furthermore, this tendency was even stronger in earlier periods of the language. Japanese appears to be no exception among the world's languages in this respect. The data presented in Haspelmath's (1993) study of 21 languages, for example, show only a slight tendency toward the anticausative pattern over the causative pattern: in 10 languages of this sample, the anticausative pattern is statistically more common than the causative pattern (Russian, German, Greek, and Rumanian exhibiting the strongest such tendency), and in 8 languages the causative pattern is statistically more common than the anticausative pattern (Indonesian, Mongolian, Turkish, and Hindi-Urdu exhibiting the strongest such tendency). In the more recent study of 84 languages in Nichols et al. (2004), by contrast, the causative pattern is dominant in twice as many languages (16) as the anticausative pattern (8).

3 The semantic markedness hypothesis

In Jacobsen (1985, 1992), the hypothesis is advanced that morphological markedness patterns in Japanese transitive-intransitive verb pairs can be accounted for at least in part by principles of semantic markedness. The notion of semantic markedness was formulated in its classic form in works of the Prague structuralist school such as Jakobson (1932), but continued to have influence well into the era of generative grammar, as seen in works such as McCawley (1978). The guiding principle in this theory is the idea that simpler linguistic forms requiring less effort to produce tend to be used when expressing situations that are relatively more normal or usual, and longer, more complex forms requiring relatively more effort to produce tend to be used when expressing situations that are relatively less normal or usual. By reserving linguistic effort for the expression of situations that are less normal, and therefore less frequent, an overall economy of effort is effected in the linguistic expression of meaning.

Transitive-intransitive verb pairs typically express events or processes that result in a change of state in some entity, attributed in the transitive case to force(s) external to the entity and in the intransitive case to force(s) internal to the entity, if any force is involved at all. In purely quantitative terms, the difference is in the number of entities involved in the event, one in the intransitive case and two in the transitive case. The semantic markedness hypothesis posits that differences arise in human experience among events of different types according to which of these two types of occurrence is seen as the more normal mode of occurrence for the event in question. Those where occurrence apart from the influence of any external force is viewed as more normal will be encoded in verb pairs where the intransitive member is the simpler, less marked member of the pair (the causative pattern). Those where occurrence under the influence of such a force is viewed as more normal will be encoded in verb pairs where the transitive member is the simpler, less marked member (the anticausative pattern).

Evidence for the plausibility of this hypothesis can be found, first, in the preponderance of verbs that express natural processes among verb pairs of the causative pattern. As illustrated in (2), this includes pairs involving the suffix *-e(ru)* illustrated earlier in (1), but is not limited to this suffix.

(2) Transitive marked (causative pattern)
    itam(u)/itam-e(ru)   'hurt/cause hurt'
    kawak(u)/kawak-as(u)   'dry$_{in}$/dry$_{tr}$'
    koor(u)/koor-as(u)   'freeze$_{in}$/freeze$_{tr}$'
    sizum(u)/sizum-e(ru)   'sink$_{in}$/sink$_{tr}$'
    sodat(u)/sodat-e(ru)   'grow/raise'
    ukab(u)/ukab-e(ru)   'float$_{in}$/float$_{tr}$'
    wak(u)/wak-as(u)   'boil$_{in}$/boil$_{tr}$'

Natural processes such as drying, sinking, and boiling do not of course literally occur apart from the influence of any forces external to the thing that dries, sinks, or boils. But those forces do not typically present themselves to the senses in a distinct, straightforward way that readily allows them to be packaged into linguistic units. Events such as these are in that sense "normally" perceived to be limited in their occurrence to the entity undergoing the change in question, apart from an external entity or force. The simpler, less complex form is therefore identified in these cases with the intransitive member of the verb pair, in line with the markedness hypothesis.

Evidence for markedness of the opposite type can be found among verb pairs exhibiting the anticausative pattern. Salient here are verbs that express either the disintegration of a solid entity into parts, or the integration of several elements into a whole.

(3) Intransitive marked (anticausative pattern)
    kir-e(ru)/kir(u)   'become cut/ cut'
    kudak-e(ru)/kudak(u)   'become smashed/smash'
    or-e(ru)/or(u)   'break$_{in}$/break$_{tr}$ (of long things)'
    sak-e(ru)/sak(u)   'tear$_{in}$/tear$_{tr}$'
    tunag-ar(u)/tunag(u)   'be connected, connect'
    war-e(ru)/war(u)   'break$_{in}$/break$_{tr}$, split$_{in}$-split$_{tr}$'
    yak-e(ru)/yak(u)   'burn$_{in}$/burn$_{tr}$'
    yabur-e(ru)/yabur(u)   'tear$_{in}$/tear$_{tr}$'

The disintegration of a solid entity into parts is an event that is normally seen to involve the exertion of an outside force, and not to occur spontaneously in an entity. Similarly, it is unintuitive to conceive of the integration of several elements into a whole, as in the meaning of 'connect', as being due to the spontaneous coordination of the several elements, a process that is more likely to be seen as being guided by an external force. Markedness considerations thus account straightforwardly for the fact that the simple, less complex member of the pair corresponds in these cases to the transitive form.

One apparent difficulty for the semantic markedness hypothesis arises in the case of verb pairs that apparently express the same meaning yet exhibit different markedness patterns. As pointed out in Jacobsen (1992), for example, the verb pairs yak-e(ru)/yak(u) and mo[y]-e(ru)/moy-as(u) both express the meaning of 'burn', but only the former exhibits the anticausative pattern; the latter is equipollent in marking. If the markedness patterns are correlated with meaning, why should verb pairs of similar meaning exhibit different markedness patterns?

Even apparent counterexamples such as this, however, turn out on close examination to involve distinctions in meaning that support the markedness hypothesis. Of the two pairs meaning 'burn', for example, only yak-e(ru)/yak(u) expresses a burning that results in the disintegration or loss of an entity; mo[y]-e(ru)/moy-as(u) by contrast refers to a type of burning that involves no such loss, such as the burning of fire itself.

(4) a. Hi   ga   moe-ru   Ie   ga   moe-ru
        fire NOM   burn-NONPST   house NOM   burn-NONPST
        'Fire burns.'   'The house burns.'

    b. *Hi   ga   yake-ru   Ie   ga   yake-ru
        fire NOM   burn-NONPST   house NOM   burn-NONPST
        'Fire burns (down).'   'The house burns (down).'

The fact that only the verb pair expressing disintegration or loss of an entity exhibits an unmarked transitive form is thus in line with the hypothesis.

Similarly, the two pairs *kowa-re(ru)/kowa-s(u)* and *war-e(ru)/war(u)* both express the meaning 'break', but only the latter pair exhibits the anticausative pattern expected with events of disintegration; the former belongs by contrast to the equipollent category. The kind of breakage involved in the two cases is, however, different. *Kowa-re(ru)/kowa-s(u)* expresses breakage that is accompanied by loss of a function, typically in a man-made or organic entity, whereas *war-e(ru)/war(u)* merely involves disintegration of a solid entity into parts, regardless of any function the entity might or might not have. This difference can be seen in the differing patterns of acceptability in (5), correlating to the degree to which the entity involved in each case can be seen inherently to possess such a function.

(5) a. *Iwa/koori/mado/omotya/?terebi   ga   ware-ru.*
       rock/ice/window/toy/television   NOM   break-NONPST
       'Rock/ice/window/toy/television breaks.'

   b. **Iwa/*koori/mado/omotya/terebi   ga   koware-ru.*
       rock/ice/window/toy/television   NOM   break-NONPST
       'Rock/ice/window/toy/television breaks.'

   c. *Onaka   o   kowas-u/*war-u.*
       stomach   ACC   break$_{tr}$-NONPST/break$_{tr}$-NONPST
       Lit. 'Break one's gut (get a stomachache).'

It is commonplace in human experience for entities possessing organic or other complex functions to lose those functions spontaneously with the passage of time, without the influence of external force, but for solid entities to spontaneously disintegrate is clearly less common. Here again, what is an apparent counterexample to the markedness hypothesis turns out in fact to support it.

Correlations between formal and semantic markedness of this kind observed in Japanese[1] are strongly confirmed across other languages as well. In Haspelmath's (1993) study of 21 languages exhibiting transitive alternations, expanding on earlier work by Nedjalkov (1969), and confirmed in subsequent studies such as Comrie (2006), the meanings that turn up most frequently in verb pairs exhibiting the causative alternation and anticausative alternation patterns, respectively, are those in (6).

---

[1] Further, more fine-grained, correlations between semantic and morphological markedness in Japanese are discussed in Matsumoto (this volume), taking into account factors such as whether the subject is human/animate vs. inanimate.

(6) Haspelmath (1993)

Derivational type:	Causative (transitive member marked)	Anticausative (intransitive member marked)
Meanings most commonly observed:	boil freeze dry wake up go out sink melt	split close break open gather change connect

These results are very much in line with Japanese, with natural processes predominant in the causative patterns and processes of disintegration or integration predominant in the anticausative pattern, providing convincing evidence that semantic markedness plays a role in accounting for formal markedness patterns in transitive-intransitive pairs universally.

Despite this widely-attested correlation, though, there are numerous transitive-intransitive verb pairs in Japanese that are difficult to reconcile with the semantic markedness hypothesis, even within the range of meanings such as (6) above. The verb pairs *tuk(u)/tuk-e(ru)* 'become attached/attach' and *narab(u)/narab-e(ru)* 'line up$_{tr}$/line up$_{in}$', for example, appear to express events involving the integration of multiple entities into one, where an unmarked transitive form might be expected on semantic grounds, yet it is the intransitive form that is unmarked here. Similarly, *ak(u)/ak-e(ru)* 'open$_{in}$/open$_{tr}$', which at least in some uses expresses the detachment of one entity from another, exhibits an unmarked intransitive, going against the cross-linguistic pattern observed in (6). And when verbs of the equipollent markedness pattern are considered, verbs that should represent processes exhibiting the equal likelihood of occurrence with or without the influence of an outside force, we find numerous pairs, particularly those with intransitive –*ar(u)*, where any notion of "normal" occurrence apart from the influence of an outside force appears grossly counterintuitive: *tasuk-ar(u)/tasuk-e(ru)* 'be helped/help', *mituk-ar(u)/mituk-e(ru)* 'be found/find', *tukama-r(u)/tukama-e(ru)* 'be caught/catch', etc.[2] While some of these pairs point to explanations other than purely semantic ones, others require a more

---

[2] Pairs such as these provide evidence for the place of a broader notion of derivation than adopted here, such as that adopted in Matsumoto (this volume), whereby -*ar(u)* represents the derived form, even though it contains no greater quantity of morphological material than the corresponding transitive form in -*e(ru)*.

careful consideration of which meaning of a verb it is that determines morphological markedness and shifts that may occur in the meaning of a form over time.

4 Semantic range and shift over time

The role played by semantic markedness in determining the formal markedness of a particular verb pair must take into account the possibility of a range of meanings in a verb, not all of which carry equal weight in determining formal markedness, and which will only be relevant at the historical stage at which the morphological forms in question take shape in the language. Given the tendency for lexical items to shift over time in meaning, or for shifts to occur in which of several meanings is considered the dominant meaning, the possibility arises that over time the original relationship between semantic and formal markedness may become skewed. Though it is clear that the causative pattern was dominant historically in intransitive-transitive verb pairs in Japanese (see Narrog this volume), exactly what the nature and extent of historical shifts were that have occurred in the meaning of Japanese transitive-intransitive pairs over time must await further research. Two examples are considered here that are at least suggestive of how such skewing might occur.

We noted earlier that Japanese *ak(u)/ak-e(ru)* 'open$_{in}$/open$_{tr}$' exhibits the causative pattern (intransitive unmarked), going against the broader cross-linguistic tendency observed in Haspelmath (1993) for verbs of opening to exhibit the anticausative pattern, reflecting the expected presence of an outside force in "typical" events of opening. Another such pair where the formal markedness pattern appears to counter the predictions of semantic markedness is *todok(u)/todok-e(ru)* 'be delivered/deliver'. If we assume that the uses of the intransitive members of these pairs in (7) represent the most salient usage of these verbs in the modern language, it would indeed be counterintuitive to argue that the events expressed here are "normally" seen to occur independently of the action of an outside force.

(7) a. *Doa   ga   ak-u.*
      door NOM open-NONPST
      'The door opens.'

   b. *Nimotu   ga   todok-u.*
      luggage NOM be.delivered-NONPST
      'The luggage is delivered.'

In fact, however, the uses in (7) are only one of multiple usages of these verbs. The use of the intransitive *ak(u)* in (7a) is, first of all, a special case of numerous uses that cluster around the meaning 'space/time comes into existence'.

(8) a. *Zikan ga ai-ta node eiga o mi-ta.*
 time NOM *aku*-PST because movie ACC see-PST
 'Because I had some time (lit., time came about), I saw a movie.'

 b. *Hune no soko ni ana ga ai-ta.*
 boat GEN bottom LOC hole NOM *aku*-PST
 'A hole formed in the bottom of the boat.'

While it is true that the use of *aku* in (7a) and the uses in (8) are rendered by orthographically distinct Chinese characters in modern Japanese, and for that reason may be considered in popular consciousness to constitute "different" lexical items, it is clear that all these uses are of a common provenance. The point is that events in (8) are much more easily, and "normally," conceived of as occurring without the influence of an outside force. It is plausible to assume that the meanings of *aku* that were dominant in the historical generation of the morphology of *aku* as a lexical item more closely approximate those in (8), overshadowing the use in (7a), and that the form *aku* persisted even after the use in (7a) became the dominant use of this verb in the modern language.

Similarly, the use of the intransitive *todoku* in (7b) is only one alongside multiple other uses illustrated in (9).

(9) a. *Kanozyo no koe wa tooku made todok-u.*
 she GEN voice TOP distant as.far.as *todoku*-NONPST
 'Her voice carries far.'

 b. *Kare no mimi ni uwasa ga todoi-ta.*
 he GEN ear LOC rumor NOM *todoku*-PST
 'The rumor reached his ears.'

 c. *Kanozyo no seii ga kare ni todoi-ta.*
 she GEN sincerity NOM he LOC *todoku*-PST
 'Her sincerity touched (lit., reached) him.'

Considered in the context of these examples, the meaning of 'be delivered/ deliver' present in (7b) is but a special case of a larger range of meanings clustering around the notion of 'reach, move to a point as far as'. While semantic markedness might predict that the narrower meaning in (7b) considered in isolation is unmarked in its transitive occurrence, involving the presence of an external force, the larger range of meanings in (9) clearly include event types that are more intuitively seen as normally occurring without the influence of outside force, and therefore being unmarked in their intransitive occurrence.[3]

The possibility is therefore present that individual, narrower senses of the meaning of a verb pair may conflict with each other as to the predictions semantic markedness makes of what constitutes their "normal" occurrence, and that the conflict will be resolved in favor of the meaning that is central or dominant to the verb pair, a judgment that may shift over time. The larger lesson here is that the full range of a verb's meanings needs to be considered when considering the predictions of semantic markedness. There is a more practical lesson here as well, and that is that in assigning verb pairs to meaning categories across languages, the English meaning must not be allowed to cloud the judgment of the linguistic analyst, as might occur if, for example, 'open' were considered to be the sole or dominant meaning of *ak(u)/ak-e(ru)*.

The process and timing by which transitive-intransitive verb pairs evolved into the markedness patterns observed in contemporary Japanese is not clear in all details, but some form of grammaticalization of lexical forms into abstract grammatical markers (Hopper & Traugott 2003) undoubtedly played at least a partial role in this evolution. An attractive hypothesis in this regard is one that posits the verb *e-* 'get' (classical citation form *u*) as the source of the modern affix *-e(ru)* (Frellesvig & Whitman this volume), an affix capable of marking either transitive or intransitive meaning (see (1)). This hypothesis is plausible from a general semantic standpoint, in view of the ability of the verb 'get' to exhibit both causative and anti-causative (e.g. passive) functions in numerous languages, including English. An account will of course have to be provided of the fact that *-e* was not historically part of an invariant verb stem as it is in the modern language: through at least the 15th century the intransitive and transitive members of verb pairs such as *ak(u)/ak-e(ru)* (*-e(ru)* transitive) and *yak-e(ru)/yak(u)* (*-e(ru)* intransitive) had identical citation forms *aku* and *yaku*,

---

[3] A reviewer points out that the earliest citations of the verbs *aku* and *todoku* in historical dictionaries such as the *Nihonkokugo Daijiten* (2001, Shogakukan) exemplify meanings such as those given in (7a). Citations from dictionaries, however, based as they are exclusively on written sources, have only limited utility as a guide to tracing the historical genesis of word meaning, given that the earliest written sources available (in the case of Japanese, from no earlier than the 8th century) date from a relatively late period in the larger sweep of linguistic history and that the linguistic data they provide may not constitute a truly representative corpus of the colloquial language acquired by native speakers of the time. That being the case, the earliest citations of *aku* and *todoku* in the *Nihonkokugo Daijiten* in fact exhibit a range of meanings including those exemplified in (8) and (9) as well as those in (7).

the -e vowel appearing in alternation with -u only in forms other than the citation form, as determined by the distinct conjugational patterns to which the transitive and intransitive members belonged (Frellesvig 2010). It is nevertheless possible to view the presence of the e/u- alternation as constituting extra morphological material that distinguishes one of the members of each verb pair as marked with respect to the other, even within a conjugational paradigm, as noted by Narrog (this volume). *Which* member of a particular verb pair is marked in this regard is not, however, something that can be accounted for solely in terms of the semantics of 'get', a matter that requires instead an independent account of the sort made possible by the semantic markedness hypothesis.

As noted earlier, numerous affixes other than -e(ru) play a role in marking transitive-intransitive alternations in Japanese, most notably multiple affixes built on the consonant -s- marking transitive meaning and multiple affixes built on the consonant -r- marking intransitive meaning (see the Appendix). Although some of these appear to be distinguished by particular semantic characteristics (Kageyama 1996), in other cases phonological features appear to play a central role in determining their distribution (Matsumoto 2000, this volume). The semantic markedness hypothesis does not make any predictions as to which of these particular affixes is chosen to mark transitive or intransitive meaning, but applies only to cases where one member of an intransitive-transitive pair carries extra morphological weight with respect to its partner, whatever the particular makeup of the morphological form may be.

5 Semantic markedness and frequency

If a process is more normally *experienced* as occurring transitively, under the influence of an external force, than intransitively, without the influence of such a force, then it would appear to follow naturally that the process will also be *expressed* that way more often, or vice versa. In general, therefore, unmarked morphological forms, to the extent at least that their meaning reflects that of the historical stage at which the forms arose, should occur more frequently than their corresponding marked forms in actual language usage. This expectation is borne out in a study by Haspelmath et al. (2014) of 20 verb meanings in 7 languages (including Japanese), meanings that include those in (6). The quantitative data in this study show a three-way correlation between (i) verb pairs whose meaning exhibits a low level of "causative prominence" – i.e., a lower tendency for the event to be conceived of as being brought about causally by an outside force, (ii) a morphological pattern of the causative type – i.e., one where the intransitive form is unmarked, and (iii) higher frequency of occurrence of the unmarked intransitive form in actual corpus data. While these data provide strong confirmation of a correlation between morphological (un)markedness and frequency, at least within the range of data targeted in the study, frequency itself does not provide an ultimately satisfying explanation of the markedness data, counter to what the authors argue, as it begs the question of why the frequency differentials between transitive and intransitive forms occur in the first place. This is, again, something that calls for a deeper explanation of the sort that the semantic markedness hypothesis aims to provide, at least partially.

As studies such as Shibatani (this volume) show, however, when the range of meanings is broadened to a larger sample of transitive-intransitive pairs beyond the meanings in (6), a straightforward correlation between unmarked morphology and higher frequency of usage does not always obtain. This cannot however be taken at face value to disconfirm the semantic markedness hypothesis. Frequency counts are in the first place subject to numerous biases inherent in the data base, which may not reflect frequency distributions in the oral language corpus to which children are exposed at the stage of first language acquisition. In addition, frequency counts that target the contemporary language do not reflect the historical stage at which morphological markedness patterns arise (see Narrog this volume), and are therefore subject to skewing that may arise from semantic drift over time. Still, it is remarkable that for a core group of meanings such as those in (6), a correlation between semantic (un)markedness, morphological (un)markedness, and higher frequency in corpus data appears to hold consistently not only across languages, but across time as well.

6 Transitive alternations and prototypes

In accounting for the relationship between form and meaning in the expression of transitivity across languages, many linguistic studies have appealed to the concept of a transitive prototype, borrowing a concept from psychology that was articulated in its most classic form in studies such as Berlin & Kay (1969) and Rosch (1975). While semantic markedness is defined in terms of pairs of linguistic forms that are *opposed* to each other along some parameter of meaning, such as transitive and intransitive members of a verb pair, prototypes are concerned with multiple forms that *share* a meaning in common, although not all to the same degree. Membership in a prototype category is thus defined in gradient, rather than dichotomous, terms, with some members of the prototype being seen as more central to its meaning than others. The category of fruit, for example, forms a prototype defined by properties such as being edible, round, sweet in taste, and having seeds. Apples are therefore a prototypical fruit, having all these properties, whereas bananas and tomatoes are less prototypical fruits, the former lacking roundness and seeds, and the latter lacking the sweet taste of prototypical fruits, even though all three of these may be considered to fall under the general category of fruit.

As the fruit example illustrates, prototypes are meanings composed of multiple properties that do not necessarily bear a logical relationship to one another, but are seen to cohere together on the basis of common and repeated encounters with exemplars of the prototype in daily human experience. Given their familiarity in human experience, prototypes can be expected to have special linguistic forms reserved for their expression in language, and considerations of economy will predict that such expression will tend in the direction of formal simplicity rather than complexity, much as in the case of meaning that is unmarked.

Linguistic transitivity is concerned with event types, and in particular with a basic opposition between event types involving two participants and those involving one. *Each* of these two general categories comprises multiple event types, some of which can be seen to more centrally exemplify the general meaning category than others. It may seem strange to speak of event types being more or less central to a meaning category that is defined in terms of the discrete numerical values of two versus one, but as we shall see shortly, in the linguistic packaging of events into predicates with their associated noun arguments, what counts as one participant versus two is not always something that can be determined in a clear-cut arithmetic fashion.

7 A 'transitive bias' in traditional studies of transitivity

Although a broad distinction can be made in this way between event types that involve a single participant, and those that involve two participants, the linguistic study of transitivity has in the past been almost exclusively preoccupied with a prototype for events involving two participants, exhibiting what I will call a 'transitive bias'. The transitive prototype, in its classic formulation by Hopper & Thompson (1980), is defined by the properties summarized in (10).

(10) a. Two participants are involved in the transitive event – agent and patient.
b. The agent acts in an intentional manner.
c. The patient undergoes a change in state as a direct consequence of (b).
d. The event occurs in actual time.
e. The event is telic and bounded in time.

To the degree that all these properties are present, a particular event is seen to exemplify the central meaning of the prototype. This meaning is, furthermore, expressed by a special linguistic form – a grammatical prototype – reserved for that purpose. As illustrated in (11), the grammatical prototype in Japanese is characterized by two formal properties – at the level of syntax, the presence of the accusative case marker *o* and, at the level of morphology, a verb form that constitutes the transitive member of a transitive-intransitive lexical pair (here the transitive member *war(u)* of the pair *war-e(ru)/war(u)* 'break$_{in}$, split$_{in}$/ break$_{tr}$, split$_{tr}$').

(11) Kokku   ga   tamago   o   wat-ta.
     cook   NOM   egg   ACC   break$_{tr}$-PST
     'The cook broke the egg.'

Although properties such as realis modality (10d) and aspectual telicity (10e) may not bear a logical relationship to the presence of two participants, they conspire with all the properties in (10) to define an event where two participants are *maximally differentiated* (Næss 2007). Whether two distinct entities are seen to be involved in an event or not will, for example, correlate in Japanese grammar with the degree to which the event is seen as occurring in actual time. Non-actual meanings such as potential meaning typically involve a shift in the case marking of the patient from accusative *o* to nominative *ga*.

(12) (Kono yarikata de   wa)   kantanni tamago ga   war-e-ru.
     (this way   INSTR TOP) easily   egg   NOM break-POT-NONPST
     'With this method, the egg is easily broken/one can easily break the egg.'

The resulting construction is indistinct from an intransitive construction involving only one participant, representing a departure from event types where two distinct entities are maximally differentiated.

The transitive prototype has rightfully been assumed to play a central role in human experience and language. But why should events involving two participants differentiated in this way be seen to have a uniquely more central place in human experience than events involving only one participant? Previous linguistic research has provided no clear rationale for this, and the morphological patterning of transitive verb pairs in languages such as Japanese provides strong empirical evidence that calls this bias into question. Specifically, such pairs provide abundant evidence of event types that may be framed as involving *either* one participant or two, but where the alternation pattern is causative – i.e., it is the intransitive form that receives simpler unmarked morphological expression than the transitive form. In the case of Japanese such alternation patterns are in fact significantly more common than the anti-causative alternation pattern, where the transitive member receives unmarked expression. This is difficult to account for in a framework that admits only of a transitive prototype, one that by implication holds a uniquely central place in human experience to the exclusion of intransitive occurrence. The prevalence of semantically and morphologically unmarked intransitive meaning points, that is, to the need to accommodate the notion of an intransitive prototype as distinct from the transitive prototype that has held sway in past linguistic treatments of transitivity. In subsequent sections, I take up the question of how that intransitive prototype should be formulated. Before doing so, I will consider one influential treatment of transitive verb alternations that can be considered to exhibit this transitive bias.

8 The external causation hypothesis of Levin & Rappaport Hovav (1995)

Prototypically transitive meaning as proposed in Hopper & Thompson (1980) can be represented as in (13), to borrow a formulation widely adopted in influential studies such as Dowty (1979) and Kageyama (1996). This meaning can be seen to be most centrally and prototypically realized to the extent that entities x and y are maximally differentiated along the Hopper-Thompson parameters seen earlier in (10).

(13) [DO(x)] CAUSE [BECOME (STATE(y))]

In a famous study, Levin & Rappaport Hovav (1995) (hereafter LRH) posit (13) as the semantic structure underlying *both* transitive and intransitive uses of verbs that alternate transitively. In the English alternating pair in (14), for example, both sentences are seen to be manifestations of the semantic structure in (15)

(14) a. The child broke the vase.
   b. The vase broke.

(15) [DO(x)] CAUSE [BECOME (*broken*(y))]

For LRH, the difference between (14a) and (14b) is simply that the transitive version in (14a) is realized when both the slots *x* and *y* are filled by a lexical form, as in (16a), whereas in the corresponding intransitive form (14b), *x* is prevented from being filled by any surface argument through a process of 'argument binding' that generates the structure in (16b), leaving only y to appear on the surface as the subject argument *vase*.

(16) a. [DO(*child*) CAUSE [BECOME (*broken*(*vase*))]
   b. [DO(Ø)] CAUSE [BECOME (*broken*(*vase*))]

This so-called 'external causation hypothesis' assumes that the presence of an external force as formulated in (13) underlies the meaning of both members of transitive-intransitive alternating pairs. The unilateral direction of semantic derivation that this posits, from transitive to intransitive meaning, is, however, difficult to reconcile with the facts of morphological derivation seen in languages such as Japanese, where the direction of derivation is seen to go in both directions, and in fact the intransitive to transitive derivation pattern is more dominant. LRH's hypothesis thus exemplifies a transitive bias that is at odds with the morphological patterning of languages such as Japanese. Another piece of evidence for the inadequacy of this hypothesis can be seen in patterns of adverb occurrence in Japanese, which we consider next.

9 Adverb co-occurrence and the external causation hypothesis

Certain adverbs in Japanese may be taken as diagnostic of the presence or absence of an external force in the occurrence of an event.[4] Kageyama (1996) points out, for example, that the adverb *kantanni* 'easily' is diagnostic of the presence of such force. This can be seen in the ease with which it occurs in

---

4 The argument from adverb co-occurrence presented here is a slight revision of that presented in an earlier form in Jacobsen (2007).

intransitive contexts that explicitly make reference to an agentive external force that is responsible for the occurrence of the event.

(17) *Doa   o   osite-mi-tara   kantanni   ai-ta.*
door ACC   push-try-COND   easily   open$_{in}$-PST
'When I tried pushing the door, it opened easily.'

(18) *Netto   de   sagasi-tara   kantanni   apaato   ga   mitukat-ta.*
internet INST search-COND   easily   apartment NOM be.found-PST
'When I searched on the internet, an apartment was easily found.'

The verbs *aku* (past form *aita*) in (17) and *mitukaru* (past *mitukatta*) in (18) are the intransitive members, respectively, of the pairs *ak(u)/ak-e(ru)* 'open$_{in}$/open$_{tr}$', and *mituk-ar(u)/mituk-e(ru)* 'be found/find'. Given the explicit mention of an external force in the first clause of each of these examples, the meanings of the intransitive verbs here may be seen to represent the externally-caused intransitive meaning that results from LRH's 'argument binding' represented in (19).

(19) [DO(Ø)] CAUSE [BECOME (STATE(y))]

The meaning in (19) characterizes one large subclass of intransitives, those formed from the affix *-ar(u)*, such as *kimaru* 'be decided', *mitukaru* 'be found', and *tukamaru* 'be caught', etc., most of which express an exclusively externally-caused variety of intransitive meaning. This is reflected in the fact that they have no intransitive counterparts in English, where the corresponding meaning can be expressed only in a passive form. In terms of their morphological patterning, all fall under the 'equipollent' Class C in (1): *kimar(u)/kime(ru)* 'be decided/decide', *mitukar(u)/mituke(ru)* 'be found/find', *tukama(r)u/tukamae(ru)* 'be caught/catch', etc. *Kantanni* occurs easily with all the intransitive members of this class, as illustrated in (18), but also occurs more widely, including with some intransitives that are unmarked with respect to their transitive partners, such as *aku/akeru* 'open$_{in}$/open$_{tr}$,' in (17). Unlike intransitives formed with *-ar(u)*, though, verbs such as *aku* are not limited to expressing an externally-caused type of meaning.

An example of an adverb that is diagnostic of the *absence* of external cause, as opposed to *kantanni*, is seen in *katteni* 'by (it)self'. This adverb occurs most naturally in contexts where the presence of an external force is explicitly negated.

(20) Doa   o   aketa   n   zya-naku-te,
     door   ACC open_tr-PST   NMNL   COP-NEG-GER
     katteni   ai-ta   n   da.
     by.itself open_intr-NONPST NMNL   COP
     'I didn't open the door, it opened by itself.'

(21) Denki   o   kesi-ta   n   zya-naku-te,
     light   ACC turn.off-PST NMNL   COP-NEG-GER
     katteni   kie-ta   n   da.
     by.itself go.off-PST   NMNL   COP
     'I didn't turn off the light, it went off by itself.'

(22) Tyanneru   o   kae-ta   n   zya-naku-te,
     channel   ACC change_tr-PST   NMNL   COP-NEG-GER
     katteni   kawat-ta   n   da.
     by.itself change_intr-NONPST   NMNL   COP
     'I didn't change the channel, it changed by itself.'

Each of the intransitives in (20)–(22) is a member of an alternating intransitive-transitive pair. Note that *kawaru* (past *kawatta*) in (22) is exceptional in being formed from the affix *-ar(u)*, which in most cases expresses an exclusively externally-caused variety of meaning and thus resists co-occurrence with *katteni*.

(23) *Apaato   o   mituke-ta   n   zya-naku-te,   katteni
     apartment   ACC find-PST   NMNL   COP-NEG-GER   by.itself
     mitukat-ta   n   da.
     be.found-PST   NMNL   COP
     'I didn't find the apartment, it was found by itself.'

The possibility of co-occurrence of *katteni* with intransitive members of alternating pairs such as those in (20)–(22) thus provides clear evidence that at least some alternating intransitives in Japanese express events that are not caused by any external force.

One class of events that are not externally-caused would of course be those that are brought about by a force internal to the event – specifically, by a force that originates in the single participant encoded as the intransitive subject. Events brought about by the intentional agency of a human or animate subject are the clearest case of this type of meaning, and *katteni* occurs freely with verbs that express such intentional meaning.

(24) *Hito   no   heya   ni   katteni hair-u   na.*
     person GEN   room   LOC   by.self enter-NONPST   IMP-NEG
     'Don't enter someone's room without asking (lit., by yourself).'

(25) *Kenkoosindan-tyuu ni   katteni beddo kara   oki-rare-te   wa*
     healthexam-midst   TEMP   by.self bed   from   get.up-PASS-GER   TOP
     komar-u.
     be.inconvenienced-NONPST
     'Don't get up off the bed without asking (lit., by yourself) in the middle of a checkup.'

Although intentional meaning commonly arises in intransitives, including certain intransitives that alternate with transitives, as in (24) and (25), such intransitives are in many ways more transitive-like than intransitive-like in their behavior. They occur, for example, in a range of construction types that are possible with transitives, but not with non-intentional intransitives, such as imperatives (as in (24)), passives (as in (25)), potentials, and causatives.

But there is a more fundamental semantic sense in which intentional intransitives are transitive-like. As argued elegantly in Searle (1983), intentional action inherently involves two subevents: an intention by an agent to bring about an event in the outside world and the actual occurrence of that event as a result. These define two distinct semantic roles: that of the agent and that of an entity in the outside world that participates in the resulting event. In transitive constructions these roles are encoded in distinct subject and object arguments of the predicate.

(26) *Oya   ga   kodomo   o   okos-u.*
     parent   NOM   child   ACC   get.up$_{tr}$-NONPST
     'The parent gets the child up.'

But the entity targeted in an intentional act is not necessarily one distinct from the agent. It is possible for an agent to intend an event in itself, giving rise to reflexive meaning such as that in (27).

(27) *Kanzya   ga   beddo   kara   karada   o   okos-u.*
     patient   NOM   bed   from   body   ACC   get.up$_{tr}$-NONPST
     'The patient gets himself up from the bed.'

As argued in Jacobsen (1992: 99), it is this reflexive structure that characterizes the meaning of intentional intransitives, evidence for which is seen in the possibility of reflexive transitive paraphrases of certain intentional intransitive constructions. The intransitive (28), for example, can be considered a paraphrase of the reflexive-transitive (27).

(28) *Kanzya   ga   beddo   kara   oki-ru.* (cf. 27)
     patient   NOM   bed   from   get.up$_{in}$-NONPST
     'The patient gets up from the bed.'

Intentional intransitives such as *okiru* 'get up' may therefore be seen to express the transitive semantic structure in (13), with the sole difference that the roles of *x* and *y* are mutually identified, both represented in (29) as *x*.

(29)   [DO(x)] CAUSE [BECOME (STATE(x))]

The reflexive, intentional meaning in (29) does not, however, represent all uses of *okiru*, as there are also non-intentional (non-agentive) uses of this verb, as in (30).

(30) *Omowanu   zitai   ga   oki-ta.*
     unexpected situation NOM   arise-PST
     'An unexpected situation arose.'

Intransitives that alternate with transitives, as *okiru* does with *okosu*, in fact always allow such a non-intentional interpretation, and in some cases can only be interpreted in that way. By contrast, intransitives that lack transitive partners typically exhibit meanings that are inherently intentional, and therefore reflexive, in meaning. Salient among these are activity verbs such as *hasiru* 'run', *oyogu* 'swim', *odoru* 'dance', etc., illustrated in (31).

(31) *Mai-hime   ga   butai   de   odot-ta.*
     dancing-girl   NOM   stage   LOC   dance-PST
     'The dancing girl danced on the stage.'

These verbs exhibit a meaning structure such as (32), following the schema of Kageyama (1996), where the roles of intending agent and thematic entity participating in the event intended by the agent are again mutually identified, yielding a reflexive structure.

(32)   [DO(x)] CAUSE [MOVE(x)]

The inherently intentional character of activity verbs is a consequence of the fact that their meaning makes direct reference to bodily movements, and consequently to an agent controlling the bodily movements. The fact that these intransitives do *not* alternate with transitives underscores the fact that reflexive meaning is in fact transitive-like. To the extent that an intransitive verb is inherently reflexive in its meaning structure, that is, it fails to exhibit the typical intransitive characteristic of alternating with a transitive.

A reflexive meaning structure such as that in (29) and (31) extends beyond intentional meaning to any intransitive event where the subject entity is seen to exert control over the occurrence of the event. The concept of control, whether or not it originates in an animate being, itself presumes a distinction between two roles – that which controls and that which is controlled, and is therefore inherently reflexive in meaning.

All intransitive contexts in which the adverb *katteni* occurs may be seen to involve the presence of internal force or control in this sense. But does the *absence* of external force automatically entail the *presence* of internal force or control in this way? Yet a third type of adverb suggests that such is not the case, that there is a variety of intransitive meanings distinct from either external *or* internal causation. That is the class of adverbs represented by *sizenni* 'naturally' and *hitorideni* 'of own accord'.[5] As illustrated in (33)–(35), these adverbs, like *katteni*, occur in contexts where the presence of an external force is explicitly denied.

(33)   *Doa   o   ake-ta   n   zya-naku-te,*
       door   ACC   open$_{tr}$-PST   NMNL   COP-NEG-GER

   sizenni/hitorideni   ai-ta   n   da.
   naturally/of.own.accord   open$_{intr}$-NONPST   NMNL   COP

   'I didn't open the door, it opened naturally/of its own accord.'

(34)   *Denki   o   kesi-ta   n   zya-naku-te,*
       light   ACC   turn.off-PST   NMNL   COP-NEG-GER

   sizenni/hitorideni   kie-ta   n   da.
   naturally/of.own.accord   go.off-PST   NMNL   COP

   'I didn't turn off the light, it went off naturally/of its own accord.'

---

5 Other examples of members in this class would include the now antiquated adverbs *onozukara* and *onozuto* "spontaneously."

(35) Hootteoi-tara   kizu   wa   hitorideni/sizenni   naot-ta.
     leave.alone-COND   wound   TOP   naturally/of.own.accord   heal-PST
     'When I left it alone, the wound healed naturally/of its own accord.'

But unlike *katteni*, these adverbs do not occur in contexts of internal control such as intentional action.

(36) *Hitorideni/sizenni   hito   no   heya   ni   hair-u
     of.own.accord/naturally   person   GEN   room   LOC   enter-NONPST
     na. (cf. 24)
     IMP-NEG
     'Don't of your own accord/naturally enter someone else's room.'

Nor, on the other hand. do they occur in contexts of external control such as those associated with *kantanni*.

(37) *Netto   de   sagasi-tara   sizenni/hitorideni   apaato
     internet   INST   search-COND   naturally/of.own.accord   apartment
     ga   mitukat-ta.
     NOM   be.found-PST
     'When I searched on the internet, an apartment was found naturally/of its own accord.'

This third category of adverb thus singles out an event type that is distinct from events that are either externally caused, on the one hand, or internally caused, on the other. The relationship between this third type of adverb and the two considered earlier with regard to internal versus external causation can be summarized as in (38):

(38) Adverbs and event type

Event type:	Externally caused	Not externally caused	
	Not internally caused	Not internally caused	Internally caused
	kantanni	hitorideni sizenni	katteni

Evidence from adverbs thus points to the existence of event types where there is no force, external *or* internal, that is seen to bring about an event.

Such event types can be schematized in terms of the absence of the DO component of the transitive structure seen earlier in (13), leaving the structure in (39), exemplified in (40) for *Denki ga sizenni kieru* 'The lights go off of their own accord'.

(39) [BECOME (STATE (x))]

(40) [BECOME (OFF (*light*))]

The semantic structures in (39)–(40) define a type of event that occurs without the influence of any force whatsoever, a purely spontaneous form of occurrence. In the next section, we consider how event types such as this are even possible, and where they might be seen to originate in human experience.

10 An intransitive prototype and its origins

Evidence from adverb occurrence such as that considered in the previous section points to the existence of three distinct types of intransitive occurrence, summarized in (41).

(41) a. DO(x)] CAUSE [BECOME (STATE(x))]
          (e.g., agentive *hairu* 'enter', *okiru* 'get up', etc.)

      b. [DO(Ø)] CAUSE [BECOME (STATE(x))]
          (e.g., *mitukaru* 'be found', *tukamaru* 'be caught', etc.)

      c. [BECOME (STATE (x))]
          (e.g., spontaneous *kieru* 'vanish', *naoru* 'heal', etc.)

(41a), involving an internal force directed reflexively toward itself, and (41b), involving an external force that is entailed, but left unspecified by, the unfilled argument slot of DO, both share the fundamentally *transitive* meaning structure seen earlier in (13). Recall that, while alternating intransitives can be found in each of the three meaning categories, as illustrated in the parentheses above, intransitives that *fail* to alternate, such as those of the activity type, are concentrated in the transitive-like (41a) category. But (41a) and (41b) are not *prototypically* transitive in that they do not encode two entities that are maximally differentiated.

(41c), by contrast, is distinct from either of these, not only in lacking the transitive structure characterized by the predicate DO, but in allowing for only a single semantic role, and thereby encoding a participant entity that, of all the participant entities encoded in the three intransitive types, is most highly *un*differentiated. If the transitive prototype is characterized by a maximal differentiation of participating entities (Næss 2007), then, this meaning category points to a prototype that stands in polar opposition to the transitive prototype, one defined by spontaneous occurrence and maximal undifferentiation among participating entities.

Is the notion of purely spontaneous occurrence defining the intransitive prototype in this way a coherent one, and if so what specific kinds of events may be seen to exemplify the prototype? From a cognitive perspective, an event of spontaneous occurrence is one where a previously non-existing state comes into existence in the form of a sense datum impinging on the field of awareness of the perceiving self. This sense datum may represent a newly arising state in an entity that already exists in the field of awareness, but may also represent an entity that itself did not previously exist in that field of awareness – an event, that is, where the entity itself comes into existence in an event of appearing. Examples of intransitive constructions expressing this sort of meaning are those involving perceptual verbs as in (42)–(43) and related constructions such as (44). In each case the intransitive verb is one that alternates with a transitive.

(42) *A!   Huzisan   ga   mie-ta.*
look   Mt.Fuji   NOM   become.visible-PST
'Look! There's Mt. Fuji (lit., Mt. Fuji became visible)!'

(43) *Henna   oto   ga   kikoe-ta.*
strange sound NOM   become.audible-PST
'There was a strange sound (lit., a strange sound became audible).'

(44) *Denwa   ga   kakatte   ki-ta.*
phone   NOM   become.connected   come-PST
'A phone call came.'

Central to the semantic prototype in (41c), therefore, is an event type where the STATE predicate takes the form EXIST, as in (45). The entity x in such cases has no existence in the field of awareness of the self *prior* to the occurrence of the event, but the coming into existence of a state associated with an entity *already* existing in the field of awareness, as in (46), may be seen as a natural extension of this meaning. Such meaning is exemplified in examples (47)–(48).

(45) [BECOME (EXIST (x))]

(46) → [BECOME (EXIST (STATE (x)))] = [BECOME (STATE (x))]

(47) *Denki ga tui-ta.*
lights NOM come.oNONPST
'The lights came on.'

(48) *Singoo ga kawat-ta.*
traffic.light NOM change-PST
'The traffic light changed.'

The notion of events arising apart from the influence of any external or internal force may appear to run counter to a scientific world view that posits a cause of some kind for any event occurring in the real world. Avoiding the attribution of any force in the *linguistic* expression of an event (41c), however, does not necessarily reflect assumptions the speaker has about the structure of the real world. Such avoidance may, for example, be for reasons of epistemology: the speaker may not know what, if any forces, are at work in the occurrence of an event, even if s/he may believe such a force to be present. A spontaneous mode of linguistic expression allows the speaker in such cases to express the occurrence of an event free from having to identify what forces are responsible for the event, as in (49).

(49) *Denki ga tomat-ta mitai.*
electricity NOM stop-PST EVID
It appears the electricity has stopped.

(49) represents, that is, the speaker's perception pure and simple of a newly arisen state in the absence of evidence as to what real-world causes might have given rise to that state, even when the speaker may believe that such causes exist.

Factors of a pragmatic sort may also play a role in motivating spontaneous modes of expression, allowing the speaker to avoid attribution of responsibility or fault for an event, even when it may be known, for reasons of politeness or other social factors. A spontaneous expression such as (50), for example, would allow the speaker to avoid embarrassment to the hearer in a case where s/he knew that it was in fact the hearer's actions or negligence that brought about the event of the stove breaking.

(50) *Sutoobu ga   koware-ta   mitai.*
     stove   NOM   break-PST   EVID
     'It appears that the stove is (lit., has become) broken.'

Nevertheless, just as the transitive prototype and the causal chain it embodies (Croft 1991) may be seen to have ontological origins in the child's early experience of the world, the intransitive prototype may likewise be seen to have such ontological origins. The notion of causation underlying transitivity, on the one hand, is likely to originate in the awareness of a relationship between intentions in the self and events caused by those intentions in the outside world, eventually broadening to an awareness of a relationship between intentions in other people and real-world events, and ultimately to causal relationships between real-world events that involve no human intentionality. The intransitive prototype, in a distinct but parallel fashion, is likely to originate in the primal experience of sense data spontaneously impinging on the field of awareness of the self, sense data that represent either entities or states of entities, first in the perceptual realm of the self and then extending to changes of state in a world existing independently from that perceptual realm. The exploitation of the intransitive prototype for epistemological and pragmatic purposes would, under this scenario, represent derivative uses appearing at a later stage of cognitive development than that of these early experiences of the world on the ontological level.

There is evidence from first-language acquisition research (Ito 1990; Nomura & Shirai 2012), that the acquisition of intransitive modes of expression predates that of transitive modes of expression, at least in the case of Japanese. This suggests that the intransitive prototype itself is more cognitively basic, in the sense of representing an earlier stage of cognitive development, than the transitive prototype. Even apart from the facts of acquisition, however, it seems natural to assume that the experience of sense data impinging on the consciousness underlies, and precedes, any cognitive judgments regarding the real world entities and forces that those sense data represent, including relationships of causation implicit in the notion of transitive occurrence.

11 Conclusion

Japanese provides convincing evidence that patterns of morphological markedness in intransitive-transitive verb alternations have a semantic basis, evidence that is corroborated in cross-linguistic studies. These patterns point to a fundamental distinction present in human language and experience between two basic event types, one that is typically seen as occurring under the influence of an outside force, and another that is typically seen as occurring without the presence of any such force. Correlations between semantic and morphological markedness must, however, take into account historical shifts in the meaning of verb forms that may skew the effects of such semantic factors.

Past studies of transitivity have tended to assign a more basic role in human language and experience to event occurrence of the transitive type, involving an outside force, than of the intransitive type, involving no such outside force. This bias is evident in the prominence that has been accorded in linguistic analysis to a transitive prototype, formulated in its classic form by Hopper & Thompson (1980), one which involves a maximal differentiation among event participants, and which has been seen to underlie the meaning of both transitive and intransitive members of alternating verb pairs (Levin & Rappaport Hovav 1995).

Evidence from both morphological patterning and adverb collocation in Japanese provides evidence that, to the contrary, intransitive meaning, involving the presence of no external force, is basic to more verb alternations than transitive meaning. This evidence points to the existence of a separate, intransitive prototype, defined in terms of purely spontaneous occurrence wherein no force is present, either external or internal to the event, and involving a single participant entity that is maximally undifferentiated in its semantic role. The intransitive prototype may be seen to have its origins in the primal experience of sense data impinging on the consciousness, a logical and cognitive precondition to notions of causal interaction that underlie the transitive prototype, and representing an earlier stage of cognitive development than the latter.

Abbreviations

ACC accusative; COND conditional; COP copula; EVID evidential; GEN genitive; GER gerund; IMP imperative; in intransitive; INSTR instrumental; LOC locative; NEG negative; NMNL nominalizer; NOM nominative; NONPST nonpast; PASS passive; POT potential; PST past; TEMP temporal; TOP topic; tr transitive.

Acknowledgments

I am grateful to Heiko Narrog, Taro Kageyama, and an anonymous reviewer for their helpful comments on the content and style of an earlier draft of this chapter. These comments made possible considerable improvements in the presentation of the claims made in this chapter, even on points on which I may not be in full agreement with the reviewers, though I of course take responsibility for all defects that remain.

References

Berlin, Brent & Paul Kay. 1969. *Basic color terms: Their universality and evolution.* Berkeley: University of California Press.
Comrie, Bernard. 2006. Transitivity pairs, markedness, and diachronic stability. *Linguistics* 44 (2). 303–318.
Croft, William. 1991. *Syntactic categories and grammatical relations: The cognitive organization of information.* Chicago: University of Chicago Press.
Dowty, David. 1979. *Word meaning and Montague grammar.* Dordrecht: Reidel.
Frellesvig, Bjarke. 2010. *A history of the Japanese language.* Cambridge: Cambridge University Press.
Frellesvig, Bjarke & John Whitman. this volume. The historical source of the bigrade transitivity alternations in Japanese. In Taro Kageyama & Wesley M. Jacobsen (eds.), *Transitivity and valency alternations: Studies on Japanese and beyond.* Berlin & Boston: De Gruyter Mouton.
Haspelmath, Martin. 1993. More on the typology of inchoative/causative verb alternations. In Bernard Comrie & Maria Polinsky (eds.), *Causatives and transitivity* [Studies in Language Companion Series 23], 87–111. Amsterdam & Philadelphia: John Benjamins.
Haspelmath, Martin, Andreea Calude, Michael Spagnol, Heiko Narrog & Elif Bamyaci. 2014. Coding causal-noncausal verb alternations: A form-frequency correspondence explanation. *Journal of Linguistics* 50. 587–625.
Hopper, Paul J. & Sandra Thompson. 1980. Transitivity in grammar and discourse. *Language* 56 (2). 251–299.
Hopper, Paul J. & Elizabeth Traugott. 2003. *Grammaticalization.* Cambridge: Cambridge University Press.
Ito, Katsutoshi. 1990. *Kodomo no kotoba: shūtoku to sōzō* [Children's speech: acquisition and creation]. Tokyo: Keisō Shobō.
Jacobsen, Wesley M. 1985. Morphosyntactic transitivity and semantic markedness. *Chicago Linguistics Society* 21, Part 2. 89–104.
Jacobsen, Wesley M. 1992. *The transitive structure of events in Japanese.* Tokyo: Kurosio Publishers.
Jacobsen, Wesley M. 2007. The semantics of spontaneity revisited. In Susumu Kuno, Seiichi Makino & Susan G. Strauss (eds.), *Aspects of linguistics: In honor of Noriko Akatsuka*, 19–41. Tokyo: Kurosio Publishers.
Jakobson, Roman. 1932. The structure of the Russian verb. Reprinted in Linda Waugh & Morris Halle (eds.), *Russian and Slavic grammar studies, 1931–1981*, 1–14. The Hague: Mouton, 1984.
Kageyama, Taro. 1996. *Dōshi imiron: Gengo to ninchi no setten* [Verb semantics: The interface of language and cognition]. Tokyo: Kurosio Publishers.
Levin, Beth & Malka Rappaport Hovav. 1995. *Unaccusativity: At the syntax – lexical semantics interface.* Cambridge, MA: MIT Press
Matsumoto, Yo. 2000. Causative alternations in English and Japanese: A closer look. *English Linguistics* 17 (1). 160–192. Tokyo: The English Linguistics Society of Japan.
Matsumoto, Yo. this volume. Phonological and semantic subregularities in non-causative/causative verb pairs in Japanese. In Taro Kageyama & Wesley M. Jacobsen (eds.), *Transitivity and valency alternations: Studies on Japanese and beyond.* Berlin & Boston: De Gruyter Mouton.

McCawley, James D. 1978. Notes on Japanese clothing verbs. In Irwin Howard and John Hinds (eds.), *Problems in Japanese syntax and semantics*, 68–78. Tokyo: Kaitakusha.
Næss, Åshild. 2007. *Prototypical transitivity*. Amsterdam & Philadelphia: John Benjamins.
Narrog, Heiko. this volume. Japanese transitivity pairs through time – a historical and typological perspective. In Taro Kageyama & Wesley M. Jacobsen (eds.), *Transitivity and valency alternations: Studies on Japanese and beyond*. Berlin & Boston: De Gruyter Mouton.
Nedjalkov, Vladimir P. 1969. Nekotorye verojatnostnye universalii v glagol'nom slovoobrazovanii. In I. F. Vardul' (ed.), Jazykovye universalii I lingvističeskaja tipologija, 106–114. Moscow: Nauka.
Nichols, Johanna, David A. Peterson & Jonathan Barnes. 2004. Transitivizing and detransitivizing languages. *Linguistic Typology* 8. 149–211.
Nomura, Masami & Yasuhiro Shirai. 2012. Overextension of intransitive verbs in the acquisition of Japanese. Ms. Tokyo: Daito Bunka University.
Rosch, Eleanor. 1975. Cognitive representation of semantic categories. *Journal of Experimental Psychology: General* 104 (3). 192–233.
Searle, John. 1983. *Intentionality*. Cambridge: Cambridge University Press
Shibatani, Masayoshi. this volume. The role of morphology in valency alternation phenomena. In Taro Kageyama & Wesley M. Jacobsen (eds.), *Transitivity and valency alternations: Studies on Japanese and beyond*. Berlin & Boston: De Gruyter Mouton.

Yo Matsumoto
2 Phonological and semantic subregularities in noncausative-causative verb pairs in Japanese

1 Basic facts and questions

Japanese has more than 300 pairs of morphologically related verbs that (typically) represent an event of change and the causation of such an event. Such verb pairs, which we will refer to as noncausative-causative pairs in this chapter, present interesting challenges to morphological analysis and to the study of the interface between form and meaning (Okutsu 1967; Shimada 1979; Jacobsen 1992, this volume; Suga & Hayatsu 1995; Kageyama 1996; Matsumoto 2000a, b, c; Maruta & Suga 2000; Narrog 2007a,b). In this chapter I will examine such pairs for the semantic and phonological regularities to be found in them and discuss the nature of these regularities.

An example of a noncausative-causative verb pair in Japanese is given in (1).

(1) a. Noncausative
    Roopu   ga   kir-e-ru
    rope   NOM cut-DA-NONPST   (DA= Decausativizing affix)
    'The rope gets cut.'

  b. Causative
    Kare ga   roopu o   kir-u
    he   NOM rope   ACC cut-NONPST
    'He cuts a rope.'

An important feature of the members of such pairs is that they are morphologically related, one morphologically more complex than the other, with causativity or noncausativity morphologically marked (Haspelmath 1993) or overtly coded (Haspelmath et al. 2013). The causative verb *kir(-u)* 'cut' in (1b), for example, is a morphologically unaffixed or unmarked verb, while the noncausative verb *kir-e(-ru)* 'become cut' in (1a) is morphologically marked, suffixed by *-e*.

There are three "markedness types" of noncausative-causative verb pairs. Type I is noncausative-basic or causativizing; here the noncausative members

---
Yo Matsumoto, Kobe University

are morphologically unmarked, while the causative ones are marked with the addition of a causativizing affix (CA). Type II is causative-basic or decausativizing; in this case the causative members are unmarked, while the noncausative ones are marked with the addition of a decausativizing affix (DA). Type III is neither, with the two members related by an alternation of stem final sounds (corresponding to Haspelmath's (1993) equipollent pattern). These are shown in (2)–(4).

(2) Type I: Causative verbs affixed with -e, -as, -os, -ase, -akas, or -se
    a. *tat-u*   'stand$_{vi}$ up'   *tat-e-ru*   'stand$_{vt}$ up'
    b. *ugok-u*   'move$_{vi}$'   *ugok-as-u*   'move$_{vt}$'
    c. *mi-ru*   'see'   *mi-se-ru*   'show'

(3) Type II: Noncausative verbs affixed with -e, -ar, -or, -are, or -ore
    a. *kir-e-ru*   'get cut'   *kir-u* 'cut'
    b. *hasam-ar-u*   'be caught between'   *hasam-u* 'catch between'

(4) Type III: Stem-ending alternation with contrasting /r/~/s/, /re/~/s/, /ri/~/s/
    a. *toor-u*   'go through'   *toos-u*   'let through'
    b. *taore-ru*   'fall over'   *taos-u*   'topple'

Several different affixes are found for both causativization and decausativization, and they all have limited productivity. Notably, one of the major affixes, -e, is ambivalent, functioning both as a causativizing and as a decausativizing affix (see (2a) and (3a)). Also notable is the fact that all causativizing affixes except -e contain a phoneme /s/, and all decausativizing affixes except -e contain /r/. Together with the fact that pairs with stem-ending alternation have /r/ for the noncausative members and /s/ for the causative members, all noncausative-causative pairs can be said to involve the /r/ and /s/ contrast whenever a consonant is involved in marking the semantic contrast, a generalization first noted, to my knowledge, by Sakuma (1936).[1]

Note that the /r/ and /s/ endings in Type III pairs are not suffixes (at least in the same sense as -e, -ar and -as are), given that there is no evidence for the morpheme status of the stems minus those stem-final sounds (e.g., *too* in (4a)).

---

[1] This generalization appears to have been independently reached by Jacobsen (1992:59), and is referred to by Nishiyama (2000) as Jacobsen's generalization.

It is nevertheless true that /r/ and /s/ in (4a) mark noncausativity and causativity, respectively. In this sense they convey some kind of meaning, and they are therefore affix-like (I will discuss this issue in Section 5).

The causativizing affixes seen in (2) are crucially different from the -*sase* causative affix, which creates a syntactic biclausal structure at some abstract level of syntactic representation (e.g., Shibatani 1976; Inoue 1976; Matsumoto 1996). In contrast, sentences headed by causative verbs in (2) are purely monoclausal, and so are the causative verbs in (3) and (4). These causative verbs are called *lexical causatives* (Shibatani 1976), and those in (2) are often treated without sublexical morphological analysis. The present chapter, however, takes the view that these forms are morphologically complex.

The purpose of this chapter is two-fold. First, we will look for semantic and phonological regularities in noncausative-causative verb pairs. These include regularities in the choice of markedness patterns, an issue taken up by Jacobsen (1992, this volume) and Narrog (2007a, b), as well as by Haspelmath (1993) and Nichols et al. (2004) in their typological surveys of noncausative-causative alternation and related phenomena. We will also look at regularities in affix choices, which have been discussed by Kageyama (1996) and Matsumoto (2000a, b, c). I will base my discussion on a close examination of a comprehensive list of noncausative-causative verb pairs. The second purpose is to ask what kind of theory is needed to capture the regularities observed. I will point out that Japanese noncausative-causative pairs exhibit layers of phonological and semantic subregularities, which can be best captured by a hierarchy of schemas such as those proposed in Booij (2007, 2010) in the framework of Construction Morphology.

Before proceeding further, some general comments on the range of noncausative-causative verb pairs found in Japanese may be in order. The criterial features of such pairs are that (i) one member has a theme or theme-like argument in the subject, and (ii) the other has the corresponding theme or theme-like argument in the object and has a causer as the subject. The majority of such verb pairs involve one member representing a change of state in the subject, and the other representing a causatively instigated change of state in the object. However, there are some pairs that are somewhat different from such prototypical cases. Some indicate a change of location (rather than state), including *nagare(-ru)/nagas(-u)* 'flow'/'cause to flow' and *ugok(-u)/ugok-as(-u)* 'move'/'cause to move'. In other cases the noncausative verb indicates a state but less clearly its change; e.g., *kanasim(-u)* 'be sad over'. However, all participating verb pairs can be said to represent a change or a changeable state of the subject/object, and therefore can be said to have a theme or theme-like subject/object.

The range of such paired verbs in Japanese is somewhat broader than causative alternation pairs found in languages the reader may be more familiar with (e.g., English, as described in Levin & Rappaport Hovav 1995). For example, unlike what is claimed to be true in English, changes of state necessarily brought about by human beings may be realized in noncausative-causative verb pairs in Japanese. Thus, Japanese not only exhibits pairs of verbs with meanings such as *koware(-ru)/kowas(-u)* 'break/cause to break', but also pairs such as *sir-e(-ru)/sir(-u)* 'become known'/'know', and *tasuk-ar(-u)/tasuke(-ru)* 'become saved (rescued)'/'save (rescue)' (see Jacobsen 1992; Kageyama 1996).

In other cases, noncausative verbs may involve agentivity in addition to change of state. Consider the case of *dok(-u)* 'get out of the way' and *dok-e(-ru)* 'put ... out of the way'. The former represents a change of location in its subject, while the latter represents the causing of such a change in its object. However, *dok(-u)* also encodes the fact that such a change is agentively brought about by the undergoer. Such agentivity of the undergoer is suppressed in the causative counterpart. While verbs representing such agentively caused changes-of-state do not participate in noncausative-causative alternation in some languages, Japanese allows such a possibility.

Another point to note is that Japanese exhibits transitive/ditransitive pairs that can be regarded as variants of noncausative-causative pairs (see Matsumoto 2000a, b). Examples include the following (see Appendix A (pp. 479ff.) for a complete list).

(5) a. *ki(-ru)/ki-se(-ru)* 'get dressed, put ... on one's own body'/'dress, put ... on someone else's body'[2]

b. *abi(-ru)/abi-se(-ru)* 'be covered with (bathed in)'/'pour (over ...)'

c. *mi(-ru)/mi-se(-ru)* 'see'/'show'

d. *azuk-ar(-u)/azuke(-ru))* 'be entrusted with'/'entrust'

---

[2] Members of some of these verb pairs may be regarded as differing in "directedness" rather than causativity. For example, *ki(-ru)* represents a self-directed dressing action while *ki-se(-ru)*, an other-directed dressing action. However, these pairs can also be interpreted as noncausative-causative pairs. *Ki(-ru)* represents a change in state of the subject, in that it comes to be covered with clothing, while *ki-se(-ru)* represents the causing of such a change in the referent of the dative NP. What complicates the picture here is that the change of state represented by *ki(-ru)* is usually brought about by the agentive action of the subject himself/herself. In the process of causativization by which the verb *ki-se(-ru)* is derived, the agentivity of the undergoer is suppressed. This is simply a special case of the kind of agentive suppression mentioned above in connection with *dok(-u)/dok-e(-ru)*.

The transitive members of these pairs encode a change of state in the subject (often instigated by the subject itself), while their ditransitive counterparts encode the causing of such a change in the (dative-marked) object argument, in the same way as intransitive/transitive verb pairs do. These pairs also involve the same affixes as those in causativity-based intransitive/transitive pairs, calling for a unified treatment.³

Finally, two notes on terminology are in order. I have chosen to use the terms *noncausative* and *causative* partially in keeping with the sense in which they are currently used widely among linguists, but they are not without problems. The term causative poses no problem as all "causative" member verbs in fact encode causation of some sort. The term noncausative, on the other hand, is problematic in two respects. First, it is too broad a term, covering action verbs involving no causation of change, such as *hit*, which behave differently from the verbs in question. Second, some "noncausative" verbs in fact represent a change of state brought about by the undergoer (e.g., *dok(-u)* 'get out of way' and *ki(-ru)* 'put ... on one's own body,' discussed above). Although strictly speaking involving causation, such verbs need not be excluded from the "noncausative" category if "noncausative" is taken to mean the absence of an external causer independent of the theme (or undergoer) encoded in the subject of the verb, in contrast to its causative counterpart. The distinction here might alternatively be expressed as "subject-theme" versus "object-theme" verbs, except that the crucial notion of causation in one of the members is left unmentioned in this case. The term inchoative is also often used in the literature to designate noncausative verbs (e.g., Levin & Rappaport Hovav 1995), but this term is better avoided as it carries with it an aspectual sense that may be misleading.

It should also be noted that I use the terms "decausativization" and "causativization" in place of the more commonly-used "intransitivization" and "transitivization". The reason is two-fold. The present study is concerned with causativity-based verb alternations, and such pairs include more than just intransitive and transitive pairs, as noted above. In addition, not all variations in transitivity are causativity-based (Kishimoto, Kageyama & Sasaki 2015). Non-causativity-based alternation, however, falls outside the scope of this chapter.⁴

---

3 Japanese is not the only language that has transitive/ditransitive pairs. Examples of such are also found in Korean, Hindi, and Hebrew.
4 Japanese does have a handful of "labile" verbs, which have identical forms for noncausative and causative meanings (e.g., *hirak(-u)* 'open$_{vi,vt}$', *tozir(-u)* 'close$_{vi,vt}$', *mas(-u)* 'increase$_{vi,vt}$'). These verbs fall outside the scope of this chapter.

2 Preliminaries

2.1 Identifying alternation types

Prior to looking for regularities in verb alternation, we must first clarify how different alternation types are to be identified. Not all scholars agree as to the types of causative alternation that are involved in Japanese. One question concerns the status of pairs like the following.

(6) a. *e/-as*:   *de(-ru)* 'go out'   *d-as(-u)* 'make ... go out'
    b. *e/-akas*: *obiye(-ru)* 'be frightened'   *obiy-akas(-u)* 'threaten'
    c. *i/-as*:   *miti(-ru)* 'fill$_{in}$'   *mit-as(-u)* 'fill$_{tr}$'
    d. *i/-os*:   *oki(-ru)* 'get up, wake up$_{in}$' *ok-os(-u)* 'make ... get up, wake up$_{tr}$'
    e. *-ar/e*:   *ag-ar(-u)* 'go up, rise'   *age(-ru)* 'make ... go up, raise'

The pairs exemplified in (6a–e) may appear to involve common roots like *d*, *mit*, *ok*, and *ag*, with something added to both member verbs. Among these, (6a) (6e) are very common, but cases like (6b, c, d) are also found.

Some scholars treat such pairs as equipollent in terms of directionality or markedness (e.g. Jacobsen 1992, this volume; Haspelmath 1993). There are two possible subvarieties to this view. One is to treat such pairs as involving stem-final sound alternation, similar to the Type III pairs in (4) above; the other is to treat both verbs as containing affixes attached to hypothetical roots that are themselves neutral in causativity (i.e., in this view the root for (6a) is *d*, and the noncausative verb is analyzed as *d-e(-ru)*, with decausativizing *-e*, and the causative verb as *d-as(-u)*, with causativizing *-as*). In contrast, other scholars treat such pairs as involving directionality or difference in markedness, so that (6a, b, c, d) are considered as noncausative-basic, and (6e) as causative-basic (Okutsu 1967; Inoue 1976; Kageyama 1996; Matsumoto 2000a, b, c; Narrog 2007a, b, 2014). On this view, the examples in (6) involve the affixation of *-as/-os/-akas* and *-ar* with the deletion of the final vowel of the base stem.

The present study takes the differential markedness view. The reasons are as follows. First, treating the pairs in (6) as cases of stem-final sound alternation misses the fact that /as/, /os/ and /ar/ are phonologically and semantically identical to *-as*, *-os*, and *-ar* used as affixes. Second, treating both noncausative and causative verbs as containing causativity-changing suffixes encounters a problem in the case of verb pairs where the noncausative member has the stem-final vowel /i/, which allegedly contrasts with *-as* and *-os* in (6b, c). Unlike /e/, the vowel /i/ does not have any use as a decausativizing affix, making the bidirectional derivation account implausible. Third, the status of hypothetical causativity-neutral roots is unclear. There is no evidence for recognizing causativity-neutral roots like *ag* for *ag-ar(-u)* and *age(-ru)*. There *are* cases where the segments without /e/ and /i/ are roots, but, interestingly, in such cases they are not neutral in causativity but are rather either clearly noncausative or clearly causative. Consider the verb pair *more(-ru)* 'leak$_{vi}$' and *mor-as(-u)* 'leak$_{vt}$'. There is in fact a verb without /e/, namely *mor(-u)*, but this is noncausative only, meaning 'leak$_{vi}$', with a slightly more restricted meaning than *more(-ru)*.[5] (Thus /e/ in *more(-ru)* is an affix that does not alter causativity.) Or consider the verb pair *kire(-ru)* 'get cut, run out' and *kir-as(-u)* 'make/let ... run out'. There is a verb form without /e/, *kir(-u)* (cf. (1) above) but this verb is clearly causative, meaning 'cut' (so the derivation is *kir(-u)* → *kir-e(-ru)* → *kir-as(-u)*, and /e/ in *kir-e(-ru)* is the decausativizing *-e*). These are situations difficult to account for in a view that posits hypothetical causativity-neutral roots.

In the present account, when *-as* and other affixes are suffixed, the preceding vowel /e/ or /i/ drops out regardless of its nature. /e/ may be simply a stem-final vowel (as in *de(-ru)*), or a nonalternating affix (as in *mor-e(-ru)*, < *mor-u*), or a decausativizing affix (as in *kir-e(-ru)* < *kir-u*). This view does not run into any of the problems pointed out above with respect to the equipollence analysis.

The reason some researchers are drawn to the equipollence analysis may be the predominance of /e/ ending in base member verbs in (6) and the use of *-e* as an affix. Why is it that most of the morphologically unmarked verbs of the types in (6) end with /e/? This is merely a reflection of a more general tendency in Japanese verb endings. /e/ and /i/ are the only vowels allowed in stem-final position with Japanese verbs, and between the two, /e/ is much more common.

2.2 Data for the present study

The data in this study are based on my own list of 306 noncausative-causative verb pairs in contemporary Japanese. This list is based on a reexamination of

---

5 While *mor(-u)* can only be used for the leakage of liquid, *mor-e(-ru)* can be used for that of gas and certain other entities in addition. The causative verb *mor-as(-u)* can take both gas and liquid as its object, and so it is the causative form of *mor-e(-ru)*, though it can also be the causative of *mor(-u)*. Other pairs involving nonalternating *-e* are listed in the List of Additional Pairs in Appendix B. See Matsumoto (2007) for more on the semantic differences between *mor(-u)* and *mor-e(-ru)* and other similar pairs involving nonalternating *-e*. Pairs like these exist because of the fluctuation of certain verbs between the so-called *godan* and *shimoichidan* verb conjugation classes.

Jacobsen's (1992) list as well as on a close examination of verbs listed in *Iwanami Goitaikei*. The list is given in Appendix A on pp. 479ff. (List of Core Pairs). This list is an improvement over Jacobsen's in the following respects. 1) pairs missing in Jacobsen's list are added (e.g., *kanaw(-u)/kanaw-e(-ru)* 'come true'/'make ... come true'; 2) mistakes in classification are corrected (e.g., *nor(-u)/nose(-ru)* 'ride'/'mount' now classified as Type III with a correct morpheme boundary on *nor(-u)*); 3) transparently complex verbs such as compound verbs and deadjectival verbs with -*m(-)ar/-me* are excluded (e.g., *ara-dat(-u)/ara-dat-e(-ru)* 'become rough'/'make rough', and *taka-m-ar(-u)/ taka-me(-ru)* 'become higher'/'make higher')[6]; 4) pairs involving archaic and rare verbs are excluded (e.g., *aki(-ru)/*ak-as(-u)* 'get bored, get satisfied'/*'make ... bored of, satisfy'); 5) pairs whose status as noncausative-causative pairs is dubious are excluded. This last point is the result of a finer systematic examination of the semantics and morphology of these pairs. Pairs that synchronically exhibit a remote semantic correspondence are excluded (e.g., *mukaw(-u)/mukaw-e(-ru)* 'head for'/'welcome'). Judgments concerning semantic relatedness are due to the present author. The morphology of verb pairs is also more systematically examined, and pairs that are not synchronically directly related are excluded (e.g. *hair(-u)/ire(-ru)* 'go in'/'put in'). Along with the List of Core Pairs (Appendix A, pp. 479ff.), a list of verbs omitted from this list is also provided in Appendix B (pp. 489ff.) under the List of Additional Pairs.

The data in the present study also differs from those used in previous studies in the following respects. It differs from Jacobsen (1992, this volume) and the treatment of Japanese in Haspelmath (1993) in that a different analysis is adopted of apparently equipollent pairs. As noted earlier, Jacobsen and Haspelmath adopt an equipollence analysis for pairs like *de(-ru)* and *d-as(-u)* in (6), and the majority of pairs in their database belong to the equipollent type. Adopting a differential markedness analysis for pairs exemplified in (6), our database contains more examples of causativizing and decausativizing pairs than Jacobsen's and Haspelmath's. It also differs from Haspelmath (1993) and Nichols et al. (2004) in that it includes *all* verb pairs in Japanese rather than a select few. Narrog's (2007a, b) diachronic study of Japanese noncausative-causative alternation is similar to the present one in many respects, but the present study is purely synchronic. The database used in the present chapter

---

[6] Most deadjectival verb pairs involve the suffixation of -*ar* to causative verbs formed from an adjective root (e.g., *taka* 'high') and a verbalizing suffix -*m(e)* (see Sugioka 2002). There are, however, forms like *tika-m-ar(-u)* (near-Vblz-DA-NONPST) 'become near', which do not have "source" causative counterparts, suggesting that -*mar(-u)* may have become a verbalizing affix for creating noncausative verbs from an adjective directly.

will thus make possible thorough and accurate statistical analyses of the type frequencies of the relevant verb pairs in modern Japanese, yielding new insights into the morphology and semantics of these alternation patterns.[7]

3 Markedness types and semantics

3.1 Backgrounds

Directionality or differing markedness in noncausative-causative pairs has been discussed in the typological literature from two perspectives. One is how skewed a particular language is in terms of its preference toward decausativization or causativization. Nichols et al. (2004) claim that languages may differ in terms of this preference: some languages tend to make greater use of causativization, and others decausativization. (Nichols et al.'s observation is based on a much wider range of alternations than those seen in "lexical causatives" considered in this chapter, such as those involving syntactic causativization.) In this regard, Narrog (2007a,b) claims that Japanese exhibits more cases of causativization (of noncausative verbs) than decausativization (of causative verbs), based on a count of type frequencies of both patterns at different stages of the history of Japanese, and treats Japanese as a "transitivizing" language, concurring with Nichols et al. (2004).

The second issue that has received attention in the typological literature is whether there exist semantic correlations to the morphological markedness types when a language allows more than one type. It is often claimed that the choice of markedness types is based on whether a given process is typically brought about by an external force, or is due to a cause internal to the undergoer. Such tendencies are pointed out in various forms by Nedjalkov (1969), Haspelmath (1993), and Comrie (2006). A related but different view is taken by Nichols et al. (2004: 172), who observe that languages tend to "lexicalize actions or states of human (or animates more generally) as primary." On this view, noncausative verbs with human undergoers can be basic even if they represent changes not internally caused.

---

[7] See Plag (2006) for the view that productivity of an affix can be measured by counting the number of attested different words with the particular affix (i.e., type-frequency). He claims that type frequency may be indicative of past productivity. The phenomena targeted in the current study are not synchronically productive, at least in most cases, and so it is not unreasonable to use type frequencies for identifying the productivity of an affix.

Previous studies on Japanese causative alternation have presented related findings. Morphological markedness types in Japanese have been claimed to be semantically motivated, at least partially (Jacobsen 1992, this volume). It is claimed by Jacobsen (1992: 75) that many of the Type I verb pairs express "changes normally seen to occur either spontaneously or as being brought about by [the referent of the subject] in itself". He notes that noncausative verbs in Type I typically include animate motion verbs (e.g., 'fly'), verbs of bodily pain (e.g., 'suffer', 'hurt'), and verbs expressing events that typically happen without any apparent causative source (e.g., 'grow', 'sink'). Type II pairs, on the other hand, are claimed to involve "changes normally seen to occur under the influence of an outside agent." Many Type II causative verbs, he notes, are verbs of destruction and violence (e.g., 'break', 'cut', crush', 'tear').

However, it is also known that these are mere tendencies and counterexamples are easy to find (Jacobsen 1992; Matsumoto 2000b). For example, there are Type I verbs representing events that do not normally occur spontaneously.

(7) Exceptions to typical Type I semantics
 totonow(-u) 'become ready'   totonow-e(-ru) 'make ready, put in order'
 todok(-u) 'be delivered, reach'   todok-e(-ru) 'deliver'

The existence of such verbs necessitates a statistical analysis of the tendencies observed.

In addition, it is not entirely clear if all major verbs of the Type I class can in fact be characterized as expressing events that occur spontaneously or as being brought about in the subject by itself. It is not clear, for example, why verbs of bodily pain above can be characterized as such. Psych verbs are also known to be primarily of the Type I class, but these do require an outside cause or stimulus. Interestingly, these are verbs that have human undergoers, suggesting that this factor may also be relevant in Japanese, at least in certain cases.

3.2 Correlations between undergoer type and causal nature of the change

In our database, the numbers of Type I, Type II, and Type III pairs amount to 145, 117 and 44, respectively. There are more cases of causativization than of decausativization, although application of the Sign Test shows that the difference does not reach a level of statistical significance at the 0.05% level ($p = 0.08$).

We examined all of these verbs for two factors that appear to contribute to the choice of markedness type. The first factor is the *nature of the undergoer*.

Verb pairs can be classified according to whether they represent a change of state [A] in a human being or other higher animate (including its group or its part), or [B] in an inanimate entity or any entity in general (i.e., human/animate undergoers vs. inanimate/neutral undergoers). The first category includes both psychological changes of state and changes in bodily condition (e.g., 'become tired') and other characteristics of human or animate beings. The second factor is the *causal nature of the change*. Verb pairs can be classified into [1] those representing changes that are necessarily brought about by a human being or some other external force or stimulus (inherently caused changes), [2] those representing changes that can occur naturally (naturally occurring changes), and [3] those that are neutral in this respect. See Appendix A for how each verb pair is classified.[8]

3.2.1 Undergoer type and markedness type

Table 1 shows the relationship between undergoer type and markedness type.

Table 1: Undergoer type and markedness type

undergoer	markedness type		
	Type I	Type II	Type III
Human/Animate	58	14	8
Inanimate/Neutral	87	103	36

The difference between verb pairs with human/animate undergoers and those with inanimate/neutral undergoers is statistically significant ($\chi^2(2) = 28.04$, $p < 0.001$). A residual analysis suggests that human/animate undergoers are associated significantly more often with Type I and less often with Type II, and the tendency is opposite with inanimate/neutral undergoers ($p < 0.001$). At the same time, there are many Type I pairs that do not have human/animate undergoers. This means that human/animate undergoer is one important feature for Type I pairs, but is not the only factor determining the markedness type.

A further analysis was conducted based on a finer semantic subcategorization of verb pairs. Human/animate changes were subdivided into [A-1] human/animate motion, and [A-2] human/animate change of state. Inanimate/neutral

---

8 All judgments regarding classification of verbs are due to the author. When members of a verb pair do not have the same range of meanings, the judgment is based on the most common meaning shared by the members of a verb pair.

changes were subdivided into [B-1] inanimate/neutral motion, [B-2] inanimate/ neutral change of state, and [B-3] degree change .

Motion categories [A-1] and [B-1] were then further classified into those representing [1a] manner of motion (e.g., 'fly', 'drip'), [1b] path of motion (e.g., 'go into', 'pass'), and [1c] location change accompanied by a state change (e.g., 'soak in', 'get buried') (see Matsumoto 1997). Changes in human/animate state [A-2] were subdivided into [A-2a] change in outer physical state (e.g., 'stand up'), [A-2b] change in inner bodily condition (e.g., 'wake up'), [A-2c] change in psychological state (e.g., 'become surprised'), [A-2d] biological change ('be born'), [A-2e] change with respect to the possession of concrete or abstract entities (e.g., 'be entrusted with'), and [A-2f] change in abstract status (e.g., 'be saved').[9] Changes in state of inanimate entities [B-2] were subcategorized into [B-2a] disintegration (e.g., 'break', 'become cut'), [B-2b] change of shape (e.g., 'bend'), [B-2c] change in other physical properties (e.g., 'melt'), [B-2d] "spatio-relational" change, in which a (spatial) relationship between objects or parts of an object changes (e.g., 'be connected', 'open'), [B-2e] existential change (e.g., 'appear', 'become exhausted (run out)'), [B-2f] change in semi-abstract status (e.g., 'be put in order'), [B-2g] purely abstract change associated with human activity (e.g., 'be sold'), and [B-2h] aspectual change (e.g., 'begin'). A detailed classification of verb pairs is given in the appendix.

Markedness patterns with these various subcategories of verb pairs are as shown in Table 2.

Almost all subtypes of motion and change with human/animate undergoers are noncausative-basic (Type I), confirming that not just psych predicates but almost all predicates involving change of state in human/animate beings are predominantly Type I. Different subtypes of motion and change with inanimate/ neutral undergoers exhibit different tendencies, suggesting that other factors are at work (see below). As noted earlier by Jacobsen (1992), manner of motion is predominantly noncausative-basic, and interestingly this is true even when the undergoer is inanimate/neutral.

3.2.2 Causal nature of change and markedness types

Some changes are necessarily induced by human beings or some external force or stimulus, and other changes can occur in nature without human intervention.

---

9 Initially, attempts were made to classify verbs in terms of *Bunrui Goihyō* (NINJAL thesaurus of Japanese words) and Levin's (1993) verb class categories in English. These classifications turn out to miss some important distinctions relevant to our discussion and so a new classification was adopted.

Table 2: Semantic subcategories of verb pairs and markedness type

Broad and narrow categories		Markedness type		
		Type I	Type II	Type III
Motion (human/animate)	Manner	2	0	1
	Path	2	0	1
	Location+state change	4	0	0
Change of state (human/animate)	Outer state	13	1	1
	Inner state	9	2	1
	Psychological	13	2	0
	Biological	3	1	1
	Possessional	3	3	2
	Abstract	2	4	1
	Other	7	0	0
Motion (inanimate/neutral)	Manner	4	0	3
	Path	10	5	9
	Location+state change	7	19	5
	Other	4	4	1
Change of state (inanimate/neutral)	Disintegration	2	17	4
	Shape	7	5	0
	Physical properties	14	7	4
	Spatio-relational	7	16	2
	Existential	6	0	2
	Semi-abstract	7	6	3
	Abstract	7	10	2
	Aspectual	3	2	0
	Other	1	5	1
Degree Change		7	5	0

How does this contrast correlate with markedness type? Table 2 above presents evidence for the relevance of the role of the causal nature of change to markedness type. Among verbs expressing a change of state in inanimate entities, verbs of disintegration are predominantly causative-basic. Since disintegration requires an outer force, this is a reflection of inherently caused change favoring Type II (as noted by Jacobsen). However, the relevance of causal nature to markedness types is not clear in other subcategories.

In order to clarify the relevance of causal nature of the change to markedness type, all verb pairs were individually analyzed for their causal nature. Some changes are by their very nature brought about by a causative force – i.e., are inherently caused. Among these, some require a strong external force (human or nonhuman) to occur; e.g., 'break' and 'be scraped'. Other changes necessarily require an external stimulus of some kind; e.g., 'become surprised' and 'become thrilled'. Still other inherently caused changes are necessarily brought about by human beings. These include 1) changes brought about with the use of a tool, including fire (implying the presence of human activity); e.g., 'become sharpened' and 'get fried/sautéed'; 2) changes brought about with the use of human body parts; e.g., 'be born'; 3) changes brought about with carefulness, effort, or planning attributed to human beings; e.g., 'become orderly'; 4) changes presupposing human perception or cognition (e.g., 'become visible' and 'become known'); and 5) changes presupposing social convention (e.g., 'become sold').

In contrast, some changes are naturally occurring, arising due to atmospheric changes (e.g., 'melt'), gravity (e.g., 'fall'), movement of the earth or sun (e.g., 'dawn breaking'), or the normal functioning of organisms (e.g., 'grow'). Changes that are not clearly categorizable in terms of the causal nature of change are grouped in the "Other" category. See the appendix for how particular verbs are classified.

The identification of verb pairs representing inherently caused changes and naturally occurring changes was done with the assistance of three native speakers of Japanese who were asked to judge the acceptability of Japanese sentences meaning 'Things usually do not [Verb] of themselves' and 'Things usually [Verb] naturally (when they [Verb])', respectively, where a noncausative verb appears in the [Verb] slot. Only those pairs passing these judgment tests were regarded as inherently caused or naturally occurring.[10]

Markedness types found among verb pairs classified according to the causal nature of the change they express are shown in Table 3.

This table shows that naturally occurring changes are exclusively noncausative-basic (causativizing), while inherently caused changes are predominantly causative-basic (decausativizing), except for those involving external stimuli. Application of the chi-square test to the totality of verbs expressing naturally occurring changes, inherently caused changes, and other changes revealed a level of statistical significance (Yates' $\chi^2 = 86.19$, dif. = 4, $p < 0.001$). There are a sizable number of verbs in the "Other" category which are predominantly noncausative-basic, suggesting that some other factor may also be at work here.

---

10 The actual steps taken were as follows. For inherently caused changes three native speakers were asked to judge the acceptability of the sentence *Futsuu X-wa {katte-ni/hitoride-ni} Y-suru koto-wa nai* "Normally X does not do Y of itself," in which a noncausative verb is inserted in Y, and an appropriate general nominal is inserted in X. For naturally occurring changes, the sentence form employed was *Futsuu X-ga Y-suru toki {hitoride-ni/shizen-ni} Y-suru* "Normally X does Y {of itself/naturally} when it does Y." If at least two of the three native speakers said yes to the acceptability of the sentence and the third did not say absolutely no, then the sentence was considered to have passed the test.

Table 3: Causal nature of change and markedness type

causal nature of change			Type I	Type II	Type III
			\multicolumn{3}{l}{markedness type}
Naturally occurring			20	0	2
Inherently caused	External stimulus		9	1	0
	External force		10	24	3
	Humanly induced	tool use	5	15	2
		body part use	0	4	1
		care, effort, plan, etc.	8	24	1
		cognition	0	7	0
		social background	6	9	2
Other			96	34	33

Table 4: Type I vs. Type II ratio of verb pairs according to undergoer type and causal nature type

	Causal nature				
		\multicolumn{3}{l}{Inherently caused}	
Undergoer	Naturally occurring	External stimulus	External force	Humanly induced	Other
Human/Animate	7:0	9:1	3:1	4:10	44:3
Inanimate/Neutral	13:0	0:0	7:23	15:49	52:31

The findings in this and the previous sections suggest that undergoer type and causal nature of the change both contribute to the choice of markedness types in noncausative-causative verb pairs. The data cannot be accounted for by any single one of these factors, so that both factors appear to be relevant. This becomes clearer when the interaction of the two factors is considered. What would be the markedness type when a humanly induced change of state has a human undergoer (e.g., 'be born'/'give birth to' and 'learn'/'teach') or when a naturally occurring change has an inanimate/neutral undergoer? Table 4 shows the ratio between Type I and Type II verb pairs according to undergoer type and causal nature type.

This table confirms that verb pairs representing naturally occurring changes are noncausative-basic, whether or not they involve a human undergoer. The influence of either factor of inherent causation or human vs. animate undergoer may be overridden by the other factor. Verb pairs representing inherently caused changes tend to be causative-basic but tend not to be so in verb pairs with human/animate undergoers, especially when an external stimulus is involved.

Verb pairs with human/animate undergoers tend to be noncausative-basic except for those representing humanly caused changes. The preference for causativization with changes involving a human/animate undergoer is clearly seen in "other" changes, where the causal nature of the change is irrelevant.

The two factors favoring causativization, i.e., natural occurrence and human/animate undergoer, do not commonly pattern together. There are only 7 verb pairs (e.g., *sodat(-u)/sodat-e(-ru)* 'grow'/'raise') in which the two factors are consistent, suggesting that the two may not together form a clear prototype.

3.2.3 Markedness types and affixes

Are these tendencies generalizations at the level of markedness type, and not at the affix level? Tables 5 and 6 show the relationship between undergoer and causal nature type, respectively, and affix type.

Table 5: Undergoer type and markedness type/affix

	markedness/affix				
	Type I		Type II		Type III
undergoer	-e	-as, etc	-e	-ar, etc	
Human/animate	15	43	1	13	8
Inanimate/neutral	23	64	37	66	36

Table 6: Causal nature and markedness types/affix

	markedness/affix				
	Type I		Type II		Type III
causal nature	-e	-as, etc	-e	-ar, etc	
Inherently caused	11	18	32	51	9
Naturally occurring	3	17	0	0	2
Other	24	72	6	28	33

Table 5 shows that human/animate undergoer pairs prefer Type I over Type II, and that this is true regardless of affix used. Table 6 also shows that inherently caused changes prefer Type II, again regardless of affix used. The only exception is naturally occurring changes, which predominantly use *-as*. Thus, except for this last case the tendencies observed in this section tend to hold regardless of the particular affix used. I will discuss the case of naturally occurring changes below.[11]

4 Choice of affix

How, then, are particular affixes chosen for decausativization or causativization? There are two opposing views on this issue in the previous literature.

4.1 Previous accounts: Semantic or phonological?

It has been claimed that different causativizing and decausativizing affixes are associated with different semantic operations. For example, in his influential work Kageyama (1996) claims that causativizing -e and -as/-os are associated with different semantic structures, which he formulates as follows in his theory of lexical conceptual structure.

(8) -e: [x CONTROL [EVENT ...]]

 -as, -os; [[EVENT x ACT] CAUSE [EVENT...]]

However, the semantics of -e verbs and that of -as/-os verbs in fact vary considerably within each verb group, and it is not realistic to suppose that all verbs with the same affix have the same semantic structure (Matsumoto 2000b). For example, the above semantic structure for -as/-os posits an event as the first argument of CAUSE, which is based on the observation that -as/-os verbs (mostly causative psych verbs in Kageyama's study) can take an event as subject. However, this is not true of all -as/-os verbs. -As/-os verbs representing a physical change of state, for example, generally cannot take an event as subject. This is true of verbs like *megur-as(-u)* 'surround, fence' *tob-as(-u)* 'fly$_{vt}$', *d-as(-u)* 'take out', *kog-as(-u)* 'scorch', *hekom-as(-u)* 'dent', *tar-as(-u)* 'drip', *mak-as(-u)* 'defeat', *mor-as(-u)* 'leak$_{vt}$', *tizir-as(-u)* 'curl', *or-os(-u)* 'bring down', *ot-os(-u)* 'drop$_{vt}$', and *mit-as(-u)* 'fill'. On the other hand, psych verbs can take an event

---

[11] It is worth examining whether "apparently Type III" pairs discussed in Section 2.1 are semantically similar to Type III pairs. Table A shows the relationship between markedness types and the nature of undergoers, with Type I pairs divided into those to which a suffix is placed on a consonant stem (clear Type I), and those to which it is placed on a vowel stem with a vowel deleted (apparently Type III). The former include verbs with any suffixes (the number of those with suffixes other than -e is indicated in the parentheses), while the latter can only have

suffixes other than -e. The table shows that the apparently Type III pairs exhibit a pattern slightly different both from clear Type I pairs and from Type III pairs, though neither difference reaches the 0.05% significance level by Fischer's Exact test.

Table A: markedness types and nature of undergoers with two subtypes of Type I pairs

undergoer	markedness type		Type III
	Type I		
	suffixed to Cons. stems	suffixed to Vowel stems	
Human/Animate	37 (22)	21	8
Inanimate/Neutral	44 (21)	43	36

Table B shows the relationship between markedness types and nature of undergoers, with Type II pairs divided into those to which a suffix is placed on a consonant stem (clear Type II), and those to which it is placed on a vowel stem with a vowel deleted (apparently Type III). The former include verbs with any suffixes (the number of verbs with suffixes other than -e is indicated in the parentheses), while the latter can only have suffixes other than -e. The table shows that apparently Type III pairs exhibit a pattern similar both to clear Type II pairs and to Type III pairs (the differences are nonsignificant at 0.01% level by Fischer's Exact test).

Table B: markedness types and nature of undergoers with two subtypes of Type II pairs

undergoer	markedness type		Type III
	Type II		
	suffixed to Cons. stems	suffixed to Vowel stems	
Human/Animate	4 (3)	10	8
Inanimate/Neutral	45 (8)	57	36

Table C shows the relationship between markedness types and causal nature, with Type I pairs divided into clear Type I pairs, and apparently Type III pairs. The latter shows a pattern similar to clear Type I pairs as well as Type III pairs (the differences are nonsignificant at 0.01% level by Chi-square test).

Table C: markedness types and causal nature with two subtypes of Type I pairs

causal nature	markedness type		Type III
	Type I		
	suffixed to Cons. stems	suffixed to Vowel stems	
inherently caused	16 (5)	13	9
naturally occurring	11 (8)	9	2
other	54 (30)	42	33

as subject regardless of the affix used (e.g., *kurusim-e(-ru)* 'torture' can take an event as subject). Based on these observations, Matsumoto (2000b) argues that semantic classes of verbs (or conceptual domains of the events that verbs represent) are a better predictor of whether the subject can be an event or not.

In contrast to the semantic view above, Matsumoto (2000a, b) claims that the choice of an affix is phonologically restricted, at least partially (cf. Kuginuki 1996). He points out that suffixation of causativizing *-e* and decausativizing *-e* is restricted to base verb stems ending in a consonant or the vowel /i/ (i.e., stems that do not end in /e/), while that of causativizing *-as* and decausativizing *-ar* is not conditioned by phonology. Other causativizing affixes are also phonologically conditioned: *-os* is used for base verb stems containing the vowel /o/;[12] *-se* is used mostly for single-syllable base verb stems ending in the vowel /i/; and *-akas* is for base stems ending in /ye/ (and /re/). These affixes differ in the specificity of their phonological environments, and those with a more specific range of application tend to be given priority. Thus, since *-se* is used for single-syllable base stems ending in /i/, there are no clear cases in Modern Japanese where *-as* or *-os* is applied to such base stems. This kind of "phonological habitat segregation" also involves /r/~/s/ stem-final sound alternation. Decausativizing affixes are rarely applied to causative verb stems ending in /s/, since the /r/~/s/ alternation takes precedence in such cases. (Noncausative stems ending

---

Table D shows the relationship between markedness types and causal nature, with Type II pairs divided into clear Type II pairs and apparently Type III pairs. The latter shows a pattern somewhat different from clear Type II pairs (significant at 0.005 level by Fischer's Exact test) but more clearly different from Type III pairs (significant at 0.0001% level).

Table D: markedness types and causal nature with two subtypes of Type II pairs

causal nature	markedness type		
	Type II		Type III
	suffixed to Cons. stems	suffixed to Vowel stems	
inherently caused	43 (11)	40	9
naturally occurring	0 (0)	0	2
other	7 (1)	27	33

Thus, those apparently Type III pairs often exhibit a pattern clearly different from Type III pairs, though they tend to lie between Type III pairs and clear Type I or Type II pairs in terms of semantics.

12 Mabuchi (1999) claims that the choice between *-as* and *-os* in Old Japanese was based on vowel harmony.

in /r/ also have the option of -*as* suffixation; see below.) Based on these observations, Matsumoto (2000b) claims that suffix choices are essentially phonological in nature.

In the following sections we will examine the phonological and semantic nature of affix choices in terms of our data, which will suggest that affixes do exhibit both phonological and semantic differences.

4.2 The phonology of affixation

Let us begin with an examination of the phonological environments in which affixes appear. Our data confirm the view that affixes differ in the phonological environments in which they occur. Among decausativizing affixes, -*e* is attached to 38 causative verb stems, 36 of which end in a consonant, and the other two in /i/. -*Ar* is attached to 68 base verb stems, 60 of which end in /e/ and the rest in a consonant. As for causativization, the suffix -*e* is attached to 37 noncausative verb stems, all of which end in a consonant. (There are two cases where -*e* is attached to base verb stems ending in /i/ among verb pairs whose semantic relations are opaque; e.g., *iki(-ru)* 'live' and *ik-e(-ru)* 'arrange (living flowers)'.) -*As* is suffixed to 32 consonant base stems and 50 vowel base stems.

One important question remains, however, for the phonology view: how an affix is chosen for base verb stems ending in a consonant, where both -*e* and -*as* should be possible for causativization and -*e* and -*ar* for decausativization. Our data show that there are phonological conditions again: the choice is largely predictable from the particular final sounds of the base verbs to which affixes are attached (I owe this idea to Kuginuki's (1996: 307–335) description of Old Japanese verb morphology). This is very clear in the case of decausativization, as seen in Table 7, which shows the number of Type II base (unmarked) causative verb endings in each consonant and the available choices for decausativizing affix in each case.

Table 7: Stem-final consonants of Type II causative verbs and decausativizing affixes

affix	final cons.						
	m	w	b	r	k	g	other
-e	0	0	0	19	13	4	2
-ar, -are, etc.	5	1	0	0	0	3	2

The table shows that all of those causative stems ending in /k/ and /r/ are suffixed by -*e* (as in *kudak-e(-ru)* and *kir-e(-ru)*), while all of those ending in

/m/ are suffixed by -ar (as in hasam-ar(-u) 'be caught between'). The numbers here confirm that the choice of affix is determined by the stem-final consonant of the base verb, except in the case of /g/.

Table 8 shows the number of Type I base noncausative verbs ending in each consonant and the choices for causativizing affix in each case.

Table 8: Stem-final consonants of Type I noncausative verbs and causativizing affixes

affix	final cons						
	m	w	b	r	k	g	other
-e	19	4	2	0	8	2	3
-as, -os, etc.	6	5	5	8	12	1	0

This table shows that there is one consonant -e clearly avoids. Noncausative verb stems ending in /r/ are all suffixed by -as (as in her-as(-u) 'decrease'); -e is not an option in that case.[13] In contrast, there is no consonant that -as and its variants completely avoid. In stems ending in consonants other than /r/, -e or -as may be weakly preferred over the other; those ending in /k/ weakly prefer -as or its variants, while those ending in /m/ weakly prefer -e, though cases involving other affixes are also found.

Why is causativizing -e disfavored for /r/-ending base verbs? A key to the answer is found in the patterns of decausativization, in which -e also participates. As Table 7 above shows, causative stems ending in /r/ (and also /k/) all select -e for decausativization. It appears that causativizing -e is avoided for noncausative stems ending in /r/ since the addition of -e for /r/ base stems is reserved for decausativization.

This preference for decausativizing -e for /r/ causative stems is also related to a tendency observed in the phonological shapes of noncausative verbs which are not marked with a decausativizing affix. /re/ is a very common stem ending among noncausative verbs in Type I (noncausative-basic) pairs (to which -as and other suffixes are attached to derive causative verbs). Table 9 shows the phonological shapes of Type I noncausative verb stems ending in /e/.

Table 9: Final syllables of Type I noncausative verb stems ending in /e/

Final syllable	me	we	be	re	ke	ge	ye	other
# of verbs	2	1	0	21	10	3	11	2

---

[13] The verb ir-e(-ru) 'put in' may be an exception, but the base noncausative verb ir(-u) is now obsolete as an independent verb and is not included in our core list of verb pairs.

Table 9 shows that basic noncausative verbs ending in /e/ exhibit an uneven distribution of final syllables. There are many ending in /re/ (e.g., *nure(-ru)* 'get wet'), accounting for 42% of the total; many also end in /ke/ (e.g., *make (-ru)* 'be defeated') and /ye/ (e.g., *obiye(-ru)* 'be terrified'). This means that /re/ is a very common final syllable for basic noncausative verbs. The affixation of *-e* to causative stems ending in /r/ would result in a verb shape preferred for noncausative verbs.[14]

In contrast, /re/ is an utterly unfavored stem-final syllable for causative verbs, even among those which are not marked with a causativizing affix. Table 10 shows the stem-final syllables of the basic causative verbs among Type II (causative-basic) verb pairs (to which *-ar* and other suffixes are attached to derive noncausative verbs).

Table 10: Final syllables of Type II causative verb stems ending in /e/

Final syllable	me	we	be	re	ke	ge	ye	other
# of verbs	34	9	0	0	10	5	0	8

This table shows that there are no attested basic causative verb stems ending in /re/. Thus affixation of *-e* to noncausative stems ending in /r/ would create this nonexisting verb shape for causative verbs.[15]

This situation is summarized in Figure 1.

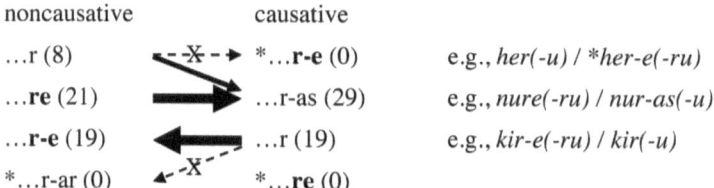

Figure 1: Suffix choice and noncausative-causative verb stems ending in /r/ and /re/

---

14 Those stems ending in /ke/ invariably take *-as* as causativizing affix (e.g., *mak-as(-u)* 'defeat'). The high number of causative verbs ending in /kas/ appears to be related to the fact that *-akas* has developed into an affix (see Aoki 2010: Part II). It is also to be noted that Old Japanese preferred *-e* as a causativizing rather than decausativizing suffix for verbs ending in /k/ (Kuginuki 1996), whereas this form is more commonly used for decausativization than causativization in present-day Japanese. Perhaps the increased number of cases of *-as* suffixation for stems ending in /k/ is related to this change in the character of *-e* suffixation.

15 The tendency for *-as* to be used exclusively on base verb stems ending in /r/ is reinforced by the commonality of causative verbs ending in /ras/, which may originate in another source. As shown in Table 9, there are many base noncausative verb stems ending in /re/. These take *-as*, and less commonly *-os*, for causativization, with /e/ deleted, resulting in a high number of causative verbs ending in /ras/ (*nur-as(-u)* 'make wet').

One may note here that /re/ as a preferred stem-final syllable for noncausative verbs goes much further than discussed above. /re/ stem endings are found among those verbs suffixed by decausativizing -are and -ore (variants of -ar; e.g., wakat-are(-ru) 'become divided'), and those that exhibit a /re/~/s/ stem-final sound alternation (e.g., koware(-ru) 'break$_{vi}$'). The number of /re/ noncausative verb stems totals 64, combining those with -e added to an /r/-final causative verb stem, those ending in /re/ among basic noncausative verbs for Type I pairs (Table 9), those with affixes ending in /re/ (e.g., with -are, -ore), and those ending in /re/ exhibiting stem-final sound alternation (i.e., /re/~/s/), accounting for as much as 57% of all noncausative verbs whose stems end in /e/![16]

A similar situation is found for base verb stems ending in /m/. The suffix -e is used to causativize noncausative verb stems ending in /m/ (see Table 8), but not to decausativize causative verb stems ending in /m/ (Table 7). This is consistent with the fact that /me/ is a very common ending in basic causative verb stems (Table 10), and that there are only a limited number of basic /me/ noncausative verb stems (Table 9). This situation is summarized in Figure 2.

noncausative   causative

...m (25)   ...m-e (19)   e.g., *sizum(-u) / sizum-e(-ru)*
...**me** (2)   ...m-as (8)   e.g., *same(-ru) / sam-as(-u)*
*...**m-e** (0)   ...m (5)   e.g., **tukam-e(-ru) / tukam(-u)*
...m-ar (39)   ...**me** (34)   e.g., *atum-ar(-u) / atume(-ru)*

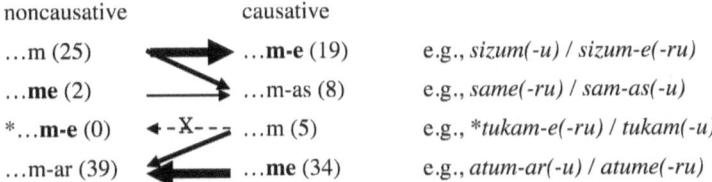

Figure 2: Suffix choice and noncausative-causative verb stems ending in /m/ and /me/

The discussion in this section has shown that choice of affix is phonologically governed to a high degree. Causativizing and decausativizing -e is restricted to verbs ending in a consonant (or /i/), and moreover the suffixation of -e to certain consonant base stems is avoided when it would create a phonological shape nonexistent or disfavored among the basic verbs in the target meaning.

Differential preferences for affixes in different phonological environments may also lead to a phonologically-based, differential productivity in causativizing and decausativizing affixes. Such affixes have been generally regarded as unproductive. However, there are a limited number of attested new forms with -as used to produce favored phonological forms. In the language of young

---

[16] This commonality of /re/ endings may give one an impression that both *nure(-ru)* 'get wet' and *kir-e(-ru)* 'get cut' have the same /re/, leading to an analysis of /e/ as a decausativizing affix in *nure(-ru)*; see my discussion of apparently Type III pairs in Section 2.1.

people in recent years there are many innovative verbs having a stem-final /r/.[17] The following form based on such an innovative verb is one that I have directly observed: *nanamer-as(-u)* 'make ... slanted' < *nanamer(-u)* 'become slanted' (< *naname* 'slanted'). Such a form is congruent with the earlier observation that /r/-ending base stems exclusively select *-as* for causativization. Another interesting case is the verb *habur(-u)* 'exclude from a friendship group', for which the suffixed form *habur-as(-u)*, used in the same causative meaning, is also attested. It is possible that this is derived via noncausative *habur-e(-ru)*, (i.e., *habur(-u)* > *habur-e(-ru)* > *habur-as(-u)*, in a way parallel to *kir(-u)* > *kir-e(-ru)* > *kir-as(-u)*).[18] These examples suggest that *-as* may have some degree of productivity, at least when favored forms result (see Booij (2010) for the view that affixes exhibit differential productivity in different environments).

4.3 Reexamination of the semantics of the two causativizing affixes

In spite of my discussion above, a close examination of our database suggests that there are also semantic tendencies associated with certain affixes, although in ways different from Kageyama's (1996) claims. Even though affixes differ in phonological environment, it does not follow from this that they do not differ in their semantics. Affixes in fact appear to differ in the range of meanings that they can express. Considering first the case of causativizing affixes, these appear to differ not only in the nature of the change involved, but also in the nature of the causation expressed.

Causation occurs in various forms (Talmy 1976, 1986; Shibatani 1976; Shibatani & Pardeshi 2002, among others). It can differ in terms of how it is enacted: whether by neural operation (e.g., moving one's own fingers), physical manipulation (e.g., picking up a cup), assisting an agent (e.g., helping someone to stand up), directive order (e.g., telling someone to come), noncontact influencing (e.g., surprising someone), nonprevention of motion or occurrence (so-called 'let'-causation, as in letting water drip), or in an abstract chain of cause and result (e.g., boosting the economy).

Causativizing affixes differ in the range of causation types they represent. Causativizing *-e*, for example, is in most cases restricted in its meaning to direct causation of some type, although restrictions vary slightly among verbs. Some *-e* verbs are restricted to "causer-internal" causation, as exemplified in (9).

---

17 See Tsujimura & Davis (2011) for innovative verbs with stem-final /r/ in recent Japanese.
18 *Habur-e(-ru)* is attested, but not judged acceptable by my informants.

(9) *causer-internal causation vs. physical manipulation*
   a. *Kare wa hiza o {kagam-e-ta/mage-ta/nob-asi-ta}.*
      he TOP knee ACC {bend$_{vi}$-CA-PST/bend$_{vt}$-PST/get.extended-CA-PST}.
      'He {bent/bent/straightened} his knees.'

   b. *Kare wa ningyoo no hiza o {??kagam-e-ta/mage-ta/nob-asi-ta}.*
      he TOP doll GEN knee ACC {bend$_{vi}$-CA-PST/bend$_{vt}$-PST/
      get.extended-CA-PST}
      'He {bent/bent/straightened} the doll's knees.'

(9a) is an example of causer-internal causation, in which the causer produces a change in his/her own body parts (e.g., one's own knees) through his/her own motor nervous system connected to the parts: the causation here occurs within the causer. (9b), on the other hand, is a case of physical manipulation, in which the causer acts on something (e.g., a doll's knee) outside his/her body, using his/her body parts (e.g., one's hands). (Causer-internal causation is not simply reflexive action or causation with one's own body part as a causee. It crucially involves one's own motor nervous system *connected to the body part*. Thus, using the right hand to lift the left hand does not count as causer-internal causation, since the change is not effected through the nervous system connected to the left hand.[19])

Examples in (9) suggest that *kagam-e(-ru)* 'bend (one's own body)' can be used only for causer-internal causation, while *mage(-ru)* 'bend' and *nob-as(-u)* 'stretch' are not so restricted Other verbs that are similarly restricted include *sukum-e(-ru)* 'shrug (one's shoulder), duck (one's head)', and *hisom-e(-ru)* 'hide (one's body)'. In our database, 5 out of 6 such verbs are causativized with *-e*: the only exception is the somewhat peculiar *sobiy-akas(-u)* 'make (one's shoulders) tower over'. Restriction to such internal causation is not seen in *-as* verbs.[20] Interestingly, *-e* used to express such causativization is observed with five noncausative verb stems ending in /m/, where *-e* is preferred for causativization, but (importantly) *-as* suffixation is phonologically possible as well. Still, all the causative verbs specialized for causer-internal causation have chosen *-e* rather than *-as*. Note that *-as can* express causer-internal causation in the range of causation it represents, as shown by *nob-as(-u)* (get.extended-CA) 'stretch'

---

[19] In this respect causer-internal causation is narrower than "auto-causation" sometimes encountered in the typological literature (Geniušienė 1987).

[20] Sometimes judgments are subtle. Almost all uses of *ugomek-as(-u)* 'wriggle' we found in a certain corpus appear to involve causer-internal causation, but the use of this verb to express the wriggling of something other than one's own body parts is certainly acceptable.

in (9) and *d-as(-u)* (go.out-CA) 'take out' in *sita-o d-as(-u)* 'stick out one's tongue'. However, these *-as* verbs are not *restricted* to causer-internal causation, being able to represent manipulative, assistive, and directive causation as well.[21]

Other *-e* verbs can express manipulative as well as internal causation but no other types of causation. Consider the semantics of posture verbs with *-e* and other suffixes. Causativized posture verbs with other affixes, such as *ok-os(-u)* 'get (someone) up', *ne-kas(-u)* 'make (someone) lie down (for sleep)', *ne-se(-ru)* 'make (someone) lie down (for sleep)', can be used in a broad range of causative situations, including causer-internal, manipulative, assistive, and directive causation. The verb *ok-os(-u)*, for example, can be used for events like raising up one's own body from a lying position (causer-internal), raising up a bottle that is lying down (manipulative), helping a child lying down to his/her feet (assistive), or telling a person lying down to rise (directive). However, the *-e* verb *tat-e(-ru)* (stand-CA) 'stand$_{vt}$ up' is restricted to either causer-internal or manipulative causation; it can be used for drawing one's own knee up to the chest (causer-internal), or standing a book up (manipulative), but not for helping a child to stand (assistive) or telling someone to stand (directive). Similarly, verbs like *muk-e(-ru)* 'turn ...' and *narab-e(-ru)* 'line ... up' cannot express directive causation.[22]

The suffix *-e* tends to be disfavored in representing nondirect causation. This suffix rarely expresses 'let'-causation, in which the causer allows a change to occur: for example, *susum-e(-ru)* (advance-CA) 'advance$_{vt}$' and *sirizok-e(-ru)* (retreat-CA) 'drive away' cannot mean 'let ... advance' or 'let ... retreat'. The only *-e* verbs representing 'let'-causation in our list are *yasum-e(-ru)* 'make/let (one's body) rest' and *akaram-e(-ru)* 'let (one's face) redden, blush', both of which are interestingly restricted to 'let'-causation of a change in one's own body.[23] In contrast, *-as* can more freely express 'let'-causation, as seen in examples such as *tar-as(-u)* 'let drip', *ot-os(-u)* 'drop, let fall', *kir-as(-u)* 'let ... run out', *nig-as(-u)* 'let ... escape', and *hay-as(-u)* 'let ... grow'. Note that many of these represent naturally occurring processes.

---

[21] There are, however, some *-as* verbs that are primarily used to express the 'let' causation of a process involving one's own body parts and other self-related entities.

[22] Shibatani (1976) uses the semantics of *tat-e(-ru)* to illustrate the existence of semantic restrictions on lexical causative verbs. His presentation of the data is somewhat skewed because of the choice of this *-e* verb.

[23] The verb *ir-e(-ru)* 'put in' can express 'let' causation, but again *ir(-u)/ir-e(-ru)* is not included in our core list of verb pairs because of the obsolete nature of the noncausative verb. The verb *sodat-e(-ru)* 'grow$_{vt}$' may seem to represent 'let' causation. However, the event of *sodat-e(-ru)* involves repetitive care of a growing being over the period of growth and is in that sense different from 'let' causation, in which the causer sanctions a process of development by refraining from any direct involvement in it.

How about other causation types? There are only a limited number of examples where *-e* expresses the causing of a psychological change, with no physical action exerted on the causee (noncontact influencing). The verb *kanasim-e(-ru)* 'sadden' is the only clear example; *kurusim-e(-ru)* 'torture' is the only other psych verb but this verb has a flavor of physical causation. Causation of abstract change that cannot be brought about by physical action is rarely coded by *-e*, the only clear examples I have been able to find being *kanaw-e(-ru)* 'make ... come true' and perhaps *yawarag-e(-ru)* 'soften, mitigate'. Notably, the *-e* causative form of *sitagaw-u*, which means both 'obey' and '(spatially) follow in obedience', involves only the latter meaning: *-e* has a strong flavor of physical causation.

All these restrictions are reflected in the use of *-e* across the subcategories of change seen in Section 2: 82% of *-e* causative verbs represent purely concrete changes (disintegration, change in shape, physical change, spatio-relational change, existential change, outer physical change and biological change in humans). There are only 7 examples involving nonconcrete change (change in inner bodily condition, psychological change, possessional change, semi-abstract change, and abstract change). In contrast, purely concrete changes account for a much lower 66% of *-as* causative verbs.

Earlier I pointed out that naturally occurring change (e.g., 'dry out', 'fall') requires *-as/-os* for causativization. These are changes not brought about by physical manipulation or assistance but ones that are allowed to develop, which is why *-e* is disfavored in such cases.

All this suggests that *-e* is more restricted than *-as/-os* in terms of causation type. The difference between these two affix types is represented in the semantic map (cf. Haspelmath 2003) in Figure 3. The particular meanings that *-e* marks cannot go outside the domain indicated, often restricted to causer-internal type as in *kagam-e(-ru)* above.

The question to consider now is how such semantic and phonological restrictions on a causativizing affix are able to coexist. In the case of causativizing affixes, *-e* is more restricted semantically and phonologically, and *-as* has a broader range of uses. Whenever *-e* is not possible semantically and/or phonologically, *-as* is there to fill the gap. The use of productive *-sase* is also available to fill such gaps.

The situation is somewhat different in the case of decausativization, where phonological conditioning is stricter. In most cases *-e* is used for change in an inanimate entity brought about by physical manipulative causation (e.g., *war-e(-ru)* 'become broken'). *-Ar* appears to be much less restricted. However, as noted above, these affixes are to a large degree phonologically conditioned. There are no instances of decausativizing *-ar* applied to verbs ending in /r/ and /k/, as

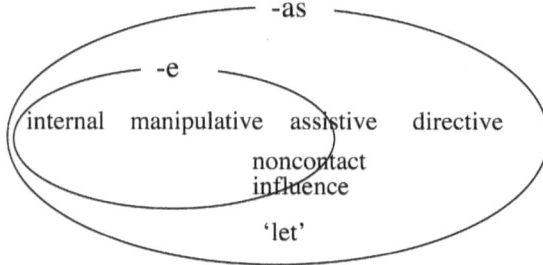

Figure 3: Difference between causation types expressed by -e and -as

shown in Table 7 (unlike -as which is applied to verb stems ending in all major consonants). For such verbs -e is the only option and in fact allows in such cases meanings not favored by this suffix in other environments (e.g., changes not brought about by physical manipulation, as in *ur-e(-ru)* 'be sold', *sir-e(-ru)* 'become known', and *sabak-e(-ru)* 'become sold out').

4.4 Summary

Sections 3 and 4 have confirmed that the morphological markedness of non-causative-causative verb pairs is correlated with the semantics of the event described, and that phonological restrictions on the choice of suffixes exist alongside the semantic restrictions. Our discussion has also shown that regularities are found at different levels of generality: some at the level of markedness type, others at the level of the affix used. Still others are based on verb classes (or semantic domains) regardless of the affix or markedness type (e.g., event subjects are in general allowed for causative psych verbs). The regularities are not expressible in terms of a single meaning associated with a given form or pattern, but in terms of a range of preferred meanings. There are also phenomena that make reference to particular phonological environments (e.g., the degree of productivity of an affix).

All this means that generalizations are not always affix-based, nor are affixes associated with a single meaning. A theory of morphology that is able to account for this is called for and will be discussed in the next section.

5 A schema-based analysis

5.1 Construction Morphology

What kind of morphological theory can capture the generalizations found in noncausative-causative verb pairs in Japanese? The kinds of causativization and decausativization considered above are very limited in productivity (as is quite common in morphology), and therefore any regularities that are found are best stated primarily in terms of generalizations over existing lexical items. Such a situation is clearly not amenable to treatment in terms of derivational rules, but calls for nonprocedural statements about related lexical items. In this section I will show that the notion of hierarchical schema in Construction Morphology (Booij 2007, 2010) is well suited to capturing such generalizations.

Construction Morphology is an application of Fillmore's notion of construction (Fillmore, Kay & O'Connor 1988; Goldberg 1995) to morphology. In this framework, word formation patterns are seen as abstract schemas that generalize over sets of existing complex words having a systematic correlation between form and meaning. Such abstract schemas and the individual complex words instantiating them together form a part of the lexicon that is hierarchically organized into layers of subgeneralizations.[24]

Schemas are exemplified in (10), which describes properties of English words ending in -*ist* (Booij 2010: 31). Schemas have the "form" part on the left, representing the morphological structure of words, and the "meaning" part on the right, representing their semantics. These are paired to constitute two poles of a construction.

(10) a. $[x\text{ -}ist]_{Ni}$ ↔ [PERSON WITH ABILITY, IDEOLOGY, DISPOSITION Y]$_i$
 (If x=N_j, A_j, then Y is related to SEM_j)

 b. $[[x]_{Nj}\text{ -}ist]_{Ni}$ ↔ [PERSON WITH ABILITY, IDEOLOGY, DISPOSITION Y related to $SEM_j]_i$

 c. $[[x]_{Aj}\text{ -}ist]_{Ni}$ ↔ [PERSON WITH ABILITY, IDEOLOGY, DISPOSITION Y related to $SEM_j]_i$

Schemas are hierarchically organized: (10a) is a general schema that has subschemas (10b,c) representing two of its subtypes (e.g., N-based *accordeonist*, and A-based *activist*).

The relationship between two complex words can be stated in terms of a correspondence between two word schemas, as shown in (11), which captures the relationship between -*ist* and -*ism* (e.g., *communism/communist*) (Booij 2010:33).

(11) <$[x\text{-}ism]_{Ni}$ ↔ SEM_i> ~ <$[x\text{-}ist]_{Nj}$ ↔ [person with property Y related to $SEM_i]_j$>

---

[24] See Matsumoto (2012) for an application of Construction Morphology to Japanese compound verbs.

5.2 A schema-based analysis of alternation

In a schema-based constructional view of morphology, regularities of Japanese noncausative and causative verb pairs are captured in the form of a schema that relates two verb schemas such as that represented in skeleton form in (12). I will refer to this schema as an *alternation schema*.

(12)   <[NCaus Form]$_i$ ↔ [NCaus Sem]$_i$> ~ <[Caus Form]$_j$ ↔ [Caus Sem]$_j$>

There are three major types of alternation schemas corresponding to markedness types, I, II, and III. The schemas are shown in (13), each differing from the others in the morphological structure specified in the form part of the verb schemas. The semantic part of verb schemas will be elaborated below.

(13) Type I   <[x(...)]$_{vi}$ ↔ [NCaus Sem]$_i$> ~ <[[x]$_{vi}$-Aff]$_{vj}$ ↔ [Caus Sem]$_j$>

Type II   <[[x]$_{vj}$-Aff]$_{vi}$ ↔ [NCaus Sem]$_i$> ~ <[x(...)]$_{vj}$ ↔ [Caus Sem]$_j$>

Type III <[x+ending$_l$]$_{vi}$ ↔ [NCaus Sem]$_i$> ~ <[x+ending$_m$]$_{vj}$ ↔ [Caus Sem]$_j$>

These alternation schemas capture the relationship between noncausative verb forms and causative verb forms nonderivationally – none is derived from any other in terms of order. However, the existence of an affix in only one of the verb schemas in Type I and II alternation schemas reflects the notion of markedness we have discussed earlier. Note also that the verb schemas in Type III involve particular endings, and the segments to which they are attached do not have morpheme status, unlike the case of roots and affixes in Types I and II. It is possible to represent such forms in schemas like these without positing the existence of hypothetical roots. The fact that such endings convey noncausative and causative meaning is ensured by their participation in this schema.

These three alternation schemas are general schemas, each having various subschemas capturing different affixation patterns, as in (14). In these schemas, phonological properties of the forms are indicated by a phonological substructure linked to the FORM part of the schema.[25]

---

[25] Here I am departing slightly from Booij (2010), who uses the tripartite structure (<[PHON] ↔ [SYN] ↔ [SEM]>).

(14) I(-e) <[x]$_{vi}$ ↔ [NCaus Sem]$_i$> ~ <[[x]$_{vi}$-e]$_{vj}$ ↔ [Caus Sem]$_j$>
          | |
       [...C]$_i$ [...C]$_i$

   I(-as) <[x...]$_{vi}$ ↔ [NCaus Sem]> ~ <[[x]$_{vj}$-as]$_{vk}$ ↔ [Caus Sem]$_k$>
          | |
       [...C$_l$(V)]$_i$ [...C$_l$]$_j$

   II(-e) <[[x]$_{vi}$-e]$_{vj}$ ↔ [NCaus Sem]$_i$> ~ < [x]$_{vi}$ ↔ [Caus Sem]$_i$>
          | |
       [...C(i)]$_j$ [...C(i)]$_i$

   II(-ar) <[[x]$_{vi}$-ar]$_{vk}$ ↔ [NCaus Sem]$_k$> ~ <[x...]$_{vj}$ ↔ [Caus Sem]$_j$>
          | |
       [...C$_l$]$_i$ [...C$_l$(V)]$_j$

   III(/re/~/s/) <[x$_k$+ending$_l$]$_{vi}$ ↔ [NCaus Sem]$_i$> ~ <[x$_k$+ending$_m$]$_{vj}$ ↔ [Caus Sem]$_j$>
          | |
       [re]$_l$ [s]$_m$

The subschemas in (14) have further subordinate subschemas that contain more specific information on the phonological environments in which each affix can occur. For example, Schema I(-e) is linked to the lower schema I(/m/-e) in (15a), among others, and Schema II(-e) to II(/r/-e) in (15b), among others. In contrast, Schema I(-e) is not linked to any lower schema involving stem-final /r/.

(15) a. I(/m/-e) <[x]$_{vi}$ ↔ [NCaus Sem]$_i$> ~ < [[x]$_{vi}$-e]$_{vj}$ ↔ [Caus Sem]$_j$>
              | |
           [...m]$_i$ [...m]$_i$

     b. II(/r/-e) <[[x]$_{vj}$-e]$_{vi}$ ↔ [NCaus Sem]$_i$> ~ <[x]$_{vj}$ ↔ [Caus Sem]$_j$>
              | |
           [...r]$_j$ [...r]$_j$

Similarly, Schema I(-as) is linked to the following schema (instantiated by verbs like *nure(-ru)* 'get wet' and *nur-as(-u)* 'make wet').

(16) I(/r(e)/-as) <[x...]$_{vj}$ ↔ [NCaus Sem]$_j$> ~ <[[x]$_{vi}$-as]$_{vk}$ ↔ [Caus Sem]$_k$>
              | |
           [...r(e)]$_j$ [...r]$_i$

Such schemas are ultimately linked down to, or satisfied by, the form and meaning of individual verb pairs.

Subschemas can be instances of more than one superordinate schema. This helps to capture the contrast between /r/ and /s/ seen in Section 1: Noncausative forms tend to contain /r/ at the end and causative forms, /s/ at the end. Schemas I(-*as*) and III(/*re*/~/*s*/) in (14) are instances of the S-CausV schema given in (17a), and Schemas II(-*ar*) and III(/*re*/~/*s*/), of the R-NCausV schema given in (17b).

(17) a. S-CausV schema
 <[x...]$_{vi}$ ↔ [NCaus Sem]$_i$> ~ <[x...]$_{vj}$ ↔ [Caus Sem]$_j$>
 |
 [...s(V)]$_j$

 b. R-NCausV schema
 <[x...]$_{vi}$ ↔ [NCaus Sem]$_i$> ~ <[x...]$_{vj}$ ↔ [Caus Sem]$_j$>
 |
 [...r(V)]$_i$

In these schemas, the internal structure of the verb is unspecified, and the whole verb is linked to the phonological structure ending in r(V) or s(V). In this way, a generalization can be stated in a way neutral to the distinction between "morpheme+aff" in Schemas I and II and "nonmorpheme+ending" in Schema III.

Other crossclassifying general schemas involve common phonological shapes for noncausative or causative meaning. The one for the /*re*/ ending for noncausatives is given below.

(18) /*re*/-NCaus V Schema
 <[x...]$_{vi}$ ↔ [NCaus Sem]$_i$> ~ <[x...]$_{vj}$ ↔ [Caus Sem]$_j$>
 |
 [...*re*]$_i$

This schema is instantiated by all verb pairs whose noncausative members end in /re/, whatever the morphemic status of /re/, and whatever the form of the causative member, covering such pairs as *kir-e(-ru)/kir(-u)* 'get cut'/'cut', *wak-are(-ru)/wake(-ru)* 'get divided'/'divide', *koware(-ru)/kowas(-u)* 'become broken'/'break', and *nure(-ru)/nur-as(u)* 'get wet'/'make wet'. There is no schema in which /re/ is linked to the morphological structure of causative verbs, as pointed out in 4.2 above.

Schemas linked to a large number of words have the potential to expand (i.e., to be productive). The schemas in (15), (16) and (18), for example, have many instances and are productive, albeit to a limited extent, as pointed out earlier.

The meaning part of verb schemas can be specified in the following way. The most common, general semantic specification of an alternation schema can be represented as in (19). Here, GO represents a change in general, spatial or otherwise. CAUSE has two arguments: a cause and a caused event.

(19) <[NCaus Form]$_i$ ↔ [... GO ...]$_i$> ~
<[Caus Form]$_j$ ↔ [... CAUSE [... GO ...]$_i$]$_j$>

The semantic specifications portions indexed by i and j in (19) can be alternatively represented in terms of image schemas such as those in (20).

(20) a.   b.

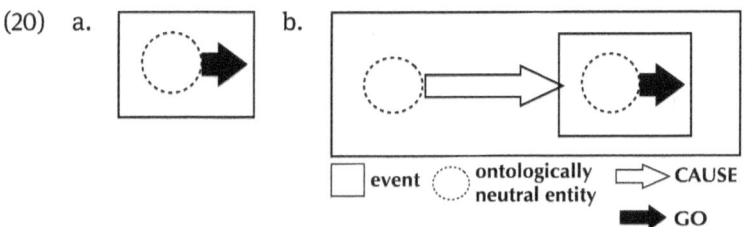

Subschemas of the general schema in (19) have different specifications according to 1) causation type (e.g., causer-internal, manipulative, assistive, etc.), 2) ontological nature of the participants (e.g., event, human being, inanimate entity, etc.), and 3) change type (change of state or location, psychological change, physical change, etc.). (21a) is a subschema for causer-internal causation of a physical change-of-state in a body part of the causer; (21b) represents noncontact causation giving rise to a psychological change-of-state in a human being. These causative semantic structures can alternatively be schematized as in (22).

(21) a. Causer-internal causation of a change-of-state in a body part
<[NCaus Form]$_i$ ↔ [$_{physic}$ y GO [...]]$_i$> ~
<[Caus Form]$_j$ ↔ [x CAUSE [$_{physic}$ y GO [...]]$_i$ BY [x ACT-ON$_{neuro}$ y]]$_j$>
(where x=human being, y = x's body part)

b. Noncontact causation giving rise to a psychological change
<[NCaus Form]$_i$ ↔ [$_{psych}$ y GO [TO ...]$_i$> ~
<[Caus Form]$_j$ ↔ [[$_{event}$ ...] CAUSE [$_{psych}$ y GO [TO ...]]$_i$]$_j$>
(where y = human being)

(22) a.

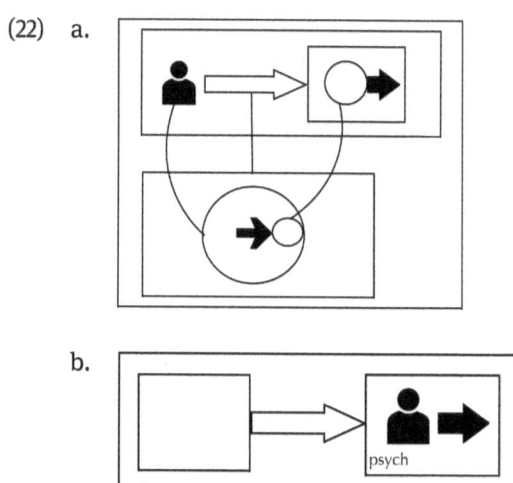

b.

In these representations, causation types differ in how their causing events and means substructures are specified. Causer-internal causation (and manipulative causation) necessarily has a human or animate entity as its cause, and the means of causation specifies how the causation is executed. In contrast, non-contact causation giving rise to a psychological change has an event as the cause, and has no such means substructure involving ACT-ON, indicating no contact. Such schemas capture verb-class specific characteristics of meaning in a way independent of the affixes involved, such as the occurrence of an event subject with psychological causative verbs, but not with internal and manipulative causative verbs.

Constraints are placed on the association of morphological and semantic structures within verb alternation schemas. Previous approaches tended to associate a specific affix with a specific meaning. Our discussion above, however, suggests that a better solution is to state tendencies in the range of possible association of forms and meanings. This can be done by associating a given morphological structure with a set of semantic structures, often at different levels of generality. Generalizations involving markedness types such as seen in Section 2 can be captured by combining different markedness-type schemas (I, II) with a set of multiple semantic structures. For example, the Type I schema is (preferably) associated with a semantic structure involving a human undergoer, etc. Generalizations involving the semantics of each affix are captured by combining each structural schema with a set of multiple semantic schemas sanctioned (and preferred) by the affix. For example, the structural schema for causativizing -e is combined with a set of semantic structures indicating causer-internal causation and manipulative causation but not 'let'-causation.

The preferred or default alternation schema for decausativizing *-e* is thus formulated as in (23).

(23)

<[α]$_{vi}$ ↔ [$_{physcl}$ y GO...]$_i$> ~ <[[α]$_{vi}$-e]$_j$ ↔ [x CAUSE [$_{physcl}$ y GO...]$_i$ BY [x ACT-ON$_{neuro/physcl}$ y]]$_j$>
   | |
[...C]$_i$ [...C]$_i$

(x=human, y=x's body part)

Hierarchies of schemas can be used in this way to capture in a satisfying way generalizations observed in noncausative-causative verb pairs in Japanese.

6 Conclusion

Japanese noncausative-causative verb pairs present interesting challenges to morphological analysis and to the study of the interface between form and meaning. A close semantic and phonological examination of all existing noncausative-causative verb pairs was conducted to uncover any semantic and phonological subregularities associated with the choice of markedness types and affixes, adopting a morphological analysis of certain pairs differing from that in Jacobsen (1992). It was statistically confirmed that markedness types are correlated with semantics (Jacobsen 1992), with certain classes of paired verbs (e.g., verbs representing events with a human undergoer) predominantly noncausative-basic, and other classes (e.g., verbs representing events brought about forcefully or by human agency) predominantly causative-basic. Furthermore, there are both phonological and semantic restrictions on, or preferences for, particular suffixes; even though there are real phonological restrictions on suffix choice, affixes do exhibit semantic preferences as well. An analysis was presented that utilizes the notion of hierarchical schema in a constructional theory of morphology (Booij 2010) which is able to capture the regularities and tendencies we have observed for noncausative-causative verb pairs at different levels of generality.

Abbreviations

ACC accusative; CA causativizing affix; DA decausativizing affix; GEN genitive; NOM nominative; NONPST nonpast; PST past; TOP topic

Acknowledgments

This work is a revised version of the paper presented at the NINJAL International Symposium on Valency Classes and Alternations in Japanese, held in August 2012, which traces back to one given much earlier at Tohoku University in February 2000. I would like to thank Yoko Sugioka, Naoyuki Ono, Heiko Narrog, Prashant Pardeshi, Geert Booij, Clemens Poppe, Natsuko Tsujimura, Anna Bugaeva, Hirotaka Nakajima, Yasuhito Kido, Bjarke Frellesvig, Stephen Horn, Wesley Jacobsen, and Taro Kageyama, for their comments and encouragement at various stages over those years. I would also like to thank Shi Chunhua, Hirotaka Nakajima, Akinori Ito and Yuzo Morishita for their help in creating the verb lists used in this chapter. All errors are of course mine.

References

Aoki, Hirofumi. 2010. *Gokeisei-kara mita Nihongo-bunpō-shi* [History of Japanese grammar from the perspectives of word-formations]. Tokyo: Hituzi Syobo.
Booij, Geert. 2007. Construction morphology and the lexicon. In Fabio Montermini, Gilles Boyé & Nabil Harbout (eds.), *Selected proceedings of the 5th Décembrettes. Morphology in Toulouse*, 34–44. Somerville MA.: Cascadilla Press.
Booij, Geert. 2010. *Construction morphology.* Oxford: Oxford University Press.
Comrie, Bernard. 2006. Transitivity pairs, markedness, and diachronic stability. *Linguistics* 44 (2). 303–318.
Fillmore, Charles J., Paul Kay & Mary Catherine O'Connor. 1988. Regularity and idiomaticity in grammatical constructions: The case of let alone. *Language* 64. 501–538.
Geniušienė, Emma. 1987. *The typology of reflexives.* Berlin & New York: Mouton de Gruyter.
Goldberg, Adele E. 1995. *Constructions: A construction grammar approach to argument structure.* Chicago: University of Chicago Press.
Haspelmath, Martin. 1993. More on the typology of inchoative/causative verb alternations. In Bernard Comrie & Maria Polinsky (eds.), *Causatives and transitivity*, 87–120. Amsterdam & Philadelphia: Benjamins.
Haspelmath, Martin. 2003. The geometry of grammatical meaning: Semantic maps and cross-linguistic comparison. In Michael Tomasello (ed.) *The new psychology of language*, volume 2, 211–243. New York: Erlbaum.
Haspelmath, Martin, Andreea Calude, Michael Spagnol, Heiko Narrog & Elif Bamyacı. 2014. Coding causal-noncausal verb alternations: A form-frequency correspondence explanation. *Journal of Linguistics* 50. 587–625.
Inoue, Kazuko. 1976. *Henkei-bunpō to Nihongo, ge: Imi-kaishaku o chūshin ni* [Transformational grammar and Japanese, 2: Semantic interpretation]. Tokyo: Taishukan.
Jacobsen, Wesley M. 1992. *The transitive structure of events in Japanese.* Tokyo: Kurosio Publishers.

Jacobsen, Wesley M. this volume. The semantic basis of Japanese transitive-intransitive derivational patterns. In Taro Kageyama & Wesley M. Jacobsen (eds.), *Transitivity and valency alternations: Studies on Japanese and beyond*. Berlin & Boston: De Gruyter Mouton.
Kageyama, Taro. 1993. *Bunpō to gokeisei* [Grammar and word formation]. Tokyo: Hituzi Syobo.
Kageyama, Taro. 1996. *Dōshi imiron: Gengo to ninchi no setten* [Verb semantics: The interface of language and cognition]. Tokyo: Kurosio Publishers.
Kishimoto, Hideki, Taro Kageyama & Kan Sasaki. 2015. Valency classes in Japanese. In Andrej Malchukov & Bernard Comrie (eds.), *Valency classes in the world's languages*, 765–805. Berlin & Boston: De Gruyter Mouton.
Kuginuki, Tooru. 1996. *Kodai Nihongo no keitai henka* [Morphological changes in Old Japanese]. Osaka: Izumi Shoin.
Levin, Beth. 1993. *English verb classes and alternations: A preliminary investigation*. Chicago: University of Chicago Press.
Levin, Beth & Malka Rappaport Hovav. 1995. *Unaccusativity: At the syntax–lexical semantics interface*. Cambridge, MA: MIT Press.
Mabuchi, Kazuo. 1999. *Kodai Nihongo no sugata*. Tokyo: Musashino Shoin.
Maruta, Tadao & Kazuyoshi Suga (eds.). 2000. *Nichi-eigo no jita no kōtai* [Intransitive/transitive alternation in Japanese and English]. Tokyo: Hituzi Syobo.
Matsumoto, Yo. 1996. *Complex predicates in Japanese: A syntactic and semantic study of the notion 'word'*. Stanford: CSLI, and Tokyo: Kurosio Publishers.
Matsumoto, Yo. 2000a. Nihongo ni okeru tadōshi-nijūtadōshi pea to nichieigo no shieki-kōtai [Transitive/ditransitive pairs in Japanese and causative alternation in English and Japanese]. In Tadao Maruta & Kazuyoshi Suga (eds.), *Nichieigo no jita no kōtai* [Transitivity alternation in Japanese and English], 167–207. Tokyo: Hituzi Syobo.
Matsumoto, Yo. 2000b. Causative alternation in English and Japanese: A closer look. Review article on Taro Kageyama's *Dōshi imiron: Gengo to ninchi no setten*. *English Linguistics* 17. 160–192. The English Linguistic Society of Japan.
Matsumoto, Yo. 2000c. *Osowaru/oshieru* nado no tadooshi/nijuutadooshi-pea no imiteki-seishitsu [Semantic properties of transitive/ditransitive pairs like *osowar-u* 'learn' and *osie-ru* 'teach']. In Susumu Yamada (ed.), *Kunihiro Tetsuya-kyooju koki-kinen ronbunshu* [Collected papers presented to Professor Tetsuya Kunihiro on his seventieth birthday], 79–95. Tokyo: Hituzi Syobo.
Matsumoto, Yo. 2003. A reexamination of the crosslinguistic parameterization of causative predicates: Evidence form Japanese and other languages. In Miriam Butt & Tracy Holloway King (eds.), *Argument realization*, 135–169. Stanford: CSLI.
Matsumoto, Yo. 2007. Go-ni okeru metafā-teki-imi-no jitsugen-to sono seiyaku [Realizations of metaphorical meanings in words and their constraints]. In Masaaki Yamanashi (ed.), *Ninchigengogaku Ronkō* 6. 49–93. Tokyo: Hituzi Syobo.
Matsumoto, Yo. 2012. A Constructional account of compound verbs in Japanese. Paper presented at the Seventh International Conference of Constructional Grammar, Seoul.
Narrog, Heiko. 2007a. Nihongo jita-dōshi ni okeru yūhyōseisa no dōkizuke [Motivation for the markedness contrast between intransitive/transitive pairs in Japanese]. In Mie Tsunoda, Kan Sasaki & Tōru Shiotani (eds.), *Tadōsei no tsūgengoteki kenkyū* [Crosslinguistic study of transitivity] Tokyo: Kurosio Publishers.
Narrog, Heiko. 2007b. Nihongo jita-dōshi-tsui no ruikeiron-teki ichizuke [Typological status of intransitive/transitive pairs in Japanese]. In Taro Kageyama (ed.), *Lexicon Forum No. 3*, 161–193. Tokyo: Hituzi Syobo.

Narrog, Heiko. 2014. Japanese causative alternation verb data. Shieki-kootai gengo-chizu [Linguistic maps of causative alternation]. National Institute for Japanese Language and Linguistics. (http://watp.ninjal.ac.jp)

Nedjalkov, Vladimir P. & Georgij C. Silnitsky. 1973. The typology of morphological and lexical causatives. In Ferenc Kiefer (ed.), *Trends in Soviet theoretical linguistics*, 1–32. Dordrecht: Reidel.

Nichols, Johanna, David Peterson & Jonathan Barnes. 2004. Transitivizing and detransitivizing languages. *Linguistic Typology* 8. 149–211.

Nishiyama, Kunio. 2000. Jitakōtai-to keitairon [Intransitive-transitive alternation and morphology]. In Tadao Maruta & Kazuyoshi Suga (eds.), *Nichieigo no jita no kōtai* [Transitivity Alternation in Japanese and English], 145–165. Tokyo: Hituzi.

Okutsu, Keiichiro. 1967. Jidōshika, tadōshika oyobi ryōryokuka-henkei [Transitivization, intransitivization and bipolarization of Japanese verbs] *Kokugogaku* 70. 46–66.

Plag, Ingo. 2006. Productivity. In Bas Aarts & April McMahon (eds.), *The handbook of English linguistics*, 537–557. Oxford: Blackwell.

Sakuma, Kanae. 1936. *Gendai Nihongo no hyōgen to gohō* [Expressions and usage of Modern Japanese]. Tokyo: Kooseisha Kooseikaku.

Shibatani, Masayoshi. 1976. Causativization. In Masayoshi Shibatani (ed.), *Syntax and semantics, volume 5: Japanese Generative Grammar*, 239–294. New York: Academic Press.

Shibatani, Masayoshi & Prashant Pardeshi. 2002. The causative continuum. In Masayoshi Shibatani (ed.), *The grammar of causation and interpersonal manipulation*, 85–126. Amsterdam & Philadelphia: John Benjamins.

Shimada, Masahiko. 1979. *Kokugo ni okeru jidōshi to tadōshi* [Intransitive and transitive verbs in Japanese]. Tokyo: Meiji Shoin.

Suga, Kazuyoshi & Emiko Hayatsu (eds.). 1995. *Dōshi no ji-ta* [Intransitive/transitive distinction of verbs]. Tokyo: Hituzi Syobo.

Sugioka, Yoko. 2002. Keiyōshi-kara hasei-suru dōshi-no jita-kōtai-o megutte [On the intransitive/transitive alternation of verbs derived from adjectives]. In Takane Ito (ed.), *Bunpō-riron: Rekishikon to tōgo* [Grammatical theory: Lexicon and syntax], 91–116. Tokyo: University of Tokyo Press.

Talmy, Leonard. 1976. Semantic causative types. In Masayoshi Shibatani (ed.), *Syntax and semantics 6: The grammar of causative constructions*, 47–116. New York: Academic Press.

Talmy, Leonard. 1988. Force dynamics in language and cognition. *Cognitive Science* 12 (1). 49–100.

Tsujimura, Natsuko & Stuart Davis. 2011. A construction approach to innovative verbs in Japanese. *Cognitive Linguistics* 22 (4). 797–823.

Taro Kageyama
3 Agents in anticausative and decausative compound verbs

1 Introduction

Recent cross-linguistic studies on transitivity alternations have brought it to light that human languages exhibit a repertoire of at least five types of intransitivization from transitive verbs, which Alexiadou & Doron (2012: 4) summarize as in (1).

(1) a. Anticausatives of the *break/open* type, denoting spontaneous events.

  b. Lexical reflexive verbs (*wash, shave*) and reciprocal verbs (*meet, kiss*)

  c. Dispositional middles (*This book sells well.*)

  d. Medio-passives, typically underdetermined for passive and anticausative.

  e. Passives (*The door was opened by the guard.*)

To this list may be added adjectival (stative) passives like *distinguished* and *well-known*. Of these, anticausatives (1a), having a complex nature crosscutting the lexicon, morphology, semantics, and syntax, are one of the most hotly debated topics in recent research whether theoretical or typological in orientation. This chapter addresses theoretical and descriptive issues involving phenomena of intransitivization from the standpoint of Verb-Verb (V-V) compound verbs in Japanese. Novel data for compound verbs presented in this chapter will shed fresh light on issues that have so far been discussed almost exclusively on the basis of simplex or derived verbs.

Anticausative verbs of the *break/open* type are commonly regarded as involving no volitional agent across languages (Horvath & Siloni 2011). On the empirical side, the non-involvement of agents in such verbs has been confirmed by in-depth studies on European languages such as Levin & Rappaport Hovav (1995) on English and Schäfer (2008) on German, and on the theoretical side, the question of how agent arguments of causative verbs become invisible to syntax upon anticausativization has provoked much discussion (Levin & Rappaport

Taro Kageyama, National Institute for Japanese Language and Linguistics

Hovav 1995; Reinhart 2002; Schäfer 2008; Alexiadou 2010; Koontz-Garboden 2012; Rappaport Hovav & Levin 2012, among others).

Researchers on Japanese, however, have frequently noted cases in which an agent appears to be retained in intransitive verbs derived from their causative transitive counterparts. Jacobsen (1992) and Kageyama (1996) observe that a large number of Japanese intransitive variants in the causative/inchoative pairs have no way of being translated into English apart from using the passive construction. These intransitives, sometimes called "lexical passives", are typically coded by the suffix *-ar* added to a transitive stem, as in *mituk-ar-u* 'be found/discovered' < *mituke-ru* 'find/discover' (classical transitive *mituk-u*), and *tasuk-ar-u* 'be saved' < *tasuke-ru* 'save' (classical tr. *tasuk-u*). The events described by such intransitive verbs cannot happen naturally or spontaneously without volitional instigation by a human agent. Based on this kind of data, Kageyama (1996) differentiates two distinct operations of lexical intransitivization, called "anticausativization" and "decausativization":

TWO TYPES OF INTRANSITIVIZATION

A. Anticausativization: Agents are erased.

The agent argument is totally absent from intransitive variants. Technically, the agent (or a whole causing event) may be erased, or be lexically bound by the theme argument in the manner of counter-reflexivization (cf. also Koontz-Garboden 2009).

B. Decausativization: Agents are preserved in lexical semantic structure.

The agent argument of the transitive base undergoes existential binding, thereby being rendered invisible to syntax though semantically understood to refer to some unidentified person.

Decausative verbs, which retain agents, contrast sharply with anticausative verbs, which totally lack agents. Lexical decausativization is thus a new addition to the inventory of intransitivization processes shown in (1).

According to Kageyama (1996), anticausative and decausative verbs are diagnosed by their cooccurrence relations with particular kinds of adjuncts. One group of adjuncts including *katteni* '(all) by itself' and *sizenni* 'naturally' correlates with non-involvement of an external causer (see also Jacobsen this volume). These adjuncts are compatible with anticausatives, but not with decausatives. Another group of adjuncts such as *nannaku* 'without difficulty', *te o tukusite* 'with great effort', and *kuroo no sue* 'after all the effort' expresses the physical endeavor or mental state of a human agent in carrying out the action.

This latter group of adjuncts is rejected by anticausatives but is congruent with decausatives.

(2) a. Anticausatives
   Kami   ga   {katteni / *te o tukusite yatto}   yabur-e-ta.
   paper   NOM   {all.by.itself / *with.great.effort} tear-ANTICAUS-PST
   'The paper tore {by itself /*with great effort}.'

  b. Decausatives
   Takaramono   ga   {te o tukusite yatto / *katteni}   mituk-at-ta.
   treasure   NOM   {with.great.effort / *all.by.itself} find-DECAUS-PST
   'The treasure was found {with great effort / *all by itself}.'

This chapter will develop novel arguments for the validity of this distinction based on fresh data on transitivity alternations in V-V compound verbs. In the course of our discussion, the question of whether detransitivized verbs include non-human causers such as natural or mechanical force (cf. Schäfer 2012) will also be addressed. Since anticausative and decausative compound verbs exhibit considerable variation in acceptability and lexical entrenchment, the feasibility of our proposed analyses will be empirically tested by statistical data on the frequencies of actually occurring examples calculated from web searches. The results will be discussed in light of Haspelmath's (2008) hypothesis concerning the frequency/basicness correspondence.

The chapter is organized as follows. With a view to laying a foundation for our discussion of compound verb alternations, Section 2 will first provide an overview of lexical V-V compound verbs classified into two types, thematic compounds and aspectual compounds, and then introduce the Transitivity Harmony Principle (Kageyama 1993, 1999), a combinatory restriction on lexical V-V formation, which makes a crucial prediction concerning the availability of compound verbs for intransitivization. Section 3 reveals that intransitivization is generally prohibited from applying to thematic compound verbs because of a robust restriction imposed by the Transitivity Harmony Principle, whereby only a limited number of thematic compounds can be shown to be intransitivized, due to their agent arguments being obliterated by semantic reanalysis. By contrast, Section 4, focusing on a particular head verb, *-agaru* 'go up, be finished', demonstrates that aspectual compound verbs participate productively in intransitivization while maintaining the agent arguments of their transitive counterparts. The discussion in these two sections thus uncovers a neat correlation between a thematic/aspectual distinction among V-V compound verbs, on the one hand, and the distinction between anticausativization and decausativization, on the other. The intransitivization involved in thematic compound verbs is identified as anticausativization, whose application is semantically motivated, whereas intransitivization in aspectual compound verbs is identified as decausativization, which is triggered by a particular verb *agaru*. Section 5 concludes the chapter, pointing out theoretical implications of the compound verb data for general theories of lexical transitivity alternations.

2 The Transitivity Harmony Principle and the thematic/aspectual distinction among V-V compound verbs

Preliminary to a more detailed discussion in subsequent sections, this section introduces the core properties of lexical V-V compound verbs: the Transitivity Harmony Principle (Section 2.1) and the distinction between thematic and aspectual compound verbs (Section 2.2).

2.1 The Transitivity Harmony Principle

The Transitivity Harmony Principle (THP) is a descriptive generalization, discovered by Kageyama (1993, 1999), that captures the basic combinatory patterns of lexical V-V compound verbs in terms of the argument structure types of their component verbs.

(3) The Transitivity Harmony Principle (THP)
Given the three argument structure schemas below, lexical compound verbs are built by combining two verbs of the same type of argument structure.
(a) transitive verbs (Tr.): (Ag <Th>)
(b) unergative intransitive verbs (Unerg.): (Ag < >)
(c) unaccusative intransitive verbs (Unacc.): <Th>
N.B. "Ag" represents an agent argument, and "Th" a theme argument.

The sameness of argument structure type here hinges on the presence of an agent argument. Transitive and unergative verbs, equipped with an agent argument, count as the same type whereas unaccusative verbs, lacking an agent, form a disparate type. The THP thus allows the combinations of "Tr + Tr", "Tr

+ Unerg", "Unerg + Tr", "Unerg + Unerg", and "Unacc + Unacc" while disallowing the combinations of "Tr + Unacc", "Unacc + Tr", "Unerg + Unacc", and "Unacc + Unerg" (see Kageyama (2016) for concrete examples of these grammatical and ungrammatical combinations). Traditional Japanese grammarians sometimes noticed the strong tendency for a transitive verb to combine with another transitive verb while an intransitive verb tends to be combined with another intransitive verb, and Jacobsen (1992) dubs this tendency "transitive parity". The THP, defined in terms of a verb's argument structure, is more restrictive and hence more explanatory than transitive parity, which counts only a verb's valency or adicity.

The crucial effect of the THP manifests itself most clearly in the disparity of grammaticality between causative transitive compounds as in (4a) and anticausative compounds as in (4b).

(4) a. Transitive + Transitive
 uti-otosu 'shoot (tr.) + drop (tr.)' = 'shoot down', *musiri-toru* 'pluck (tr.) + remove (tr.)' = 'pluck off', *naguri-korosu* 'strike (tr.) + kill (tr.)' = 'strike dead'

 b. *Transitive + Unaccusative
 **uti-otiru* 'shoot (tr.) + fall (intr.)', **musiri-toreru* 'pluck (tr.) + come.off (intr.)', **naguri-sinu* 'strike (tr.) + die (intr.)'

From the perspective of transitivity alternations, the THP effect in (4b) will be rephrased as follows: Compound verbs of the form "Tr + Tr" cannot undergo anticausativization because the resultant form "Tr + Unacc" violates the THP. This is because lexical transitivity in Japanese is specified for individual simplex verbs. Since compound verb formation applies to simplex verbs whose transitivity is already established lexically, it is theoretically impossible to change the transitivity of a V-V compound verb as a whole. Consequently, valency change in an entire compound verb is generally consigned to syntactic passive and causative structures.

2.2 Thematic and aspectual compound verbs

Based on the observation that some of the second members (V2s) of V-V compounds have lost their original verbal meanings and bear auxiliary-like meanings, Kageyama (2013, 2016) differentiates two types of lexical compound verbs, as follows:

(5) a. Lexical thematic V-V compound verbs

Both the first (V1) and the second member (V2) of a compound verb have their own argument structure and lexical meaning, and the argument relations of the compound as a whole are determined by the head verb V2, with V1 semantically modifying V2's eventuality.

b. Lexical aspectual V-V compound verbs

The argument relations of a compound as a whole are basically determined by the first member (V1), with the second member (V2) supplying a variety of lexical aspectual (*Aktionsart*) meanings to the eventuality denoted by V1.

Since the V-V compound verbs discussed in this chapter are all "lexical" in the lexical-syntactic distinction among compound verbs (Kageyama 1989, 1993), the term "lexical" will hereafter be omitted in referring to compound verbs.

A heuristic guideline for identifying the type of a given compound verb is whether it can be paraphrased as "V1-*te* V2" (V1 and then V2). This paraphrase is generally applicable to thematic compound verbs, as in *nigiri-tubusu* (grasp-squash) 'crush in one's hand', which is paraphrased as *nigit-te tubusu* 'grasp and squash', and *aruki-tukareru* (walk-get.tired) 'get tired from walking', paraphrased as *arui-te tukareru* 'walk and then get tired'. Aspectual compound verbs cannot be paraphrased in this manner; most of them are instead paraphrased by inverting the order of the two member verbs, as in *huri-sikiru* (fall-occur. repeatedly) 'rain incessantly', which may be rendered as *sikirini huru* 'fall incessantly', and *(hana ga) saki-kisou* (bloom-compete) '(flowers) be in full blossom', which can plausibly be paraphrased as *kisot-te saku* 'bloom competitively'. A reliable diagnosis is thus that the argument relations and selectional restrictions of a whole compound are determined by V2 in the case of thematic compounds and by V1 in the case of aspectual compounds.

Based on a database of about 2,500 lexical compound verbs (NINJAL 2014), Kageyama (2016) examined to what degrees the THP is observed in the two types of lexical compound verbs and found that although the THP applies with a statistically significant degree of precision overall (83.39%), it exhibits a non-trivial disparity in applicability between these two classes of compound verbs.

Table 1: The Transitivity Harmony Principle in thematic/aspectual compound verbs

Types of compounds	Total	THP congruence	THP incongruence
Thematic compounds	1,621	1,450 (89.45%)	171 (10.55%)
Aspectual compounds	818	584 (71.39%)	234 (28.61%)
Grand total	2,439	2,034 (83.39%0)	405 (16.61%)

As depicted in Table 1, thematic compounds showed a THP congruence of 89.45% (1,450 cases) and a THP incongruence/violation of 10.55% (171 cases) among 1,621 cases, whereas aspectual compounds showed a lesser degree of THP congruence of 71.39% (584 cases) and a higher degree of THP incongruence of 28.61% (234 cases) among 818 cases. The difference in the degrees of THP congruence between thematic and aspectual compounds was examined by a 2 (types of compounds) × 2 (THP congruence and incongruence) Chi-squared test of independence. The result suggested that the two categorical variables of thematic/aspectual compound types and THP congruence/incongruence were significantly associated with each other [$\chi^2(1)$ = 128.01, p < .001]. More precisely, the degree of THP congruence among thematic compounds was significantly higher than among aspectual compounds. Converseley, the degree of THP incongruence/violation among thematic compounds was significantly less than among aspectual compounds. In conclusion, thematic compound verbs tend to conform to the THP more strictly than aspectual compound verbs.

In subsequent sections, we attempt to offer a principled explanation of the conspicuous disparity revealed in Table 1, and demonstrate that it is this disparity that accounts for variations in the applicability of valency alternations across compound verbs.

3 Anticausativization in thematic compound verbs

Since lexical distinctions of transitivity are coded on simplex verbs only, the alternating pair of simplex verbs *tubusu* 'crush (tr.)' and *tsubureru* 'crush (intr.)', for example, ceases to exhibit this alternation when appearing in the position of the head (V2) of a compound verb, as shown by the ungrammaticality of (6b).

(6)   a.   *Inu   ga   hana   o   humi-tubusi-ta.*
             dog   NOM flower ACC trample(tr.)-crush(tr.)-PST
           'The dog crushed the flowers by trampling; He trampled the flowers down.'

       b. **Hana   *ga*   *humi-tubure-ta.*
           flower NOM trample(tr.)-crush(intr.)-PST
           'The flowers were trampled down.'

Humi-tubusu 'trample down' in (6a) is a thematic compound verb because each of the two members is equipped with its own argument structure and these jointly determine the thematic relations of the compound as a whole. Due to the right-hand head structure of Japanese, the meaning of a thematic compound verb can be represented as the first verb (V1) modifying the second verb (V2) in certain fixed semantic relations such as means of action ('V2 by V1-*ing*': *arai-otosu* [wash-remove] 'wash (dirt) off'), manner of action or motion ('V2 while V1-*ing*': *asobi-kurasu* [play-live] 'idle a day away'), reason for a result ('V2 because of V1': *hataraki-tukareru* [work-get.tired] 'get tired from working'), purpose of action ('V2 for the purpose of V1-*ing*': *kui-tuku* [eat-jump.at] 'jump at something to eat'), and coordination ('V1 and V2': *nayami-kurusimu* [worry-be.troubled] 'be distressed'). Regardless of their internal semantic relations, thematic compound verbs are prohibited by the THP from participating in transitivity alternations, in particular the intransitivization of a transitive verb to "Tr + Unacc" (6b).

The THP as it was presented earlier in (3) was formulated as a kind of formal matching between two argument structure patterns. The question we must now address is: how is this principle functionally motivated? We maintain that the essential function of the THP is to identify the agent arguments (external arguments, to be precise) of the two member verbs, V1 and V2, for the purpose of semantic integration of the two subevents. In order for the whole compound *humi-tubusu* 'trample down' to coherently express the meaning of someone crushing something by trampling it, the agent of V1 must necessarily be identical to the agent of V2. More generally, if there is an agent argument in either member of a compound verb, that agent must be identified with the agent of the other member. If V1 were represented by a transitive verb and V2 by an unaccusative verb, then the agent of V1 could not extend its control over the spontaneous subevent in V2, thus yielding an ungrammatical compound like *humi-tubureru (6b), whose argument relations are schematically shown in (7).

(7) Argument structure of *humi-tubureru 'trample (tr.) + crush (unacc.)'
    humi <Ag, Th$_i$>   tubureru <Th$_i$>
         ↓ |_____|
    Ag: unsaturated   Th: identified and projected to syntax as subject

In (7), the agent of V1 *humi-* 'trample' remains unidentified or "unsaturated", violating the general principle that all arguments must be saturated (cf. Higginbotham 1985). Note incidentally that there is no identity restriction on themes (internal arguments), as shown by *me o naki-harasu* (cry [unerg.]-make.

swell [tr.]) 'cry one's eyes out', where V1 *naki* 'cry' lacks an object argument corresponding to that of V2 *harasu* 'make swell'.

The ungrammaticality of the pattern "transitive V1 + unaccusative V2" holds pervasively for Japanese lexical compound verbs, regardless of how V2s are coded morphologically, as illustrated in Table 2. The irrelevance of morphological shape strongly indicates that anticausativization is a semantic rather than morphology-induced operation.

Table 2: Anticausative suffixes in compound verbs

anticausative suffixes on V2	causative (tr. + tr.)	anticausative (tr. + unacc.)
-re	*tataki-kowasu* 'knock + break'	**tataki-kowareru* 'kick + break (intr.)'
-e	*kiri-toru* 'cut + remove'	**kiri-toreru* 'cut + come off'
-i	*yuri-okosu* 'shake + wake'	**yuri-okiru* 'shake + wake (intr.)'
-ar	*yobi-atumeru* 'call + gather'	**yobi-atumaru* 'call + gather (intr.)'
labile (same form)	*osi-hiraku* 'push + open'	**osi-hiraku* (* as intransitive)

Now, given that the ban on anticausativization of compound verbs derives from the unsaturated status of the agent of V1, it is predicted that anticausativization will become feasible if V1 loses its agent argument for some reason or other (or even its entire argument structure due to grammaticalization to prefixes), thereby evading the saturation problem. This prediction proves correct.

Let us start with the pair *bura-sageru* 'dangle' (tr.) and *bura-sagaru* 'dangle' (intr.), where the first element *bura-* is not a verb but a mimetic adverb designating the swaying movement of a hanging entity. Since this is not a V-V compound and its first member does not have an argument structure, it is not immediately clear which variant is basic and which is derived. Native speakers' intuition, coupled with the historical fact that the intransitivizing suffix *-ar* was added to the transitive *-sage(ru)* or its classical form *sag(u)* (cf. Narrog this volume), suggests that the transitive variant is basic and the intransitive variant derived. In fact, according to my informal search of Japanese websites using the Google engine (20 December 2012; the same date applies to all search results hereafter reported in this chapter), the intransitive/transitive frequency ratio (hereafter abbreviated as "I/T ratio") for this pair is about 0.776, which means that the total number (2,890,000) of occurrences of the intransitive variant amounts to about 77.6% of that of the transitive variant (3,726,000). The high frequency of the intransitive variant is understandable in view of the fact that it is fully lexicalized and listed in dictionaries. Also, the asymmetry in frequency between transitive and intransitive alternants is in line with the claim of Haspelmath (2008) that the less coded forms (in this case, the transitive variant) should be consistently more frequent than the more coded forms (Zipf's law). It should be stressed, however, that the frequency/basicness correspondence is to be regarded as a reflection of semantic (un)markedness (Haspelmath 1993; Comrie 2006) rather than morphological complexity. Compelling evidence derives from the pair *tateru* 'build' (tr.) and *tatu* 'be built' (intr.). Although the morphological criterion identifies the intransitive *tatu* as basic, the actual frequencies of these two variants run counter to Haspelmath's (2008) prediction. The transitive variant *tateru* (141,830,000) far outnumbers the intransitive variant *tatu* (15,550,000), where the I/T ratio is only 0.11. This striking asymmetry obviously stems from the fact that building a house is par excellence an agentive volitional activity, so that the transitive variant, the longer form, is semantically basic.

What we observed above with mimetic compounds could be extended to full-fledged V-V compound verbs by taking into account the degree of weakening of agency in V1. Several verbs in the V1 position are known to have lost their verbal meaning and become grammaticalized as "prefixes". Representative examples are *kaki-* lit. 'scratch' as in *kaki-kesu* (tr.) (scratch-delete) 'delete completely' vs. *kaki-kieru* (intr.) 'disappear completely', *hiQ-*, the phonetically eroded form of *hiki-* 'pull', as in *hik-komu* (intr.) 'withdraw' vs. *hik-komeru* (tr.) 'draw in', *kut-*, presumably originating from *kui-* 'eat, bite', as in *kut-tuku* (intr.) 'stick' vs. *kut-tukeru* (tr.) 'put together', and *buti-* 'beat', from *uti* 'beat', as in *buti-ateru* (tr.) 'bump' vs. *buti-ataru* (intr.) 'bump'.

In addition to historical grammaticalization, similar phenomena can also be found in current Japanese, especially in informal language, where deviant combinations of transitive and unaccusative verbs are created from time to time. Previous studies (Kageyama 1996; Matsumoto 1998; Nishiyama 1998; Yumoto 2005; Zhu 2009; Chen 2010) went no further than a mere enumeration of exceptional cases without going into the critical question of whether those exceptions are equally acceptable or occur with equal frequency, or of why they emerge in the first place. I will show that such deviant anticausative compounds, which display considerable variation in acceptability and stability, emerge from reanalyzing the meaning of V1 as an event that has no agentive source.

To grasp the current state of affairs in statistical terms, I used the Google search engine to count the actual number of attested examples of both transitive and intransitive compound verbs inflected for past (*-ta*), non-past (*-ru*), and gerundive (*-te*) and calculated their intransitive/transitive frequency ratios (I/T ratios). The I/T ratio is taken as a rough indicator of the relative acceptability of the "ungrammatical" intransitive variants as compared with the immaculate transitive variants. Our prediction is that the theoretically ungrammatical intransitive variants will gain increased acceptability according as their agent argument, in particular the meaning of volitional control, becomes less perceptible and the event of V1 is reinterpreted as a cause or manner adverbial that involves no volitional agent. The examples in (8) illustrate how the reanalysis of transitive compound verbs as intransitive verbs takes place as a result of the reinterpretation of the meaning of their first member (V1) as designating a manner of change or resulting state of the subevent V2. In the examples, each I/T ratio is followed by the absolute numbers of attested examples in the Google search.

(8) a. *tuki-nuku* (tr.) (thrust-pierce) 'pierce through' / *tuki-nukeru* (intr.) 'go through', where V1 *tuki-* 'thrust' is reinterpreted as emphasizing the straight-line movement of the theme. I/T ratio = 0.935 [intr. 6,967,000 / tr. 7,450,000]

b. *tsuki-sasu* (tr.) (thrust-stick) 'stick (a pin) in' / *tuki-sasaru* (intr.) (thrust-stick.in) '(a pin) be stuck in', where V1 *tuki-* 'thrust' is reinterpreted as emphasizing violent movement of the theme. I/T ratio = 0.785 [intr. 5,580,000 / tr. 7,110,000]

c. *hiki-simeru* (tr.) (pull-fasten) 'tighten up' / *hiki-simaru* (intr.) (pull-be.fastened) 'be tightened and compact', where V1 *hiki* 'pull' is reinterpreted as stressing the tightness and compactness of the resulting state. I/T ratio = 0.411 [intr. 8,730,000 / tr. 21,220,000]

d. *hiki-tigiru* (tr.) (rip-tear (tr.)) 'tear forcibly by ripping' / *hiki-tigireru* (intr.) (rip-tear (intr.)) 'be ripped off', where V1 *hiki-* 'rip' is reinterpreted as stressing the violent manner of the separation. I/T ratio = 0.104 [intr. 76,800 /tr. 736,000]

Three points deserve special mention about such intransitivized compounds. First, they have varying degrees of acceptability, as demonstrated by a lack of uniformity in their I/T frequency ratios. Second, no systematic coding property is detected that triggers anticausativization, with a multiplicity of V1s and V2s randomly participating in the process. This morphological idiosyncrasy suggests that the intransitivization at stake is not a rule-governed morphological process but is arbitrarily motivated by semantic reanalysis.

The third point to be noted is that these anticausative variants have not completely shifted to pure intransitives (unaccusatives) that denote autonomous events, as shown by their incompatibility in (9) with *katteni* 'by itself' and *sizenni* 'naturally', which indicate the lack of an external cause.

(9) a. *Supootu-sensyu no karada wa katteni/sizenni
sports-athlete GEN body TOP by.itself/naturally
hiki-simatte iru.
pull-be.tight is
lit. 'Athletes' bodies are firm by themselves/naturally.'

b. *Naihu ga katteni/sizenni ringo ni tuki-sasat-ta.
knife NOM by.itself/naturally apple DAT thrust-stick.in-PST
lit. 'A knife stuck in the apple by itself/naturally.'

Designating 'the absence of an external cause or force' (Levin & Rappaport Hovav 1995; Kageyama 1996; Rákosi 2012), the adverb *katteni* or its English counterpart *by itself* is compatible with canonical unaccusative verbs of the *break/open* type and the *happen* type but turns out to be incongruous with the intransitivized compounds in (9), suggesting that the semantically reanalyzed intransitive compounds like those in (8) somehow preserve a causative semantic structure. The same holds for *sizenni* 'naturally'. This observation will raise an empirical problem for those theories of intransitivization that deny the existence of agent and cause components in anticausatives altogether (Reinhart 2002, among others). This problem is aggravated if we turn our attention to anticausatives with inanimate causers.

Let us compare the transitive *uti-ageru* (hit/shoot-send.up) 'shoot off, launch' (e.g. *Nihon ga zinkoo-eisei o uti-ageta.* 'Japan launched an artificial satellite.') with the anticausative alternant *uti-agaru* (shoot-go.up) 'shoot up into the sky, be launched' (e.g. *Zinkoo-eisei ga uti-agatta.* 'An artificial satellite shot up in the sky'). The anticausative compound *uti-agaru*, commonly listed in dictionaries along with the transitive variant, is attested on the Internet with a high I/T ratio of 0.896. Crucial to our discussion is the semantic function the V1 *uti-* 'hit, shoot' serves in the anticausative alternant. I will argue that V1 *uti-* 'hit, shoot' has different semantic properties between transitive and anticausative compounds, with respect to its agency.

First, the transitive verb *utu* 'hit, strike, knock, shoot, etc.' itself exhibits multiple ambiguity with a core meaning of severe physical impact on the object entity, as typically seen in 'hitting a homerun', 'shooting fireworks', or 'launching an artificial satellite', and when used as V1 in the transitive compound *uti-ageru* 'hit-send.up', it retains this original ambiguity, with a core meaning of sending something high in the sky by hitting/shooting/launching it. The theme objects of transitive *uti-ageru* range from fly balls in baseball to fireworks to rockets and artificial satellites, and in all these acts of hitting and shooting, involvement of a human agent is a prerequisite. Curiously, however, the anticausative variant *uti-agaru* 'hit-rise' is restricted to a narrower semantic range of themes, disfavoring, in particular, fly balls in baseball games. Compare the grammatical *Hanabi/roketto ga uti-agatta*. 'Fireworks/a rocket shot up.' with the unacceptable ?**Huraibooru ga uti-agatta*. 'A fly ball was hit'. The reason is that the act of shooting off fireworks or rockets can be executed by an appropriate device made for that purpose, whereas the act of hitting a fly ball in baseball must necessarily be brought about by a human agent using a bat. This state of affairs can be represented in a simplified semantic structure involving a causal chain, as follows.

(10) ACTOR   CAUSER   THEME
      Agent   →   Device   →   Change ...
      [x DO   [y:device ACT]]   CAUSE [BECOME ...

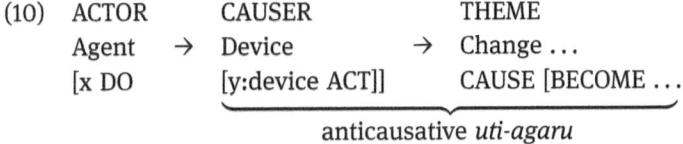
anticausative *uti-agaru*

In (10), the meaning of the anticausative *uti-agaru* is represented as covering the inanimate causer (device) and the caused event, to the exclusion of the volitional agent (actor). As is the case with the other anticausative compound verbs exemplified earlier, the lack of a human agent is the distinctive trait of the intransitive *uti-agaru*. Because anticausativization projects the theme argument to the subject in syntactic structure, the causer (mechanical device) in (10) can only be realized as an adjunct. Contrast the behavior of adjuncts marked with *de* 'by, with' in (11a) and (11b).

(11) a. *Atarasii   sooti   de   roketto/hanabi   ga   uti-agat-ta.*
         new   device   INST   rocket/fireworks NOM   hit-go.up-PST
         'A rocket/Fireworks shot up by means of a new device.'

   b. **Atarasii batto   de   hurai   ga   uti-agat-ta.*
         new   bat   INST   fly.ball   NOM   hit-go.up.PST
         lit. 'A fly ball shot up with a new bat.'

The ungrammaticality of (11b) is attributed to the appearance of the instrument 'bat', which calls for a human agent who swings it.

In the literature, V-*ageru* 'raise' and V-*agaru* 'rise' are often cited as representative examples of alternating compound verbs. The alternation, however, is far from free. Additional evidence indicating that the alternation is severely restricted by the perceptibility or imperceptibility of a volitional agent in V1 derives from the extremely low I/T ratios of the examples in (12):

(12)   a.   *turi-ageru* 'fish up (in angling)' / ??*turi-agaru* 'be caught in angling'
            I/T ratio = 0.0936 [intr. 222,100 / tr. 2,374,000]

       b.   *keri-ageru* 'kick (a ball) high' / *keri-agaru 'be kicked high'
            I/T ratio = 0.00277 [intr. 23,670 / tr. 8,547,000]

       c.   *nage-ageru* 'throw (a ball) up' / *nage-agaru 'be thrown up in the sky'
            I/T ratio = 0.000562 [intr. 493 / tr. 877,300]

       d.   *hippari-ageru* 'pull up'/ *hippari-agaru 'be pulled up'
            I/T ratio = 0.000438 [intr. 1,863 / tr. 4,251,160]

The anticausative variants in (12) are judged virtually ungrammatical because the actions designated by their V1s necessarily involve a human agent directly.

A more restrictive view would hold that the anticausative is devoid not only of an agent but also of a secondary causer like a device. On this view, *uti-agaru* would have the same semantic structure as a purely spontaneous (unaccusative) intransitive like *haeru* '(hair) grow' or *aku* 'open' (intr.) that covers only the "change" event in the causal chain of (10). This view, however, conflicts with the incompatibility of *uti-agaru* with *katteni* 'all by itself', *sizenni* 'naturally', and similar adjuncts that indicate that the event happens without any external causer. Compare the two sentences in (13).

(13)   a.   *Doa ga katteni/sizenni aita.* 'The door opened by itself/naturally.'

       b.   **Hanabi ga katteni/sizenni uti-agatta.* 'Fireworks shot up all by themselves/naturally.'

It is thus necessary to postulate an inanimate causer like an artificial device in the semantic structure of *uti-agaru*. The inanimate causer of this compound may be extended to natural forces as in (14).

(14)   *Nyuuzii-rando   no   kaigan   ni   kuzira   ga   uti-agat-ta.*
       New-Zealand   GEN   shore   LOC   whale   NOM   hit-go.up-PST
       'A whale was washed ashore in New Zealand.'
       http://blogs.yahoo.co.jp/jukukou_maru2006/43564475.html
       (searched 21/12/ 2012)

In (14), the causer that brought about the event of a whale getting ashore is a natural force like 'waves', which can be expressed by an adjunct *ookina nami de* 'by big waves'. Even more intriguing is *moti-agaru* (hold.in.hand-go.up) 'lift up'. The V1 *moti-* 'hold in hand' by itself requires a human agent who uses his hand to lift something up, and the transitive variant *moti-ageru* has this literal meaning. The anticausative variant, however, displays a different semantic range of causers, as shown by (15), where an earthquake is responsible for the lifting up of the ground.

(15) {*Zisin de* / **Katteni*} *zimen ga moti-agat-ta.*
{earthquake by / all.by.itself} ground NOM hold-go.up-PST
'The ground lifted up {because of the earthquake / *all by itself}.'

The causer is even more vague in example (16).

(16) *Totuzen yosoogai no mondai ga moti-agat-ta.*
suddenly unexpected GEN problem NOM hold-rise-PST
'Suddenly an unexpected problem cropped up for some unknown reason.'

Lacking a transitive counterpart, *moti-agaru* in (16) seems to be lexicalized as an intransitive verb with the meaning of 'crop up' or 'arise'. Nonetheless, when compared with an unequivocally unaccusative verb like *syooziru* 'emerge', it still appears to retain in its semantic structure an unknown cause or reason that led to the emergence of the problem, as suggested by the contrast between *katteni syooziru* 'emerge by itself' and **katteni moti-agaru* 'arise by itself'.

The usage of *moti-agaru* in (15) and (16) as an anticausative compound should not be confused with the same verb used as a dispositional middle, as in (17).

(17) *Kono zitensya wa katate de moti-agaru hodo karui.*
this bicycle TOP single.hand INST hold-go.up so.much.so light
http://detail.chiebukuro.yahoo.co.jp/qa/question_detail/q1055863345
'This bicycle is so light it lifts up with a single hand.'

In its middle usage, the intransitive *moti-agaru* denotes an adjectival notion equivalent to 'light, not too heavy' and, as is the case with English middles like *The lid lifts up easily*, implies the presence of a human agent, as seen in the naturalness of adding to (17) a human adjunct like *kodomo demo* 'for even small children'.

Our analysis of Japanese compound verbs might also be extended to English resultative constructions like those in (18).

(18) a. Witnesses said that the ground **lifted up** to one metre in places, with widespread liquefaction.
http://news.monstersandcritics.com/asiapacific/news/article_1621004.php/Buildings-down-injuries-reported-in-big-Christchurch-quake-2nd-Lead

b. An unidentified creature **washed ashore** dead, on a beach near the business district of Montauk, New York in July 2008.
http://en.wikipedia.org/wiki/Montauk_Monster

c. The Sky Rocket is powered by water pressure, so when you pull the trigger the rocket will **shoot off** into the air.
http://www.lazyboneuk.com/products/Sky-Rocket-%252d-Water-Powered.html

The intransitive verbs *lift*, *wash*, and *shoot* in (18) are not dispositional middles but anticausatives, because they refer to dynamic events that take place at a particular time. Their apparent parallelism with Japanese anticausative compounds suggests that English intransitivized resultative constructions such as these might be derived by an analogous semantic mechanism, triggered by resultative predicates such as *up*, *ashore*, and *off*, whereby the agentive action of a main verb (*lift*, *wash*, *shoot*) is converted to that of a non-human causer. Interestingly, causer adjuncts representing natural forces in (18a, b) are coded by the preposition *with*, as in *The ground lifted up with/*by/*from the earthquake* and *The creature washed ashore dead with/*by/*from the tsunami*, whereas the mechanical device in (18c) is marginally representable by *by*, as in *The rocket shot off into the air ?by/*with/*from air pressure* (John Whitman, p.c.). Compare this observation with the discussion on *from* (e.g. *The vase broke from the draught.*) in Schäfer (2012) and Rákosi (2012). Rákosi (2012) argues, based on Hungarian data, that anticausatives are intransitives from the beginning without underlying causative semantics and it is rather causer PPs that introduce the interpretation of causation to spontaneous events. This argument, however, does not apply to Japanese compound verbs or English resultative constructions, which have transitive sources.

The foregoing considerations lead us to the following well-formedness condition on the semantic reanalysis of causative to anticausative compound verbs as was schematically represented earlier in the semantic structure of (10).

(19) Well-formedness condition on anticausative compound verbs
Anticausative compound verbs gain increased acceptability to the degree that the meaning of V1 is conceptualized as representing the manner of occurrence of or state resulting from the subevent in V2 or a mechanical or natural force that brings about a change in V2 without direct manipulation by a human agent.

Formulated as a relative rather than absolute constraint, the condition in (19) enables us to measure the degree of acceptability of non-conventional anticausative compound verbs that are created sporadically. A reasonable hypothesis is that the acceptability of reanalyzed anticausative compounds correlates with the extent to which agency is perceived in V1. The less perceptible the agency of V1, the more acceptable the anticausative will be; conversely, an anticausative compound will be less acceptable if V1 is interpreted as maintaining its agency. The acceptability of reanalyzed anticausative compounds can be evaluated statistically by their I/T ratios, as demonstrated by the remarkable disparity between the illustrative examples in (20) and (21).

(20) Relatively high acceptabilities observed with compounds whose V1 may change to an adverbial meaning as a result of diminished agency.
   a. *uti-ageru* (strike-send.up) / *uti-agaru* (strike.-go.up) 'shoot up in the sky' I/T ratio = 0.896 [intr. 2,652,000 / tr. 2,959,000]
   b. *tuki-sasu* (thrust-stick (tr.)) / *tuki-sasaru* (thrust-stick (intr.)) 'stick firmly in' I/T ratio = 0.785 [intr. 5,580,000 / tr. 7,110,000]
   c. *huki-tobasu* (blow-fly (tr.)) / *huki-tobu* (blow-fly (intr.)) 'blow away, disappear altogether' I/T ratio = 0.58 [intr. 900,000 / tr. 1,551,000]
   d. *ii-tutaeru* (say-hand.down) / *ii-tutawaru* (say-be.handed.down) 'be passed down from generation to generation orally' I/T ratio = 0.463 [intr. 26,640 / tr. 57,590]
   e. *hiki-simeru* (pull-tighten (tr.)) / *hiki-simaru* (pull-tighten (intr.)) 'be tightened' I/T ratio = 0.411 [intr. 8,730,000 / tr. 21,220,000]
   f. *hiki-tigiru* (tr.) (rip-tear (tr.)) / *hiki-tigireru* (intr.) (rip-tear (intr.)) 'rip off' I/T ratio = 0.104 [intr. 76,800 / tr. 736,000]
   g. *hari-tukeru* / *hari-tuku* 'stick firmly to' I/T ratio = 0.0928 [intr. 13,733,000/ tr. 148,050,000]

(21) Extremely low acceptabilities observed with compounds whose V1 cannot be diminished in agency.

    a. *ami-awaseru* (knit-combine) 'knit together' / *ami-awasaru (knit-be.combined) 'be knitted together' IT-ratio = 0.0039 [intr. 533 / tr. 136,070]

    b. *kui-tirakasu* (eat-mess.up) 'leave a mess after eating' / *kui-tirakaru (eat-become.messy) 'get messy after eating' I/T ratio = 0.0027 [intr. 1,172 / tr. 429,800]

    c. *nui-tukeru* (sew-attach) 'sew onto' / *nui-tuku (sew-be.attached) 'be attached by sewing' I/T ratio = 0.0012 [intr. 14,490 / tr. 12,645,000]

    d. *kudoki-otosu* (persuade-obtain) 'persuade and acquire' / *kudoki-otiru (persuade-be.obtained) 'fall into one's hands by persuading' I/T ratio = 0.00091 [intr. 2,187 / tr. 2,411,000]

    e. *nage-ageru* (throw-send.up) 'throw up high' / *nage-agaru (throw-go.up) 'go up by throwing' I/T ratio = 0.00056 [intr. 493 / tr. 877,300]

    f. *yobi-atumeru* (call-gather) 'call together' / *yobi-atumaru (call-get.together) 'get together by calling' I/T ratio = 0.00037 [intr. 519 / tr. 1,404,900]

    g. *yobi-tomeru* (call-stop (tr.)) 'call and make stop' / *yobi-tomaru (call-stop (intr.)) 'be called and stop' I/T ratio = 0.000 [intr. 0 / tr. 1,231,000]

V1s in those anticausative variants in (20) that exhibit relatively high I/T ratios are amenable to reinterpretation as causer or manner adverbials modifying their host V2s, in conformity with the well-formedness condition in (19). In some examples like *uti-agaru* 'shoot up in the sky' (20a), *huki-tobu* 'blow away' (20c), and *hiki-tigireru* 'rip off' (20f), V1 is understood as representing a non-human force that directly brings about the resulting event in V2. In the other examples, the meaning of V1 is construed as an adverbial representing the manner of occurrence of or state resulting from the subevent in V2. In *ii-tutawaru* (speak-be.handed.down) 'be handed down by word of mouth' (20d), for example, the V1 *ii-* 'speak' takes on an adverbial meaning 'by word of mouth, orally'. Although this anticausative variant is not listed in dictionaries, it sounds fairly acceptable to my ear. Likewise, in the anticausative variant of the pair *hari-tukeru* 'stick with paste' and *hari-tuku* 'stick firmly' (20g), *hari-* lit. 'stick with paste' has lost the literal meaning of 'pasting' and instead depicts the firmness of the state of being stuck.

In stark contrast to these relatively acceptable anticausatives are the anticausatives illustrated in (21), which all sound bizarre and in fact have extremely low I/T ratios. The unacceptability of these examples naturally follows from the indispensability of a human agent in the execution of the actions denoted by their V1s, such as throwing, eating, sewing, coaxing, and calling.

To recapitulate, this section has shown that anticausative V-V compounds that violate the Transitivity Harmony Principle gain increased acceptability if V1 is semantically reanalyzed as a causer or manner adverbial modifying the event of V2 or its result. The relative acceptability of anticausative compounds that lack volitional agency is empirically demonstrated by their high I/T ratios as compared with the negligibly low I/T ratios of the barely acceptable examples where agency is retained, and this result tallies with the common view that (non-compound) anticausative verbs in general do not involve a volitional agent.

The findings of this section have interesting implications for general theories of valency change. The observation that Japanese anticausative compound verbs as well as English intransitivized resultative constructions co-occur with non-human causers such as mechanical or natural forces is at odds with the currently popular view that anticausatives are devoid of animate and inanimate causers (Reinhart 2002; Neeleman & van de Koot 2012; Schäfer 2012; Rappaport Hovav & Levin 2012; and others). In our view, anticausativization only defocuses the agency of the transitive base, and need not erase the causer or the entire causing event altogether. Another possible analysis would be to assume that anticausative compounds are not directly intransitivized from their transitive sources but have separate lexical entries of their own, in which case the correspondence with their transitive counterparts is to be captured by a lexical redundancy rule in the style of Jackendoff (2010). On this view, the anticausative compound *ii-tutawaru* 'be handed down orally', for example, would be formed by directly compounding the transitive stem *ii-* lit. 'speak' and the unaccusative *tutawaru* 'be passed on'. To circumvent the effect of THP under this analysis, it would be necessary to assume that the V1 *ii-* 'speak' has a lexical entry as a kind of adverbial, and not as an ordinary transitive verb. Postulation of such a lexical entry, however, lacks independent motivation and is hardly justifiable, given that such a verb stem never shows up as an independent adverbial with the meaning of 'orally' or 'by word of mouth'. In conclusion, evidence from Japanese anticausative compounds reinforces the view that anticausativization, where no volitional agent is involved, is a lexical operation of a semantic nature.

4 Decausativization in aspectual compound verbs

In this section we turn our attention to aspectual compound verbs and make the following two observations: (i) a fairly regular alternation takes place with certain aspectual V2s, presenting a systematic exception to the THP; and (ii) unlike the semantically reanalyzed intransitive compounds discussed in Section 3, intransitive variants of aspectual compound verbs maintain their agents in V1, just like the decausativized simplex verbs introduced in Section 1. Observation (i), the systematic violation of THP, is correctly predicted from our assumption that the THP effect basically applies to thematic compound verbs, whose agent arguments require co-identity. In theory, the THP is immaterial to aspectual compound verbs because their V2s lack argument structure, and in fact this class of compounds is more liberal in allowing exceptions to the THP (cf. Table 1). Observation (ii), the persistence of the agent in V1, is attributed to a particular V2, -*agaru* 'be finished', which contains the characteristic suffix -*ar* found on the simplex decausative verbs discussed in Section 1.

4.1 Valency-changing function of aspectual verbs

The central claim of this chapter is that the possibility of transitivity alternations in V-V compound verbs pivots on a distinction between two types of lexical compound verbs, thematic and aspectual. Since argument relations and selectional restriction in thematic compound verbs are collaboratively determined by the two members, it is generally impossible to change the transitivity of only the second member in violation of the THP. Because argument relations in aspectual compound verbs, on the other hand, are generally determined by V1, their V2 is not directly involved in identifying the agent as is essential in the case of thematic compound verbs. This allows aspectual V2s to undergo transitivity alternations on their own. This point manifests itself most clearly in the discrepancy between thematic and aspectual usages of V-*ageru* (V-raise/send.up) and V-*agaru* (V-rise/go.up) with respect to the possibility of transitivity alternations.

Although the V-*ageru*/V-*agaru* alternation is observed in the domains of both thematic compound and aspectual compound verbs, its applicability differs in the two cases. As shown in Section 3, alternations in thematic compounds, as exemplified by *Hanabi/roketto ga uti-agat-ta*. 'Fireworks/a rocket shot up', take place irregularly as a result of semantic reanalysis, whereas alternation between aspectual V-*ageru* and V-*agaru* is a rule-governed lexical operation whose application can be lucidly delimited by reference to event semantics, as discussed in

4.2. However, regularity is not the only feature of the V-*ageru*/V-*agaru* alternation. Its more significant feature is the preservation of the agent argument of V1 in the intransitive variant. The intransitive sentence *Seetaa ga ami-agat-ta* 'A sweater is knit/done', for example, entails that a human agent was voluntarily engaged in the act of knitting. The existence of a volitional agent is demonstrated by compatibility with adverbs like *kuroo-site* 'with great effort' and *doryoku no sue* 'as a result of effort' that depict the mental attitude of an agent, versus incompatibility with such adverbs as *katteni* 'by itself' and *hitorideni* 'of its own accord', which exclude involvement of an external cause.

(22) a. *Seetaa ga kuroo-site/*katteni ami-agat-ta.*
sweater NOM with.great.effort/*by.itself knit-go.up-PST
'The sweater was knit with great effort/*by itself.'

b. *Ronbun ga doryoku no sue / *hitorideni kaki-agat-ta.*
article NOM effor GEN after / *of.its.own.accord write-go.up-PST
'The article was written {after all the effort/*of its own accord}.'

Even more telling evidence comes from compatibility with adjuncts that overtly refer to a human agent, as exemplified by the actually attested examples in (23).

(23) a. *Oyazisan no te niyotte yaki-agat-ta okonomiyaki wa ...*
old.man GEN hand by bake-rise-PST flat.pancake TOP
'The *okonomiyaki* baked by the hand of the old man was ...'
http://blogs.dion.ne.jp/thayato210/archives/6980118.html

b. *Eiga no sutoorii wa wakai zyosei no te de si-agat-ta.*
movie GEN story TOP young woman GEN hand by do.rise-PST
'The plot of the movie was created by a young woman.'
http://www.ryuken.info/about/president

In (23), the implied agents are realized indirectly through mediation of the noun *te* 'hand', which appears to be non-omissible. This restriction can be attributed to the fact that the agent argument is existentially bound and hence cannot show up as such.

The data in (22) and (23) bring to light a decided contrast between agent entailment in aspectual compounds and the total absence of volitional agents in thematic compounds discussed in Section 3. To make this distinction explicit, we will hereafter restrict the term "anticausative compounds" to those intransitivized compounds that involve no volitional agent, as exemplified in thematic compound verbs, and refer to the intransitivized compounds of the aspectual class that imply a volitional agent as "decausative compounds", on a par with simplex decausative verbs like *tasukaru* 'be saved' and *mookaru* 'be earned' introduced in Section 1. The remainder of this section will be devoted to an elucidation of the nature of decausative V-*agaru* compounds.

4.2 Aspectual conditions on V-*ageru* compounding

As aspectual verbs, the transitive -*ageru* 'raise, send up' and the intransitive -*agaru* 'rise, go up' both denote successful completion of an event giving rise to a new state in the theme, and this meaning is by and large correlated with that seen in the independent use of these verbs, as illustrated by (24).

(24) a. *sigoto o ageru* lit. 'raise a task' = 'put a task to completion'

　　 b. *sigoto ga agaru* lit. 'a task rises' = 'a task comes to completion'

Jacobsen (1992: 234) suggests that a compound V-*agaru* (intr.) is possible only if it corresponds to the simplex intransitive *agaru* used to mean completion or production with the same subject nouns.

(25) a. *Yuukan　　　ga　　suri-agat-ta /　　agat-ta.*
　　　　evening.paper　NOM　print-go.up-PST /　go.up-PST
　　　　'The evening paper has come off the press.'

　　 b. *Zyagaimo　ga　　ni-agat-ta /　　agat-ta.*
　　　　potato　　　NOM　boil-go.up-PST /　go.up-PST
　　　　'The potatoes are done (boiling).'

While *suri-agaru* 'be done, printing' and *agaru* 'come off the press' in (25a) are both commonly used, the single verb *agaru* in (25b) is hardly acceptable to me. The paraphrasability in (25a) is not so much the norm as an exception because in most cases the V-*agaru* compound is grammatical but the simplex verb *agaru* is not. It is thus safe to assume that the alternation between compounds V-*ageru*/V-*agaru* should be discussed on its own without directly associating it with such behavior in independent verbs.

　　The alternation of aspectual V-*ageru*/V-*agaru* is not entirely automatic. Three groups of base verbs, as shown in Table 3, are differentiated with respect to their compatibility with -*ageru* and -*agaru*. This table shows that only a subset of base verbs that cooccur with transitive *-ageru* 'finish' have acceptable decausative alternants in *-agaru*.

Table 3: Compatibility with V-*ageru*/V-*agaru*

base verbs	V-*ageru* (tr.)	V-*agaru* (intr.)
Group I	✓	✓
Group II	✓	*
Group III	*	*

Verbs in group I compound felicitously with both *-ageru* and *-agaru*, as exemplified in (26). Due to space limitations, each of the examples in (26b–e) is accompanied only with an English gloss of V1 and a simplified translation of the intransitive sentence as a whole. Note that in the example sentences of (26), (27), and (28) the object nouns marked by the accusative particle *o* are to be associated with the transitive verbs shown in the braces, and the subject nouns marked by nominative *ga* with the intransitive variants.

(26) a. *Ronbun {o/ga}   {kaki-age-ta/kaki-agat-ta}*. cf. *kaki-* 'write'
       article   {ACC/NOM} {write-raise-PST/write-go.up-PST}
       (intr. meaning) 'An article is written/done (and ready for publication).'

   b. *Pan {o/ga} {yaki-age-ta/yaki-agat-ta}*. cf. *yaki-* 'bake' 'Bread is baked.'

   c. *Gohan {o/ga} {taki-age-ta/taki-agat-ta}*. cf. *taki-* 'cook' 'Rice is cooked.'

   d. *Seetaa {o/ga} {ami-age-ta/ami-agat-ta}*. cf. *ami-* 'knit' 'A pullover is knit.'

   e. *Turu {o/ga} {ori-age-ta/ori-agat-ta}*. cf. *ori-* 'fold, make origami'
      'A paper crane is folded/made.'

V1s in this group also include *koneru* 'knead (pie dough)', *iru* 'roast (coffee beans)', *itameru* 'fry (vegetables and other food)', *niru* 'boil (food)', *musu* 'steam (food), *nuu* 'sew (clothing)', *oru* 'weave', *someru* 'dye', *horu* 'carve, inscribe', *hosu* 'dry (to make dried food)', *nuru* 'paint', and *sitateru* 'tailor (suits)'. Some of these V1s have a morphologically paired intransitive (e.g. *yaku* 'bake'/*yakeru* 'be baked'), but the others lack such a paired intransitive (e.g. *amu* 'knit'), so the morphological pairing is irrelevant.

Verbs of group II, exemplified by (27), can be successfully compounded with transitive *-ageru*, but not with intransitive *-agaru*.

(27) a. *Uta {o/*ga} {utai-age-ta/*utai-agat-ta}.* cf. *utai-* 'sing' (transitive meaning 'He sang the song to the end'; intended intransitive meaning 'The song was created as a result of singing.')

b. *Sankasya no ninzuu {o/*ga} {kazoe-age-ta/*kazoe-agat-ta}.* cf. *kazoe-* 'count' (transitive meaning 'He counted up the number of participants'; intended intransitive meaning 'The number of participants was created as a result of counting.')

c. *Karada {o/*ga} {kitae-age-ta/*kitae-agat-ta}.* cf. *kitae-* 'train, build up (one's body)' (transitive meaning 'He built up his body'; intended intransitive meaning 'His body was created as a result of training.')

d. *Syuei {o/*ga} {sibari-age-ta/*sibari-agat-ta}.* cf. *sibari-* 'tie with a rope' (transitive meaning 'He tied the guard up with a rope.'; intended intransitive meaning 'The guard was created as a result of tying.'

e. *Kodomo {o/*ga} itininmae ni {sodate-age-ta/* sodate-agat-ta}.* cf. *sodate-* 'raise, bring up' (transitive meaning 'She raised her child to a full-fledged man'; intended intransitive meaning 'The child was created by raising.')

Also belonging to this group are verbs like *katameru* 'harden' (**katame-agaru* 'be hardened'), *tutomeru* 'work for a company' (**tutome-agaru* 'work for a company until retirement'), *yomu* 'read' (**yomi-agaru* 'be read through'), and *uru* 'sell' (**uri-agaru* 'be sold out').

Verbs of group III, such as *umu* 'give birth to', *tateru* 'build', *naosu* 'repair', *kowasu* 'smash', *korosu* 'kill', and *kesu* 'delete', are rejected in both transitive *-ageru* and intransitive *-agaru* compounds, as exemplified in (28).

(28) a. **Kodomo {o/ga} {umi-age-ta/umi-agat-ta}.* cf. *umi-* 'give birth to' (intended meaning 'complete giving birth to a baby')

b. **Ie {o/ga} {tate-age-ta/tate-agat-ta}.* cf. *tate-* 'build' (intended meaning 'complete building a house')

c. **Kowareta tokei {o/ga} {naosi-age-ta/naosi-agat-ta}.* cf. *naosi-* 'repair' (intended meaning 'finish repairing a broken watch.')

d. **Gaityuu {o/ga} {korosi-age-ta/korosi-agat-ta}.* cf. *korosi-* 'kill' (intended meaning 'finish killing the harmful insects.')

One could easily conjecture that it is aspectual properties of V1 that determine compatibility with -*ageru*/-*agaru*. However, the traditional classification of lexical aspect into five categories – state (*be, know, belong*), activity (*shout, push a cart*), achievement (*notice, die*), accomplishment (*build a house, walk to the bridge*), and semelfactive (*flash, hit*) – does not provide a straightforward solution to this question. In particular, the accomplishment category, which might at first glance appear to provide the most likely source of an explanation, turns out not to do so, since all three groups of base verbs belong to this category (see Rappaport Hovav 2008 for the heterogeneous nature of the accomplishment category). We will attempt to pinpoint the crucial factors by decomposing the notion of accomplishment into several components.

Rothstein (2004: 107) suggests an intuitively appealing conceptualization of accomplishments as consisting of "an activity, e, and a BECOME event which is an incremental event which 'accompanies' it". Rothstein calls this accompanying event "an incremental process", and adds that "the culmination of the accomplishment is the final minimal event in this incremental process" (p. 107), which embraces the resultant state of a theme argument. The verbs that appear to fit in with this definition most naturally are those of group I. Take *imo o yaku* 'bake potatoes', for example. This event consists of an agent's activity of applying heat to the potatoes and a concomitant incremental process of the potatoes' changing into a baked state. The incremental process has a specific point of culmination, namely the state of being baked, which constitutes the inherent upper bound of the change and its attainment induces telicity, as shown by the compatibility with time-delimiting adverbials as in *Imo o sanzyuppun de yaita* 'I baked the potatoes in 30 minutes'. Because the event includes a continual process, however, the baking event in Japanese can also accommodate a durative time adverbial perfectly, as shown by *Imo o sanzyuppunkan yaita*. 'I baked the potatoes for 30 minutes'. Accomplishments are also compatible with adverbs like *yukkuri* 'slowly' which describe the speed with which the potatoes change into the baked state, as well as with adverbs like *kanzenni* 'completely' which depict attainment of the upper bound. Compounds with the syntactic auxiliary verb -*sugiru* 'do excessively, go beyond a certain limit', as in *imo o yaki-sugita* 'I baked the potatoes too much', explicitly state that the change proceeded beyond the inherent bound. These diagnoses of accomplishment apply to group I verbs.

Verbs in group II are similar to those in group I in some respects but different in others. Like group I verbs, group II verbs freely cooccur with durative time adverbials (*Karada o sankagetukan kitaeta*. 'I trained my body for three months'), but unlike group I verbs, they have difficulty with time-delimiting adverbials (**Karada o sankagetu de kitaeta*. 'I trained my body in three months') unless a resultant state is explicitly shown. This indicates that group II verbs do not have an inherent upper bound, which can also be demonstrated by their incompatibility with the adverb *kanzenni* 'perfectly', as in **Kodomo o kanzenni sodateta*. 'I raised my child completely', or with *-sugiru* 'change beyond a certain limit', as in **Hitori no kodomo o sodate-sugita*. 'I brought up my only child too much'. Modification by *yukkuri* 'slowly' is possible, but the semantic interpretation seems to be different from when the same adverb modifies group I verbs. In the case of group I verbs, *yukkiri* 'slowly' depicts how the change in the theme progresses (i.e. the potatoes changed slowly), whereas in the case of group II verbs, the same adverb appears to refer to the slowness of the agent's action, as in *Karada o yukkuri kitaeta*. 'I trained my body slowly.' This contrast suggests that what is incremental (i.e. scalar) is the process in the case of group II verbs but is the result state itself in the case of group I verbs, reminiscent in the latter case of so-called "degree achievements" in English (e.g. *The soup cooled for/in ten minutes*). The preceding observations on group I and group II verbs can be summarized in terms of simplified causal chain schemas as in Table 4:

Table 4: Aspectual properties of V1 and compatibility with *-ageru/agaru*

	V1's causal chain schemas	Compounds with *-ageru*	Compounds with *-agaru*
Group I	activity → incremental change of state → lexically specified result	✓	✓
Group II	activity → incremental process (→ pragmatically inferred result)	✓	*
Group III	activity → transition → lexically specified result	*	*

Examples: A. *ronbun o kaku* 'write an article', *pan o yaku* 'bake bread'

B. *kodomo o sodateru* 'raise a child', *karada o kitaeru* 'build up one's body'

C. *ie o tateru* 'build a house', *tokei o naosu* 'repair a watch'

Group III verbs form a striking contrast to both group I and group II verbs, in that they are strictly telic and reject durative time adverbials, as in **Ie o ikkagetukan tateta* 'I built a house for a month', **Kodomo o sanzikan unda* 'I gave birth to a baby for three hours', **Tokei o itizikan naosita* 'I repaired the watch for an hour'. While the events described by *ie o tateru* 'build a house', *kodomo o umu* 'give birth to a child', and *tokei o naosu* 'repair a watch' are commonly conceived of as accomplishments, they actually do not involve an incremental process that continues over a period of time, as also shown by the fact that *yukkuri* 'slowly' indicates the speed of the agent's action rather than the speed with which the change progresses. It was pointed out to me by Wesley Jacobsen (p.c.) that the adverb *sukosi-zutu* 'little by little' is compatible with *ie o tateru* 'build a house' and *tokei o naosu* 'repair a watch'. This adverb, however, describes how the component parts of a theme object change, rather than how the change event itself progresses incrementally. Note that *sukosi-zutu* 'little by little' is impossible, for example, with the act of giving birth to a baby (*kodomo o umu*). There is thus no solid empirical evidence for postulating incrementality in the semantic structure of group III verbs.

Given the causal chain schemas in Table 4, the cooccurrence restriction with transitive *-ageru* can be generalized as follows: Only those transitive verbs that involve incremental processes or incremental changes of state are qualified for compounding with aspectual *-ageru*. This restriction is a natural reflection of the semantic structure of *ageru* used as an independent verb with the meaning of physical motion 'raise, lift up', which also progresses incrementally along a path.

Such aspectual properties, however, are not sufficient to characterize precisely the compatibility of intransitive *-agaru* with group I verbs and its incompatibility with group II verbs. Why does intransitive *-agaru* impose a more complex restriction on its base verbs than transitive *-ageru*? The next subsection will argue that this increased complexity is attributable to the intransitivizing suffix *-ar*, which emerges from decomposition of *-agaru* into a root *-ag* and ending *-ar(u)*.

4.3 V-*agaru* decausatives and the notion "product"

Co-composition, proposed by Pustejovsky (1995: 122–125), is a generative operation that lends a new understanding to the notion of verb in the lexicon. Consider the ambiguity of *bake* that arises in combination with different types of object nouns: a change-of-state meaning in *She baked the potato* and a creation meaning in *She baked a cake*. Pustejovsky regards the change of state meaning ('apply heat') as the basic sense of *bake*, with the creation sense generated by co-composition. The co-composition proceeds as follows. First, the Agentive quale of the verb *bake* – an act that gives rise to the baked state of an object – is specified as a 'baking' act. Second, this meaning is identical to the one specified in the Agentive quale of the noun *cake*, namely the act of baking that gives rise to a product entity 'cake'. The creation sense of the verb *bake* thus obtains by co-composition of the Agentive quale of *bake* and that of *cake*.

The notion of co-composition provides a clue to solving the question of why only group I verbs in Table 4 are eligible for -*agaru* intransitivization. Recall the grammatical V-*agaru* intransitives in (26), where typical combinations of V1 and object noun include *ronbun o kaku* 'write an article', *pan o yaku* 'bake bread', *seetaa o amu* 'knit a sweater', and *origami o oru* 'make origami by folding paper'. The 'product' interpretation of all these object nouns can be attributed to co-composition, and the meaning of co-compositional products can be seen to be highlighted by V-*agaru*. As pointed out by Himeno (1999: 41), transitive V-*ageru* may take either a material noun or a (co-compositional) product noun as its object, whereas intransitive V-*agaru* is limited to (co-compositional) product nouns. Consider (29).

(29) a. *nuno o ori-ageru* 'finish weaving a piece of cloth' [product noun]
          ito o ori-ageru 'finish weaving threads' [material noun]

      b. *nuno ga ori-agaru* 'A piece of cloth is woven' [product noun]
          *ito ga ori-agaru lit. 'Threads are done (weaving)' [material noun]

The causal chain schemas of *ito o oru* 'weave threads' and *nuno o oru* 'weave a piece of cloth' thus look as follows.

(30) a. *ito o oru* 'weave threads' (OK with -*ageru*, * with -*agaru*)
          weaving activity → incremental change of state → result state

      b. *nuno o oru* 'weave cloth' (OK with both -*ageru* and -*agaru*)
          weaving activity → incremental change of state → result state ∧ **product**

Transitive -*ageru* focuses on the last segment of 'result state', whereas intransitive -*agaru* makes crucial reference to a product entity, denoted by a result noun, that comes into being as a direct result of the incremental change of state.

A perplexing problem with this analysis is posed by *tukuru* 'make', a verb of creation par excellence. Although this verb meets the aspectual condition in the last section and is indeed compounded with the transitive -*ageru* to form *tukuri-ageru* 'finish making', it is, surprisingly, resistant to intransitivization with -*agaru*, as shown by the extremely low I/T ratio of *tukuri-ageru* and ?*tukuri-agaru: 0.0038.

(31) a. *Kare wa sekai-iti no daikigyoo o tukuri-ageta.*
          'He succeeded in building a top world enterprise.'

      b. ?**Sekai-iti no daikigyoo ga tukuri-agatta.*
          'A top world enterprise was made.'

I suggest that the ill-formedness of *tukuri-agaru (make-go.up) can be ascribed to suppletion by deki-agaru (become-go.up) 'be done, come out'. The suppletion analysis is supported by the fact that although the verb dekiru 'become, come out' is non-volitional in itself, the compound verb deki-agaru, as a semantic counterpart to tukuri-ageru, implies the existence of an agent, which is hinted at by cooccurrence with such agent-oriented adverbs as kuroo no sue 'as a result of great effort by the agent'.

Why does intransitive -agaru impose the 'product' condition on V1s? The reason, I contend, can be sought in a lexical property of the suffix -ar in -ag-ar-u. Although the morphological contrast between ageru and agaru superficially suggests an equipollent derivation, it appears that historically the suffix -ar was attached to the classical transitive form ag(u) to derive intransitive ag-ar(u).

The hypothesis I propose is that, as opposed to the lexical passive -ar in tukam-aru 'be caught/arrested' and other similar decausative verbs, which would presumably be associated with the syntactic passive -rare, the aspectual suffix -ar considered above reflects properties of the existential verb aru 'be', in particular its intransitivizing function when used as a syntactic auxiliary verb attached to the gerundive (-te) form of a main verb.

(32) Suitti   ga   ire-te   aru.
      switch   NOM   turn.on-GER   be
      'The switch is turned on. The switch is in the state of having been turned on.'

Matsumoto (1990) characterizes this resultative -te aru construction as denoting a state that has been purposefully produced by the action of an agent associated with the main verb. As Matsumoto correctly points out, the well-formedness of this construction is determined by interactions of both semantic and pragmatic factors.

Three characteristic properties of syntactic -te aru construction should be noted. First, the main verb (V1) must be transitive (but see Tsujimura [this volume] for variation on this in contemporary Japanese). Second, the action denoted by V1 is volitionally carried out to bring about a certain intended result in the object noun (though the result need not be a product that is brought into existence). Third, it involves an implicit agent that is syntactically active and can function as the controller of a purpose clause. Of these, the first property and the 'product' part of the second property are shared with aspectual -agaru. The third property of a syntactically active implicit agent seems to be lacking in aspectual -agaru. However, V-agaru semantically implies the presence of a volitional agent, as evidenced by compatibility with adverbs indicating mental attitude of an agent.

These similarities indicate a close relationship between the syntactic auxiliary *aru* and the suffix *-ar* in V-*agaru*. Of prime importance is their theme-profiling effect on the argument structure of the base verb.

(33) Theme profiling by the intransitivizer *ar(u)*
Base verb: (x <y>) → λy∃x(x <y>)

In (33), the intransitivizer *ar(u)* extracts the theme argument (y) and links it to the subject of a sentence, with the consequence that the agent argument (x) is existentially bound. When this operation takes place in syntax, the defocused agent is syntactically present in the form of a null pronoun (PRO) that is capable of acting as the controller of a purpose clause. The agent argument that is existentially bound in lexical structure, by contrast, is syntactically invisible though semantically implied.

The existence of an agent in intransitive V-*agaru* compounds is confirmed by a unique interpretation that arises, namely that the action in V1 is done purposefully – an entailment that is shared by the syntactic *-te aru* construction. Indeed, both syntactic *-te aru* and lexical V-*agaru* strongly imply that a resultant state or product intended by the agent is attained for the purpose of further use. Just as *Onigiri ga nigit-te aru* 'A rice ball is made (and is available)' implies that the rice ball is ready for someone to eat, so *Gohan ga taki-agatta* 'Rice is cooked (and is available)' means that the rice is ready to serve.

These observations lead us to assume that aspectual *agaru* is decomposed into a transitive stem *ag-* and an intransitivizing suffix *-ar*. The stem *ag-* designates the successful completion of an accomplishment eventuality denoted by V1, and the suffix *-ar* picks out a 'product' entity that comes about as a direct result of the accomplishment expressed in V1, aided by co-composition. The semantic structure of *kaki-ag-ar(u)* 'be done, writing' can be diagrammatically represented as in (34).

(34)

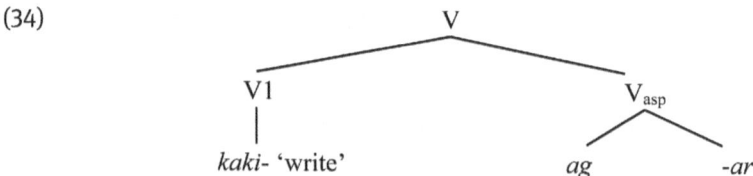

e: activity → incr. change of state → **product**   FINISH(e)   λy∃x(x <y>), y:**product**

The semantic interpretation of the whole compound proceeds compositionally. The stem *ag-* emphasizes the completion of the incremental process of V1, from which the suffix *-ar* extracts the product entity (the theme argument of V1 *kaki-*) by lambda abstraction. As a side effect of this, the agent argument of V1 is defocused (existentially bound), thus yielding the valency reduction effect of aspectual *-agaru*.

The proposed analysis of aspectual intransitive V-*agaru* explicitly predicts that there should be a marked difference in I/T ratios between those V1s that entail a product entity and those V1s that entail only a change of state in the theme argument. This prediction is well borne out in our web search.

(35) a. Verbs that imply a product (with the assistance of co-composition)
taki-agaru 'be cooked' (I/T ratio = 0.55: intr. 3,177,000 / tr. 5,752,000)
nui-agaru 'be sewed' (I/T ratio = 0.70: intr. 99030 / tr. 142,000)
ami-agaru 'be knit' (I/T ratio = 0.58: intr. 99,030 / tr. 142,000)
kaki-agaru 'be written' (I/T ratio = 0.53: intr. 1,214.900 / tr. 2,099,000)
musi-agaru 'be steamed' (I/T ratio = 0.53: intr. 610,000 / tr. 1,153,100)
nuri-agaru 'be painted' (I/T ratio = 0.21: intr. 78,970 / tr. 378,700)
sitate-agaru 'be tailored' (I/T ratio = 0.26: intr. 3,992,000 / tr. 15,302,000)

b. Verbs of change of state that entail no product entity
kitae-agaru '(body) be trained' (I/T ratio = 0.031: intr. 30,514 / tr. 987,000)
matome-agaru 'be put into a unified whole' (I/T ratio = 0.0034: intr. 30,622 / tr. 8,936,800)
sibari-agaru 'be tied up' (I/T ratio = 0.00005: intr. 30 / tr. 563,200)
yomi-agaru 'be read through' (I/T ratio = 0.00: intr. 0 / tr. 4,113,000)
utai-agaru 'be sung to the end' (I/T ratio = 0.00: intr. 0 : tr. 1,202,000)

Our analysis makes the additional prediction that decausativization with *-agaru* does not extend to other aspectual uses of *ageru*, such as spatial aspect (*mi-ageru* 'look upward'), social deixis (*moosi-ageru* 'tell a person of higher rank'), and adverbials (*yomi-ageru* 'read aloud'), which lack any entailment that an entity is produced. No decausative form is possible with any of these compounds (*mi-agaru, *moosi-agaru, *yomi-agaru).

Before closing this section, we hasten to add that the V-*ageru*/V-*agaru* pair is not alone in undergoing decausativization by the *-ar* suffix. Another fairly systematic pair can be seen in V-*kaeru* 'change, replace' and V-*kawaru* 'be changed, be replaced', as in (36).

(36) a. *Tookyoo eki o tate-kaeta.* 'They rebuilt the Tokyo Station building.'

b. *Tookyoo eki ga tate-kawatta.* 'The Tokyo Station building was rebuilt.'

Used as an aspectual verb, the transitive *kaeru* in V2 denotes performing an action again. Thus, the transitive version (36a) means that a new building came into existence as a direct result of reconstruction. Only when a new product emerges as a direct result of an activity can the intransitive V-*kawaru* be used. Examples of the same type are *tuke-kaeru* / *tuke-kawaru* 'be renewed by setting again', *nuri-kaeru* / *nuri-kawaru* 'be renewed by painting again', and *ire-kaeru* / *ire-kawaru* 'be renewed by changing the contents'. On the other hand, if a new entity does not arise as a direct result of V1's activity, the intransitive variant will be unavailable, even though the transitive variant is well-formed. Consider *kutu o haki-kaeru* 'take off one's shoes and put on a new pair instead'. Here the act of taking off and putting on shoes does not result in the creation of a new pair of shoes. Because the 'product' requirement of the -*ar* suffix is not satisfied, the decausative compound in **Kutu ga haki-kawatta* lit. 'New shoes were created by putting on again' is ungrammatical.

This section has shown that in distinct contrast to anticausativization, which takes place only sporadically with V-V compound verbs through semantic re-analysis (section 3), decausativization applies to V-V compounds rather productively by virtue of lexical semantic properties of the particular suffix -*ar*. Note that the same morphological coding appears systematically on non-compound decausative verbs like *kim-aru* (decidedecaus) 'be decided', *mook-aru* (earn-DECAUS) 'be earned', and many others discussed by Jacobsen (1992) and Kageyama (1996).

5 Concluding remarks

Based on a distinction between thematic and aspectual compounds, this chapter has developed a lexical-semantic analysis of transitivity alternations exhibited by V-V compound verbs and uncovered the systematic contrasts summarized in Table 5 between anticausativization, which takes place only irregularly with thematic compound verbs, and decausativization, which is triggered by particular aspectual verbs.

From these findings, new perspectives open up on the nature of lexical intransitivization. While anticausativization, characterized by non-involvement of human agency, has been recognized as a universal phenomenon, Japanese presents another way of intransitivizing transitive verbs, namely decausativi-

Table 5: Differences between anticausativization and decausativization

	anticausativization	decausativization
types of compounds	thematic compound verbs	aspectual compound verbs
triggers	semantic reanalysis	particular aspectual verbs
regularity	very low	high
I/T frequency ratios	low	high
semantic transparency of intransitive alternants	idiosyncratic	transparent
implied agent	no	yes

zation. The crucial difference between the two, empirically demonstrated by co-occurrence relations with adjuncts of various types, is that decausatives preserve the agent argument of the transitive base verb, whereas anticausatives are devoid of any human agent, though accompanied by natural or mechanical causers. One original contribution of this chapter has been to substantiate the relevance of these two lexical valency-decreasing operations with data from V-V compound verbs where the first member (V1) overtly expresses the presence of a human agent or non-human causer – a phenomenon that has been ignored in previous studies, which have solely targeted simplex verbs. We propose therefore that decausativization be added to the universal repertoire of lexical intransitivization operations (cf. the list in (1).)

The theoretical implications of compound verb alternations may be better appreciated if the distinction between anticausatives and decausatives is recast against the background of the old debate, going back to the 1980s, concerning the nature of passivization. One view, championed by Perlmutter & Postal (1984) and others, holds that the primary function of passives is to "promote" the object argument to subject position, whereas the other view, advocated by Shibatani (1985) and others, maintains that passivization functions primarily to demote the subject argument to adjunct status. While current research appears to favor the demotion analysis, centering on the question of how the agent is erased (cf. Reinhart 2002; Schäfer 2008; Koontz-Garboden 2009; inter alia), the Japanese data suggest that both views have validity, with anticausative compounds best regarded as a case of agent demotion and decausative compounds as a case of theme promotion. V1s in anticausative compounds denote the total lack of a human agent, whereas the -*ar* suffix in V-*agaru* decausative compounds explicitly singles out the theme argument as the subject predicated by the whole compound while maintaining the agent argument of V1 at the same time. This distinction may further be compared to that of English middle verbs and adjectival passives, which are both considered lexical. Adjectival passives like *distinguished (person)* and *cooked (food)* are like anticausatives in that they completely lack a volitional agent, whereas middle verbs like *This book reads easily (even for children)* behave like decausatives in keeping their agent arguments, though they are syntactically inactive.

Theme promotion and agent demotion may also be correlated with two types of *-ar* suffix: aspectual *-ar*, which promotes a theme (product) argument to subject, as argued in this chapter, and lexical passive *-ar*, which presumably functions to demote an agent argument. Only the latter allows syntactic realization of a defocused agent with the dative particle, as in *Yoogisya ga keisatu ni tukamatta* 'The suspect was arrested by the police'. An agent argument cannot be overtly manifested with aspectual *-ar* because aspectual *-ar* specifically highlights a product argument and binds the agent argument existentially.

Abbreviations

ACC accusative; ANTICAUS anticausative; DAT dative; DECAUS decausative; GEN genitive; GER gerundive; INST instrumental; LOC locative; NOM = nominative; PST = past; TOP = topic

Acknowledgments

This work originates from the collaborative research project "Syntactic, semantic, and morphological characteristics of the Japanese lexicon" (Project leader: Taro Kageyama), carried out at the National Institute for Japanese Language and Linguistics from 2010–2015. I am grateful to Wesley Jacobsen, Natsuko Tsujimura, and Volker Gast, chief editor of the Trends in Linguistics series, for pertinent suggestions on an earlier draft of the chapter. Special thanks go to Katsuo Tamaoka, who helped me work out the analysis of the statistical data shown in Table 1.

References

Alexiadou, Artemis. 2010. On the morphosyntax of (anti)causative verbs. In Malka Rappaport Hovav, Edit Doron & Ivy Sichel (eds.), *Lexical semantics, syntax, and event structure*, 177–203. Oxford: Oxford University Press.

Alexiadou, Artemis & Edit Doron. 2012. The syntactic construction of two non-active voices: Passive and middle. *Journal of Linguistics* 48 (1). 1–34.
Chen, Jie-Yi. 2010. Goiteki fukugōdōshi no jitakōtai to gokeisei [Transitivity alternation and word formation of lexical compound verbs]. *Nihongo Bunpō* [Journal of Japanese grammar] 10 (1). 37–53. Tokyo: Kurosio Publishers.
Comrie, Bernard. 2006. Transitivity pairs, markedness, and diachronic stability. *Linguistics* 44 (2). 303–318.
Haspelmath, Martin. 1993. More on the typology of inchoative/causative verb alternations. In Bernard Comrie & Maria Polinsky (eds.), *Causatives and transitivity*, 87–111. Amsterdam & Philadelphia: John Benjamins.
Haspelmath, Martin. 2008. Frequency vs. iconicity in explaining grammatical asymmetries. *Cognitive Linguistics* 19 (1). 1–33.
Higginbotham, James. 1985. On semantics. *Linguistic Inquiry* 16. 547–594.
Himeno, Masako. 1999. *Fukugōdōshi no kōzō to imi-yōhō* [The structure and meaning/usage of compound verbs]. Tokyo: Hituzi Syobo.
Horvath, Julia & Tal Siloni. 2011. Causatives across components. *Natural Language & Linguistic Theory* 29. 657–704.
Jackendoff, Ray. 2010. *Meaning and the lexicon: The parallel architecture 1975–2010*. Oxford: Oxford University Press.
Jacobsen, Wesley M. 1992. *The transitive structure of events in Japanese*. Tokyo: Kurosio Publishers.
Jacobsen, Wesley M. this volume. The semantic basis of Japanese transitive-intransitive derivational patterns. In Taro Kageyama & Wesley M. Jacobsen (eds.), *Transitivity and valency alternations: Studies on Japanese and beyond*. Berlin & Boston: De Gruyter Mouton.
Kageyama, Taro. 1989. The place of morphology in the grammar: Verb-verb compounds in Japanese. In Geert Booij & Jaap van Marle (eds.) *Yearbook of Morphology* 2: 73–94. Dordrecht: Foris.
Kageyama, Taro. 1993. *Bunpō to gokeisei* [Grammar and word formation]. Tokyo: Hituzi Syobo.
Kageyama, Taro. 1996. *Dōshi imiron: Gengo to ninchi no setten* [Verb semantics: The interface of language and cognition]. Tokyo: Kurosio Publishers.
Kageyama, Taro. 1999. Word formation. In Natsuko Tsujimura (ed.), *The handbook of Japanese linguistics*, 297–325. Oxford: Blackwell.
Kageyama, Taro. 2013. Goiteki-fukugōdōshi no shin-taikei [A new architecture of lexical compound verbs]. In Taro Kageyama (ed.), *Fukugōdōshi kenkyū no saisentan* [Frontiers of compound verb studies], 3–49. Tokyo: Hituzi Syobo.
Kageyama, Taro. 2016. Verb-compounding and verb-incorporation. In Taro Kageyama & Hideki Kishimoto (eds.), *Handbook of Japanese lexicon and word formation*, 273–310. Berlin & Boston: De Gruyter Mouton.
Koontz-Garboden, Andrew. 2009. Anticausativization. *Natural Language & Linguistic Theory* 27. 77–138.
Koontz-Garboden, Andrew. 2012. The monotonicity hypothesis. In Violeta Demonte & Louise McNally (eds.), *Telicity, change, and state: A cross-categorial view of event structure*, 139–161. Oxford: Oxford University Press.
Levin, Beth & Malka Rappaport Hovav. 1995. *Unaccusativity: At the syntax – lexical semantics interface*. Cambridge, MA: MIT Press.
Matsumoto, Yo. 1990. Constraints on the 'intransitivizing' resultative *-te aru* construction in Japanese. In Hajime Hoji (ed.), *Japanese/Korean Linguistics*, 269–283. Stanford: CSLI.

Matsumoto, Yo. 1998. Nihongo no goiteki fukugōdōshi niokeru dōshi no kumiawase [Combinatorial possibilities in Japanese V-V lexical compounds]. *Gengo Kenkyu* 114. 37–83.

Narrog, Heiko. this volume. Japanese transitivity pairs through time – a historical and typological perspective. In Taro Kageyama & Wesley M. Jacobsen (eds.), *Transitivity and valency alternations: Studies on Japanese and beyond*. Berlin & Boston: De Gruyter Mouton.

Neeleman, Ad & Hans van de Koot. 2012. The linguistic expression of causation. In Martin Everaert, Marijana Marelj & Tal Siloni (eds.), *The theta system: Argument structure at the interface*, 20–51. Oxford: Oxford University Press.

NINJAL (Taro Kageyama & Kyoko Kanzaki). 2014. *Compound Verb Lexicon* (online database). Tokyo: National Institute for Japanese Language and Linguistics. http://vvlexicon.ninjal.ac.jp/

Nishiyama, Kunio. 1998. V-V compounds as serialization. *Journal of East Asian Linguistics* 7. 175–217.

Perlmutter, David & Paul Postal. 1984. The 1-advancement exclusiveness law. In David Perlmutter & Carol Rosen (eds.), *Studies in relational grammar 2*, 81–125. Chicago: University of Chicago Press.

Pustejovsky, James. 1995. *The Generative Lexicon*. Cambridge, MA: MIT Press.

Rákosi, György. 2012. In defence of the non-causative analysis of anticausatives. In Martin Everaert, Marijana Marelj & Tal Siloni (eds.), *The theta system: Argument structure at the interface*, 177–199. Oxford: Oxford University Press.

Rappaport Hovav, Malka. 2008. Lexicalized meaning and the internal structure of events. In Susan Rothstein (ed.), *Theoretical and crosslinguistic approaches to the semantics of aspect*, 13–42. Amsterdam & Philadelphia: John Benjamins.

Rappaport Hovav, Malka & Beth Levin. 2012. Lexicon uniformity and the causative alternation. In Martin Everaert, Marijana Marelj & Tal Siloni (eds.), *The theta system: Argument structure at the interface*, 150–176. Oxford: Oxford University Press.

Reinhart, Tanya. 2002. The Theta system: An overview. *Theoretical Linguistics* 28 (3). 229–290.

Rothstein, Susan. 2004. *Structuring events: A study in the semantics of lexical aspect*. Oxford: Blackwell.

Schäfer, Florian. 2008. *The syntax of (anti-)causatives: External arguments in change-of-state contexts*. Amsterdam & Philadelphia: John Benjamins.

Schäfer, Florian. 2012. Two types of external argument licensing – the case of causers. *Studia Linguistica* 66 (2). 128–180.

Shibatani, Masayoshi. 1985. Passives and related constructions: A prototype analysis. *Language* 61. 821–848.

Tsujimura, Natsuko. this volume. The role of lexical semantics in the reorganization of the resultative construction. In Taro Kageyama & Wesley M. Jacobsen (eds.), *Transitivity and valency alternations: Studies on Japanese and beyond*. Berlin & Boston: De Gruyter Mouton.

Yumoto, Yoko. 2005. *Fukugōdōshi, haseidōshi no imi to tōgo* [Semantics and syntax of compound verbs and derived verbs]. Tokyo: Hituzi Syobo.

Zhu, Chunri. 2009. Fukugōdōshi no jita-taiō ni tsuite [Concerning the transitive-intransitive correspondences in compound verbs]. *Sekai no Nihongo Kyōiku* [Japanese-language education in the world] 19. 89–106. Tokyo: Bonjinsha.

Hideki Kishimoto
4 Valency and case alternations in Japanese

1 Introduction

Valency alternations may be divided into two major types: "coded alternations", which involve some change in verb form, and "uncoded alternations", which do not. Japanese has both coded alternations (e.g. passive, causative, potential, and lexically-governed transitivity alternations) and uncoded alternations (e.g. locative, substance/source, plural-agent, source-argument and possessor-raising alternations (see Kishimoto et al. 2015). Some alternations involve changes in the meanings they carry (e.g. locative and potential alternations) or changes in construction type (e.g. passive and causative alternations), but others retain their core meanings as well as their structural type (e.g. plural-agent and source-argument alternations). In Japanese, alternations are always flagged in the sense that they are reflected in the morphological marking of arguments, regardless of whether they may be categorized as coded or uncoded alternations (Malchukov et al. 2010).

Not all theoretically possible alternation patterns are available in Japanese, due to certain grammatical constraints. In this article, I will take up one such constraint, often referred to as the nominative-case constraint (NCC), and show that while valency alternations are generally constrained by the nominative-case constraint, there are nevertheless cases where this constraint does not apply. I propose to attribute this to the property of tense, which can be reduced to the question of whether tense is identified as operative or inoperative with regard to the case licensing of arguments. I suggest that when tense bears case features that license arguments, the clause is constrained by the nominative-case constraint; on the other hand, when tense bears no case feature licensing an argument, the clause is not subject to the nominative-case constraint. In the literature, there is a controversy over what gives rise to the grammatical requirement that there be a subject in the clausal subject position (Spec-TP), which is often referred to as the EPP requirement. The Japanese data pertaining to valency alternations suggest that the EPP requirement is also attributable to the property of tense.

Hideki Kishimoto, Kobe University

The discussion in this chapter proceeds as follows. In section 2, I show how the nominative-case constraint affects case-marking patterns in valency alternations if it is in force. Section 3 discusses cases where the nominative-case constraint does not apply, and shows that when tense has no case features licensing arguments, the clause is exempt from the nominative-case constraint. This section also discusses some facts that lend empirical support to a proposal on subject raising. Section 4 presents the conclusion.

2 The nominative-case constraint

One of the general case-marking constraints that has been observed in Japanese grammar is the nominative-case constraint.[1]

(1) a. *Ken ga ronbun {o/ga} kak-e-ru.*
Ken NOM paper {ACC/NOM} write-POTEN-PRS
'Ken can write a paper.'

b. *Ken ni ronbun {ga/*o} kak-e-ru.*
Ken DAT paper {NOM/ACC} write-POTEN-PRS
'Ken can write a paper.'

Potential verbs suffixed with *-(r)e* or *-(r)are* allow their subjects to bear either dative or nominative case. As seen in (1), when the subject has nominative case, the object can be marked with either accusative or nominative case. When the subject is marked with dative case, the object can only be marked with nominative case; the logical possibility of marking the object with accusative case is excluded here. The lack of a fourth possibility leads to the formulation of the nominative-case constraint.

(2) The nominative-case constraint (NCC):
A finite clause must have at least one nominative argument in it.

---

[1] When an adverbial particle is added to an argument, its case marking often does not appear on the surface. Nevertheless, a case marker can sometimes appear even with an adverbial particle, which shows that arguments are case-marked even when a case marker is suppressed in the presence of an adverbial particle. This is a situation distinct from cases where structural case markers are replaced by oblique case markers (or semantic case markers), as in the plural-agent and source-argument alternations to be discussed below.

In Japanese, the nominative-case constraint applies quite persistently. It constrains many different valency alternations, so that not all conceivable argument realization patterns are observed.[2] This can readily be confirmed by considering a certain class of transitive stative predicates where various differing case alternations can be invoked for the same predicate. For the purpose of illustrating how valency alternations are constrained by the nominative-case constraint, I will discuss three distinct types of case alternation below (i.e. dative-nominative, nominative-accusative, and dative-genitive alternations).

The first case alternation type, which I refer to as dative-nominative alternation, is realized on the subject of a transitive stative predicate such as *wakaru* 'understand, recognize'. As seen in (3), *wakaru* takes a dative subject when its object is marked with nominative case, and in such cases, its subject can be marked with nominative case as well.

(3) Ken   {ni/ga}   kono   imi   ga   wakar-u.
     Ken   {DAT/NOM}   this   meaning   NOM   understand-PRS
     'Ken understands this meaning.'

The class of dative-subject predicates that allow nominative case as an alternative subject marker includes predicates expressing perception (e.g. *mieru* 'see'), necessity (e.g. *hituyoo-da* 'necessary'), potentiality (e.g. *kanoo-da* 'possible'), existence (e.g. *aru* 'be'), and the like (see Shibatani 2001).

The second type of case alternation, referred to here as nominative-accusative alternation, applies to the objects of stative predicates. Non-verbal predicates normally do not allow accusative marking on their objects, but there is a special group of predicates, such as *suki-da* 'like', that can assign accusative case, as well as nominative case, to their objects (Shibatani 1978, Sugioka 1986).

(4) Ken   ga   tyokoreeto   {ga/o}   suki-da.
     Ken   NOM   chocolate   {NOM/ACC}   fond-PRS
     'Ken likes chocolate.'

---

2 When a finite clause is embedded in another clause, the nominative-case constraint is often not observed, as seen from the well-known case of nominative-genitive conversion.

(i) [Ken   no   kai-ta]   ronbun
    Ken   GEN   write-PST   paper
    'a paper which Ken wrote'

Since some restrictions other than the nominative-case constraint apply in embedded contexts, our discussion is limited to cases where a finite clause appears in non-embedded contexts.

The nominative-accusative alternation affects the case marking of objects rather than subjects. The class of predicates marking objects with accusative as well as nominative case includes predicates of (dis)liking (e.g. *suki-da* 'be fond of', *kirai-da* 'hate'), wanting (e.g. *hosii* 'want') and understanding (e.g. *wakaru* 'understand, recognize').[3] (Predicates like *suki-da* and *hosii* do not allow their subjects to be marked with dative case.)

Another type of valency alternation, which has not received much attention in the literature on Japanese, has to do with possessor raising, which can be invoked with certain (idiomatic) predicates including a nominal element that can host a possessor.[4]

(5) a. Sore ga [John no ki] ni sawat-ta.
    that NOM John GEN mind LOC offend-PST
    'John did not like that.'

  b. John ni wa sore ga ki ni sawat-ta.
    John DAT TOP that NOM mind LOC offend-PST
    'John did not like that.'

As shown in (5), the idiomatic predicate *ki ni sawaru* 'not like' allows its experiencer argument to appear either within the component noun *ki* 'mind' or as a clausal argument. The experiencer argument, if marked with dative case, appears as a clausal argument; when marked with genitive case, the experiencer argument appears on the inalienable noun. There are two major classes of predicates that allow this alternation, as seen in the non-exhaustive list of such predicates in (6).

(6) a. *ki ni sawaru* [mind LOC offend] 'not like' *o-ki ni mesu* [HON-mind LOC call] 'like (honorific form)' *ki ni kuwa-nai* [mind LOC eat-NEG] 'not like'

  b. *nayami no tane* [worry GEN seed] 'source of worry' *o-ki-ni-iri* [HON-mind-LOC-enter] 'favorite', *yuiitu no ziman* [only GEN pride] 'one's only source of pride'

---

3 With a non-verbal predicate like *hituyoo-da* 'necessary', accusative marking is not available for its object, but *wakaru* 'understand, recognize', which is a verbal predicate, can mark its object with accusative case when the subject is marked with nominative case (see Shibatani 1978; Koizumi 1999). As Shibatani (1978) notes, it appears that there is idiolectal variation as to whether predicates like *hosii* 'want', *wakaru* 'understand, recognize' and *suki-da* 'like' allow accusative marking on their objects.
4 The possessor-raising construction discussed here differs from often-discussed types of possessor-raising constructions that give rise to a major subject in addition to the thematic subject (Kuno 1973).

The first class of predicates in (6a) includes idiomatic predicates consisting of an inalienable noun and the verb, and the second class in (6b), nominal predicates (Kishimoto 2013, 2014).⁵ In both classes of predicates, the experiencer – generated as a possessor to a noun – can undergo possessor raising and hence participate in the possessor-raising alternation. (For the first class of predicates, I assume that the body-part noun constitutes part of the idiomatic predicate, rather than an argument.)

The three types of alternations noted above involve no change in transitivity, so the grammatical status of the arguments of the transitive stative predicates that participate in these alternations, i.e. *wakaru, suki-da,* and *ki ni sawaru,* is unvarying regardless of their case marking; in all the variants in question, the predicates take experiencer arguments as subjects, and theme arguments as objects. This fact is readily confirmed by applying subject and object tests available in Japanese.

First, the distribution of reflexive binding allows us to confirm that the experiencer arguments are construed as subjects. Reflexive *zibun* 'self' has subject orientation, as is widely recognized (e.g. Shibatani 1978; Katada 1991). With a non-stative predicate like *sikaru* 'scold', reflexive *zibun* can take a nominative subject, but not an accusative object, as its antecedent, as illustrated in (7).

(7) Ken$_i$ ga   Mari$_j$ o   zibun$_{i/*j}$ no   heya   de   sikat-ta.
    Ken   NOM   Mari   ACC   self   GEN   room   in   scold-PST
    (lit.) 'Ken$_i$ scolded Mari$_j$ in self$_{i/*j}$'s room.'

For transitive stative predicates like *wakaru* 'understand, recognize,' and *suki-da* 'be fond of', the experiencer argument, but not the theme argument, qualifies as the antecedent of reflexive *zibun*, and the possibility of reflexive binding remains

---

5 The following examples illustrate the possessor-raising alternation patterns with a nominal predicate.

(i) a. *John ni   wa   sore ga   o-ki-ni-iri   dat-ta.*
       John DAT TOP   that NOM   HON-mind-LOC-enter   COP-PST
       'John likes that.'
    b. *Sore ga   [John no   o-ki-ni-iri]   dat-ta.*
       that NOM John GEN   HON-mind-LOC-enter   COP-PST
       'That is John's favorite.'

In (ib), the predicate itself serves as a host for the possessor/experiencer argument. The predicate *o-ki-ni-iri (da)* 'favorite' also allows dative-nominative alternation on the subject when the subject counts as a clausal argument (see Kishimoto 2014).

constant regardless of the case marking of the experiencer argument, as shown in (8).

(8) a. *John$_i$ {ni wa/ ga} zibun$_i$ no kodomo ga wakara-na-i.*
John {DAT TOP/NOM} self GEN child NOM understand-NEG-PRS
'John cannot recognize his child.'

b. *John$_i$ ga zibun$_i$ no kuruma ga suki-da.*
John NOM self GEN car NOM fond-PRS
'John likes his own car.'

With a possessor-raising predicate like *ki ni sawaru* 'not like', the experiencer argument appears within an inalienable noun when marked with genitive case. This genitive experiencer serves as the antecedent of the reflexive *zibun*, in much the same way as an experiencer marked with dative case, which counts as a clausal argument, as in (9).

(9) a. *Zibun$_i$ no musuko no taido ga [John$_i$ no ki] ni sawat-ta.*
self GEN son GEN attitude NOM John GEN mind LOC offend-PST
'John did not like his son's attitude.'

b. *John$_i$ ni wa zibun$_i$ no musuko no taido ga ki ni sawat-ta.*
John DAT TOP self GEN son GEN attitude NOM mind LOC offend-PST
'John did not like his son's attitude.'

This fact shows that the experiencer argument has subject properties irrespective of whether it is marked with genitive case or dative case.[6]

Secondly, the so-called 'formal noun insertion' test provides a way of checking which argument counts as an object. As discussed by a number of researchers (e.g. Kuno 1976; Sasaguri 1999; Kishimoto 2004; Takubo 2010), the formal noun *koto* – losing its usual lexical meaning of 'fact, matter' – can be added to a nominal in direct object position, but not in subject position, as exemplified in (10).

---

[6] This fact raises the question of how reflexive *zibun* can be bound by a genitive experiencer. Although I do not discuss this point in this chapter, a genitive experiencer residing in a nominal host on the surface should be able to serve as the antecedent of *zibun* if it undergoes A-movement to a subject position via Spec-vP at the LF level. See Kishimoto (2013) for arguments that a subject positioned in Spec-TP having passed Spec-vP via A-movement at some point in the derivation can serve as the antecedent of *zibun*.

(10) a. *John ga Ken (no koto) o sikat-ta.*
    John NOM Ken (GEN fact) ACC scold-PST
    'John scolded Ken.'

   b. *John (*no koto) ga Ken o sikat-ta.*
    John (GEN fact) NOM Ken ACC scold-PST
    'John scolded Ken.'

   c. *Ken (*no koto) ga John ni sikar-are-ta.*
    Ken (GEN fact) NOM John by scold-PASS-PST
    'Ken was scolded by John.'

In (10a), the object *Ken no koto* can refer to a human individual even in the presence of *koto*, but in (10b), *John no koto* cannot; *koto* here can only be interpreted as a substantive noun referring to an abstract entity. Not even the nominative subject of a passive clause like (10c), which has been promoted from an erstwhile direct object, can refer to a human if it occurs with *koto*. This shows that formal noun insertion is sensitive to the surface grammatical function of arguments, and can be applied only to direct objects.

Bearing in mind this generalization on formal noun insertion, let us consider stative predicates like *wakaru* 'understand, recognize' and *suki-da* 'be fond of'. These stative predicates allow theme arguments to occur with the formal noun *koto*, regardless of their case-marking pattern.

(11) a. *Ken {ni wa/ga} ano ko (no koto) ga wakara-na-i.*
    Ken {DAT TOP/NOM} that child (GEN fact) NOM understand-NEG-PRS
    'Ken cannot recognize that child.'

   b. *Ken ga ano ko (no koto) {ga/o} suki-da.*
    Ken NOM that child (GEN fact) {NOM/ACC} fond-PRS
    'Ken likes that child.'

This fact shows that the theme argument of transitive stative predicates like *wakaru* and *suki-da* is construed as an object whether it is marked with accusative or nominative case. By contrast, the formal noun *koto* cannot be added to an experiencer argument, regardless of whether it is marked with dative or nominative case.

(12) a. *Ken (*no koto) {ni wa/ga} ano ko ga wakar-u.*
    Ken (GEN fact) {DAT TOP/NOM} that child NOM understand-PRS
    'Ken can recognize that child.'

b. *Ken (*no koto) ga ano ko {ga/o} suki-da.*
  Ken (GEN fact) NOM that child {NOM/ACC} fond-PRS
  'Ken likes that child.'

The examples in (12) are not acceptable when the experiencer argument occurs with *koto*, showing that *koto* cannot be interpreted here as a formal noun. This fact also shows that the experiencer argument never counts as an object, regardless of its case marking.

For the predicate *ki ni sawaru* 'not like', which allows possessor-raising alternation, however, a theme argument marked with nominative case allows the insertion of the formal noun *koto* whether the experiencer is marked with genitive or dative case.

(13) a. *Musuko (no koto) ga [John no ki] ni sawat-ta.*
    son (GEN fact) NOM John GEN mind LOC offend-PST
    'John did not like his son.'

  b. *John ni wa musuko (no koto) ga ki ni sawat-ta.*
    John DAT TOP son (GEN fact) NOM mind LOC offend-PST
    'John did not like his son.'

Importantly, in the genitive-experiencer variant (13a), the theme counts as the sole clausal argument, but still behaves as an object. On the other hand, the experiencer argument resists formal insertion in both variants.[7]

(14) a. *Musuko ga [John (*no koto) no ki] ni sawat-ta.*
    son NOM John (GEN fact) GEN mind LOC offend-PST
    'John did not like his son.'

  b. *John (*no koto) ni wa musuko ga ki ni sawat-ta.*
    John (GEN fact) DAT TOP son NOM mind LOC offend-PST
    'John did not like his son.'

In the light of the data in (14), coupled with the facts from reflexivization, it is reasonable to conclude that possessor-raising alternation, just like the two other types of alternation, is a valency alternation that does not effect a change in transitivity.

---

[7] As Sasaguri (1999) observes, an argument cannot be accompanied by *koto* if it appears in a nominal, regardless of its grammatical relation. This does not affect the argument here. The nominative theme argument tolerates *koto*-insertion, so we would not expect the experiencer argument to occur with the formal noun *koto*.

It is worth noting here that there exist transitive stative predicates like *(o-)ki ni mesu/mesa-nai* '(not) like' that are able to trigger any of the three types of alternation, as seen in (15).

(15) a. *Sensei {ni wa/ ga} ano ko ga o-ki ni mesa-na-i.*
  teacher {DAT TOP/NOM} that child NOM HON-mind LOC call-NEG-PRS
  'The teacher does not like that child.' <DAT, NOM> or <NOM, NOM>

  b. *Sensei ga ano ko {ga/o} o-ki ni mesa-na-i.*
  teacher NOM that child {NOM/ACC} HON-mind LOC call-NEG-PRS
  'The teacher does not like that child.' <NOM, NOM> or <NOM, ACC>

  c. *Ano ko ga [sensei no o-ki] ni mesa-na-i.*
  that child NOM teacher GEN HON-mind LOC call-NEG-PRS
  'That child is not the teacher's darling.' <GEN, NOM>

The idiom *(o-)ki ni mesu/mesa-nai* counts as a transitive stative predicate that selects either a dative or a nominative subject (15a). This idiomatic predicate falls under the category of predicates of (dis)liking as well, so that the nominative-accusative alternation applies to its object (15b). The predicate also qualifies as a possessor-raising predicate, allowing its experiencer argument to occur within the inalienable noun, marked with genitive case (15c). When the experiencer is a clausal argument, the predicate serves as a transitive predicate that allows the dative-nominative alternation on the subject and the nominative-accusative alternation on the object. Accordingly, *o-ki ni mesu/mesa-nai* allows three different kinds of case marking on the experiencer subject, i.e. dative, nominative, and genitive marking, and two kinds of case marking on the theme object, i.e. accusative and nominative marking.

Logically speaking, *o-ki ni mesu/mesa-nai* should allow six different combinations of subject and object marking <DAT, NOM>, <NOM, NOM>, <NOM, ACC>, <GEN, NOM>, <DAT, ACC> and <GEN, ACC>. However, the logically possible case frames <DAT, ACC> and <GEN, ACC> do not in fact occur, as can be seen in (16).

(16) a. **Sensei ni wa ano ko o o-ki ni mesa-na-i.*
  teacher DAT TOP that child ACC HON-mind LOC call-NEG-PRS
  'The teacher does not like that child.' *<DAT, ACC>

  b. **Ano ko o [sensei no o-ki] ni mesa-na-i.*
  that child ACC teacher GEN HON-mind LOC call-NEG-PRS
  'That child is not the teacher's darling.' *<GEN, ACC>

The data illustrate that the composite predicate *o-ki ni mesu/mesa-nai* allows only the four case frames <DAT, NOM>, <NOM, NOM>, <NOM, ACC>, and <GEN, NOM>. Since the illegitimate case frames *<DAT, ACC> and *<GEN, ACC> both lack nominative case, it would appear that the unavailable frames are ruled out by the nominative-case constraint.

Recall that the three types of case alternation trigger no change in transitivity. In the case of *o-ki ni mesu/mesa-nai* as well, the experiencer counts as subject and the theme as object in all the variants. In the first place, the experiencer argument consistently behaves as a syntactic subject, for it can serve as the antecedent of subject-oriented *zibun* regardless of its case marking.

(17) a. Sensei$_i$ ga zibun$_i$ no gakusei {ga/o}   o-ki   ni   mesa-na-i.
       teacher NOM self   GEN student {NOM/ACC} HON-mind LOC call-NEG-PRS
       'The teacher does not like his own student.'

   b. Sensei$_i$ ni wa zibun$_i$ no gakusei ga o-ki   ni mesa-na-i.
      teacher DAT TOP self   GEN student NOM HON-mind LOC call-NEG-PRS
      'The teacher does not like his own student.'

   c. Zibun$_i$ no gakusei ga [sensei$_i$ no o-ki]   ni mesa-na-i.
      self   GEN student NOM teacher GEN HON-mind LOC call-NEG-PRS
      'His own student is not the teacher's darling.'

Secondly, the formal noun *koto*, which is possible only with object arguments, is allowed to occur with the theme argument here.

(18) a. Sensei ni wa kare (no koto) ga   o-ki   ni   mesa-na-i.
       teacher DAT TOP he   (GEN fact) NOM HON-mind LOC call-NEG-PRS
       'The teacher does not like him.'

   b. Sensei ga   kare (no koto) {ga/o}   o-ki   ni mesa-na-i.
      teacher NOM he   (GEN fact) {NOM/ACC} HON-mind LOC call-NEG-PRS
      'The teacher does not like him.'

   c. Kare (no koto) ga [sensei no o-ki]   ni mesa-na-i.
      he   (GEN fact) NOM teacher GEN HON-mind LOC call-NEG-PRS
      'He is not the teacher's darling.'

Needless to say, the insertion of the formal noun *koto* is not allowed with the experiencer argument, which counts as the subject of *o-ki ni mesu/mesa-nai*.

(19) a. *Sensei (*no koto) ni wa kare ga o-ki ni mesa-na-i.*
teacher (GEN fact) DAT TOP he NOM HON-mind LOC call-NEG-PRS
'The teacher does not like him.'

b. *Sensei (*no koto) ga kare {ga/o} o-ki ni mesa-na-i.*
teacher (GEN fact) NOM he {NOM/ACC} HON-mind LOC call-NEG-PRS
'The teacher does not like him.'

c. *Kare ga [sensei (*no koto) no o-ki] ni mesa-na-i.*
he NOM teacher (GEN fact) GEN HON-mind LOC call-NEG-PRS
'He is not the teacher's darling.'

The data show that the grammatical relations of the two arguments of *o-ki ni mesu/mesa-nai* are invariant regardless of their case marking (even when the experiencer is embedded under the inalienable noun *ki* 'mind').

In summary, the predicate *o-ki ni mesu/mesa-nai* can invoke three different types of valency alternation: (1) the dative-nominative alternation (available for subjects of transitive stative predicates), (2) the nominative-accusative alternation (available for objects of predicates of (dis)liking), and (3) the possessor-raising alternation. The experiencer (i.e. the subject) can be marked with nominative, dative, or genitive case, and the theme (i.e. the object) with nominative or accusative case. Theoretically, the predicate should allow six different patterns of argument marking, but some of the logical possibilities are missing, by virtue of the nominative-case constraint.

3 Tense and the NCC

The previous section has shown that valency alternations, such as the dative-nominative, nominative-accusative, and possessor-raising alternations, are constrained by the nominative-case constraint. In this section, I will show that other valency alternations, such as the plural-agent and source-argument alternations, are apparently exempt from this constraint. I argue that the nominative-case constraint is not in force when tense is rendered inoperative for the case licensing of arguments because of oblique-case replacement. I also show that even when oblique-case replacement takes place, the nominative-case constraint is enforced if tense participates in the case licensing of arguments.

3.1 Two valency alternations exempt from the NCC

Let us begin by discussing the source-argument alternation. This alternation involves the ablative marker *kara* 'from' which alternates variously with nominative, dative, and accusative case markers, as shown in (20).⁸

(20) a. Watasi {ga/kara} sono koto o hanasi-mas-u.
     1.SG.   {NOM/ABL} that fact ACC talk-POL-PRS
     'I will be the one to talk about (bring up) that matter.'

   b. Ken {ga/kara} Eri ni hon o atae-ru.
      Ken {NOM/ABL} Eri DAT book ACC give-PRS
      'Ken will give the book to Eri.'

   c. Ken ga Eri {ni/kara} hon o morat-ta.
      Ken NOM Eri {DAT/ABL} book ACC get-PST
      'Ken got the book from Eri.'

   d. Otoko ga ie {o/kara} de-ta.
      man NOM house {ACC/ABL} depart-PST
      'The man left (from) the house.'

Kara-replacement is possible insofar as an argument can be characterized as a source. In (20a), the subject can be characterized as playing both the role of source and agent, thus allowing nominative case on the subject to be replaced with ablative *kara*. As shown in (20b) and (20c), source arguments with change-of-possession verbs, including verbs of communication, are also compatible with ablative marking. Similarly, verbs of departure, such as *deru* 'go out', allow the accusative-ablative alternation on their complements, as in (20d), because such verbs focus on the starting point of a motion, i.e. source. This type of

---

8 The present discussion concerns only cases where arguments receive oblique marking. Incidentally, note that a phrase marked with the ablative marker *kara* 'from' is used as an adjunct rather than an argument when it designates ordering, as in (ia).

(i) a. *John ga ringo kara tabe-ta.*
       John NOM apple ABL eat-PST
       'John ate, starting from apples.' (OK with an 'ordering' sense)

   b. *John ga huruutu o ringo kara tabe-ta.*
      John NOM fruit ACC apple ABL eat-PST
      'John ate fruit, starting from apples.'

The adjunct status of the *kara*-phrase in (ia) can be verified by (ib), where an accusative argument is expressed independently of the *kara*-marked expression.

alternation is found with English verbs as well, such as *leave* and *depart* (see e.g. Levin 1993). Note, however, that when *deru* takes an inherently non-sentient subject like *kemuri* 'fume', no accusative marking is available, leaving ablative marking as the only possible marking on the path argument, as seen in (21).

(21) Kemuri   ga   entotu   {*o/kara}   de-ta.
     fume   NOM   chimney   {ACC/ABL}   depart-PST
     'The fume went out from the chimney.'

This is presumably because *deru* in (21) is construed as an unaccusative verb, which takes an internal argument realized as a surface subject (Miyake 1996; Levin & Rappaport Hovav 1995).

In (20a) and (20b), the agent argument retains subject status even if nominative case is replaced by ablative *kara*. This can be seen from the fact that in both examples, the agent can be construed as the antecedent of the subject-oriented reflexive *zibun*, irrespective of whether it is marked with nominative *ga* or ablative *kara*.[9]

(22) a. Ken_i {ga/kara wa} $zibun_i$ no koto o hanasa-nakat-ta.
        Ken {NOM/ABL TOP} self GEN fact ACC talk-NEG-PST
        'Ken did not talk about himself.'

    b. Ken_i {ga/kara mo} seito ni $zibun_i$ no koto o osie-ta.
        Ken {NOM/ABL also} pupil DAT self GEN fact ACC teach-PST
        'Ken (also) told his pupils things about himself.'

---

9 Subject honorification provides another form of verification, since it has subject orientation (Harada 1976; Shibatani 1978). As shown in (i), the agent/source argument of *hanasu* 'talk' can be targeted for subject honorification regardless of whether it receives oblique *kara* or nominative *ga* marking via the source-subject alternation.

(i) *Suzuki-sensei   {ga/kara}   kekka o   **o**-hanasi-**ni**-**nat**-ta.*
    Suzuki-teacher   {NOM/ABL}   result ACC HON-talk-DAT-become-PST
    'Prof. Suzuki talked about the result.'

The same holds true for the plural-agent alternation. Example (i) shows that the plural agent argument of *tateru* 'draw up' can be targeted for honorification, whether it is marked with *ga* or *de*.

(ii) *Sensei-tati {ga/de}   keikaku o   **o**-tate-**ni**-**nat**-ta.*
     teacher-PL {NOM/INST} plan   ACC HON-make-DAT-become-PST
     'The teachers drew up the plan.'

These data illustrate that neither the source-argument nor plural-agent alternation has an effect on the transitivity of a clause.

The examples in (22) show that the source-argument alternation does not alter the subject status of the experiencer argument. What is important is that the ablative-subject sentences taking the case frame <ABL, ACC> or <ABL, DAT, ACC> are acceptable, as in (20a) and (20b), even though they lack nominative arguments (see Inoue 1998, 2005), showing that the ablative-subject construction is exempt from the nominative-case constraint.

Before proceeding, two remarks are in order. First, the subject of a ditransitive verb like *ataeru* 'give' can be identified as a source when the verb denotes a change of possession or transmission of a message (see Kishimoto 2001a). Thus, in (20b), the subject can be assigned ablative marking. The subject of *ataeru* does not always count as a source, however, in which case *kara*-replacement is blocked, as seen in (23).

(23) *Tikyuu-ondanka {ga/*kara} noogyoo ni eikyoo o atae-te i-ru.*
global-warming {NOM/ABL} agriculture DAT influence ACC give-GER be-PRS
'Global warming is causing bad effects on agriculture.'

In (23), the subject is understood to be no more than a cause that exerts an influence on the causee – the indirect object – with no conceivable transfer of possession from the former to the latter. Thus, (23) is unacceptable if nominative *ga* is replaced by *kara*.

Secondly, the teaching verb *osieru* 'teach' can take the two distinct case frames <NOM, DAT, ACC> and <NOM, ACC>, which are not available for other predicates carrying similar meanings, like *kyooiku-suru* 'educate'.

(24) a. *Abe-sensei ga seito ni eigo o osie-ru.*
Abe-teacher NOM pupil DAT English ACC teach-PRS
'Prof. Abe teaches English to the pupils.'

b. *Abe-sensei ga koko no seito o osie-ru.*
Abe-teacher NOM here GEN pupil ACC teach-PRS
'Prof. Abe teaches the pupils here.'

The case-marking pattern in (24a) is typically found among verbs denoting transfer of possession, while (24b) involves typical transitive marking. (Interestingly, the corresponding 'teaching' verb in other languages including English often shows the same kind of alternation.) These two different case-marking patterns are available for the verb *osieru* 'teach' due to its distinct meanings. Indeed, the fact that the two alternants show a difference in the possibility of *kara*-replacement suggests that they should have two distinct meanings.

(25) a. *Abe-sensei   {ga/kara}   seito   ni   kaitoo   o   osie-ru.*
   Abe-teacher {NOM/ABL} pupil DAT answer ACC teach-PRS
   'Prof. Abe teaches answers to the pupils.'

b. *Abe-sensei   {ga/*kara}   koko   no   seito   o   osie-ru.*
   Abe-teacher {NOM/ABL} here GEN pupil ACC teach-PRS
   'Prof. Abe teaches the pupils here.'

When the teaching verb takes the case frame <NOM, DAT, ACC>, the subject can receive alternative ablative marking, as in (25a). In (25a), the subject is identified as a source, since *osieru* 'teach' denotes transfer of possession, as is the case with the ditransitive verb *ataeru* 'give' in (20b). On the other hand, when the same verb takes the <NOM, ACC> case frame, as in (25b), the subject cannot receive ablative marking (in the intended sense), as it is not conceived of in that case as a source.

The case frame <NOM, ACC> is found among activity verbs like *sidoo-suru* 'supervise', *kyooiku-suru* 'educate', and *homeru* 'praise', which describe an action directed toward theme, with no entailment of a change of state. Given this fact, it is reasonable to hypothesize that when *osieru* takes the <NOM, ACC> frame, it counts as an activity verb, but that it counts as an accomplishment verb when it takes the <NOM, DAT, ACC> frame, since in that case it denotes transfer of possession. In fact, the distribution of time adverbs in (26) confirms that the verb *osieru* appearing in the <NOM, ACC> frame is construed as an activity verb, while the same verb with the <NOM, DAT, ACC> frame is an accomplishment verb.

(26) a. *Abe-sensei   ga   {*iti-zikan de/iti-zikan}   koko   no   seito   o   osie-ta.*
   Abe-teacher NOM {one-hour in/one-hour} here GEN pupil ACC teach-PST
   'Prof. Abe taught the pupils here {*in one hour/for one hour}.'

b. *Abe-sensei   ga   {iti-zikan de/iti-zikan}   seito   ni   kaitoo   o   osie-ta.*
   Abe-teacher NOM {one-hour in/one-hour} pupil DAT answer ACC teach-PST
   'Prof. Abe taught the answers to the pupils {in one hour/for one hour}.'

Moreover, the verb *osieru* 'teach' exhibits a transitivity alternation with *osowaru* 'be taught'. A clause headed by *osowaru* displays a case-marking pattern akin to that found in passive clauses, as seen in (27).

(27) a. *Gakusei   ga   sono sensei   {ni/kara}   eigo   o   osowat-ta.*
   student NOM that teacher {DAT/ABL} English ACC be.taught-PST
   'The students learned English from that teacher.'

b. *Gakusei ga sono sensei {ni/kara} eigo o osie-rare-ta.*
   student NOM that teacher {DAT/ABL} English ACC teach-PASS-PST
   'The students were taught English by that teacher.'

In (27a), just like (27b), the dative phrase is construed as a source, and hence can be replaced by ablative *kara*.

To return to our earlier discussion, another case of apparent exceptions to the nominative-case constraint is found in the plural-agent alternation, which gives rise to the possibility of subject marking either with nominative *ga* or instrumental (possibly locative) *de* (see Takubo 2010).

(28) *Sensei-tati {ga/de} keikaku o tate-ta.*
     teacher-PL {NOM/INST} plan ACC make-PST
     'The teachers drew up the plan.'

This alternation is possible with verbs taking agentive subjects that refer to more than one individual (or to a group of individuals).[10] Thus, the subject cannot be marked with *de* if it refers to a single individual, such as *Ken*.

The *de*-marked agent argument in (28) retains its grammatical status as subject even though nominative case has been replaced here by an oblique marker, and is therefore able to act as the antecedent for the reflexive *zibun*.

(29) *Sensei-tati$_i$ {ga/de} zibun(-tati)$_i$ no keikaku o tate-ta.*
     teacher-PL {NOM/INST} self(-PL) GEN plan ACC make-PST
     'The teachers drew up their own plan.'

The agent argument serves as subject whether it is marked with nominative *ga* or oblique *de*. Notably, no nominative argument appears in (28) when the subject is marked with instrumental *de*. The acceptability of the variant formed by replacing nominative case with oblique *de* illustrates that the plural-agent alternation is not constrained by the nominative-case constraint.

One important question that immediately arises here is why the nominative-case constraint does not apply to the source-argument and plural-agent alternations, unlike the other alternations discussed in section 2. A key to understand-

---

10 No semantic plurality is required of *de*-marked adjuncts, unlike subjects marked with oblique *de*, as shown in (i).

(i) *Watasi ga zibun de sono keikaku o tate-ta.*
    1.sg. NOM self INST that plan ACC make-PST
    'I myself drew up that plan.'

ing this issue lies in the fact that T enters into a case-licensing relation with a nominative argument, as discussed by Takezawa (1987), Koizumi (1999), and Kishimoto (2001b) (see also Kuno 1973; Tada 1992). Given this, I suggest that the nominative-case constraint is enforced when T is operative (i.e., T is operative if it carries a formal case feature that needs to be deleted in agreement with an argument), but that this nominative-case constraint is not in force when T is deactivated. I propose here that while inoperative T bears no case feature licensing arguments, operative T always bears [+NOM] as its most prominent case feature.

From the theoretical perspective of implementing "feature agreement" (see Chomsky 1995, 2000, 2001, 2004, and others), the facts regarding variant source-subject and plural-agent clauses with no nominative argument can be accounted for in the following way. To begin with, it is reasonable to assume that T can be deactivated if nominative case on the subject is replaced by an oblique marker, since two distinct types of T are available in Japanese, one without any case feature and another, more ordinary, type that is equipped with case features. The existence of T without case features is motivated independently by so-called avalent (or zero-place) predicates. While many clauses require the presence of at least one nominative argument in Japanese, meteorological verbs like *sigureru* 'shower' and *hubuku* 'snow storm', as noted by Kuroda (1978), as well as the time-denoting verb *suru* 'pass', do not select any argument, as seen in (30).

(30) a. *Kinoo   hubui-ta.*
yesterday snow.storm-PST
'It snow-stormed yesterday.'

   b. *Iti-zikan si-tara, (watasi wa   kaer-u).*
one-hour do-if   1.sg.   TOP return-PRS
'When one hour has gone by, (I will go home).'

Although no nominative argument appears in the clauses headed by *hubuku* 'snow-storm' or *suru* 'pass' in (30), these clauses are fully acceptable. This fact illustrates that T associated with these predicates has no case feature that case-licenses a nominative argument. Since Japanese allows inoperative T to appear in certain contexts, as exemplified in (30), I suggest that when a subject is marked with oblique case as a result of the source-argument or plural-agent alternation, T without any case feature is merged with the clause, and hence the nominative-case constraint does not apply.

More concretely, in nominative-subject constructions, T comprises [+NOM], as in $T_{[+NOM]}$.[11] (Note that case features need to be deleted in the derivation; if they fail to be deleted, the derivation is illegitimate.) In (31a), which has a nominative subject, the case feature [+NOM] on T is deleted by agreement with the case feature on the nominative subject. If the clause has an object, the case feature [+ACC] on V is deleted along with the case feature of the object by agreement.

(31) a. [SBJ~~[+NOM]~~ OBJ~~[+ACC]~~ V~~[+ACC]~~ T~~[+NOM]~~]

 b. [SBJ ABL/INST OBJ~~[+ACC]~~ V~~[+ACC]~~ T]

In (31a), the nominative-case constraint applies, for T is operative, and the derivation is legitimate only when a nominative argument is present in the clause. On the other hand, obliquely-marked arguments do not require an external licenser, so that if nominative case on the subject is replaced by an oblique marker, T is rendered inert (or inactive). This means that inoperative T, but not operative T, is merged with this type of clause, as in (31b). In (31b), the derivation is legitimate (without a nominative argument), because the case feature [+ACC] on V is deleted via agreement with the case feature on the accusative object. Since T does not include any case features that need to be deleted in the derivation, (31b) is exempt from the nominative-case constraint, and hence the sentence is acceptable even if it contains no nominative argument.

Under the view espoused here, the difference between nominative-subject and oblique-subject clauses in applicability of the nominative-case constraint is accounted for, relying on the tense-type distinction between operative and inoperative T. Alternatively, one might say that the nominative-case constraint is voided if nominative case is simply replaced by an oblique (or semantic) case marker. Even though the core cases – (20a) and (28) – can be accounted for in this way, this cannot be the whole story, as the clauses in (32) are constrained by the nominative-case constraint.

(32) a. Ken ga kono heya {ga/kara} de-rare-nakat-ta.
 Ken NOM this room {NOM/ABL} leave-POTEN-NEG-PST
 'Ken could not leave (from) this room.'

---

[11] According to Chomsky (2000, 2001), the structural case feature on an argument is valued as nominative if T is the probe. Since, in Japanese, finite T is not always capable of valuing the case feature on a nominative argument, it is reasonable to state that only when T bears [+NOM] can it participate in the case valuation of nominative arguments.

b. *Ken ni wa kono heya {ga/*kara} de-rare-nakat-ta.*
    Ken DAT TOP this room {NOM/ABL} leave-POTEN-NEG-PST
    'Ken could not leave (from) this room.'

While nominative case on the locative argument can be replaced by *kara* in (32a), this replacement is not allowed in (32b). The sole difference between (32a) and (32b) lies in the marking of the subject. These alternation patterns are comparable to those found in (33).

(33) a. *Ken ga kono heya {ga/o} de-rare-nakat-ta.*
        Ken NOM this room {NOM/ACC} leave-POTEN-NEG-PST
        'Ken could not leave this room.'

   b. *Ken ni wa kono heya {ga/*o} de-rare-nakat-ta.*
        Ken DAT TOP this room {NOM/ACC} leave-POTEN-NEG-PST
        'Ken could not leave this room.'

Just as accusative case cannot replace nominative case in (33b), so too oblique *kara* cannot replace nominative case in (32b). It should be apparent then that in (32b), the nominative-case constraint rules out the ablative-source variant where nominative case is replaced with *kara*.

The same holds true for the plural-agent alternation. The dative-subject causative sentence in (34b) results in unacceptability if the nominative case on the object is replaced by dative *ni*, accusative *o*, or instrumental *de*.

(34) a. *Ken ga kodomo-tati {ga/ni/o/de} asob-ase-rare-nakat-ta.*
        Ken NOM child-PL {NOM/DAT/ACC/INST} play-CAUS-POTEN-NEG-PST
        'Ken could not {let/make} the children play.'

   b. *Ken ni wa kodomo-tati {ga/*ni/*o/*de} asob-ase-rare-nakat-ta.*
        Ken DAT TOP child-PL {NOM/DAT/ACC/INST} play-CAUS-POTEN-NEG-PST
        'Ken could not {let/make} the children play.'

Both sentences in (34) fall into the class of potential constructions, where the subject has the option of bearing either nominative or dative marking. The two variants in (34) are derived from (35) by adding the potential suffix *rare* to the causative predicate.

(35) *Ken ga kodomo-tati {ni/o/de} asob-ase-nakat-ta.*
     Ken NOM child-PL {DAT/ACC/INST} play-CAUS-NEG-PST
     'Ken did not {let/make} the children play.'

When the subject is marked with dative case, as in (34b), the causee cannot take oblique *de*, just as it cannot take accusative or dative case. This fact suggests that in (34b), the nominative-case constraint prevents *de* from substituting for nominative *ga* when the subject is marked with dative case.[12]

The data illustrate that, due to the nominative-case constraint, it is not always possible to derive a clause with no nominative argument by means of oblique-case replacement. The generalization that emerges here is that the nominative-case constraint cannot be voided in constructions where the subject is marked with dative case. These facts naturally fall out if tense is responsible for sanctioning dative case, as well as nominative case, in dative-subject constructions, i.e. if T is furnished with [+DAT] alongside [+NOM], as in $T_{[+DAT], [+NOM]}$ (see Kishimoto 2001b). In dative-subject constructions, the dative case feature [+DAT] appearing on T is deleted in agreement with the case feature on the dative subject, and the nominative case feature [+NOM] is deleted by the case feature on the nominative object, as illustrated in (36a).

(36) a. [SBJ$_{[+\text{DAT}]}$ OBJ$_{[+\text{NOM}]}$ Vv   T$_{[+\text{DAT}] [+\text{NOM}]}$]

   b. *[SBJ$_{[+\text{DAT}]}$ OBJ$_{[+\text{ACC}]}$ Vv$_{[+\text{ACC}]}$ T$_{[+\text{DAT}] [+\text{NOM}]}$]

   c. *[SBJ$_{[+\text{DAT}]}$ OBJ-ABL Vv   T$_{[+\text{DAT}] [+\text{NOM}]}$]

In dative-subject constructions, even if nominative case on the object is replaced by an oblique marker such as *kara*, T bears the case feature [+DAT] that needs to be deleted in agreement with the case feature on the dative subject, which means that T cannot be deactivated, and that [+NOM] consequently must also appear on T. In (36b–c), the derivation is ruled out because [+NOM] on T remains undeleted in the absence of a nominative argument. In other words, owing to the presence of operative T, the derivation of dative-subject sentences is not

---

[12] A causative clause can be embedded in *tough*-predicates like *yasui* 'easy' and *nikui* 'hard'. Here, the same pattern of distribution with regard to oblique *de* replacement is observed.

(i) a. *Ken ga   kodomo-tati {ga/de}   asob-ase-yasukat-ta.*
       Ken NOM child-PL   {NOM/INST} play-CAUS-easy-PST
       'It was easy for Ken to {let/make} the children play.'

   b. *Ken ni   kodomo-tati {ga/*de}   asob-ase-yasukat-ta.*
       Ken DAT child-PL   {NOM/INST} play-CAUS-easy-PST
       'It was easy for Ken to {let/make} the children play.'

When the subject is marked with nominative case, the causee can take oblique *de*, via the plural-agent alternation, as in (ia). Oblique *de* replacement is not allowed, however, when the subject is marked with dative case, as (ib) shows.

possible unless they contain a nominative argument.[13] Thus, a violation of the nominative-case constraint is incurred in dative-subject constructions if nominative case on the object is replaced by an accusative or oblique case marker.

The present analysis taking tense as responsible for the nominative-case constraint rests on the assumption that T licenses dative case on the dative subject (Chomsky 2001, 2004, 2008). It is sometimes assumed (see e.g. Ura 2000), however, that dative case is to be treated as inherent case, which does not require the presence of an external licenser. Nevertheless, there is good reason to believe that the dative subject has its dative case licensed by T. To see this, consider (37).

(37) a. [PRO$_{arb}$ hon o yom-u] koto wa ii koto da.
　　　　　　　book ACC read-PRS fact TOP good thing COP
　　　'It is a good thing [PRO$_{arb}$ to read books].'

　　b. *[Kodomo ga PRO$_{arb}$ yom-u] koto wa ii koto da.
　　　　child NOM read-PRS fact TOP good thing COP
　　　'It is a good thing [for children to read PRO$_{arb}$].'

---

[13] When a potential predicate is intransitive, its sole argument must be marked with nominative rather than dative case, owing to the nominative-case constraint.

(i) Kono uma {ga/*ni} hasir-e-ru.
　　this horse {NOM/DAT} run-POTEN-PRS
　　'This horse can run.'

Despite this generalization, it appears that a dative-subject clause without any nominative argument is sometimes fairly acceptable (see Shibatani 1978).

(ii) (Kare wa oyog-e-na-i ga) ano hito ni wa oyog-e-ru.
　　he TOP swim-POTEN-NEG-PRS but that man DAT TOP swim-POTEN-PRS
　　'(He cannot swim, but) that man can swim.'

To my ear, the dative-subject clause in (ii) sounds acceptable when the subject receives a contrastive interpretation. Given that dative marking can often be replaced by a complex postposition like *nitotte* 'for', perhaps for the purpose of adding emphasis, as in (iii), I surmise that *ni* appearing on the dative subject could be a postposition.

(iii) Kare {ni/nitotte} wa sore ga hituyoo-da.
　　he DAT/for TOP that NOM necessary-PRS
　　'That is necessary for him.'

Provided postpositional *ni* is available for certain dative-subject clauses, it is plausible to say that in (ii), postpositional *ni*, instead of dative *ni*, is assigned to the subject *ano hito* 'that man', given a contrastive context. If *ni* is a postposition, T does not enter into a case-licensing relation with any argument. In this case, T appears without any case feature. Accordingly, the dative-subject clause in (ii) is found to be fairly acceptable, even if it does not contain any nominative argument.

As shown in (37), with a non-stative predicate, the nominative subject – but not an accusative object – can be turned into PRO$_{arb}$. According to Chomsky and Lasnik (1993), PRO is licensed by receiving null case from infinitival T. As discussed by Kuroda (1983), in Japanese, a verb in the present form can be associated with infinitival T, and thus, (37a) can receive a PRO$_{arb}$ interpretation. (No PRO$_{arb}$ interpretation is available if the verb appears in the past form.) In dative-subject constructions, it is the dative rather than the nominative argument that is turned into PRO$_{arb}$.

(38) a. [PRO$_{arb}$ hon ga yom-e-ru] koto wa ii koto da.
book NOM read-POTEN-PRS fact TOP good thing COP
'It is a good thing [PRO$_{arb}$ to be able to read books].'

b. *[Kodomo ni PRO$_{arb}$ yom-e-ru] koto wa ii koto da.
child DAT read-POTEN-PRS fact TOP good thing COP
'It is a good thing [for children to be able to read PRO$_{arb}$].'

Given that PRO$_{arb}$ occurs by replacing an argument in subject position whose structural case is licensed by finite T, it is reasonable to say that T is what licenses the case of dative subjects in dative-subject constructions.

There are cases where a dative argument is licensed by the verb, rather than T. When T does not enter into a case-agreement relation with a dative argument, nominative case can be replaced by an oblique marker without affecting acceptability, as in (39).

(39) a. John {ga/kara} sensei ni soodan-su-ru.
John {NOM/ABL} teacher DAT consult-do-PRS
'John consults the teacher.'

b. Kodomo-tati {ga/de} tomodati ni soodan-si-ta.
child-PL {NOM/INST} friend DAT consult-do-PST
'The children consulted their friends.'

The complex predicate *soodan-suru* 'consult', which selects a dative-marked argument, allows both the source-argument and plural-agent alternations. When the subject has either of the two oblique markers (i.e. *kara* or *de*), no nominative argument shows up in the clause, but even so the sentence is acceptable. This is obviously due to the fact that the dative case found on the indirect objects in (39) is not licensed by T. Evidence in support of this view can be adduced from (40).

(40) a. *Tomodati ga sono koto o soodan-s-are-ta.*
friend NOM that matter ACC consult-do-PASS-PST
'Friends were consulted about that matter.'

b. *Sono koto ga tomodati ni soodan-s-are-ta.*
that matter NOM friend DAT consult-do-PASS-PST
'That matter was consulted about to a friend.'

As shown in (40), the dative-marked object, just like the accusative object of *soodan-suru* 'consult', can be promoted to a passive subject. Since passivization is made possible by suppressing a case feature of the verb, it must be the case that in (39), dative case is licensed by the verb. If a dative argument is not case-licensed by T, inoperative T can appear. Accordingly, (39) is not ruled out by the nominative-case constraint even if nominative case is replaced by an oblique marker.

In essence, the nominative-case constraint arises from the property of tense. In unmarked cases, T bears [+NOM], and the clause requires at least one nominative argument, which is used to delete the case feature [+NOM] on T. The derivation is legitimate when [+NOM] is successfully deleted by a nominative argument. If nominative case on the subject is replaced by an oblique case marker, inoperative T (without [+NOM]) can be merged. In such cases, the nominative-case constraint is not implemented, as T does not contain [+NOM], and the sentence is legitimate even without a nominative argument. In dative-subject constructions, T must be operative, because it needs to contain [+DAT] to be deleted by agreeing with the case feature on the dative subject. Thus, T must carry [+NOM], and the nominative-case constraint is enforced; the dative-subject sentence is rendered unacceptable if nominative case on a non-subject argument is replaced by an oblique marker.

3.2 The significance of subject raising in valency alternations

In Japanese, as suggested by Kishimoto (2001b, 2010), ordinary clauses are subject to the grammatical (EPP) requirement that Spec-TP be filled by a subject. This suggests that when T is operative, the EPP requirement is imposed on T, so that it carries [+EPP]. Conversely, given the distinction between operative and inoperative T, it is plausible to hypothesize that when T is inoperative, it lacks an EPP feature, and hence, does not attract a subject, as in (41b).

(41) a. [$_{TP}$ SBJ [$_{vP}$ ~~SBJ~~ OBJ V-v] T$_{[+EPP]}$]
     b. [$_{TP}$ [$_{vP}$ SBJ OBJ V-v] T]

In (41a), T has an EPP feature, and thus, the subject is raised to Spec-TP. From the present perspective, if T is inoperative, as in oblique-subject constructions, it is expected that the subject will remain in base position without subject raising, as in (41b). This is in fact the case, as I will discuss below.

Kishimoto (2010) argues, based on focus association with *bakari*, that subjects are not raised to Spec-TP in oblique-subject constructions, i.e. non-nominative subject constructions formed by the plural-agent or source-argument alternation. To make this point, let us consider (42).

(42) *Ken ga [manga o yon-de] bakari i-ru.*
     Ken NOM comics ACC read-GER only be-PRS
     'Ken is doing nothing but reading comics.'

In (42), the emphatic particle *bakari* 'only' can be associated with the object, but not with the subject. Thus, (42) can be interpreted as 'Ken is reading nothing but comics', but not 'No one but Ken is reading comics.' According to Kishimoto (2010), this difference arises from the fact that the object remains in vP-internal position, which falls under the scope of *bakari*, while the subject is raised to Spec-TP outside its scope.

The present analysis leads to the prediction that *bakari* can be associated with oblique subjects appearing in clauses where inoperative T appears. This is in fact the case. In (43a) as well as (43b), *bakari* can be associated with the obliquely-marked subject, and the interpretations indicated by the translations are available.

(43) a. *Kodomo-tati de ason-de bakari i-ru.*
        child-PL INST play-GER only be-PRS
        'No one but children are playing.'

     b. *Kodomo kara Ken ni hanasikake-te bakari i-ru.*
        child ABL Ken DAT talk-GER only be-PRS
        'No one but children are talking to Ken.'

By contrast, when the subjects are marked with nominative case, as in (44), *bakari* cannot be associated with them. Thus, in (44), the interpretations indicated by the translations are not available.

(44) a. *Kodomo-tati ga   ason-de   bakari i-ru.
        child-PL   NOM   play-GER only   be-PRS
        'No one but children are playing.' (* on the intended interpretation)

   b. *Kodomo ga   Ken ni hanasikake-te bakari i-ru.
        child NOM Ken DAT talk-GER   only   be-PRS
        'No one but children are talking to Ken.'
                                      (* on the intended interpretation)

The data show that in (43), unlike (44), the subjects remain in vP-internal position without raising to Spec-TP. Note that the examples in (43) represent cases where the nominative-case constraint is not in force, and thus, it is reasonable to state that when T is deactivated, no subject raising to Spec-TP occurs.

The presence or absence of subject raising is verified by considering sentences formed on the conjectural evidential *sooda* 'likely' as well (not to be confused with the hearsay evidential *sooda* 'I hear'). As discussed by Takezawa (2004), the conjectural evidential *sooda* can be converted into the subject honorific form *soode-irassyaru*. When the subject appears in the nominative case, either the main predicate or the evidential *sooda* can appear in subject-honorific form.

(45) a. Sensei   ga   suguni hanasi-soode-**irassyar**-u.
        teacher NOM soon   speak-likely-HON-PRS
        'The teacher is likely to speak soon.'

   b. Sensei   ga   suguni **o**-hanasi-**ni**-**nari**-sooda.
        teacher NOM soon   HON-speak-DAT-become-likely
        'The teacher is likely to speak soon.'

In both sentences in (45), subject honorification can be construed to target the nominative subject.[14] On the other hand, the sentences containing an honorific evidential are not acceptable when the subject is marked with the oblique *de* or *kara*, as shown in (46).

---

[14] In the 'hearsay' evidential construction, the subject honorific form of *sooda* is not possible, as in (i).

(i) *Sensei ga   hanasi-ta soode-**irassyar**-u.
    teacher NOM speak-PST hear-HON-PRS
    'I hear that the teacher spoke.'

In (i), an independent tensed clause is embedded under *sooda*. Since the honorific target is located in the embedded clause, subject honorification fails.

(46) a. *Sensei-tati de atumari-soode-***irassyar**-u.
　　　　teacher-PL INST gather-likely-HON-PRS
　　　　'The teachers are likely to get together.'

　　b. *Sensei kara Ken ni hanasikake-soode-***irassyar**-u.
　　　　teacher ABL Ken DAT speak-likely-HON-PRS
　　　　'The teacher is likely to speak to Ken.'

The sentences with the oblique subjects are fine, however, when the main predicate is turned into a subject-honorific form, as in (47).

(47) a. Sensei-tati de o-atumari-***ni-nari***-sooda.
　　　　teacher-PL INST HON-gather-DAT-become-likely
　　　　'The teachers are likely to get together.'

　　b. Sensei kara Ken ni o-hanasikake-***ni-nari***-sooda.
　　　　teacher ABL Ken DAT HON-speak-DAT-beocome-likely
　　　　'The teacher is likely to speak to Ken.'

Kishimoto (2012) suggests that subject honorification is an instance of vP-level agreement (cf. Harada 1976; Shibatani 1978). The difference in acceptability of the subject-honorifics in (45), (46) and (47) follows naturally from this, given that the oblique subjects remain in vP-internal position without subject raising to Spec-TP.

(48) a. [TP SBJ-NOM [vP S̶B̶J̶ [TP S̶B̶J̶ [vP S̶B̶J̶　　　　V-v-HON]]-likely-HON]]

　　b. [TP　　　　[vP　　　　[TP　　　　[vP SBJ-{ABL/INST} V-v-HON]]-likely-*HON]]

I assume that *sooda* selects an infinitive TP complement, and projects vP, which accommodates a copy of the subject raised to the upper Spec-TP. The higher honorific form in the nominative-subject sentence in (45a) is legitimate because the nominative subject is raised to the matrix Spec-TP via the Spec-vP projected from the conjectural evidential *sooda*, as illustrated in (48a). Subject honorification at the level of the main predicate is legitimate as well, as in (45b), since the honorific verb agrees with a copy of the subject in the lower vP. In the oblique-subject constructions, by contrast, the higher honorific form for *sooda* is not possible, as in (46), because the subject remains unmoved, without raising to the matrix Spec-TP via the upper vP projected from the conjectural evidential, as (48b) illustrates. On the other hand, the subject-honorific form of the main verb is legitimate, as in (47), since it can agree with the unmoved subject in the lower vP. These data suggest that clauses that have no nominative argument do not allow subject raising to Spec-TP.[15]

To summarize, the nominative-case constraint is imposed on a finite clause when T carries the case feature [+NOM] to be deleted in agreement with a nominative argument. In nominative-subject constructions, T is made inoperative when nominative case on the subject is replaced by *de* or *kara* (i.e., via the plural-agent or source-argument alternation). In dative-subject constructions, T bears [+DAT] alongside [+NOM]. In such cases, T cannot be made inoperative, i.e., T necessarily bears [+NOM] to be deleted via agreement with a nominative argument. Since the nominative-case constraint is enforced in dative-subject constructions, unacceptability results if nominative case on the object is replaced with an oblique case marker via the plural-agent or source-argument alternation.

4 Concluding remarks

In this chapter, a number of valency alternations available in Japanese have been examined, including the dative-nominative alternation for transitive stative predicates, the nominative-accusative alternation for predicates of (dis)liking, the possessor-raising alternation, the source-subject alternation, and the plural-agent alternation. It has been shown that the first three alternations are governed by the nominative-case constraint, so that these alternations are restricted in such a way that the resulting clause has at least one nominative argument, in accordance with this constraint. In contrast, the nominative-case constraint

---

[15] The present analysis leads to the expectation that subjects are raised when a clause contains a nominative argument. This expectation is indeed correct.

(i) a. Sensei   ga   {hasiri-soode-***irassyar***-u/taore-soode-***irassyar***-u}.
    teacher NOM {run-likely-HON-PRS/fall-likely-HON-PRS}
    'The teacher is likely to {run/fall down}.'

  b. {Sensei   ni/Sensei-tati   de}   keisan   ga   deki-soode-***irassyar***-u.
     {teacher DAT/teacher-PL INST} calculation NOM can.do-likely-HON-PRS
     'The teachers are likely to be able to make a calculation.'

  c. Sensei   {ni/kara}   sono   ko   ga   mie-soode-***irassyar***-u.
     teacher {DAT/ABL}   that   child NOM see-likely-HON-PRS
     'The teacher is likely to see that child.'

Example (ia) shows that a nominative subject is raised to Spec-TP regardless of whether the verb is unergative or unaccusative. (ib) shows that a dative subject as well as a *de*-marked subject undergoes subject raising, and (ic) illustrates that an ablative subject is also raised to Spec-TP. Crucially, all of these clauses have a nominative argument.

does not apply to the source-subject and plural-agent alternations, which involve replacement of nominative case on the subject with an oblique marker.

The difference in applicability of the nominative-case constraint between the two types of valency alternations is attributed to the property of tense. The nominative-case constraint is enforced when T is operative, because it contains a nominative case feature to be deleted by agreement with a nominative argument. The nominative-case constraint is voided, however, if T is rendered inoperative by replacement of the nominative case. This is precisely because T does not in that case enter into a case-licensing relation with any argument in the clause. Nevertheless, the nominative-case constraint is imposed if T cannot be deactivated, as is the case with dative-subject constructions, where T has both dative and nominative case features. In dative-subject constructions, T cannot be deactivated by replacing nominative case on the object with an oblique (or semantic) case marker, since it carries a dative case feature even after oblique-case replacement. The data we have considered illustrate that the nominative-case constraint is imposed on clauses when operative T is associated with them.

Abbreviations

1.sg. first person singular; ABL ablative; ACC accusative; CAUS causative; COP copula; DAT dative; GEN genitive; GER gerundive; HON honorific; INST instrumental; LOC locative; NEG negative; NOM nominative; PASS passive; PL plural; POL polite; POTEN potential; PRS present; PST past; TOP topic

Acknowledgments

An earlier version of the present chapter was presented at the NINJAL International Symposium "Valency Classes and Alternations in Japanese" (August 4–5, 2012). I am grateful to Yukinori Takubo, Taro Kageyama, Koichi Takezawa, Hiroshi Aoyagi, Kan Sasaki, Mamoru Saito, Keiko Murasugi, Jiro Abe, and the audience for comments and suggestions. I am thankful to a reviewer for directing my attention to some points that need to be clarified, and also to Wesley Jacobsen for suggestions on style and presentation. Needless to say, all remaining errors and inadequacies are my own responsibility.

References

Chomsky, Noam. 1995. *The minimalist program*. Cambridge, MA: MIT Press.
Chomsky, Noam. 2000. Minimalist inquiries: The framework. In Roger Martin, David Michaels & Juan Uriagereka (eds.), *Step by step: Essays on minimalist syntax in honor of Howard Lasnik*, 89–155. Cambridge, MA: MIT Press.
Chomsky, Noam. 2001. Derivation by phase. In Michael Kenstowicz (ed.), *Ken Hale: A life in language*, 1–52. Cambridge, MA: MIT Press.
Chomsky, Noam. 2004. Beyond explanatory adequacy. In Adriana Belletti (ed.), *Structures and beyond: The cartography of syntactic structures, volume 3*, 104–131. New York: Oxford University Press.
Chomsky, Noam. 2008. On phases. In Robert Freidin, Carlos P. Otero & Maria Luisa Zubizarreta (eds.), *Foundational issues in linguistic theory: Essays in honor of Jean-Roger Vergnaud*, 133–166. Cambridge, MA: MIT Press.
Chomsky, Noam & Howard Lasnik. 1993. The theory of principles and parameters. In Joachim Jacobs, Arnim Von Stechow & Wolfgang Sternefeld (eds.), *Syntax: An international handbook of contemporary research, volume 1*, 506–569. Berlin: Walter de Gruyter.
Harada, S. I. 1976. Honorifics. In Masayoshi Shibatani (ed.), *Syntax and semantics 5: Japanese generative grammar*, 499–561. New York: Academic Press.
Inoue, Kazuko. 1998. Sentences without nominative subjects in Japanese. *Grant-in-Aid for COE Research Report (2A): Researching and verifying an advanced theory of human language*, 1–34. Chiba: Kanda University of International Studies.
Inoue, Kazuko. 2005. Case (with special reference to Japanese). In Martin Everaert & Henk van Riemsdijk (eds.), *The Blackwell companion to syntax, volume I*, 295–373. Oxford: Blackwell.
Katada, Fusa. 1991. The LF representation of anaphors. *Linguistic Inquiry* 22. 287–314.
Kishimoto, Hideki. 2001a. The role of lexical meanings in argument encoding: Double object verbs in Japanese. *Gengo Kenkyu* 120. 35–65.
Kishimoto, Hideki. 2001b. Binding of indeterminate pronouns and clause structure in Japanese. *Linguistic Inquiry* 32. 597–633.
Kishimoto, Hideki. 2004. Transitivity of ergative case-marking predicates in Japanese. *Studies in Language* 18. 105–136.
Kishimoto, Hideki. 2010. Subjects and constituent structure in Japanese. *Linguistics* 48. 629–670.
Kishimoto, Hideki. 2012. Subject honorification and the position of subjects in Japanese. *Journal of East Asian Linguistics* 21. 1–41.
Kishimoto, Hideki. 2013. Covert possessor raising in Japanese. *Natural Language & Linguistic Theory* 31. 161–205.
Kishimoto, Hideki. 2014. Dative/genitive subjects in Japanese: A comparative perspective. In Mamoru Saito (ed.), *Japanese syntax in comparative perspective*, 228–274. New York: Oxford University Press.
Kishimoto, Hideki, Taro Kageyama & Kan Sasaki. 2015. Valency classes in Japanese. Andrej Malchukov & Bernard Comrie (eds.), *Valency classes in the world's languages, volume 1: Introducing the framework and case studies from Africa and Eurasia*, 765–805. Berlin & Boston: De Gruyter Mouton.
Koizumi, Masatoshi. 1999. *Phrase structure in minimalist syntax*. Tokyo: Hituzi Syobo.
Kuno, Susumu. 1973. *The structure of the Japanese language*. Cambridge, MA: MIT Press.

Kuno, Susumu. 1976. Subject raising. In Masayoshi Shibatani (ed.), *Syntax and semantics 5: Japanese generative grammar*, 17–49. San Diego: Academic Press.

Kuroda, S.-Y. 1978. Case marking, canonical sentence patterns, and counter equi in Japanese (A preliminary survey). In John Hinds & Irwin Howard (eds.), *Problems in Japanese syntax and semantics*, 30–51. Tokyo: Kaitakusha.

Kuroda, S.-Y. 1983. What can Japanese say about government and binding. *Proceedings of the west coast conference on formal linguistics* 2. 153–164. Stanford CA: Stanford Linguistics Association, Stanford University.

Levin, Beth. 1993. *English verb classes and alternations*. Chicago: University of Chicago Press.

Levin, Beth & Malka Rappaport Hovav. 1995. *Unaccusativity: At the syntax–lexical semantics Interface*. Cambridge, MA: MIT Press.

Malchukov, Andrej, Martin Haspelmath & Bernard Comrie. 2010. Ditransitive constructions: A typological overview. In Andrej Malchukov, Martin Haspelmath, and Bernard Comrie (eds.), *Studies in ditransitive constructions: A comparative handbook*, 1–64. Berlin & New York: De Gruyter Mouton.

Miyake, Tomohiro. 1996. *Nihongo no idō-dōshi no taikaku-hyōji ni-tsuite* [On accusative marking on Japanese motion verbs]. *Gengo Kenkyu* 110. 143–168.

Sasaguri, Junko. 1999. Meishiku no modaritii toshiteno *koto* [*Koto* as noun phrase modality]. In Yukiko Alam Sasaki (ed.), *Gengogaku to nihongokyōiku* [Linguistics and Japanese Education], 161–176. Tokyo: Kurosio.

Shibatani, Masayoshi 1978. *Nihongo no bunseki* [An analysis of Japanese]. Tokyo: Taishukan.

Shibatani, Masayoshi. 2001. Non-canonical constructions in Japanese. In Alexandra Y. Aikhenvald, R. M. W. Dixon & Masayuki Onishi (eds.), *Non-canonical marking of subjects and objects*, 307–354. Amsterdam: John Benjamins.

Sugioka, Yoko. 1986. *Interaction of derivational morphology and syntax in Japanese and English*. New York: Garland.

Tada, Hiroaki. 1992. Nominative objects in Japanese. *Journal of Japanese Linguistics* 14. 91–108.

Takezawa, Koichi. 1987. *A configurational approach to case marking in Japanese*. Seattle, WA: University of Washington dissertation.

Takezawa, Koichi. 2004. Nihongo-hukugōjutsugo ni-okeru hiteiji no ichi to setsu-kōzō [The position of negation and clause structure in Japanese complex predicates]. *Nihongo bunpō gakkai dai-go-kai happyō ronbun shū* [Papers from the 5th annual meeting of the Society of Japanese Grammar]. 175–184.

Takubo, Yukinori. 2010. *Nihongo no kōzō: Suiron to chishiki-kanri* [Japanese structure: Inference and knowledge management]. Tokyo: Kurosio Publishers.

Ura, Hiroyuki. 2000. *Checking theory and grammatical functions in universal grammar*. New York: Oxford University Press.

Natsuko Tsujimura
5 The role of lexical semantics in the reorganization of the resultative construction

1 Introduction

One of the most frequently discussed topics of transitivity alternations in Japanese is morphologically related transitive-intransitive verb pairs such as *ageru-agaru* 'raise (tr.) – rise (intr.)', *kowasu-kowareru* 'break (tr.) – break (intr.)', and *otosu-otiru* 'drop (tr.) – fall (intr.)', as many of the chapters in this volume attest to. This topic has been analyzed from multiple standpoints, ranging from morphology, morpho-phonology, and morpho-syntax, to dialectal variation and diachronic change. Although predated by other equally important work on the topic, the seminal work of Jacobsen (1981, 1992) has played a particularly significant role as a stepping stone to subsequent research that has furthered our understanding, both in breadth and in depth, of the nature of transitive-intransitive verb pairs and of the important repercussions they have for other related phenomena. For example, there are at least two resultative constructions in Japanese – one formed from *-te aru* and the other formed from *-te iru*, where *-te* is the gerundive verb suffix – that generally exhibit collocational restrictions on the transitivity of the verb. That is, in the case of a morphologically related transitive-intransitive verb pair, *-te aru* is expected to appear with the transitive verb and *-te iru* with its intransitive counterpart when the interpretation is resultative. This is illustrated in (1–2), where the verb pairs, *tukeru–tuku* 'turn on, attach' and *yaburu–yabureru* 'tear', are morphologically related, sharing a common root, *tuk-* and *yabur-*, respectively (cf. Tsujimura 1989).

(1) *tukeru* (tr.) – *tuku* (intr.) 'turn on, attach'
    a. *Denki ga   tuke-te   ar-u.* (← *tukeru* – tr.)
       light NOM turn.on-GER be-NONPST
       'The light has been turned on.'

    b. *Denki ga   tui-te   iru.* (← *tuku* – intr.)
       light NOM turn.on-GER be-NONPST
       'The light is turned on.'

Natsuko Tsujimura, Indiana University

(2) *yaburu* (tr.) – *yabureru* (intr.) 'tear'
    a. *Hyoosi ga yabut-te ar-u.* (← *yaburu* – tr.)
       cover NOM tear-GER be-NONPAST
       'The cover has been torn.'

    b. *Hyoosi ga yabure-te iru.* (← *yabureru* – intr.)
       cover NOM tear-GER be-NONPST
       'The cover is torn.'

Both constructions have been considered to express resultative states, describing the state of an entity as a result of the event denoted by the verb, but there are some semantic and morpho-syntactic differences between them. The (a) examples involving *-te aru* "carry the implication that the state in question was brought about intentionally and for a specific purpose" (Jacobsen 1992: 195). As such, the presence of an agent is assumed as a part of the meaning, although overt reference to it is not allowed. In contrast, the (b) examples with *-te iru* lack either overt or covert reference to any agent that brought about the event, allowing the interpretation that the described state resulted from a natural cause beyond human control. Another difference is that the *-te aru* construction involves a reduction in the valency of the verb whereas the *-te iru* construction does not change the valency of the verb. In the (a) examples of (1–2) above, the verb bases are transitive, taking agent and theme arguments, but in the *-te aru* construction, only the theme argument can surface as subject of the sentence. The contrast in (3–4) shows the effect of the reduction in valency involved in the *-te aru* resulatative.

(3) *Akira ga denki o tuke-ta.*
    Akira NOM light ACC turn.on-PST
    'Akira turned on the light.'

    Cf. *Denki ga tuke-te ar-u.* (=1a)
        light NOM turn.on$_{tr}$-GER be-NONPST
        'The light has been turned on.'

(4) *Gakusei ga hyoosi o yabut-ta.*
    student NOM cover ACC tear-PST
    'The student tore the cover.'

    Cf. *Hyoosi ga yabut-te ar-u.* (=2a)
        cover NOM tear$_{tr}$-GER be-NONPST
        'The cover has been torn.'

The promotion of the direct object to the subject in this valency-reducing operation is reminiscent of the passive construction, except that the agent of the action can be overtly expressed in the passive construction, unlike the *-te aru* resultative. The contrast is shown in (5).

(5) a. passive construction
    Hyoosi   ga   gakusei   ni (yotte)   yabur-are-ta.
    cover   NOM   student   by   tear-PASS-PST
    'The cover was torn by the student.'

  b. *-te aru* resultative construction
    Hyoosi   ga   (*gakusei   ni (yotte))   yabut-te   ar-u.
    cover   NOM   (student   by)   tear-GER   be-NONPST
    'The cover has been torn (*by the student).'

The relation between the morphologically related transitive-intransitive verb pairs in the two resultative constructions and the passive construction is interesting in that once passivized, the transitive verb of the pair (or transitive verbs in general) can appear in the *-te iru* construction. That is, resultative state can be expressed in three ways, as illustrated in (6).

(6) *yaburu* (tr.) – *yabureru* (intr.) 'tear'
  a. transitive verb + *-te aru*
    Hyoosi   ga   yabut-te   ar-u.
    cover   NOM   tear-GER   be-NONPST
    'The cover has been torn.'

  b. intransitive verb + *-te iru*
    Hyoosi   ga   yabure-te   ir-u.
    cover   NOM   tear-GER   be-NONPST
    'The cover is torn.'

  c. transitive verb: passive + *-te iru*
    Hyoosi   ga   yabur-are-te   ir-u.
    cover   NOM   tear-PASS-GER be-NONPST
    'The cover has been torn.'

There has been much discussion in the literature on the *-te iru* and *-te aru* resultatives and their interaction with each other as well as with the passive construction, but it is commonly agreed that the *-te aru* resultative construction is restricted to transitive verbs, as seen in the fact that this construction is commonly referred to as an "intransitivizing" construction or a valency-reducing operation. For instance, resultative sentences like (7–8) are inconsistent with the valency-reducing nature of the *-te aru* construction, and have been considered ungrammatical.

(7) **Denki ga tui-te ar-u.* (← *tuku* – intr.)
 light NOM turn.on-GER be-NONPST
 'The light has been turned on.'

(8) **Hyoosi ga yabure-te ar-u.* (← *yabureru* – intr.)
 cover NOM tear-GER be-NONPST
 'The cover is torn.'

As I have pointed out elsewhere (Tsujimura 2009, 2010, 2011, 2012a, 2012b), however, ungrammatical sentences like (7–8) that violate the transitive requirement for the *-te aru* construction are not absolutely rejected by all native speakers, but are more highly accepted by speakers fitting certain sociolinguistic profiles. Furthermore, such speakers do not accept just any intransitive verb in the *-te aru* construction, but show a preference for certain intransitive verbs that form a semantically coherent cluster. The following are actual examples from a recent literary work by the young award-winning author, Mieko Kawakami.

(9) *Menyuu ga kakat-te ar-u kabe no atari o mitume…*
 menu NOM hang-GER be-NONPST wall GEN area ACC gaze
 'I gazed at the wall where the menu was hung…'

(10) *Sutekina omoide ga ippai tumat-te ar-u.*
 nice memory NOM much fill-GER be-NONPST
 'It's filled with a lot of nice memories…'

(11) *Sekai ga hirogat-te ar-u.*
 world NOM spread.out-GER be-NONPST
 'The world is spread out…'

The underlined *-te aru* expressions in (9–11) are all formed from intransitive verbs: *kakaru* 'hang', *tumaru* 'fill', and *hirogaru* 'spread'. These verbs all have transitive morphological partners, *kakeru*, *tumeru*, and *hirogeru*, respectively, which are the forms expected to occur in the *-te aru* construction. Kawakami uses these types of non-standard *-te aru* sentences frequently throughout her literary works, against what is the prescriptively accepted pattern. As we shall elaborate on in more detail in section 3, a close examination of one of her books reveals that non-standard *-te aru* sentences with intransitive verbs are in fact used even more commonly than the standard pattern with transitive verbs, both by token and type count. This tendency observable in Kawakami's writing demands an explanation that we will seek in this chapter. Furthermore, we aim to show by a comparison of this non-standard use of the *-te aru* resultative with the *-te iru* resultative that a different principle is emerging in the way resultative expressions are organized and catalogued in the language from what has conventionally been the case. After providing an overview of traditional characterizations of the *-te aru* resultative construction, primarily in meaning, I will move on to a case study drawn from Mieko Kawakami's literary work to illustrate how lexical semantic properties interact with the transitivity continuum, i.e. the transitive-passive-intransitive continuum, in the distinction observed in her writings between the *-te aru* and *-te iru* resultative constructions.

An important caveat should first be mentioned. In discussing the "resultative" *-te aru* construction as an instance of a valency-changing operation, it is necessary to exclude another normative *-te aru* construction where there is no change in the original valency of the verb. As we have noted for (3–4) above, the hallmark of the valency-changing *-te aru* construction is that the object of a transitive verb surfaces as subject of the construction with no possibility of the subject of the original transitive verb appearing, overtly or covertly. There is another construction involving *-te aru* morphology, however, where there is no change in the valency of the transitive verb – the type Hasegawa (1996) calls the "valence-maintaining" *-te aru* construction (as opposed to "valence-changing" *-te aru* construction). The valency-maintaining *-te aru* construction generally expresses a volitional action that is taken preparatory to some future purpose, as illustrated in (12–13) (cf. Masuoka 1984).[1]

(12) a. *Otto   ga   biiru o   kat-ta.*
husband NOM beer ACC buy-PST
'My husband bought beer.'

b. *Otto   ga   biiru o   takusan kat-te   ar-u*
husband NOM beer ACC a.lot   buy-GER be-NONPST

(kara   moo   kau   hituyoo wa   nai.)
(because any.longer buy need   TOP there.isn't)

'Since my husband bought a lot of beer [in preparation for a party, for instance] (there is no need to buy any more).'

---

[1] What Hasegawa calls the "valence-maintaining" *-te aru* construction corresponds to Masuoka's (1987) Pattern B.

(13) a. *Kyaku   ga   atarasii kutu   o   tyuumonsi-ta.*
    customer NOM new   shoes ACC order-PST
    'A customer ordered a new pair of shoes.'

  b. *Kyaku   ga   raisyuu   no   reesu no   tameni*
    customer NOM next.week GEN race GEN for

    atarasii kutu   o   tyuumonsi-te ar-u.
    new   shoes ACC order-GER   be-NONPST
    'A customer ordered a new pair of shoes [in preparation] for the race next week.'

There is no change in the distribution of the subject (marked with the Nominative *ga*) and the object (marked with the Accusative *o*) between the simple transitive sentences in the (a) examples and their *-te aru* counterparts in the (b) examples. Furthermore, since there is no manipulation of the arguments associated with the verb, which remain the same in number and type as well as in their alignment with grammatical functions (i.e. subject-agent, object-theme), this type of *-te aru* construction can be formed with intransitive verbs as well, as in (14), involving the intransitive verb, *neru* 'sleep'.

(14)   *Yuube   zyuubun   ne-te   ar-u   kara   kyoo   no*
    last.night enough   sleep-GER be-NONPST because today GEN

    siken   wa   daizyoobu   da.
    exam   TOP   all.right   COP
    'Because I slept enough last night [to prepare for the test], I should [be awake enough] do well in the test today.'

Although the case study reported on in section 3 highlights a set of valency-maintaining sentences as exemplified in (9–11), they differ from (12–13) in that they involve an intransitive verb whose sole argument, which surfaces as subject, bears the theme role.

2 Characterization of the *-te aru* resultative construction – previous observations

The most distinctive grammatical property of the *-te aru* resultative construction that has drawn linguists' attention is the change in valency of the verb that appears in the construction: from agent *cum* theme/patient to theme/patient alone. As mentioned above, this property has led to the construction being called alternatively an "intransitivizing" construction. Beyond this morpho-syntactic characterization, however, much of the discussion in the relevant literature has focused on grammaticality judgments that pertain to the meaning or interpretation of the *-te aru* resultative construction. Various conditions have been proposed for the felicitous interpretation, ranging from the semantic nature of the subject argument of the construction (Teramura 1984, Masuoka 1987, Miyagawa 1989, Jacobsen 1992) to the (lexical) aspectual property of the transitive verb (Toratani 2007) and pragmatic conditions that must be met by the construction as a whole (Matsumoto 1990; Toratani 2007).[2]

As for the subject of the *-te aru* resultative construction (i.e. the object argument of the transitive verb), Jacobsen (1992: 194) characterizes the verb as one belonging to "the transitive prototype" and the subject of the *-te aru* construction as one that therefore "clearly undergo[es] a change of state".[3] The *-te aru* construction cannot, for instance, be used with what Martin (1987) calls "emotion transitive verbs", since the object with such verbs, which surfaces as subject of the *-te aru* construction, undergoes no recognizable change of state. Martin's emotion transitive verbs include *aisuru* 'love', *iwau* 'celebrate', *homeru* 'praise', *kirau* 'dislike', *konomu* 'like', *matu* 'wait',[4] *nageku* 'lament', and *donaru* 'yell at', among others. Examples of the unacceptable use of the *-te aru* resultative construction with these verbs are shown in (15–16), taken from Martin (1987: 187) with minor modification in the English glosses.

(15) *Haru   ga   mat-te   ar-u.
     spring   NOM   wait-GER   be-NONPST
     'Spring has been waited for.'

(16) *Kodomo   ga   aisi-te   ar-u.
     child   NOM   love-GER   be-NONPST
     'The child has been loved.'

A further semantic restriction on the *-te aru* resultative construction is that human subjects are inappropriate, as seen in (17) and (18): in both these examples *-te aru* is attached to the identical transitive verb, *naraberu* 'arrange

---

2 A detailed literature survey is found in Toratani (2007).
3 Both Miyagawa (1987) and Jacobsen (1992) relate this semantic restriction to the theme role.
4 It is not clear why this verb is classified as an "emotion" transitive verb, but it likely has to do with the fact that the verb has a sense of waiting with hope.

something in a line' but the use of the human subject in (17) is odd or unacceptable, while the use of the inanimate subject in (18) is fully natural.

(17) *Takarakuzi no uriba ni takusan no hito ga
    lottery GEN ticket.counter LOC many GEN person NOM
    narabe-te ar-u.
    form.in.a.line-GER be-NONPST
    'Many people have been formed in a line at the lottery ticket counter.'
    (Teramura 1984: 149)

(18) Misesaki ni kireina hosiika ga narabe-te ar-u.
    storefront LOC pretty dried.squid NOM arrange-GER be-NONPST
    'Good looking dried squid has been arranged at the storefront.'
    (Teramura 1984: 149)

Although less committed to the exclusion of human subjects from the -te aru resultative construction, Masuoka (1987) points to a weaker restriction, citing the examples in (19–20) (the judgments are his).

(19) Inu/?Hito ga kusari ni tunai-de ar-u.
    dog/?person NOM chain LOC tie-GER be-NONPST
    'A dog/?person has been tied to a chain.'
    (Masuoka 1987: 221)

(20) ?Seito ga rooka ni tatase-te ar-u.
    student NOM hallway LOC make.stand-GER be-NONPST
    'A student has been made to stand in the hallway.' (Masuoka 1987: 221)

Recognizing the lower acceptability of *hito* 'person' than *inu* 'dog' as the subject in (19) and a similarly low degree of acceptability of the human subject in (20), Masuoka concludes that while it may not be appropriate to restrict the subject exclusively to nouns that denote a non-sentient being/entity, the "typical" subject is nevertheless one that is non-sentient. He further notes that the acceptability of (19) with *hito* 'person' as subject and of (20) is improved when the verb is replaced by the passive form of the verb followed by *-te iru* (Masuoka 1987: 234): that is, *tunag-are-te iru* ('tie-passive' + *iru*) for (19) and *tatas-are-te iru* ('make stand-passive' + *iru*) for (20).

A second semantic characterization of the -*te aru* resultative construction is discussed in Toratani (2007) with regard to the aspectual property of the transitive verb that appears in the construction. Building upon Hasegawa's (1996) analysis of the -*te aru* resultative construction, which takes it to be an operation over Logical Structure (LS) in the framework of Role and Reference Grammar, Toratani examines transitive verbs of various LS types to see which LS patterns result in acceptable interpretations with the -*te aru* construction. She observes that transitive verbs that are aspectually characterized as active accomplishments (e.g. *kaku* 'write'), causative achievements (e.g. *tukuru* 'make'), and causative accomplishments (e.g. *kowasu* 'break') are compatible with the construction, whereas states (e.g. *konomu* 'like'), activities (e.g. *donaru* 'shout at'), and achievements (e.g. *okoru* 'get angry at') are not. As a common denominator among verbs compatible with the -*te aru* construction, Toratani proposes the Lexical Aspectual Condition (LAC) in (21).[5]

(21) To be able to be combined with -*te aru*, the verb must be syntactically transitive and its LS must contain an activity component [**do'** (x, Ø)] and a change-of-state component [BECOME/INGR **pred'** ((z,) y) where z ≠ EXPERIENCER]   (Toratani 2007: 62)

Both Hasegawa's (1996) original formulation of the LS for the -*te aru* construction and Toratani's elaboration of it in (21) appear to be attempts to account for the following three observations: (i) the presence of an agent that brings about an action, as pointed out in the earlier quote from Jacobsen (1992: 195) that "[there is an] implication that the state in question was brought about intentionally and for a specific purpose", (ii) the presence of a clear change of state, as also noted by Jacobsen (1992), and (iii) the incompatibility of Martin's (1987) "emotion transitive verbs" with the construction. The activity component of [**do'** (x, Ø)] ensures the presence of an agent of the action; BECOME/INGR **pred'** ((z,) y) indicates that change of state is a part of the meaning of the verb; and [BECOME/INGR **pred'** ((z,) y) where z ≠ EXPERIENCER] excludes verbs that express a psychological change in an individual (i.e. experiencer).

---

5 Toratani quotes Van Valin & LaPolla (1997:104) for the difference between "BECOME" and "INGR" in (21): these encode "change over some temporal span" and "instantaneous changes", respectively.

Finally, Matsumoto (1990) argues that the *-te aru* resultative construction is bound by two pragmatic conditions, the Purposefulness Condition and the Describability Condition.⁶

(22) Purposefulness Condition
      An agent must have purposefully produced the situation being described by *-te aru*.

(23) Describability Condition
      It must be evident that the state being described in the *-te aru* construction have resulted from a previous action of an agent.

The Purposefulness Condition is in line with Jacobsen's observation cited above: "[there is] the implication that the state in question was brought about intentionally and for a specific purpose". That is, the presence of the agent's intentionality and of a specific purpose is assumed to be central to the interpretation of the *-te aru* construction, whether this aspect of the construction is considered to be of a semantic or pragmatic nature. According to Matsumoto, the Purposefulness Condition accounts for the unnaturalness of sentences like (15–16) because they do not denote an underlying purposeful action by the agent. Furthermore, he explains that the example in (24) can only be interpreted as resulting from purposeful action by an agent, even though the fallen state of a

---

6 Toratani (2007: 71) proposes a different type of pragmatic condition: "the speaker must be able to take an objective epistemological stance to use a sentence with *-te-ar* in a presentational context". This condition is built upon Ezaki's (2001) observation that empathy, in the sense of Kuno & Kaburaki (1977), must be present for the *-te aru* construction to be used felicitously. To illustrate the relevance of this condition, Toratani explains the oddity that some speakers feel in the example below.

(i) *Omotya ga   kowasi-te   ar-u.*
     toy   Nom break-GER   be-NONPST
    'A toy has been broken.'

She comments on (i) as follows: "[(i)] is awkward as a plain introduction of the toys to discourse because the broken condition would evoke the speaker's empathy. But if the broken toys are seen to exist on the set of a TV studio and understood to be used as a prop in a TV program, the sentence's felicity improves.... Furthermore, using *-te-ar* has the implication that the speaker is portraying the scene and distancing him/herself from the scene" (71). Setting aside the question of whether this pragmatic condition is valid or not, it seems that her explanation quoted above could well be interpreted to follow from Jacobsen's observation that "the state in question was brought about *intentionally and for a specific purpose*" (emphasis mine). That is, toys are generally for children and nobody would think of breaking them unless there is "a specific purpose" for doing so, such as the TV studio scenario Toratani refers to in her explanation.

tree could also result from a natural force like a strong wind (p. 274). (24) cannot in fact be used to describe a situation where the tree has been toppled by a storm or a strong wind.

(24) Ki   ga   taosi-te   at-ta.
     tree   NOM   topple-GER   be-PST
     'A tree was in the state of having been toppled.'

The Describability Condition is proposed to explain the oddity of (25) and (26).[7]

(25) #Doa   ga   tatai-te   ar-u.
     door   NOM   beat-GER   be-NONPST
     'The door is in the state of having been knocked upon.' (intended)
     (Matsumoto 1990: 275)

(26) #Isi   ga   nigit-te   ar-u.
     stone   NOM   grasp-GER   be-NONPST
     'The stone is in the state of having been grasped (e.g. its shape is changed).' (intended)   (Matsumoto 1990: 276)

His explanation for (25) is that under normal circumstances, a door that has been knocked on does not show any sign of the knocking action. Similarly, in (26), it is not ordinarily possible to detect any state arising in a stone as a result of somebody having grasped it. Thus, the unnaturalness of (25–26) is due to the lack of any evidence allowing one to conclude that an action of knocking on a door or of grasping a stone has taken place from observing the state of the entity denoted by the subject NP. To support the validity of the Describability Condition, Matsumoto contrasts (25–26) with the minimally different sentences in (27–28). Information clearly pointing to the occurrence of a relevant action leading to the described state is provided by *itamu hodo* 'to the degree of being damaged' in (27) and by the replacement of the subject *isi* 'stone' in (26) with *nendo* 'clay' (an entity on which the impression of a hand can more easily be made) in (28).

---

[7] Matsumoto (1990: 275) comments that the notation of "#" in (25-26) "is used to indicate semantic/pragmatic anomaly". This suggests that he does not make a precise distinction between semantic and pragmatic properties relevant to the way in which the *-te aru* resultative construction is interpreted.

(27) *Doa ga itamu hodo tatai-te ar-u.*
door NOM be.damaged degree beat-GER be-NONPST
'The door is in the state of having been beaten to the degree of being damaged.'

(28) *(?)Nendo ga nigit-te ar-u.*
Clay NOM grasp-GER be-NONPST
'The clay is in the state of having been grasped (i.e. its shape is changed).'
(Matsumoto 1990: 276)

We have given a brief summary of primarily semantic and pragmatic characterizations of the *-te aru* resultative construction. I will conclude this section with Masuoka's (1987) analysis of the semantic properties of the *-te aru* construction, based on which he classifies the construction into two groups. Although his classification does not seem to be taken up in the later literature to any considerable degree, I wish to introduce his analysis since a subset of one of his groups will be shown to have a significant relevance to our discussion of the non-conventional use of the construction briefly mentioned at the outset. One of these groups corresponds to valency-maintaining *-te aru* sentences like (11b) and (12b), which I will not discuss further here. The other group, the valency-changing *-te aru* construction, is further divided into two patterns, Pattern A_1 and Pattern A_2. Examples of each pattern, taken from Masuoka (1987: 221–223), are given in (29) and (30).

(29) a. *Bonsai ga ikuhatika narabe-te at-ta.*
bonsai NOM several.pots line.up-GER be-PST
'Several pots of bonsai had been lined up.'

b. *Ribingu-teeburu ni wa hana ga kazat-te ar-u.*
living.room.table LOC TOP flowers NOM arrange-GER be-NONPST
'The living-room table has been decorated with flowers.'
[lit. "Flowers have been arranged on the living-room table."]

(30) a. *Sore ga itunomanika migai-te ar-u...*
that NOM at.some.time.or.other polish-GER be-NONPST
'That has been polished at some time or other...'

b. *Iriguti ni tikai katasumi ga... ake-te ar-u.*
entrance LOC near corner NOM open-GER be-NONPST
'Some space has been opened at the corner near the entrance.'
[lit. "The corner (area) near the entrance has been opened.".]

The A_2 pattern exemplified by the sentences in (30) represents the standard resultative -*te aru* construction fitting the description of Jacobsen (1992) that "[there is an] implication that the state in question was brought about intentionally and for a specific purpose". What is unique about Masuoka's classification is his identification of the -*te aru* sentences of the type in (29) as an independent pattern, i.e. the A_1 Pattern. He characterizes this group as "a type that describes the existence of an object at a certain location, as a result of an action" (p. 221; translation mine). The reason for this two-way distinction has to do with a subtle meaning difference that Masuoka notes. While the A_1 pattern depicts a concrete resulting state associated with the existence of an object, the resulting state described in the A_2 pattern is of a more abstract nature (p. 231). Emphasizing the existence of an object as the principal semantic characteristic of the A_1 pattern, Masuoka goes on to say that the verbs that appear in this pattern are primarily transitive verbs of "placement" such as *oku* 'put', *naraberu* 'line up, arrange', *kazaru* 'decorate', *noseru* 'put (x) on (y)', *kakeru* 'hang', *haru* 'paste', *siku* 'spread', and *tomeru* 'stop'. Masuoka's category of verbs of placement will turn out to shed important light on the non-standard variant of the -*te aru* construction observed in our case study of Mieko Kawakami's writing.[8]

---

[8] Masuoka presents two arguments for treating the A_1 pattern as an independent meaning class of the -*te aru* construction. First, sentences of the A_1 type can be conjoined with the existential verb *aru* 'be', as in (i).

(i) *Heya ni wa ... ikebana ga kazat-**te** **ari**,*
    room LOC TOP   flower.arrangement NOM decorate-GER be

   *kamidana ni mo butudan ni mo osonaemoti ga **at-ta**.*
   Shinto.altar LOC also Buddhist.altar LOC also an.offering.of.rice.cakes NOM be-PST

   'The room had been decorated with a flower arrangement and there were rice cakes both at the Shinto altar and at the Buddhist altar.' (Masuoka 1987: 222)

Second, he claims that -*te aru* sentences can serve as an answer to a question that contains the existential verb *aru* 'be', as in (ii).

(ii) Q: *Sono heya ni wa donna mono ga **arimasi-ta**-ka.*
       that room LOC TOP what.sort.of things NOM be-PST-Q
      'What sort of things were in the room?'

   A: *Huukeiga ga kazat-**te** **ari**, piano ga oi-**te** **ari**, tooki*
      landscape NOM decorate-GER be piano NOM place-GER be pottery
      *ga narabe-**te** **arimasi-ta**.*
      NOM line.up-GER be-PST
      'There were a landscape, a piano, and a pottery piece.".
      (Masuoka 1987: 222–223)

His justification for treating the A_1 type as an independent meaning class is that it has a strong collocational relation to the existential verb *aru* 'be', but he does not provide examples to show that the A_2 pattern (i.e. sentences like those in (30)) with *aru* leads to awkward or infelicitous interpretations, making the contrast between the two patterns inconclusive.

3 An innovative use of the *-te aru* construction

The type of *-te aru* resultative that formed the center of our discussion in section 2 is valency-reducing, and as such only transitive verbs are expected to appear in the construction. The use of intransitive verbs in this construction, such as (9–11), repeated below, would therefore be dismissed as erroneous from a prescriptive point of view that limits the construction to transitive verbs. That is, although the subjects in (9–11) are indeed theme arguments of their verbs, the sentences as a whole in which they appear, formed as they are from intransitive verbs, are not the products of a valency-reducing operation.

(9) Menyuu ga   kakat-te   ar-u   kabe no   atari o   mitume...
    menu   NOM hang-GER   be-NONPST   wall GEN   area ACC   gaze
    'I gazed at the wall where the menu was hung...'

(10) Sutekina omoide   ga   ippai   tumat-te   ar-u.
     nice   memory   NOM   much   fill-GER   be-NONPST
     'It's filled with a lot of nice memories...'

(11) Sekai ga   hirogat-te   ar-u.
     world NOM   spread.out-GER   be-NONPST
     'The world is spread out...'

As I mentioned in the introduction, however, these examples are taken from the literary works of a winner of the prestigious Akutagawa prize, Mieko Kawakami. It is not that professional writers are always expected to use prescriptively "correct" language while non-professionals are prone to using "erroneous" forms. Nevertheless, our case study will hopefully suggest a potential path through which a valency-changing resultative construction could be related to, or developed into, a valency-maintaining resultative construction in a non-trivial way. Furthermore, Kawakami's use of the non-standard *-te aru* pattern exhibits an interesting regularity of its own, shedding light on the nature of an emerging form of the construction in the language. I will take up this issue not only as an intriguing example of linguistic variation itself, but as an example of how lexical semantic factors play a critical role in such variation.[9]

---

[9] The editors of this volume point out to me that speakers of the Osaka dialect, especially male speakers, use a contracted form of *-te aru*, i.e. *-taaru*, as a type of aspectual auxiliary, and that the *-taaru* form "is used only in friendly colloquial language, and sounds definitely dialectal and even vulgar.". The non-standard *-te aru* pattern under discussion in this section seems to be distinct from the *-taaru* form in that it has no such "vulgar" tone associated with it.

Mieko Kawakami was born in Osaka in 1976. While she became a public figure for her singing career, she quickly also gained a reputation as a talented writer. Her 2008 book, *Titi to Ran* "Breast and Egg", written in the Kansai dialect, won the 138th Akutagawa prize, one of the most esteemed prizes awarded in Japan for contemporary literary work. Examples of *-te aru* sentences used with intransitive verbs in her published work include (31–33) in addition to (9–11) seen earlier.

(31) *Makkana kuruma ga   tuzukete   sandai mo*
    red   car   NOM one.after.another three as.many.as
    naran-de ar-u.
    line.up be-NONPST
    'As many as three red cars are lined up in sequence.'

(32) *Biirubin   ga yama   to   natte   ware-te   at-tari...*
    beer.bottles NOM mountain QUOT forming break-GER be-for.example
    'Beer bottles are broken into a pile.'

(33) *Honma wa watasi ga hait-te   ar-u   noni...*
    truth TOP I   NOM go.in$_{in}$ -GER be-NONPST but
    'To tell you the truth, I am in(side) [the human-sized figure], but...'

Kakaru 'hang', *tumaru* 'stuff', and *hirogaru* 'spread out' in (9–11) and *narabu* 'line up', *wareru* 'break', and *hairu* 'enter, put in' in (31–33) are all intransitive verbs. It is a crucial factor to keep in mind that the subject of these sentences assumes the theme role. These verbs all have morphologically related transitive counterparts, *kakeru, tumeru, hirogeru, naraberu, waru,* and *ireru*, respectively; and it is these transitive verbs that are expected to appear in the *-te aru* resultative construction in its normative use.

In order to determine whether there is a systematic pattern to Kawakami's use of intransitive verbs with *-te aru*, particularly focusing on the semantic nature of these verbs, five published works by Kawakami were surveyed and example sentences of the emerging pattern with intransitive verbs were collected, as in (9–11) and (31–33). The literary works include two novels, two essays, and one poetry book. 40 tokens of 27 types of intransitive verbs in the *-te aru* construction were found. Included in the 40 tokens are *tuku* 'attach' (5 tokens), *narabu* 'line up' (3 tokens), *tumaru* 'stuff' (3 tokens), *haeru* 'grow' (2 tokens), *kakaru* 'hang' (2 tokens), *kuttuku* 'attach' (2 tokens), *harituku* 'attach (by pasting)' (2 tokens), and *mitiru* 'be filled' (2 tokens). Interestingly, many of these verbs and others among the 27 types show lexical semantic regularity in that they fall under Levin's (1993) classes of "verbs of spatial configuration" and "verbs of contiguous location", both subsets of verbs of existence. Verbs of spatial configuration are defined as "specify[ing] the spatial configuration of an entity with respect to some location" (255–256). Members of this category in English include *bend, dangle, hang, lean, lie, open, protrude, rest, stand*, and *tilt*, among many more. Levin also explains that "verbs of contiguous location" are supposed to "describe a spatial relation between two entities that are contiguous in space" (257). English verbs that fall under this class are *adjoin, border, contain, cover, cross, fill, line, precede, straddle, surround, top*, and *underline*, among others. Relevant examples of the 40 tokens that range over 27 types of intransitive verbs in Kawakami's works were further categorized into these two lexical semantic classes. As a result it was found that 16 out of the 27 types (56%) of the intransitive verbs used in Kawakami's *-te aru* sentences belong to either verbs of spatial configuration or verbs of continuous location. In terms of token count, this amounts to 28 of the 40 tokens (70%). The high rate of appearance of these two semantically coherent classes of intransitive verbs – 56% types and 70% tokens – among Kawakami's *-te aru* sentences suggests a certain degree of uniformity in her use of the non-standard resultative pattern, and further indicates that the semantic nature of the intransitive verbs may be a factor significant to their appearance in the non-standard pattern.

The two lexical semantic classes that characterize Kawakami's non-standard *-te aru* sentences, i.e. verbs of spatial configuration and verbs of contiguous location, are in fact reminiscent of Masuoka's A_1 *-te aru* construction pattern. Recall that Masuoka characterizes this as a pattern that "describes the existence of an object at a certain location, as a result of an action". Verbs appearing in this pattern, which he calls "placement verbs," include *oku* 'put', *naraberu* 'line up, arrange', *kazaru* 'decorate', *noseru* 'put (x) on (y)', *kakeru* 'hang', *haru* 'paste', *siku* 'spread', and *tomeru* 'stop'. While these are all transitive verbs, the intransitive verbs that enter into the non-standard *-te aru* resultative sentences in Kawakami's literary works share this semantic nature with Masuoka's "placement verbs". In fact, some of Kawakami's intransitive verbs find their morphologically related transitive counterparts in Masuoka's list of "placement verbs": for example, *narabu* (intr.) vs. *naraberu* (tr.) 'line up, arrange', *kakaru* (intr.) vs. *kakeru* (tr.) 'hang', and *nokkaru* (intr.) vs. *noseru* (tr.) 'put (x) on (y)', although in the last pair, *noseru* (tr.) is more strictly to be paired with *noru* (intr.). While Masuoka does not make clear the reason for his distinction between the two types of meaning associated with the *-te aru* resultative construction (see footnote 8), the specific isolation of existential or locational meaning as characterizing the construction allows us to capture systematically the semantic nature of Kawakami's non-standard *-te aru* sentences.

We have thus far focused on non-standard variants of the *-te aru* resultative construction that are found in Kawakami's literary works, i.e. *-te aru* sentences with intransitive verbs. We now consider whether the normative *-te aru* pattern with transitive verbs can also be found in her works, and if so, whether there is any systematic contrast between transitive *-te aru* sentences and intransitive *-te aru* sentences. Furthermore, a comparison of *-te aru* sentences with *-te iru* resultative sentences may shed light in a broader context on the question of whether and how Kawakami differentiates among the various resultative expressions available in Japanese. To this end, I have examined sentences from Kawakami that exemplify the three construction patterns in (34).

(34) a. Theme-*ga* + transitive verb + *aru*

b. Theme-*ga* + intransitive verb + *aru*

c. Theme-*ga* + intransitive verb + *iru*

As was briefly mentioned in connection with examples (1–2) in the introduction, the resultative constructions in (34a) and (34c) are similar in meaning, and raise the question of how, if at all, Kawakami differentiates among the three patterns. To answer this, I will consider some examples from her most representative novel, *Titi to Ran* "Breast and Egg", for which she received the Akutagawa Prize in 2008.

The results seem to show some distinction among the three patterns in (34). As before, token and type numbers reported below refer to verbs. First, the standard *-te aru* resultative construction with transitive verbs in (34a) is underrepresented in this novel: examples can be found of only 11 verb tokens of 4 types. The 4 types are *kaku* 'write', *tate-kakeru* 'lean (x) against (y)', *kesu* 'erase', and *oku* 'place'. It is noteworthy, however, that 7 of the 11 tokens involve the verb *kaku* 'write', as in *kai-te aru* 'it has been written'; of the remaining types, *oku* exhibits 2 tokens while *tate-kakeru* and *kesu* exhibit only one token each. It is also of note that *tate-kakeru* and *oku* correspond to what Masuoka calls "placement verbs"; the former certainly falls under verbs of spatial configuration and the latter arguably does as well. The frequent use of the verb *kaku* 'write' in this pattern is of further interest. Teramura (1984: 151) comments that verbs of description and inscription such as *kaku* 'write' and *syomei-suru* 'sign' are frequently used in the *-te aru* form, as in *kai-te aru* 'it has been written' and *syomei-si-te aru* 'it has been signed', but that these instances do not imply intentionality (of the sort that Jacobsen alludes to) as do prototypical resultative sentences in the *-te aru* form such as (1a) and (2a). If we follow Teramura's intuition and set aside the 7 tokens of *kai-te aru* in *Titi to Ran* as belonging to a semantically different group, we are left with 4 tokens of 3 types of verbs. Since 2 of the 3 remaining verb types imply existence of an object in general terms, the verb *kesu* 'erase' in *kesi-te aru* counts as the only instance of the *-te aru* construction that fits the normative pattern, i.e. describing a state resulting from an intentional action for a specific purpose. It seems appropriate to conclude, then, that the normative *-te aru* resultative construction is greatly underrepresented in *Titi to Ran*, especially in comparison with examples such as (34b) and (34c), as we will see shortly.

The second pattern of (34b) is the non-standard *-te* construction that we observe in Kawakami's writing. A total number of 20 tokens of 12 types of verbs are found of this type. The verbs in this group can further be divided into three kinds: (i) intransitive verbs of spatial configuration or contiguous location (9 tokens; 6 types), (ii) intransitive verbs of other lexical semantic classes (5 tokens; 5 types), and (iii) passivized transitive verbs (6 tokens; 5 types). Examples of (iii) are included under (34b) rather than (34a) because they have been considered "undesirable" from a prescriptive point of view (e.g. Nishio 1962).[10] That is, neither intransitive verbs nor passive verbs are strictly speaking transitive verbs of the type required in the normative *-te aru* pattern, and as such their use may be considered "non-standard". Actual examples of the three groups comprising (34b) are given in (35–37); the number in parentheses indicates token count.

(35) verbs of spatial configuration and contiguous location (9 tokens; 6 types)
narabu 'line up' (3), *kakaru* 'hang' (2), *tuku* 'attach' (1), *kuttuku* 'attach' (1), *umaru* 'be buried' (1), *osamaru* 'be contained' (1)

(36) intransitive verbs of other lexical semantic classes (5 tokens; 5 types)
wareru 'crack' (1), *haeru* 'grow' (1), *butikireru* 'cut' (1), *okoru* 'happen' (1), *nokoru* 'remain' (1)

(37) passivized transitive verbs (6 tokens; 5 types)
ok-are-ru (oku) 'be put' (2), *tum-are-ru* (tumu) 'be piled' (1), *kak-are-ru* (kaku) 'be written' (1), *tome-rare-ru* (tomeru) 'be held, be tightened to' (1), *s-are-ru* (suru) 'be done' (1)

---

[10] Teramura (1984) notes that passivized transitive verbs, in theory, should not appear in the *-te aru* construction especially given the existence of the passive+*te iru* form, but this pattern does in fact appear in literary works by writers during the Taisho and Meiji periods, citing Takahashi (1969). Included among these writers is Seicho Matsumoto. Teramura observes that the passive+*te aru* form seems to lack the same degree of intentionality underlying the event as is exhibited by the *-te aru* construction with transitive verbs. As I have reported elsewhere (cf. Tsujimura 2010, 2011, 2012a, 2012b), the *-te aru* construction with passivized verbs is tolerated quite freely by native speakers of Western (Kansai) dialects.

A comparison of the total number of -*te aru* constructions in the two patterns in (34a) and (34b) clearly shows that the non-standard pattern is more frequent, both in token and type. Although the statistics are not fully robust, it is nevertheless clear that lexical semantic properties of the intransitive verbs play a contributing role in giving rise to the non-standard form. Note, incidentally, that the majority of even the passivized verbs listed in (37) belong to the categories of spatial configuration or contiguous location (*tumu* 'pile', *tomeru* 'hold'), and "placement" (*oku* 'put'). Although passive in form, these verbs share common lexical semantic properties with the verbs in (35).

Finally, the -*te iru* resultative construction in (34c) also occurs widely in *Titi to Ran*: there are 80 token sentences that appear in this construction. The range of meaning exhibited by these tokens seems to be random, but three observations can be made about them relevant to our discussion so far. First, verbs of spatial configuration and verbs of contiguous location, such as *katamuku* 'lean', *tuku* 'attach', and *tunagaru* 'link', are used in the -*te iru* resultative construction, but the majority of these appear in the contracted form -*teru* of -*te iru*, such as *katamui-teru*, *tui-teru*, and *tunagat-teru*. The only verbs from these lexical semantic classes that take the full form -*te iru* are *tumaru* 'pack' (*tumat-te iru*) and possibily *sorou* 'become complete' (*sorot-te iru*).[11] Second, passive forms appear in this construction, but similarly to the examples above, they occur in the contracted form -*teru*. Examples include *kak-are-teru* (*kaku* 'write'), *tozikomer-are-teru* (*tozikomeru* 'confine'), and *torikom-are-teru* (*torikomu* 'take in'). The only exception to this is *settis-are-te-iru* (*settisuru* 'set up'), which takes the full -*te iru* form. It should be noted that verbs of spatial configuration and verbs of contiguous location as well as passivized verbs constitute approximately 25% of the 80 tokens of the -*te iru* resultative construction in *Titi to Ran*. Third, the remainder, and majority, of the -*te iru* sentences correspond roughly to change of state verbs (e.g. *ookikunaru* 'become big', *hieru* 'cool', *tuku* 'turn on', *heru* 'reduce') and emission verbs (*nizimu* 'ooze out', *hikaru* 'shine', *hibiku* 'resonate'). Verbs of emission in the -*te iru* form are often ambiguous between the resultative and progressive interpretations (Tsujimura 2014), and if these are excluded, the -*te iru* resultative construction in this novel can be said to cooccur most typically with change of state verbs.

To summarize, the distribution of -*te aru* resultative constructions, both normative and non-standard, and -*te iru* resultative constructions that occur in

---

11 The English translational equivalent of *sorou* 'become complete' does not fully convey the sense of spatial configuration or contiguous location conveyed by the Japanese verb. In Kawakami's novel, though, *sorot-te iru* refers to the neatness of a person's handwriting and may in that sense be reasonably seen fall under either of these verb classes.

our sample from Kawakami's novel, *Titi to Ran*, show that the *-te aru* construction is under-used and the *-te iru* construction seems to be the preferred construction for expressing resultative states. When *-te aru* sentences do appear, however, they show a relatively strong tendency to co-occur with verbs of spatial configuration and verbs of contiguous location as well as passive verbs (some of which also fall under these two lexical semantic classes). As pointed out earlier in our discussion of Masuoka's semantic classification of *-te aru* constructions, one meaning (the A_1 pattern) associated with the construction is to describe "the existence of an object at a certain location, as a result of an action", and this semantic characterization seems to correspond generally to the primary use of Kawakami's *-te aru* sentences although they take the non-standard pattern with intransitive verbs. Kawakami's use of the two resultative construction types may suggest that for her, the *-te iru* construction is the primary, if not sole, linguistic apparatus for describing a state resulting from an action, whether or not the presence of an agent or intentionality of an agent is implied. In contrast, the *-te aru* construction is reserved for describing the existence of an entity where the presence of an agent in an event of bringing about the entity's existence, or even the occurrence of such an event at all, is possibly irrelevant. That is, the contrast between the two is that a state is captured in its connection with a dynamic event in the *-te iru* construction whereas a state is perceived simply as static in the *-te aru* construction; and the role of agent or intentionality is moot, at least as an integral semantic factor distinguishing between the two constructions.

Two observations can be drawn from this case study of Kawakami's writing as to the form and meaning of the non-standard *-te aru* resultative construction. Formally, the transitive verb requirement is violated, and hence, the *-te aru* construction ceases to be valency-reducing, even though the themehood of the subject is maintained. Semantically, *-te aru* sentences are used to describe the existence of an entity in some definable location or spatial configuration. Such a characterization of *-te aru* sentences departs substantially from the formal and semantic nature as traditionally understood in the sense summarized in section 2 – i.e. as a valency-reducing construction that describes a state resulting from an intentional action.

Kawakami's non-standard use of the *-te aru* construction may be indicative of a wider phenomenon of language change than is observable in the writing of a single author. It is common knowledge that languages change over time, but it is often difficult to discern linguistic change as it is actually taking place. One way of observing linguistic change is through sociolinguistic examination using real-time data. Real-time studies are conducted by surveying speakers either longitudinally or cross-sectionally. The former type of survey tracks a small number of individual speakers over an extended period of time. The latter targets a given speech community at two distinct points in time using the same fieldwork methodology. A third approach to observing language change in progress, distinct from either of these, was pioneered by Labov (1963, 1972) in his seminal study of Martha's Vineyard. Labov (1972: 23) observed that "shifting frequencies of usage in various age levels" which may be reflected in data from different age groups tested at one and the same point in time, is a significant sign of language change in progress. This innovative view has come to be known as the apparent-time construct and has been widely applied in a number of sociolinguistic investigations. Under the premise of the apparent-time construct, Tsujimura (2010, 2011, 2012a, 2012b) investigates the speech of younger speakers in the western Kansai region of Japan (i.e. Osaka and neighboring prefectures) and reports that they accept, with statistical significance, the non-standard *-te aru* pattern with intransitive verbs more readily than do speakers in Tokyo and its surrounding prefectures in eastern Japan and that within the Kansai region, younger speakers accept the non-standard *-te aru* pattern of the type observed in Kawakami (i.e. involving intransitive verbs having the specific lexical semantic properties discussed earlier in this section) more readily than do older speakers (i.e. 50 years of age and older).[12] An anonymous reviewer pointed out that "this usage is not new at all, and as far as I can tell, it has been constant in the dialect for a long time" (i.e. this pattern is normal for this dialect and involves no innovation). If *-te aru* with intransitive verbs has been standard "in the dialect for a long time," then it raises the question as to why the older generation in my earlier study did not accept *-te aru* with intransitive verbs to the same or higher degree as did the younger speakers. More importantly, even if what I have been referring to as a non-standard pattern (i.e. *-te aru* with intransitive verbs) were more solidly rooted in a particular geographical community of speakers than I have portrayed here and elsewhere, the case study of Kawakami's writing that I have presented in this chapter, complemented by Tsujimura (2010, 2011, 2012a, 2012b), demonstrates that the *-te aru* structure does not occur with just any intransitive verb. And if the non-arbitrary nature of verbs that appear in the non-standard pattern, as I have attempted to elucidate here, is new to the speakers of the dialect to which the reviewer refers, then that would serve as a contributing factor to the change observed in

---

[12] Tsujimura (2010, 2011, 2012a, 2012b) reports that in addition to the lexical semantic properties of intransitive verbs, frequency of verb use – particularly low frequency – turns out to be another crucial factor contributing to the relative acceptability of *-te aru* with intransitive verbs: that is, the less frequent an intransitive verb, the higher its degree of acceptability in the *-te aru* construction.

our study using the apparent-time construct. That is, the formal shift from a valency-changing operation to a valency-maintaining construction coupled with the semantic property that accompanies it may be captured as an on-going change that is currently in progress.

4 Conclusion

A re-examination of the -*te aru* resultative construction in Japanese, discussions of which are often framed in terms of a transitivity dichotomy, has been motivated by the emergence of a non-standard pattern that departs from the traditional valency-changing character of this so-called "intransitivizing" construction. While this construction has traditionally been analyzed to be restricted to transitive verbs, whose arguments are reduced to one, a violation of the constraint on transitivity is observed in cases where intransitive verbs appear instead of transitive verbs. Such a "violation", if regarded as a general phenomenon of ongoing language change, could reflect a construction change (or extension) from valency-changing to valency-maintaining. I have argued, however, that this violation should not be seen as an idiosyncrasy or anomaly that is "erroneous" or "ungrammatical", but instead as a phenomenon that exhibits a systematic character triggered by a coherent lexical semantic factor. It is hoped that our discussion of the phenomenon of the non-standard -*te aru* variant, as exemplified in our case study of the literary works of Meiko Kawakami, illuminates aspects of the -*te aru* resultative that go beyond what have been considered undisputable linguistic analyses of this construction, as mentioned in the introduction. I would like to close this chapter with a brief note that might point to the morpho-semantic nature of the -*te aru* resultative construction, focusing on the particular question of how "resulting states" can be expressed in a more general sense.

It is well documented that languages employ different means in expressing resulting states, either lexically or periphrastically. (cf. Nedjalkov [ed.] 1988; Kageyama 1996) The lexical marking of resulting states is exemplified by the Japanese verb *korosu* "kill" and the English verb *redden*, where the states of being dead and being red, resulting from intentional events, constitute an integral component of the lexical semantic representation of these verbs. Resulting states can also be expressed periphrastically, as in English resultative constructions like *John painted the wall red*, where the resulting state is stated by the secondary predicate *red*. A large number of morphologically related transitive-intransitive verb pairs, at least in some analyses (Kageyama 1996; Tsujimura

2003), show a "division of labor" between an action that is intended to bring about a resulting state and the actual attainment of that state. The intended result implied in a statement made with a transitive verb can be cancelled by its morphologically related intransitive verb – a phenomenon originally observed by Ikegami (1985) and later discussed by Miyajima (1985), Kageyama (1996), and Tsujimura (2003). Relevant examples here are taken from Tsujimura (2003: 393).

(38) Mado   o   ake-ta   kedo (sabituiteite) ak-anakat-ta.
     window ACC open$_{tr}$-PST but   (rusty)   open$_{in}$-NEG-PST
     'I opened the window, but it didn't open (because it was rusty).'

(39) Tukue o   ugokasi-ta   kedo (omosugite) ugok-anakat-ta.
     desk   ACC move$_{tr}$-PST but   (too.heavy) move$_{in}$-NEG-PST
     'I moved the desk, but it didn't move (because it was too heavy).'

In both examples, the verbs in the first and second clause form a morphologically related transitive-intransitive pair: *akeru* vs. *aku* 'open' in (38), and *ugokasu* vs. *ukogu* 'move' in (39). The fact that the intended goal can be cancelled in these examples indicates that transitive verbs may not include attainment of the intended resulting state as a part of their meaning, although such meaning is an essential component of the meaning of their morphologically related intransitive counterparts. (See Tsujimura (2003) for a detailed discussion of this analysis; also see Kageyama (1996) for issues related to this.)

Yet another mechanism for expressing resultative states in Japanese is by way of a morphological complex like *-te iru* and *-te aru*, as we have discussed in this chapter. One of the environments in which the *-te iru* construction induces a resultative interpretation is when the attached verb belongs to the aspectual class of achievements, which is typically the case with intransitive verbs of the unaccusative type, which in turn generally correspond to the intransitive member of a morphologically related transitive-intransitive verb pair. This can be seen in the (b) sentences of (1–2). The *-te aru* construction has likewise been customarily analyzed as inducing a resultative meaning, and as doing so in general by requiring a transitive verb that subsequently undergoes a valency-changing operation. It is this long-held generalization that has been demonstrated in our case study above to be violable in certain environments, namely, when the attached verb is intransitive and belongs to the class of spatial configuration verbs or contiguous location verbs. I have suggested a parallel between this non-standard *-te aru* pattern and Masuoka's A_1 pattern, in which the *-te aru* pattern describes the existence of an entity in some location. This observation by Masuoka, together with new data drawn from the literary works of Meiko Kawakami, is indeed important when viewed in the larger context of the typology of resultative constructions. Kozinskij's (1988) discussion of the universals of resultative formation, for one, proposes a hierarchy of resultatives in terms of semantic classes. Put simply, crucial for our purpose is that the "bivalent locational" class[13] (e.g. "attached to", "situated upon", "enclosed in") is included in the hierarchy as one of the most fundamental semantic notions relevant to resultative formation. From this, it can be interpreted that verbs describing the existence or location of an entity form a natural class that is subsumed under the larger rubric of resultatives. It is not clear to me at this point whether existential or locational states should always be viewed as resulting from a (dynamic) event that temporally leads to that state. To the extent that bivalent location serves as a conceptual notion relevant to resultative formation in general, however, it provides an important thread connecting Masuoka's A_1 pattern, one consistent with the traditional requirement limiting this construction to transitive verbs, to the non-standard *-te aru* construction involving intransitive verbs observed in Kawakami's literary works. That is, the difference in transitivity notwithstanding, the verbs in these two constructions share the same lexical semantic character. The existential meaning of the *-te aru* construction may well be reinforced by the fact that the verb *aru* in *-te aru* is itself an existential verb.[14]

Although Kawakami's use of *-te aru* with intransitive verbs is still likely to be judged as non-standard or even unacceptable by many native speakers, if it can be understood to represent an emerging variant of the normative *-te aru* construction, as I believe to be the case, then its emergence can be expected to follow a path that is not random, but exhibits a linguistic logic of its own. As mentioned at the end of section 3, the emergence of this pattern may have non-trivial repercussions for the overall organization of resultative expressions in Japanese. The case study of Kawakami's writing presented in this chapter suggests that an account of such a reorganization of resultative strategies should make reference to the lexical semantics of the participating verbs, especially when considered in connection with the morphological and morpho-syntactic dimensions of transitivity and valency alternation phenomena as traditionally understood.

---

[13] The bivalent locational class is contrasted with the "monovalent" class, which includes resulting states such as "swollen", "frozen", and "exposed". Both are further subsumed under the larger semantic rubric of "observable" results.

[14] In view of our discussion of the existential/locational function of *-te aru* in this chapter, it seems plausible to analyze *aru* as a main verb in the *-te aru* construction and the preceding verb in the gerundive *-te* form as supplying additional information as to how an entity exists or is located. Under such a view, the morphological complex of V-*te aru* would be analyzed as two morphologically separate units, rather than a single unit.

Abbreviations

ACC accusative; COP copula; GEN genitive; GER gerund; intr. intransitive; LOC locative; NEG negative; NOM nominative; NONPST nonpast; PASS passive; PST past; Q question; QUOT quotative; TOP topic; tr. transitive

Acknowledgments

Various parts and versions of the research materials discussed in this chapter have been presented at the annual conferences of NWAV 37 (Houston, 2008) and of NWAV 39 (San Antonio, 2010), Harvard University (2011), the National Institute of Japanese Language and Linguistics's (NINJAL) colloquium series (2011), and the NINJAL International Symposium on valency classes and alternations in Japanese (2012). I would like to thank the audiences for their comments and suggestions. I am particularly indebted to Wesley Jacobsen, whose meticulous editing has made the final version of this chapter far more coherent and readable than it would otherwise have been.

References

Ezaki, Motoko. 2001. *Stativization of verb semantics in modern Japanese: A pragmatic approach*. Los Angeles: UCLA dissertation.
Hasegawa, Yoko. 1996. *A study of Japanese clause linkage: The connective TE in Japanese*. Stanford: CSLI Publications.
Ikegami, Yasuhiko. 1985. 'Activity' – 'accomplishment' – 'achievement' – a language that can't say 'I burned it, but it didn't burn' and one that can. In Adam Makkai & Alan K. Melby (eds.), *Linguistics and philosophy: Essays in honor of Rulon S. Wells*, 265–304. Amsterdam: John Benjamins.
Jacobsen, Wesley M. 1981. *Transitivity in the Japanese verbal system*. Chicago: University of Chicago dissertation.
Jacobsen, Wesley M. 1992. *The transitive structure of events in Japanese*. Tokyo: Kurosio Publishers.
Kageyama, Taro. 1996. *Dōshi imiron* [Verb semantics]. Tokyo: Kurosio Publishers.
Kozinsky, Isaak. 1988. Resultative: Results and discussion. In Vladimir P. Nedjalkov (ed.), *Typology of resultative constructions*, 498–525. Amsterdam: John Benjamins.
Kuno, Susumu & Etsuko Kaburaki. 1977. Empathy and syntax. *Linguistic Inquiry* 8. 627–672.
Labov, William. 1963. The social motivation of a sound change. *Word* 19. 273–309. Revised as Ch.1 in *Sociolinguistic patterns*, 1–42. Philadelphia: University of Pennsylvania Press.
Labov, William. 1972. *Sociolinguistic patterns*. Philadelphia: University of Pennsylvania Press.
Levin, Beth. 1993. *English verb class and alternations: A preliminary investigation*. Chicago: The University of Chicago Press.

Martin, Samuel E. 1987. *A reference grammar of Japanese*. Rutland: Charles E. Tuttle Company.
Masuoka, Takashi. 1987. *Meidai no bunpō: Nihongo bunpō josetsu*. [Propositional grammar: A preface to Japanese grammar.] Tokyo: Kurosio Publishers.
Matsumoto, Yo. 1990. Constraints on the 'intransitivizing' resultative *-te aru* construction in Japanese. In Hajime Hoji (ed.), *Japanese/Korean linguistics*, 269–283. Stanford: CSLI Publications.
Miyagawa, Shigeru. 1989. *Structure and case marking in Japanese*. San Diego: Academic Press.
Miyajima, Tatsuo. 1985. 'Doa o aketa ga, akanakatta' dōshi no imi ni okeru <kekkasei> [The nature of <result> in 'I opened the door but it didn't open']. *Keiryōkokugogaku* 14 (8). 335–353.
Nedjalkov, Vladimir P. (ed.). 1988. *Typology of resultative constructions*. Amsterdam: John Benjamins.
Nishio, Toraya. 1962. Te iru to te aru [-te iru and –te aru]. *Kōgo bunpō no mondaiten*. [Problems in colloquial grammar], 289–293. Tokyo: Meiji Shoin.
Takahashi, Taro. 1969. Sugata to mokuromi [Appearance and intention]. Kyōiku kagaku kenkyūkai bunpō kōza tekisuto. Reprinted in Haruhiko Kindaichi (ed.), *Nihongo dōshi no asupekuto* [The aspect of Japanese verbs], 316–337. Tokyo: Mugi Shobō, 1976.
Teramura, Hideo. 1984. *Nihongo no shintakusu to imi II* [Syntax and meaning of Japanese II]. Tokyo: Kurosio Publishers.
Toratani, Kyoko. 2007. A semantic and pragmatic account of the *te-ar* construction in Japanese. *Journal of Japanese linguistics* 23. 47–75.
Tsujimura, Natsuko. 1989. Some accentuation properties in Japanese and lexical phonology. *Linguistic inquiry* 20. 334–338.
Tsujimura, Natsuko. 2003. Event cancellation and telicity. In William McClure (ed.), *Japanese/Korean linguistics* 12, 388–399. Stanford: CSLI.
Tsujimura, Natsuko. 2009. Kōbun to goi no "yure" ni tsuite [Lexical and constructional variation]. In Yoko Yumoto and Hideki Kishimoto (eds.), *Goi no imi to bunpō* [Lexical meaning and grammar], 415–431. Tokyo: Kurosio Publishers.
Tsujimura, Natsuko. 2010. The role of lexical semantics in the innovative construction. Paper presented at the 39th meeting of New Ways of Analyzing Variation (NWAV). San Antonio, Texas.
Tsujimura, Natsuko. 2011. Innovation and language change: The case of the intransitivizing construction in Japanese. Talk given at Harvard University.
Tsujmura, Natsuko. 2012a. Frequency effects on constructional variation in Japanese. Paper presented at New Ways of Analyzing Variation (NWAV) Asia-Pacific 2, NINJAL, Tokyo, Japan.
Tsujimura, Natsuko. 2012b. Variation in valency-changing operation. Paper presented at NINJAL Internation Symposium: Valency Classes and Alternations in Japanese, Tokyo, Japan.
Tsujimura, Natsuko. 2014. *An introduction to Japanese linguistics*, 3rd edn. Oxford: Wiley-Blackwell.
Van Valin, Robert D. Jr. & Randy J. LaPolla. 1997. *Syntax: Structure, meaning and function*. Cambridge: Cambridge University Press.

II Dialects and Ryukyuan

Kan Sasaki
6 Anticausativization in the northern dialects of Japanese

1 Introduction

In recent typological studies of transitivity alternations, languages have been classified into several types according to whether the causative or anticausative alternation is more dominant. Haspelmath (1993) classifies Japanese as a non-directed alternation type language where neither causativization nor anticausativization is dominant. This classification is based on observation of a limited number of standard Japanese verbs including alternating lexical verb pairs. When we consider productive morphology, a different picture appears. Viewed from this perspective, standard Japanese is a causativization dominant language that has productive causative morphology but lacks productive anticausativization.

In the northern dialects of Japanese, mainly spoken in the Tōhoku and Hokkaidō areas, there is less reason to view causativization as the dominant pattern in productive morphology. One of the most prominent grammatical features of these dialects is the productive use of the spontaneous suffix as a morphological marker for anticausativization. The range of anticausativization in the northern dialect is wider not only than lexical anticausativization in other Japanese dialects, but also than that of languages employing the reflexive morpheme to express anticausative meaning.

The aim of this chapter is two-fold: to introduce anticausative data from the northern dialects and to propose an analysis compatible with the wide range of anticausativization observed in these dialects. The structure of this chapter is as follows. Section 2 introduces the basic assumptions in this chapter, presenting the definition of terms and theoretical background we adopt in our study of anticausativization. Section 3 describes some basic facts about anticausativization in Japanese dialects, in particular, the distribution of productive anticausatives and the range of uses of the spontaneous suffix. Syntactic and semantic properties of anticausative constructions are illustrated in section 4, contrasting anticausative constructions with passive constructions on the one hand and with resultative constructions on the other. Section 5 describes the wide range over which anticausativization occurs in the Hokkaidō dialect, on which the

---

Kan Sasaki, Sapporo Gakuin University

data in sections 4 and 5 is based. An analysis compatible with the anticausative data from the northern dialects is proposed in section 6. Section 7 concludes the discussion.

2 Basic assumptions of this chapter

Before presenting the data from the northern dialects, a short discussion of the terms used in the following sections is in order.

Anticausative is the term used to refer to the morphologically marked non-causative member in a causative/non-causative opposition. This term was introduced by Nedjalkov & Sil'nickij (1969) in their typological study of causative constructions. Anticausativization shares with passivization the property that it is an intransitivization process resulting in demotion of the external argument. However, the manner of demotion differs in the two cases. In passive sentences, the external argument can be expressed in oblique (or adpositional) form, while in anticausative sentences, the external argument cannot be expressed even in oblique form. The Modern Greek examples in (1) and (2), from Alexiadou & Anagnostopoulou (2004: 122), illustrate this difference. I follow the original glossing, where "Nact" stands for the non-active verb form. Modern Greek employs the non-active verb form for both passive and anticausative. The passive sentence (1) is compatible with an agentive prepositional phrase (corresponding to the English *by*-phrase), while the anticausative sentence (2) is not. When the agentive prepositional phrase *apo to Jani* is removed, the sentence (2) becomes grammatical.

(1) To   vivlio   diavastike   apo   ton   Petro.   (passive)
    the   book.NOM   read.Nact   by   the   Peter
    'The book was read by Peter.'

(2) *I   supa   kaike   apo   to   Jani.   (anticausative)
    the   soup   burnt.Nact   by   the   John
    Lit. 'The soup burned by John.'

The removal of the external argument (at least in surface syntactic form) is found not only in anticausativization but also in middle formation. The middle sentence (3) in English, for example, contains no agentive phrase.

(3) Bureaucrats bribe easily.   (middle)

Anticausative constructions and middle constructions differ semantically, however: anticausative constructions are eventive while middle constructions are not.

Subsequent lexical semantic studies of causative and non-causative verb pairs introduced the subdivision of anticausativization (in the classical sense) into decausativization and anticausativization in a narrower sense. Kageyama (1996) argues that the semantic operation responsible for decausativization is existential binding of the external argument and that responsible for anticausativization is the co-indexing of the external argument and the internal argument, i.e., reflexivization. Although this distinction is important, it is not accepted by all researchers: Kulikov (2001) points out that decausativization and anticausativization are both used to refer to the derivation of morphologically marked non-causative predicates. He also notes that the term "anticausativization" is used by some authors (Alexiadou & Anagnostopoulou 2004; Koontz-Garboden 2009) to refer to the formation of unaccusative predicates employing morphemes other than the reflexive morpheme. In this chapter, I will use the term "anticausativization" as a cover term referring in general to the formation of morphologically marked non-causative eventive predicates.

The term "lexical anticausative" (abbreviated as LAC in our glosses) refers to intransitive predicates that are morphologically derived from unmarked transitive counterparts by means of a set of (nonproductive) suffixes such as -e in or-e(-ru) (break$_{tr}$-LAC) 'break$_{in}$', derived from or(-u) 'break$_{tr}$'. Note that despite the involvement of the same -e suffix, alternation pairs like intransitive ak(-u) 'open' and transitive ak-e(-ru) 'open' are not categorized as anticausatives because the intransitive member ak(-u) is morphologically unmarked and the transitive one ak-e(-ru) is derived. The transitive verb ak-e(-ru) 'open' is regarded as a lexical causative derived from the intransitive ak(-u) by the suffix -e functioning, this time, as a morpheme of lexical causation (LCAUS). See Matsumoto (this volume) and Frellesvig & Whitman (this volume) for the nature of the dual function of the suffix -e in Modern and Old Japanese.

Lexical aspect plays a central role in the analysis of anticausativization in the northern Japanese dialects. I adopt the aspectual classification found in Dowty (1979) and Foley & Van Valin (1984), where verbs are classified into four aspectual types: state, activity, achievement and accomplishment. The generalized representation of the four aspectual types obtained through lexical decomposition is illustrated in (4), where **pred'** and **do'** stand for stative predicate and activity predicate, respectively.

(4) State   **pred'** (x)
     Activity   **do'** (x)
     Achievement   BECOME **pred'** (x)
     Accomplishment   [**do'** (x)] CAUSE [BECOME **pred'** (y)]

Anticausative predicates tend to exhibit the aspectual character of achievements. It is worth noting that, in this framework, accomplishment is the causative counterpart of achievement, a fact that will be relevant for the analysis proposed in this chapter.

The interpretation of the progressive form is important for understanding the event structure of anticausative predicates in the Hokkaidō dialect. In some Japanese dialects, notably western Japanese dialects including those in Chūgoku and Shikoku, different auxiliary verbs are used to distinguish between progressive (V-*yor(-u)*) and perfect (V-*tor(-u)*). On the other hand, eastern Japanese dialects employ one and the same auxiliary -*te iru* to represent both progressive aspect and perfect (or resultative) aspect. As in other eastern Japanese dialects, in the dialects with productive anticausativization, the verbal complex V-*te i-ru* (V-GER-NONPST, or its contracted form V-*te-ru*) is interpreted as denoting progressive aspect when the verb's lexical aspect type is activity or accomplishment, and as denoting a resultant state when the verb's lexical aspect type is achievement.

Several types of analysis have been proposed to account for the semantic effects of anticausativization. Some linguists, such as Grimshaw (1982), consider that the deletion of the causing event is responsible for anticausativization. Other researchers, in particular Koontz-Garboden (2009), suggest that anticausativization is an operation of co-indexing the external argument with the internal argument. I will refer to this latter approach as the reflexive analysis and will examine the applicability of previously proposed analyses to the northern Japanese dialect data in 5.2.

3 Dialectal distribution of anticausative constructions

An auxiliary-like suffix that indicates spontaneous (non-externally caused) occurrence of an event is widely used across Japanese dialects to mark anticausativization. This suffix has two regional variants, namely -*(r)asar* and -*(r)ar*, both considered to be derived from the Old Japanese spontaneous suffix -*(r)ar*. But whereas Old Japanese -*(r)ar* inflects as a bi-grade verb, the spontaneous suffix in most contemporary dialects inflects as a quadrigrade (*yodan*) verb with consonant stem, with the exception of certain dialects spoken in the Kyūshū area, where the spontaneous suffix maintains a bi-grade inflection.

3.1 Anticausativization with -(r)asar

Dialects using the spontaneous suffix -(r)asar as a morphological marker for anticausativization are found in Hokkaidō, the northern Tōhoku area (Aomori Prefecture and Iwate Prefecture), the northern Kantō area (Tochigi Prefecture) and the Ōi River region in Shizuoka prefecture. The following examples of anticausative constructions are from previous studies of spontaneous voice morphology in Japanese dialects.[1] The suffixation of -(r)asar in these dialects has usages other than anticausativization, in particular unintentionality and middle (property description). I will illustrate these usages in section 3.3. "SP" in the glosses stands for spontaneous suffix.

(5) Hokkaidō dialect (Yamazaki 1994)
 Kugi ga ita kara nuk-asar-u.
 Nail NOM board ABL pull-SP-NONPST
 'The nail is pulled out of the board.'

(6) Morioka dialect (Iwate Prefecture, Takeda 1998)
 Kikko ga ue-rasar-u.
 tree.diminutive NOM plant-SP-NONPST
 'A tree is planted.'

(7) Utsunomiya dialect (Tochigi Prefecture, Katō 2000)
 Sakana-nga yak-asaQ-ta.
 fish-NOM grill-SP-PST
 'The fish was grilled.'

(8) Ikawa dialect (Shizuoka prefecture, Nakada 1981)
 Huton ga kireeni tatam-a(a)sat-te-ru.
 futon NOM neatly fold.up-SP-GER.be-NONPST
 'The futon is neatly folded up.'

Dialects employing the spontaneous suffix -(r)asar are more widely distributed than those employing -(r)ar. The northern edge of this distribution coincides with the geographical northern edge of Japan in Hokkaidō. The southern

---

[1] Most of the original data has been recorded in Japanese *kana* and Chinese characters. Data transcription follows the transcription rules of the style sheet for this volume, except for the Utsunomiya dialect in example (7). Data for this dialect was originally recorded in alphabetic form, and I follow the original transcription here.

edge of the distribution is the Ōi River region in Shizuoka Prefecture. Example (8) is from the Ikawa dialect spoken in the upper reaches of the Ōi River.

3.2 Anticausativization with -(r)ar

Dialects employing the spontaneous suffix -(r)ar as a morphological marker for anticausativization are spoken in the southern Tōhoku area (Yamagata and Fukushima Prefectures) and Gifu Prefecture (Yamada 2007). The following examples are from the southern Tōhoku dialects.

(9) Yamagata dialect   (Yamagata prefecture, Shibuya 2006)
     Tukue   no   ue   ni   bin   ga   og-a-t-ta.[2]
     desk   GEN   above DAT   bottle NOM   put-SP-PROG-PST
     'The bottle has been put on the table.'

(10) Fukushima dialect   (Fukushima prefecture, Shiraiwa 2012)
     Heya   ni   huton   ga   sik-at-te-ru.
     room   DAT   futon   NOM   lay-SP-GER.be-NONPST
     'The futon has been laid out in the room.'

Two peculiarities of the anticausative use of the spontaneous suffix in the Fukushima dialect bear noting. First, as pointed out by Shiraiwa (2012), this suffix can be used to express resultative meaning only in the form gerund plus existential verb (corresponding to V-te i-ru in standard Japanese), but not in the simple past form as in other dialects.[3] For example, in the Yamagata dialect, the past form of an anticausative with -(r)ar, such as *yag-a-ta* 'burn-SP-PST', is grammatical. The dialects mentioned in the previous subsection also permit the past form of the anticausative with the spontaneous suffix.

The use of the spontaneous suffix to effect intransitivization through removal of the agent is also found in the Saga dialect, spoken in Kyūshū. Example (11) is provided by Toshio Hidaka (p.c.). The Saga dialect has a perfect suffix distinguished from the progressive suffix, similarly to other western Japanese dialects. The predicate in example (11) is a non-past perfective form of the spontaneous predicate and denotes a resultant state. The theme argument is

---

2 *ogatta* is a truncated form of /og-a(r)-te-ta/ 'put-SP-PROG-PST', having undergone deletion of /e/ in the progressive suffix.
3 The existential verb root is often truncated in the Fukushima dialect, as in example (10). Truncation of this root in the progressive form is also found in other dialects.

case-marked in the nominative and the agent is removed. These semantic and syntactic properties indicate that sentence (11) can be regarded as an anticausative construction.

(11) Ika   no   hos-at-to?.
     squid   NOM   dry-SP-PFV.NONPST
     'The squid have been hung to dry.'

Agent removal with spontaneous suffixation is also found in the Ōmura dialect spoken in Nagasaki prefecture, but it is uncertain whether the construction with spontaneous predicates in this dialect can be regarded as an instance of anticausative. In example (12), from the Ōmura dialect, affixation of the spontaneous suffix -ar results in the agent being removed and the theme argument being promoted into subject position.

(12) Ōmura dialect   (Nagasaki prefecture, Hayashida 1962)
     Natuyasumi   no   hidoo   mat-ar-u?.
     summer.vacation   NOM   really   wait.for-SP-NONPST
     'Summer vacation is really looked forward to.'

Although the argument coding in (12) resembles the anticausative pattern, the status of sentence (12) as an anticausative is doubtful. This is because the derived intransitive sentence in (12) differs in its semantic properties from typical anticausative constructions. As will be shown in section 3.3, active predicates and their anticausative counterparts typically exhibit the aspectual properties of accomplishment and achievement, respectively. However, in (12) the transitive verb mat- 'wait for' is aspectually an activity predicate and its spontaneous counterpart mat-ar-u? 'wait.for-SP-NONPST' a state. Such a correspondence between activity and stative aspect lacks any implication of deletion or suppression of a causing event, as we would expect in an anticausative construction.

As seen from the examples adduced above, some western dialects exhibit anticausative-like constructions. Overall, however, anticausativization is considered a characteristic feature of the northern dialects.

3.3 Uses of spontaneous forms to express anticausative and other meanings

As shown in the previous subsection, the spontaneous suffix is primarily used as a morphological marker for anticausativization in the Fukushima dialect. By contrast, in most other dialects, the spontaneous suffix has three usages: to mark unintentional, potential (middle), and anticausative meaning. These three usages are illustrated below for a dialect in Hokkaidō. Example (13) illustrates its use as an unintentional marker, where the object optionally receives nominative case-marking instead of the expected accusative marking, with no change in the valency of the verb. Its use as a potential (middle) marker is illustrated in (14), where the agent is removed and the form of the predicate is limited to the non-past form. The subject in this usage corresponds not only to internal arguments but also to adjuncts, as in (14), where the subject derives from an instrument. Example (15) illustrates its anticausative usage, with the agent removed.

(13) Unintentional
 Watasi wa gohan ga tabe-rasar-u.
 1SG TOP rice NOM eat-SP-NONPST
 'I can't stop myself from eating rice.'

(14) Potential (middle)
 Kono pen wa yoku kak-asar-u.
 this pen TOP well write-SP-NONPST
 'This pen writes well.'

(15) Anticausative
 (*dareka niyotte) kootei ni ookina maru ga
 (*someone by) playground DAT big circle NOM
 kak-asat-te-ru.
 draw-SP-GER.be-NONPST
 'A big circle has been/was drawn on the playground (by someone).'

These three usages share the semantic property of reduced agentivity, although the degree of reduction differs from usage to usage. This common property is the key to understanding anticausativization in the northern dialects.

4 Syntactic and semantic properties of anticausative constructions

This section examines syntactic and semantic properties of the anticausative construction based on data from the Hokkaidō dialect, comparing the anticausative construction with two detransitive constructions, namely the passive and resultative constructions. Anticausativization through suffixation of -(r)asar and passivization through suffixation of -(r)are are both valency reducing operations, but these differ in manner of promotion and demotion of arguments, compatibility with the intentional adverbial *wazato* and aspectual interpretation. Similarly, anticausativization and the V-*te ar-u* resultative constructions are both detransitivization operations resulting in removal of the agent, but these differ with respect to compatibility with the intentional adverbial *wazato* and aspectual properties.

4.1 Demotion of agent and promotion of object

Although anticausative constructions with -(r)asar share with passive constructions derived with -(r)are the syntactic properties of demotion of agent and promotion of object to subject, the two constructions differ in the manner of demotion and the range of promotion.

In the passive construction, the demoted agent may be expressed in oblique form. The nominative agent in the active construction (16), for example, corresponds to the oblique agent phrase marked with the particle *ni* in the passive construction (17).

(16) Active (transitive)   (Sasaki & Yamazaki 2006)
Oziisan   ga   taroo   o   situke-ta.
grandfather NOM   Taro   ACC   discipline-PST
'His grandfather disciplined Taro.'

(17) Passive, S → Obl., DO → S   (Sasaki & Yamazaki 2006)
Taroo   wa   oziisan   ni   situke-rare-ta.
Taro   TOP   grandfather   DAT   discipline-PASS-PST
'Taro was disciplined by his grandfather.'

In the anticausativized construction, on the other hand, the agent is removed. As illustrated in the pair (18) and (19), expressing the agent even in oblique form is unacceptable in the anticausative construction.

(18) Active (transitive)   (Sasaki & Yamazaki 2006)
Dareka   ga   ookina   maru   o   kai-ta
Someone   NOM   big   circle   ACC   write-PST
'Someone drew a big circle.'

(19) Anticausative, S → Ø, DO → S (Sasaki & Yamazaki 2006)
    Kootei   ni   ookina   maru ga   (*dareka   niyotte)
    playground DAT   big   circle NOM (*someone   by)
    kak-asat-te-ru.
    write-SP-GER.be-NONPST
    'A big circle has been drawn on the playground (by someone).'

Promotion to subject is possible not only from direct object but also from indirect object in passive constructions. In the passive construction (21), the subject corresponds to the direct object in (20). In example (22), the subject corresponds to the indirect object in (20).

(20) Active (ditransitive)
    sono   musume ga   sensee   ni   hon   o   okut-ta
    that   girl   NOM   teacher DAT book ACC send-PST
    'That girl presented a book to the teacher.'

(21) Passive, S → Obl., DO → S
    musumesan niyotte hon   ga   sensee no   tokoro ni
    girl   by   book NOM teacher GEN place   DAT
    okur-are-ta
    send-PASS-PST
    'A book was presented to the teacher by the girl.'

(22) Passive, S → Obl., IO → S
    sensee   wa   musumesan niyotte hon   o   okur-are-ta
    teacher   TOP   girl   by   book ACC send-PASS-PST
    'The teacher was presented with a book by the girl.'

In the case of anticausativization, the element undergoing promotion to subject is limited to the direct object. The subject of an anticausative construction corresponds to the direct object in its active counterpart, as illustrated in the pair (23) and (24). On the other hand, example (25) illustrates that promotion from indirect object is unacceptable.

(23) Active (ditransitive) (Sasaki & Yamazaki 2006)
    Dareka   ga   sinseisyo   o   taroo ni   okut-ta.
    Someone NOM application ACC Taro   DAT send-PST
    'Someone sent Taro an application.'

(24) Anticausative, DO → S   (Sasaki & Yamazaki 2006)
 Sinseisyo   ga   taroo   ni   okur-asat-ta.
 Application NOM   Taro   DAT   send-SP-PST
 'An application was sent to Taro.'

(25) Anticausative, *IO → S   (Sasaki & Yamazaki 2006)
 *Taroo   ga   sinseisyo   o   okur-asat-ta.
 Taro   NOM   application ACC   send-SP-PST
 'Taro was sent an application.'

Promotion to subject by anticausativization is not limited to theme arguments. In anticausative constructions formed from locative alternation verbs, the derived subject corresponds to the locative direct object of the active sentence. Examples (26) and (27) illustrate that both locative direct objects and theme objects are candidates for promotion.[4]

(26) Locative subject in anticausative formed from a locative alternation verb
 線画の黒部分が塗らさってたり...
 http://a2y.skr.jp/pict/make/05.html
 senga   no   kuro-bubun ga   nur-asat-te-tari ...
 line drawing GEN   black-part NOM   paint-SP-GER.be-and
 'The black part of the line drawing is painted and ...'

---

4 A reviewer suggested that both of the subjects in (26) and (27) are theme because the referent of the subject undergoes a change of state in both constructions. However, there is another view on the semantic interpretation of locative alternation constructions. Foley & Van Valin (1984) regards *the paint* as theme and *the wall* as location in both (i) and (ii) below. In both cases the Undergoer corresponds to the internal argument, but the internal argument is theme in (i) and locative in (ii).

(i) Harry sprayed paint on the wall.
(ii) Harry sprayed the wall with paint.

This type of analysis is found not only in Role and Reference Grammar, a monostratal grammatical theory advocated by Foley & Van Valin (1984), but also in multistratal grammatical theories such as Relational Grammar. Channon (1982) argues that pairs of locative alternation constructions like (i) and (ii) above share a common representation of grammatical relations in the initial stratum although they differ with respect to the representation of grammatical relations in the final stratum. The present article adopts this type of analysis for locative alternation constructions.

(27) Theme subject in anticausative formed from a locative alternation verb
ポテチにチョコが塗らさってるものを....
http://blogs.dion.ne.jp/zero_cat/archives/2856058.html

poteti	ni	tyoko	ga	nur-asat-te-ru	mono o
potato chips	DAT	chocolate	NOM	paint-SP-GER.be-NONPST	thing ACC

'... potato chips with chocolate coating'

V-*te ar-u* resultative constructions exhibit the same patterns of change in grammatical functions as anticausative constructions. As illustrated in (28) and (29) below, the agent in this construction is removed and the direct object in the corresponding active transitive sentence is promoted into subject position. However, the two de-agentivizing constructions differ with respect to their syntactic and semantic properties as shown in subsequent subsections.

(28) Active (transitive)
Karera wa sono tsukue ni haizara o oi-ta
3PL TOP that desk DAT ashtray ACC put-PST
'They put an ashtray on that desk.'

(29) Resultative (V-*te ar-u*)
Sono tukue ni haizara ga oi-te ar-u
that desk DAT ashtray NOM put-GER be-NONPST
'An ashtray is on that desk.'

4.2 Incompatibility with intentional adverbial *wazato*

Anticausative, passive and resultative constructions exhibit different degrees of agentivity as revealed by restrictions on their co-occurrence with intentional adverbials. Examples (30), (31) and (32) illustrate that the passive and resultative constructions are compatible with the intentional adverbial *wazato* 'intentionally', like the corresponding active construction, while the anticausative construction in (33) is not.

(30) Transitive with *wazato*
dareka ga genkan no mae ni yuki o wazato oi-ta
someone NOM entrance GEN front DAT snow ACC intentionally put-PST
'Someone intentionally dumped snow in front of my entrance.'

(31) Passive with *wazato*
 Genkan no mae ni yuki ga wazato
 entrance GEN front DAT snow NOM intentionally
 ok-are-te i-ta
 put-PASS-GER be-PST
 'Snow was dumped in front of my entrance (by someone) intentionally.'

(32) Resultative with *wazato*
 Genkan no mae ni yuki ga wazato oi-te at-ta
 entrance GEN front DAT snow NOM intentionally put-GER be-PST
 'Snow was dumped in front of my entrance intentionally.'

(33) Anticausative with *wazato*
 ?Genkan no mae ni yuki ga wazato ok-asat-te i-ta
 entrance GEN front DAT snow NOM intentionally put-SP-GER be-PST
 'Snow was dumped in front of my entrance intentionally.'

Constructions compatible with *wazato* require the presence of agent at some level. The transitive sentence (30) has the agent as overt subject. The passive sentence in (31) does not have an overt subject, but the passive construction can potentially co-occur with an oblique agent as shown in (17), (21) and (22) in 4.1. Matsumoto (1990b) proposed an analysis of resultative constructions where V-*te ar-u* is a complex predicate with a mono-clausal functional (syntactic) structure and a bi-clausal argument structure, based on data from Standard Japanese. In his analysis, the agent exists as logical subject of the embedded predicate but it is not mapped onto any grammatical function because the theme argument of the main predicate *ar-u*, which is shared with the logical object of the embedded predicate, is mapped onto subject in the functional structure. The compatibility of *wazato* with the resultative construction in (32) indicates that, although the agent is not expressed, it is syntactically accessible in the Hokkaidō dialect if it exists at the level of argument structure. The compatibility of *wazato* with anticausative constructions is lower than that with other detransitive constructions. Two thirds of my consultants judged the sentence in (33) as unacceptable. This tendency indicates that the anticausative construction does not have an agent in its syntactic structure or argument structure. However, the meaning of the sentence compels us to assume that an agent exists in the lexical conceptual structure of the anticausative construction since the dumping of snow presupposes the existence of an agent.

4.3 Aspectual properties of anticausatives and passives

Passive constructions and anticausative constructions also exhibit differences with respect to their aspectual properties. Only accomplishment verbs can serve as the base for either passivization or anticausativization, although certain transitive activity verbs undergo anticausativization when they take on the aspectual property of accomplishment at the phrasal level, as shown in 5.3. Passive constructions formed from transitive accomplishment verbs generally exhibit the same aspectual properties as their corresponding active construction, although passive forms also sometimes exhibit state-like properties not shared by their active counterparts. On the other hand, anticausative constructions based on transitive accomplishment verbs have different aspectual properties from their corresponding active constructions. In this subsection, I will examine aspectual differences between the two detransitive constructions, based on co-occurrence restrictions with time adverbials and the semantic interpretation of the progressive form, and will show that the aspectual opposition between active and anticausative pairs is the same as that between members of corresponding lexical transitive-intransitive alternation pairs.

Before considering the aspectual properties of passive and anticausative constructions, let us review the behavior of the four aspectual classes of state, achievement, activity, and accomplishment in their underived form. Stative verbs, e.g., *ar-* 'exist', which do not take the progressive form (**at-te (i-)ru*), are compatible with durative time adverbials like *itizikan* 'for an hour' but incompatible with completive adverbials like *itizikan de* 'in an hour'. Achievement verbs, e.g., *sin-* 'die', are compatible with completive adverbials but incompatible with durative adverbials. The progressive form of an achievement verb, such as *sin-de (i-)ru* 'die-GER be-NONPST', is interpreted as a resultant state '(someone) is dead'. Activity verbs, such as *asob-* 'play', can co-occur with durative adverbials but are incompatible with completive adverbials. The progressive form of an activity verb, such as *ason-de (i-)ru* (play-GER be-NONPST) 'be playing', is interpreted as progressive. Accomplishment verbs, such as *situke-* 'discipline, teach manners', are compatible with both durative and completive adverbials. The progressive form of an accomplishment verb, such as *situke-te (i-)ru* (discipline-GER be-NONPST) 'be teaching manners', is interpreted as a progressive event. Table 1 summarizes these properties of the various aspectual classes.

The passive construction exhibits the same properties as its corresponding active construction in terms of compatibility with time adverbials. The passive form of an accomplishment verb, such as *situke-rare-* (discipline-PASS) 'be trained', is compatible with both durative and completive time adverbials, as shown in (34) and (35).

Table 1: Semantic tests for aspectual classification

	State	Achievement	Activity	Accomplishment
Co-occur with durative time adverbials	yes	no	yes	yes
Co-occur with completive time adverbials	no	yes	no	yes
Interpretation of progressive form	—	resultant state	progressive	progressive

(34) Durative adverbial   (Sasaki & Yamazaki 2006)
 Itinenkan   situke-rare-ta.
 for a year   discipline-PASS-PST
 '(Someone) was disciplined (by someone) for a year.'

(35) Completive adverbial   (Sasaki & Yamazaki 2006)
 Itinenkande   situke-rare-ta.
 in a year   discipline-PASS-PST
 '(Someone) was disciplined (by someone) in a year.'

The progressive form of a passive formed from an accomplishment verb, such as *situke-rare-te (i-)ru* (discipline-PASS-GER be-NONPST) 'be trained', allows either the progressive or the resultative interpretation, as shown in (36), although the preferred interpretation is progressive with both active and passive forms.

(36) *Situke-rare-te-ru.*   (Sasaki & Yamazaki 2006)
 discipline-PASS-GER.be-NONPST
 '(Someone) is being disciplined (by someone).'
 '(Someone) has been disciplined (by someone).'

Anticausativization, on the other hand, differs from the passive in its co-occurrence restrictions with time adverbials and interpretation of the progressive form. Anticausative constructions are compatible with completive time adverbials but not with durative time adverbials, as shown in (37) and (38). The progressive form of an anticausative is, furthermore, interpreted as a resultant state, not a progressive event, as shown in (39).

(37) Durative adverbial   (Sasaki & Yamazaki 2006)
 **Itinen-kan   situke-rasat-ta.*
 one.year-for   discipline-SP-PST
 '(Someone) was disciplined for a year.'

(38) Completive adverbial   (Sasaki & Yamazaki 2006)
    Itinenkan   de   situke-rasat-ta.
    one.year   in   discipline-SP-PST
    'It took one year (for him) to be disciplined.'

(39) Spontaneous (resultant state reading)   (Sasaki & Yamazaki 2006)
    Situke-rasat-te-ru.
    discipline-SP-GER.be-NONPST
    '(Someone) has been disciplined.'

The behavior illustrated above is that typically seen with achievement predicates, not accomplishment predicates, even though anticausativizes are generally based on transitive accomplishment verbs. I will return to this problem in the next section and discuss some apparent exceptions, but it is clear that in general anticausativization is accompanied by a change in aspectual property from accomplishment to achievement. Passivization can also be accompanied by a change in aspectual property, but this is not obligatory as in the case of anticausativization. This difference between anticausativization and passivization indicates that the two valency reducing processes operate at different levels of grammatical structure, a point I will take up in section 6.

The accomplishment-achievement correspondence is also found in lexical transitive-intransitive alternation pairs, such as *or-* 'break$_{tr}$' and *or-e-* (break-LAC) 'break$_{in}$'. The aspectual opposition seen in active-anticausative pairs is thus parallel to this, but the parallelism is only partial, as will be shown in Section 5.

4.4 Aspectual properties of anticausatives and resultatives

Anticausativization and V-*te ar-u* resultative formation are both detransitivization operations that remove the agent and foreground a change of state, but their aspectual properties are different. Although both anticausative and resultative constructions are used to express the state resulting from an event, the V-*te ar-u* resultative construction can express only resultant state, while the anticausative construction formed from the spontaneous suffix can express other aspectual meanings too. Resultant state is expressed by anticausatives in the progressive form, but with the past tense form they refer to the moment of change, as shown in (40).

(40) Bottan   ga   os-asat-ta
     Button   NOM   push-SP-PST
     'The button was pushed (just now).'

Anticausatives can also refer to an ongoing change of state when they enter into the V-*te ku-ru* complex predicate construction, as shown in (41).

(41) Mata   zassi   ga   tum-asat-te   ki-ta.
     Again magazine NOM   pile-SP-GER   come-PST
     'Magazines have again started piling up (lit., come to pile up).'

V-*te ar-u* resultative predicates cannot express the moment of change or an ongoing change of state. The past form of resultative predicates, like (32) in 4.2, does not refer to the moment of change but to a resultant state established before the time of utterance. Resultative predicates cannot co-occur with the V-*te ku-ru* complex predicate construction, as shown in (42).

(42) *Mata   zassi   ga   tun-de   at-te   ki-ta
     Again magazine NOM   pile-GER be-GER come-PST
     'Magazines have again come to be piled up.'

The progressive form of the anticausative with *-(r)asar* can usually be translated with the V-*te ar-u* resultative in Standard Japanese, although the two constructions are not syntactically equivalent (see 4.2). However, the situation for the past form and the V-*te ku-ru* form is different. The sentences (40) and (41) do not have semantically equivalent intransitive expressions in Standard Japanese.

5 Range of morphological anticausativization in the Hokkaidō dialect

As seen in 4.3, the aspectual opposition between active and anticausative is the same as that between the transitive and intransitive members of lexical alternation pairs. However, the semantic conditions required for anticausativization with *-(r)asar* are different from those for lexical anticausative formation with *-e* or *-ar*. This is reflected in the fact that the range of predicates allowing anticausativization with *-(r)asar* is wider than that of those allowing lexical anticausative formation. This section will demonstrate that anticausativization with *-(r)asar* applies beyond certain semantic restrictions pointed out in crosslinguistic studies of anticausativization. The semantic restrictions examined in this section include those concerning manner specification and restrictions on expression of agent. Information provided at the phrasal level is also relevant to the range of anticausativization with -(r)asar. Despite the wide range of its application, anticausativization with -(r)asar is not unrestricted.

5.1 Irrelevance of manner specification

As argued by Hayatsu (1989) and Satō (2005), lexical transitive-intransitive alternation in standard Japanese is possible only when the transitive member expresses a change of state in the referent of the object and the manner of activity of the agent is not specified. Thus, the transitive verb *nur-u* 'paint', which denotes the iterative application of liquid to the surface of an object entity, has no intransitive counterpart. This restriction is basically the same as the following crosslinguistic generalization of Haspelmath (1993) regarding semantic restrictions on anticausativization:

(43) A verb meaning that refers to a change of state or going-on may appear in an inchoative/causative alternation unless the verb contains agent-oriented meaning components or other highly specific meaning components that make the spontaneous occurrence of the event extremely unlikely. (Haspelmath 1993: 94)

In the Hokkaidō dialect, the range of the lexical transitive-intransitive alternation is the same as that in standard Japanese. However, the range of anticausativization with -(r)asar is wider than that of the lexical transitive-intransitive alternation. For example, verbs that specify the manner of activity such as *nur-u* 'paint,' and therefore fail to meet Haspelmath's (1993) condition, are able to function as a base for anticausativization with -(r)asar, as in *nur-asar-u* (paint-SP-NONPST).

In order to ascertain the range of anticausativization with -(r)asar in the Hokkaidō dialect, I conducted an internet search of spontaneous verb forms used in this dialect between July 31st, 2007 and March 11th, 2008, using Yahoo! API. For details of this study, see Nakamura, Sasaki & Nose (2015). The verb roots listed in (44) are the derivational bases for the anticausatives formed with -(r)asar that were collected in this research.[5] Forms produced by speakers of

---

5 Our internet research program found several anticausative forms of verbal noun (VN) + light verb, such as the following.

other dialects are excluded. The number of tokens is expressed in parentheses for each verb root. Verbs with fewer than 5 tokens are omitted. The list includes three transitive verbs that have lexical anticausative counterparts, *yak-* 'burn, grill', *kir-* 'cut' and *or-* 'break, bend'. However, the majority of transitive verbs in the list have no lexical anticausative counterpart. Transitive verbs specifying manner include not only *nur-* 'paint' but also *hos-* 'dry' (classified as a manner specifying verb in Hayatsu 1989) and *ok-* 'put' (classified as a manner specifying verb in Sato 2005). The wide range of application of anticausativization with *-(r)asar* thus reflects the laxity of semantic restrictions it places on the specificity of manner of activity.

(44) Transitive roots serving as a base for anticausativization (Total: 1,542)
mak- 'roll, wind' (223), *tum-* 'load' (181), *okur-* 'send' (131), *dak-* 'hold' (104), *har-* 'stick' (99), *kak-* 'write' (88), *tutum-* 'wrap' (61), *musub-* 'tie' (50), *tak-* 'boil' (43), *hos-* 'dry' (41), *ok-* 'put' (40), *nur-* 'paint' (37), *sik-* 'lay' (37), *tor-* 'take (a picture/video)' (35), *kum-* 'assemble, program' (34), *har-* 'stretch' (30), *nuw-* 'sew' (29), *tak-* 'kindle' (20), *kak-* 'draw' (19), *mor-* 'fill, pile' (14), *hum-* 'step on' (11), *sas-* 'stab' (11), *yak-* 'burn, grill' (10), *kir-* 'cut' (9), *hor-* 'dig' (8), *hor-* 'carve' (8), *kitae-* 'train' (8), *migak-* 'polish' (8), *tatam-* 'fold' (7), *or-* 'break, bend' (7), *hak-* 'put on, wear' (7), *tozi-* 'close' (6), *sibor-* 'squeeze' (6), *hurikom-* 'transfer (money)' (6), *am-* 'knit' (6), *kaw-* 'buy' (6), etc. (83).

5.2 Applicability of anticausativization to agentive predicates

In this subsection, I examine the relevance of agentive restriction in anticausativization in the Hokkaidō dialect. Koontz-Garboden (2009) argues that transitive verbs

---

(i) 携帯から送った奴が反映ささってない
http://sarimeri.blog32.fc2.com/blog-date-200612.html
Keitai kara okut-ta yatu ga   han'ei   s-asat-te-nai
cellular ABL send-PST thing NOM reflection do-SP-GER.be-NEG.NONPST
'Things sent from cellular phones are not reflected.'

The anticausative form VN + *s-asar-u* is a form reported in the previous literature (Igarashi 1950) but which is not accepted by all speakers. Yamazaki (1994) pointed out that there is another form of the anticausativized light verb, *si-rasar-u*, where the host is not the verb root but an irrealis-infinitive common stem. One of my informants also used a third form, namely *si-sasar-u*. According to another informant, the passive form *s-are-ru* is the form preferred for intransitivizing light verbs.

selecting an agent as their external argument are excluded from anticausativization. This generalization does not hold in the Hokkaidō dialect.

Anticausativization is often realized crosslinguistically by means of reflexive morphology. Based on this, Koontz-Garboden (2009) advocates a reflexive analysis for anticausativization, where the co-indexing of an external argument with an internal argument renders the external argument unrealized syntactically. Koontz-Garboden does not argue that reflexivization always results in an anticausative reading, but shows that the possibility of such a reading is conditioned by the verb's selectional restrictions on its external argument. The Spanish examples below illustrate that the reflexive construction may take not only an anticausative reading, as in (45), but also an agentive reflexive as in (46), where the overt NP is interpreted as an agent.

(45) *El vaso se rompió.*
 the cup REFL broke
 'The cup broke.'

(46) *Kim se cortó.*
 Kim REFL cut
 'Kim cut himself.'

Koontz-Garboden argues that the anticausative reading of a reflexive construction is restricted to cases where the external argument is an effector, a generalized semantic role corresponding not only to agent but also instrument, natural force, and so on (Van Valin & Wilkins 1996), while agentive reflexive constructions like *Kim dressed herself* occur in those cases where the external argument is an agent. This generalization is based on the fact that verbs for which reflexivization results in anticausativization, e.g. *romper* 'break', co-occur with non-agent external arguments, and that verbs not undergoing anticausative reflexivization select only agents as their external arguments. Koontz-Garboden's reflexive analysis of anticausativization is mainly based on Spanish, a language employing reflexive pronouns as morphological markers of anticausativization, but "[the] analysis is intended not simply as one of a particular language, but as one that covers anticausativization in general" (Koontz-Garboden 2009: 80). The universal characterization ("in general") of the reflexive analysis is supported by the fact that this analysis is applicable to anticausativization in Ulwa, a Misumalpan language spoken in Nicaragua. Likewise, Kageyama (1996) advances a similar "counter-reflexization" analysis to account for a set of verb pairs exhibiting lexical anticausativization with the lexical transitivity alternation suffix *-e* in Japanese.

If the reflexive analysis is available for anticausativization "in general" as argued by Koontz-Gardboden, all languages with anticausativization should obey the same agentive restriction. In other words, Koontz-Garboden's reflexive analysis predicts that no language will permit anticausativization from a verb selecting only agent as its external argument. If there is a language allowing anticausativization from verbs selecting only agent as their external argument, the universality of Koontz-Garboden's reflexive analysis is called into question.

The verb *kak-* 'write' undergoes anticausativization with *-(r)asar* as illustrated in (47). This example is obtained from a blog article written by a speaker of the Hokkaidō dialect. According to my informant, the corresponding active sentence is acceptable when the semantic role of the subject is agent as illustrated in (48), but it is not acceptable when the semantic role of the subject is instrument or cause as illustrated in (49) and (50).

(47) 何故か同じ記事が3つも書かさっていました...。
http://blog.livedoor.jp/nuvo/archives/2006-01.html
Nazeka   onazi kizi   ga   3-tu   mo   kak-asat-te   i-masi-ta.
somehow same article NOM 3-NC even write-SP-GER be-POL-PST
'Somehow as many as three identical articles are written.'

(48) *Watasi wa   onazi kizi   o   3-tu   mo   kai-te   simat-ta.* (agent)
1SG   TOP same article ACC 3-NC even write-GER finish-PST
'I unintentionally wrote as many as three identical articles.'

(49) **Zitaku no   konpyuutaa ga   onazi kizi   o*
home   GEN computer   NOM same article ACC
3-tu   mo   kai-te   simat-ta. (instrumental)
3-NC even write-GER finish-PST
'My home computer unintentionally wrote as many as three identical articles.'

(50) **Hutyuui   ga   onazi kizi   o   3-tu   mo   kai-te*
carelessness NOM same article ACC 3-NC even write-GER
simat-ta. (cause)
finish-PST
'Carelessness unintentionally wrote as many as three identical articles.'

The fact that a verb selecting agent as its external argument can undergo anticausativization in the Hokkaidō dialect casts doubt on the universality of the reflexive analysis for anticausativization.

The relaxation of restrictions on the semantic role of the external argument does not guarantee the universality of the reflexive analysis. If the reflexive analysis is correct, it would follow that, irrespective of the tightness of the semantic restriction on the external argument, a verb will never undergo anticausativization when the application of reflexive morphology to it results in an agentive reflexive reading. However, this prediction fails. The crucial data for this comes from active sentences taking the reflexive pronoun *zibun* and the possibility of anticausativization with the verb *tor-* 'take a picture'.

Example (51) is an active sentence with the reflexive pronoun *zibun* in direct object position (the subject is dropped in this sentence). This sentence has an agentive reflexive and therefore co-indexing of the external argument with the internal argument of *tor-* does not result here in an anticausative reading.

(51) *Sakki   keitai   de   zibun   o   tot-ta.*
     short.while.ago cellular.phone   INST   self   ACC   take.picture-PST
     '(I) just took a picture of myself with a cellular phone.'

There is in fact no form of reflexivization with *tor-* 'take (a picture)' that results in an anticausative reading. On the other hand, suffixation with *-(r)asar* does result in an anticausative reading, as shown in (52).

(52) *Henna   mono   ga   tor-asat-ta.*
     Strange thing   NOM   take.picture-SP-PST
     'A picture of a strange thing has been taken.'

The agentive reflexive sentence and the anticausative sentence above indicate that anticausativization with *-(r)asar* is obtained by a semantic operation other than co-indexing of the external argument with the internal argument. The semantic operation responsible for anticausativization with *-(r)asar* will be discussed in the next section.

5.3 Phrasal information

Most verbs that appear in the anticausativization construction in the Hokkaidō dialect are accomplishment verbs. However, transitive activity verbs can appear in this construction when there are elements in the verb phrase that impose an aspectually accomplishment reading.

For example, the verb *os-u* 'push' often appears in the anticausativation construction even though it does not always imply a change of state and is generally classified as an activity verb. When the verb phrase as a whole implies no change of state, anticausativization with *-(r)asar* fails to occur, as seen in (53).

(53) *Senaka   ga   os-asat-te-ru.
     back   NOM   push-SP-GER.be-NONPST
   ← Senaka   o   os-
     back   ACC   push
     'to push someone's back'

On the other hand, when the verb phrase as a whole indicates a change of state, as in (54), anticausativization is possible.

(54) Saiseibotan   ga   os-asat-te-ru.
      replay.button NOM   push-SP-GER.be-NONPST
      'The replay button is on (by having been pushed).'

    ← Saiseibotan   o   os-
      replay.button ACC   push
      'to push the replay button'

The above contrast indicates that phrasal information is relevant to anticausativization in this dialect.[6] Anticausativization with *-(r)asar* can thus be regarded as a syntactic process, while that with *-e* and *-ar* is a lexical process. As syntactic processes tend to be more productive than lexical processes, the productivity of anticausativization with *-(r)asar* can be seen as reflecting its syntactic status.

5.4 A restriction on verbs of giving and exchanging

The range of anticausativization with *-(r)asar* is wide, but there are some restrictions we can point out. Verbs of giving such as *yar-u* and *kure-ru* and the

---

[6] Matsumoto (1990a) points out that a similar semantic condition is relevant for the V-*te ar-u* resultative: the V-*te ar-u* resultative is not acceptable when the subject is not a theme argument affected by the event conducted by the agent.

verb of exchanging *bakur-u* 'exchange' do not undergo anticausativization, even though aspectually they are accomplishments.

(55) Unacceptability of anticausatives formed from verbs of giving
    a. *kure-ru* 'give (to me)' → **kure-rasar-u* 'give-SP-NONPST'
    b. *yar-u* '(I) give' → **yar-asar-u* 'give-SP-NONPST'

The unacceptability shown in (55) indicates that anticausativization is blocked when the person of the argument is specified as part of the lexical meaning of the verb. The verbs *yar-u* and *kure-ru* are distinguished by deixis (Hidaka 2007) or the directionality of giving (Newman 1996). For the verb *yar-u*, the direction of the giving is from speaker to non-speaker. For the verb *kure-ru*, it is from the non-speaker to the speaker. The directionality of giving is a matter of specification of the person of agent and recipient, and such specification cannot be overridden by the semantic operation responsible for anticausativization with *-(r)asar*.

Semantic structures of verbs of giving are schematized in (56) and (57). For the verbs *yar-u* and *kure-ru*, semantic features relating to person are prespecified.

(56) *yar-u* (give, from speaker to other(s))
    [**do'** (x)] CAUSE [BECOME **be-at'** (y, z)] (x = giver, y = theme, z = recipient)
       | |
    [+ego]   [−ego]

(57) *kure-ru* (give, from other(s) to speaker)
    [**do'** (x)] CAUSE [BECOME **be-at'** (y, z)] (x = giver, y = theme, z = recipient)
       | |
    [−ego]   [+ego]

Not all 3-place verbs are excluded from anticausativization. Verbs without a person restriction on their arguments, such as *okur-u* 'send-NONPST', can participate in anticausativization, as illustrated earlier in example (24) of section 3.1.

Another accomplishment verb incompatible with anticausativization is the dialectal verb *bakur-u* 'exchange'. Example (59) illustrates that anticausativization is ruled out with this verb, even though its active counterpart (58) is acceptable.

(58) Kare ga tomodati to CD o bakut-ta.
3SG NOM friend COM CD ACC exchange-PST
'He exchanged CD's with his friend.'

(59) *CD ga tomodati to bakur-asat-te-ru.
CD NOM friend COM exchange-SP-GER.be-NONPST
'The CD was exchanged with his friend.'

However, when *bakur-u* is used as a verb of replacement and does not take a human internal argument, anticausativization is possible.

(60) Kare no CD to tomodati no CD ga
3SG GEN CD COM friend GEN CD NOM
bakur-asat-te-masi-ta.
exchange-SP-GER.be-POL-PST
'His CD was replaced with his friend's CD.'

The verb *bakur-u* has two semantic structures. When it means 'exchange', the semantic structure is reciprocal as shown in (61). On the other hand, when it means 'replace', the semantic structure is not reciprocal, as shown in (62).

(61) Reciprocal *bakur-u* (informal characterization)
X hands Y1 to Z; Z hands Y2 to X
Y1 and Y2 are the same kind of thing.
Subject: X; Object: Y(1, 2); Oblique: Z

(62) Non-reciprocal
[**do'** (x)] CAUSE [BECOME **replaced-with'** (y, z)]
The variables y and z refer to the same kind of thing.

For the reciprocal verb 'exchange', removal of the external argument obscures the core of the lexical meaning, namely, the bi-directional transfer of possession. On the other hand, for the non-reciprocal verb 'replace', removal of the external argument does not affect the core of the lexical meaning, namely, the replacement of one thing with something similar. Blockage of anticausativization with the reciprocal verb 'exchange' can thus be accounted for as a strategy for avoiding the loss of core lexical meaning.

There is a semantic property shared by the verbs of giving *yar-u* and *kure-ru* and the reciprocal verb 'exchange.' For all three of these verbs, the relationship between external argument and internal argument is to a high degree fixed lexically, and removal of the external argument thus blurs this semantic relationship. Although anticausativization in the Hokkaidō dialect has a wide scope, it cannot delete semantic information specifying relationships between arguments.

6 The semantics of anticausativization with the spontaneous suffix

This section examines the semantic operation underlying anticausativization with the spontaneous suffix and addresses the following questions: at what level does the semantic operation occur, and what type of operation is responsible for the removal of agent?

Contemporary grammatical studies recognize multiple layers of sentence structure: syntactic structure describing phrase structure and/or grammatical relations; argument structure describing the semantic/thematic roles of nominals; and lexical semantic structure (Levin & Rappaport Hovav 1995) or logical structure (Foley & Van Valin 1984) encoding aspectual properties of sentences. Passivization is considered to be an operation affecting the organization of syntactic structure (Perlmutter & Postal 1977; Chomsky 1981; Bresnan 1982) or the mapping between argument structure and syntactic structure (Bresnan & Kanerva 1989; Foley & Van Valin 1984). The non-obligatoriness of aspectual change between the active and passive form in Japanese dialects observed in 4.3 indicates that this type of analysis is suitable for these dialects. On the other hand, anticausativization with the spontaneous suffix obligatorily imposes a change in aspect from accomplishment to achievement, indicating that the operation responsible for anticausativization takes place at a level where aspectual properties are specified, or at least affects how aspectual properties are mapped onto argument structure.

Our proposal that anticausativization should be seen as operating at a level where aspect is specified is not new. Grimshaw (1982) proposes an analysis for anticausativization with reflexive morphology in the Romance languages where anticausativization is seen as an operation involving deletion of the causing event. Recent studies of anticausativization, by contrast, assume operations of various kinds on variables appearing in lexical semantic structure, rather than deletion of the causing event, in order to capture semantic restrictions on anticausativization. As mentioned in 5.2, Koontz-Garboden (2009) argues that co-indexing of the external argument and the internal argument is responsible for anticausativization. Levin & Rappaport Hovav (1995) regard lexical transitivity alternation in English as an instance of anticausativization, arguing that existential binding of the external argument is responsible for such alternation. Kageyama (1996) argues that two types of operation on these variables are required to account for lexical intransitivization in standard Japanese, i.e., co-indexing of the external argument and the internal argument and existential binding of the external argument.

Suffixation of *-(r)asar* does not result in wholesale deletion of the causing event. As shown in 5.3, activity verbs such as *os-* 'push' undergo anticausativization when there are elements present in the verb phrase that impose a change of state reading. For such cases, deletion of the causing event would blur lexical information contained in the verb root. The reflexive analysis is, for its part, contradicted by the anticausativization data involving spontaneous suffixes presented in 5.2. The remaining operation proposed in previous studies to account for anticausativization is existential binding of the external argument. The range of intransitivization phenomena analyzed as instances of existential binding in previous literature is narrower than that of anticausativization with *-(r)asar*. The lexical intransitivization process with *-ar* analyzed by Kageyama (1996), for example, does not apply to transitive verbs specifying manner of activity, and English transitive verbs providing specific information about the nature of the external cause do not undergo lexical intransitivization (Levin & Rappaport Hovav 1995: 108). Anticausativization with the spontaneous suffix, by contrast, applies more broadly. This difference does not necessarily mean that the existential binding analysis is invalid for anticausativization with *-(r)asar*; it may simply reflect the fact that the range of lexical operations is narrower than that of syntactic operations. For example, while lexical causativization with *-as* or *-e* applies to a limited number of intransitive verbs, syntactic causativization with *-(s)ase* (or *-(r)ase ~ -(r)ahe* in some dialects) applies to almost all the verbs. The difference in the range of application between anticausativization with lexical transitivity alternating suffixes and that with *-rasar* found in the northern dialects may reflect this general tendency.

The existential binding analysis also has the advantage of accounting for the exclusion of verbs of giving and exchange from anticausativization, a restriction that may be regarded as a consequence of the non-recoverability of lexical meaning. The existential binding of the external argument would obscure the lexical meaning of these verbs because the referent of the external argument is pre-specified for verbs of giving. Likewise, the existence of agent and recipient is necessary to ensure reciprocality in the case of verbs of exchange.

The most plausible semantic account for anticausativization with *-rasar* is therefore provided by existential binding. This is the operation responsible for decausativization in Kageyama's (1996) terminology. Kageyama (1996) advocates decausativization, i.e., the existential binding of the external argument, for intransitivization with the lexical suffix -*ar* in Standard Japanese. As shown in 3.2, some dialects employ the spontaneous suffix -*(r)ar* for anticausativization. In these dialects, the spontaneous suffix exhibits the same form as the Standard Japanese lexical suffix -*ar* when it attaches to consonant-final verb stems. The spontaneous suffix -*(r)asar* used in the Hokkaidō and northern Tōhoku area partially overlaps in form with -*ar*. The connection between the Standard Japanese lexical suffix -*ar* and the spontaneous suffix in the northern dialects is obvious not only from their semantic properties but also from their phonological shape.

Assuming existential binding to be the semantic operation responsible for anticausativization with the spontaneous suffix is also useful for capturing the semantic commonality among the various usages of the spontaneous suffix. As shown in 3.3, the spontaneous suffix has three usages: unintentionality, potential (middle) and anticausativization. Intentionality is expressed in lexical decomposition analyses along the lines of Dowty (1979) by means of the operator DO, a two place predicate taking a volitional participant and an event argument. Unintentionality can therefore be characterized by lack of or suppression of this operator. When the target of existential binding is not the external argument of certain eventive predicates, but the first argument of DO, the subsequent suppression of DO will result in a non-volitional reading. Potential usage can be regarded as a type of construction used for property description. In this usage, the form of the predicate is limited to the non-past form, as mentioned in 3.3, indicating that the spontaneous predicate is in such cases not eventive. Kageyama (2006) argues that the suppression of the external argument (or, in some cases, of the internal argument) occurring in property description constructions is a by-product of the suppression of the event argument. The removal of agent in potential usage can be analyzed as a collateral effect of event argument suppression. The three usages of the spontaneous predicate thus share the semantic characteristic of suppression of the outermost variable of semantic structure.

7 Concluding remarks

This chapter has introduced data from northern Japanese dialects where anticausativization is expressed by attachment of a spontaneous suffix and has argued that the semantic operation responsible for such anticausativization is existential binding of the external argument. This phenomenon is observed mainly in the northern area of the Japanese Archipelago, such as northern Tōhoku and Hokkaidō, but is not seen to occur as a productive phenomenon in the southern dialects of Japan, including the Ryukyuan dialects. As suggested in Sasaki, Okuda & Shiraishi (2014) the northern dialects of Japan appear to participate in this respect in an areal feature shared by other, genetically unrelated, languages in the vicinity of Hokkaidō, such as Ainu and Nivkh. Concerning the lexical transitivity alternation, the northern Japanese dialects exhibit the same pattern as Japanese dialects spoken in other areas in that they have anticausative, equipollent and causative alternations, while Ainu and Nivkh have only equipollent and causative alternations but lack anticausative alternations. However, in transitivity alternations with productive morphology, a different picture arises: Ainu, Nivkh and the northern Japanese dialects all exhibit both anticausativization and causativization when such productive morphological alternations are taken into account. On the other hand, Japanese dialects spoken in areas other than Tōhoku and Hokkaidō have only causativization. While Ainu and Nivkh exhibit anticausativization as a productive morphological phenomenon, the specific morphological marker for anticausativization varies from language to language: Ainu employs reflexive and 1st person plural prefixes, Nivkh employs reflexive and reciprocal prefixes, and the northern Japanese dialects employ the spontaneous suffix to express this meaning. Areal linguistic considerations may thus be key to understanding the development of the use of the spontaneous suffix as a marker of anticausativization in northern Japan.

Abbreviations

1SG first person singular; 3PL third person plural; 3SG third person singular; ABL ablative; ACC accusative; COM comitative; DAT dative; GEN genitive; GER gerundive; INST instrumental; LAC lexical anticausative; LCAUS lexical causative; NC noun classifier; NEG negation; NOM nominative; NONPST non-past; PASS passive; PFV perfective; POL polite; PROG progressive; PST past; REFL reflexive; SP spontaneous; TOP topic

Acknowledgements

The data included in this chapter on the Hokkaidō dialect were mainly provided by Keisuke Sanada and Yukari Nagayama, to whom I wish to express my appreciation. I have benefited from discussions with Daniela Caluianu. I express my thanks to Wesley Jacobsen and Taro Kageyama for their invaluable comments on earlier drafts of this chapter. This research was supported by JSPS Grant-in-Aid for Scientific Research (C) 17520273 and (C) 22520405. All errors and shortcomings are my own.

References

Alexiadou, Artemis & Elena Anagnostopoulou. 2004. Voice morphology in the causative-inchoative alternations: Evidence for a non-unified structural analysis of unaccusatives. In Artemis Alexiadou, Elena Anagnostopoulou & Martin Everaert (eds.), *The unaccusative puzzle: Explorations of the syntax-lexicon interface*. 114–136. Oxford: Oxford University Press.

Bresnan, Joan. 1982. The passive in lexical theory. In Joan Bresnan (ed.), *The mental representation of grammatical relations*, 3–86. Cambridge, MA: MIT Press.

Bresnan, Joan & Jonni M. Kanerva. 1989. Locative inversion in Chichewa: A case study of factorization in grammar. *Linguistic Inquiry* 20. 1–50.

Channon, Robert. 1982. 3 → 2 advancement, beneficiary advancement, and *with*. *Proceedings of the Eighth Annual Meeting of the Berkeley Linguistic Society*, 271–282.

Chomsky, Noam. 1981. *Lectures on government and binding*, Dordrecht: Foris.

Dowty, David. 1979. *Word meaning and Montague grammar*, Dordrecht: Reidel.

Foley, William & Robert Van Valin Jr. 1984. *Functional syntax and universal grammar*. Cambridge: Cambridge University Press.

Frellesvig, Bjarke & John Whitman. this volume. The historical source of the bigrade transitivity alternations in Japanese. In Taro Kageyama & Wesley M. Jacobsen (eds.), *Transitivity and valency alternations: Studies on Japanese and beyond*. Berlin & Boston: De Gruyter Mouton.

Grimshaw, Jane. 1982. On the lexical representation of Romance reflexive clitics. In Joan Bresnan (ed.), *The mental representation of grammatical relations*, 87–148. Cambridge, MA: MIT Press.

Haspelmath, Martin. 1993. More on the typology of inchoative/causative alternations. In Bernard Comrie & Maria Polinsky (eds.), *Causatives and transitivity*, 87–120. Amsterdam & Philadelphia: John Benjamins.

Hayashida, Akira. 1962. Ōmura hōgen no hyōgen [Expressions in the Ōmura dialect]. *Kokubun Gakukō* 28. 374–385.

Hayatsu, Emiko. 1989. Yūtsui-tadōshi to mutsui-tadōshi no chigai ni tsuite [On the semantic difference between paired and unpaired transitive verbs in Japanese]. *Gengo Kenkyu* 95. 231–256.

Hidaka, Mizuho. 2007. *Juyo-dōshi no taishō-hōgengaku-teki kenkyū* [Cross-dialectal study on verbs of giving and receiving]. Tokyo: Hituzi Syobo.

Igarashi, Fukuo. 1958. Hokkaidō hōgen ni okeru dōshi no katsuyō ni tsuite. [On verb conjugation in the Hokkaidō dialect of Japanese]. *Kokugogaku* 34. 1–12.

Kageyama, Taro. 1996. *Dōshi imiron: Gengo to ninchi no setten* [Verb semantics: The interface between language and cognition]. Tokyo: Kurosio Publishers.

Kageyama, Taro. 2006. Property description as a voice phenomenon. In Tasaku Tsunoda & Taro Kageyama (eds.), *Voice and grammatical relations*, 85–114. Amsterdam & Philadelphia: John Benjamins.

Katō, Atsuhiko. 2000. Utsunomiya hōgen ni okeru iwayuru jihatsu o arawasu keishiki no imi-teki keitaitōgo-teki tokuchō [Semantic and morphosyntactic characteristics of the so-called spontaneous form in the Utsunomiya dialect of Japanese]. *Kokuritsu Minzokugaku Hakubutsukan Kenkyū Hōkoku* 25 (1). 1–58.

Koontz-Garboden, Andrew. 2009. Anticausativization. *Natural Language & Linguistic Theory* 27. 77–138.
Kulikov, Leonid. 2001. Causatives. In Martin Haslepmath, Ekkehard König, Wulf Oesterreicher & Wolfgang Raibe (eds.), *Language typology and language universals*. 886–898. Berlin & New York: Walter de Gruyter.
Levin, Beth & Malka Rappaport Hovav. 1995. *Unaccusativity*, Cambridge: MIT Press.
Matsumoto, Yo. 1990a. Constraints on the 'intransitivizing' resultative *-te aru* construction in Japanese. In Hajime Hoji (ed.), *Japanese/Korean linguistics* 1, 269–283. Stanford: CSLI.
Matsumoto, Yo. 1990b. On the syntax of Japanese "intransitivizing" *-te aru* construction: non-lexical function changing. *Papers from the 26th Regional Meeting of the Chicago Linguistic Society* 26. 277–292.
Matsumoto, Yo. this volume. Phonological and semantic subregularities in noncausative-causative verb pairs in Japanese. In Taro Kageyama & Wesley M. Jacobsen (eds.), *Transitivity and valency alternations: Studies on Japanese and beyond*. Berlin & Boston: De Gruyter Mouton.
Nakada, Toshio. 1981. Shizuoka-ken Ōigawa-ryūiki hōgen ni okeru saru-kei dōshi [The *saru*-form verbs in the dialect spoken in the area along the Ōigawa river in Shizuoka prefecture]. *Todai Ronkyū* 18. 1–13.
Nedjalkov, Vladimir & Georgij Sil'nickij. 1969. Tipologija morfologičeskogo I leksičeskogo kauzativov. In Aleksandr Xolodovič (ed.), *Tipologija kauzativnyx konstrukcij: Morfologičeskij kauzativ*, 20–50. Leningrad: Nauka.
Newman, John. 1996. *Give: A cognitive linguistic study*. Berlin & New York: Mouton de Gruyter.
Perlmutter, David & Paul Postal. 1977. Toward a universal characterization of passivization. *Proceedings of the Third Annual Meeting of the Berkeley Linguistic Society*, 394–417.
Nakamura, Wataru, Kan Sasaki & Masahiko Nose. 2015. *Ninchi ruikeiron* [Cognitive typology]. Tokyo: Kurosio Publishers.
Sasaki, Kan & Akie Yamazaki. 2006. Two types of detransitive constructions in the Hokkaidō dialect of Japanese. In Werner Abraham & Larisa Leisiö (eds.), *Passivization and typology: Form and function*, 352–372. Amsterdam & Philadelphia: John Benjamins.
Sasaki, Kan, Osami Okuda & Hidetoshi Shiraishi. 2014. Hokkaidō shūhen gengo no tadōsei kōtai [Transitivity alternations in the languages around Hokkaidō]. In Yoneichi Ono, Yasuo Suga & Kan Sasaki (eds.), *Seikatsugo no sekai* [The world of everyday words]. 128–135. Sapporo: Hokkaidō Hōgen Kenkyūkai.
Satō, Takuzō. 2005. *Jidōshi-bun to tadōshi-bun no imiron* [The semantics of transitive and intransitive sentences], Tokyo: Kasama Shoin.
Shibuya, Katsumi. 2006. Jihatsu – kanō [Spontaneous and potential]. In Takashi Kobayashi (ed.), *Hōgen no bunpō* [A grammar of Japanese dialects], 47–92. Tokyo: Iwanami Shoten.
Shiraiwa, Hiroyuki. 2012. Fukushima hōgen no jihatsu hyōgen [On spontaneous form in Fukushima dialect of Japanese]. *Handai Nihongo Kenkyū* 24. 35–53.
Takeda, Kōko. 1998. Iwate-ken Morioka hōgen ni okeru *saru*-keishiki no imi-teki tokuchō [The semantic properties of *-saru* forms in the Morioka city dialect of Iwate prefecture]. *Kokugogaku Kenkyū* 37. 33–44.
Van Valin, Jr., Robert & David Wilkins. 1993. Predicting syntactic structure from semantic representations: Remember in English and its equivalents in Mparntwe Arrernt. In Robert Van Valin (ed.), *Advances in Role and Reference Grammar*, 499–534. Amsterdam & Philadelphia: John Benjamins.

Yamada, Toshihiro. 2007. Nihongo ni okeru jita no yūtaisei to tadōsei: Gifu-ken hōgen no jidōshi *obowaru*, *kitawaru*, *nosaru*, *dokasaru* o rei to shite [Transitive/intransitive pairs and transitivity in Japanese: a case study of the intransitive verbs *obowaru*, *kitawaru*, *nosaru*, *dokasaru* in the Gifu dialect]. In Mie Tsunoda, Kan Sasaki & Tōru Shionoya (eds.), *Tadōsei no tsūgengoteki kenkyū* [Crosslinguistic studies in transitivity], 271–282. Tokyo: Kurosio Publishers.

Yamazaki, Akie. 1994. Hokkaidō hōgen ni okeru jihatsu no jodōshi -*rasaru* no yōhō to sono imi-bunseki [Usages of the spontaneous auxiliary -*rasaru* in the Hokkaidō dialect and its semantic analysis]. In Hokkaidō Hōgen Kenkyūkai (ed.), *Kotoba no sekai* [The world of words], 227–237. Sapporo: Hokkaidō Hōgen Kenkyūkai.

Michinori Shimoji
7 Aspect and non-canonical object marking in the Irabu dialect of Ryukyuan

1 Introduction

This chapter approaches transitivity alternations from a different perspective from most other chapters in this volume, which are primarily concerned with transitivity alternations as lexical or derivational operations. In this chapter, transitivity alternations are examined in terms of 'variation in case-marking of the core participants in a transitive clause' (Malchukov 2006).[1] In particular, this chapter examines case alternation on O in the Irabu dialect of Ryukyuan, a Southern Ryukyuan dialect of the Japonic Family. Irabu is a nominative-accusative language in which S and A are canonically marked by nominative *ga* or *nu* (an alternation largely based on animacy) whereas O is canonically marked by accusative *u*. Unlike most other Ryukyuan languages, however, Irabu and some other Miyako dialects (Koloskova 2007; Hayashi 2010; Lawrence 2012) have another, non-canonical object marker *a*, which I henceforth call 'partitive', based on functional similarities with the Finnish partitive, to be discussed below. In (1), the object NP *mm* 'potato' is marked by the accusative marker *mu* (underlyingly *u*), while in (2) the same object NP is marked by the partitive marker *ma* (underlyingly *a*), occurring in a dependent (narrative converbal) clause marked here in brackets.

(1) mm=mu=du   pur-tar.
    potato=ACC=FOC dig-PST
    '(I) dug (the) potatoes.'

(2) [mm=ma   pur-ii]=du   if-tar.
    potato=PRT dig-CVB.NRT=FOC   go-PST
    'Digging potatoes (here and there), (I) went.'

---

[1] Following standard practice, S is used in this chapter as an abbreviation for intransitive subject, A for transitive subject (agent), and O for direct object.

Michinori Shimoji, Kyushu University

As will be shown later in this chapter, the Irabu partitive exhibits several salient syntactic and semantic-pragmatic features, as summarized in (3).

(3) Syntactic and semantic-pragmatic features of partitive marking
    (a) its occurrence is almost always restricted to narrative converbal clauses,
    (b) it occurs mostly in clauses with imperfective aspect, and
    (c) the partitive O tends to be (though not always) non-specific.

In this chapter, I will argue that the partitive case marker primarily serves to mark imperfective aspect in the clause in which it occurs. In (2) above, for example, the partitive *a* encodes imperfective aspect in a narrative converbal clause, yielding the interpretation that the act of digging potatoes is an (iterative) event overlapping with the act of going expressed in the main clause. This analysis straightforwardly explains why partitive O's primarily occur in narrative converbal clauses: this is the only type of clause that lacks aspect morphology on its verb.

This analysis might seem at odds with the general view that case has a distinguishing function (whereby the core arguments of a clause are distinguished from each other) and/or an identifying one (whereby the semantic role of an NP is identified), both of which are concerned with the grammatical role of the argument being encoded (cf. Mallison & Blake 1981; Kibrik 1985; Comrie 1981; Malchukov 2006; De Hoop & Malchukov 2008; Malchukov & De Hoop 2011). However, in many languages such as the Slavic and Finno-Ugric languages, case morphology appears to encode the aspect of a clause as well as the referential status of O. Finnish partitive marking is a well-known example (Kiparsky 1998). The present study aims to contribute to the typology of case yet another example of interfacing among case, aspect and reference through a detailed description of the partitive in Irabu.

This chapter is organized as follows. In Section 2, I give a typological overview of case, with particular reference to the interface among case, reference and aspect. In Section 3 I provide a brief overview of the morphosyntax of Irabu. In Section 4 I describe partitive marking in terms of clause type, aspect, and referential status of O. In Section 5 I propose an analysis of Irabu partitive marking that coherently explains its behavior, according to which partitive marking functions primarily to encode imperfective aspect, disambiguating the aspectual character of the narrative converbal clause. Section 6 forms the conclusion.

2 Case, reference and aspect

In many languages, referential status (e.g. definiteness and animacy), grammatical roles, and aspect are encoded using distinct formal strategies, most commonly determiners, case marking strategies (including case inflection, case adposition, cross-referencing, and word order), and verbal morphology, respectively. In most European languages, articles are used to encode the referential status of NPs and verbal morphology to encode aspect (Fischer 2005). Case has been widely held to be essentially a system of marking dependent nouns for the type of relationship they bear to their heads (Blake 2001). The 'relationship' here is either a structural/core relationship (i.e. related to core argument roles) or an inherent/peripheral one (related to semantic roles), both of which have to do with grammatical roles that NPs bear to the governing predicate. De Hoop & Malchukov (2008) state that 'case can help to distinguish one argument from the other (e.g. the subject and the object in a transitive clause) or it can encode specific semantic or pragmatic properties of the argument under consideration'. The two functions of 'distinguishing' and 'identifying,' in De Hoop & Malchukov's terms, primarily concern the grammatical role of the NP being case-marked.

The above-mentioned tripartition of form-function pairings is a somewhat idealized and simplistic view of language, as such pairings are often blurred and complicated depending on the availability of morphosyntactic strategies for the three functions in individual languages. For example, Finnish is a notorious example of a language system where case morphology may encode aspect and referential status (De Hoop 1992; Krifka 1992; Kiparsky 1998; Aissen 2003; Fischer 2005; Malchukov & De Hoop 2011), and Fischer (2005) argues that the referential and aspectual functions of case morphology 'apparently [are] due to the lack of an aspectual and a determiner system.' Fischer also notes other kinds of interfacing among case, aspect and reference. Thus in Russian and other Slavic languages there is a complex interface among case morphology, aspect, and reference, whereby both case morphology and aspect morphology encode aspect and reference.

The following pair of examples (taken from Malchukov & De Hoop 2011: 35) illustrate the aspectual function of case in Finnish, where there is a choice for marking O between partitive case -*a* and accusative -*n*.

(4)   *Anne   rakensi   talo-a.*
      Anne   built   house-PRT
      'Anne was building a/the house.'

(5) Anne   rakensi   talo-n.
    Anne   built   house-ACC
    'Anne built a/the house.'

In the literature on Finnish partitive marking, there is agreement that partitive case has two basic functions: aspectual function and NP-related (i.e. referential) function (Kiparsky 1998). On the one hand, partitive marking explicitly marks atelic aspect in the verb. For example, if the event denoted by the verb *ammuin* 'shoot (1st person singular past)' is construed as an atelic activity 'shoot at', the patient is marked with partitive O, but if the event is construed as a telic accomplishment 'shoot dead', the patient is marked with accusative O (the Finnish examples are taken and adapted from Kiparsky 1998):

(6) ammu-i-n   karhu-a.
    shoot-PST-1SG   bear-PRT
    'I shot at the/a bear.'

(7) ammu-i-n   karhu-n.
    shoot-PST-1SG   bear-ACC
    'I shot the/a bear.'

Note here that the verb form in the two examples is identical, and it is aspect that the partitive marking explicitly marks. The definiteness of O is ambiguous in either of these two examples.

On the other hand, partitive marking may explicitly mark definiteness in O, indicating that the O so marked is quantitatively indeterminate. For example, the telic verb *saan* 'get (1st person singular)' co-occurs with a partitive-marked O if the patient is quantitatively indeterminate, otherwise with an accusative-marked O.

(8) saa-n   karhu-j-a.
    get-1SG   bear-PL-PRT
    'I'll get bears.'

(9) saa-n   karhu-n.
    get-1SG   bear-ACC
    'I'll get the/a bear.'

Thus, in Finnish case morphology mediates the interface between reference and aspect. There are also other ways in which reference and aspect interface. It is well known that in English the referential status of O may affect the telicity of the verb, as formally reflected in the incompatibility of definitely-marked O with temporal adverbials such as 'for X time': *John pushed (*the) carts for an hour* (cf. Dowty 1979, Verkuyl 1993, Smith 1997, Tenny 1987). In Standard German, the lack of aspect morphology is compensated for by determiners encoding aspect (Leiss 2000), demonstrating an interface between reference and aspect mediated by a determiner system when aspect morphology is absent.

A theoretical account for this interface between referential status of O and aspect is possible based on a semantic affinity between the two: completeness of a transitive event is construed as having an effect on the patient, which is usually definite and bounded. Dowty (1979), Verkuyl (1993), and many others argue that it is the VP that determines (situation) aspect, which suggests that referential status of O and verbal aspect constitute grammatical concepts that are tightly knit together. Kiparsky (1998) argues that partitive marking in its aspectual and NP-related functions denotes a single aspectual meaning of *unboundedness* (non-completeness, irresultativity) that is manifested at the VP level.

Note that in Finnish accusative versus partitive marking is a more reliable indicator of aspect than referential status of O, a fact that is evident from the free translations of example (6) above for partitive and (9) for accusative. This has led many linguists to conclude that Finnish case marking of O primarily encodes aspect (Kiparsky 1998; Aissen 2003; Fischer 2005). I will argue in this chapter that Irabu has a similar system in which the partitive marking of O primarily functions to encode imperfective aspect, and, as a side effect of the aspectual interpretation, may function to encode non-specificity of O. For example, in (2), the imperfective interpretation arises from the fact that the action of digging is not yet completed. The action of digging, which is telic (i.e. has an inherent endpoint) in nature, is construed as a non-complete event if, among other things, there is no specification of delimitation (quantity) of the referent, i.e. if the O is non-specific. Thus, the tendency toward a non-specific interpretation of O may be seen as an indirect consequence of imperfectivity.

Like Finnish, the referential function of partitive in Irabu may be explained by the absence of a morphosyntactic strategy specialized for reference (i.e. a determiner system). However, the aspectual function of partitive cannot be argued to reflect the absence of aspect morphology, given that Irabu has rich predicate aspect morphology, as seen below. The aspectual function of partitive is crucially related to the fact that partitive marking is limited to a specific type of subordinate clause, the narrative converbal clause. I will argue that this syntactic restriction is due to the fact that narrative converbs resist aspectual marking. That is, just as in the case of Finnish, the unavailability of aspect morphology leads to a bifunctionality in case morphology. Thus, distributional peculiarities of the Irabu partitive may be straightforwardly explained by mechanisms independently proposed for other languages.

3 Preliminary notes on Irabu grammar

3.1 Topic marker and partitive

In Irabu, the partitive case marker is homophonous with the topic marker, as illustrated in (10) below.

(10) kari=a   [tigami=a   jum-ii]=du   par-tar.
     3SG=TOP   letter=PRT read-CVB.NRT=FOC   leave-PST
     'S/he left reading a letter.'

Morphophonemic alternation rules for the two morphemes are identical, and can be summarized as follows. These morphemes occur as *ja* when following a long vowel or diphthong (*kuu* 'powder' + *a* → *kuu=ja*; *kui* 'voice' + =*a* → *kui=ja*). They carry an onset consonant when following the coda consonant of the noun stem (*kan* 'crab' + *a* → *kan=na*; *paz* 'fly' + *a* → *paz=za*). They occur as *u* when following a light syllable with /u/ (*kadu* 'corner' + *a* → *kadu=u*). Elsewhere, they occur as *a*.

Given this identical morphophonemic behavior, it seems evident that they must have developed historically from the same morpheme (probably a topic marker, considering its cognate forms in Ryukyuan in general), which later split into a topic marker on the one hand and an object marker on the other, arguably in proto-Miyako Ryukyuan. Synchronically, however, there are strong grounds for them to be treated as distinct morphemes (a similar argument is given in Koloskova 2007: 288 for Hirara). First, the two morphemes have very different, in fact opposite, functions. Whereas the topic marker =*a* marks a sentential topic or a contrasted element and typically occurs in a main clause, the partitive *a* marks elements that are little topic-worthy (e.g. inanimate and non-specific referents) and almost always occurs in a subordinate clause. For example, in (10) above, the NP *tigami* is a non-specific NP in a subordinate clause (indicated by square brackets) and cannot be interpreted as the topic of the sentence, which corresponds rather to the subject *kari*.

Second, there is a complementary distribution in topic marking whereby the topical object is uniquely marked by *ba(a)* and all other topical NPs are marked by *a*. If the object NP of (10), *tigami* 'letter', is topic-marked, for example, it receives the topic marker *ba(a)* as in (11).

(11) tigami=u=baa   jum-ii=du   par-tar.
     letter=ACC=TOP read-CVB.NRT=FOC leave-PST
     'With respect to the letter, (s/he) left reading it.'

Based on these two distributional characteristics, I treat the partitive *a* and the topic marker *a* as synchronically homophonous morphemes.

Before concluding this section, it is worth mentioning that the topic marker and the direct object marker are identical in a number of genetically unrelated languages. Such languages typically have so-called Differential Object Marking (DOM: Bossong 1985; Aissen 2003), in which a highly topical O, often fronted to sentence-initial position, is marked by a special marker that is identical to the topic marker. This situation is naturally explained by assuming a historical process through which topicalization of the object NP in such languages resulted in DOM (Iemmolo 2011). This may hold true for some Northern Ryukyuan languages and Kyushu dialects as well, where the object marker is *ba*, historically developed from a topic marker. By contrast, in Irabu the partitive typically (but not necessarily) marks Os that are low in referential status (Section 4.5), and partitive Os are never fronted for topicalization. Thus, it seems unreasonable to assume that the partitive developed from a topicalization structure as in the case of DOM languages. It is at this stage still unclear why the partitive and topic markers are formally identical and how the former developed from the latter. This is an important future research topic, which will require a thorough synchronic description of the partitive in a range of Miyako Ryukyuan dialects. It is hoped that this chapter will contribute to this topic through a detailed synchronic description of the partitive in Irabu.

3.2 Verb inflection

Three verb forms are distinguished in Irabu based on their inflectional morphology: independent verbs, adnominal verbs and converbs. Independent verbs occur as predicates of independent sentences, comprising realis and irrealis forms. Realis forms carry tense and mood suffixes, as in *mii-ta-m* (look-PST-RLS) 'looked (for sure)'. Irrealis forms carry only mood suffixes with future time reference, such as the intentional (e.g. *mii-di* 'will look'), the optative (e.g. *mii-baa* 'want to look'), and the imperative (e.g. *mii-ru* 'look'). Adnominal verbs may occur as predicates of independent sentences or as predicates of adnominal clauses or of concessive clauses (a later development from adnominal clauses). These mark tense only, as in *mii-tar* (look-PST) 'looked'.

Converbs head adverbial/adsentential dependent clauses. They morphologically fall into the categories of tenseless converbs such as (12) and (13) and tensed converbs such as (14). Most converbs are tenseless.

(12) Purpose (supine) converb (tenseless)
 zzu=u   tur-ga   ik-adi.
 fish=NOM   catch-CVB.PUR   go-INT
 "Let's go catch fish."

(13) Circumstantial converb (tenseless)
 jaa=nkai   ngi-utui   vva=u=du   mac-iu-tar=dara.
 house=ALL   go-CVB.CIR   2SG=ACC=FOC   wait-PROG-PST=ASR
 'I was waiting for you (at home), having gotten home ahead of time.'

(14) Causal converb (tensed)
 ffa=nu   naf-ta-iba   daki-u-tar.
 child=NOM   cry-PST-CVB.CSL   hold-PROG-PST
 'Because the child cried, (I) held (him).'

3.3 The narrative converb and its aspectual meanings

The narrative converb is a tenseless converb that ends in -*(i)i*. Unlike all other converbs, it does not designate a specific adverbial/adsentential relationship, the exact relationship being inferred from context. That is, it is a contextual rather than specialized converb in Nedjalkov's (1995) typology of converbs. The narrative converb thus designates a wide range of meanings, including the following:

(15) Temporal sequence (narrative)
 [pzsara=nkai   ik-ii]=du   agu=n   idjav-tar=dara.
 Hirara=ALL   go-CVB.NRT=FOC   friend=DAT   meet-PST=ASR
 '(I) went to Hirara, and saw a friend.'

(16) Temporal overlap (simultaneous or circumstantial)
 [saz=za   kav-vii]=du   uma=n   biz-iu-r.
 towel=PRT   wear-CVB.NRT=FOC   there=DAT   sit-PROG-NONPST
 '(She) is sitting there wearing a towel (with her head covered by a towel).'

(17) Temporal overlap (manner adverbial)
   [nuuma=n   nuur-ii]=du   par-tar.
   horse=DAT   ride-CVB.NRT=FOC   leave-PST
   '(S/he) left riding on a horse.'

(18) Temporal overlap (manner adverbial; part of an iterative macro-event)
   [fsa=a   fmck-ii]   saba=u=du   ara-iu-r.
   plant=PRT   tread-CVB.NRT   sandal=ACC=FOC   wash-PROG-NONPST
   'As they tread seaweed (they) are washing (their) sandals.'

(19) Recitation (temporality is irrelevant)
   samsin-gama=a   pzk-ii=mai,
   samsin.guitar-DIM=PRT   play-CVB.NRT=too

   mata   aagu-gama=a   s-ii=mai=du...
   and   song-DIM=PRT   do-CVB.NRT=FOC

   '(Men and women in the past) would play the Samsin guitar, sing songs, and so on,' [Data taken from Shibata 1972: 203]

This conflation of a range of meanings, especially the narrative sequential meaning and non-sequential, modificational meaning is typologically very common in Asian languages, instantiating the 'Asian converb' type in Bickel's 1998 typology. What is crucial to the discussion in the following sections is that these various usages of narrative converbs can be classified into two broad types according to their aspectual properties: perfective (as in (15)) vs. imperfective (as in (16) to (19)).

3.4 Perfective aspect

Perfective aspect treats an event as a delimited whole with no explicit reference to its internal temporal constituency (Comrie 1976: 16; Smith 1997: 66). As a delimited event, the perfective event is construed as one that invariably entails a termination (a characteristic that is called 'event boundedness'; see Croft 2012). In (15) the action/event '(I) went to Hirara' is taken as a delimited whole with no reference to its internal temporal structure. The two clauses denote mutually independent and separable events, i.e. two macro-events, that are ordered in temporal sequence. Since the act of going to Hirara is a bounded macro-event that is completed before the act of buying, the clause that denotes the former event can co-occur with the anterior particle =kara 'after (doing something)', which helps make explicit termination of the event being described. But it should be emphasized that this particle expresses more than simple perfectivity, so it is not the usual means to mark perfectivity in the narrative converbal clause: the particle =*kara* 'after (doing something)' expresses an additional meaning of 'primarily' or 'first', so that the the action denoted in a clause so marked is a preliminary or necessary action for what follows (Shimoji 2008: 435).

3.5 Imperfective aspect

Imperfective aspect construes an event as unbounded with no clear endpoint. Examples (16) to (19) may all be seen to encode imperfective aspect, as the events/states denoted are not treated as bounded wholes, but as temporally overlapping with the action denoted in the following clause, the two events together constituting a single macro-event. This unboundedness is evident from the fact that the anterior particle =*kara* cannot co-occur with the first clause. If it does co-occur, a perfective reading obtains.

In (16), the narrative converbal clause presents a circumstance that persists over the duration of the action denoted in the main clause, much like a circumstantial or manner adverbial clause. The situation type (Smith 1997) of the verb root *kav-* 'put on' is achievement (i.e. telic and punctual), but the viewpoint aspect (i.e. perfectivity) of the clause is clearly imperfective, since the state resulting from putting a towel on one's head persists over the duration of the event denoted in the main clause, an imperfective interpretation that is reflected in the free translation of (16).[2]

In (17), the action denoted in the narrative converbal clause functions like a manner adverbial, just as in the case of (16). Here, the act of getting on a horse is a telic event, and the completion of this act is followed by the act of leaving. Thus, it might first appear that the two events are construed as two perfective events in sequence. However, in (17) the resulting state of riding the horse is construed as persisting through the event denoted in the main clause.

In (18), the events of the narrative converbal clause and of the main clause constitute sub-events of a single macro-event that occurs iteratively, the two

---

[2] The construal of an event as a resulting state is clearly related to the concept of perfect (not perfective). The so-called 'Perfect of result (Comrie 1976: 56) designates the persistence of a state resulting from an event that occurred previously. In many languages, the perfect may co-occur with either perfective or imperfective predicates, demonstrating that the two notions of perfect and perfective are distinct. Comrie notes that the perfect of result is in many languages encoded in the same way as the stative (thus imperfective).

sub-events occurring one after another in a back-and-forth fashion. The act of treading seaweed is incorporated into the act of washing sandals as the former is a manner which enables the achievement of the latter. Thus, the two sub-events are presented as a single act of washing sandals *by* treading seaweed (rather than *after* treading seaweed), with the two sub-events interpreted as occurring simultaneously.

In (19), the events denoted by the two narrative converbal clauses are ordered as they come into the mind of the speaker, not reflecting the actual temporal sequence of the two events, as would be crucial in the case of perfective clauses. In (19) the speaker recites a list of things that people in old times would do, of which the speaker picks out as examples playing the *Samsin* guitar and singing songs. This recitation function of the narrative converbal clause is extremely common in Irabu, as it lacks a specialized form for recitation such as the converb *-tari* in Japanese (*eiga=o mi-tari ongaku=o kii-tari* 'watching movies, listening to music, and so on'). Recited events are imperfective since they lack a clear endpoint and are not situated on an actual time line (i.e. they are atemporal), making event boundedness irrelevant.

3.6 The auxiliary verb construction

In addition to appearing as a clausal head, the narrative converb is employed in the auxiliary verb construction (AVC), which can be broadly defined as a 'monoclausal structure minimally consisting of a lexical verb element that contributes lexical content to the construction and an auxiliary verb element that contributes some grammatical or functional content to the construction' (Anderson 2006: 7). In Irabu, major aspectual relations are encoded by the AVC: progressive, resultative, prospective, and perfect.

(20) Progressive
 ba=a   tigami=u   [kak-ii=du   u-tar].
 1SG=TOP letter=ACC write-CVB.NRT=FOC   PROG-PST
 'I was writing a letter'

(21) Resultative
 tigami=u=ba   [kak-ii=du   ar].
 letter=ACC=TOP   write-CVB.NRT=FOC   RSL.NONPST
 '(I) have written the letter.'

(22) Prospective
 ba=a   tigami=u   [kak-ii   uk-adi].
 1SG=TOP   letter=ACC write-CVB.NRT   PROS-INT
 'I will write a letter (in advance).'

(23) Perfect
 ba=a   tigami=u   [kak-ii   njaa-n].
 1SG=TOP   letter=ACC write-CVB.NRT   PRF-NEG.NONPST
 'I have written a letter.'

The AVC consists of a lexical verb, which must be inflected as a narrative converb, and an auxiliary verb, which functions as a clausal head and inflects according to the syntactic environment in which it is placed (see Section 2.3). Different AVCs take different auxiliaries: the stative verb *ur* for the progressive AVC (20), another state verb *ar* for the resultative AVC (21), the verb *uf* 'put' for the prospective AVC (22), and *njaan* 'not exist' for the perfect AVC (23).

Thus, a narrative converb may appear as the lexical verb element in a monoclausal AVC structure as well as the predicate head of a dependent clause, as discussed in Section 2.4. The AVC in fact developed from a biclausal structure where the first clause consisted of a narrative converbal clause and the second consisted of a main clause of which the predicate has now become the auxiliary verb element. For example, the progressive AVC developed from a dependent narrative converbal clause followed by a stative main clause. In contemporary Irabu, however, the AVC is clearly mono-clausal in that the two verbs (i.e. the lexical verb element and the auxiliary element) share the same argument(s), show a fixed internal structure (i.e. LEX (+FOC) + AUX) as a single predicate phrase, and behave as a single intonational unit (see Shimoji 2008 for a detailed discussion of the mono-clausality of the AVC). In the sections to follow, the term 'narrative converbal clause' is used to indicate a dependent clause headed by a narrative converb, exclusive of the AVC.

4 Partitive marking in Irabu

This section examines distributional and semantic-pragmatic characteristics of partitive marking in Irabu. The data were obtained both through direct elicitation and from a corpus of texts that I recorded and transcribed. The total number of words in the corpus is 10,066. The total number of NPs with accusative case and those with partitive case in the corpus is 249 and 49, respectively.

As mentioned in the introduction, the canonical case marking for O is accusative; partitive case marking of O is more restricted and non-canonical, something that can be initially confirmed by the ratio of accusative to partitive occurrences in the corpus. Another feature pointing to the non-canonicity of the partitive is that the partitive can be replaced by the accusative in any environment, but not vice versa. For example, in (2) above, partitive *a* can be replaced by accusative *u*, but in (1) accusative *u* cannot be replaced by partitive *a*. Furthermore, there is no restriction on the occurrence of accusative O whereas there are two strong restrictions on the occurrence of partitive O.

(24) Restrictions on Irabu partitive marking

Restriction on clause type: the partitive occurs mostly in narrative converbal clauses.

Restriction on aspect: the partitive occurs mostly in imperfective clauses.

These two restrictions will be examined in detail in Sections 4.1 and 4.2 below. We will see that there are exceptions to the two restrictions if one looks closely at the text corpus, but they are clearly restrictions relevant to partitive marking. The optimal environment for the occurrence of partitive marking is therefore in a narrative converbal clause that has imperfective aspect, a situation that accounts for most of the occurrences of partitive marking. In addition to these restrictions, there is a weak tendency for partitive Os to be non-specific, as will be discussed in Section 4.3. Unlike the restrictions in (24), however, I will argue that this referential feature of O is a concomitant feature of the aspectual feature.

4.1 Partitive and clause type

The restriction of partitive marking to narrative converbal clauses is pervasive to all the dialects of Irabu (Lawrence 2012 for the Nakachi dialect), and is also found to varying degrees in Miyako Ryukyuan in general. While in Gusukube non-canonical O marking appears to be restricted to narrative converbal clauses just as in the case of Irabu (Mika Sakai, p.c.), Hirara (Koloskova 2007) and Ikema (Hayashi 2010) allow non-canonical marking to occur in other clause contexts, even though there is a clear tendency for it to occur in narrative converbal clauses (see Section 5.1 for further discussion).

Table 1 shows the distribution of the partitive in Irabu. The numbers here demonstrate clearly that, whereas the accusative (ACC) occurs in a wide range of clauses, the partitive (PRT) is primarily restricted to narrative converbal clauses (94%). The other 6% of PRT clearly constitute marginal uses of the partitive.

Table 1: Object marking in texts

Clause type (categorized by predicate head)	ACC	PRT
Narrative converbal clause	56 (22%)	46 (94%)
Converbal clause (other)	28 (11%)	1 (2%)
Clause headed by adnominal form	125 (50%)	1 (2%)
Clause headed by independent realis form	17 (7%)	0 (0%)
Clause headed by independent irrealis imperative form	8 (3%)	1 (2%)
Clause headed by other independent irrealis form	7 (3%)	0 (0%)
Verb-less (with O stranded)	8 (3%)	0 (0%)
Total	249	49

It should be emphasized here that this biased distribution of the partitive does not reflect the relative frequency of the narrative converbal clause itself. In my text database, by far the most frequently observed clause types are those headed by an adnominal form. Indeed, the distribution of the ordinary accusative in the text actually parallels this overall distributional pattern (see Table 1). Thus, it is necessary to examine why the partitive occurs mostly in narrative converbal clauses.

Example (25) illustrates partitive marking occurring in a narrative converbal clause, where the bracketed converbal clause and the main clause together constitute a single iterative macro-event.

(25) Narrative converbal clause (in brackets)
 [miz=za fm-ii] waagi=nkai nuur-ii ff?
 water=PRT get-CVB.NRT upward=ALL climb-CVB.NRT come

 '(Did people) used to get water (down there) and come upward (over and over)?'

Examples (26) to (28) are the attested examples of partitive marking found in clauses other than the narrative converbal clause.

(26) Conditional converbal clause (in brackets)
    [bura=a   mak-ii   u-tigaa]   unu   suncjuu=ja=i,
    band=PRT   wear-CVB.NRT   PROG-CVB.CND   that mayor=TOP=DSC

    kaee=tti   gusjan=na   nci-i,
    ONM=QT   stick=PRT   put-CVB.NRT

    tii-gama   kacmi-i   c-cii,
    hand-DIM   get-CVB.NRT   come-CVB.NRT

    zjautu=n=tii   fz-gama=u=mai   mjaanai=i,
    nice=DAT=QT   sleeve-DIM=ACC=too   fix.CVB.NRT=DSC

    'The mayor wore a band, and, leaning his stick against the wall, he would take (my) hand and fix up (my) sleeves to make (me) look nicer.'

(27) Adnominal clause (in brackets)
    [jaa=ja   njaan]   su=u   ukukazifc-nagi=n=mai   ik-ii...
    house=PRT   not.exist   person=TOP   typhoon-APRX=DAT=too   go-CVB.NRT
    'Those who did not have their own houses left in the middle of the typhoon...'

(28) Independent clause (imperative mood)
    vva=mai   hoogen=na   az-zi.
    2SG=too   vernacular=PRT   say-IMP
    'Speak the Irabu language like us.'

4.2 Aspect and partitive marking

The other restriction on partitive marking in Irabu concerns aspect. That is, partitive Os occur mostly in imperfective clauses. In this section, I focus on narrative converbal clauses in which the partitive occurs, examining their aspectual value (perfective vs. imperfective). Note that all the examples of the partitive occurring in clauses other than narrative converbal clauses (26–28) can be considered to have imperfective aspect: specifically, progressive (26), stative (27) and non-completed future (28).

Elicitation revealed that partitive Os never occur with the anterior clitic *kara* 'after (doing something)' (Section 3.4), which explicitly marks perfectivity. In texts, however, there are several exceptions in which partitive Os did occur in perfective clauses. As is shown in Table 2, among all tokens of narrative converbal clauses in which the accusative (ACC) occurs, perfective use is slightly outnumbered by imperfective uses (which include circumstantial, iterative, habitual, etc.). By contrast, among all instances of the partitive (PRT) that occurred in the narrative converbal clause, 90% occurred in clauses that have imperfective aspect.

Table 2: Object marking and aspect in narrative converbal clauses

	ACC	PRT
Perfective	23 (41%)	2 (4%)
Imperfective	29 (52%)	41 (90%)
Ambiguous	4 (7%)	3 (7%)
Total	56	46

As mentioned in Section 3.3, a narrative converb is unmarked for aspectual distinctions, its exact aspectual interpretation being determined contextually. One useful test for the perfectivity of a narrative converbal clause is to see whether it accepts the anterior particle *kara* 'after (doing something)' (Section 3.4). If this can be attached without changing the aspectual construal of the denoted event, the clause must have perfective aspect. Otherwise, it must have imperfective aspect. Except in those cases where the aspectual value was clear from the context, I conducted a follow-up elicitation to see whether a given instance of a narrative converbal clause with partitive marking was perfective or imperfective by this test.

4.3 The perfective aspect

There were two clear instances of perfective aspect co-occuring with partitive marking. In (29), the event in the narrative converbal clause (Event 1) can be treated as a perfective event, which must occur and be completed before Event 2.

(29) nkjaan=du [nudu-ffu-vcca=tu mii-vcca=tu
old.times=FOC neck-black-quail=COM female-quail=COM

tunuka-gama=a nasi-i]
egg-DIM=PRT give.birth.to-CVB.NRT
Event 1

uri=u jama=nu mnaka=n
that=ACC mountain=GEN middle=DAT

usui-i u-tarjaa=du,
hide-CVB.NRT PROG-CVB.RSL=FOC
Event 2

'Once upon a time, a black-neck quail and a female quail gave birth to an egg (Event 1); (they) hid it in the middle of a mountain (Event 2);'

A later elicitation confirmed that my consultants all agreed that the anterior clitic *kara* 'after (doing something)' can be attached to the bracketed clause without any change in the meaning denoted by the sentence.

In the following example, the perfective aspect of the clause is evident from the anterior particle *kara* 'after (doing something)', which makes clear that Event 1 has reached its endpoint before Event 2 occurs.

(30) *assuga*   *[tus=sa*   *tur-ii]=kara,*   *ffa-mur*   *as=saa.*
      but   age=PRT   take-CVB.NRT=after   child-caring   do.NONPST=DSC
                                Event 1   Event 2

  'But, after getting old (Event 1), (I) have been baby-sitting (Event 2).'

In both cases, Event 1 is clearly bounded in such a way that the completion of Event 1 is taken as a pre-requisite or condition for the occurrence of Event 2. The two events are delimited separate events, thus perfective events in sequence.

4.4 Imperfective aspect

As noted in Section 3.5, the term 'imperfective' subsumes various situations that appear to lack perfective characteristics. In the case of Irabu narrative converbal clauses, imperfective clauses typically exhibit temporal overlap with the clause that follows, so that the event denoted lacks a clear endpoint.

4.4.1 Temporal overlap

The most common usage of narrative converbal clauses with the partitive is as a circumstantial or manner adverbial that temporally overlaps with the action denoted by the main clause. As already noted in Section 3.5, the event denoted by an imperfective narrative converbal clause lacks a clear endpoint, constituting a larger macro-event with the event denoted by the main clause. This event unboundedness is reflected in the inability of such clauses to co-occur with the anterior particle *kara* 'after (doing something)'. In (31) below, the clause is a manner adverbial clause that denotes an event (Event 1) temporally overlapping with the event denoted by the clause that follows (Event 2).

(31) [paz=za   nbi-i]   bizi-u-tigaa
     leg=PRT   stretch-CVB.NRT   sit-PROG-CVB.CND
               Event 1   Event 2

   daizna   munu=tii   kangair=dara.
   awful   thing=QT   think.NONPST=DSC

   'If (you) sit stretching (your) legs, (people) would think (it's) awful.'

In (32), the event of watching the dance in the narrative converbal clause (the converbal suffix here is zero rather than -(i)i, due to a morpho-phonemic alternation) is imperfective in aspect, as evidenced by the fact that it persists during the occurrence of the event in the main clause (the act of thinking about the dance) and modifies its meaning. The first event, in other words, functions as a circumstantial or simultaneous event that overlaps with the main clause event, the two events together constituting a macro-event.

(32) [budur=ra   mii]   agai   kagi-munu=i
     dance=PRT   watch.CVB.NRT   INTJ   nice-thing=DSC
                 Event 1

   aparagi-munu=i=ti   umuv-tar.
   beautiful-thing=DSC=QT   think-PST
                              Event 2

   'Watching the dance, (I) thought like, "Wow, (it's) nice, beautiful!"'

The following example might at first appear to be an instance of the perfective use of a narrative converbal clause, in the sense that Event 1 occurs before Event 2.

(33) vvadu=u   [uri=a   nara-ii]   nau-hu-di=ga?
     2PL=TOP   that=PRT   learn-CVB.NRT   what-VLZ-INT=Q
                             Event 1   Event 2

   'Learning it (i.e. the Irabu language), what are you going to do (with it)?'

However, it is also possible to interpret Event 1 as a circumstantial state during which Event 2 occurs, giving rise to the interpretation 'What are you going to do while learning the Irabu language?' Here, the speaker assumes no particular endpoint to the act of learning the Irabu language. A later elicitation confirmed that this possibility is correct, as the anterior particle *kara* 'after (doing something)' cannot co-occur with the first clause, unless the partitive is replaced by the accusative. That is, the partitive blocks the perfective interpretation here. Another piece of support for the imperfective analysis of (33) is that it can be paraphrased as in (34), where the narrative converb is replaced by a circumstantial converb clearly denoting imperfective aspect 'while/during the time of (doing something)'.

(34) vvadu=u [uri=u nara-iutui] nau-hu-di=ga?
 2PL=TOP that=ACC learn-CVB.CIR what-VLZ-INT=Q
         Event 1   Event 2
 'While learning it (i.e. the Irabu language), what are you going to do (with it)?'

Note that the partitive is here replaced by the accusative. As will be discussed in Section 5.2, this incompatibility of the partitive with converbs that explicitly designate aspectual meaning provides an important insight into the nature of partitive marking. Assuming a general strategy in language for avoiding redundancy, the partitive can be seen as being blocked in contexts where the converb is explicitly marked for aspect, as the aspectual information provided by the partitive would in that case be redundant.

In (35), the narrative converbal clause and main clause together denote an iterative event made up of the two sub-events of turning over rocks and catching crabs. These two sub-events occur alternately in a back-and-forth fashion, with the result that they are each construed as lacking an endpoint.

(35) uku-zii=ja kais-ii kan=mai tur.
 big-stone=PRT turn.over-CVB.NRT crab=too catch.NONPST
 'While turning over rocks (those guys keep) catch(ing) crabs, too.'

This is in contrast to cases where two events constitute a series of distinct macro-events (i.e. two perfective events in a chain), as in (36), where the perfectivity of the narrative converbal clause is explicitly marked by the anterior particle =kara 'after'.

(36) uku-zii=ju kais-ii=kara=du kan=mai tur.
 big-stone=ACC turn.over-CVB.NRT=after=FOC crab=too catch.NONPST
 'After turning over rocks, (those guys) catch crabs, too.'

It should be noted here that the object NP *ukuzii* in the narrative converbal clause is marked by the accusative rather than the partitive.[3]

4.4.2 Recitation

Recitation is the function of enumerating a list of things as they come to the mind of the speaker (see Section 3.5), as illustrated in (37). The order in which the events are enumerated in (37) does not reflect their actual sequence in time, as would be crucial in the case of perfective clauses, but simply the random order in which the speaker remembers and lists them. Note that the two narrative converbal clauses here contain the partitive.

(37) [mm=ma   cf-fii]   [buuz=za   ibi-i]
      potato=PRT   make-CVB.NRT   sugarcane=PRT   plant-CVB.NRT
                    Event 1   Event 2

   mata   kan=mai   tumi-i   ff.
   and   crab=too   search-CVB.NRT   come.NONPST
                                         Event 3

   '(We did) things such as making potatoes, planting sugarcane and catching crabs.'

4.5 Referential status and partitive marking

As discussed in Section 2, it is the case in many languages that the referential status of O (variously called 'prominence of O' or 'individuation of O' in different theoretical frameworks) may be encoded by case morphology. Definiteness, in particular, is often encoded by case morphology, especially if the language lacks a determiner system. A scale of definiteness is commonly seen to be formed by personal pronouns > proper names > definite nouns > indefinite specific nouns > non-specific nouns (Aissen 2003: 437). In Irabu, however, the prominence of O cannot itself be seen as the determining factor governing partitive marking, but is better seen as an indirect reflection of the overwhelming tendency of clauses with partitive marking to have imperfective aspect.

---

[3] My subjects all agreed that use of the Partitive in (36) is acceptable, but when they were asked to actually repeat (36) as is with the Partitive instead of the accusative, they invariably replaced the Partitive with the accusative.

An analysis of our text data reveals no skewed distributional pattern with respect to the definiteness scale, even though there is a weak tendency for the partitive to mark non-specific objects: definite/specific nouns (including pronouns and proper names, N = 13) make up 27% of the nouns marked partitively, indefinite/specific nouns (N = 3) 6%, and indefinite non-specific nouns (N = 33) 67%. The following example contains a pronominal O marked with the partitive, even though pronouns occur at the top of the definiteness scale.

(38) ba=ga   ffa-gama-mmi,   pai=kara   c-cii,
      1SG=GEN   child-DIM-PL   field=ABL   come-CVB.NRT
      [uri=a   mii],   nac-tuurii=du u-tar.
      that=PRT   look.CVB.NRT   cry-ITR=FOC   PROG-PST
      '(I was thinking about) my children; (I) returned from the field, and looking at them, (I) cried over and over again.'

Here, the bracketed narrative converbal clause contains the demonstrative *uri* 'that (i.e. 'my children')', which is definite and specific, and is even human. In fact, unlike the tendency towards imperfectivity, which showed a correlation with partitive marking both in text-counts and in elicitation (as seen, for example, in the fact that insertion of the anterior particle *kara* 'after (doing)' resulted in lower acceptability or ungrammaticality of the partitive, as discussed in Section 4.2), the weak tendency towards non-specificity of partitively-marked nouns in our analysis of the text database turned out to be irrelevant in elicitation. That is, it was possible to elicit numerous grammatical sentences with the partitive O that refer to a definite, specific and human referent, as in the following example.

(39) [uttu-gama=a   mac-ii]=du   saihoo   as-iu-tar.
      younger.sibling-DIM=PRT   wait-CVB.NRT=FOC   sewing   do-PROG-PST
      'Waiting for (my) younger brother, (I) was sewing.'
      [Definite, Specific, Human]

It is also possible for the accusative to mark O of low prominence, since every instance of the partitive can be replaced by the accusative (see the introduction to Section 4).

It is impossible therefore to claim that there is a direct relationship between low referential status of O and occurrence of partitive marking. The text-count only suggests a relatively high frequency of non-specific Os in the partitive case, but this is not sufficient to show that referential status is the determining factor for partitive marking. As will be discussed in Section 5.3, this weak tendency for partitive Os to be low in prominence should be regarded as a side effect of the imperfective aspect that induces the occurrence of the partitive marking.

5 A functional account of Irabu partitive marking

This section aims to provide a principled analysis of partitive marking in Irabu that coherently accounts for the features of partitive marking observed in the texts, namely that (a) partitive marking is restricted almost totally to occurring in narrative converbal clauses (94%), (b) it occurs mostly in clauses with imperfective aspect (90%), and (c) partitive Os tend to be (but not necessarily) non-specific (67%). I will argue that these facts can be explained in a principled way if one considers that the primary function of partitive marking is to encode imperfective aspect in the clause in which it occurs.

Before presenting my analysis in Section 5.2, it is worth examining a previous analysis of partitive marking in Miyako Ryukyuan that notes two of the above-mentioned features ((a) and (c)) but proposes a different principle to explain non-canonical marking of O.

5.1 Previous analysis

In her description of partitive marking in Hirara (a north-west variety of Miyako Ryukyuan), Koloskova (2007) notes three major features of the non-canonical O case marker corresponding to partitive case in Irabu. First, non-canonical Os tend to occur in non-finite (i.e. dependent) clauses. Second, non-canonically marked Os tend to be low in referential status. Third, they tend to be less affected. She argues that these features reflect low transitivity of the clauses in which the differentially marked Os occur. Her analysis is largely based on the Transitivity Hypothesis proposed by Hopper & Thompson (1980), who claim that transitivity alternations such as differential marking of subjects and objects are sensitive to the various parameters summarized in (40).

(40) Transitivity parameters (Hopper & Thompson 1980)

		High	Low
(A)	**participants**	2 or more participants	1 participant
(B)	**kinesis**	action	non-action
(C)	**aspect**	telic	atelic
(D)	**punctuality**	punctual	non-punctual
(E)	**volitionality**	volitional	non-volitional
(F)	**affirmation**	affirmative	negative
(G)	**mode**	realis	irrealis
(H)	**agency**	A(gent) high in potency	A low in potency
(I)	**affectedness of O**	O totally affected	O not affected
(J)	**individuation of O**	O highly individuated	O non-individuated

Even though these transitivity parameters, at least some of them ((C), (I) and (J)), do contribute to non-canonical marking of O in Irabu and in Hirara, appealing only to the transitivity parameters fails for the following two reasons. First, attributing non-canonical marking to reduced transitivity fails to predict the exact conditions under which the marking occurs. Since this analysis predicts that non-canonical marking will occur in any type of clause that has lower transitivity of some sort or another, it cannot explain why non-canonical marking is concentrated in a specific type of subordinate clause, namely the narrative converbal clause. For example, in the following pair of sentences, the subordinate clauses (in brackets) should be equally low in transitivity in terms of the ten parameters above, since the two clauses are a near minimal pair differing only in the form of the converb.

(41) *[mm=ma   tum-ii]=du   if-tar.*
     potato=PRT search.for-CVB.NRT=FOC go-PST
     '(I) went looking for potatoes.'

(42) *[mm=mu   tumi-ccjaaki]=du   if-tar.*
     potato=ACC search.for-CVB.SIM=FOC go-PST
     '(I) went looking for potatoes.'

Both clauses involve two participants (A), denote action (B), construe an event as imperfective (C) and non-punctual (D), involve volitional agents (E)/(H), occur in an affirmative (F) and realis mood (G) and have non-specific (I) and less affected O (J). As indicated in the free translations, the two converbal clauses are very similar in meaning, in that both clauses denote an event of looking for potatoes that is simultaneous and temporally overlapping with the event of the main clause. However, in Irabu at least, partitive marking is not permitted in (42). This asymmetry would require the transitivity-based analysis to maintain that narrative converbal clauses such as that in (41) are somehow lower in transitivity than other converbal clauses such as the simultaneous converbal clause in (42). However, this is difficult to argue based on transitivity parameters alone.

Apart from transitivity parameters, a conspicuous difference between (41) and (42) is that in the narrative converbal clause the imperfective, simultaneous meaning is not marked on the verbal morphology, whereas in the simultaneous converbal clause it is explicitly marked by the converb suffix -ccjaaki.

5.2 An alternative analysis

To explain our observation that partitive marking occurs most frequently in imperfective clauses, on the one hand, and that it is restricted to narrative converbal clauses, on the other, I propose the following pair of rules that predict and constrain the occurrence of partitive marking in Irabu.

(43) Basic function of partitive: The partitive case marker functions to encode imperfective aspect.

(44) Principle of economy: The partitive O occurs only where necessary, i.e. if there is no other means available for explicitly marking imperfectivity.

In principle, the basic function (43) predicts that partitive case is assigned to *all* imperfective clauses, but the principle of economy (44), by which avoidance of redundancy is taken as the norm, restricts partitive marking to occurrence in clauses that lack aspectual marking, i.e. in narrative converbal clauses.

With regard to the basic function of the partitive in Irabu, I argue that it is aspect, not the referential status of O, that determines the occurrence of partitive case. While the partitive is fully compatible with a definite, specific and human O, the occurrence of the partitive is blocked when the anterior particle *kara*, which explicitly marks perfective aspect, is attached to the clause in which O occurs (Section 5.1). Since imperfectivity entails low referential status of O in the ways explained in the following section, the encoding of imperfective aspect through partitive case also entails low referential status of O.

The principle (43) can be demonstrated in a number of ways. First, let us consider (45), where the aspect of the bracketed narrative converbal clause is ambiguous in the absence of context.

(45) [mm=mu   tum-ii]=du   if-tar.
     potato=ACC search.for-CVB.NRT=FOC go-PST

   a. '(I) went while looking for potatoes.' (imperfective reading)

   b. '(I) looked for potatoes (at some place), then went (to somewhere else).'
      (perfective reading)

Now if accusative *u* is replaced by partitive *a*, this sentence can only be interpreted as in (45a), with the partitive marking serving to resolve the ambiguity. If the ambiguity is resolved through other means such as morphological marking of aspect on the verb, partitive marking does not occur, as it would be redundant. This is illustrated in (46), where the same meaning as (45a) is expressed by the simultaneous converb without partitive marking.

(46) mm=mu(/*=ma)   tumi-ccjaaki=du   if-tar.
     potato=ACC(/*=PRT) search.for-CVB.SIM=FOC go-PST
     '(I) went while looking for potatoes.'

In (46), the verb inflection *-ccjaaki* (simultaneous converb) indicates that the act of searching for potatoes is simultaneous with the act of going. Aspect is in this case morphologically encoded on the verb. Note that the transitivity-based analysis discussed in Section 5.1 would by itself be insufficient to account for the ungrammaticality of the partitive here.

As noted in Section 3.6, the AVC developed from a combination of the narrative converbal clause plus existential verb. In some dialects such as Ikema (Hayashi 2010: 180), the partitive occurs in matrix clauses with the AVC, as well as in narrative converbal clauses. This might seem natural, given the distributional tendency for the partitive to occur in narrative converbal clauses. However, in Irabu the partitive is *not* found in the AVC (an exception for this is (26), where the conditional clause has a progressive AVC as its predicate). Elicitation reveals that examples such as the following are not accepted.

(47) *mm=ma   tumi-i=du   u-tar.
     potato=PRT search.for-CVB.NRT PROG-PST
     '(I) was looking for potatoes.'

This seemingly puzzling distributional fact is naturally explained by an appeal to the principle of economy. That is, since the AVC is clearly imperfective due to the presence of the progressive auxiliary, the partitive is not needed in this case to mark imperfective aspect.

A similar constraint on case marking and aspect is found in Russian, where the choice for O is between accusative and genitive. The genitive case, which is associated with imperfective aspect, is blocked if the verb morphology explicitly marks imperfective aspect, a situation that likewise can be explained in terms of avoidance of redundancy (De Hoop & Malchukov 2008: 1653). Thus, principle (44) does not seem to be language-particular, but is based on a cross-linguistic tendency to avoid redundancy in encoding meaning.

5.3 Revisiting the referential status of O

If we assume that imperfective aspect is the determining factor for predicting the occurrence of partitive marking, it is readily possible to correlate partitive marking with the observed weak (but not perfect) tendency towards non-specific O. For example, if a telic verb like *pur* 'dig' is interpreted as imperfective (i.e., as an unbounded, incomplete process) in some way or another, the action of digging cannot be exhaustive, and the patient cannot therefore be exhaustively affected. This imperfective construal is possible if, among other things, the referent of O is non-specific, with no specific quantity subject to the act of digging (See Kiparsky 1998 for a similar discussion of the partitive case in Finnish). This situation is illustrated in (2), repeated as (48) here for convenience.

(48) mm=ma   pur-ii=du   if-tar.
     potato=PRT dig-CVB.NRT=FOC   go-PST
     'Digging potatoes (here and there), (I) went.'

In (48), what is being dug is an unspecified quantity of potatoes that are planted here and there. If the referent of O here were specific, such as 'the potato' or 'the potatoes planted in that particular field', an imperfective construal would be impossible. The same holds for (49), where the action denoted in the narrative converb clause occurs iteratively, so that the patient in that clause (*ukuzii* 'rocks') cannot be construed as a specific set of rocks in a specific place.

(49) uku-zii=ja   kais-ii   kan=nu   tur.
     big-stone=PRT   turn.over-CVB.NRT   crab=ACC   catch.NONPST
     'Turning over rocks (those guys) caught crabs.'

If the demonstrative *uma=nu* 'of that place' is added to *ukuzii* 'rock' in (49) to delimit its specific reference, the accusative becomes acceptable in place of the partitive, as shown in (50), something confirmed by all of the subjects in our study.

(50) *uma=nu   uku-zii=ju   kais-ii*
    that.place=GEN big-stone=ACC   turn.over-CVB.NRT

   kan=nu   tur.
    crab=ACC catch.NONPST
    '(They) turned over the rock over there, and caught crabs.'

There is thus a clear interface between imperfective meaning and non-specificity on the one hand, and between perfective reading and referentiality on the other. This interface is something commonly observed cross-linguistically (Langacker 1987; Abraham 1997; Fischer 2003), although it is not without exception, as one can easily think of imperfective events that involve specific sets of patients. For example, the action of turning over a specific rock can be incomplete if it is in progress, such as when the rock is held in a half-overturned position as in (51).

(51) *uma=nu   uku-zii=ja   kais-ii*
    that.place=GEN big-stone=PRT   turn.over-CVB.NRT

   kan=nu   tur.
    crab=ACC catch.NONPST
    'Keeping that rock over there slightly upturned, those guys caught crabs.'

I conclude therefore that the weak tendency observed in our data toward non-specific O's with partitive marking is partially (though not exclusively) due to the effect of the imperfective aspect of the clauses in which they occur.

5.4 Summary and discussion

As mentioned in Section 2, the typological literature suggests that a complex interface exists between function and form, whereby case marking morphology often serves to mark aspect and the referential status of O's. Assuming the three major functions of grammatical role, reference, and aspect, on the one hand, and three corresponding formal methods of encoding of accusative, partitive and verbal morphology, on the other, the form-function correspondence relevant to O marking in Irabu can be summarized as in (52) and (53).

(52) Form-function correspondences in narrative converbal clauses

	Grammatical role	Reference	Aspect
Accusative	+	–	–
Partitive	+	(+)	+
*Verbal ASP morphology			

(53) Form-function correspondences elsewhere

	Grammatical role	Reference	Aspect
Accusative	+	–	–
*Partitive			
Verbal ASP morphology	–	(+)	+

As the default choice for O marking, accusative marking does not encode anything other than that the NP so marked is an O, as indicated in (52) and (53), where '+' occurs only under grammatical role. By contrast, partitive marking encodes imperfective aspect ('+' for Aspect in (52)) and hence may entail a low referential status for O ('(+)' for Reference in (52)). This aspectual effect on referential status is also observed when verbal morphology is available for marking aspect, hence (+) for Aspect in (53). For example, the simple past marks perfectivity and the progressive form imperfectivity, and these may entail that O is high or low in referential status respectively. As indicated by the asterisk in (52), verbal aspectual morphology is not available in narrative converbal clauses, so partitive marking serves to mark aspectual value in that environment. In other clauses, the partitive is unnecessary as its functions (grammatical role, on the one hand, and reference and aspect, on the other) can be encoded by accusative and verbal morphology, respectively. That is, the partitive is absent in such cases because it is redundant (due to the principle of economy suggested in (44)).

This way of understanding partitive marking allows us to provide an explanation of two classes of exceptions in a unified way. First, we have seen several examples in which partitive marking occurs in imperfective clauses other than narrative converbal clauses (Section 4.2). Second, we have seen several other examples in which partitive marking occurs in narrative converbal clauses that have perfective aspect (Section 4.3). For the first class of exceptions, it might be possible to simply state that the principle of economy is violated in these cases. That is, we could argue that aspect marking is here encoded by both partitive and verbal aspectual morphology. However, this explanation does not work for the second class of exceptions. For these, we may say that there is a functional shift, whereby the Reference function, normally a secondary function of the partitive (indicated by '(+)' in (52)), becomes the primary function and the Aspect function falls to secondary status ('(+)' → '+' for Reference and '+' → '(+)' for Aspect in (52)). The first class of exceptions may also be explained in this way. Note that the attested exceptions in both cases involve indefinite or non-specific O's: *bora* '(wearing) a band' (26), *jaa* '(there is no) house' (27), *hoogen* '(you speak) a dialect' (28), *tunukagama* '(gave birth to) eggs' (29) and *tus* '(getting) age(d)' (30).

Such a functional shift is well-motivated, since it allows case marking morphology to be directly linked to an NP-related, reference function. The question is whether such a shift can be reconstructed diachronically from data from other Miyako Ryukyuan dialects. Even though such syntactic reconstruction may be difficult at this stage, largely due to a lack of synchronic data from Miyako Ryukyuan, there is supporting evidence for this hypothesis. Considering the widespread pattern of partitive marking in Miyako Ryukyuan, whereby the partitive is restricted to narrative converbal clauses (attested in all dialects of Irabu and many other mainland Miyako dialects such as Gusukube), the partitive in proto Miyako must have had a similar aspect-oriented function to that found in contemporary Irabu. Such is not the case in Ikema, however. Hayashi (2010: 179–180) clearly states that the partitive ('topic marker' in her terms) is not restricted to narrative converbal clauses, occurring both in independent and dependent clauses of various types. It is interesting to see that her examples all involve non-specific O's (even one example of S). This may indicate that the aspect function of the partitive is much less salient than in Irabu. Koloskova (2007) shows that in Hirara the reference function of the partitive is pervasive, much more so than in Irabu. Given these facts, it is reasonable to hypothesize that the functional shift of partitive from aspect-oriented function to reference-oriented function occurred in some dialects of Miyako, with Irabu representing the initial stage of this process.

6 Concluding remarks

In this chapter I have examined partitive case marking in Irabu, and argued that it primarily functions to encode imperfective aspect in the clause in which it occurs. The partitive case thus exhibits in its behavior an interface between case morphology, aspect, and reference. The restriction of the partitive to narrative converbal clauses, which might appear to be a language-particular restriction, is in fact based on a cross-linguistically recurrent pattern whereby a lack of verb morphology marking aspect leads to a proliferation of functions in case morphology.

Abbreviations

ABL	ablative	NRT	narrative
ACC	accusative	ONM	onomatopoeia
ALL	allative	PL	plural
APRX	approximative	PRF	perfect
ASR	assertive	PROG	progressive
CIR	circumstantial	PROS	prospective
CND	conditional	PRT	partitive
COM	comitative	PST	past
CSL	causal	PUR	purposive
CVB	converb	Q	question
DAT	dative	QT	quotative
DIM	diminutive	RLS	realis
DSC	discourse marker	RSL	resultative
FOC	focus	SG	singular
GEN	genitive	SIM	simultaneous
IMP	imperative	TAG	tag marker
INT	intentional	TOP	topic
INTJ	interjection	VLZ	verbalizer
ITR	iterative	1SG	first person singular
NEG	negative	2SG	second person singular
NOM	nominative	3SG	third person singular
NONPST	non-past	2PL	second person plural

References

Abraham, Werner. 1997. The interdependence of case, aspect and specificity in the history of German: the case of the verbal genitive. In Ans van Kemenade & Nigel Vincent (eds.), *Parameters of morphosyntactic change*, 29–61. Cambridge: Cambridge University Press.

Aissen, Judith. 2003. Differential object marking: iconicity vs. economy. *Natural Language & Linguistic Theory* 21. 435–483.

Anderson, Gregory D.S. 2006. *Auxiliary verb constructions*. Oxford & New York: Oxford University Press.

Bickel, Balthasar. 1998. Review article: Converbs in cross-linguistic perspective. *Linguistic Typology* 2 (3). 81–397.

Blake, Barry J. 2001. *Case*. 2nd edn. Cambridge: Cambridge University Press.

Bossong, Georg. 1985. *Differentielle Objectmarkierung in den Neuiranischen Sprachen*. Tubingen: Narr.

Comrie, Bernard. 1976. *Aspect*. Cambridge: Cambridge University Press.

Comrie, Bernard. 1981. *Language universals and linguistic typology: Syntax and morphology*. Oxford: Blackwell.

Croft, William. 2012. *Verbs: Aspect and causal structure*. Oxford: Oxford University Press.

Dowty, David R. 1979. *Word meaning and montague grammar. The semantics of verbs and times in generative semantics and in Montague's PTQ*. Dordrecht: Reidel.

Fischer, Susann. 2003. Partitive vs. genitive in Russian and Polish: An empirical study on case alternation in the object domain. In Susann Fischer, Ruben van de Vijver & Ralf Vogel (eds.), *Experimental studies in linguistics*, 123–137. Potsdam: Institut für Linguistik.

Fischer, Susann. 2005. Interplay between reference and aspect. In Klaus von Heusinger, Georg A. Kaiser & Elisabeth Stark (eds.), *Proceedings of the workshop 'specificity and the evolution/emergence of nominal determinations systems in Romance'*. Universität Konstanz.
Hayashi, Yuka. 2010. Ikema Ryukyuan. In Michinori Shimoji & Thomas Pellard (eds.), *An introduction to Ryukyuan languages*, 167–188. Tokyo: ILCAA.
De Hoop, Helen. 1992. *Case configuration and noun phrase interpretation*. Groningen: Univeristy of Groningen dissertation. Published: New York: Garland Publishing, 1996.
De Hoop, Helen & Andrej Malchukov. 2008. Case-marking strategies. *Linguistic Inquiry* 39. 565–587.
Hopper, Paul. J. & Sandra A. Thompson. 1980. Transitivity in grammar and discourse. *Language* 56. 251–299.
Iemmolo, Giorgio. 2011. Towards a typological study of differential object marking and differential object indexation. Pavia, Italy: University of Pavia dissertation.
Kibrik, Andrej E. 1985. Toward a typology of ergativity. In Johanna Nichols & Anthony Woodbury (eds.), *Grammar inside and outside the clause*, 268–324. Cambridge: Cambridge University Press.
Kiparsky, Paul. 1998. Partitive case and aspect. In Miriam Butt & Wilhelm Geuder (eds.), *The projection of arguments*, 265–307. Stanford: CSLI Publications.
Koloskova, Yulia. 2007. Ryūkyūgo Miyako hōgen no chokusetsu mokutekigo no hyōshiki to tadōsei [The direct object marker in Miyako Ryukyuan and transitivity]. In Mie Tsunoda, Kan Sasaki & Toru Shionoya (eds.) *Tadōsei no tsūgengogakuteki kenkyū* [Crosslinguistic studies in transitivity], 283–294. Tokyo: Kurosio Publishers.
Krifka, Manfred. 1992. Thematic relations as links between nominal reference and temporal constitution. In Ivan A. Sag & Anna Szabolcsi (eds.), *Lexical matters*, 29–53. Stanford: CSLI Publications.
Langacker, Ronald. 1987. *Foundations of cognitive grammar, volume I: Theoretical prerequisites*. Stanford: Stanford University Press.
Lawrence, Wayne P. 2012. Southern Ryukyuan. In Nicholas Tranter (ed.) *Languages of Japan and Korea*, 381–411. London: Routledge.
Leiss, Elisabeth. 2000. *Artikel und Aspekt. Die grammatischen Muster von Definitheit*. Berlin & New York: De Gruyter.
Malchukov, Andrej L. 2006. Transitivity parameters and transitivity alternations: Constraining co-variation. In Leonid Kulikov, Andrej Malchukov & Peter de Swart (eds.), *Case, valency and transitivity*, 329–359. Amsterdam & Philadelphia: John Benjamins.
Malchukov, Andrej L. & Helen de Hoop. 2011. Tense, aspect, and mood based differential case marking. *Lingua* 121. 35–47.
Mallinson, Graham & Barry J. Blake. 1981. *Language typology: Cross-cultural studies in syntax*. Amsterdam: North Holland.
Næss, Åshild. 2007. *Prototypical transitivity*. Amsterdam & Philadelphia: John Benjamins.
Nedjalkov, Vladimir P. 1995. Some typological parameters of converbs. In Martin Haspelmath & Ekkehard König (eds.), *Converbs in cross-linguistic perspective*, 97–136. Berlin & New York: Mouton de Gruyter.
Shimoji, Michinori. 2008. *A grammar of Irabu, a Southern Ryukyuan language*. Canberra: Australian National University dissertation.
Smith, Carlota. 1997. The Parameter of aspect. 2nd edn. Dordrecht: Kluwer Academic Publishers.
Tenny, Carol. 1987. *Grammaticalizing aspect and affectedness*. Cambridge, MA: MIT dissertation.
Verkuyl, Henk J. 1993. *A theory of aspectuality: The Interaction between temporal and atemporal Structure*. Cambridge: Cambridge University Press.

III History

Heiko Narrog
8 Japanese transitivity pairs through time – a historical and typological perspective

1 Transitivity pairs and the typology of their morphological patterns

This paper has two major goals. The first is to determine the typological status of Japanese with respect to its lexical inventory of transitive-intransitive verb pairs, according to the typology proposed by Haspelmath (1993) and Nichols et al. (2004). The second is to test the hypothesis of Comrie (2006) that the verb vocabulary of languages tends to be stable with respect to this typology.

I understand 'transitivity pairs' to refer to lexicalized pairs of causal and non-causal verbs (Haspelmath et al. 2013). One verb is less transitive and the other more transitive, i.e., commonly one verb is intransitive and the other transitive, or, much less commonly, one is transitive and the other ditransitive. The two verbs express the same event but a participant is added or deleted in the valency of one verb compared to the other verb. The two verbs also usually share the same morphological root. Verb pairs with an equal number of arguments are not included. While some earlier research (e.g. Haspelmath 1993; Comrie 2006) limited the scope of transitivity pairings to so-called inchoative-causative verb pairs in order to ensure cross-linguistic comparability, the scope of this paper encompasses all types of causal – non-causal verb pairs in the entire transitivity pair vocabulary of Japanese. It therefore also includes a few stative and activity verbs, and some transitive verbs, as the non-causal counterpart.

Research on transitivity pairs from a cross-linguistic perspective goes back at least to Nedjalkov & Silnitsky (1973), who proposed a typology of lexical causatives based mainly on an analysis of Eurasian languages. The typologies relevant to our purposes are those put forward by Haspelmath (1993) and Nichols et al. (2004). The actual classification of types of verb pairs is essentially identical across these papers except for the terminology[1]. In both papers, the following four patterns of transitivization were posited.

---
[1] Concepts expressed as inchoative verbs in one language may be expressed as state verbs in other languages; e.g. E. *know* (state) vs. J. *sir-u* (inchoative). This is the reason that Nichols et al. (2004) do not include inchoative verbs in their survey.

Heiko Narrog, Tohoku University

(a) Transitivization: transitive verbs are derived from intransitive ones. Haspelmath (1993) labeled this pattern as 'causative alternation'.
E.g. Nanai *ajaktala-* 'be angry' (itr.) > ajaktala-wa:n 'make angry' (tr.)[2] (cf. Nichols 2004: 199)

(b) Detransitivization: intransitive verbs are derived from transitive ones. Haspelmath (1993) labeled this pattern as 'anticausative alternation'.
E.g. Russian *serdit'* 'make angry' (tr.) > *serdit'-sja* 'be angry' (itr.) (cf. Nichols 2004: 198)

(c) Indeterminate formation: One form expresses both the transitive and the intransitive event. Haspelmath (1993) and others labeled this as 'labile alternation'. Suppletion and change of inflectional class are also commonly included in this pattern.
E.g. Mandarin Chinese *shāo* 'burn' (itr.) < > *shāo* 'burn' (tr.) (cf. Nichols 2004: 206)

(d) Neutral formation: Both verbs are phonologically and morphologically equally 'heavy' or 'marked'. This includes formation with auxiliary verbs and phonological alternation. Haspelmath (1993) labels this pattern as 'equipollent'.
E.g. Ingush *kag-lu* 'break' (itr.) < > *kag-d.u* 'break' (tr.) (cf. Nichols 2004: 201)

The research question that immediately arises from this typology is how the four transitivization patterns are distributed in individual languages and among the languages of the world.[3] For example, for each of the languages from which an example was provided in (a) to (d), the pattern illustrated is characteristic of that language. According to Nichols et al. (2004), Nanai is transitivizing, Russian is detransitivizing, Mandarin Chinese favors indeterminate formation, and Ingush favors neutral formation. Cross-linguistically, in Nichols et al.'s sample of 84 languages, languages characterized by neutral formation were most frequent (24), followed by languages characterized by indeterminate formation (17), transitivization (16), and detransitivization (8).[4] Furthermore, if the world's languages are classified by area, the distributions in Table 1 emerge.

---

[2] ">" indicates a relationship of derivation from the verb on the left to the verb on the right.
[3] In order to determine the cross-linguistic patterns, Haspelmath (1993) investigated 31 verb pairs in 21 languages, and Nichols et al (2004) 18 verb pairs in 84 language.
[4] Nichols et al. 2004: 181. 18 languages could not be classified according to a specific pattern.

Table 1: Distribution of transitivity patterns by area (excerpt from Nichols et al. 2004: 181)

	transitivizing	detransitivizing	neutral	indeterminate	none
Africa	3	1	5	3	0
Europe	2	3	4	1	1
North Asia	3	0	2	1	2
South & Southeast Asia	2	0	2	2	2
Australia	0	1	5	1	1
North America	5	0	0	1	6

The data in Table 1 suggest that, for example, in Europe the rare 'detransitivization' pattern is common, while in North Asia, the region to which Japan belongs, transitivization is most frequent. However, given the low numbers, such generalizations can only be tentative.

These lexicalization patterns as such deserve attention. They may even have deeper repercussions beyond the lexicon. For example, Nichols (1993; Nichols et al. 2004: 177–178) points out that these may be reflected in syntactic, stylistic and historical features of a language. Also, in terms of Ikegami's (1981) typology of 'do' vs. 'become' languages, transitivization (that is, where non-causal verbs are the basis of derivation) would point to membership in the 'become' language category, and detransitivization to membership in the 'do'-type language category.

2 Japanese transitivity pairs

Although Haspelmath (1993) and Nichols et al. (2004) proposed a similar typology of transitivization patterns, their actual conclusion with respect to Japanese, which both included in their sample, differs. According to Haspelmath (1993: 101–102), Japanese has mostly equipollent (neutral) verb pairs, while according to Nichols et al. (2004: 190, 194), Japanese belongs to transitivizing languages with verbs with animate subjects/objects (causees) and to no particular type with verbs with inanimate subjects/objects. However, even with 'inanimate' verbs, transitivization is slightly more frequent than other types of formation. Nichols et al. (2004) do not present an analysis of their Japanese data, but Haspelmath (1993: 116) does. According to him, the four patterns are illustrated in Japanese as follows:

(a) Causative alternation (transitivization): *ak-u* 'open$_{in}$'/*ak-e-ru* 'open$_{tr}$'

(b) Anticausative derivation (detransitivization): *or-e-ru* 'break$_{in}$'/*or-u* 'break$_{tr}$'

(c) Labile alternation (indeterminate pattern) *hirak-u* 'open$_{in/tr}$'

(d) Equipollent alternation (neutral pattern): *ok-i-ru* 'wake$_{in}$ up'/*ok-os-u* 'wake$_{tr}$ up'; *kaw-ar-u* 'change$_{in}$'/*ka-e-ru* 'change$_{tr}$'

Haspelmath's analysis may appear appropriate on first sight but a look at specialized research on Japanese verb pairs soon reveals that it may not be adequate. Specifically, there is a problem with the 'equipollent' pairs, which may not in fact be equipollent. Crucially, transitivity pairs in Japanese are not the result of productive morphological processes in the modern language but were already lexicalized in the earliest historically documented stage of Japanese. If their morphological components are extracted by a simple linear analysis of their present shape, it is difficult to explain the morphological processes by which they were formed, and the resulting analysis may not reflect the actual derivational relationship between the members of each pair.[5] It is thus necessary to analyze them according to their status as lexicalizations, that is, historical fossils of erstwhile morphologically productive word formation patterns.

In the specialized Japanese literature, a number of complex analyses have been proposed for these verb pairs. For example, Brannen (1967) applied a 'lexical template' method, and Okutsu (1967) proposed 'euphonic form change rules' in order to arrive at a synchronically adequate analysis.[6] Nishio (1954 and others) already pointed out early on that in verb pairs ending in ~*e-ru* vs. ~*ar-u* that may superficially appear equipollent, the ~*e-ru* form as a rule has diachronic primacy and the ~*ar-u* form is derived. Okutsu (1967) applied this insight to his synchronic analysis and classified the ~*e-ru* vs. ~*ar-u* alternation as a pattern of 'intransitivization', for example, positing the derivation *age-ru* 'raise' > *ag-ar-u* 'rise'.

In other words, if it is known that one group of verbs is systematically derived from another, one cannot say that the two groups are equal or equipollent even if they appear to be so in their phonological surface structure. In order to

---

[5] If, for example, the pair *oki-ru/okos-u* would be analyzed as *ok-i-ru/ok-os-u*, it would not be possible to explain why there is an opposition –*i*- vs. –*os*-. Also, it would be a mistake to consider *oki-ru/okos-u* as equipollent, when from a historical perspective it is clear that *oki-ru* is the basic verb and *okos-u* the derived verb.

[6] The analysis of Japanese transitivity pairs goes at least back to Moto'ori (1902(1828)). Suga & Hayatsu (1995) present a comprehensive bibliography of research up to 1995.

determine their actual relationship, it is important to look at their diachronic genesis, that is, at their derivational relationship at the time when the underlying pattern was still productive, or at a time as close as possible to that. A similar stance has been expressed by Jacobsen (1992: 76), who writes that:

> "To achieve optimal objectivity in observing relationships between the morphological and semantic markedness of a form, it is therefore necessary to consider the meaning a form had at the point it originally took hold in the language, a historical investigation of the sort we have neither sufficient data nor space to undertake here."

This is the position taken in this paper, although my goal is more modest since it is limited to verb morphology and does not include meaning. The goal is thus to analyze lexical patterns of transitivization in Japanese diachronically, based on their original morphological structure at the time when these formations were still productive and transparent.

I will include as many verb pairs as possible, not only intransitive~transitive ones,[7] but also transitive~ditransitive verb pairs that exhibit similar morphological patterns. Also, while both members of a verb pair as a rule must share a core event, I also include pairs where the semantic relationship between the two verbs has lost transparency over time, due to abstract and metaphorical uses. Haspelmath (1993) and Nichols et al. (2004) are primarily concerned with the morphology of verbs rather than a deeper semantic or syntactic analysis. Morphology is also the primary concern of this paper, but I include a diachronic perspective, which for a number of reasons is difficult to apply in a cross-linguistic study covering dozens of languages. By including a diachronic perspective, it should be possible to arrive at a more comprehensive analysis of Japanese as an individual language, on the one hand, while pointing out aspects of transitivity pairs that go unnoticed in a purely synchronic typological analysis, on the other.

To start with the conclusion, transitivization, with intransitive verbs as the base of derivation, is the dominant morphological pattern in Japanese. But the transitivizing pattern has been receding historically, giving way to the other patterns. Additionally, due to changes in overall verb morphology, patterns of transitivization and detransitivization have increasingly come to superficially resemble equipollent patterns. Also, although the dominant morphological pattern is transitivization, due to processes such as backformation, actual historical derivation is observed to occur more equally between transitivization and detransitivization (cf. section 4.4).

---

[7] In Japanese the number of stative verbs is small, and many verbs that are stative in English are inchoative in Japanese. As a result, most transitivity pairs contain an inchoative verb.

I will proceed as follows. The next section, Section 3, is devoted to explaining the basics of the morphological analysis adopted in this paper and its application to Japanese verb pairs. In section 4, the core section of this paper, a diachronic analysis of the Japanese lexicon of transitivity pairs is presented. Section 4.4 deals with historical derivation, and the last section, Section 5, offers a summary and conclusion.

3 A historically-motivated analysis of Japanese transitivity pairs

3.1 Basic assumptions about morphological analysis

This paper adopts the structuralist morphological analysis as developed in Rickmeyer (1995) and applied to Japanese verb morphology in Narrog (1998). Morphemes are identified on the basis of phonological transcription and systematic distributional analysis. In this type of analysis, we distinguish between derivation in the lexicon, that is, fossilized forms, and derivation through synchronically productive morphemes. If a word form contains elements that are only found in a limited number of words and not productively applicable to other stems to form a new derivation, the whole word form is considered as lexicalized. Only if an element can be productively applied to new stems is it considered to be a morpheme. While the borderline between productive and non-productive may sometimes be fluid across languages, in the case of Japanese verb morphology the distinction is clear-cut. On the one hand, there is valency-related productive verb morphology such as the causative suffix -(s)ase-ru and the passive suffix -(r)are-ru. These suffixes started to develop in Old Japanese and were already productive by Early Middle Japanese. On the other hand, there are lexicalized verb pairs such as *war-u* 'break (tr)' ~*ware-ru* 'break (itr)' or *sugi-ru* 'pass (itr)' ~ *sugos-u* 'pass (tr)', most of which have existed from the earliest documented stages of Japanese. These are the formations dealt with in this paper. They are clearly fossilized and are generally not applicable to new stems.[8]

Despite their fossilized status, phonological elements contained in these lexicalized verb pairs, such as /e/ or /ar/ are considered as morphemes on a

---

[8] Interestingly, though, new verb pairs have been added, but at an extremely slow pace. In the case of the *war-u* ~ *ware-ru* type of formation, two new pairs were added in the 19th century and one in the 20th century.

par with productive morphology in some research. From the perspective adopted here, this is a confusion of lexical and morphological elements. Instead, we consider lexemes such as *war-* 'break (tr)', *ware-* 'break (itr)', *sugi-* 'pass (itr)' and *sugos-* 'pass (tr)' as monomorphemic. However, it is only reasonable to assume that these patterns that are fully lexicalized in Modern Japanese, and were already lexicalized by Old Japanese, go back to productive morphology at an earlier stage. A full morphological analysis of these formations thus requires reconstruction of the morphology at the stage when these formations were productive.

Alongside productivity, morphological transparency is another main factor distinguishing lexical and morphological formations. The productive suffix *-(s)ase-ru*, for example, is added completely regularly as *sase-ru* to vowel stems and as *-ase-ru* to consonant stems. In contrast, the lexical pair *sugi-ru* and *sugos-u*, for example, have no common stem in Modern Japanese, nor can *-os* be added to any other stem by means of a phonological rule. One may very abstractly posit *-s-* for transitivization and *-r-* for detransitivization (e.g. Nishiyama 2000: 146–147) but this still does not render morphologically transparent stems and endings. In order to obtain these one must go back to the time when such formations were productive.[9]

3.2 Aspects of derivation

Derivation in the lexicon of at least three types can be posited: derivation in form, derivation in meaning, and diachronic derivation.

If one lexical item is derived from another, there is first a diachronic relationship between them, then a morphological-phonological relationship between them, typically involving the addition, subtraction or alternation of phonemes, and thirdly a contrast in meaning between them, often related to a contrast in syntax, for example one involving the addition or deletion of arguments. The default expectation is that the directionality of derivation will agree in all three of these respects. For example, given the verb pair *hasir-u* 'run' and (classical) *hasirakas-u* 'let run', we recognize that *hasir-u* is morphologically simpler than *hasirakas-u*, that it is the historical basis for the derivation of *hasirakas-u*, and that *hasirakas-u* is semantically more complex, adding an element of causation.

---

9 There are also pairs in English, where the original derivational relationship is obscured by phonological changes. Pairs like *lie ~ lay*, for example, go back to the addition of the causativizing suffix **-jan* to verb stems in Germanic (cf. García 2005: 74).

Haspelmath (1993) and Nichols et al. (2004) understand derivation in a purely morphological sense. Comparing pairs of intransitive (inchoative, stative) and transitive (causative) verb pairs across languages, they consider the morphologically 'unmarked', i.e. shorter and simpler, form as the basis of derivation, and the marked, i.e. longer and more complex, form as derived. This is of course also due to constraints in working with a large set of data from many languages. As a result, derivation is analyzed purely on the basis of synchronic morphological surface structure, tacitly assuming that derivation in morphology, semantics (and syntax), and diachrony are congruent. That is, iconicity between form, meaning and history is presupposed.

While it is plausible to assume iconicity as a default, some examples where iconicity does not hold are well-known from English language history. For instance, the ending *-er/-ar/-or* generally derives nouns from verbs, e.g. *print* (V) > *printer* (N), *survive* (V) > *survivor* (N). However, there are also cases such as *burglar* (N) > *burgle* (V), *swindler* (N) > *swindle* (V) (Hansen et al. 1990: 134–136), which are known under the label 'backformation' (e.g. Beard 1998: 56). Semantically as well, the iconicity assumption does not necessarily hold. Thus, depending on the noun-verb pair, the derived verb can be considered as more complex than the noun, as in the case of *burgle* vs. *burglar*, or less complex than the noun, as in the case of *swindle* vs. *swindler* (cf. Hansen et al. 1990: 135–136)[10]. Thus, there are cases in which the historical and semantic direction of derivation conflict with the morphological direction, or where the historical direction conflicts with the morphological and semantic direction.

The possibility of such cases of non-iconicity also holds for the Japanese verbs covered in this research. Additionally, there is the case of the labile (neutral) verbs, where there is no formal opposition at all but still historical and semantic derivation. For example, with the verb *hirak-u* 'open', according to the *Nihon kokugo daijiten* (*Shogakukan unabridged dictionary of the Japanese language*), the transitive use here is historically prior. Likewise, with equipollent verb pairs, it is not necessarily the case that both verbs arose simultaneously, or are semantically equal. Here as well, in spite of formal equality, some directionality of derivation holds, historically and/or semantically.

Analyzing derivation from all possible perspectives is beyond the scope of this paper. Our focus is rather on morphology. An analysis of semantic derivation would be complex and potentially controversial, (cf. Hansen et al. 1990:

---

[10] Hansen et al. (1990: 135) argue that the derived verb *burgle* means 'act as a burglar' and is therefore semantically more complex than *burglar*. In contrast *swindle* behaves in every respect like a regular derivation, i.e., *swindler* would be 'someone who swindles' and more complex than *swindle*. However, admittedly, the evidence for making such fine semantic distinctions is not very strong.

135) and is thus not undertaken here. We will, on the other hand, consider in section 4.4 historical data available that make it possible for us to study the historical aspects of derivation in Japanese.

3.3 Morphological structure of verb pairs in Old Japanese and proto-Japanese

As mentioned above, Japanese transitivity pairs were already lexicalized in Old Japanese (OJ). From a synchronic OJ perspective, roughly two patterns can be distinguished.[11]

A. Change of inflection: consonant-stem verbs V_c vs. *e*-base verbs V_e[12]
   E.g. *war-u* (V_c; tr.; stem *war-*; base *war•i-*) vs. *war-u* (V_e; itr.; stem *war-*; base *war•e*)

B. Stem extension
   a) stem extension through –*Vr*; e.g. *sas-u* 'sting (tr)' vs. *sasar-u* 'be stung (itr)'
   b) stem extension through –*Vs*; e.g. *wak-u* 'boil (itr)' vs. *wakas-u* 'boil (tr)'
   c) other stem extensions; e.g. *mi(ru)* 'see (tr)' vs. *miy-u* 'be visible (itr)'

The only process among those listed above that is arguably still to some extent productive in OJ is the suffixation of *-(r)(a)y-u* as in *miy-u* (Bc). The other formations are already lexicalized, but we try to reconstruct here their presumptive structure at the stage when they were still productive.

As for pattern (A), a common assumption is that the vowel *-e* in the verb base goes back to a morpheme *-Ci* (e.g. Unger 2000: 664, 667) that Robbeets (2007, 2010) labels as 'causative-passive' and identifies as *-(k)i*. Traditionally it has been assumed that this is related to causative-passives in Korean and other Transeurasian languages (cf. also Robbeets 2007, 2010). Whitman (2008) and

---

[11] In A. and B. and below, 'stem' of a verb refers to the naked stem, which ends on a consonant with athematic stem verbs, and which is a morphologically dependent morpheme that has to be combined with inflectional and derivational morphemes in order to form a word. It is not a unit found in traditional Japanese school grammar. The 'base' refers to the *ren'yōkei* in traditional grammar, that is, the stem combined with an /i/ in the case of athematic stem verbs, but identical with the stem in the case of thematic stem verbs. The 'base' alone can form an independent word but can also combine with other morphemes (suffixes).

[12] Abbreviations are used in this chapter as follows: Vc for verbs with consonant-stem inflection, Ve for verbs with e-base inflection, Vi for verbs with i-base inflection, and Vv for verbs with pure vowel-stem inflection.

Frellesvig & Whitman (this volume) propose an alternative hypothesis in terms of derivation from the verb *e-* 'get'. Although the non-past form of the derived verbs, which is the common citation form in dictionaries, has the same length as the un-derived non-past form (e.g. *war-u* vs. *war-u*), the derived form is phonologically heavier in many other inflectional forms (cf. Table 3 below). It is therefore rather uncontroversial in Japanese linguistics that the Ve verb is a derivation of the Vc verb, and that this derivation took place through the addition of morphological material. The same holds for Vi verbs, that is, verbs whose base ends with an /i/ rather than an /e/.

As for pattern (Ba), we assume here that it is the result of suffixation of the suffix *-r-u* (Robbeets 2010; Unger (p.c.)). Due to limitations of space we are unable to go into detail here, but it seems that there are parallels to this suffix across the Trans-Eurasian languages (Robbeets 2010). Furthermore, the phonological parallelism to the pattern in (Bb), including verbs with a final vowel different from /a/, cannot be explained if we assume that the existential verb **ari/ar-u* 'be' is the source, as has been sometimes claimed.[13] For pattern (Bb), to my knowledge it is rather uncontroversial that it goes back to the addition of the verb **s-u* 'do' (cf. Yoshida 1973: 170, 202). An alternative would be to consider it as a phonologically changed form of the older suffix *-t-u*, perhaps in analogy to **s-u*. Overall, one can thus reconstruct the following derivations:

(1)   **sasa + r- > sasa•r-*

(2)   **waka + s- > waka•s-*

Besides the transitivizing *-s-* and the intransitivizing *-r-*, which are very frequent, there are also a number of other rather infrequent suffixes that appear in the various word formation patterns. *-T-*, which may be reconstructed to proto-Japanese (pJ) **-ta-* and proto-Transeurasian **-ti-* (Robbeets 2007, 2010), is causative, and alternates with *-s-* in some word forms. Apparently it was confounded with *-s-* from early on due to phonological similarity. Another element *-p-* may either derive from an intensifying suffix *-(a)p-*, that was still productive in OJ, but not later, or go back to a pJ anticausative suffix **-pa-* with reflexes in other Transeurasian languages (Robbeets 2010).

---

[13] It has also been pointed out to me by Wesley Jacobsen (p.c.) that there is a conflict between the stative aspect of *ari* and the non-stative nature of the *-r-u* verbs.

In any case, the important point is that not only the patterns in (B) but also the one in (A) are derivations with a direction, and not equipollent.[14] Table 2 shows which members in a verb pair are basic, and which are derived.

Table 2: Basic verbs and derived verbs in Japanese transitivity pairs

Basic verbs	Derived verbs
Vc	Ve
Vc, Ve, Vi, Vv	Verbs extended through -Vs-, -Vr, and similar elements

Table 3 shows an example of a verb stem that participated in both major patterns of derivation, *tum-* 'pile'. The base Vc verb is labile, the Ve verb is transitive, and the V+*Vr*- verb is intransitive. Bold letters indicate the longest, i.e., morphologically most marked verb of the set.

Table 3: Vc vs. Ve vs. V+*Vr*- in Old Japanese

Form	Vc	Ve	V+*Vr*-
Finite present	tum-u	tum-u	**tumor-u**
Adnominal present	tum-u	tum-uru	**tumor-u**
Nominal	tum-aku	tum-uraku	**tumor-aku**
Present real conditional	tum-e	tum-ure	**tumor-e**
Present hypothetical conditional	tum-aba	tume-ba	**tumor-aba**
Negative future	tum-azi	tume-zi	**tumor-azi**
Desiderative	tum-ana	tume-na	**tumor-ana**
Finite Preterite	tumi-ki/si	tume-ki/si	**tumori-ki/si**
Nominal preterite	tumi-keku	tume-keku	**tumori-keku**
Preterite conditional	tumi-sika/seba/kyeba	tume-sika/seba/kyeba	**tumori-sika/seba/kyeba**
Imperative	tum-e	tume-yo	**tumor-e**

The V+*Vr*- verb is clearly longer than the base verb in all inflectional forms, the V_e verb in only some forms, but in no form is the base verb longest. There are thus three grades of morphological heaviness or markedness in the word formation patterns: V_c are the least marked, V+Vr/s- are the most marked, and V_e

---

[14] Unger (p.c.) assumes that the formation of verbs ending on -*Vr*- and -*Vs*-was entirely parallel. According to Unger, *sasar-u*, for example, goes back to *sasa•r-u* rather than *sasa•ar-u*, and is not the product of suffixation of the existential verb to a verb stem. If *ari/ar-u* was actually added to the verb stem, it would be necessary to assume that the initial /a/ was deleted.

are in the middle. In the rest of this paper we view, in accordance with iconicity, the marked verb as "derived" from the less marked verb. That is, in short, V_c forms the basis of derivation for the other two verb formations, while conversely V+*Vr/Vs-* can be derived from the other two patterns.[15]

4 Historical data survey

Haspelmath (1993), Haspelmath et al. (2014) and Nichols et. al. (2004) present conclusions on the basis of a relatively small number of verb pairs (18, 20, and 31, respectively) in a large number of languages. This survey aims at the converse, namely the analysis of a large number of verb pairs in one language. If the number of verb pairs is limited, the question naturally arises which verbs are to be selected. Haspelmath (1993: 96) chose "verbs with a rather basic meaning that can be easily identified by means of a dictionary", and Nichols et al. (2004: 156) likewise verb pairs that "involve basic lexical semantics and [...] are relatively likely to be attested in lexical sources", aiming for a "wide spread in lexical semantics". Whether their selection of verb pairs is truly representative is inevitably open to question. In this study, I have tried to include the entire diachronic Japanese vocabulary of transitivity pairs, based on the diachronic verb list of Martin (1987: 665–789), and supplemented by verb pairs that I have additionally found in reference works such as the NKD, the Kōjien, and specialized studies such as Kuginuki (1996) and Shimada (1979). Martin's (1987) list does not show correspondences between verbs that fall into pairs, so these I have identified myself.

4.1 Premises of the study

The morphological status of verbs in OJ, as discussed in 3.3, remained basically unchanged until Early Modern Japanese (EModJ) in the early 18th century. Regularly inflecting consonant-stem verbs, the largest verb class throughout Japanese language history, have remained stable in their inflection up through Contemporary Japanese. In contrast, other verb classes have undergone changes. As the result of a protracted process culminating around 1750, V_e and V_i were

---

[15] The validity of this assumption was basically confirmed by Narrog (2007b), who investigated transitivity pairs documented in the *Man'yōshū*, the largest and most important source of data for OJ, and showed that in 101 out of 119 verb pairs in which only one verb of a verb pair was documented, it is usually the basic (underived) verb according to the classification here.

integrated into a general vowel-stem class V$_v$. A number of inflectional forms in this class underwent change, and as a result, the markedness relationship between members of verb pairs where one is of the V$_e$ or V$_i$ class and the other a verb extended by -Vr- and -Vs- is not always transparent.

Table 4 shows how the same verbs formed from the root *tum-* that were presented in Table 3 above are inflected in Modern Japanese (note that *tum-*, *tume-* and *tumor-* no longer form a set of semantically corresponding verbs in Modern Japanese). As before, bold letters indicate the longest, i.e., morphologically most marked verb of the set.

Table 4: Vc vs. Vv vs. V+Vr- in Modern Japanese

Form	Vc	Vv	V+Vr-
Non-past	tum-u	**tume-ru**	tumor-u
Future	tum-oo	**tume-yoo**	**tumor-oo**
Conditional	tum-eba	**tume-reba**	**tumor-eba**
Imperative	tum-e	**tume-ro**	tumor-e
Negative participle	tum-azu	tume-zu	**tumor-azu**
Gerund	tuN-de	tume-te	**tumot-te**
Past	tuN-da	tume-ta	**tumot-ta**
Temporal-conditional	tuN-dara	tume-tara	**tumot-tara**
Exemplative	tuN-dari	tume-tari	**tumot-tari**

Modern Japanese has fewer inflectional forms than Old Japanese had, but the basic markedness relationship between verbs remains the same. Vv (erstwhile Ve) are more marked than Vc, and V+Vr- are the most marked. In detail, (1) Vv have a number of new inflectional forms that are heavier than the corresponding Vc forms, but (2) the non-past, i.e. the dictionary citation form, is now equipollent to the V+Vr- non-past. Fact (2) has led Haspelmath (1993) and a number of other researchers not familiar with Japanese verb inflection to conclude that Vv and V+Vr/s-formations are equipollent.

Based on changes in the vowel-stem verb classes, I propose that the development of Japanese transitivity pairs be divided into three periods as in Table 5.

While it is reasonable to assume that the verb pairs go back to a productive and transparent morphological pattern of suffixation in pJ, already by OJ the pattern had become partially nontransparent. For example, the pair *sug-u* ~ *sugus-u/sugos-u* are already at this point unanalyzable as regular agglutination. However, the derivational relationship is still clearly visible in surface structure. From EModJ on, not only is the original morphological structure nontrans-

Table 5: Historical periods in the development of the surface forms of Japanese transitivity pairs

Period	Status of V_e/V_i verbs	Transparency of original morphological structure of verb pairs	Original derivational relationship maintained in surface structure
pJ	Formation through addition of a suffix (-Ci).	Semi-transparent e.g. *sugu-u ~ *sugu-s-u/sugo-s-u	yes
OJ~EModJ	Vowel-stem inflection V_e/V_i	Nontransparent e.g. sug-u ~ sugus-u/sugos-u	yes e.g. sug-u/sug-uru ~ sugus-u/sugos-u
EModJ~	General vowel-stem inflection V_v	Nontransparent; e.g. sugi-ru ~ sugos-u	no e.g. sugi-ru ~ sugos-u

parent, but the original derivational relationship also becomes difficult to discern in surface structure.[16]

Based on this observation, I will divide the historical data in my paper into pre-modern, i.e., up to mid 18th-century, and modern, and will compare the pre-modern with the modern period. The original directionality of derivation is reconstructed from the time when this derivation was presumably productive. We will see later in section 4.4 that the directionality of derivation in fact holds up through modern times.

4.2 The pre-modern verb inventory

Based on the periodization proposed in the previous section, I provide in Table 6 all verb pairs that have been documented prior to the mid 18th century. There are cases where a single verb participates in more than one verb pair (e.g. *mi-ru* 'see' ~ *mie-ru* 'be seen', and *mi-ru* ~ *mise-ru* 'show'). Verbs are displayed in their historical form. Slashes connect two verb forms that I believe to be variants of the same lexeme. This includes not only purely phonological variants but also variants with a slightly different shape, such as *nigoras-u* and *nigorakas-u* 'make muddy' as the causative counterparts of *nigor-u* 'become muddy'. If one verb member of a pair is documented in the NKD a hundred or more years

---

[16] Before V_e verbs were absorbed into the pure vowel-stem V_v verbs, the adnominal form of verbs had already taken over from the clause-final form (e.g. *sug-u* > *sug-uru*). This meant that the final form had already become longer, but the verb-stem had not changed yet.

earlier than the other one, this is noted in the "early use" column. Those verb pairs that are already documented in OJ are marked with a "#" in this column. If one verb of a pair, or both verbs are not recorded after 1750, I have indicated so in bold type. I give only one meaning gloss per pair, namely the one for the morphologically basic verb, and in the case of labile verbs, the historically earlier, or, if unknown, the intransitive use. I cite every verb in the non-past finite -(r)u-form. This means that there is no visible difference in morphological shape between V_c and $V_{e/i}$ verbs.[17]

4.2.1 Transitivization pairs

Transitivization is realized through four patterns of derivation:

1) $V_c > V_e$
2) $V_c > V+Vs/t$
3) $V_{e/i/v} > V+Vs/t$
4) $V > V+Vp$

Verb pairs exhibiting these patterns are listed in Table 6 below.

Table 6: List of pre-modern Japanese transitivizing pairs

Vc (itr) vs. Ve (tr)			E.g. *itam-u* (Vc; itr) ~ *itam-u* (Ve; tr)		
verb	early use	gloss	verb	early use	gloss
ap-u	#	fit	pukuram-u	itr	swell
ik-u	#	live	pus-u	#	lie face down
ikop-u		rest	sakap-u		oppose
imas-u	#	be, come (honorific)	sakidat-u	itr	precede
irop-u	tr	be colorful/shiny	sakipap-u	#	thrive
ir-u	#	enter	sidum-u	#	sink
isam-u	#	be excited	sikam-u	itr	get wrinkled
itam-u	itr	hurt	**sim-u**	#	dye
kagam-u	tr	bend	sirizok-u	itr	retreat
kaduk-u	#	dive	sitagap-u	itr	follow
kamap-u	tr	care for	siwam-u	itr	get wrinkled

---

[17] I have included transitive-ditransitive verb pairs such as *mi-ru~mise-ru* in the list, because they involve the addition of an argument (transitivization). In contrast, verb pairs such as *osie-ru~osowar-u* 'teach' vs. 'learn from' that merely express a change of perspective, and compound verbs, were not included.

kanap-u	itr	accord with	**sobam-u**		turn to the side	
kap-u	#	do mutually	*sodat-u*	itr	grow up	
karam-u	tr	twine around	**sok-u**	#	retreat	
karom-u		get light	*somuk-u*	itr	turn one's back	
kasum-u	#	grow hazy	*sop-u*	#	accompany	
kataduk-u	itr	be put in order	*sorop-u*	tr	get complete	
katamuk-u	itr	lean (towards)	*subom-u*	itr	grow narrow	
kawarag-u		dry	*sukum-u*		shrink	
kom-u	tr	enter	**sum-u**	itr	get clear	
kugum-u	tr	bend	**susam-u**	itr	get rough/wild	
kukum-u	itr	contain (in the mouth)	*susum-u*	itr	proceed	
kuram-u	itr	get dark	*tagap-u*	#	differ	
kurom-u	itr	get black	**tapira-g-u**	tr	get flat/peaceful	
kurusim-u	#	suffer	**tar-u**	#	hang down/drop	
mak-u	#	be sent	**tasinam-u**	itr	suffer	
maturop-u	#	follow	*tat-u*	#	stand up	
matop-u	itr	wrap around	*tawam-u*	itr	bend	
mit-u	#	get full	**tayum-u**	itr	get loose/tired	
mukap-u	#	face/move towards	*tidim-u*	itr	shrink	
muk-u	#	face towards	*tigap-u*		differ	
modorok-u	tr	get speckled	*tikaduk-u*	itr	come near	
nabik-u	#	flutter	**tiribam-u**	itr	be covered with dust	
naduk-u		be named	*todok-u*	itr	reach	
nagom-u	tr	calm down	*totonop-u*	tr	be completed	
nagusam-u	#	be comforted	**toyom-u**	#	resound	
nam-u	#	form a line	**tudop-u**	#	come together	
natuk-u	#	get attached to	*tuduk-u*	#	continue	
narab-u	#	form a line	*tugap-u*	itr	form a pair	
nayam-u	itr	be troubled with	*tuk-u*	#	soak in	
nigipap-u	#	flourish, be crowded	*tuk-u*	#	stick to	
nipop-u	#	be dyed	*tum-u*	#	pile up	
nok-u	itr	leave	**tum-u**	tr	fill, stuff	
nok-u	tr	look up	*tutap-u*	#	move along	
nurum-u	itr	get tepid	*ukab-u*	#	hover	
omomuk-u	itr	turn towards	**uk-u**	#	float	
pap-u	#	crawl	*urup-u*	itr	get wet	
paruk-u		clear up	*yam-u*	#	stop	
pedat-u	#	get distant	*yasum-u*	#	rest	
pigam-u		get twisted	**yasura-p-u**	itr	hesitate	
pirog-u	tr	extend	*yawarag-u*	#	get soft	
pisom-u	tr	be latent	*yugam-u*	itr	be bent	
pisom-u		be distorted	*yurum-u*		get weak/loose	
			yurup-u/yurub-u	#	get loose	

Total: 107 pairs

Japanese transitivity pairs through time – a historical and typological perspective

Vc (itr) vs. V+Vs/t (tr) Vc (tr) vs. V+Vs/t (ditr)		E.g. *ap-u* (Vc, itr) ~ *apas-u* (V+Vs-, tr), *tor-u* (Vc, tr) ~ *toras-u* (V+Vs-, ditr)	
Vc	V+Vs/t-	gloss	
ap-u	*apas-u*	fit	itr
ari	**aras-u**	be	
isog-u	*isogas-u*	hurry	itr
kap-u	*kapas-u*	do mutually	itr
kawak-u	*kawakas-u*	dry	#
kayop-u	*kayopas-u*	commute	#
kik-u	*kikas-u*	hear, ask	itr
kir-u	**kiras-u**	get misty	#
korob-u	*korobas-u*	tumble	tr
kor-u	*koras-u*	be absorbed in	itr
kuram-u	*kuramas-u*	get dark	tr
kusar-u	*kusaras-u/kusarakas-u*	rot	
magirap-u	**magirapas-u/magirapakas-u**	be mixed in	#
marob-u	**marobas-u**	tumble	
matop-u/madop-u	*matopas-u/madopas-u*	be puzzled	itr
matop-u/matup-u	*matopas-u/matupas-u*	wrap around	#
mayop-u/mayup-u	*mayopas-u*	be perplexed	itr
megur-u	*meguras-u*	go around	
modorok-u	**modorokas-u**	get speckled	#
nabik-u	*nabikas-u*	flutter	#
nar-u	*naras-u*	sound	itr
nayam-u	*nayamas-u*	be troubled with	#
nigor-u	*nigoras-u/nigorakas-u*	get muddy	itr
nipop-u	*nipopas-u/nipopos-u*	dye, smell	itr
nug-u	*nugas-u*	take off	itr
numer-u	**numerakas-u**	be slippery	#
odorok-u	*odorokas-u*	be surprised	#
op-u	**opos-u/opus-u**	carry	#
oyob-u	*oyobos-u*	reach	itr
pagem-u	*pagemas-u*	make efforts	itr
pasir-u	**pasirakas-u**	run	
per-u	*peras-u*	decrease	
pibi-ku	*pibikas-u*	reverberate	itr
ponome-ku	*ponomekas-u*	be barely perceptible	
pur-u	*puras-u*	fall	
sek-u	*sekas-u*	hurry	itr
sibuk-u	**sibukas-u**	stagnate	#
siger-u	**sigeras-u**	grow thick	itr
sir-u	*siras-u*	come to know	itr
sobiy-u	*sobiyakas-u*	rise skywards	itr
sop-u	*sopas-u*	accompany	itr

sor-u/ser-u	soras-u	be curved	itr
suber-u	suberas-u/suberakas-u	slip	itr
suk-u	sukas-u	get transparent	#
sum-u	sumas-u	get clear	#
tadayop-u	tadayopas-u	drift	#
tarap-u	**tarapas-u**	be sufficient	#
ter-u	teras-u	shine	#
tir-u	tiras-u	fall, scatter	itr
tob-u	tobas-u	fly	itr
todorok-u	todorokas-u	thunder	#
togar-u	togaras-u	get pointed	#
tor-u	toras-u	take	#
toyom-u/doyom-u	toyomos-u/doyomos-u	resound	#
tuk-u	tukas-u	pierce	#
tuk-u	tukas-u	soak	itr
ugok-u	ugokas-u	move	
uk-u	ukas-u	float	
wak-u	wakas-u	boil	
yurug-u	yurugas-u	waver	

Total: 60 pairs

Ve, Vi, Vv (itr) vs. V+Vs (tr) — E.g. *sam-u* (Ve, itr) ~ *samas-u* (V+Vs-, tr),
Ve, Vi, Vv (tr) vs. V+Vs (ditr) — *mi(r-u)* (Vv, tr) ~ *mis-u* (V+Vs-, ditr)

ab-u	abus-u/abis-u/amus-u	bathe	itr
ak-u	akas-u	get light	
amay-u	amayakas-u	depend on	itr
ar-u	aras-u	get rough	
ay-u	**ayas-u**	drop	#
bak-u	bakas-u	turn into	itr
(i)d-u	(i)das-u	exit	#
ik-u	ikas-u	live	#
iy-u	iyas-u	be healed	itr
kar-u	karas-u	whither	itr
katan-u	**katanas-u**	tie up	#
kir-u	kiras-u	snap, come apart	tr
ki-ru	kis-u	dress	tr
kog-u	kogas-u	be scorched	#
kok-u	kokas-u	fall, stumble	itr
kor-u	koras-u	get cautious	#
koy-u	koyas-u	grow fat	#
kur-u	kuras-u	grow dark, advance in time	#
kut-u	**kutas-u**	decay	itr
kuy-u	**kuyas-u**	fall apart	#
magir-u/magur-u	magiras-u/magirakas-u	get mixed up	itr
mi-(ru)	mis-u	see	#
midar-u	**midarakas-u**	go out of order	itr

mit-u	mitas-u	get full	#
mor-u	moras-u	leak	itr
moy-u	moyas-u	burn	itr
moy-u	moyas-u	sprout	
nar-u	naras-u	get accustomed to	itr
nay-u	nayas-u	droop	#
nig-u	nigas-u	escape	itr
ni-ru	nis-u	resemble	#
nob-u	nobas-u	stretch	itr
n-u	**nas-u**	sleep	#
nuk-u	nukas-u	come off	#
nur-u	**nuras-u**	come loose	itr
nur-u	nuras-u	get wet	#
obiy-u	obiyas-u/obiyakas-u	be afraid	itr
ok-u	okos-u	get up	#
op-u	**oyas-u**	grow	itr
or-u	oros-u	come down	tr
ot-u	otos-u	fall	itr
pag-u	pagas-u	come off	tr
par-u	paras-u/parukas-u	clear up	#
pas-u	**pasas-u**	run	#
pat-u	patas-u	come to an end	itr
pay-u	payas-u	grow	#
piy-u	piyas-u/piyakas-u	cool down	itr
porob-u	porobos-u	go to ruin	#
potob-u	**potobas-u/potobos-u**	swell	itr
p-u	pos-u	dry	itr
puk-u	pukas-u	grow late	#
pukur-u	pukuras-u	swell	itr
pur-u	**purus-u**	grow old	
sakay-u/sakap-u	**sakayakas-u**	flourish	#
sam-u	samas-u	get cold	
sam-u	samas-u	come awake	itr
sar-u	**saras-u**	get exposed to	
sobiy-u	sobiyakas-u	rise skywards	#
sor-u	soras-u	escape, deviate	tr
sug-u	sugus-u/sugos-u	pass	itr
suk-u	sukas-u	get transparent	itr
tadar-u	**tadarakas-u**	be sore	itr
tar-u	taras-u	drop	tr
tay-u	tayas-u	cease	itr
torok-u	torakas-u/torokas-u/torokos-u	melt	#
tukar-u	tukaras-u	get tired	#
tuk-u	tukus-u	get exhausted	tr
tupiy-u	tupiyas-u	wear down	#

uk-u/ug-u	ukat-u/ugat-u	hole be formed	tr
urag-u	uragas-u	enjoy	tr
yur-u	yuras-u	shake	tr
yur-u	yurus-u	get pardoned	tr

Total: 73 pairs

Transitivizing pairs on -ap-

us-u (Ve)	usinap-u	lose	#
ter-u (Vc)	terap-u	shine	#

Total: 2 pairs
Transitivizing total: 242 pairs

Detransitivization is realized through 4 patterns of derivation:

1) $V_c > V_e$
2) $V_c > V + Vr$
3) $V_{e/i/v} > V + Vr$
4) $V > V + Vy$

Verb pairs exhibiting these patterns are listed in Table 7 below.

Table 7: List of pre-modern Japanese detransitivizing pairs

Vc (tr) vs. Ve (itr)			E.g. kir-u (Vc; tr) ~ kir-u (Ve; itr)		
verb	early use	gloss	verb	early use	gloss
kak-u	itr	lack	pirak-u	#	open
kir-u	tr	cut	podok-u	tr	untie
kubir-u	#	grasp, strangle	por-u	tr	make a hole
kudak-u		crush	sabak-u	tr	put into order/get sold
kuzik-u	tr	sprain	sak-u	#	tear apart
makur-u	tr	turn/roll up	sir-u	#	come to know
midar-u	#	put into disorder	sog-u	tr	split
modir-u		twist	sugur-u	itr	select
mog-u	tr	wrench off	sur-u	tr	rub
mot-u	tr	hold	tok-u	#	(dis)solve
muk-u		peel off	tor-u	tr	take
ner-u	tr	knead	war-u	#	split
nezir-u		twist	wor-u	tr	break
nug-u	tr	take off	yabur-u		defeat
nuk-u	tr	pull out	yak-u	#	burn
pag-u	tr	peel off	yar-u	itr	destroy
papur-u	tr	let go	yodir-u	#	twist
pik-u	tr	pull			

Total: 35 pairs

Vc (tr) vs. V+Vr (itr)

E.g. *sas-u* (Vc, tr) ~ *sasar-u* (V+Vr, itr)

Vc	V+Vr-	gloss	early use
kukum-u	*kukumor-u/kugumor-u*	contain (in the mouth)	#
matag-u	*matagar-u*	straddle	
matup-u/matop-u	*matupar-u/matopar-u*	wrap	#
musub-u	*musubor-u/musubopor-u*	tie up	#
pasam-u	*pasamar-u*	put in between	#
pusag-u/putag-u	*pusagar-u/putagar-u*	obstruct	#
sas-u	*sasar-u*	pierce	tr
tog-u	*togar-u*	grind, sharpen	tr
tum-u	*tumor-u*	pile up	#
um-u	*umar-u*	give birth to	#

Total: 10 pairs

Ve (tr) vs. V+Vr (itr)

E.g. *ag-u* (Ve, tr) ~ *agar-u* (V+Vr, itr)

Ve	V+Vr- (itr)	gloss	early use
ag-u	*agar-u*	lift	#
aratam-u	*aratamar-u*	change	#
atatam-u	*atatamar-u*	warm up	tr
at-u	*atar-u*	hit	
atum-u	*atumar-u*	collect	#
kabus-u	*kabusar-u*	cover	tr
kagam-u	*kagamar-u*	bend	#
kak-u	*kakar-u*	hang	#
kap-u	*kapar-u*	change	#
karam-u	*karamar-u*	entangle	itr
kasan-u	*kasanar-u*	pile up	#
katam-u	*katamar-u*	harden	#
kipam-u	*kipamar-u*	study thoroughly	#
kiyom-u	*kiyomar-u/kiyomapar-u*	purify	tr
kom-u	*komor-u*	put inside, insert, load	#
kupap-u	*kupapar-u*	add	#
mag-u	*magar-u*	bend	#
mak-u	**makar-u**	make leave	#
marog-u	**marogar-u/marokar-u**	round up	itr
marum-u	*marumar-u*	make round	
mazip-u	*mazipar-u*	mix	#
pam-u	*pamar-u*	insert	tr
pas-u	*pasir-u*	let run	#
payam-u	*payamar-u*	quicken	tr
pazim-u	*pazimar-u*	begin	tr
pedat-u	*pedatar-u*	separate	#
pirog-u	*pirogar-u*	extend	tr
pirom-u	*piromar-u*	spread	tr

pisom-u	pisomar-u	conceal	tr
sadam-u	sadamar-u	determine	#
sag-u	sagar-u	lower	#
sak-u	**sakar-u**	avoid	#
sap-u	sapar-u	cut off, inhibit	#
sem-u	semar-u	attack	#
sidum-u	sidumar-u	sink, calm	#
sim-u	simar-u	tie up	tr
som-u	somar-u	dye	#
sonap-u	sonapar-u	prepare	
sop-u	sopar-u/sopor-u	attach to	
subom-u/tubom-u	subomar-u/tubomar-u	make narrower	tr
sukum-u	**sukumar-u**	shrink	
sut-u	sutar-u	discard	tr
su-u/suy-u	suwar-u	put into position	tr
tadusap-u	tadusapar-u	take along	#
tam-u	tamar-u	accumulate	#
tasuk-u	tasukar-u	rescue	tr
tidim-u/sizim-u	tidimar-u/sizimar-u	shrink, shorten	tr
todom-u	todomar-u	stop	#
tom-u	tomar-u	stop	#
totonop-u	**totonopor-u**	prepare	#
tudum-u	tudumar-u	shorten	itr
tuk-u	tukar-u	soak	tr
tum-u	tumar-u	fill in, stuff	#
turan-u	turanar-u	put things in a row	itr
tutap-u	tutapar-u	convey	
tutom-u	tutomar-u	serve	tr
udum-u	udumor-u	cover, fill	itr
um-u	umar-u	bury	tr
um-u	umor-u	bury	#
u-u	uwar-u	plant	tr
wak-u	wakar-u	divide	#
wop-u	wopar-u	end	#
wosam-u	wosamar-u	rule	#
yasum-u	yasumar-u	give rest to	#
yokotap-u/yokodap-u	yokotapar-u	lay down	tr
yos-u	**yosor-u/yosar-u**	bring near	#
yud-u	yudar-u	boil	tr

Total: 67 pairs

detransitivizing pairs with -Vy-			
kik-u	kikoy-u	hear	#
mi(r-u)	miy-u	see	#
ni-ru	niy-u	boil	tr
omop-u	omopoy-u/obopoy-u/ omopay-u	think	#

Total: 4 pairs
Detransitivizing total: 116 pairs

Equipollent pairs exhibit the following patterns:

1) V+Vs/t < > V+Vr/y
2) Various other patterns unsystematically involving a variety of elements

Verb pairs exhibiting these patterns are listed in Table 8.

Table 8: List of pre-modern Japanese equipollent pairs

V+Vs/t (tr) vs. V+ Vr/y (itr)		E.g. *amas-u* (V+Vs-, tr) ~ *amar-u* (V+Vr-, itr)	
V+Vr/y (itr)	V+Vs/t- (tr)	gloss	early use
amar-u	ama-su	be left over	#
arapar-u	arapas-u	appear	#
damar-u	damas-u	get silent	
hotur-u	**hotus-u**	come loose	itr
itar-u	itas-u	reach	#
kabur-u	kabus-u	put on	itr
kakur-u	kakus-u	hide	#
kapar-u	kapas-u	exchange	#
kaper-u	kapes-u	turn around, return	#
kegar-u	kegas-u	be defiled	tr
kitar-u	kitas-u	come	#
kiy-u	kes-u/ket-u	disappear	itr
kobor-u	kobos-u	spill	tr
kogar-u	kogas-u	get scorched	itr
konar-u	konas-u	get broken up into pieces, be well-digested	tr
kopar-u/kopor-u	kopas-u/kopos-u/ kopot-u/kobot-u	break	#
koy-u	kos-u	pass, cross	#
kudar-u	kudas-u	go down	#
kutugaper-u	kutugapes-u	overturn	#
kuzur-u	kuzus-u	fall apart	itr

mapar-u	mapas-u	revolve	itr
marokar-u/marogar-u	**marokas-u**	get round	tr
matupar-u/matopar-u	matupas-u/matopas-u	get entangled with	#
midar-u	midas-u	get out of order	itr
modor-u	modos-u	return	itr
motopor-u/motoporop-u	**motopos-u**	go around	#
nagar-u	nagas-u	flow	#
napor-u	napos-u	get well	itr
nar-u	**nas-u**	sound	#
nar-u	nas-u	become	#
nigor-u	nigos-u	get muddy	itr
nobor-u	nobos-u	go up	#
nogar-u	nogas-u	escape	itr
nokor-u	nokos-u	remain	#
nor-u	nos-u	get on	
obor-u	**obopos-u**	drown	#
okor-u	okos-u	spring up, happen	#
otor-u	otos-u	be inferior	itr
padur-u	padus-u	come off	
pagar-u	pagas-u	peel off	tr
panar-u	panat-u/panas-u	part from	#
payar-u	**payas-u**	be in fashion	tr
per-u	pes-u	decrease	tr
pirugaper-u	pirugapes-u	turn around	itr
pitar-u	pitas-u	soak	tr
podar-u	**podas-u**	get tied up	tr
pogur-u	pogus-u	go astray	tr
sator-u	satos-u	realize	#
sim-u	simes-u	get damp	itr
suber-u	**subes-u**	slip	
sugur-u	**sugus-u/sugos-u**	pass	#
tapur-u	tapus-u	stumble, fall	itr
tar-u	tas-u	suffice	#
tay-u	tat-u	cease	#
tobor-u/tomor-u	tomos-u/tobos-u	become alight	tr
topor-u	topos-u	pass through	#
tubur-u	tubus-u	be crushed	
tukar-u	**tukas-u**	soak	tr
ukar-u	ukas-u	float, get excited	itr
utur-u	utus-u	move to	#
wakar-u	wakat-u	part from	
wasir-u	**wasis-u**	run	tr
watar-u	watas-u	go across	#
yatur-u	yatus-u	get haggard	
yogor-u	yogos-u	get dirty	tr
yor-u	yos-u	come near	#

Total: 66 pairs

Other equipollent pairs			
ik-u (V$_i$)	ik-u (V$_e$)	live	tr
kirap-u	**kiras-u**	get misty	#
kisim-u	**kisir-u**	creak	itr
mazir-u	mazip-u	mix	#
nigipap-u	nigipas-u	be crowded	itr
sin-u	**sis-u**	die	#
sin-u	**sos-u**	die	itr
urupop-u	urupos-u	get moist	itr

Total: 8 pairs
Equipollent total: 74 pairs

Note that equipollent pairs already extant in OJ could originally be transitivizing pairs, since verbs formed with the 'fientive' -Vr- are most likely an inheritance from proto-Transeurasian (cf. Robbeets (2007, 2010) while verbs formed with -Vs- are Japanese-internal formations.

Lastly, there are 41 labile pairs and one suppletive pair, as presented in Table 9.

Table 9: List of pre-modern Japanese indeterminate pairs

Labile verbs (conjugational class varies verb by verb)					
verb	early use	gloss (early use)	verb	early use	gloss (early use)
ak-u	itr	open	pirak-u	tr	open
ak-u	#	get bright	pur-u	#	move
ayamar-u	itr	be mistaken	purup-u		shake
ikop-u		rest	**sakap-u**		be opposed to
kagir-u	tr	limit	sar-u	itr	go away
karam-u		entwine	sek-u	tr	hurry
kipam-u	tr	reach the limit	**sik-u**	#	spread out
kisir-u	itr	creak	sop-u	tr	attach to
kom-u	itr	enter, get crowded	sosog-u/sosok-u	#	flow into
kozor-u		do together	s-u	#	do
mas-u	itr	increase	tar-u	tr	drop
matop-u/matup-u	itr	wrap around	tatam-u/tatan-u	tr	fold up
moyopos-u	tr	arouse	tod-u	tr	close
nagusam-u	#	get comfort	tomonap-u	tr	accompany
nos-u		stretch	**totonop-u**	tr	complete
nukind-u	tr	select	tugap-u	tr	mate with
okonap-u	tr	carry out	**tum-u**		pile up
pan-u	tr	let bounce	**tum-u**	tr	stuff, fill
par-u	#	stretch out	wop-u		end
pas-u	tr	let run	**yusur-u**	tr	shake
pikap-u		wait			

Total: 41 pairs

Suppletive pair			
V (itr)	V (tr)	gloss (itr)	early use
sin-u	koros-u	die	#
			Total: 1 pairs
			Indeterminate total: 42 pairs

The identification of the indeterminate (labile) verbs is the most difficult task. In Japanese arguments are frequently deleted. This holds even more for historical stages than for Modern Japanese (ModJ), and verbs can change their transitivity in particular contexts (cf. Morita 1994: 246, 248). Moreover, we may be dealing with homophones. I thus limited this list to verbs that I consider as unambiguous examples of labile verbs.

There are also verbs which are only labile if used in compounds (e.g. *kaes-u* 'return (tr)' as in *mori-kaes-u* 'recover/rally back'; cf. Morita 1994: 240), but I have ignored these here. Suppletive verb pairs are also difficult to determine. I did not include *s-u* 'do' ~ *nar-u* 'become' here although it is another possible candidate for this category.

4.2.2 Typological classification of the pre-modern verb inventory

If the verb pairs listed in Table 6 to Table 9 are divided into transitivizing, detransitivizing, equipollent, and indeterminate classes, the numbers in each class are as in Table 10.

Table 10: Premodern Japanese transitivity pairs divided by typological pattern

Type	Pattern of derivation	# of verb pairs	ratio
transitivizing	$V_c > V_e$	107	51%
	$V_c > V+Vs/t$-	60	
	$V_{e/i} > V+Vs/t$-	73	
	$V_{c/e} > V+Vp$-	2	
detransitivizing	$V_c > V_e$	35	24%
	$V_{c/v} > V+Vr/y$	14	
	$V_{e/i} > V+Vr$	67	
equipollent	$V+Vs/t <\ > V+Vr/y$ (and others)	74	16%
indeterminate	labile verbs	41	9%
	suppletive pairs	1	
	total	474	

Table 10 shows that transitivizing pairs make up about half of the verb inventory. It can thus be said that, at least originally, Japanese is a language in which transitivization dominates, as claimed by Nichols et al. (2004), and in harmony with other North Asian languages. In the next section I will extend this analysis to the modern verb inventory.

4.3 The Modern Japanese verb inventory

As stated above, most patterns of transitivity alternation were already established as lexical patterns at the time of OJ. An exception are the verb pairs with suffixes -(r)(a)y-u (passivizing) and -(a)p-u (intensifying), which can be considered as still productive in OJ, and then later became fossilized. Nevertheless, a number of transitivity pairs seem to have emerged during subsequent historical periods (although there is always the possibility that they have simply escaped documentation thus far), including EModJ and ModJ. Conversely, a fair number of verb pairs fell out of use. Furthermore, the change in verb inflection described in section 4.1 may influence not only how linguists analyze verb pairs but also the way they are perceived by speakers of the language themselves. In our discussion below, each of these factors will be taken into account.

4.3.1 Addition of Japanese verb pairs

The number of transitivity pairs that emerged in EModJ and ModJ is comparatively small. They are listed in Table 11. Most of them date to the 18th and the first half of the 19th century, that is, to EModJ. New verb pairs after the late 19th century are extremely rare. By contrast, Sino-Japanese vocabulary and Western loanwords increased exponentially during that period. The former occupy a unique place in the Japanese verbal lexicon and will therefore be treated in a section of their own (4.3.2). Since language materials for the period from the 18th to 20th century are plentiful, I have reduced the time span for one member of a verb pair to qualify as earlier than the other to ten years from a hundred for this period. The transcription of verbs is unified to modern phonology, even if one of the verbs is of pre-modern origin.

Table 11: New transitivity pairs in Early Modern and Modern Japanese

Transitivization: Vc (itr) > Ve (tr)

Vc	Ve	gloss (intransitive meaning)	early use
dok-u	doke-ru	move aside	
kasig-u	kasige-ru	tilt towards	tr
utumuk-u	utumuke-ru	face downwards	itr
yasurag-u	yasurage-ru	get peace of mind	itr
yodom-u	yodome-ru	stagnate	itr

Total: 5 pairs

Transitivization: Vv (itr) > V+Vs/t (tr)

Vv	V+Vs-	gloss	early use
bare-ru	baras-u	come to light	itr
hagure-ru	hagurakas-u	go astray	itr
hake-ru	hakas-u	flow	
hare-ru	haras-u	get swollen	itr
hue-ru	huyas-u	increase	tr
koroge-ru	korogas-u	stumble, fall	
make-ru	makas-u	be defeated	itr
ne-ru	nekas-u	sleep	itr
toke-ru	tokas-u	melt	itr
toke-ru	tokas-u	get solved	itr
tuki-ru	tukas-u	get exhausted	itr
zire-ru	ziras-u	get impatient	
zure-ru	zuras-u	get out of position	tr

Total: 13 pairs

Detransitivization: V_c > V_v

Vc	Vv	gloss	early use
hazik-u	hazike-ru	snap	tr
ur-u	ure-ru	sell	tr

Total: 2 pairs

Detransitivization: V_c > V+Vr-

Vc	V+Vr-	gloss	early use
tukam-u	tukamar-u	catch	tr

Total: 1 pair

Detransitivization: V_v > V+Vr-

Vv	V+Vr-	gloss	early use
butuke-ru	butukar-u	bump against	
hukame-ru	hukamar-u	deepen	tr
kime-ru	kimar-u	decide	tr

kurome-ru	kuromar-u	blacken	tr
kurume-ru	kurumar-u	lump together	
make-ru	makar-u	lower (price)	tr
matome-ru	matomar-u	complete	tr
maze-ru	mazar-u	mix	tr
mituke-ru	mitukar-u	find	tr
sebame-ru	sebamar-u	narrow	tr
tukamae-ru	tukamar-u	catch, seize	tr
tunage-ru	tunagar-u	connect	tr
tuyome-ru	tuyomar-u	strengthen	tr
uke-ru	ukar-u	receive	tr
udume-ru	udumar-u	cover, fill	tr
yowame-ru	yowamar-u	weaken	tr
butuke-ru	butukar-u	bump against	tr
			Total: 16 pairs

Equipollent: V+Vr- < > V+Vs-

V+Vr-	V+Vs-	gloss	early use
ibur-u	ibus-u	smolder	tr
mure-ru	mus-u	get musty	tr
nomer-u	nomes-u	fall forward	itr
tirakar-u	tirakas-u	be scattered	tr
			Total: 4 pairs

Labile verbs (Vc)

owar-u* 'end' *itr*, *hakob-u* 'transport' *tr

verb	early use	gloss (early use)	verb	early use	gloss (early use)
hakob-u (V$_c$)	tr	transport	owar-u (V$_c$)	itr	end
					Total: 2 pairs

As Nishio (1954) hypothesized (but did not actually show), the detransitivizing Vv > V+*Vr* pattern of derivation is the most frequently occurring pattern in modern times. The transitivizing V$_v$ > V+*Vs* pattern follows. In most cases, the V$_v$ verb still forms the actual basis for derivation. This is interesting since one might assume that now that verb pairs tend to superficially, that is, on the basis of the comparison of the -*(r)u* form alone, look more equipollent, the directionality of derivation would be random, that is, occurring with about equal frequency in both directions. Instead, the actual directionality of derivation (cf. Table 4 above) is maintained.

4.3.2 Sino-Japanese verbal nouns

Especially from Middle Japanese on, Sinitic vocabulary began to permeate everyday language use, and in ModJ, Sino-Japanese vocabulary has increased dramatically in response to the need to express new social and technical concepts. So-called verbal nouns are a major subclass of this new vocabulary. They can be used either as nouns, or as verbs by adding the light verb *s-uru* 'do'. Since the inventory of nouns is potentially unlimited in number, it is much more difficult to capture and measure than the inventory of verbs. A study of the 1989 Asahi newspaper by Kobayashi (2004: 24) found as many as 1750 different Sino-Japanese verbal nouns. However, these do not form transitivity pairs, and, judging from their actual usage in the extant literature, most of them seem to be limited to either transitive or intransitive use. Adding or deleting participants is achieved by adding the productive causative *-ase-ru* or the passive suffix *-are-ru* on the verb *s-uru* as in (3) and (4).

(3) *zyuku~s-uru* 'ripen' > *zyuku~s-ase-ru* 'let ripen'

(4) *niNsiki~s-uru* 'perceive' > *niNsiki~s-are-ru* 'be perceived'

Thus, most Sino-Japanese verbal nouns need not be included in this study. However, a small number of labile Sino-Japanese verbal nouns have been identified in the literature. There are both originally transitive ones that have acquired intransitive uses (cf. Kageyama 1996: 203–204), and intransitive ones that have acquired transitive uses (cf. Kim 2004)[18]. They are listed in (5) and (6), respectively.

(5) Transitive > intransitive (13): *kakudai~s-uru* 'expand', *syukusyoo~s-uru* 'reduce', *heNkei~s-uru* 'transform', *kaNbi~s-uru* 'equip with', *kaNsei~s-uru* 'complete', *seizyooka~s-uru* 'normalize', *kaiteN~s-uru* 'rotate', *kaiteN~s-uru* 'open shop', *teNkai~s-uru* 'develop', *kaisaN~s-uru* 'dissolve', *zitugeN~s-uru* 'materialize', *kaisyoo~s-uru* 'dissolve', *gutaika~s-uru* 'concretize' (Kageyama 1996: 202)

---

18 According to Kim (2004:89, 98), the transitive use of these verbal nouns is generally limited to cases where there is a reflexive relationship between subject and object of the verb.

(6) Intransitive > transitive (14) *kaihuku~s-uru* 'recover', *ippeN~s-uru* 'change completely', *soositu~s-uru* 'lose', *huNsitu~s-uru* 'lose', *zeNsyoo~s-uru* 'burn completely', *syuutyuu~s-uru* 'concentrate', *hassyoo~s-uru* 'develop symptoms', *kaisaN~s-uru* 'get dissolved', *tyuudaN~s-uru* 'be interrupted', *teishi~s-uru* 'stop', *kessoku~s-uru* 'unite', *kaNryoo~s-uru* 'complete', *syuuryoo~s-uru* 'end', *hukkatu~s-uru* 'come back' (Kim 2004: 97)[19]

As mentioned above, the Sino-Japanese verbal noun inventory is large, and it is therefore difficult to exhaustively identify those verbal nouns that are labile. It is possible that there are actually more Sino-Japanese labile verbal nouns, but for this study we consider the above list as exhaustive. Sino-Japanese verbal nouns have not yet infiltrated the basic verb vocabulary to a large extent. The *Usage Dictionary of Japanese Basic Verbs* lists 728 verbs, and only 154 of these are Sino-Japanese verbs or verbal nouns. 262 Japanese verbs in the dictionary form 131 verb pairs. There are 25 more that belong to a verb pair, but where the other verb was not included in the list of basic verbs. In contrast, only 2 of the 154 basic Sino-Japanese verbal nouns are labile (*kaNsei~s-uru* 'complete' and *zitugeN~s-uru* 'materialize'). This is due to the fact that Sino-Japanese verbal nouns, as shown in (3) and (4), tend to use productive morphology to indicate the deletion or addition of arguments instead of the ambiguous labile pattern.

4.3.3 Loss of vocabulary

In Table 6 through Table 9, those verbs for which it can be assumed, based on the information given in the NKD and the Kōjien, that they were no longer used in EModJ and ModJ, are rendered in bold type. Their number is recorded in the fourth column of Table 12 in the following subsection 4.3.4.

4.3.4 Typological classification of modern vocabulary

If we combine the data on increase and loss in verb vocabulary during EModJ and ModJ as described above, we obtain the numbers in Table 12. These are classified according to the same typological patterns as those appearing in Table 10.

---

[19] It is impossible to determine whether the intransitive or the transitive use was first using current dictionaries. Therefore, I am not able to provide data here on the historical sequence in which these uses emerged.

Table 12: Modern Japanese transitivity pairs categorized by typological pattern

type	Pattern of derivation	# of verb pairs (pre-modern)	# of verb pairs lost in EModJ and ModJ	# of verb pairs added in EModJ and ModJ	Resulting number of pairs in ModJ	ratio
transitivization	Vc > Ve	107	54	5	58	42%
	Vc > V+Vs/t-	60	11	0	49	
	Ve/i > V+Vs/t-	73	17	13	69	
	Vc/e > V+Vf	2	0	0	2	
detransitivization	Vc > Ve	35	4	2	33	29%
	Vc/v > V+Vr/y	14	1	1	14	
	Ve/i > V+Vr	67	6	16	77	
equipollent	V+Vs < > V+Vr etc.	74	15	4	63	15%
indeterminate	Labile verbs	41	12	29	58	14%
	suppletion	1	0	0	1	
	total	474	120	70	424	

Note first that, in this study, I have identified 424 transitivity pairs and labile verbs in Modern Japanese compared to 220 in Hayatsu (1995 (1987): 192), 419 in Nishio (1988 (1982): 199), and Shimada (1979: 608) who has 292 plus 43 labile verbs. This shows that the verbs and verb pairs targeted in this study are closer to being comprehensive than those in previous studies, and furthermore offer the advantage of ease of comparison with previous studies.

Secondly, concerning change in the overall number of verb pairs, it is clear that they have decreased in number compared to pre-modern times. This may be due to the following reasons: 1) There is always some change and loss in vocabulary in any period of a language, but replacement and additions in modern times no longer take place in indigenous Japanese vocabulary, but rather in Sino-Japanese vocabulary and loanwords. These usually do not form transitivity pairs. 2) To some extent this may be an artifact of how data has been presented in this study. The pre-modern period in Table 10 covers a broad time range, and not all verb pairs were necessarily in use simultaneously. However, it is technically difficult to divide the pre-modern period into sub-periods equivalent in length to the modern period in Table 12.

The biggest loss of vocabulary took place in the '$V_c > V_e$ transitivization' pattern. Furthermore, the transitivization patterns as a whole declined. It appears that in the modern period a preference developed for marking the addition of arguments analytically through productive morphology, as in the case of Sino-Japanese verbal nouns. Another factor leading to the avoidance of the formation of V_e verbs from V_c verbs may be the emergence of the so-called 'potential verbs' (that is, verbs to which the potential morpheme *-(r)e-ru*, originally having only the allomorph *-e-ru* is suffixed) in Middle and Early Modern Japanese. The potential form has a detransitivizing effect, and thus the presence of *-e-* has become increasingly associated with detransitivization.

Compared to the loss of transitivizing verb pairs, the loss of detransitivizing verb pairs is small, and the number of labile verbs has even increased. The latter is mainly due to the emergence of Sino-Japanese verbal nouns (cf. 4.3.2).

4.4 Historical derivation

In the preceding sections, I have analyzed Japanese transitivity pairs morphologically from a typological perspective, based on their original morphological structure at the time of derivation. The analysis was historical in the sense of reflecting the historical morphology of Japanese but the actual historical derivation is not necessarily iconic to historical morphological structure. This problem is resolved in the present section. Table 13 summarizes the numbers for actual historical derivation to the extent that it can be inferred from available historical materials. Concrete information about each verb pair has already been presented in Table 6 through Table 9 and Table 11.

Table 13: Historical derivational relationship in Japanese transitivity pairs

	Historical derivation		
Morphological derivation	Non-causal > causal	Causal > non-causal	Equal or unknown (existing from OJ)
Vc > Ve (transitivization)	37	19	58 (45)
V > V+Vs/t (transitivization)	61	15	71 (54)
Vc > Ve (detransitivization)	3	20	14 (8)
V > V+Vr/y etc. (detransitivization)	6	39	53 (45)
V+Vs <> V+Vr (equipollent)	20	19	40 (33)
Labile verbs + suppletion (indeterminate)	22	33	17 (8)
total	149	145	253 (193)

As stated in section 3.2, the prediction is that morphological, historical and semantic derivation coincide in their directionality. Otherwise we are seeing backformation, which should be exceptional. Equipollent and indeterminate pairs should exhibit no specific directionality of derivation.

For about half of the Japanese transitivity pairs, we have no idea about the directionality of their derivation because both verbs of the pair were already present in OJ, or both verbs appear in the documents roughly simultaneously. The other pairs, which make their first appearance in documents from Early Middle Japanese on, roughly confirm the above prediction. Especially in the case of transitivization through the extension of the root by -*Vs/t*, and detransitivization through extension of the root through -*Vr/y*-, and through conversion from V_c to V_e, the basic verb is documented earlier in the overwhelming number of cases. Similarly, equipollent pairs display no directionality in their derivation, as expected. There are two patterns, however, that somewhat confound expectations. In the case of transitivization through derivation from Vc to Ve, about 30% of the pairs are apparently due to backformation, and the labile verbs are double as likely to be the result of detransitivization as of transitivization. The lexical inventory of Japanese verbs invites backformation since there are a large number of V_e verbs and verbs ending with -*Vr*- that have no counterpart.

There may also be some semantic explanation for these exceptions, which is not within the scope of this study. From a morphological point of view, it can be said that the markedness difference (difference in phonological heaviness) between V_c and V_e verbs is smaller than if a verb is derived through -*Vs/t*-. Also, *e*-base verbs as such are neutral with respect to transitivity. A total of 202 *e*-base verbs can be identified diachronically that do not belong to a transitivity pair, and of these 92 are intransitive while 101 are transitive. Some verbs oscillated between consonant-stem inflection and *e*-base inflection in historical times without changing their meaning. Thus it is not surprising that the directionality between *e*-base and consonant-stem verbs is less pronounced. I stated earlier in 4.3.4 that through the emergence of the -*(r)e*- potential suffix -*e* became increasingly associated with intransitivity from Middle Japanese on. This may partly explain why *e*-based verbs have historically functioned more frequently as markers of detransitivization than transitivization.

As for the labile verbs, it may be generally easier to subtract an argument without changing the verb form than to add an argument. But this is a cognitive rather than a language-specific explanation and should be checked with other languages.

Overall, while morphologically transitivization is the dominant pattern in Japanese, historically speaking the difference between transitivization (148 verb pairs) and detransitivization (139 verb pairs) is negligible. This is the result of two factors, namely (1) detransitivization having been the dominant pattern with labile verbs in historical times, as discussed in the preceding two paragraphs, and (2) the fact that there were many more transitivizing pairs already present in OJ than detransitivization ones. Additionally, many of the equipollent pairs already extant in OJ may actually be the product of historical transitivization, since the -*Vr*- 'fientive' suffix is likely historically older than the -*Vs*- transitivizing suffix. Overall then, in pre-historical times, Japanese was apparently very strongly transitivizing and this strong tendency increasingly gave way to detransitivizing and indeterminate patterns in historically documented times.

5 Summary and conclusions

In this paper, I have analyzed Japanese transitivity pairs from a historical-morphological perspective. I have shown that Japanese patterns with other North Asian languages in leaning towards transitivization, with intransitive (or less transitive) verbs constituting the basis for verb pair formation.

The dominant pattern of transitivization in the lexicon may also have reflexes in other areas of a language. Ikegami (1981 and elsewhere) proposed a typology of 'do' vs. 'become' languages. The fact that in Japanese transitivity pairs the intransitive verb is more often basic and the transitive verb derived than vice versa, agrees with the overall characterization of Japanese as a 'become' type language. Relatedly, in first language acquisition research it has been found that Japanese children acquire transitive clauses later than German children (Miura 2005).

On the other hand, in that portion of the lexical inventory of Japanese transitivity pairs that emerged in historical times, transitivization is not significantly more frequent than detransitivization. Furthermore, transitivization patterns have decreased as the result of historical changes, while labile verbs and detransitivizing patterns have increased. One reason for this is the attrition of indigenous Japanese verb vocabulary and the increase in Sino-Japanese verbal noun vocabulary, which does not form pairs but instead generates labile verbal nouns. Also, $V_e \sim V\text{-}Vr/s$ pairs became equipollent in their non-past form through the absorption of V_e verbs into the class of general vowel-stem verbs (V_v). Note, though, that this equipollence only holds if one focuses exclusively on the -(r)u form, for which there is no particular theoretical or empirical basis. For example, historically many dictionaries took the verb base, the so-called *ren'yōkei* in traditional grammar as the most basic form of the verb, and not the -(r)u form (*shūshikei*). A comparison across inflectional forms shows that the V-Vr/s forms are still morphologically clearly heavier (cf. Table 4), even in Modern Japanese. So it is no surprise that this change in verb morphology did not also influence the actual (historical) directionality of derivation in these patterns for those verb pairs that newly appeared in the past 250 years. They are still transitivizing (V+*Vs*) and detransitivizing (V+*Vr*), respectively.

If these changes continue, the ratio of labile verbs and equipollent verb pairs to the total corpus of verb pairs may further increase in Japanese, and transitivizing pairs decrease. This would be in accordance with a cross-linguistic tendency, since according to Nichols et al. (2004) neutral and indeterminate patterns are most frequent across the world's languages. Interestingly, in English as well, labile verbs have increased significantly over time. Möhlig & Klages (2002) present many examples of erstwhile transitive verbs acquiring intransitive use (e.g. *dry, close, fill, clean, wash*). The reverse pattern is also found (e.g. *cook, walk*), leading to the overall saliency of the indeterminate pattern in Modern English. The rise of labile verbs with no markedness distinction in Japanese may be a tendency towards a typologically more general pattern, or even towards a sort of entropy in the lexicon. The verb vocabulary as a whole has remained transitivizing, though, confirming Comrie's (2006) hypothesis.

Acknowledgments

I wish to thank the editors of this volume for providing me with the opportunity to publish this research in a revised, and hopefully improved, version in English, and for their hard work on editing this paper. All remaining errors remain my own.

Abbreviations

C consonant; EModJ Early Modern Japanese; itr intransitive; ModJ Modern Japanese; OJ Old Japanese; tr transitive; V vowel (if in italics); Vc consonant-stem verb; Ve e-base verb; Vi i-base verb; Vv vowel-stem verb

References

Beard, Robert. 1998. Derivation. In Andrew Spencer & Arnold M. Zwicky (eds.), *The handbook of morphology*, 44–65. London: Blackwell.

Brannen, Noah S. 1967. Nihongo ni okeru tsui o nasu ji-ta dōshi to matorikkusu [Japanese intransitive-transitive verb pairs and the matrix], *Kokugogaku* 70. 67–75.

Comrie, Bernard. 2006. Transitivity pairs, markedness, and diachronic stability. *Linguistics* 44 (2). 303–318.

Drossard, Werner. 1998. Labile Konstruktionen. In Leonid Kulikov & Heinz Vater (eds.), *Typlogy of verbal categories: Papers presented to Vladimir Nedjalkov on the occasion of his 70th birthday*, 73–83. Tübingen: Narr.

Frellesvig, Bjarke & John Whitman. this volume. The historical source of the bigrade transitivity alternations in Japanese. In Taro Kageyama & Wesley M. Jacobsen (eds.), *Transitivity and valency alternations: Studies on Japanese and beyond*. Berlin & Boston: De Gruyter Mouton.

García, Luisa García. 2005. *Germanische Kausativbildung. Die deverbalen jan-Verben im Gotischen*. Heidelberg: Vandenhoeck & Ruprecht.
Hansen, Barbara, Klaus Hansen, Albrecht Neubert & Manfredet Schhentke. 1990. *Englische Lexikologie. Einführung in Wortbildung und lexikalische Semantik*. Dritte Auflage. Leipzig: VEB Verlag Enzyklopädie.
Haspelmath, Martin. 1993. More on the typology of inchoative/causative verb alternation. In: Bernard Comrie & Maria Polinsky (eds.), *Causatives and transitivity*, 87–120. Amsterdam: John Benjamins.
Haspelmath, Martin, Andrea Calude, Michael Spagnol, Heiko Narrog & Elif Bamyacı. 2014. Coding causal-noncausal verb alternations: A form-frequency correspondence explanation. *Journal of Linguistics* 50 (3). 587–625.
Hayatsu, Emiko. 1995. Yūtsui dōshi to mutsui dōshi no chigai ni tsuite – imiteki na tokuchō o chūshin ni [On the difference between paired and non-paired verbs – semantic characteristics]. Originally published in *Gengo Kenkyū* 95 (1989); reprinted in Kazuyoshi Suga & Emiko Hayatsu (eds.), *Nichieigo no jita no kōtai* [Transitivity alternations in Japanese and English], 179–197. Tokyo: Hituzi Syobo.
Ikegami, Yoshihiko. 1981. *Suru to naru no gengogaku – Gengo to bunka no taiporojii e no shiron* [The linguistics of doing and becoming. An attempt at a typology of language and culture]. Tokyo: Taishūkan.
Jacobsen, Wesley M. 1992. *The transitive structure of events in Japanese*. Tokyo: Kurosio Publishers.
Kageyama, Tarō. 1996. *Dōshi imiron: Gengo to ninchi no setten* [Verb semantics: The interface of language and cognition]. Tokyo: Kurosio Publishers.
Kim, Yong-Suk. 2004. VN *suru* no jita kōtai to saikisei [Intransitive-transitive alternation in VN *suru* and reflexivity]. *Nihongo Bunpō* 4 (2). 89–102.
Kobayashi, Hideki. 2004. *Gendaigo no kango dōmeishi no kenkyū* [A study of Sino-Japanese verbal nouns in Modern Japanese]. Tokyo: Hitsuji Shobō.
Koizumi, Tamotsu, Michio Funaki, Kyōji Honda, Yoshio Nitta & Hideki Tsukamoto (eds.). 1989. *Nihongo kihon dōshi yōhō jiten* [Usage dictionary of Japanese basic verbs]. Tokyo: Taishūkan Shoten.
Kōjien = Niimura, Ide (ed). 1991. *Kōjien*. 4th ed. Tokyo: Iwanami Shoten.
Kuginuki, Tōru. 1996. *Kodai Nihongo no keitai henka* [Morphological change in Classical Japanese]. Tokyo: Izumi Shoin.
Martin, Samuel E. 1987. *The Japanese language through time*. New Haven: Yale University Press.
Miura, Yūki. 2005. Nihongo tadōshibun no kakutoku – dōshi ippanteki na chishiki e no dankaiteki hattatsu [The acquisition of the Japanese transitive clause – the gradual development of general knowledge about verbs]. *Nihon Gengo Gakkai Dai-130-kai Taikai Yokōshū*, 128–133. The Linguistic Society of Japan.
Möhlig, Ruth & Monika Klages. 2002. Detransitivization in the history of English from a semantic perspective. In Teresa Fanego et al. (eds.) *English historical syntax and morphology (Selected papers from 11 ICEHL, Santiago de Compostela, 7–11 September 2000)*, 231–254. Amsterdam: John Benjamins.
Morita, Yoshiyuki. 1994 (1990). Jita dōkei dōshi no mondai [The problem of homomorphous intransitive-transitive verbs]. Originally published in *Kokubun Kenkyū* 102; reprinted in Yoshiyuki Morita. *Dōshi no imironteki bunpō kenkyū* [Studies on the semantic grammar of verbs], 232–252. Tokyo: Meiji Shoin, 1994.

Moto'ori, Haruniwa. 1902 (1828). Kotoba no kayoiji [Ways to words]. Originally published 1828. Reprinted in *Motoori Nobunaga zenshū* [Collected works of Motoori Nobunaga] 11, 55–122. Tokyo: Yoshikawa Kōbunkan.
Narrog, Heiko. 1998. Nihongo dōshi no katsuyō taikei [The inflection system of Japanese verbs]. *Nihongo Kagaku* 4. 7–30.
Narrog, Heiko. 2004. From transitive to causative in Japanese: Morphologization through exaptation. *Diachronica* 21 (2). 351–392.
Narrog, Heiko. 2007a. Nihongo no jita dōshi-tsui no ruikeironteki ichi-zuke [The typological position of Japanese transitivity pairs]. In Taro Kageyama (ed.), *Lexicon Forum No. 3*, 161–193. Tokyo: Hituzi Syobo.
Narrog, Heiko. 2007b. Nihongo jita dōshi ni okeru yūhyōsei-sa no dōki-zuke [On the motivation for markedness differences in Japanese transitivity verb pairs]. In Mie Tsunoda, Kan Sasaki & Tooru Shionoya (eds), *Tadōsei no tsūgengoteki kenkyū – Tsunoda Tasaku Hakase kanreki kinen ronbunshū* [Cross-linguistic studies of transitivity – A festschrift for the 60th birthday of Dr. Tsunoda Tasaku], 295–306. Tokyo: Kurosio Publishers.
Nedyalkov, Vladimir P. & Georgij G. Silnitsky. 1973. The typology of morphological and lexical causatives. In Ferenc Kiefer (ed.), *Trends in Soviet theoretical linguistics*, 1–32. Dordrecht: D. Reidel.
Nichols, Johanna. 1993. Transitive and causative in the Slavic lexicon: Evidence from Russian. In Bernard Comrie and Maria Polinsky (eds.), *Causatives and transitivity*, 69–86. Amsterdam: Benjamins.
Nichols, Johanna, David A. Peterson & Jonathan Barnes. 2004. Transitivizing and detransitivizing languages. *Linguistic Typology* 8. 149–211.
Nishio, Toraya. 1988 (1954). Dōshi no hasei ni tsuite – jita tairitsu no kata ni yoru [On the derivation of verbs, based on the patterns of intransitive-transitive verbs]. Originally published in *Kokugogaku* 17 (1954); reprinted in Toraya Nishio: *Gendai goi no kenkyū* [Studies on the contemporary lexicon], 149–170. Tokyo: Meiji Shoin.
Nishio, Toraya. 1988 (1982). Jidōshi to tadōshi – taiō suru mono to shinai mono [Intransitive verbs and transitive verbs – verbs with corresponding verbs and verbs without]. Originally published in *Nihongo Kyōiku* 42; reprinted in Toraya Nishio: *Gendai goi no kenkyū* [Studies on the contemporary lexicon], 192–206. Tokyo: Meiji Shoin, 1988.
Nishiyama, Kunio. 2000. Jita kōtai to keitairon [The morphology of intransitive-transitive alternations]. In Tadao Maruta & Kazuyoshi Suga (eds.), *Nichieigo no jita no kōtai* [Transitivity alternations in Japanese and English], 145–165. Tokyo: Hituzi Syobo.
NKD = *Nihon kokugo daijiten* [Shogakukan unabridged dictionary of the Japanese language]. 2000–2002. 14 vols. 2nd edn. Edited by the Nihon Kokugo Daijiten Henshū Iinkai. Tōkyō: Shōgakukan.
Noda, Hisashi. 1991. Bunpōteki na voisu to goiteki na voisu no kankei [The relation between grammatical and lexical voice]. In Yoshio Nitta (ed.), *Nihongo no voisu to tadōsei* [Japanese Voice and Transitivity], 211–232. Tokyo: Kurosio Publishers.
Okutsu, Keiichirō. 1967. Jidōka, tadōka oyobi ryōkyokuka tenkei – ji-tadōshi no taiō [Intransitivization, transitivization and bi-directionality – the correspondences of intransitive-transitive verbs]. *Kokugogaku* 70. 46–66.
Rickmeyer, Jens. 1995. *Japanische Morphosyntax*. Heidelberg: Julius Groos.
Robbeets, Martine. 2007. The causative-passive in the Trans-Eurasian languages. *Turkic Languages* 11. 235–278.

Robbeets, Martine. 2010. Trans-Eurasian: Can verbal morphology end the controversy? In Lars Johanson & Martine Robbeets (eds), *Verbal morphology and the historical comparison of the Transeurasian languages*, 81–114. Wiesbaden: Harrassowitz.

Shimada, Akihiko. 1979. *Kokugo ni okeru jidōshi to tadōshi* [Intransitive and transitive verbs in the Japanese Language]. Tokyo: Meiji Shoin.

Suga, Kazuyoshi & Emiko Hayatsu (eds.). 1995. *Dōshi no jita* [Intransitive and transitive in verbs]. Tokyo: Hituzi Syobo.

Unger, J. Marshall. 2000. Reconciling comparative and internal reconstruction: The case of Old Japanese /ti, ri, ni/. *Language* 76 (3). 655–681.

Whitman, John. 2008. The source of the bigrade conjugation and stem shape in pre-Old Japanese. In Bjarke Frellesvig & John Whitman (eds.), *Proto-Japanese: Issues and prospects*, 159–173. Amsterdam & Philadelphia: Benjamins.

Yoshida, Kanehiko. 1973. *Jōdaigo jodōshi no shiteki kenkyū* [Historical studies on the Old Japanese auxiliaries]. Tokyo: Meiji Shoin.

Bjarke Frellesvig and John Whitman
9 The historical source of the bigrade transitivity alternations in Japanese

1 Introduction

A well-known feature of the Japanese verbal lexicon is the existence of transitivity alternations associated with differences in stem shape. Alternations between vowel (Old Japanese bigrade) and consonant (OJ quadrigrade) stems are of particular interest, because the valency of the stem is not predictable by its shape: some transitive vowel stem verbs (such as *tate-* 'stand it up') are paired with an intransitive consonant stem (*tat-* 'stand'), but at the same time some intransitive vowel stems (such as *sake-* 'split') are paired with a transitive consonant stem (*sak-* 'split it'). In each case the vowel stem appears derived, but which stem is transitive and which is intransitive is unpredictable. As Murasugi (this volume) shows, these alternations are mastered only at a later stage of first language acquisition, but the alternations occur with mostly slight variation across Japanese languages and dialects, and they appear in the oldest attested form of Japanese, Old Japanese of the 8th century. In this chapter we reconstruct a diachronic source for the stem shape-based transitivity alternation in Japanese.

Our account revives an insight that dates back at least 60 years among Japanese historical linguists, but that has gone unnoticed in the typologically informed literature on Japanese transitivity alternations. This is that the transitivity alternations originate as an **acquisitive** pattern, involving grammaticalization of the verb 'get'. The account also contributes to a revised understanding of reconstructed post-proto Japanese; specifically, that an older layer of verbal derivation in Japanese resulted from V1–V2 patterns where V2 was attached directly to the basic stem (root) of V1, unlike later stages of the language where verbal derivation requires a derived stem (primarily the infinitive) of V1. We call this pattern in post-proto Japanese *direct stem affixation*. We argue that the consonant stem – vowel stem alternation derives from combination of the basic stem (root) of V1 with the verb *e-* 'get'. This combination results in the subregularities that survive to this day: transitive accomplishment verbs from the combination of 'get' with intransitive achievements, and a smaller number of anticausative intransitives from the combination of 'get' with transitives. We

Bjarke Frellesvig, University of Oxford
John Whitman, Cornell University

also discuss the relationship of the 'get' derivation with other patterns of direct stem affixation at the proto-Japanese level. Combinations of Vstem1 + *ar- (probably cognate with the verb ar- 'exist') derive stative intransitives. Combinations of Vstem1 + *s- (possibly cognate with *sə- 'do') derive causative transitives. *-s- was used primarily to derive transitives from stative roots, but also, we argue, was subject to phonological restrictions on its use. *e- 'get' was used in part to supplete for transitivizing *-s- after consonant stems. Some of the semantic overlap between transitives derived by *-s- and *-e- results from their original suppletive relation, as discussed in 5.4.

We show that direct stem affixation related to transitivity alternations involves two distinct layers. The pattern with intransitive *ar- and transitivizing *s- is older. The -(a)r-/-s- alternation is already fully lexicalized by Old Japanese, and probably was well before that period. It is fully attested in all Japonic varieties, including Ryukyuan.

The alternation involving *e- 'get' is more recent. Prior to OJ, *-e- replaced *-s- as a transitivizer. We see some evidence of the expansion of transitivizing -e- even in OJ, although -e- too has ceased to be fully productive by the OJ stage.

The relation between transitivizing and detransitivizing *-e- is complex, but we present an account compatible with the relatively limited scope of the latter pattern. Our central point is that all functions of this morpheme are compatible with well-known grammaticalization paths for 'get'.

For this chapter we use data from the earliest attested stage of Japanese, Old Japanese (abbreviated OJ; in Japanese *jōdaigo* 上代語), which mainly reflects the language of the 8th century spoken in and around the then capital, Nara, in the Kansai region.[1] Texts from the OJ period also comprise material that pre-dates the 8th century, but is included in texts written or compiled in the 8th century, and also some eastern dialect material. The majority of texts from the OJ period are poetry, which is also the only written genre from the time with significant amounts of phonologically written text; needless to say, only phonographically written text can give reliable information about the actual shapes of words, and therefore about the actually attested patterns of alternation between related verbs.[2] We have accessed and searched the texts through the Oxford Corpus of Old Japanese (see http://vsarpj.orinst.ox.ac.uk/corpus/), an electronic annotated

---

[1] Later periods of Japanese are as follows: Early Middle Japanese 800 – 1200 (EMJ; *chūkogo* 中古語); Late Middle Japanese 1200–1600 (LMJ; *chūseigo* 中世語); Modern Japanese from 1600 (NJ; *kindaigo* 近代語, *gendaigo* 現代語). See further Frellesvig 2010.

[2] The main poetic texts are: *Kojiki kayō* (古事記歌謡, abbreviated KK; 712), *Nihon shoki kayō* (日本書紀歌謡; 720), *Fudoki kayō* (風土記歌謡; 730s), *Bussukoseki-ka* (仏足石歌; after 753), *Man'yōshū* (万葉集, MYS; after 759); *Shoku nihongi kayō* (続日本紀歌謡; 797).

corpus of Old Japanese which comprises all poetic texts from the Old Japanese period, approximately 90,000 words.

2 Transitivity alternations in Old Japanese

A well known feature of the Japanese verbal lexicon is the existence of transitivity alternations associated with differences in stem shape. We briefly review the main alternations found in OJ. The same alternations are mostly also found in NJ (Modern Japanese), but the lexical distribution, frequency and balance differ in some important respects; we summarize the distribution of the different patterns in section 2.1 below. As in NJ, some of these alternations involve derivational morphology with positively defined transitivity value, in particular transitive *-s-* and intransitive *-r-*, sometimes in alternation with simple stems, sometimes alternating with each other, e.g. (1).

(1) Simple   -s- Transitive   -r- Intransitive
     tir-   *tiras-*
     'scatter (i)'   'scatter (t)'
               watas-   *watar-*
               'make go across'   'go across'
               nas-   *nar-*
               'make'   'become'

A pattern of particular interest involves alternations between a simple quadrigrade verb and a derived bigrade verb.[3] In these cases the transitivity of the members of each derivational pair is not strictly predictable from the shape of the stems. See (2).

(2)   <u>Quadrigrade</u>   <u>Bigrade</u>
      Intransitive   Transitive
      tat-   *tate-*
      'rise, set out'   'raise'

      Transitive   Intransitive
      yak-   *yake-*
      'burn'   'burn'

---

3 Quadrigrade (*yodan*) and bigrade (*nidan*) refer to the two major conjugations of OJ. See Frellesvig (2010) for a description of these conjugations and OJ verbal morphology more generally. Quadrigrade and bigrade verbs are the ancestors of NJ consonant and vowel stem verbs respectively.

However, of these two alternations, the one exemplified in (4)–(5), between an intransitive quadrigrade verb and a transitive bigrade verb, is the main pattern, fairly well attested for OJ.[4]

(4) *tat-* 'rise, set out'
能許　乃　宇良　奈美　多多奴　日　者
*noko　no　ura　nami　tata-nu　*pi　pa
Noko　GEN　bay　wave　rise-NEG　day　TOP
'a day when the waves are not rising in the Noko Bay' (MYS 15.3670)

(5) *tate-* 'raise (trans.)'
世　　　人　　能　多都流　許等
yo　　　no　pito　no　taturu　koto
world　GEN　people　GEN　raise　word
'what people say' (MYS 18.4106)

The second pattern of alternation is between a transitive quadrigrade verb and an intransitive bigrade verb, exemplified in (6)–(7). However, although their number increases in following periods of the language, there are in fact only a few examples of this pattern in OJ.

(6) *yak-* 'burn (trans.)'
加良怒　　　　袁　志本　爾　夜岐
karanwo　　　wo　sipo　ni　yaki
karano(boat)　ACC　salt　into　burn
'burn the *Karano* boat to make salt' (KK 74)

(7) *yake-* 'burn (intr.)'
夜気牟　　　志婆加岐
yake-mu　　sibakaki
burn-CONJ　brushwood.fence
'the brushwood fence which will burn' (KK 109)

In addition to these two morphologically simple alternation patterns, other, more frequent, alternating patterns include bigrade verbs alternating with verbs

---

4 When citing textual examples from OJ we include original script. Our transcription is phonemic and follows the Frellesvig & Whitman system (see Frellesvig & Whitman 2008). Text which is phonographically written is transcribed in *italics* (e.g. '*noko*' in (4)), whereas logographically written text is transcribed in plain type (e.g. 'pi' in (4)).

that themselves involve derivational transitivity material, for example transitive bigrade verbs alternating with intransitive -r- derivatives, (8), or intransitive bigrade verbs alternating with transitive -s-, (9).

(8) Bigrade transitives   -r- intransitives
    kasane- 'pile up'   *kasanar-* 'increase'
    tome- 'stop'   *tomar-* 'stop'

(9) Bigrade transitives   -s- transitives
    ide- 'emerge'   *idas-* 'take, put out'
    kure- grow dark'   *kuras-* 'spend (time)'

There is also a binary transitivity alternation pattern involving intransitive -r- alternating with transitive -s-, with no bigrade verb involved.

(10) -r- intransitives   -s- transitives
      amar- 'remain'   *amas-* 'leave over'

Finally, in addition to these simple, binary alternations, there are some examples of a fuller set of alternating verbs, such as (11), although these are very few.

(11) Simple quadrigrade *kap-*   'mix (intr.), buy, change (intr.)'
     Bigrade   *kape-*   'change (tr.)'
     -r-   *kapar-* 'change (intr.), succeed'
     -s-   *kapas-* 'switch (tr.)'

2.1 Lexical distribution of transitivity patterns

The volume of text from the Old Japanese period is not great and generalizations based on numbers must often be treated with some caution. However, as mentioned above, the distribution of the different patterns of derivation and alternation is in some respects discernibly unequal in the OJ lexicon. Based on the poetic texts in the Oxford Corpus of Old Japanese, the figures for the main binary (two-member) patterns in Old Japanese are as shown in Table 1.[5] The first number for each pattern is the number of alternating pairs where both members are phonographically attested; the number in brackets is the additional number

---

[5] Incidentally, there are no clear OJ examples of the type ...CVC => ...CVCVr-, where -(a)r- derives an intransitive verb from a transitive consonant base verb. Rather, derivations in -(a)r- seem first and foremost to be stative and not primarily related to transitivity.

of pairs where only one member is phonographically attested, but attestation of the other reflects reading tradition of logographically written text.[6]

Table 1: Main patterns of transitivity alternations in Old Japanese

types	alternating patterns			number of pairs
a.[7]	Intransitive …CVC- e.g. *tat-* 'rise, set out'	=>	Transitive …CVCe- *tate-* 'raise'	23 (9)
b.	Transitive …CVC- e.g. *sak-* 'split it'	=>	Intransitive … CVCe- *sake-* 'split'	5 (2)
c.	…CVC- e.g. *ter-* 'shine (intr.)'	=>	…CVCVs- *teras-* 'light it up (tr.)'	5 (2)
d.	…CVCe- e.g. *age-* 'raise'	~	…CVCVr- *agar-* 'rise'	6 (5)
e.	…CVCe- e.g. *ide-* 'go out'	~	…CVCVs- *idas-* 'put out'	7 (1)
f.	…CVCr- e.g. *kudar-* 'go down'	~	…CVCVs- *kudas-* 'take down'	8 (2)

3 Basic facts about the bigrade conjugation class

Before discussing the origin of the bigrade conjugation class, and in particular the transitivity alternations involving bigrade verbs, we outline basic facts about the bigrade classes in OJ (see for details further Frellesvig 2008, 2010: 96 ff.; Whitman 2008). There are two distinct bigrade conjugation classes, upper bigrade (in Japanese *kami nidan* 上二段), whose stems end in *-(w)i-*, and lower bigrade (*shimo nidan* 下二段) with stems ending in *-e-*. The two subclasses are very different in distribution and with regard to transitivity alternations.

First, the lexical distribution of the three main OJ verb conjugation classes is as shown in (12). As shown, the lower bigrade class is lexically far more frequent than the upper bigrade class.

---

[6] Kuginuki (1996: 247) gives 50 OJ examples of the intransitive quadrigrade : transitive bigrade pattern in (4–5) (his pattern I.1) and 10 examples of the transitive quadrigrade : intransitive pattern in (6–7) (his I.2). The literature includes several lists of OJ transitivity alternation patterns, including Kida (1988) and Narrog (this volume), but such lists usually uncritically cite verbs as attested in OJ, regardless of whether they are in fact phonographically attested in OJ or not.

[7] This pattern includes causative derivations from transitive verbs, e.g. *mot-* 'hold' => *mote-* 'make hold'.

(12) Quadrigrade (stems ending in consonants):   c. 75% of OJ verbs
    Lower bigrade (stems ending in -*e*-):   c. 20% of OJ verbs
    Upper bigrade (stems ending in -*(w)i*-):   less than 4% of OJ verbs

Second, not all bigrade verbs take part in transitivity alternations. Only (but far from all) lower bigrade verbs take part in transitivity alternations with simple quadrigrade verbs, whereas upper bigrade verbs do not. Finally, it must be mentioned that the bigrade conjugation is a fairly young conjugation type in the language that emerged only fairly shortly before the OJ period (see Frellesvig 2008 for details).

4 Previous accounts of the origin of the bigrade conjugation

A number of accounts of the origin of the bigrade conjugation class(es) have been proposed. The main previous accounts that we will mention here are by Ohno (1953 [discussed in Section 4.1]) and Unger (1977 [Section 4.2]). See Frellesvig (2008) for a more detailed overview than the one presented here.

4.1 Ohno 1953

In Ohno's (1953) seminal study on the origin of verb inflection in Japanese he proposed that the difference between bigrade and quadrigrade conjugations corresponds to differences in root shape, such that quadrigrade verbs reflect closed (consonant final, *CVC-) roots, whereas bigrade verbs reflect open (vowel final, *CV- and *CVCV-) roots. Ohno's account has been influential,[8] but it gives no account of the transitivity alternations in which the bigrade verbs participate.

4.2 Unger 1977

The first significant alternative to Ohno's account was proposed by Unger in his Yale University dissertation (available as Unger 1977/1993). According to Unger

---

[8] Not least in disseminating within the scholarly community in Japan the synchronic analysis of verb stems, also in NJ, as consonant or vowel final, an analysis which cannot be expressed in the traditional *katsuyōkei* system.

all pJ verb roots were open (of the shape *CV- or *CVCV-). On this proposal, OJ quadrigrade verbs represent a reanalysis of *CVCV- roots as CVC-, whereas bigrade verbs reflect CV- and CVCV- roots augmented with a derivational morpheme whose function was to switch or flip the transitivity of the root. Unger reconstructs this morpheme, affectionately known as the 'transitivity flipper', as *-gi, and proposes to account for the OJ shape of bigrade verbs by various sound changes (consonant loss and vowel contraction): *CVCV-gi > *CVCVi > CVCV-, thereby also accounting for the transitivity alternations which bigrade verbs participate in, e.g.

(13)   *tata 'rise' + -gi- =>   *tatagi- 'raise' >   *tatai- >   tate-
       *yaka 'burn (tr.)' + -gi- =>   *yakagi- 'burn (intr.)' >   *yakai- >   yake-

The proposal that bigrade vebs incorporate and lexicalize additional morphological material has become widely accepted, but both the hypothesis that all pJ roots were open as well as the proposed identity and function of the additional derivational material have since been rejected. We follow here the view that pJ roots could be both open and closed (Unger 2000; Whitman 2008 for details). More central to this chapter is the observation that the 'transitivity flipper' hypothesis does not work as an account of the origin of the bigrade conjugation. Several facts tell us this: first, upper bigrade verbs do not take part in transitivity alternations with simple quadrigrade verbs, and only a minority of lower bigrade verbs do so, making clear that transitivity flipping is not an essential part of the bigrade conjugation. Second, some auxiliaries which belong to the bigrade conjugation are morphologizations of derivational suffixes with the same valency, e.g. the passive auxiliary -re- which diachronically derives from the intransitivizing derivational suffix -r-; or the causative auxiliary -se- which comes from the transitivizing derivational morpheme -s-, again showing that there is no bi-unique relation between bigrade conjugation and transitivity flipping.[9]

5 The GET hypothesis

We turn now to a proposal articulated by Whitman (2008), that the transitivity alternating bigrade verbs originate in the suffixation of the verb e- 'get' to the

---

9 Further difficulties with the *gi "transitivity flipper" hypothesis are discussed in Whitman 2008. An additional problem raised for this hypothesis by the facts discussed in this chapter is that it has no account for bigrade -e- stems such as those in (24), which are derived from noun, not verb stems. The acquisitive hypothesis accounts for these straightforwardly.

basic stem (or root) of quadrigrade verbs,[10] as in (14). It should be noted that the idea that bigrade verbs originate from *e- 'get' has a long history. Both Takeda (1953) and Yoshida (1973) make this suggestion, Yoshida making the point that both the form and meaning of *e- 'get' fit, without elaborating further.

(14) tat- 'rise' + e- 'get' =>   tate- 'raise'
      yak- 'burn (tr.)' + e- 'get' => yake- 'burn (intr.)'

5.1 The GET hypothesis: Form

First of all, e- 'get' and other lower Bigrade verbs conjugate identically. More significantly, e- 'get' is identical to the ending of all lower bigrade verbs. In this sense, e- 'get' **is** the lower bigrade conjugation, see (15).

(15)

	'get'	'raise'	'burn'
Basic stem (語幹)	e-	tate-	yake-
Infinitive (連用形)	e	tate	yake
Conclusive (終止形)	u	tatu	yaku
Adnominal (連体形)	uru	taturu	yakuru
Exclamatory (已然形)	ure	tature	yakure
Imperative (命令形)	eyo	tateyo	yakeyo

On the direct stem affixation hypothesis, e- 'get' attached directly to the basic stem (root) of another verb. This is different from most later patterns of compounding or affixation to a verb stem, where a derived stem of V1 in a V1–V2 compound generally was used. There are, however, other examples in Japanese of synchronic direct stem affixation, including (a) the affixation of the OJ stative auxiliary -yeri to consonant stem verbs: sak- 'come into bloom' + -yeri => sakyeri 'be in bloom';[11] or (b) in pre-OJ, affixation of the negative auxiliary *-anu: *sak- 'come into bloom' + *-anu => *sakanu 'doesn't bloom' (Ohno 1953).[12] Our hypothesis here is that V+e- is a further example of direct stem affixation. We show

---

[10] Frellesvig (2008) and Whitman (2008) present different accounts of the origin of the bigrade conjugation as such, but both incorporate Whitman's proposal of the origin of the transitivity alternating bigrade verbs.
[11] As is well known, the OJ Stative auxiliary –yeri diachronically derives from contraction and resegmentation of a construction involving the ancestor of the OJ infinitive followed by the existential verb ari, e.g., *saki ari 'be in bloom' > *sakyeri, but synchronically in OJ the morphological structure was clearly sak-yeri, i.e., an example of synchronic direct stem affixation.
[12] Negative forms like sakanu were later, still in pre-OJ, resegmented and in OJ had the structure saka-nu; see Frellesvig 2008:184f for details.

in 5.3 that V+*e* instantiates a well-established pattern in OJ: incorporation of a secondary predicate into a main verb.

5.2 The GET hypothesis: Function

OJ *e*- functioned as a transitive lexical verb 'get, acquire', and as a potential auxiliary verb in both pre- and postverbal position. The latter two exemplify a widely attested modal development from acquisitives (see van der Auwera et al. 2009), but here we are interested in the first function.

Our hypothesis requires a clarification of the meaning and structure associated with acquisitive verbs such as *get*. The syntax/semantics literature analyzes *get* as an aspectual variant of *have* (Gronemeyer 1999; Richards 2001; Harley 2004; McIntyre 2005). For the sake of explicitness, we adapt the view of Richards and Harley, that *get* decomposes into an aspectual predicate BECOME and *have*:

(16) [$_{AspP}$ BECOME [$_{vP}$ Naomi has a new house]]
'Naomi gets a new house.'

Using this basic approach, we represent the three basic meanings of *get* distinguished by Gronemeyer (1999):

(17) a. Agentive 'obtain'
          $_{AspP}$[BECOME $_{vP}$[NP$_{AGENT}$ *v* $_{VP}$[HAVE NP$_{THEME}$]]]

      b. Locative 'acquire'
          $_{AspP}$[BECOME $_{vP}$[*v* $_{VP}$[NP$_{GOAL}$ *v'*[HAVE NP$_{THEME}$]]]]

      c. Secondary predication '*get* NP XP'
          $_{AspP}$[BECOME $_{vP}$[NP$_{AGENT/GOAL}$ *v* $_{VP}$[NP$_{THEME}$[HAVE XP]]]]

(17a) is the case of agentive *get* in "Naomi got a dog." (b) is the case of non-agentive "Naomi got a cold." Both of these patterns are attested in OJ, as shown by examples (18) and (19) below. Pattern (c) is the case of *get* NP plus a secondary predicate (XP), *Kei gets Naomi out of the house/drunk* and intransitive *Naomi gets drunk/out of the house*. As we show in section 6, this pattern is the crosslinguistic source of diathetic aquisitives (valency altering combinations with *get* and similar verbs of acquisition). Acquisitives combine with secondary predicates to derive patterns like transitive *get NP out of the house/drunk* and intransitive *NP gets drunk/out of the house*. The OJ lexical verb *e-* attests the secondary predication pattern in (c) as well (see (20)). Thus, as an independent lexical verb OJ *e-* 'get' had all three of the basic patterns in (17).

(18) 須理夫久路　伊麻波　衣天之可
　　 suri-bukurwo   ima pa   e-tesika
　　 suri-bag   now TOP   get-OPT
　　 'Would that (I) had gotten a *suri* bag!' (MYS 18.4133)

(18) is agentive transitive *get*: the *pro* subject actively wants to get the bag.

(19) 山人　　　　　乃　和礼　爾　衣志米之
　　 yamabito   *no* *ware* *ni*   *e-sime-si*
　　 mountain.person GEN I   DAT   get-CAUS-PST
　　 夜麻都刀　　　曾
　　 yamadutwo   *so*
　　 mountain.souvenir FOC
　　 'This is the mountain souvenir which the mountain dweller made me get (gave me)' (MYS 20.4293)

(19) is non-agentive transitive *get*: *ware* 'I' is a recipient/goal, who acquires a souvenir through the agency of the mountain dweller.

(20) 可里乎　　都可比　　尓　　　衣弖之　可母
　　 kari wo   *tukapi*   *ni*   *e-tesika* *mo*
　　 goose ACC messenger   be.INF get-OPT   even
　　 'Would that I had gotten the wild geese as messengers!' (MYS 15.3676)

(20) is agentive transitive *get* with a secondary predicate, *tukapi ni* 'as messenger'. The secondary predicate is formed from *tukapi* 'messenger' and the infinitive of the defective copula *ni* 'to be'. Note that the speaker/subject in this example does not actually want to get the geese; s/he wants to *get them to be messengers*. The sentence renders perfectly as an English *get* causative. The pattern in OJ is analytic, formed from a nominal predicate and the infinitive of the copula, but the example shows that *e-* as an independent verb continued to have the transitive secondary predication pattern of (17c) in OJ. This is exactly the pattern we want for transitivizing **e-*.

5.3 Incorporated secondary predicates in OJ

OJ had a second strategy in addition to the infinitive of the copula for licensing secondary predicates: incorporation into the lexical verb. For example, the noun *yoko* 'side' is incorporated in the verbs *yokosarap-* 'go sideways' and *yokotape-* 'put on its side'.[13] The first verb is derived from the verb *sar-* 'go' plus the activity verb derivative *-ap-*, incorporating *yoko* 'side'.[14] Similar examples are *sakanobor-* 'go against the current' from *nobor-* 'climb' incorporating *saka* 'backward', and *sakapagi-* 'flay inside out', from *pag-* 'flay' incorporating *saka*.[15] All of these verbs involve the pattern NP_{THEME} XP V, where XP is the secondary predicate that incorporates into the verb.

A similar pattern of incorporation can be found with secondary predicates like *kata* 'one of a pair, alone,' as in *katasik-* 'lay out alone', from *sik-* 'lay out' incorporating *kata*:

(21) 其呂母蘇弖　加多思吉弖
koromoswode　kata+siki-te
robe　　　　　alone lay.out-GER
'laying out (my) robe alone' (MYS 15.3625)

Here *kata* 'alone' is predicated of the theme object *koromoswode* 'robe.'

Finally, we can find examples of uninflected adjectives as incorporated secondary predicates. Examples include *takasik-* 'administer high and grand', from *sik-* 'spread out, rule' incorporating *taka* 'high', and *takasir-* 'build, establish high and grand', from *sir-* 'know, rule' and *taka*:[16]

(22) 此　山　　乃　弥　高思良珠　　　　水　　激
kono yama　no　iya　taka+sira-su　　midu tagitu
this mountain GEN very tall+build-RESP water flow.fast

瀧　　　　之　宮子
taki　　　no　miyakwo
waterfall GEN palace

'the palace in these mountains, which (the emperor) built very tall, with water running in its waterfalls' (MYS1.36)

---

13 Only the first of these verbs is attested phonographically in OJ.
14 For the activity verb derivative *-ap-*, see Frellesvig (2010: 52). The basic verb *sar-* 'go, depart' does not appear with *-ap-*, presumably because it is difficult to generate an activity reading for 'go'. 'Go sideways', on the other hand, is a robust activity verb.
15 Only the first of these verbs is attested phonographically in OJ.
16 Only the second of these verbs is attested partly phonographically in OJ.

In (22) it is the palace which is tall, just as in (21) it is the robe that is by itself. In all of the above cases, the incorporated item is predicated of the innermost argument.

Given that the lexical verb *e-* 'get' occurs in the transitive secondary predicate pattern of (20), we should not be surprised to find that it also occurs in the incorporated secondary predicate pattern. As we pointed out at the end of section 4, the bigrade formative *-e-* is not restricted to attaching to lexical verbs. Even among verb pairs involving a transitivity alternation one of whose members is formed with, *-e-*, the stem cannot always be traced back to a verb stem. This is particularly true of pairs built on intransitive *-(a)r* and transitive *-e-*, as in (8). Let us look at some additional examples of this type:

(23) | *Bigrade transitives* | *-r-* intransitives | Related stem |
| --- | --- | --- |
| *mage-* 'curve' | *magar-* 'curve' | *maga* 'curved, curve' |
| *wope-* 'end' | *wopar-* 'end' | *wo* 'tail' |
| *ate-* 'touch' | *atar-*[17] 'touch' | *ata* 'span between thumb and middle finger' |

There is no evidence for verb stems *mag-* 'curve', *wop-* 'end', or *at-* 'touch', and if such verb stems existed, it is not clear what they would mean, since the intransitive state sense is expressed by the *-r-* intransitives. Given that *-(a)r- was the standard device for deriving stative verbs from noninflecting stems, it makes more sense to posit a noninflecting stem as the source for the pairs in (8) and (23). On this view, the source for transitive *mage-* and intransitive *magar-* is as in (24), where noninflecting stems are incorporated secondary predicates:

(24) | Stem | Bigrade intransitive | *-r-* intransitive |
| --- | --- | --- |
| *maga* 'curve' | *maga+e-* 'get a curve, get curved' | *maga+r-* 'have a curve' |
| **wop* 'tail, end' | *wop+e-* 'get an end, get ended' | *wop+ar* 'have an end' |
| *ata* 'touch' | *ata+e-* 'get a touch' | *ata-r* 'have a touch' |

5.4 The GET hypothesis: A diachronic scenario

We have shown that *-e-* 'get' derived some transitivizing bigrade verbs by incorporating noninflecting stems as secondary predicates. The underlying pattern is the transitive secondary predicate pattern in (17c), synchronically attested by the OJ analytic or nonincorporated structure in (20). It is but a short step from

---

[17] *Atar-* is not phonographically attested in OJ.

incorporating noninflecting stems to incorporating uninflected verb stems, the core of the GET hypothesis in (14). It is difficult to tell which derivation came first, but the typological evidence on diathetic acquisitives discussed in section (6) suggests that the pattern incorporating noninflecting (nonverbal) stems came first.

One of the biggest challenges for diachronic and synchronic analyses of the Japanese transitivity alternations is specifying the factors distinguishing transitivizing -e- and transitivizing -s- (see Jacobsen 1988, 1992 for a treatment of this opposition in Modern Japanese). From a diachronic standpoint, the difference between these two strategies is that (a) -s- is older (b) -s- is phonologically more restricted.

The -s- pattern appears to have been the standard way of deriving transitive verbs from uninflected adjective stems.

(25) Uninflected adjective stem -s- transitive
   kura 'dark, red'   *kuras-* 'make dark, redden'
   opo 'big'   *opos-* 'raise, bring up'
   ara 'rough, barren'   *aras-* 'lay waste to'

Examples where bigrade -e- derives a transitive from an adjectival root, in contrast, are nonexistent.[18]

However, transitivizing -s- appears to have been phonologically restricted. It attaches to vowel stems, such as the uninflected adjectives in (25). Since OJ disallows consonant clusters, attachment to consonant stems would have required some phonological adjustment. There is evidence that -s- also derived transitives from simple *r*-stems, with deletion of final /r/. This is provided by examples like *yos-* 'bring near'. It is unlikely that the corresponding intransitive *yor-* 'approach' is derived, as there is no stem *yo-* in this meaning. Similar examples are *kas-* 'lend' : *kar-* 'borrow' and *tas-* 'add'[19] : *tar-* 'suffice, be full'.

If this idea is correct, -s- derived transitives in at least the two patterns in (26) in pre-OJ:

(26) Transitivization by -s- (Pre-OJ)
  a. (CVC)V- + -s- > (CVC)Vs *kura* 'dark' + -s- > *kuras-* 'make dark'
  b. (CVC)Vr- + -s- > (CVC)Vs *yor-* 'approach' + -s- > *yos-* 'bring near'

---

[18] Transitive *mage-* 'curve, bend': *maga* 'curve(d), bent' is the only clear, potential example. But as pointed out in 5.3, *maga* was a noun, with the meaning 'curve, bend'.
[19] *Tas-* 'add' is not attested in OJ.

The derivational option in (26b) explains the (admittedly small) number of sets in OJ involving a consonant stem, an *-r-* intransitive, and an *-s-* transitive, such as those built on *kap-* 'mix, buy, change' in (11). The root verb *kap-* is quintessentially labile, with transitive and intransitive meanings. *Kapar-* (intr.) is derived by affixation of intransitivizing *-ar-*, which gives the meanings 'change, change places with, succeed (chronologically)'.[20] Transitive *kapas-* is derived from *kapar-* by the process in (26b), deleting stem-final *r before *-s-. This example shows the relationship between pre-OJ intransitivizing *-ar- and transitivizing *-s-. From the original labile stem *kap-, intransitivizing *-ar- derives the intransitive meaning 'change, switch (intr.)'. Transitivizing *-s- derives 'switch (tr.)' from the latter; were *kapas-* derived directly from *kap-*, we might expect it to mean 'make buy' or 'make mix'.

Transitive *kape-* 'change (tr.)', on the other hand, directly incorporates the stem **kap-* into *-e- 'get'. Its meaning is composed from the meaning 'change' of the original stem. This example gives us a glimpse of the original division of labor between *-s- and *-e-: the restriction of *-s- to vowel and -r- stems had the result that it transitivized primarily statives, particularly uninflected adjectives. Transitivizing -e-, on the other hand, was subject to no restriction. It therefore suppleted for *-s- as a transitivizer after consonant stems. As predicted by its origin as an acquisitive, its function was valency increasing, not merely transitivizing. Thus we find ditransitive formations in -e- such as *pame-* 'throw into' from *pam-* 'eat' + -e-, and *aduke-* 'entrust to' from *aduk-* 'take into one's care' + -e-.

There is a diachronic link between the original suppletive relation between *-s- and *-e- and Matsumoto's (2000) argument that the distribution of transitivizing -s versus -e in Modern Japanese is phonologically, rather than semantically determined. Matsumoto observes for modern Japanese that "-e can be suffixed only to intransitive stems which end in a consonant. The affix -as is more productive... it can be placed both on vowel-final stems ... and on consonant-final verbs" (2000: 181). The restriction of transitivizing -e to consonant stems is a direct reflex of the original suppletive pattern, where *e- served as a transitivizer where *-s- could not attach, after consonant stems. The freer distribution of transitivizing -as- in the modern language is a post-OJ development. As Matsumoto

---

20 Examples such as this, with a clear original CVC- root, provide good evidence that the original shape of the intransitivizing suffix was -ar-, identical to the stem shape of *ar-* 'exist, be'. In such cases the shape of the suffix is invariably -ar-. An even more compelling case is provided by examples like *tomar-* 'stop (intr.)'. The stem is a violation of the strong version of Arisaka's law, suggesting that there was originally a morphological boundary between *tom-* and -ar-.

(2000: 181) notes, Jacobsen (1992; 264–265) lists 38 NJ transitives in *-as-* corresponding to intransitive consonant stems. However only 5 of these have phonogrammatic attestations in OJ. In some cases NJ transitivizing *-as-* has spread at the expense of OJ transitivizing *-e-*, such as *nakas-* 'make cry' : OJ *nake-* 'make cry' and *naras-* 'make ring' : OJ *nare-* 'make ring'.

The fact that *-e-* could attach freely to consonant stems accounts for one of the distinctive properties that bigrade transitives display at the OJ stage. Bigrade transitives function as transitivity reinforcers in alternation with transitive consonant stem verbs:

(26) Consonant stem transitive   *-e-* (Bigrade) transitive
  kak- 'hang, attach (tr.)'   *kake-* 'hang, attach'
  mak- 'depute'   *make-* 'depute'
  sak- 'expel, send away'   *sake-* 'expel, send away'
  nam- 'line up (tr./intr.)'   *name-* 'line up (tr.)'

In the case of the first verb, the bigrade transitive has completely replaced the consonant stem transitive in NJ. Examples such as this suggest that *-e-* had become a salient marker of transitivity by the OJ stage. Transitivizing *-e-* also functioned to reduce the lability of verbs such as *kap-* and *nam-* 'line up'. The transitive ('buy') and intransitive ('mix, change') meanings of *kap-* are certainly related to an original meaning 'change', unspecified for transitivity, but with the development of bigrade *kape-*, the transitive meaning of *kap-* specializes to 'buy'.

The final question to be clarified under the GET hypotheis is the genesis of the quadrigrade transitive : bigrade intransitive pattern in (6–7). The typological evidence we consider in section 6 suggests that diathetic acquisitives first produce the transitive (causative) pattern from the transitive secondary predicate source in (17c). The intransitive pattern arises as a result of suppressing the goal argument in the transitive pattern.

The Japanese historical and diachronic evidence is consistent with this scenario. As we saw, the intransitive bigrade: transitive quadrigrade pattern is rare in OJ (cf. section 2.1). Comparative Ryukyuan evidence indicates that this pattern may not be reconstructible to proto-Japanese. For example, while transitive *yak-* 'burn (tr.)' and *tak-* 'burn/cook (tr.)' have corresponding verbs in Yonaguni (Ikema 2003) and prewar Yaeyama (Miyara 1930), their bigrade intransitive counterparts appear to be unattested.

Pairs such as *kure-* 'grow dark' and *kuras-* 'spend (time)' suggest a scenario for the development of the intransitivizing function. These verbs coexist with the adjectival root *kura-* 'dark', a pattern which is also seen with the pair *are-* 'become rough' and *aras-* 'lay waste':

(27) Adjective root   Bigrade intransitive   -s- Transitive
     kura 'dark'   *kure-* 'grow dark'   *kuras-* 'pass the day, make dark'
     ara 'rough, barren'   *are-* 'become rough'   *aras-* 'lay waste'

Despite the difference in transitivity, the meaning of the bigrade and -s- transitive is quite close:

(28) 晝羽裳   浦不樂   晩之
     piru *pa mo*   urasabwi   kurasi
     day TOP also sadly   darken
     '(I) spend the day sadly' (MYS 2.210)

(29) 日能   久礼由氣婆   家乎之曽   於毛布
     pi *no*   kure yukeba   ipye *wo si zo*   omopu
     day GEN   darken go.when home ACC EMPH FOC   think
     'When the day ends I think of nothing but my home.' (MYS 17.3895)

In transitive (28) the experiencer is realized as a *pro* subject; in intransitive (29) the experiencer is suppressed and the theme is realized as subject. The bigrade intransitivizing pattern in (6–7), which as we noted above is rare in OJ and appears not be reconstructable to proto-Japanese-Ryukyuan, may be the result of analogy with suppressed experiencer intransitives like (29). This idea is supported by the fact that OJ examples of intransitiving bigrades such as *yake-* 'be burned' often appear as psychological predicates, parallel to (29)[21]:

(30) 所燒   吾   下情
     yakuru   wa ga   sita.gokoro
     burn.ADN   1P GEN   under.heart
     'The bottom of my heart burns.' (MYS 1.5)

Summarizing, bigrade transitives are the product of the incorporation of a secondary predicate into the verb **e-* 'get'. The first instance of this type is likely to have involved noninflecting secondary predicates, as in (24). Combination of the lexical verb with secondary predicate XP to derive a causative with the

---

21 This attestation is not phonographic.

meaning 'get NP to XP' survives into OJ (see (20)). The secondary predicate + -*e*- pattern is extended to uninflected verb stems, the main pattern attested in OJ. Suppression of the nonagentive experiencer/goal in secondary predicate + -*e*- results in bigrade intransitives such as (30).

6 Typology

A survey and review of the treatment of the Japanese transitivity alternations in the typological literature is provided by Narrog (this volume, 2007a, 2007b). Narrog makes the important point that the two most influential studies in this line of research, Haspelmath (1990) and Nichols et al (2004), reach opposite conclusions about whether Japanese is a "primarily transitivizing" or "primarily detransitivizing" language. These conflicting results highlight the risks inherent in "whole language typology" classifications without detailed analyses of the language in question. From the standpoint of such an attempt as applied to Japanese, classification of Japanese as primarily "transitivizing" or "detransitivizing" obscures two facts: (i) two of the widely cited formations, intransitive -*(a)r*- and transitive -*as*-, for the most part derive verbs from noninflecting stems, not other verbs (ii) the third formation, in -*e*-, has both transitiving and intransitivizing outcomes because this is a typical development of 'get', the lexical verb from which it is derived.

Our typological focus here is on the crosslinguistic behavior of acquisitives, formations based on verbs of acquisition such as 'get'. Taking *e*- 'get' as the source for the bigrade transitivity alternations fits the general pattern of acquisitive derivations (van der Auwera et al. 2009). These divide into two basic types, modal derivations (such as the potential function of *e*- in OJ) and diathetic derivations. The latter involve a change in valency, either transitivizing or detransitivizing. Below we give just a few broadly distributed examples.

(31) Diathetic Aquisitive Derivations
    a. Estonian *saama* 'get' causative (Tragel & Habicht 2012: 1385)
        Sa-i-n   saapa-d pori-st   puhta-ks.
        Get-PST-1SG boot-PL   mud-ELA clean-TRAN
        'I got the boots clean of mud.'

    b. Southern Min *chhoa7* causative < 'haul' 拽 (Chen 2008)
        只   景   拽   人   憔悴
        Chi2 keng2 chhoa7 lang5 chiau5–chui7.
        this   scene pull   people emaciated
        'This scene makes people emaciated.'

c. Seychelles Creole *Ganny* passive < Fr. *gagner* 'win' (Haspelmath 1990; Michaelis & Rosalie ND)

Bidze	2005	ti	ganny	approve	menm	zour.
budget	2005	PST	PASS	approve	same	day

'The budget for 2005 was approved the same day.'
(example cited from Michaelis & Rosalie)

d. German *kriegen* 'get' (McIntyre 2005)
Transitive (causative)   Intransitive (passive)
Er *kriegt* das Problem *gelöst*.   Er *kriegt geholfen*.
'He gets the problem solved.'   'He gets helped.'

Diathetic acquisitive derivations are particularly common in the languages of Western and Northern Europe (see the papers in van der Auwera et al 2012). The best documented case is in fact English, where diathetic derivations involving *get* developed over a very short time, from the 14th to the 17th century.

A detailed description of the development of the English diathetic acquisitive pattern is given by Gronemeyer (1999). *Get* first appears in combination with secondary predicate adverbs and PPs in the 14th century:

(32) a. that a man coveyte to geten alle thise thynges togidre
'that a man wants to get all these things together'
(Chaucer, *Boethius* 11425 (c. 1380), cited from Gronemeyer 1999: 24)

b. For with that orison sche getyth to God ful many soules þat were in oure power fast beforn.
'For with that prayer she gets to God many souls that were firmly in our power.'
(Reynes, *The Commonplace Book of Robert Reynes of Acle* (1470–1500), cited from Gronemeyer 1999: 24)

Causative *get* + infinitive is the next extension. It emerges in the 16th century:

(33) and I wyll see yf that I can gete another to be bownd with me
'and I will see if I can get another to be bound with me'
(Mowntayne, *The Autobiography of Thomas Mowtayne* (1553), cited from Gronemeyer 1999: 24)

According to Gronemeyer (1999: 23), *get* in all usages is primarily agentive (87% of tokens) in 1350–1420. In the contemporary English corpus she examines, *get* is primarily not agentive (58% recipient or ambiguous vs 42% agentive). The rise of nonagentive *get* coincides with the emergence of nonagentive diathetic patterns. Gronemeyer characterizes the English diathetic development as from lexical *get* to "movement" → causative → permissive. A separate development, exploiting nonagentive *get*, leads from the "movement" function to inchoative → passive. Modal *get* develops from lexical *get* to stative possession → obligation. For a broadly similar description focusing on the emergence of passive *get*, see Fleisher (2006).

This overall picture coincides with the scenario we have sketched for pre-OJ. *e- combines first with nonverbal (uninflected) secondary predicates. The first verbal diathetic derivation is causativizing. The detransitivizing pattern emerges later, and remains a minority pattern throughout the history of Japanese. It seems likely that morphological factors both limit and lead to the characteristic bivalence of the Japanese bigrade transitivity alternations. While English and other Western and Northern European languages develop detransitivizing constructions by combining *get* with a passive particle, Japanese has only the *e- + root combination. The acquisitive pattern built on nonfinite root + *-e- is comparable to *get* + infinitive in English and other languages, and has the same causative function. We suggested a more restricted source for detransitivizing -e- in section (5), from roots allowing a nonagentive (experiencer) external argument, which is eventually suppressed.

7 Conclusions

This chapter has focused on the transitivity alternations involving the lower bigrade conjugation in premodern Japanese, with stem final -e-. We argued for the hypothesis that this is a diathetic acquisitive pattern built on the lexical verb *e-* 'get'. We showed how lexical *e-* occurs with secondary predicates that might give rise to such a pattern in Old Japanese. We demonstrated that pre-OJ had a process of secondary predicate incorporation, a species of direct stem affixation, that could produce the secondary predicate + *e- combination. We pointed to specific cases of upper bigrade transitives that appear to involve such a source. We discussed the differentiation between causativizing *-e- and transitivizing *-s-, and suggested that it was partly phonologically conditioned. We presented a scenario for how the original verb stem + *e- causative pattern might have been extended to intransitives in limited cases. Finally, we briefly compared the development of the Japanese pattern to diathetic acquisitives in other languages.

Abbreviations

1P 1st person; 1SG 1st person singular; ACC accusative; ADN adnominal; CAUS causative; CONJ conjectural; DAT dative; ELA elative; EMPH emphatic; FOC focus; GEN genitive; GER gerund; INF infinitive; NEG negative; OPT optative; PASS passive; PL plural; PST past; RESP respect; TOP topic; TRAN translative.

Acknowledgments

We would like to thank the audience at the International Symposium on Valency Classes and Alternations in Japanese, held 4–5 August, 2012, at the National Institute for Japanese Language and Linguistics, Tokyo, for valuable feedback. We are also grateful to an anonymous reviewer for demonstrating to us our shortcomings, which we hope to have addressed in the version of the chapter included here, in setting out our proposal for a non-specialist reader.

References

van der Auwera, Johan, Petar Kehayov & Alice Vittrant. 2009. Acquisitive modals. In Lotte Hogeweg, Helen de Hoop & Andrej Malchukov (eds.), *Cross-linguistic semantics of tense, aspect, and modality*, 271–302. Amsterdam & Philadelphia: John Benjamins.

van der Auwera, Johan, Alexandra Lenz & Gudrun Rawoens (eds.). 2012. *The art of getting*: Get verbs in European languages from a synchronic and diachronic point of view. Special issue of *Linguistics* 50(6).

Chen, I-Hsuan. 2008. Grammaticalization of causative verbs in Earlier Southern Min texts: A comparison between Southern Min and Mandarin. Paper given at *NRG 4 New reflections on Grammaticalization 4*. University of Leuven 16–19/7/2008.

Fleisher, Nicholas. 2006. The origin of passive *get*. *English Language and Linguistics* 10(2). 225–252.

Frellesvig, Bjarke. 2008. On reconstruction of proto-Japanese and pre-Old Japanese verb inflection. In Bjarke Frellesvig & John Whitman (eds.), *Proto-Japanese: Issues and prospects*, 185–203. Amsterdam & Philadelphia: John Benjamins.

Frellesvig, Bjarke. 2010. *A history of the Japanese language*. Cambridge: Cambridge University Press.

Gronemeyer, Claire. 1999. On deriving complex polysemy: The grammaticalization of *get*. *English Language and Linguistics* 3. 1–39.

Harley, Heidi. 2004. Wanting, having and getting. *Linguistic Inquiry* 35. 355–392.

Haspelmath, Martin 1990. The grammaticization of passive morphology. *Studies in Language* 14 (1). 25–71.

Kida, Akiyoshi. 1988. Katsuyōkei no seiritsu to jōdai kanazukai [The formation of the katsuyōkei system and jōdai special kana usage]. *Kokugo kokubun* 57 (1). 1–24.

Kuginuki, Toru. 1996. *Kodai Nihongo no keitai henka* [Morphological change in earlier Japanese]. Osaka: Izumi Shoin.
Jacobsen, Wesley. 1988. Tadōsei to purototaipu ron. In Susumu Kuno & Masayoshi Shibatani (eds.), *Nihongogaku no shintenkai* [New developments of Japanese linguistics], 213–248. Tokyo: Kurosio Publishers.
Jacobsen, Wesley. 1992. *The transitive structure of events in Japanese*. Tokyo: Kurosio Publishers.
Matsumoto, Yo. 2000. Causative alternation in English and Japanese: A closer look. Review article on Taro Kageyama's *Dōshi imiron: Gengo to ninchi no setten*. *English Linguistics* 17. 160–192. The English Linguistic Society of Japan.
McIntyre, Andrew. 2005. The semantic and syntactic decomposition of *get*: An interaction between verb meaning and particle placement. *Journal of Semantics* 22 (4). 401–438.
Michaelis, Susanne and Rosalie, Marcel. ND. Seychelles Creole. Accessed at http://lingweb.eva.mpg.de/apics/images/2/21/SurveySeychelles.pdf
Miyara, Tōsō. 1930. *Yaeyama goi*. Tokyo: Tōyō Bunko.
Murasugi, Keiko. this volume. Children's 'erroneous' intransitives, transitives, and causatives: Their implications for syntactic theory. In Taro Kageyama & Wesley M. Jacobsen (eds.), *Transitivity and valency alternations: Studies on Japanese and beyond*. Berlin & Boston: De Gruyter Mouton.
Narrog, Heiko. 2007a. Nihongo no jita dōshi-tsui no ruikeironteki ichi-zuke [The typological position of Japanese transitivity pairs]. In Taro Kageyama (ed.), *Lexicon Forum No. 3*, 161–193. Tokyo: Hituzi Syobo.
Narrog, Heiko. 2007b. Nihongo jita dōshi ni okeru yūhyōseisa no dōkizuke [Motivating the markedness differences in Japanese transitivity verb pairs]. In Mie Tsunoda, Kan Sasaki & Tōru Shionoya (eds.), *Tadōsei no tsūgengoteki kenkyū – Tsunoda Tasaku hakase kanreki kinen ronbunshū* [Cross-linguistic Studies of Transitivity – A Festschrift for the 60th birthday of Dr. Tsunoda Tasaku], 295–306. Tokyo: Kuroshio Publishers.
Narrog, Heiko. this volume. Japanese transitivity pairs through time – a historical and typological perspective. In Taro Kageyama & Wesley M. Jacobsen (eds.), *Transitivity and valency alternations: Studies on Japanese and beyond*. Berlin & Boston: De Gruyter Mouton.
Nichols, Johanna, David Peterson & Jonathan Barnes. 2004. Transitivizing and detransitivizing languages. *Linguistic Typology* 8 (2). 149–211.
Ohno, Susumu. 1953. Nihongo no dōshi no katsuyōkei no kigen ni tsuite. *Kokugo to Kokubungaku* 350. 47–56.
Richards, Norvin. 2001. An idiomatic argument for lexical decomposition. *Linguistic Inquiry* 32. 183–192.
Takeda, Yūkichi. 1957. *Man'yōshū zenchūshaku* 2: Gengo. Tokyo: Kadokawa Shoten.
Tragel, Ilona & Külli Habicht. 2012. Grammaticalization of Estonian *saama* 'to get'. *Linguistics* 50 (6). 1371–1412.
Unger, James Marshall. 1993 [1977]. *Studies in early Japanese morphophonemics*, 2nd edition. Bloomington: IULC.
Unger, James Marshall. 2000. Reconciling comparative and internal reconstruction: The case of Old Japanese /ti ri ni/. *Language* 76 (3). 655–81.
Whitman, John. 2008. The source of the bigrade conjugation and stem shape in pre-Old Japanese. In Bjarke Frellesvig & John Whitman (eds.), *Proto-Japanese: Issues and prospects*, 168–182. Amsterdam & Philadelphia: John Benjamins.
Yoshida, Kanehiko. 1973. *Jōdai jodōshi no shiteki kenkyū*. Tokyo: Meiji Shoin.

IV Acquisition

Keiko Murasugi
10 Children's 'erroneous' intransitives, transitives, and causatives: their implications for syntactic theory

1 Introduction

"Erroneous" transitive-intransitive alternations are universally observed in children's speech across languages (Marcotte 2005, among others). English- and Portuguese-speaking children, for example, produce such erroneous sentences as (1) and (2), respectively.

(1) a. *Mommy, can you **stay** this open?*[1]
 (Bowerman 1974)

 b. *Don't **giggle** me.* (3;0)
 (Bowerman 1974, 1982)

 c. *Come and see what Jenny got today. **Pull**. **Pull**!* (3;01)
 (Lord 1979)

(2) *Quem **morreu** ele?*
 'Who died him?'
 (Figueira 1984)

In (1a), the context requires a transitive verb such as *keep*, but the child uses the intransitive verb *stay* instead. In (1b), the intransitive verb *giggle* is used as a transitive verb. (1c), by contrast, shows the child using a transitive verb (*pull*) as an intransitive verb: the child utters this while pulling at his reluctant mother and demanding that she come along with him. The example from Portuguese in (2) similarly shows a child using an intransitive verb (*die*) where a transitive verb (*kill*) would be expected in adult speech.

"Erroneous" transitive-intransitive alternations produced by children speaking Japanese, an agglutinative language with rich case marking, are observed

---
[1] The boldfaced form indicates non-adult-like usage.

Keiko Murasugi, Nanzan University

most frequently from ages 2 to 4. Japanese clearly shows that celebrated "verbal errors" of this type made by children can be considered as morphological in nature since there is no change in the number of arguments at issue and the case marking on the arguments is adult-like.

(3) a. *To   o   **aite*** (Sumihare (=S), 2;01)
       door ACC open(vi)
       'Please open the door.'

   b. *Nee, ati o   **hirogatte***. (Akkun (=A), 3;07)
       INT legs ACC spread(vi)-GER
       'Please spread your legs.'

   c. ***Todokok**-ka, ano hito ni   **todok-(y)oo**   **todok-(y)oo***. (A, 4;08)
       arrive(vi)-let's that person DAT arrive(vi)-let's arrive(vi)-let's
       'Let's send (it). Let's send (it) to that person.'

Okubo (1975) also reports that children have difficulties in using the adult form of the causative verbs as well. For instance, children at around two of age produce *haite* (vi-GER) in place of *hakasite* 'wear-CAUS', *nureta* (vi) in place of *nurasita* 'wet-CAUS' and *anyo-suru* 'walk-do (vi)' in place of *anyo saseru* 'walk-do-CAUS'.

Murasugi & Hashimoto (2004) provide a uniform account of such verbal errors following Larson's (1988) *v*-VP frame or VP-shell hypothesis, according to which: (i) the predicate-argument structures of large V's and small *v*'s are acquired early, (ii) children assume [±cause] *v* to be phonetically null at one stage, and (iii) what requires time is the acquisition of the lexical form of each V and the forms in which [±cause] small *v*'s are realized. Their analysis of the acquisition of complex predicates provides evidence supporting the VP-shell hypothesis.

In this chapter, Murasugi & Hashimoto's (2004) *v*-VP frame analysis of acquisition of Japanese verbs and complex predicates is developed and modified based on new empirical evidence from an analysis of common errors made by Japanese-speaking children that have been widely observed in longitudinal studies.

2 Descriptive adequacy

Before we discuss our analysis of the children's 'errors' in question, we consider in this section if it is descriptively adequate to view these as a typical phenomenon found at the intermediate stage of first language grammar acquisition.

The fact that this phenomenon has been observed widely by various researchers clearly points to a positive answer to this question. See, for example, the conversational data given in (4).

(4) Child (3;11): *otootyan, mado   **ai-te**.*
  daddy   window open(vi)-GER
  Intended meaning: 'Daddy, please open the window.'

  Father: *Mado   ake-te,   daro.*
   window open(vt)-GER, isn't it?
   'You mean, open the window.'

  Child: *Un,   mado   **ai-te**   yo.*
   yeah window open(vi)-GER SFP
   Intended meaning: 'Yeah, Daddy, please open the window.'

  Father: *Mado   ake-te,   da   yo.*
   window open(vt)-GER COP SFP
   'It should be "Open the window".'

  Child: *Iikara,   mado   **ai-te**   yo,   Otootyan.*
   anyway window open(vi)-GER SFP daddy
   Intended meaning: 'Anyway, please open the window, Daddy.'
   (Otsu 2002: 185 [our translation])

In (4), in attempting to ask his father to open the window, the child produces the erroneous intransitive request form *ai-te* 'open (vi)' instead of the expected transitive form *ake-te* 'open (vt)', despite direct negative evidence to the contrary given by the father. Similarly, Ito (2005) and Noji (1973–1977), among others, observe that the intransitive form *ai-te* 'open (vi)' is used in place of the transitive form *ake-te* 'open (vt)' by children in their studies, as illustrated in (5).

(5) a. *Oniityan ga   **aka**   nai.* (2;09)
   brother   NOM open(vi) NEG
   Literal meaning: Brother is not opened (the door).
   Intended meaning: Brother does not open (the door).
   (Ito 2005: 3)

  b. *Baatyan   **aite**.* (S, 2;00)
   grandma   open (vi)
   Intended meaning: Grandma, please open (the door).

The question that arises next is whether such overextension in the usage of intransitives and transitives always occurs in one direction. The answer is, in fact, negative. Just as in the English example (1c), Japanese-speaking children also use transitives instead of intransitives, as shown in (6). In (6a), the child (2;1) uses the past form *nui-ta* 'pull.out-PST' of the transitive verb *nuk-u* instead of the expected past form *nuke-ta* 'come.out-PST' of the intransitive verb *nuke-ru*. In (6b), the child (2;1) likewise uses the transitive verb *ak-en* 'open(vt)-NEG' instead of the intransitive verb *ak-an* 'open(vi)-NEG', even though the intended meaning is 'The door does not open.'

(6) a. **Nui-ta**   *koko*. (S, 2;01)
    pull.out(vt)-PST here
    Literal meaning: 'I pulled (this) out here.'
    Intended meaning: '(This) came out here.'

  b. SUM: **Ak-en**   *ak-en*. (S, 2;01)
        open(vt)-NEG open(vt)-NEG
        Literal meaning: '(I) don't open it. (I) don't open it.'
        Intended meaning: '(It) doesn't open. (It) doesn't open.'

      FAT (to MOT): *Ak-an*   *tte*   *osiete yari nasai*. (unaccusative)
                     open(vi)-NEG COMP tell   give IMP
                 'Tell him that it should be "akan (vi)".'

      SUM: *Ak-an*.
           open(vi)-NEG
           '(It) doesn't open.'

      SUM: **Ak-en**   *ak-en*   *ak-en*   *wa* **ak-en**   *ga*.
           open(vt)-NEG open(vt)-NEG open(vt)-NEG SFP open(vt)-NEG SFP
           Literal meaning: '(I) don't open it. (I) don't open. (I) don't open it.'
           Intended meaning: '(It) doesn't open. (It) doesn't open.
                             (It) doesn't open.'

      FAT: *Ak-anai*   *yo*.
          open(vi)-NEG SFP
          'It doesn't open.'

      SUM: **Ak-en**   *yo*.
           open(vt)-NEG SFP
           Literal meaning: '(I) don't open it.'
           Intended meaning: '(It) doesn't open.'

Although the child is able to parrot his father's direct correction once, he subsequently keeps producing the transitive form *ak-en* (vt) for the intransitive form *ak-an* (vi). These examples illustrate that overextension of intransitives and transitives is not always in one direction.

Are such errors, then, Japanese-specific and only found in transitive-intransitive verbs? The answer is clearly negative. As noted above, "errors" involving causatives by children have also been widely observed in the acquisition of various languages. As we have seen in the previous section, Bowerman (1974) and Figueira (1984), for example, report that there is a stage where children are unable to produce the adult form of the causative in English and Portuguese, respectively. In (7a), the child tells his or her mother to let (or help) him or her drink milk. However, the causative verb is omitted. Similar examples can be found in Portuguese, as shown in (8).

(7) a. *You can **drink** me the milk.* (Jennifer 3;08)
    (Lord 1979)

   b *I'm **singing** him.* (Christy 3;01)
      (Bowerman 1974, 1982)

(8) *(...) este balanco vai te **cair**.*
    'This swing is going to fall you.'
    Intended meaning: 'This swing will make you fall'
    (Figueira 1984)

Japanese-speaking children, at around 2 to 5 years of age, also produce such erroneous verb forms as in (9).

(9) Child (2;02): *Papa* **huusen hukuran-de**.
                  Daddy balloon swell(vi)-GER
                  Intended meaning: 'Daddy, please blow up the balloon.'

   Father: *Hukuran-de zyanai desyo hukuram-as-ite desyo.*
           swell-GER   not   isn't it swell-CAUS-GER isn't it
           'It's not *hukurande* 'swell'. It should be *hukuramas-ite* 'blow up'.'

   Child: **Hukuran-de**.
          swell(vi)-GER
          Intended meaning: 'Blow up (the balloon).'
          ...(omitted)...

Father: *Hukuram-as-ite.*
  swell-CAUS-GER
  '(You should say) blow up (the balloon).'

Child: **Hukuran-de. Hukuran-de.**
  swell(vi)-GER swell-GER
  Intended meaning: 'Blow up (the balloon)! Blow up (the balloon)!'
  (Suzuki 1987:172 [our translation])

The child asks his father to blow up the balloon. The father provides the child with the "correct" lexical causative form *hukuram-as-ite* 'blow up (vt)', but to no avail. The child continues to produce repeatedly the erroneous intransitive imperative form *hukuran-de* 'swell (vi)'.

The examples given above indicate not only that errors of this type are commonly observed in complex predicates across languages, but also that direct negative evidence is ineffective in grammar acquisition.

3 VP-shell analysis of transitive-intransitive alternations revisited

Murasugi & Hashimoto (2004), based on their longitudinal study of the acquisition of verbs – in particular, transitive-intransitive verb pairs and causatives – propose that there are four steps to acquiring verbs and morphological -(s)ase causatives in Japanese.

(10) Stage I: Small *v* is *tiyu/tita/tite* 'do/did/doing'.
  Stage II: Small *v* is null.
  Stage III: Acquisition of lexical causatives and transitive verbs; occasional erroneous lexical realization of *v*.
  Stage IV: Acquisition of syntactic causatives; occasional erroneous lexical realization of V.

In what follows, we present their analysis and further empirical evidence supporting their proposal.[2]

---

[2] This analysis is supported by Murasugi, Hashimoto & Kato (2005). They report, based on Murasugi & Hashimoto's longitudinal study of the child Akkun, that lexical *-(s)ase* causatives are acquired earlier than syntactic causatives. The same results are obtained in an experimental

Before Stage I, according to Murasugi & Hashimoto (2004), Japanese-speaking children produce sentences without overt verbs beginning around the age of 2. Some examples of this are shown in (11a) and (11b).

(11) a. *Motto koe buubu* Ø (2;01) Ø= *age-ru* (give)
more this water
'(I will give) more water to this.'

b. *Koe Papa hai doozyo* Ø (2;00) Ø= *suru* (do)
this Daddy yes please
'This one. (I want to give it) to Daddy.'
(Murasugi & Hashimoto 2004:3)

In (11a), the expected verb *age-ru* 'give' is missing. In (11b), Akkun produces *hai doozyo*. *Hai* means 'yes' and *doozyo* means 'please,' but in combination the phrase *hai doozyo* means 'Here you are.' Murasugi & Hashimoto (2004) consider that before Stage I, the child initially uses *hai doozyo* to express the meaning of 'give' or possibly the transfer of an item from one person to another in general. The child does not use an actual verb in the ditransitive construction here.

Akkun's Stage I (2;05–2;09) begins at around 2;05, at which point he starts to place *tiyu/tita/tite*[3] in sentence-final position quite productively, as shown in (12a) through (12c).

(12) a. *Mama Akkun hai doozyo **tiyu**.* (A, 2;05)
Mommy yes please do
'Akkun (/I) will give it to Mommy.'

b. *Mama Akkun paku **tiyu**.* (A, 2;07)
Mommy onomatopoeia do
'Mommy, please let Akkun(/me) eat this.'

---

study conducted by Fuji (2006), a corpus analysis by Murasugi, Hashimoto & Fuji (2007), and a longitudinal study by Nakatani (2010). These findings of the two stages in acquiring -(s)ase causatives suggest that there are two types of -(s)ase causative in adult Japanese: syntactic and lexical. This is because they are clearly distinguished and there is no reason to suppose that the later acquisition of syntactic causatives results in the loss of lexical causatives. See also Okabe (2007).
3 *Tiyu/tita/tite* are *suru/sita/site* in adult speech and correspond in meaning to '*do/did/doing*' in English (Murasugi & Hashimoto 2004: 4).

c. *Akkun nezi kuyukuyu* **tite,** *konoko syabeyu.* (A, 2;09)
   screw turn around doing this one talk
   'When Akkun (/I) turns this screw around, it talks.'

d. *Tootyan, ozityan ga dondon* **si-ta** *yo.* (S, 1;11)
   Daddy   a man NOM beat (*onomatopoeia*) do-PST SFP
   'Daddy, a man beat (a wall).'

A parallel pattern is found in the longitudinal observation of the child Sumihare reported in Noji (1973–1977) (Murasugi, Hashimoto & Fuji 2007). Although Sumihare's Stage I (1;11–2;1) begins at around 1;11, 6 months earlier than Akkun's, Sumihare starts putting *tiyu/tita/tite* (*suru/sita/site*) in sentence-final position at this stage just as Akkun does. An example of this is cited in (12d).

It should be noted that *tiyu/tita/tite* never appears before Stage I. The "predicates" that occur with *tiyu/tita/tite* are typically onomatopoeic or mimetic expressions. For example, *paku* in (12b) is the sound that describes a person putting food into his/her mouth. The utterance in (12b) means, 'Please, Mommy, put this in Akkun's mouth' or more literally, 'Mommy makes this food go into Akkun's mouth.' *Kuyukuyu* in (12c), which corresponds to *kurukuru* in adult speech, is a mimetic word describing things turning around. The child is trying to say that he will turn the screw, or more literally that he will cause the screw to turn around, and as a result the toy will talk.

The same pattern is observed in the Sumihare corpus. It is at 1;11 that *suru (tyuru,* or *'do')* appears in this corpus, as shown in (12d). At this point, almost without exception, the *sita* form is used, but at 2;0, other conjugational forms of *suru (tyuru)* appear. *Suru (tyuru)*-forms can be considered to be one of the main "verbal" forms a child uses at this stage. The frequent use of *suru*-forms beginning around the age of two, under the *v*-VP frame analysis, indicates that children at this stage have acquired the *v*-VP frame, and that *v* is realized in their speech as *suru/sita/site*.

Murasugi & Hashimoto (2004) propose that children at this stage use *tiyu/tita/tite* to describe an activity that brings about a certain event or change of state. The adult counterpart to *tiyu/tita/tite, suru/sita/site,* is able to assign the agent role, like the English verb *do/did/doing*. The rest of the utterance describes the event or change of state brought about. Thus, *tiyu/tita/tite* seems to correspond exactly to small *v*.[4] The structure proposed by Murasugi & Hashimoto (2004) to the sentence (12c) is shown in (13).

---

4 Note here that the hypothesis that *tiyu/tita/tite* corresponds to small *v* can be confirmed in the adult grammar of Malayalam. The *-(i)kk* suffix in this language introduces a new argument into the syntactic frame of the verb to which it attaches (Madhavan, 2006). According to

(13)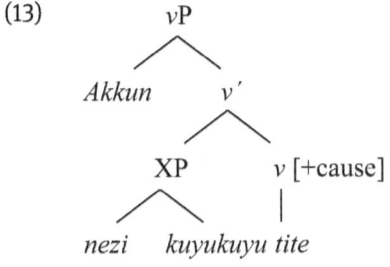

(Murasugi & Hashimoto 2004: 5)

In (13), *tite* describes an activity that causes a screw to turn around, and *Akkun* is the agent. The complement of small *v* is indicated not as VP but as XP because it lacks the categorical status of verb at this stage. Again, *kuyukuyu* (*kurukuru*)

Madhavan (2006), Malayalam has regular intransitive- transitive pairs, in which the suffix -*(i)kk* functions as a transitivizer, as in (i).

(i) a. *muŋŋ-uka* / *mukk-uka*
       sink(vi)-inf   sink(vt)-inf

   b. *poTT-uka* / *poTT-ikk-uka*
      break(vi)   break(vt)
      (Madhavan 2006:1)

This -*(i)kk* suffix also functions as a causativiser.

(ii) *kara-y-uka* / *kara-y-ikk-uka*
     cry   make cry
     (Madhavan 2006:1)

However, the -*(i)kk* suffix is not allowed on loan (foreign) words in Malayalam: *cey* 'do' is used instead in such cases, as in (iii).

(iii) a. *John Mary e   kkonta   ezut -ipp-ikk-iccu* (-ikk + -ikk → -ipp + -ikk)
              ACC Postposition write-CAUS-CAUS-PST
         'John made Mary write.'

     b. *John Mary e   kkonta   type ceyy-ikk-iccu*
              ACC Postposition do-CAUS-PST
         'John made Mary type.'

     c. **John Mary e   kkonta   type-ipp-ikk-iccu*
              ACC Postposition -CAUS-CAUS-PST
     (Hany Babu, M.T. p.c.)

(iiic) is ill-formed since the causative -*ikk* is attached to the loan word *type*. Under Murasugi & Hashimoto's *v*-VP Frame analysis, in adult Malayalam, small *v* is realized as *do* in forming causatives on loan (foreign) words; in Stage I of Japanese child grammar, likewise, small *v* is realized as *do*. Thus, Stage I, where Japanese-speaking children use *suru* (do) to describe activities, corresponds to one type of causative formation in, say, adult Malayalam. Intermediate stages of grammar acquisition are thus restricted to what count as possible human grammars.

is a mimetic word describing things turning around, and the XP expresses the meaning of 'the screw turns.' At this stage, the child has begun utilizing the v-VP frame, and small v is phonetically realized as *tiyu/tita/tite*. Crucially, this indicates that the child grammar projects the functional category of small v, which is responsible for the assignment of an external theta-role (Chomsky 1995: 315).

However, Stage I is still several steps away from adult grammar: actual lexical items to insert in the v-V combination have not yet been acquired. As for Akkun, intransitive and ditransitive verbs are acquired at around 2;09, which we call Stage II (A: 2;09–4;08). The sentences in (14) are examples of the 'correct' usage of these verbs.

(14) a. *Dango   ga   huta pakan   tite,   dango*
     dumpling NOM lid   onomatopoeia do-GER dumpling
     ga   atta. (A, 2;09)
     NOM exist-PST
     'There was a dumpling (when I) opened the lid of the dumpling (box).'

   b. *Mama   tyotto   ageyu.* (A, 2;07)
      Mommy a little give
      'Mommy, (I will) give you a little bit.'
      (Murasugi & Hashimoto 2004:6)

In (14a), the intransitive verb *atta* 'exist-PST' appears, and in (14b), the ditransitive verb *ageru* 'give' is used in an adult-like way.

At the same time, Akkun exhibits interesting and consistent "errors" as he acquires actual lexical verbs. Note first that, in adult English, transitive and intransitive (unaccusative) verbs often take the same phonetic form, giving rise to alternations as in (15).

(15) a. *John passed the ring to Mary.*

   b. *The ring passed to Mary.*

If the argument structures of these sentences are realized as in (16), then v is a "zero morpheme" without phonetic content whether it is [+cause], as in the case of (15a), or [-cause], as in the case of (15b).

(16)   *v*P (v [+cause] + PASS = *pass*, v [-cause] + PASS = *pass*)

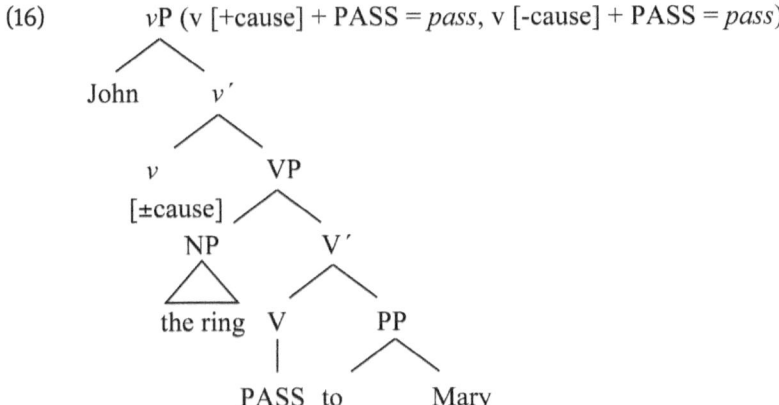

Consequently, 'v [+cause]+PASS' and 'v [-cause]+PASS' are both realized as *pass*.
In adult Japanese, by contrast, transitivity and intransitivity (unaccusativity) are often marked by distinct suffixes, as illustrated in (17).

(17)   Transitive   Unaccusative
   a.   *watas-u* (pass.CAUS-PRS)   *watar-u* (pass.INTR-PRS)
   b.   *ak-e-ru* (open-CAUS-PRS)   *ak-u* (open-PRS)
   c.   *hirog-e-ru* (spread-CAUS-PRS)   *hirog-ar-u* (spread-INTR-PRS)

These examples show that the forms of the suffixes are idiosyncratic and probably have to be learned individually. It is plausible to assume that these suffixes occupy the *v* position. For example, [+cause] *v* is realized as *-s* and [-cause] *v* as *-r* in the case of (17a).

In the process of acquiring such lexical items that stand for V-*v* combinations, children often produce transitive sentences with intransitive (unaccusative) verbs. The examples in (18a) through (18d) are data produced by Akkun, and the examples in (18e) through (18g) are data produced by Sumihare (Murasugi, Hashimoto & Fuji 2007).

(18) a. *Koe ziityan   ni **miyu**.*[5] (A, 2;09)
        this grandfather to see(vi)
        'I show this to Grandfather.'

---

5 *Mi-yu* is *mi-ru* in adult usage.

b. *Nee, ati o* **hirogatte**. (A, 3;07)
   INT legs ACC spread(vi)-GER
   'Please spread your legs.'

c. *Kore,* **ai-toku** *kara saa.* (A, 4;05)
   this open(vi)-keep as SFP
   '(I will) open this and keep it open.'

d. **Todokok**-*ka, ano hito ni* **todok-oo** **todok-oo**. (A, 4;08)
   arrive(vi)-let's that person to arrive (vi)-let's arrive(vi)-let's
   'Let's send (it). Let's send (it) to that person.'

e. *Kaatyan* **ai-te**. (S, 2;01)
   mother open(vi)-GER
   Literal meaning: '(Please) be open, mother.'
   Intended meaning: '(Please) open (the door), mother.'

f. *Koko oite* **tyameru**.[6] (S, 2;01)
   here put get.cold(vi)
   Literal meaning: 'I put (a cup of tea) here and it gets cold.'
   Intended meaning: 'I put (a cup of tea) here and make it cold.'

g. *Kaatyan taitai* **agat-te**. *Boku o* **agat-te**.
   Mommy carp.streamer go.up (vi)-GER I GEN go.up(vi)-GER
   agat-te *ya.* (S, 2;02)
   go.up(vi)-GER SFP
   Literal meaning: 'Mommy, please go up my carp streamer.
                    Go up mine. Go up, please.'
   Intended meaning: 'Mommy, please make my carp streamer go up higher.
                     Make it higher. Higher, please.'

In each of these examples, children "erroneously" use the intransitive form of the verb in place of the transitive. What Akkun intends in (18b), for example, is *hirog-e-te* 'spread(vt)-GER' and not *hirog-at-te* 'spread(vi)-GER'. In adult Japanese, (18c) and (18d) literally mean 'I will remain open' and 'Let's be delivered to that person', respectively.

Murasugi & Hashimoto (2004) propose that children produce these errors because they assume [±cause] *v* to be zero. The sentences in (19) show verb pairs

---

[6] *Tyameru* is child speech for *sameru* '(something) gets cold'.

of transitive and intransitive (unaccusative) in adult grammar. (19a) and (19b) have the representations in (20a) and (20b), respectively.

(19) a. *Hanako ga   hon o   Taroo ni   todok-e-ru.*
    Hanako NOM book ACC Taro DAT deliver(vt)-PRS
    'Hanako delivers a book to Taro.'

   b. *Hon ga   Taroo ni   todok-Ø-u.*
    book NOM Taro DAT be.delivered(vi)-Ø-PRS
    'A book is delivered to Taro.'

(20) a.

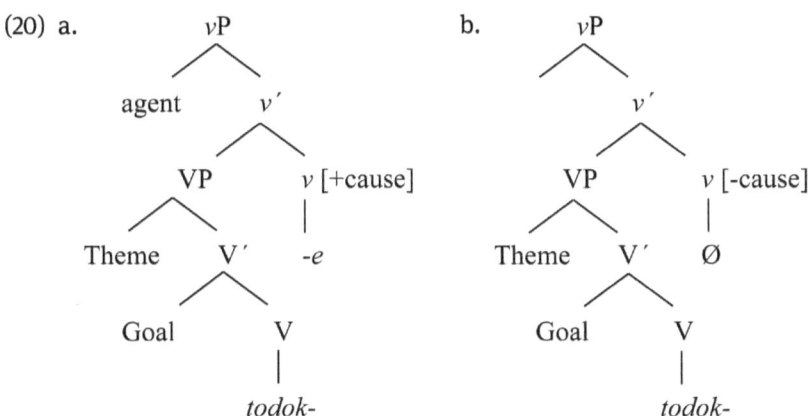

(Murasugi & Hashimoto 2004: 8–9)

In (20a), [+cause] *v* is realized as *-e*, but in (20b), [-cause] *v* is not realized phonetically.

Now let us consider the sentence in (18a), of which (21) is the adult counterpart.

(21) *Kore   ziityan   ni   miseru.*
    this   grandfather DAT show
    'I show this to Grandfather.'

In (21), the ditransitive verb, *miseru* (show) is used. The structure of the adult-grammar form in (21) is as in (22).

(22)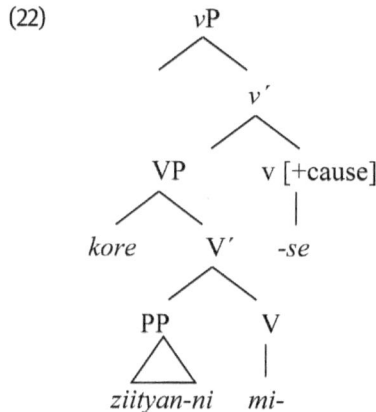

If children hypothesized that [±cause] *v* were zero, the structure which children have in mind would be as in (23) instead.

(23)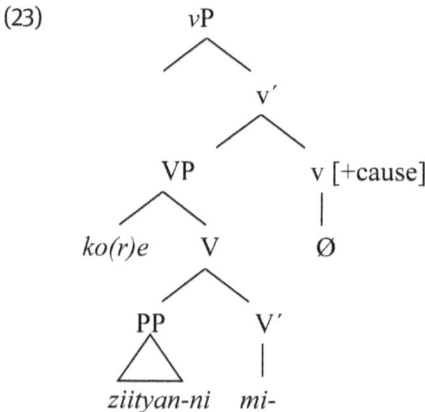

In (23), small *v* is not realized phonetically. Thus, children produce the monotransitive verb *miyu* instead of the ditransitive verb *miseru*. Their use of less transitive monotransitives for (di)transitives, is observed over a period of several months or several years, depending on the child.[7]

As mentioned above, it should be noted that children at this stage use transitives for intransitives as well. Some examples of this are seen in (24). Example (6b) seen earlier is repeated here as (24a).

---

7 Murasugi & Hashimoto (2004) observe this type of error for two years, up to 4;08.

(24) a. ***Ak-en***   ***ak-en***. (S, 2;01)
    open(vt)-NEG   open(vt)-NEG
    Literal meaning: '(I) don't open it. (I) don't open it.'

  b. *Koko kara hi ga das-u n ze* (S, 2;06)
    here from sun NOM take out COMP SFP
    'The sun comes out from here.'

These studies suggest that at Stage II children assume that pronounced verbs are Vs and that [±cause] *v* is phonetically empty. Accordingly, intransitives and their transitive counterparts are homophonous, as in English. They only later realize that surface forms of verbs are derived by suffixing *v* to the verbal root. As the actual realization of [±cause] *v* is idiosyncratic and sometimes even null (e.g., *toziru* 'shut (vt, vi)') in adult Japanese, the acquisition of verbs involves complex morphological analysis and, not surprisingly therefore, requires time.

4 VP-shell analysis of causatives revisited

During Stage II, according to Murasugi & Hashimoto (2004), children also produce lexical causative sentences without the causative suffix *-(s)ase*, as shown in (25).

(25) a. *Mama Akkun **non-de**.* (A, 2;08)
    Mommy   drink(vt)-GER
    'Mommy, please feed me (with milk).'

  b. *Mama ga pantyu **nui-da** toki.* (A, 3;02)
    Mommy NOM underpants undress(vt)-PST when
    Literal meaning: ... when Mommy took her underpants off.
    Intended meaning: ... when Mommy took my underpants off me.

  c. *Kutyu **hai-te**.* (S, 2;01)
    shoes put.on(vt)-GER
    Literal meaning: '(Please) put on (your) shoes.'
    Intended meaning: '(Please) put a pair of shoes on me.'

Children consistently omit the causative morpheme *-(s)ase* and use only the regular form of verbs instead. For example, in (25a), the causative form *nom-ase-te* should be used in this context, but Akkun omits *-(s)ase* and produces *non-de* instead. Akkun intends to say 'Mommy, please let me drink,' but the meaning of what he actually says is 'Mommy, drink Akkun.' Similarly, in (25b), the causative form *nug-ase-ta* should be used in this context, but Akkun omits *-(s)ase* and produces *nui-da* instead. He means to say '(It hurt) when Mommy took off my underwear,' but what he actually says is '(It hurt) when Mommy took off her underwear.'

(25c) further supports Murasugi & Hashimoto's (2004) analysis. According to Noji's (1973–1977) observation, in the context of (25c), the causative form *hak-(s)ase-te* should be used. However, Sumihare omits the causative suffix *-(s)ase*, and produces *hai-te* instead.[8]

The examples in (25) present additional evidence for the *v*-VP hypothesis: children hypothesize that the suffix *-(s)ase* appears in the head position of *v*P, but children omit it since [±cause] *v* is assumed to be zero at Stage II. In Murasugi & Hashimoto's (2004) analysis, both [+cause] and [-cause] small *v*'s are realized as zero morphemes (i.e., without phonological content). The 'error' can be attributed to the existence of alternations such as in (15), which are widely attested, as in English (di)transitive- intransitive (unaccusative) pairs, e.g., 'John passed the ring to Mary/ The ring passed to Mary' both involving the same surface form *pass*. Hence, we can say that Japanese-speaking children at Stage II assume that Japanese verbs are structured just like their English counterparts.

---

[8] See Murasugi, Hashimoto & Fuji (2007) for a more detailed analysis. There are some individual differences between Akkun (A) and Sumihare (S), but the order of acquisition is the same. The age for each stage can be summarized as in (i) and (ii).

(i) Akkun (A)
    Stage I: (2;05)–(2;07)
    Stage II: (2;07)–(4;08)
    Stage III: (3;06–)
    Stage IV: (5;03–)

(ii) Sumihare (S)
    Stage I: (1;11)–(2;01)
    Stage II: (2;01)–(2;05)
    Stage III: (2;05–)
    Stage IV: (3;04–)

Sumihare's Stage I is from 1;11 through around 2;01, and his Stage II is from 2;01 through around 2;05. Almost all verbs produced at around 2;00 are intransitive, or less transitive; *mi-te* 'see' for *mi-sete* 'show', and *ai-te* 'open(vi)' for *ak-ete* 'open(vt)', for example, are observed at 2;01 and 2;02. Sumihare overextends quite a few transitives as well as intransitives, but the overextension decreases after 2;03. Causatives without *-(s)ase* are also observed in Stage II, just as in the case of Akkun.

When and how, then, are the structure of causatives and causative morphemes acquired? Adult Japanese has a well-known causative verbal suffix, -sase which syntactically takes a sentential vP complement. Thus, the subject-oriented reflexive pronoun zibun can take either the causer or the causee as its antecedent in causative sentences.

(26) a. Taroo$_i$ ga   Hanako$_j$ ni   zibun$_{i/*j}$ no   koto   o   hanasi-ta.
       Taro   NOM Hanako   DAT self   GEN things ACC tell-PST
       'Taro told Hanako (things) about himself.'

   b. Taroo$_i$ ga   Hanako$_j$ ni   zibun$_{i/j}$ no   heya   o   katazuke-sase-ta.
      Taro   NOM Hanako   DAT self   GEN room   ACC clean-CAUS-PST
      'Taro made Hanako clean up her/his room.'
      (Murasugi & Hashimoto 2004:17)

This shows that causative sentences contain two subjects and, hence, an embedded clause (see Shibatani 1976, among others). The causative -sase, then, is not a realization of [+cause] v but is itself a V (or a V-v combination) under the VP-shell analysis.

Matsumoto (2000), however, proposes that there are monoclausal causatives in Japanese as well. Observe (27).

(27) Hanako$_i$ ga   umaretabakari   no   akatyan$_j$ ni   zibun$_{i/*j}$ no
     Hanako   NOM newborn   GEN baby   DAT self   GEN
     kutusita   o   hak-ase-ta.
     socks   ACC put.on-CAUS-PST
     'Hanako put self's (her) socks on a new born baby.'

As mentioned before, the Japanese reflexive pronoun zibun is subject oriented. In (27), it cannot take akatyan (the baby) as its antecedent, indicating that only Hanako plays the role of subject and (27) is monoclausal. Matsumoto (2000) calls such monoclausal -(s)ase causatives "lexical -(s)ase causatives."

Based on hypotheses advanced by Shibatani (1976) and Matsumoto (2000), Murasugi & Hashimoto (2004) propose (28a) and (28b) as the structural representations for these two types of -(s)ase causatives in the v-VP framework.

(28) a.

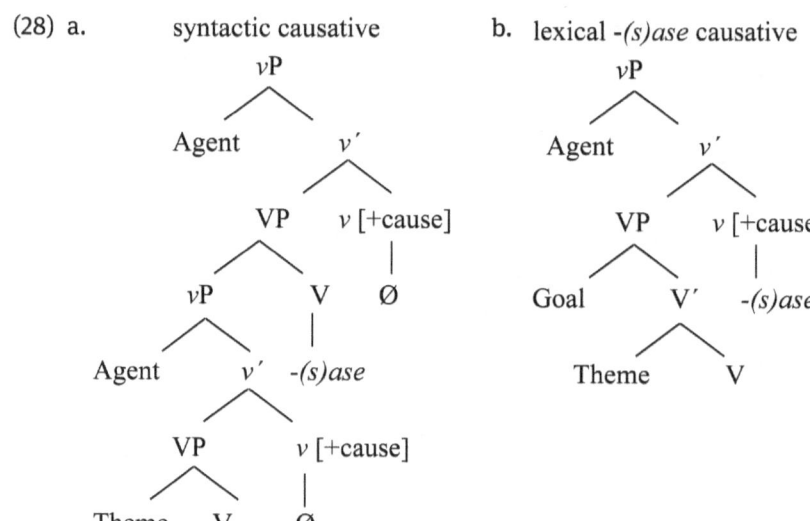

According to this analysis, *-(s)ase* is ambiguous in the adult grammar of Japanese. Under one interpretation, it is an independent large V taking a *v*-projection as its complement and yielding a complex structure. In this case, the dative argument is interpreted as agent. Under the other interpretation, it combines with a large V and forms a complex verb to yield a simple sentence with no embedding. The dative argument is in this case interpreted as a goal. In Murasugi & Hashimoto's terms, *-(s)ase* can here be analyzed as a realization of [+cause] *v*. For syntactic causatives having the structure in (28a), since both causer and causee function as subjects, they are both assigned the role of agent, the former by the higher small *v* and the latter by the lower small *v*. For lexical *-(s)ase* causatives having the structure in (28b), on the other hand, *-(s)ase* is the realization of [+cause], and the causee functions as goal, appearing not in the Spec of *v*P, but rather in the Spec of VP.

Akkun started uttering syntactic causative sentences quite productively around the age of five, but sporadic uses of *-sase* can also be observed in his speech much earlier.

Stage III, where sentences with an overt causative suffix *-(s)ase* are observed, begins at around age 3, although there are individual differences in the age of onset of this stage.[9] Some relevant examples are shown in (29).

---

[9] As for Akkun, it is around age 3;05 to 3;06 that Stage III begins, while Sumihare's Stage III begins much earlier. Sumihare starts producing the adult form of lexical causatives consistently at around 2;05.

(29) a. *Akkun ni   tabe-sase-tee.* (A, 3;06)
         DAT eat-CAUS-GER
   'Please feed Akkun (/me) (food).'

b. *Nomi-tyatye-te.* (*-tyatye* appears to correspond to adult *-sase*) (A, 3;07)
   drink-CAUS-GER
   'Please feed me (miso soup.)'

c. *Seizi-kun boku ga   ne   nak-asi-tan   zyanai   noyo.* (S, 2;07)
              I   NOM INT cry-CAUS-PST-COMP was-not SFP
   'I'm not the one who made Seiji cry.'

d. *Okaatyan hak-asi-te.* (S, 3;00)
   Mommy   put on-CAUS-GER
   'Mommy (please) put (a pair of shoes) on me.'

e. *Okaatyan kore Teruki-tyan ga   sin-asi-tan   yo.* (S, 3;04)
   Mommy   this   NOM die-CAUS-PST SFP
   'Mommy, Teruki-chan made this die.'

Interestingly, in all these examples, the causee is non-agentive. Thus, they can all be considered instances of the lexical *-(s)ase* causative. If (29a), for example, were a syntactic causative, it would mean something like '(Please) permit me to eat some food,' but it means rather 'Feed me some food' with *Akkun (me)* interpreted as a goal rather than agent. Therefore, (29a) is a lexical *-(s)ase* causative, where *-(s)ase* is a realization of [+cause] *v*. The same applies to (29b).

Murasugi, Hashimoto & Fuji (2007) argue that the examples given in (29c) through (29e) taken from Noji's longitudinal study are further supporting evidence for Murasugi & Hashimoto (2004). The context of (29c) is that Seizi is crying and Sumihare is under pains to explain that it was not Sumihare who made Seizi cry. Here, *Seizi* is not an agent, as his action, crying, was coerced by someone else. The agent is *boku* (I, or Sumihare), and the object *Seizi-kun* is scrambled (or topicalized) to sentence initial position. Hence, (29c) can be considered to have monoclausal structure. In (29d), Sumihare is asking his mother to put a pair of shoes directly on him, with Sumihare functioning as a covert indirect object, interpreted however as goal, not as agent. (29d) can therefore likewise be seen to have monoclausal structure. In (29e), *kore* (this) refers to a fly that, needless to say, died unintentionally. Thus, it is not an agent, and (29e) also has monoclausal structure. As these utterances occur at a stage when children struggle with the idiosyncratic realization of [±cause] *v*, one can conjecture that they are using *-sase* as one realization of [+cause] *v*.

Fuji, Hashimoto & Murasugi (2008) also report cases of overgeneration of the causative morpheme at Stage III. This overgeneration occurs in one of two ways: one in the form "verb + -(s)ase", and the other in the form "causative verb + causative morpheme". Examples of the first type of overgeneration are given in (30).

(30) a. *nomi-**tyatye**-te.* (-tyatye = -sase) (A, 3;07) (adult form: nom-**(s)ase**-te)
drink-CAUS-GER
Intended meaning: '(Please) feed me (miso soup.)'
(Murasugi & Hashimoto 2004)

  b. *ok-**i-sasi**-te.* (S, 3;01) (adult form: oko**si**-te)
wake.up-INTR-CAUS-GER
Intended meaning: '(Please) wake (me) up.'
(Noji 1973–1977)

The adult causative form of the verb *nom-(r)u* 'to drink' is *nom-(s)ase-ru*, formed by attaching the causative morpheme *-ase* to the verb stem, *nom*. However, (30a) shows that Akkun erroneously attaches *-tyatye*, the child's phonetic version of *-sase* to the compound form *nomi*, resulting in *nomi-tyatye-te*. In (30b), Sumihare asks someone to wake him up. Here, the IMP form of the lexical causative verb *okos-(r)u* 'to wake ... up,' or *okosi-te*, is expected in adult speech, but Sumihare erroneously attaches *-sasi* (sometimes used in place of the standard *-sase* in his dialect) to the stem of the intransitive verb *ok-i-ru* 'to get up.'

These data indicate that children know that v should be phonetically realized in forming causatives, but they fail to choose the right version among several ways of realizing the causative morpheme. Interestingly, the choice made by children tends to be the unmarked bound morpheme *-sase*.

The second type of overgeneration, "causative verb + causative morpheme," is observed at around late age three up to age five. Some relevant examples are given in (31).

(31) a. *Kuruma o   too-**si-sase**-ru.* (Taatyan, 3;10) (adult form: *too-**s**-(r)u*)
car   ACC pass-CAUS-CAUS-PRS
Intended meaning: '(I'll) let the car pass through.'

  b. *Kondo   mi-**se-si**-te   ageru   kara ne.* (Taatyan, 4;06)
next time see-CAUS-CAUS-GER give/let as   SFP
(adult form: mi-**se**-te)
Intended meaning: '(I'll) show (it to) you next time.'
(Arai 2003)

In (31a), the transitive verb *too-s-(r)u* 'to let ... pass,' which is a causative verb as well, is erroneously associated with an additional causative morpheme *-sase*. (31b) is a similar example of a doubly-marked causative. The transitive verb *mi-se-ru* 'to show' or 'to let ... see' is, in fact, a causative verb containing the transitive (or causative) morpheme *-se* in it. However, the child adds the additional causative morpheme *-si*,[10] producing *mi-se-si-te* by mistake.

Why then does the second type of overgeneration take place? Mamoru Saito (p.c.) has pointed out to us that the overgeneration in (31) can be considered morphological in nature since the number of arguments does not increase unlike well-known examples of syntactic overgeneration such as 'Don't giggle me' in (1b). This is the stage at which children still have difficulty in finding the appropriate form for verb stems as well as for bound morphemes. What children have internalized at this stage is an undifferentiated causative verb in the form of a bare verb stem, and a rule that *v* must be phonetically realized to form a causative verb. Hence, they attach additional causative morphemes *-sase* or *-si* onto the undifferentiated V, as illustrated in (32).

(32)

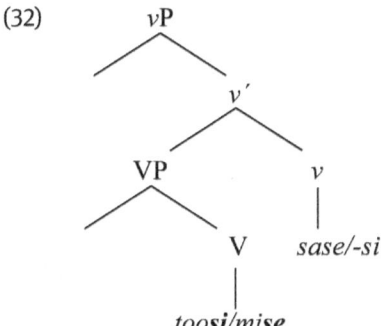

Since children regard the verbal forms *toosi* and *mise* as a whole to correspond to V, they attach additional causative morphemes in the position of *v* in order to realize causative meaning phonetically. This would account for the causative doubling phenomenon, and in particular the overgeneration phenomenon of the second type described above.[11]

---

10 The causative morphemes *-(s)ase* and *-(s)e* are often pronounced *-(s)asi* and *-(s)i* in western dialects of Japanese.

11 See Fuji, Hashimoto & Murasugi (2008) for a detailed analysis of the overgeneration of causative and potential morphemes. In Japanese, a number of syntactic phenomena, e.g., passive, causative, honorific, and so on, involve functional categories, and children have to "learn" the exact lexical realization for each functional category.

The acquisition of adult causative constructions with the full verb *-sase* takes place later than that of the lexical causatives. Some examples of Stage IV utterances are shown in (33) (Murasugi & Hashimoto 2004; Murasugi, Hashimoto & Fuji 2007).

(33) a. *Obaatyan no toko de tabe-masu. A, biiru dake*
Grandma GEN place LOC eat-PRS (formal) INT beer only

*nom-**ase**-te kudasai.* (A, 5;03)
drink-CAUS-GER please
'(I'll) eat at Grandma's place. Um, please let me drink beer (there)'

b. *Moo gohan tabe-**sase**-n yo.* (S, 4;09)
more food eat-CAUS-NEG SFP
'(I) won't let you eat anymore.'

c. *Tuke-**sase**-te age-tara funa o kure-tan yo.* (S, 5;03)
put-CAUS-GER let-COND fish ACC give-PST SFP
'When (I = Sumihare) let (the people fishing) put a net trap (in the water), (they) gave me a fish.'

In (33a), Akkun does not ask his mother to feed him, but asks her to let him drink beer. The causee *Akkun* is not overtly produced here, but is agentive. Hence, the causative in (33a) may be considered to be a syntactic causative. Sumihare's syntactic causatives appear at around 3;04, much earlier than Akkun's, but become fully productive beginning at age 4.[12] (33b) and (33c) each have two agents, one associated with each of two clauses in a biclausal structure. In (33b), for example, since Sumihare's utterance is directed to his father, the agent of the action *taberu* (eat) would be his father. Thus, (33b) can be considered an example of a syntactic causative. In (33c), the agent of the action *tuke-ru* 'put' would be the people fishing, who borrowed Sumihare's net, put it in the water, and gave Sumihare a fish they caught with it later, but not *me* (= Sumihare). On the other hand, the agent of the action *–sase-te age-ta* 'let (the people fishing put the net trap in the water)' is *I* (= Sumihare). Hence, (33c) also has two agents present and can be considered a syntactic causative as well.

---

[12] From 3;03 through 4;01 we find a few "syntactic causatives" with "wrong" lexical realization (e.g., *-se* for *-sase*). Sumihare's morphological realization of syntactic causatives can be considered to be fully acquired by the age of 4 years.

5 Implications and remaining problems

As discussed in Murasugi & Hashimoto (2004), children are equipped with the concept of a *v*-VP frame from the early stages of acquisition, but they require some time to discover the morphological makeup of the actual verbs, which are formed by combining V and *v*. The causative suffixal verb -*sase* is initially assumed to be a realization of [+cause] *v* and is only later acquired as a full verb that takes a sentential (*v*P) complement. Lexical items typically correspond to syntactic heads, but they are sometimes formed by combining two or more distinct morphemes that project phrases of their own. Children must perform morphological analysis in order to acquire such complex lexical items. We would expect such a process to take time in some cases, and that is exactly what Murasugi & Hashimoto (2004) have observed for the acquisition of verbs in Japanese.

There are two remaining questions to be addressed. One is regarding whether or not the acquisition process given in (10), repeated in (34), is empirically correct and descriptively adequate.

(34) Stage I: Small *v* is *tiyu/tita/tite* 'do/did/doing'
 Stage II: Small *v* is null
 Stage III: Acquisition of lexical causatives and transitive verbs; occasional erroneous lexical realization of *v*
 Stage IV: Acquisition of syntactic causatives; occasional erroneous lexical realization of V

In fact, an exactly parallel acquisition process has been confirmed by Murasugi, Hashimoto & Fuji (2007) based on a corpus analysis of Sumihare (Noji 1973–1977), and a longitudinal study by Nakatani (2010). Nakatani (2010) finds that a Japanese-speaking child, Yuta, follows a process of acquisition just like Akkun and Sumihare, as shown in (35).[13]

(35) 1;09 *Jyaa   suru.*
 ↓   onomatopoeia do
     'I want you to pour water in here.'

 1;11 *Naran   de.*
 ↓   line up (vi) in order
     'Please put them in order.'

---

[13] See Nakatani (2010) for a more detailed discussion.

2;03 *Yuta ga   kik-asi-te-ageru.*
↓   NOM hear-CAUS-GER-give
   'Yuta will let <u>you</u> hear (about it).'

2;07 *Tittyai ofune de   oyog-ase-tai   naa.*
   small ship with swim-CAUS-want SFP
   '(Putting a small doll on the ship) (I) want <u>the doll</u> to swim with the ship.'

Yuta starts by producing the onomatopoeia + *suru* (do) construction, followed by stages marked by verbal errors, lexical causatives, and syntactic causatives in that order. Since children brought up in different times and in different places exhibit the same acquisition process, it is quite plausible to conjecture that the data described here meet the criterion of descriptive adequacy.

The second question is regarding how children stop making 'errors' and acquire the adult system. Our recent corpus analysis of Sumihare (Noji 1973–1977) indicates that transitive-intransitives errors take place until 2;02, as far as the verbs *aku* (vi)/*akeru* (vt) are concerned.

(36) a. *Baatyan   **aite**.* (Sumihare (=S), 2;00)
         grandma   open(vi)
         Intended meaning: Grandma, please open (the door).

   b. *Tootyan   **aite**.* (S, 2;01)
      daddy   open(vi)
      Intended meaning: Daddy, please open (the door).

   c. *To   o   **aite**.* (S, 2;01)
      door ACC open(vi)
      Intended meaning: Please open the door.

   d. *Akete.   Kaatyan   **akete**.* (S, 2;01)
      open(vt) Mother   open(vt)
      Intended meaning: Mother, please open (the door).

   e. *Tootyan   **akete**.* (S, 2;02)
      Father   open(vt)
      Intended meaning: Father, please open (it).

Before around 2;01, only intransitive forms are used. However, as the data exemplified above indicate, at around 2;01, both forms, 'correct' and 'erroneous', are alternately used. Then, after around 2;02, few 'errors' are found as far as this verb pair is concerned.

The most important implication of this study is that children initially assume that pronounced verbs are Vs and that [±cause] *v* is phonetically empty, so that intransitives and their transitive counterparts should to them be homophonous, as in English.

The fact that Japanese-speaking children go through a stage corresponding to adult English would support the hypothesis that innate linguistic knowledge defines a space of possible human languages and possible linguistic variation. Linguistic errors arise in children's speech because at an intermediate stage of language acquisition, children try out possible linguistic features actually present in adult languages elsewhere in the world.

Children erroneously producing intransitive forms instead of (di)transitive forms, and intransitive/(di)transitive forms instead of causative forms are trying out languages that are not their mother tongue, yet never outside the bounds defined by the principles of possible grammar.

6 Conclusion

Children 'erroneously' produce intransitive forms instead of (di)transitive forms, and intransitive/(di)transitive forms instead of causative forms (e.g., *Daddy, I will feel you better* (meaning 'Daddy, I will make you feel better'); *Huusen hukurande* (lit. 'The balloon expands,' with the intended meaning 'Please blow up the balloon for me.')). In this chapter, well-known 'errors', which are presumably neither a response to the children's environment, nor produced due to children's limited processing ability, have been analyzed within the framework of Generative Grammar.

We have provided a uniform account of such verbal 'errors' following Larson's (1988) *v*-VP frame, or VP-shell, hypothesis, in line with Murasugi & Hashimoto (2004), namely that: (i) children making such errors as those above assume, at one stage of language acquisition, that [±cause] *v* is phonetically null, just like *pass*-type verbs in English, and (ii) what requires time is acquisition of the lexical form of each V and the forms in which [±cause] small *v*'s may be realized. We next discussed the acquisition of syntactic causatives, proposing that the causative morpheme *-sase* is used initially as a realization of [+cause] small *v*. This initial use of *-sase* entails that *-sase* is ambiguous between V and *v* in adult Japanese, and we argued that such a prediction is indeed borne out.

The evidence presented in this chapter provides, we believe, strong support for the existence of the *v*-VP frame as a syntactic structure in human language. According to our analysis, the process of acquisition of (di)transitive verbs detailed in this chapter does not necessarily reflect the acquisition of predicate-argument structures associated with verbs. The predicate-argument structures of large V's and small *v*'s are acquired quite early. What requires time is the acquisition of the lexical form of each V and, more importantly, the forms in which [±cause] small *v*'s are realized. The latter, in particular, must proceed step by step, because the realization of [±cause] small *v* depends on the associated large V in Japanese. This is part of the reason that children make transitive-intransitive-causative "errors." As this acquisition process proceeds, children start producing lexical causatives having phonetic form, e.g., -*sase* in Japanese, much before they acquire syntactic causatives.

Abbreviations

ACC accusative; CAUS causative; COMP complementizer; COND conditional; COP copula; DAT dative; GEN genitive; GER gerundive; IMP imperative; INT interjection; INTR intransitive; LOC locative; NEG negative; NOM nominative; PRS present; PST past; SFP sentence-final particle

Acknowledgments

The research presented here would not have been possible without discussions with colleagues and students involved in the activities of the Center for Linguistics at Nanzan University. Although I cannot name them all, I would like to thank Mamoru Saito, Tomoko Hashimoto, Chisato Fuji, Tomoko Kawamura, Tomomi Nakatani-Murai, Sachiko Kato, Koji Sugisaki, Luigi Rizzi, Adriana Belletti, Diane Lillo-Martin, William Snyder, Jean Crawford, Jonah Lin, Dylan Tsai, Yuji Takano, Hideki Kishimoto and Kensuke Takita for sharing their insights with me.

Deep gratitude is due to Taro Kageyama, Wesley Jacobsen, and the anonymous reviewers of this chapter for their invaluable comments.

An earlier version of this chapter was presented at the workshop on three-place predicates held at the Max Planck Institute for Psycholinguistics (Nijmegen, Holland) in May, 2003, the 2nd Yuelu Language Acquisition Workshop (Changsha, China) in September, 2005, a Lunch Talk at the University of Connecticut (Storrs, U.S.A.) in March, 2006, workshops held at Nanzan University (Nagoya, Japan) from 2002 through 2014, and the International Symposium on Valency Classes and Alternations in Japanese held at NINJAL (Tokyo, Japan) in August, 2011. At each of these I benefited from comments by participants and colleagues.

The research reported here was supported in part by a NINJAL Collaborative Research Project (Linguistic Variations within the Confines of the Language Faculty: A Study in Japanese First Language Acquisition and Parametric Syntax, Principal Investigator: Keiko Murasugi), a Nanzan University Pache Research Grant (I-A 2013–2015), and a JSPS Grant-in-Aid (2013–2016, #26370515, Principal Investigator: Keiko Murasugi and #26370708, Principal Investigator: Hiroko Tajika).

References

Arai, Fumio. 2003. Nihongo ni okeru kiin tadōshi no shūtoku dankai: kiin tadōshi -o meguru goyō no motsu imi [Developmental sequence in the acquisition of lexical causative verbs: Implications of causative errors in Japanese]. *Kyoto Sangyō Daigaku Ronshū Jinbunkagaku Keiretsu* [Kyoto Sangyo University Bulletin: Humanity Sciences] 30. 1–38.

Bowerman, Melissa. 1974. Learning the structure of causative verbs: A study in the relationship of cognitive, semantic, and syntactic development. *Papers and Report on Child Language Development* 8. 142–178.

Bowerman, Melissa. 1982. Evaluating competing linguistic models with language acquisition data: Implications of developmental errors with causative verbs. *Quaderni di Semantica* 3. 5–66.

Chomsky, Noam. 1995. *The minimalist program.* Cambridge, MA: MIT Press.

Figueira, Rosa Attié. 1984. On the development of the expression of causativity: A syntactic hypothesis. *Journal of Child Language* 11. 109–127.

Fuji, Chisato. 2006. Two types of causatives in Japanese and Japanese sign language: A study in syntax and acquisition. Nagoya: Nanzan University M.A. thesis.

Fuji, Chisato, Tomoko Hashimoto & Keiko Murasugi. 2008. A VP-shell analysis for the under-generation and the overgeneration in the acquisition of Japanese causatives and potentials. *Nanzan Linguistics* 4. 21–41.

Ito, Noriko. 2005. The longitudinal study of Jun and Shin. Unpublished ms., Nanzan University.

Larson, Richard. 1988. On the double object construction. *Linguistic Inquiry* 19. 335–391.

Lord, Carol. 1979. 'Don't you fall me down': Children's generalization regarding CAUSE and transitivity. *Papers and Reports on Child Language Development* 17. 81–89.

Madhavan, Punnappurath. 2006. Transitivity alternations and the layered VP. Paper presented at the Hyderabad-Nanzan Joint Workshop, Nanzan University, October 21–22.

Marcotte, Jean-Philippe. 2005. *Causative alternation errors in child language acquisition.* Stanford: Stanford University dissertation.

Matsumoto, Yo. 2000. On the crosslinguistic parameterization of causative predicates: Implications from Japanese and other languages. In Miriam Butt & Tracy Holloway King (eds.), *Argument realization*, 135–169. Stanford: CSLI.

Murasugi, Keiko & Tomoko Hashimoto. 2004. Three pieces of acquisition evidence for the *v*-VP frame. *Nanzan Linguistics* 1. 1–19.

Murasugi, Keiko, Tomoko Hashimoto & Chisato Fuji. 2007. VP-shell analysis for the acquisition of Japanese intransitive verbs, transitive verbs, and causatives. *Linguistics* 45 (3). 615–651.

Murasugi, Keiko, Tomoko Hashimoto & Sachiko Kato. 2005. On the acquisition of causatives in Japanese. *Nanzan Linguistics* 2. 47–60.

Nakatani, Tomomi. 2010. Shieki no kakutoku [Acquisition of causatives]. Unpublished ms. Nanzan University.

Noji, Junya. 1973–1977. *Yōji no gengoseikatsu no jittai* I–IV [A longitudinal study of a Japanese-speaking child]. Tokyo: Bunka Hyōron Shuppan.

Okabe, Reiko. 2007. Children's acquisition of causatives and bi-clausality in Japanese: An experimental study. *Proceedings of GALANA* 2. 309–319.

Okubo, Ai. 1975. *Yōji no kotoba to chie* [Children's language and knowledge]. Ayumi Shuppan.

Otsu, Yukio. 2002. Gengo no kakutoku. [Language acquisition.]. In Yukio Otsu, Masayuki Ikeuchi, Noriko Imanishi & Masanori Suikō (eds.), *Gengo kenkyuu nyuumon* [Introduction to linguistics], 179–191. Tokyo: Kenkyusha

Shibatani, Masayoshi. 1976. Causativization. In Masayoshi Shibatani (ed.), *Syntax and semantics 5: Japanese generative grammar*, 239–294. New York: Academic Press.

Suzuki, Seiichi. 1987. Yōji no bunpō nōryoku [Chidren's grammatical knowledge]. In Shūsuke Fukuzawa (ed.), *Kodomo no gengo shinri* [Children's linguistic mind], 141–180. Tokyo: Dainihon Tosho.

Ayumi Matsuo, Sotaro Kita, Gary C. Wood, and Letitia Naigles
11 Children's use of morphosyntax and argument structure to infer the meaning of novel transitive and intransitive verbs

1 Introduction

Since Quine (1960), researchers involved in children's vocabulary development have focused on the apparent difficulty children may face in vocabulary acquisition and the relative ease children have in the actual acquisition process. Many researchers found that nouns are acquired before verbs in a number of languages because children are believed to utilize constraints such as Contrast or Mutual Exclusivity (Clark 1987) or the Whole-Object Bias (Markman 1987). One exception to this is a finding in Korean where verb spurt seems to take place before noun spurt (see Choi & Gopnik 1995 for details). Since Japanese is typologically similar to Korean, Ogura (2006) entertained a possibility that Japanese children may acquire verbs before nouns; however, she found that Japanese children have noun bias unlike Korean children. In spite of noun bias reported in many languages, however, by the age of two, children seem to have general ideas on various types of verb semantics (Pinker 1984, 1989). This chapter aims to revisit the topic of verb acquisition; specifically, we will focus on current research on verb acquisition in argument drop languages and the children's uses of syntactic as well as morpho-syntactic cues in verb acquisition.

To reconcile the gap between a presumed difficulty and the actual relative ease of verb acquisition, Landau & Gleitman (1985) proposed the Syntactic Bootstrapping hypothesis as a principled guide for verb acquisition. Naigles (1990) later supported this hypothesis with her experimental findings with English-speaking 2;1 year olds. Let us consider how the Syntactic Bootstrapping hypothesis should work in both pro-drop and non-pro-drop languages.

Consider the situation where the child hears "gorping" in isolation, without a syntactic frame, while transporting a toy truck to her parent. This mystery verb can have many possible meanings such as 'bring', 'come', 'walk', 'get', 'take', 'play' and so forth. However, if the child hears "oh you are gorping the truck",

---

Ayumi Matsuo, Kobe College
Sotaro Kita, University of Warwick
Gary C. Wood, University of Sheffield
Letitia Naigles, University of Connecticut

the verb has restricted possibilities where it may mean 'taking'. In addition, when the child hears "oh you are gorping", the verb must mean something like 'coming' or 'walking'. Landau & Gleitman (1985) proposed that the frame a certain mystery verb appears in helps children narrow down plausible interpretations that the verb may have. In the examples above, the (transitive) syntactic frame "you are Xing the truck" helps children conjecture the verb must refer to some action that takes place with a causative force. On the other hand, the (intransitive) frame "you are Xing" helps children conjecture that X involves a noncausative action. If you are learning a non-pro-drop language such as English, it is generally true that a verb that appears in a transitive frame has a causative interpretation whereas a verb that appears in an intransitive frame has a noncausative interpretation (although see Naigles 1996 and Levin & Rappoport 1995 for more discussion).

Let us know consider how this hypothesis might affect Japanese children who are in the process of verb acquisition. In the same situation as above, suppose the child hears "hekitte-iru" in isolation. As mentioned, the verb may mean 'bring', 'come', 'walk', 'get', 'take', 'play' and so forth. However, when the child hears a verb in an intransitive frame such as (1), the verb has more possible interpretations than in the English case:

(1) A,   Hanako-chan,   hekitte-iru   ne.
     Oh   Hanako   gorping   tag
     'Oh Hanako, you are gorping, aren't you?'

'Hekitte-iru' in (1) can refer to a wide variety of interpretations as an isolated verb. In other words, (1) can mean 'Hanako, you are coming, aren't you?', 'Hanako, you are playing, aren't you?', or 'Hanako, you are getting something, aren't you?' to illustrate a few cases. This is because Japanese is a pro-drop language that allows pervasive argument ellipsis (Shibatani 1977, 2001). Accordingly, example (1) can be a simple intransitive construction or a transitive construction with an elided object noun. It is also possible that (1) is an intransitive construction with a dropped instrumental phrase. This means that Japanese children cannot rely on the syntactic frame that a verb appears in as English-speaking children do. This brings us to a question as to how Japanese children or children who are acquiring other pro-drop language such as Chinese, Hindi, Korean or Turkish tackle verb acquisition. It is interesting to note that there is no reported delay in lexical acquisition by children who are exposed to pro-drop languages, which makes us conjecture that these children might rely on other sources of information for learning verb meanings, such as morphological or pragmatic cues. However, it is also possible that they do make use of the

Syntactic Bootstrapping procedure, albeit in different ways (see Narasimhan et al. 2005; Rispoli 1987). This issue will be discussed again in Section 2.1.

Matsuo et al. (2012) carried out one of the first handful of studies exploring the Syntactic Bootstrapping hypothesis in a language that has possibilities of relatively free word order as well as argument ellipsis. As discussed in Section 2.2, related studies have been conducted with children learning Mandarin Chinese or Turkish; however, these latter studies have not yet investigated the *novel* verb learning that is the key test of Syntactic Bootstrapping. Matsuo et al. (2012) carried out a series of experiments using the intermodal preferential looking paradigm (IPL) in order to investigate whether Japanese two-year-olds use morpho-syntactic cues to learn meanings of novel verbs.

2 Previous studies

2.1 Naigles (1990), Naigles & Kako (1993): IPL in English

Naigles (1990) investigated whether or not English-speaking children who are learning novel verbs make use of Syntactic Bootstrapping. There were 24 participants who took part in this study and they were the youngest (between 1;11 and 2;3 with a mean age of 2;1) among the IPL studies conducted on novel verb acquisition. Naigles presented these children with multiple-action scenes composed of two simultaneous actions, one causative and the other noncausative, paired with a nonsense verb in either a transitive or intransitive frame. She found that the children who heard a transitive audio looked longer at the causative action whereas the children who heard the intransitive audio preferred to look at the non-causative action. Based on this result, she concluded that children use sentence structure to infer whether novel verbs have a causative or non-causative interpretation.

Naigles & Kako (1993) reported findings from three experiments. In all three, they modified the method used in Naigles (1990) in order to measure children's initial preferences for novel actions introduced in an experiment. They divided the participants into three groups; the first group heard a novel verb without a syntactic frame during the teaching phase (frameless group), the second group of children heard the verb in an intransitive frame and the third group of children heard the verb in a transitive frame. In Experiment 1, using the same video stimuli as Naigles (1990), Naigles & Kako (1993) found that both the children who heard novel verbs in the frameless audio and in the intransitive audio preferred looking at noncausative synchronous actions; however, the children who heard the verbs in the transitive audio again preferred the causative actions.

In Experiments 2 and 3, Naigles & Kako (1993) investigated whether or not Syntactic Bootstrapping facilitates acquisition of contact verbs such as 'rub', 'stroke', 'brush' and 'wipe'. Both causative and contact verbs appear in transitive frames but they are different in their verb semantics. In causative verb constructions, an agent makes a patient NP to do something but the same does not hold in contact verb constructions, where patient NPs are not caused to do any actions. The data gathered from 53 children averaging 27 months of age revealed that they preferred to look at the contact action when they heard the transitive audio. In sum, children are able to map contact interpretations onto novel verbs when these are introduced in the transitive frame, which was similar to what they did to the causative interpretation in Experiment 1.

The results introduced above demonstrate that although English-speaking children prefer noncausative synchronous actions in the frameless condition (when they hear novel verbs in isolation), they alter their preference when they hear verbs in a transitive syntactic frame. Naigles & Kako (1993) conclude that "the results of these three experiments fortify findings that emerged from earlier research on Syntactic Bootstrapping, showing that young children use syntactic information to constrain or alter the meanings of novel verbs" (1961; 1993). It is intriguing that children as young as two years old succeeded in assigning both causative and contact interpretations to verbs when they appeared in a transitive frame. Let us next look at how children who are acquiring pro-drop languages utilize syntactic frame in acquiring verb meanings. As mentioned above, the cues concerning argument structure are not as constant and stable in pro-drop languages.

2.2 Turkish and Chinese: the Ark studies

Naigles and her colleagues have carried out a number of studies in which children learning Turkish or Chinese have been asked to interpret sentences in 1-NP and 2-NP frames (Candan et al. 2012; Göksun et al. 2008; Lee & Naigles 2008). The paradigm was based on Naigles et al. (1993; see also Naigles et al. 1992): Children were asked to act out sentences, using a toy Noah's Ark set and small wooden animals. Crucially, approximately half of the sentences were ungrammatical, such that conventionally transitive verbs were presented in 1-NP frames (e.g., '*The zebra brings') and conventionally intransitive verbs were presented in 2-NP frames (e.g., '*The zebra goes the lion'). Naigles et al. (1993) found that 2-, 3- and 4-year-old English speakers typically enacted these sentences by following the semantics of the frames rather than the verbs. That is, they enacted 'The zebra brings' by making the zebra move by itself across a stage, and they enacted 'The zebra goes the lion' by making the zebra push or carry the lion. Thus, they treated 'transitive' verbs as noncausative when they appeared in 1-NP frames, and they treated 'intransitive' verbs as causative when they appeared in 2-NP frames. It is important to point out that the children enacted GRAMMATICAL sentences correctly at least 80% of the time; therefore, they treated 'The zebra brings the chicken' DIFFERENTLY from 'The zebra brings.' Adult speakers of English performed differently with the ungrammatical sentences: Their dominant enactments followed the semantics of the verbs, regardless of the frame. So they enacted 'The zebra brings' by making the zebra push or carry *something* (another animal, a small block), and they enacted 'The zebra goes the lion' by making the zebra move *to* the lion or *with* the lion. Interestingly, there were some age effects even within the preschoolers, in that the 3- and 4-year-olds added a patient to 'the zebra brings' around 50% of the time, whereas the 2-year-olds did so only about 35% of the time.

Naigles and her colleagues wondered how children learning Chinese or Turkish would enact similar sentences that included too many or too few NPs. Chinese is similar to Japanese in allowing NP ellipsis and relatively free word order; however, Mandarin Chinese does not use case markers to indicate thematic role assignment. SVO is the modal word order when both subject and object NPs are present; however, corpora studies have revealed that NV sentences (comprising 40% of adult utterances in Lee & Naigles 2005) are more frequent than NVN sentences (comprising 20% of adult utterances). Moreover, whereas transitive verbs appear with post-verbal NPs about 40% of the time (hence, object omissions occur about 60% of the time) intransitive verbs also occasionally appear with post-verbal NPs about 13% of the time (i.e., in sentences like 'qu4 xue2xiao4/go (to) school'). Thus, while the reliability of the *presence* of the post-verbal NP cue to indicate a transitive verb is high (about .83), the reliability of the *absence* of a post-verbal NP to indicate an intransitive verb is much lower (about .41). Chinese-learning children who relied solely on the cues in the input, then, might understand that verbs in 2-NP frames indicate causation, but should be much less likely to conjecture that verbs in 1-NP frames indicate the absence of causation.

Lee & Naigles (2008) tested these hypotheses with two groups of Mandarin learners in Singapore, who averaged 2;8 and 3;8. They were asked to enact sentences containing four transitive verbs (bring/dai4, take/na2, push/tui1, and put/fang4) and four intransitive verbs (come/lai2, go/qu4, fall/dao3, and stand/zhan4). Each verb was presented in a 2-NP frame (NVN) and a 1-NP frame (NV).

Children had to enact at least 80% of the grammatical sentences (transitive verbs in 2-NP frames, intransitive verbs in 1-NP frames) correctly in order for their enactments of the ungrammatical, or more properly 'underspecified' sentences to be coded. Enactments were coded for causativity, as described in Naigles et al. (1993; see also Naigles et al. 1992; Naigles et al. 1995).

Lee & Naigles (2008) found that the children's enactments followed the frames they were given. For example, *more* children enacted 'Xiao3zhu1 qu4 shi1zi/The pig goes the lion' causatively than 'Xiao3zhu1 qu4/The pig goes'. And *fewer* children enacted 'Xiao3gou3 dai4/The dog brings' causatively than 'Xiao3gou3 na4 shi1zi/The dog takes the lion'. Thus, when they heard transitive verbs in 1-NP frames, they enacted these noncausatively whereas when they heard intransitive verbs in 2-NP frames, they enacted them causatively. These effects held, by and large, for analyses both by subjects and by items, and the effect sizes were similar for both frames: intransitive verbs in 2-NP frames were enacted causatively about 40% *more* than the same verbs in 1-NP frames, and transitive verbs in 1-NP frames were enacted causatively about 40% *less* than the same verbs in 2-NP frames. As with the English speakers, the effects of the frame were stronger for the 2-year-olds than for the 3-year-olds; however, the Mandarin speakers performed fewer causative enactments of ungrammatical or unattested 2-NP sentences than their English-speaking peers.

Based in these findings, Lee & Naigles (2008) concluded that the number of NPs in a sentence provide a solid cue to verb meaning, even among child learners of a language in which NP ellipsis is pervasive. Two points are worth highlighting here. First, the correspondence between 1-NP frames and noncausative meanings was similar to that between 2-NP frames and causative meanings, even though Mandarin input supports the latter correspondence much more reliably than the former. Second, though, some effect of input frequency can be seen in the comparison between the two languages: the 2-NP link with causative verbs is less strong in Mandarin child learners than English child learners, and this may be related to the fact that 2-NP frames are less frequent in Mandarin than in English. Nonetheless, the robustness of the frame-meaning correspondences in Mandarin in the face of pervasive NP-ellipsis and free word order suggests that some kind of regularization is imposed upon the input by the Mandarin-learning child (Lee & Naigles 2008).

Turkish presents a somewhat different challenge to the Syntactic Bootstrapping hypothesis. Like Mandarin, Turkish allows NP ellipsis and free word order; however, unlike Mandarin – and more like Japanese – Turkish noun phrases are case-marked for thematic role. For example, compare (2) and (3) below:

(2) *Zebra kedi-yi getirsin*
    Zebra cat-ACC brings
    'The zebra brings the cat.'

(3) *Zebra-yı   kedi getirsin*
    Zebra-ACC cat   brings
    'The cat brings the zebra.'

Both of these sentences include the same NPs in the same order (SOV is the modal order for Turkish), but the presence of the accusative marker –(y)I designates the cat as the patient of the action in (2) and the zebra as the patient in (3) (Erguvanlı 1984; accusative markers are also indicators of definiteness). Moreover, dropping the subject yields a 1-NP sentence that is nonetheless grammatical and interpretable:

(4) *Kedi-yi getirsin*
    Cat-ACC brings
    '(Something/Someone) brings the cat.'

Thus, speakers of Turkish may ignore argument order and number entirely, and focus instead on the case marking of the expressed NPs, when interpreting sentences. During acquisition, the accusative case marker appears early in children's speech (Aksu-Koç & Slobin 1985); therefore, it is possible that child learners of Turkish rely on nominal morphology (morphological bootstrapping) rather than argument number and order (Syntactic Bootstrapping) in verb learning. However, recent online studies of sentence processing have suggested that word order is a useful aid to sentence comprehension by adult Turkish speakers (Demiral et al. 2008); therefore, it is possible that argument number and order are actually used by children, as well.

Göksun et al. (2008) tested these hypotheses with four groups of Turkish speakers in Istanbul, with average ages of 2;7, 3;4, 4; 5, and 5;3. They were asked to enact sentences containing six transitive verbs (bring/getir, take/gotur, push/it, pull/cek, drop/dusur and carry/tasi) and six intransitive verbs (come/gel, go/git, fall/dus, walk/yusu, run/kos, and lie-down/yat). Each verb was presented in 2-NP frame and 1-NP frames; moreover, frames either included case markers (e.g., NN$_{ACC}$V, N$_{ACC}$V) or did not (NNV, NV). Children had to enact at least 80% of the fully specified sentences (transitive verbs in 2-NP frames, intransitive verbs in 1-NP frames) correctly in order for their enactments of the ungrammatical, or more properly 'underspecified' sentences to be coded. Enactments were coded for causativity, just as with the Chinese study.

Göksun et al. (2008) found significant and independent effects of both number of NPs and presence/absence of accusative case. Effects of the accusative marker were seen with both fully specified and underspecified frames; for example, more children enacted 'Zebra kedi-**yi** getirsin/The zebra brings the cat' causatively than 'Zebra kedi getirsin/The zebra brings a cat', and more children enacted 'Zebra kedi-**yi** gelsin/The zebra comes the cat' causatively than 'Zebra kedi gelsin/The zebra comes a cat'. More children also enacted 'Kedi-**yi** getirsin/Cat-ACC brings' causatively than 'Kedi getirsin/Cat brings'. Across all verbs and both 2-NP and 1-NP frames, the presence of the accusative marker elicited more causative enactments than its absence.

Effects of the number of NPs were also seen regardless of whether the accusative marker was also present. For example, more children enacted Zebra kedi gelsin/The zebra comes a cat' causatively than 'Zebra gelsin/The zebra comes,' and fewer children enacted 'Zebra-**yi** getirsin/Zebra-ACC brings' causatively than Zebra kedi-**yi** getirsin/The zebra brings the cat.' In sum, intransitive verbs were enacted causatively more frequently when they appeared in 2-NP frames than when they appeared in 1-NP frames, and transitive verbs were enacted causatively less frequently when they appeared in 1-NP frames than when they appeared in 2-NP frames.

Based on these findings, Göksun et al. (2008) concluded that Turkish children provided evidence for *morpho-syntactic bootstrapping*, in which verb meanings are influenced by both the number of NPs of their syntactic frame and the presence/absence of case marking. They rightly pointed out, though, that the effects of the number of NPs was weaker than that observed for English speakers. Whereas English-speaking preschoolers enacted 2-NP sentences with intransitive verbs at above chance levels (e.g., 65–75%), their Turkish speaking peers enacted similar sentences at chance levels. That is, Turkish preschoolers' enactments of verbs in 2-NP frames were significantly more causative than in 1-NP frames (e.g. 40% vs. 10%), but causative enactments were rarely their dominant response for intransitive verbs.

Taken together, these studies indicate that characteristics of syntactic frames do influence verb interpretation and extension in children learning pro-drop languages, and thus, that Syntactic Bootstrapping is a viable procedure for verb learning in those languages. Children learning Turkish or Mandarin Chinese extended the meanings of familiar verbs according to the demands of the sentences in which they heard them: In both languages, intransitive verbs in 2-NP frames tended to be interpreted as including a causative component, and transitive verbs in 1-NP frames tended to be interpreted as missing their usual causative component. In Turkish, the presence of the accusative case marker also promoted more causative interpretations, even for intransitive verbs. However, these studies are limited in that they did not simulate verb learning from the beginning; i.e., by teaching the children novel verbs for novel actions as was done by Naigles (1990) and Naigles & Kako (1993). The strongest test of Syntactic Bootstrapping is one that involves novel verb acquisition, and it is this test that we applied to children learning Japanese.

3 Study on Japanese

3.1 Input Data

Before going into the details of the IPL study in Japanese, Matsuo et al. (2012) first investigated how pervasive ellipsis is in caregiver's input to a Japanese child in order to see how reliably the cues of Syntactic Bootstrapping can serve for Japanese children. The analysis of the Jun corpus from the CHILDES database (Ishii 1999; MacWhinney 2000) displayed quite a sporadic pattern of argument structures. The corpus from when Jun was 1;10 to 2;2 (a total of 13 files) was analyzed; there were 9717 lines of father-child conversation. Matsuo et al. (2012) report that both arguments and case markers are often omitted in the father's utterances. Surprisingly, it was only 11% of intransitive constructions that appeared with an overt subject and case markers such as 'ga', 'wa' and 'mo'. As for transitive constructions, there were only 1.3% of transitive utterances that appeared with overt NPs followed by a nominative and an accusative case markers. Such characteristics of parental utterances cast a question whether it is enough to create stable scaffolding for Japanese children. Similar questions have been asked by Suzuki (2000), who carried out experiments using case markers.

Suzuki (2000) reports that Japanese children have a pronounced difficulty with an accusative case marker. After seeing pictures where two animals are engaged in a hitting action, they are asked to answer questions such as (5) and (6) with missing arguments. 3- and 4-year-old children showed an error rate of 46.6% for object questions as in (5):

(5) *Dare-ga   tataita   no.*
    Who-Nom   hit   Q
    'who hit (X)?'

(6) *Dare-o   tataita   no.*
    Who-Acc   hit   Q
    'whom did (X) hit?'

Even an older group of children, namely 5- and 6-year olds, produced 27.9% of errors for answering questions such as (5).

Together with spontaneous data reported in Clancy (1985) and Morikawa (1989), there is an apparent difficulty for Japanese children in producing and interpreting NPs with correct nominative and accusative case markers. Given the results of parental utterances with pervasive argument and case marker drop and the developmental and experimental results with poor understanding of case markers, we cannot prove that the Syntactic Bootstrapping hypothesis is effective among Japanese-speaking children. The following section summarizes an experiment utilizing IPL in order to find an answer for such an investigation in Matsuo et al. (2012).

3.2 Preferential Looking Experiment

The study by Matsuo et al. (2012) investigated whether Japanese children can use number of arguments and case markers to infer the meaning of novel verbs. They used the same intermodal preferential looking paradigm and video stimuli used for a study on English-speaking children in Naigles (1990), as discussed in Section 2.1. During the teaching phase, children saw videos showing both a causative action and a non-causative action and heard a novel verb (*e.g. neketteru*) in one of three sentence frames (see (7)): transitive with case markers, transitive without case markers, and intransitive.

(7) a. Intransitive (with a coordinated subject with a case marker)
     Ahiru-san-to   usagi-san-ga   neket-teru   yo.
     duck-Mr-and   rabbit-Mr-NOM   Verb-be.ing   SFP
     'The duck and the rabbit are neketting (a novel verb).'

   b. Transitive with case makers
     Ahiru-san-ga   usagi-san-o   neket-teru   yo.
     duck-Mr-NOM   rabbit-Mr-ACC   Verb-be.ing   SFP
     'The duck is neketting (a novel verb) the rabbit.'

   c. Transitive without case markers
     Ahiru-san   usagi-san   neket-teru   yo.
     duck-Mr   rabbit-Mr   Verb-be.ing SFP
     'The duck is neketting (a novel verb) the rabbit.'

The children who had heard novel verbs in the intransitive frame in the teaching phase did not shift their gaze to the non-causative action when they were prompted to look at the referent of the verb in the test phase. Thus, these children did not infer a non-causative meaning from the sentence frame with one argument with the nominative case marker, which contrasts with English-speaking children, who do make this inference (Naigles 1990). This may be because, in Japanese, such a sentence frame is compatible with a transitive verb if one of the arguments is dropped. The children who had heard novel verbs in the transitive frame with case markers significantly shifted their gaze to the causative action when they were prompted to look at the referent of the verb in the test phase; however, such a shift was not observed for the children who heard the transitive sentence without case makers. Thus, the Japanese children used the transitive sentence frame to infer causative meaning of the novel verb, but only if the arguments had overt case markers. The importance of case marking has been reported also for Turkish children (see Section 3; Göksun et al. 2008). Just as Turkish children, Japanese children infer the meaning of novel words using Morpho-Syntactic Bootstrapping.

Morpho-Syntactic Bootstrapping in Japanese children is interesting because parental input in Japanese have a lot less information about the mapping between sentential form and verb meaning than in English. As we discussed in Section 3.1, because of argument dropping in Japanese, the number of overt arguments is much less consistently associated with transitive vs. intransitive verbs in Japanese than in English. Furthermore, overt case markers are infrequent. Thus, Syntactic Bootstrapping is robust even when the input does not provide consistent information about the number of NPs that 'go with' specific verbs.

3.3 New Proposal for Intermodal Preferential Looking Experiment and its Preliminary Result

The above results support the proposal that Japanese children are using Syntactic Bootstrapping in inferring novel verb meanings when they learn the new verbs in a canonical word order with case markings. This is a successful replication of Naigles (1990) using a Japanese audio except for issues concerning intransitive stimuli. We propose a new experiment using the same IPL method in order to alleviate the results of our 2012 paper where Japanese children did not shift significantly towards the matching screen on the intransitive trial. In the transitive trial, 21 out of 34 children demonstrated shifts towards the matching screen; however, in the intransitive condition, the children were not directed towards non-causative meanings significantly. We discussed this was possibly due to the characteristics of Japanese where arguments can be omitted freely; in other words, our intransitive stimuli were ambiguous between intransitive and transitive with object omission. We aim to investigate whether our finding in the 2012 paper with respect to the intransitive trial is a common result among 2- and 3-year-olds in our new experiment.

In Matsuo & Naigles' (2014) new movie, we only have one subject NP. Let us first revisit the original movie discussed in Section 3.2. In the non-causative movie, there were two characters involved (a duck and a bunny) and they were doing the same non-causative action with their arms; Duck and Bunny moving one of their arms in a circle in the air. There was a concern that a coordinated subject in (7a) might have been giving cues to the children such that they are choosing a screen with a coordinated movement by only processing a conjunction between two subject nouns: *to* 'and'. (7a) is repeated below in (8):

(8) Intransitive (with a coordinated subject with a case marker)
Ahiru-san-to   usagi-san-ga   neket-teru   yo.
duck-Mr-and   rabbit-Mr-NOM   Verb-be.ing   SFP
'The duck and the rabbit are neketting (a novel verb).'

In Matsuo, Kita & Naigles (2014), we changed the coordinated subject NP in (8) to a single character in (9) and paired it with a transitive stimulus as in (10):

(9) Intransitive (with a single subject with a case marker)
Ouma-san-ga   neket-teru   yo.
Horse-Mr-NOM   Verb-be.ing   SFP
'The horse is neketting (a novel verb).'

(10) Transitive (with a single subject with a case marker)
Ouma-san-ga   tori-san-o   neket-teru   yo.
Horse-Mr-NOM   Bird-Mr-ACC   Verb-be.ing   SFP
'The horse is neketting (a novel verb) the bird.'

In (9), there was only one character, a horse, who is engaged in a novel action, which should provide children with fewer cues because there is no coordinated action involved.

Our preliminary results so far with 42 children show that 27 children succeeded in our experiment and looked at matched scenes longer (non-causative actions for intransitive stimuli and causative actions for transitive stimuli). This was surprising to us because as mentioned above, the children did not shift significantly towards the matching screen on the intransitive trial in our previous paper. More detailed analyses of our results are necessary but it will be an important finding if Japanese children do indeed succeed in both transitive and intransitive trials in our new experimental conditions.

4 Future study and conclusions

This chapter reviewed evidence that children who are acquiring both pro-drop and non-pro-drop languages use Syntactic and Morpho-syntactic Bootstrapping in verb acquisition. Two experimental paradigms have been used to provide such evidence: the intermodal preferential looking paradigm for English and Japanese, and the act-out paradigm for English, Chinese and Turkish. The intermodal preferential looking paradigm uses novel verbs and measures the time children spent looking at two screens that picture the potential meaning of novel verbs. The act-out paradigm uses both grammatical and ungrammatical sentences with existing verbs and measures how young children interpret verbs presented in 1-NP vs. 2-NP frames by testing how they use toy animals. Results obtained from studies employing these two paradigms show that children use formal features indicating the argument structure of sentences to infer verb meaning.

Japanese with its flexible word order provides an opportunity to ascertain whether Japanese children adopt the '1st NP = agent' strategy proposed by Bever (1970). Both Dittmar et al. (2008) and Matsuo et al. (2012) showed that German- and Japanese-speaking two-year-olds could correctly identify the agent and patient of a sentence with a novel transitive verb when the verb was presented in a sentence frame that both had case marking and occurred in canonical word order. However, neither of these studies obtained the same results for sentences having a scrambled word order. It would be interesting to see what results would be obtained if sentences such as (11) and (12) were used in the teaching phase:

(11) *Ouma-san-ga   hekitte-iru   yo,   Tori-san-o.*
      horse-NOM   Verb-be.ing   SFP   bird-ACC
      'The horse is gorping (X), the bird'

(12) *Tori-san-o   Ouma-san-ga   hekitte-iru   yo.*
      bird-ACC   horse-NOM   Verb-be.ing   SFP
      'The bird, the horse is gorping (X).'

Both (11) and (12) involve a non-canonical word order where the object NP is post-positioned in (11) and fronted before the subject NP in (12). Matsuo et al. (2012) report that out of 144 input utterances produced with two arguments in the CHILDES Jun corpus, there were 96 instances of SOV (67%), 45 instances of post position (OV,S and SV, O) (31.2%) and three instances of scrambling (OSV) (2%). That is, even though post-position is much more common than scrambling, the dominant word-order in these child-caregiver interactions was the canonical SOV order for sentences with two arguments. Given the two input structures in (11) and (12), it is plausible to assume that young children would perform better when (11) is provided as input than when (12) is. We will leave this question to future experiments testing the validity of the Syntactic Bootstrapping Hypothesis for the acquisition of Japanese.

Acknowledgments

Part of this work was supported by the Economic and Social Research Council in the UK (RES 000-22-1398). The research described in section 2.2 was funded by NICHD R01 DC07428 and NICHD R01 HD048662 to L. Naigles, who also thanks her collaborators on those studies (Joanne Lee, Tilbe Goksun, and Aylin Küntay). We thank Yuri Shinya for her assistance with data collection and coding of the study described in section 3.2. Email address for correspondence: matsuo@mail.kobe-c.ac.jp

References

Bever, Thomas G. 1970. The cognitive basis for linguistic structures. In John R. Hayes, (ed.), *Cognition and the development of language*. New York: Wiley.
Candan, Ayse, Aylin Küntay, Ya-Ching Yeh, Hintat Cheung, Laura Wagner & Letitia R. Naigles. 2012. Age and language effects in children's processing of word order. *Cognitive Development* 27. 205–221.
Choi, Soonja & Alison Gopnik. 1995. Early acquisition of verbs in Korean: A cross-linguistic study. *Journal of Child Language* 22. 497–529.
Clancy, Patricia. 1985. The acquisition of Japanese. In Dan Isaac Slobin (ed.), *The crosslinguistic study of language acquisition*, volume 1. The Data, 373–524. Hillsdale, NJ: Lawrence Erlbaum Associates.
Clark, Eve. 1987. The principle of contrast. A constraint on language acquisition. In Brian MacWhinney (ed.), *Mechanisms of Language Acquisition*, 1–33. Hillsdale NJ: Lawrence Erlbaum.

Demiral, Şükrü Barış, Matthias Schlesewsky & Ina Bornkessel-Schlesewsky. 2008. On the universality of language comprehension strategies: Evidence from Turkish. *Cognition* 106. 484–500.

Dittmar, Miriam, Kirsten Abbot-Smith, Elana Lieven & Michael Tomasello. 2008. German children's comprehension of word order and case marking in causative sentences. *Child Development* 79. 1152–1167.

Erguvanlı, Eser. 1984. *The function of word order in Turkish grammar.* Berkeley: University of California Press.

Göksun, Tilbe, Aylin Küntay & Letitia R. Naigles. 2008. Turkish children use morphosyntactic bootstrapping in interpreting verb meaning. *Journal of Child Language* 35. 291–323.

Hirsh-Pasek, Kathy, Letitia Naigles, Roberta Golinkoff, Lila R. Gleitman & Henry Gleitman. 1988. Syntactic bootstrapping: Evidence from comprehension. Paper presented at the Boston University Child Language Conference.

Ishii, Takeo. 1999. The JUN Corpus. Unpublished.

Küntay, Aylin & Dan I. Slobin. 1996. Listening to a Turkish mother: Some puzzles for acquisition. In Dan I. Slobin, Julie Gerhardt, Amy Kyratzis, & Jiansheng Guo (eds.), *Social interaction, social context, and language: Essays in honor of Susan Ervin-Tripp*, 265–287. Mahwah, NJ: Erlbaum.

Landau, Barbara & Lila R. Gleitman. 1985. *Language and experience: Evidence from the blind child.* Cambridge, MA: Harvard University Press.

Lee, Joanne & Letitia R. Naigles. 2005. Input to verb learning in Mandarin Chinese: A role for syntactic bootstrapping. *Developmental Psychology* 41. 529–540.

Lee, Joanne & Letitia R. Naigles. 2008. Mandarin learners use syntactic bootstrapping in verb acquisition. *Cognition* 106. 1028–1037.

Levin, Beth & Malka Rappaport Horav. 1995. *Unaccusativity: At the syntax–lexical semantics interface.* Cambridge MA: MIT Press.

MacWhinney, Brian. 2000. *The CHILDES Project: Tools for analyzing talk. volume 1: Transcription format and programs; volume 2: The database.* 3rd edn. Hillsdale, NJ: Lawrence Erlbaum.

Markman, Ellen. 1987. How children constrain the possible meanings of words. In Ulric Neisser (ed.), *Concepts and conceptual development: Ecological and intellectual factors in categorization.* Cambridge: Cambridge University Press.

Matsuo, Ayumi, Sotaro Kita, Yuri Shinya, Gary C. Wood & Letitia Naigles. 2012. Japanese two-year-olds use morphosyntax to learn novel verb meanings. *Journal of Child Language* 39. 637–663.

Matsuo, Ayumi, Sotaro Kita & Letitia Naigles. 2014. Children's use of morphosyntax and the number of arguments to infer the meaning of novel transitive and intransitive verbs. A poster presented at CAPHL, Harvard University.

Morikawa, Hiromi. 1989. *Acquisition of case marking and predicate-argument structures in Japanese: A longitudinal study of language acquisition mechanisms.* Lawrence, KS: University of Kansas dissertation.

Naigles, Letitia. 1990. Children use syntax to learn verb meanings. *Journal of Child Language* 17. 357–374.

Naigles, Letitia, Anne Fowler & Atessa Helm. 1992. Developmental changes in the construction of verb meanings. *Cognitive Development* 7. 403–427.

Naigles, Letitia, Henry Gleitman & Lila R. Gleitman. 1993. Acquiring the components of verb meaning from syntactic evidence. In Esther Dromi (ed.), *Language and cognition: A developmental perspective*, 104–140. Norwood, NJ: Ablex.

Naigles, Letitia & Edward Kako. 1993. First contact in verb acquisition: Defining a role for syntax. *Child Development* 64. 1665–1687.
Naigles, Letitia, Anne Fowler & Atessa Helm. 1995. Syntactic bootstrapping from start to finish, with special reference to Down syndrome. In Michael Tomasello & William E. Merriman (eds.), *Beyond names for things: Young children's acquisition of verbs*, 299–330. Hillsdale, NJ: Erlbaum.
Narashimhan, Bhuvana, Nancy Budwig & L. Murty. 2005. Argument realization in Hindi caregiver-child discourse. *Journal of Pragmatics* 37 (4). 461–495.
Pinker, Steven. 1984. *Language learnability and language development*. Cambridge, MA: Harvard University Press.
Pinker, Steven. 1989. *Learnability and cognition: The acquisition of argument structure*. Cambridge, MA: MIT Press.
Quine, W. V. O. 1960. *Word and object*. Cambridge, MA: MIT Press.
Rispoli, Matthew. 1987. The acquisition of the transitive and intransitive action verb categories in Japanese. *First Language* 7. 183–200.
Shibatani, Masayoshi (ed.). 1976. *Syntax and semantics 5: Japanese generative grammar*. New York: Academic Press.
Shibatani, Masayoshi. 2001. Non-canonical constructions in Japanese. In Alexandra Y. Aikhenvald, R. M. W. Dixon & Masayuki Onishi (eds.), *Non-canonical marking of subjects and objects*. Amsterdam: John Benjamins.
Suzuki, Takaaki. 2000. Multiple factors in morphological case-marking errors. *Studies in Language Science* 1. 123–134.

Zoe Pei-sui Luk and Yasuhiro Shirai

12 The effect of a 'conceptualizable' agent on the use of transitive and intransitive constructions in L2 Japanese

1 Introduction

In this chapter, we examine the acquisition of Japanese transitive/intransitive verb alternation by Chinese learners, and in particular, how a 'conceptualizable' external cause (Ju, 2000) affects learners' choice. The objective is to investigate how the presence of a perceivable agent and the negative versus affirmative form of the verb affect their choice among transitive, intransitive, passive, and potential forms, and thus whether the tendency to use passive forms, which has been observed in L2 English, would also be observed in L2 Japanese. We found that Chinese learners of Japanese tend to use more transitive and passive forms under the externally-caused affirmative condition, and more potential forms under the externally-caused negative condition. We argue that the difficulty in choosing among these different verb forms in Japanese can best be explained in terms of event conceptualization, an account consistent with Ju's (2000) account explaining overpassivization in L2 English.

2 Acquisition of Verbs in L2 Japanese

2.1 The intransitive bias in Japanese

Traditionally, the intransitive unaccusative construction has been seen as one that describes an agent-less event. Guerssel, Hale, Laughren, Levin & Eagle (1985), for example, examined four typologically very different languages (English, Berber, Warlpiri, and Winnebago) and claim that in these languages verbs denoting the meaning of 'cutting' cannot be inchoative, and thus intransitive, because the act of cutting implies the use of an instrument, and thus an agent who uses it. Levin (1993) makes a similar claim in her classification of English verbs into different categories based on their meanings. She points out

---

Zoe Pei-sui Luk, The Hong Kong Institute of Education
Yasuhiro Shirai, Case Western Reserve University

that verb groups such as VERBS OF ROLLING (e.g., *roll*) and VERBS OF BREAKING (e.g., *break, crack*) allow inchoative/causative alternation, whereas VERBS OF CUTTING do not. Following Guerssel et al.'s argument, she argues that this is because VERBS OF CUTTING imply the presence of an agent, and therefore must be transitive, whereas VERBS OF ROLLING, VERBS OF BREAKING, etc. express events that may be brought about by natural forces such as wind, gravity, change of temperature, etc., without the presence of an agent.

The intransitive construction is thus often believed to contrast with the passive construction, in which the agent is not mentioned but implied. Langacker (2008), for example, argues that "an intransitive like *The door opened* construes a thematic process in absolute fashion, without reference to the force or agent that induces it", whereas "an English passive designates the entire agent-theme interaction" (p. 385).

However, Japanese allows certain actions that necessarily involve an agent to be described intransitively, as pointed out by Matsumoto (2000), for example. In fact, the transitive verb for 'cut,' *kiru*, in Japanese has an intransitive counterpart *kireru*, as illustrated in (1).

(1) *Roopu ga   kireta.*
    Rope   NOM   cut.intr
    The rope got cut (because of an extremely strong pull, wear and tear, etc.)

Matsumoto (2000: 188) stated that "the necessary involvement of a human agent does not block decausativization" in Japanese as long as the focus is on "the result of the change." To illustrate how Japanese deviates from Guerssel et al.'s claim in its pattern of lexicalization, consider the verb for 'find' in English and Japanese. In English, *find* has only a transitive use, because the act of finding must involve a person who finds, and thus, according to Guerssel et al. (1985), cannot be expressed as an intransitive. If one wishes to avoid mentioning the agent in English, a passive form such as 'a ring was found' is necessary. However, in Japanese, there exists an intransitive verb *mitukaru* morphologically distinct from the passive form *mitukerareru*. When one wishes to avoid attributing the result to a causer, the intransitive verb is more often used than the passive form, as in *yubiwa ga mitukatta* 'a ring found (intr.)'. This is thus inconsistent with Guerssel et al. (1985) and Levin (1993), because the act of finding requires a doer, in which case Guerssel et al. (1985) and Levin (1993) would predict that intransitive expression is impossible. Other examples of intransitive verbs in Japanese that involve an agent include *kimaru* 'be decided', *tukamaru* 'be caught', *tasukaru* 'be helped', *sorou* 'be complete (as a result of collecting)', *sadamaru* 'be fixed', *tunagaru* 'be connected', *mazaru* 'be mixed', *uwaru* 'be planted', *tirakaru* 'be spread', *tutawaru* 'be conveyed', *todoku* 'be delivered', *umaru* 'be buried', *somaru* 'be dyed', *hamaru* 'be fitted in', *nukeru* 'be removed', *tatu* 'be built', etc.

This kind of verb is in fact found not only in Japanese. Pardeshi (2008) points out the existence of similar verbs in four South-Asian languages–Marathi, Hindi, Telugu, and Tamil. On the basis of a comparison with Japanese examples given in Jacobsen (1992) he claims that the corresponding verbs in these languages behave similarly, and calls them "agent-implying intransitive verbs" (Pardeshi 2008: 179). (2) is an example of such a verb in Marathi.

(2) *Shukravaari sandhyaakaaLi 5 waadztaa nighaaytse Tharale*
    Friday   evening   5 o'clock   leave.of   got decided
    "It was decided to leave at 5 o'clock on Friday."
    (Pardeshi 2008: 180)

The Marathi example is parallel to the Japanese example in (1) in that the verb is intransitive (i.e., has one argument), despite the fact that the verb in both cases denotes an event that involves an agent (i.e., the person who decides).

That more verbs are able to enter into transitivity alternations in Japanese than other languages is arguably due to a more general preference in Japanese for suppressing the agent. Alfonso (1966) observes that, while English speakers show little or no preference between the use of transitive constructions (e.g., *they decided that...*) and passive constructions (e.g., *it was decided that...*), Japanese speakers show a preference for constructions where less agency is expressed (i.e., intransitive constructions)

Ikegami (1981, 1991) discusses the issue from an even wider and multi-dimensional perspective, arguing that English is a DO-language that gives prominence to human agents, whereas Japanese is a BECOME-language that prefers to suppress human agents, and express events as if they happen spontaneously. Seen in this way, the liberality of Japanese in allowing agent-involving events to be lexicalized into intransitive verbs is but one manifestation of a wider preference in the language for suppressing agents (see also Luk 2014).

Ikegami also argues that transitive, passive, and intransitive constructions can be seen to occupy three different points on a continuum. A prototypical transitive construction (e.g., *John killed Mary*) highlights both the agent and the patient. A passive construction (e.g., *Mary was killed*) highlights only the patient, but implies the presence of an agent. A prototypical (unaccusative) intransitive construction (e.g., *Mary died*) also highlights the patient, but does not imply an agent. From this we can see that there is a gradual increase in the degree of agent demotion, moving from the transitive construction to the passive construction, and finally to the intransitive construction. In other words, the intransitive construction has the highest degree of agent demotion. This is similar to Langacker's (2008) characterizations of the three constructions in terms of base and profile. The more liberal use of the intransitive construction in Japanese can thus be seen as a result of its typological characteristics (i.e. its being a BECOME-language).

2.2 Second language acquisition of transitivity alternations

Studies have indicated that the strong preference for intransitive constructions in Japanese as outlined above may pose difficulties for second language learners of Japanese in mastering transitive and intransitive verbs in Japanese. Kobayashi (1996) administered a multiple-choice test to 68 learners of Japanese as a second language with different L1 backgrounds (including Chinese, Korean, Spanish, English, and Portuguese) with 15 native Japanese speakers acting as a control group. The test investigated whether the learners were able to choose the most suitable verb form from three options, namely the intransitive (e.g., *aku* 'open'), transitive (e.g., *akeru* 'open'), and potential form (e.g., *akerareru* 'can open'). The results showed that they were not able to use these forms in a native-like manner. For example, in one test item, reproduced in (3) below, the learners were asked to choose from among the three verb forms mentioned above.

(3) *Tonari no hito ga "kagi nara arimasuyo. Koko ni otite imasu. Kore desu ka?"*
to kagi o mise masita
"ee, so desu." (gatya gatya to kagi o kagiana ni ireru)
"aa (1) ake-ta (2) ai-ta (3) ake-rare-ta"
'The person next to you says to you "(if you are looking for the key), it's here. It's here on the floor. Is this your key?' and shows you the key.
'Yes, it is.' (inserting the key into the keyhole with a clattering noise)
'Oh, (1) (I) opened (it) (2) (it) opened (3) (I) was able to open (it)'
(Kobayashi 1996: 48, translation by authors)

All native Japanese speakers preferred the intransitive verb *aku* 'open.intr', whereas the learners preferred either its transitive counterpart *akeru* 'open.tr' or the potential form *akerareru* 'can open'.

Interestingly, there seems to be some L1 influence at work in these results. Chinese-speaking (21 out of 25 participants) and Spanish-speaking learners (5 out of 5 participants) were most likely to choose the transitive counterpart or the potential form, whereas only 8 out of 20 Korean-speaking participants chose these two forms.

Yet another interesting thing to note about Kobayashi's findings is that three out of the four questions in the task were in the form of negative sentences (i.e., *ak-anai* 'not open'), and most responses from the learners for these three negative sentences involved use of the potential form (about 53% on average) (i.e., *ake-rare-nai* 'cannot open').

Kobayashi accounts for her findings (i.e., that learners did not choose intransitive forms in the way that native speakers did) in terms of the cognitive structure represented in Figure 1.

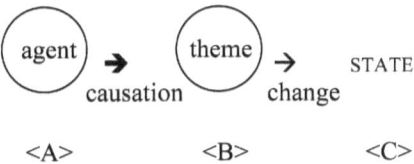

<A>　　　　　<B>　　　　　<C>

Figure 1: The transitive schema (adapted from Kobayashi 1996: 53)

Kobayashi suggests that the reason for the learners' inability to choose an appropriate form lies in the difficulty they have in deciding how much of Figure 1 is included in the scope of the meaning expressed. Citing Miyajima (1985), she argues that languages differ in terms of which part(s) of this cognitive structure is typically denoted by verbs in the language. In some languages verbs tend to include <B> and <C> but not <A>, while in other languages all three tend to be included. For example, in Japanese, *hi o kesi-ta* '(somebody) put out the fire' includes all of <A>, <B>, and <C>, whereas *hi ga kie-ta* 'the fire went out" includes only <B> and <C> (the "packaging problem," to borrow a term from Tomasello 1992). She also claims that learners showed a greater degree of indecision between transitive and intransitive in cases where there is an agent that causes the change than in cases where the change occurs naturally.

The idea that languages may differ in terms of what components of meaning they may focus on in expressing a caused event has been discussed in other studies as well, such as Kageyama (1996). He argues that, whereas English focuses on the result of an event, Japanese focuses on the process over which the change of state occurs. He cites as examples the English and Japanese sentences in (4) and (5) (Kageyama 1996: 10):

(4)　*Siroppuzyoo　ni　naru　　made　　3-4 hun　　yuderu*
　　　Syrupy.state　DAT　become　until　　minute　　boil
　　　'Boil for 3–4 mins until (it is) syrupy.'

(5) *Mae   wa   doko   made   ikimasi-ta   ka?*
    Last.time TOP where until go-past Q?
    'Where are we now?' [In the beginning of class]

Kageyama points out that both English sentences in (4) and (5) use the verb *be* to express a state without mentioning the path which the event follows in arriving at the state. In Japanese, however, the verbs *naru* 'become' and *iku* 'go' highlight the path followed by the event. This kind of cross-linguistic difference, not generally taught in L2 classrooms, may pose a challenge for second language learners of Japanese.

Building on Kobayashi's work, Nakaishi (2005) investigates further the use of transitive-intransitive verb pairs by L2 speakers of Japanese and possible reasons for the patterns of use observed. She examines production data from Chinese, English, and Korean L1 learners of Japanese in an oral proficiency interview corpus (the KY corpus, Kamada & Yamauchi 1999), and classifies verb pairs into three categories based on observed patterns of production by the learners: (1) both counterparts were used by all the learners (e.g., *hairu/ireru* 'enter/put in'), (2) only the transitive counterpart was used by all the learners (e.g., *ureru/uru* 'be sold/sell' by English-speaking learners, *tatu/tateru* 'be built/build' by Chinese-speaking learners, and *kireru/kiru* 'be cut/cut' by Korean-speaking learners), and (3) only one of the two counterparts was used by individual learners, but both counterparts were observed in the group of learners as a whole (e.g., *kimaru/kimeru* 'be decided/decide'). Nakaishi offers two explanations for the results. First, she suggests that the way Japanese textbooks present these verbs may provide one explanation for the differences observed. She shows, for example, that verbs for which both counterparts were used (i.e., category 1) were taught as pairs in most textbooks, whereas the verbs of which only one counterpart was used (i.e. categories 2 and 3) were often not introduced as pairs in textbooks. Second, following Kobayashi (1996) and Kobayashi & Naoi (1996), she suggests that verbs denoting events that must be brought about by an agent are particularly difficult. For example, all learners used *tateru* 'build' but none used *tatu* 'be built (intr.)', because the action of building is understood to be an intentional action brought about by an agent.

To summarize, there are several studies that show that learners of Japanese have difficulty using transitive/intransitive verb pairs accurately, and in particular that they erroneously tend to choose the transitive counterpart in many cases where the intransitive counterpart is preferred by the native speakers, possibly a reflection of Japanese making available more intransitive expressions than their L1s. Moreover, the preference for use of the transitive form by second language learners of Japanese appears to be associated with the perception that an agent is present.

2.3 Overpassivization and perceived agents

The avoidance of the intransitive in L2 Japanese discussed above may be seen as part of a larger problem reported in previous SLA research called overpassivization. Overpassivization refers to the non-target-like passivization of intransitive verbs. Among the first to discuss overpassivization errors was Zobl (1989). Zobl (1989: 204) reports that learners of English, regardless of their first language, often make errors such as (6) and (7):

(6) The most memorable experience of my life was happened 15 year ago (Arabic L1)

(7) Most of people are fallen in love and marry with somebody (Japanese L1)

Since Zobl (1989), overpassivization has been studied targeting learners of different language backgrounds – for example, English (Juffs 1998), English, Spanish, and Turkish (Montrul 2000), and Spanish (Zyzik 2006).

The overuse of the passive form in L2 Japanese discussed above may also be considered a case of overpassivization. For example, the use of *taterareru* 'be built' when the intransitive form *tatu* 'build.intr' is obligatory can be interpreted in this way.

Zobl proposes a syntactic explanation for the lack of overpassivization in the case of unergative verbs, noting that overpassivization errors are greater with unaccusative verbs than with unergative verbs. He regards this phenomenon as evidence in support of the Unaccusative Hypothesis (Burzio 1986; Perlmutter 1978), which states that there is a syntactic difference between unergative intransitive verbs and unaccusative intransitive verbs. He argues that learners are sensitive to whether a verb is unaccusative or unergative, and in particular that they 'know' that unaccusative verbs have an internal argument (i.e., underlying object) that moves from object position to subject position in surface structure, whereas unergative verbs have an external argument (i.e., underlying subject) that does not move in this way. Since unaccusative verbs lack an external argument, their internal argument must be raised to subject position through an operation similar to that involved in deriving a passive sentence, causing learners to produce a surface form similar to a passive sentence (i.e., *be* + *V-en*). This results in the use of the auxiliary *be* with unaccusative verbs, a case of overpassivization. Unergative verbs, by contrast, do not involve this kind of movement, as they have only an external argument. Zobl points to this syntactic difference as an explanation for the lack of overpassivization in the case of unergative verbs.

Following Zobl (1989), Balcom (1997) investigates the use of various types of verbs (e.g., experiential verbs, psych verbs, intransitive verbs with transitive counterparts, etc.) by Chinese learners of English, using a grammaticality judgment task and a cloze-type test. Adding the [+/-human] feature in the subject as a variable in the experiential and psych verb conditions (other conditions having only theme as subject) she tested the knowledge the subjects had of these subclasses of unaccusative verbs. She found that the passivized form of unaccusatives with transitive counterparts (e.g., *the door closed*), middle constructions (e.g., *this bread cuts easily*), experiential verbs with a theme subject (e.g., *the riot occurred*), and stative (e.g., *the soup tasted good*) and measure verbs (e.g., *this dress cost $40*) was often accepted by the learners in the grammaticality judgment task. In the cloze test, on the other hand, passive forms were not observed as frequently as in the grammaticality judgment test, but measure verbs, stative unaccusative verbs, and unaccusative verbs with transitive counterparts were observed to be used more often than in the grammaticality judgment test. Balcom concludes that her results support Zobl's (1989) syntactic explanation of overpassivization. She further proposes that L2 learners have correct lexical representations of unaccusative verbs in general, but they would need additional rules (e.g., "detransitivization is restricted to verbs whose action can occur without the intervention of a volitional agent" (Balcom 1997: 9)) to avoid overpassivizing unaccusative verbs.

Balcom, however, does not discuss why different subclasses of unaccusative verbs appear to have different degrees of susceptibility to overpassivization. For example, the participants were much more accurate in judging sentences with experiential verbs and human subjects (e.g., *The child underwent the operation*) than those with experiential verbs but non-human subjects (e.g., *the riot occurred*). The participants also had much less difficulty with psych verbs, regardless of whether the subject is human (e.g., *Many people like coffee*) or not (e.g., *The results pleased the students*). If overpassivization is a purely syntactic process, we would not expect to see such differences in the degree of overpassivization, because all unaccusative verbs are similar in underlying argument structure, and involve the same kind of movement.

Whereas Zobl (1989) and Balcom (1997) approach the problem of overpassivization from a generative-syntactic perspective, Ju (2000) adopts a cognitive-semantic approach.[1] Ju suggests that overpassivization is closely linked to how

---

[1] It should be noted that overpassivization has a slightly different definition in Ju (2000). Whereas Zobl referred to overpassivization as the ungrammatical passivization of intransitive verbs, Ju treated it as the non-nativelike passivization of either transitive or intransitive verbs. As English transitive/intransitive verb pairs usually do not vary in form and all the verbs that Ju used allow inchoative/causative alternations, it was not clear whether Ju was referring to passivization of the intransitive or transitive member of such pairs.

learners perceive an event, in particular whether it is perceived to involve an external cause/agent. She tested L1 Chinese learners of English using a forced-choice task (between intransitive and passive) that manipulated only the discourse context and kept the target sentences exactly the same, as in examples (8) and (9).

(8) Heavy trucks put more and more pressure on the bridge. [externally caused]
It (broke/was broken) gradually.

(9) The wooden bridge was very old. [internally caused]
It (broke/was broken) gradually.

Ju (2000) found that, regardless of whether an unaccusative has a transitive counterpart or not (contra Balcom 1997), learners made significantly more overpassivization errors when there was a conceptualizable external cause. For example, learners were more likely to overpassivize (8) than (9), because there is an external cause *heavy trucks* in (8) that causes the bridge to break, but not in (9). Native English speakers in the control group, on the other hand, chose the unaccusative option in both sentences. Ju argues that because in (8) the breaking of the bridge was perceived to be caused by "heavy trucks," the participants tended to include this information in the form of a passive construction instead of an intransitive construction.

Ju's view is similar to Kobayashi's (1996), in the sense that both adopt a semantic, rather than syntactic, explanation for why learners are inaccurate in their choice of whether or not to include agent in the constructions they produce, either explicitly with the use of a transitive verb or implicitly with the use of the passive form of a transitive verb. In contrast to Kobayashi, however, Ju does not mention any effects due to the learners' first language, treating the problem as a universal one regardless of the learner's L1 or the target L2. Kobayashi, on the other hand, argues that the problem arises because verbs corresponding in different languages to a given meaning may include different parts of a causative event (i.e., an agent/cause, a patient, and a resultative state), implying that learners may not experience this difficulty if a verb expressing a causative event in the learner's L1 includes exactly the same elements as the corresponding verb in the target language. In short, Ju's explanation is universalistic, while Kobayashi's is based on L1 transfer.

To summarize previous studies, we have seen that learners of Japanese often find it difficult to decide which verb form to use in Japanese, and they often choose a transitive form where the intransitive is deemed appropriate by native speakers. We suggest that this problem may be related to overpassivization with unaccusative verbs, something that has frequently been observed in second language learners of English and has often been explained in syntactic terms (e.g., Balcom 1997; Zobl 1989). Ju (2000), however, offers a semantic account of the phenomenon, suggesting that learners tend to overpassivize when there is a conceptualizable agent in the event. If Ju's semantic account is an adequate one, it may be that learners' difficulties with transitive versus intransitive expression are related to overpassivization in L2 acquisition in general, because both issues are associated with how much prominence the learners give to the agent/cause.

Ju's hypothesis, however, has not been tested in other L2s (including Japanese), and the difficulty that learners of Japanese face in the acquisition of transitivity alternation is seldom explained in terms of Ju's hypothesis appealing to the notion of conceptualizable agent. The present study thus looks at whether Ju's universal semantic account is also applicable to the case of second language acquisition of Japanese, a language which strongly favors intransitive verbs, and at the same time, considers whether the findings of this study are better explained by the syntactic or the semantic account. In addition, the study considers whether the affirmative or negative form of sentences has any influence on the choices made by learners, as observed in Kobayashi's study. This point is elaborated on in the next section.

The present study thus addresses the following questions:

I. Do Chinese learners of Japanese favor passive forms in Japanese (as did Chinese learners of English) when there is a conceptualizable agent (i.e., an entity that causes a change of state in another entity), as suggested by Ju (2000)?
II. What effects, if any, does affirmativity have on learner's choice?

3 The Effect of a Conceptualizable Agent on the Choice of Verb Form

The present study examines the use of transitive and intransitive verbs by Chinese learners of Japanese to test whether the presence of a conceptualizable agent affects the choices made by Chinese learners of Japanese among transitive, intransitive, passive, and potential forms in a way similar to what Ju (2000) observed for the acquisition of English and Kobayashi (1996) for the acquisition of Japanese. We hypothesized that Chinese learners of Japanese would be more likely to choose a transitive verb or passive form of a transitive verb when a conceptualizable agent is present than when it is not. More specifically, we advanced the following two hypotheses:

Hypothesis I: Chinese learners of Japanese use the passive form more often for externally caused events involving a conceptualizable (animate) agent than internally caused events.

Hypothesis II: Chinese learners use the potential form for negative sentences under the external causation condition, as observed in Kobayashi's (1996) study.

3.1 Participants

The participants were 40 Chinese learners of Japanese, whose native languages included Mandarin Chinese (N=33) and Cantonese (N=7). The Mandarin-speaking participants were all students at a university in northern Kyushu, Japan who were residing in Japan when the test was administered. The Cantonese-speaking participants were students who were studying Japanese at a university in Hong Kong. All participants confirmed orally that they were familiar with transitive/intransitive verb pairs and other verb forms (e.g., potential, passive, etc.) before they took the test. We thus considered them to be at least intermediate level learners of Japanese. In addition, 40 native Japanese undergraduate students at another university in northern Kyushu, Japan served as a control group in the study.

3.2 Materials and procedures

As in Ju (2000), the test is a forced-choice questionnaire. For each question, there were five options for the participants to choose from: (1) intransitive (e.g., *tooru* 'go through'), (2) transitive (e.g., *toosu* 'cause something to go through'), (3) potential form of the intransitive (e.g., *tooreru* '(someone) can go through'), (4) potential form of the transitive (e.g., *tooseru* 'can cause (something) to go through'), and (5) passive form of the transitive (e.g., *toosareru* 'be let through'). Because each option requires a different case particle (e.g., *ga* for the intransitive option and *o* for the transitive option), the appropriate case particles were attached to each option, as illustrated in examples (10) and (11).

There were 2 conditions, indicated by preceding discourse context: (1) internal causation condition (no animate agent involved), (2) external causation condition (an animate agent is involved, but is not mentioned in the sentence)[2]. There were also items that served as fillers, all of which were intended to elicit a transitive response. Examples of each condition are shown in (10)–(12) respectively (note that all sentences were presented in Japanese script (*kana* and *kanji*) in the actual study:

(10)   *Aki ni naru to, ha no iro (ga kawaru (intr.) / o kaeru (tr.)/ ga kawareru (intr. potential) / ga kaerareru (tr. potential)/ ga kaerareru (passive))*
When autumn comes, the color of the leaves (changes).
[Internal causation]

(11)   *Kokkai de atarasii hoorituan (ga tootta (intr.) / o toosita (tr.)/ ga tooreta (intr. potential)/ ga tooseta (tr. potential) / ga toosareta (tr. passive)*
At the congressional assembly, a new law (passed) [External causation]

(12)   *Osara o aratteiru toki, ukkari tyawan (ga warete (intr.) / o watte (tr.) / ga warerarete (intr. potential) / ga warete (tr. potential) / ga wararete (tr. passive)) simatta*
When I was washing the dishes, (I) carelessly (broke) a bowl. [distractor]

The internal and external causation conditions were further subdivided into affirmative and negative forms. In Hopper & Thompson's (1980) influential paper on transitivity, affirmativity is included as one parameter of transitivity: an affirmative transitive sentence is higher in transitivity than its corresponding negative sentence. Intuitively, a negative sentence such as *John did not break the window* is semantically much less transitive than its affirmative counterpart *John broke the window*, because in the negative sentence, the event never occurred and there was therefore no transfer of force from *John* to *the window* that caused *the window* to break. According to Hopper & Thompson (1980: 276), in some languages such as French and Finnish, the object in a negative sentence takes "a form which shows that the action of the verb is deflected and less direct". Therefore, negative sentences are believed to have lower transitivity semantically, and learners might be expected to use different forms for affirmative and negative sentences. Moreover, as mentioned above, Kobayashi (1996) observed different responses for affirmative and negative sentences: the transitive form

---

[2] We adopted the terms "external causation" and "internal causation" from Ju (2000), but in our study they are used slightly differently: the term "external causation" is used to refer to situations in which there is a perceivable animate agent, and the term "internal causation" is used to refer to situations in which there is not a perceivable animate agent.

was more frequent for affirmative[3] and the potential form more frequent for negative sentences. The factor of affirmativity was therefore added to test how this would affect learners' choice of verb forms.

There were 4 questions for each condition, for a total of 20 items in the questionnaire. One question from the external causation negative condition (number 3 in the Appendix) was removed because it was later realized that the question did not provide enough context for the participants to decide which form should be used. Therefore, the results from only the remaining 19 questions were analyzed. The conditions and number of questions are summarized in Table 1. A complete list of the questions is given in Appendix.

Table 1: Experimental design

Condition	Question type (number of questions)
1 (internally caused)	Affirmative (4) 　　prices going down 　　color of leaves changing 　　door closing 　　leaves falling Negative (4) 　　winter not continuing 　　rain not stopping 　　leaves not falling 　　clothes not drying
2 (externally caused)	Affirmative (4) 　　new law passed 　　students divided into groups 　　meat cooked 　　business trip decided Negative (3) 　　car not stopping (excluded) 　　light not working 　　book not fitting 　　salary not increasing
Fillers	Affirmative (4)

The data from the Mandarin-speaking and native Japanese participants were collected on the campuses of two different universities in northern Kyushu, Japan, by the first author. The data from the Cantonese-speaking participants

---

3 Passive was not an option in Kobayashi (1996).

were collected in a classroom in a university in Hong Kong by a Japanese language instructor without the presence of the authors. The participants took about 10 minutes to complete the questions. They were told to interpret the contexts based on information contained in the questions themselves, and were not allowed to ask questions about the task.

3.3 Results

Figures 2 (frequencies in Tables 2 and 3) and 3 (frequencies in Tables 4 and 5) show the results for the internal causation condition (no animate agent involved) with affirmative and negative items respectively. It is evident from the figures that the intransitive form is by far the most preferred option for both the Chinese learners of Japanese and the native speakers of Japanese, regardless of whether the sentence is affirmative or negative. It is noteworthy, however, that the percentage choosing the intransitive form among the native Japanese speakers (approximately 90%) is higher than that for the learners (approximately 60%) under both conditions.

Table 2: Chinese learners' results of questions of Condition 1 (Affirmative)

Question	Intransitive verb (I)	Transitive verb (T)	Potential form of Intransitive verb (PI)	Potential form of Transitive verb (PT)	Passive form of Transitive verb (PaT)	No response (N)
1	23	3	7	3	4	0
10	34	1	1	1	2	1
18	9	4	6	0	18	3
20	33	6	1	0	0	0
Total	99	14	15	4	24	4
%	61.9	8.8	9.4	2.5	15.0	2.5

Table 3: Native Japanese speakers' results of questions of Condition 1 (Affirmative)

Question	Intransitive verb (I)	Transitive verb (T)	Potential form of Intransitive verb (PI)	Potential form of Transitive verb (PT)	Passive form of Transitive verb (PaT)	No response (N)
1	38	0	0	0	1	1
10	40	0	0	0	0	0
18	34	0	0	0	5	1
20	38	0	1	0	1	0
Total	150	0	1	0	7	2
%	93.8	0.0	0.6	0.0	4.4	1.3

Note: 'I' – intransitive, 'T' – transitive, 'PI' – potential form of intransitive, 'PT' – potential form of transitive, 'PaT' – passive form of transitive, 'N' – no response

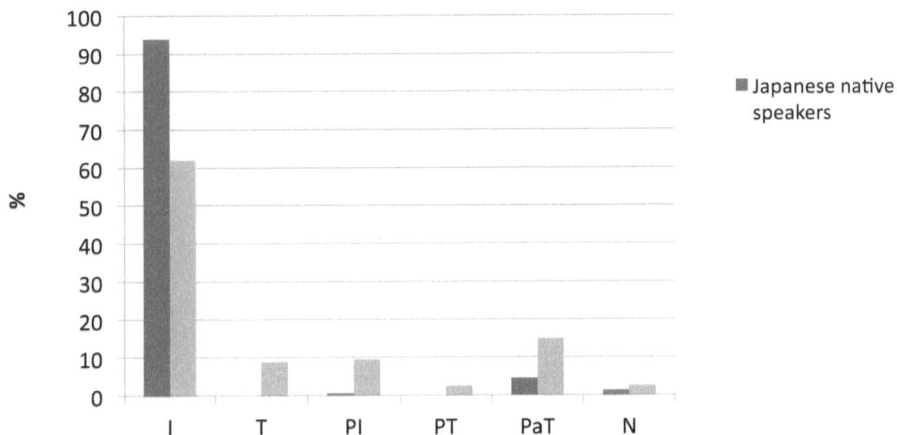

Figure 2: Percentages of verb forms chosen for the internal causation condition (affirmative sentences)

Table 4: Chinese learners' results of questions of Condition 1 (Negative)

Question	Intransitive verb (I)	Transitive verb (T)	Potential form of Intransitive verb (PI)	Potential form of Transitive verb (PT)	Passive form of Transitive verb (PaT)	No response (N)
6	23	2	5	4	0	6
7	29	1	5	3	0	2
13	27	6	1	3	1	2
15	15	1	14	6	3	1
Total	94	10	25	16	4	11
%	58.8	6.3	15.6	10.0	2.5	6.9

Table 5: Native Japanese speakers' results of Condition 1 (Negative)

Question	Intransitive verb (I)	Transitive verb (T)	Potential form of Intransitive verb (PI)	Potential form of Transitive verb (PT)	Passive form of Transitive verb (PaT)	No response (N)
6	39	0	0	1	0	0
7	40	0	0	0	0	0
13	34	6	0	0	0	0
15	29	1	0	10	0	0
Total	142	7	0	11	0	0
%	88.8	4.4	0.0	6.9	0.0	0.0

Note: 'I' – intransitive, 'T' – transitive, 'PI' – potential form of intransitive, 'PT' – potential form of transitive, 'PaT' – passive form of transitive, 'N' – no response

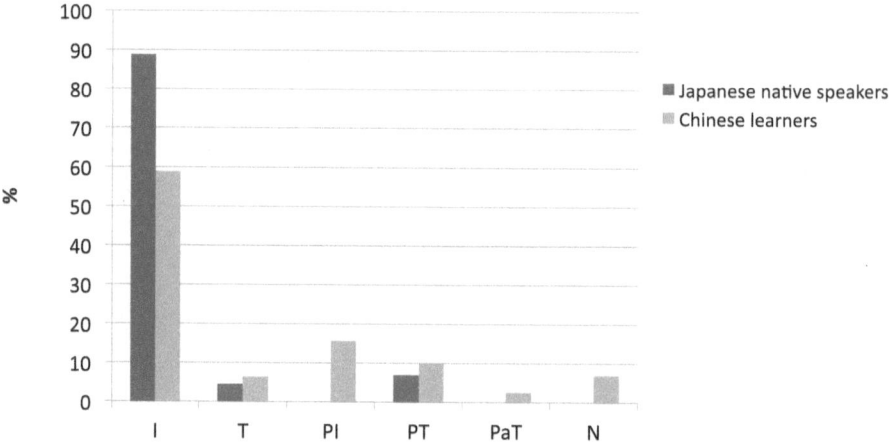

Figure 3: Percentages of verb forms chosen for the internal causation condition (negative sentences)

Figures 4 (frequencies in Tables 6 and 7) and 5 (frequencies in Tables 8 and 9) show the results in the external causation condition (involvement of agent implied). Under this condition, again, regardless of whether the sentence is affirmative or negative, the intransitive form still is the form most preferred by native Japanese speakers, by a wide margin (74%). However, the Chinese learners preferred the intransitive form less than under the internal causation condition. In fact, under the affirmative condition (see Figure 4), the intransitive form was preferred by the Chinese learners slightly less than either the passive or transitive, although the percentages for all three options were very similar (about 30%). When compared with the internal causation condition, more learners preferred the transitive form (more than 25%).

Table 6: Chinese learners' results of Condition 2 (Affirmative)

Question	Intransitive verb (I)	Transitive verb (T)	Potential form of Intransitive verb (PI)	Potential form of Transitive verb (PT)	Passive form of Transitive verb (PaT)	No response (N)
2	9	7	5	0	19	0
11	11	7	2	0	18	2
16	4	23	6	2	4	1
19	17	6	4	1	10	2
Total	41	43	17	3	51	5
%	25.6	26.9	10.6	1.9	31.9	3.1

Table 7: Native Japanese speakers' result of Condition 2 (Affirmative)

Question	Intransitive verb (I)	Transitive verb (T)	Potential form of Intransitive verb (PI)	Potential form of Transitive verb (PT)	Passive form of Transitive verb (PaT)	No response (N)
2	25	3	0	0	12	0
11	23	1	0	0	16	0
16	32	7	0	1	0	0
19	38	0	0	1	1	0
Total	118	11	0	2	29	0
%	73.8	6.9	0.0	1.3	18.1	0.0

Note: 'I' – intransitive, 'T' – transitive, 'PI' – potential form of intransitive, 'PT' – potential form of transitive, 'PaT' – passive form of transitive, 'N' – no response

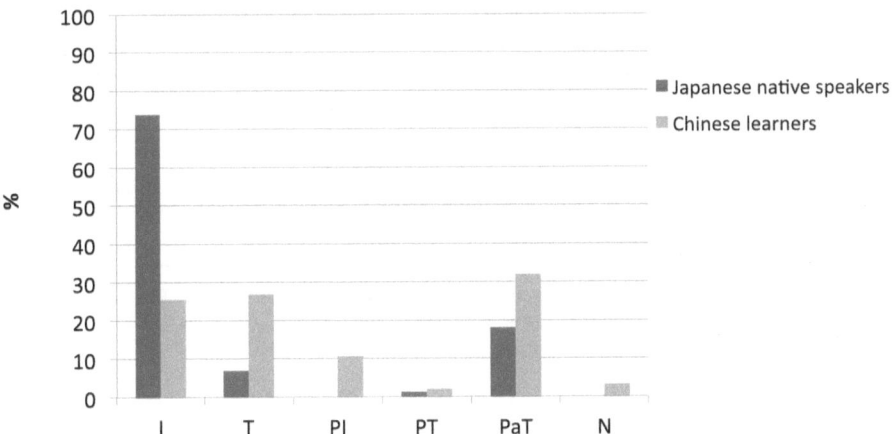

Figure 4: Percentages of verb forms chosen for the external causation condition (affirmative sentences)

For negative sentences under the external causation condition, the potential form of the transitive verb was slightly more preferred by the learners than the intransitive form (both about 20%) and their choices were spread out quite evenly over the different options (see Figure 5). In contrast, the native speakers strongly preferred intransitive verbs (95%) for the negative sentences. These results contrast greatly with results for the affirmative condition, in which the percentage of response for the potential form of the transitive verb was almost zero.

Table 8: Chinese learners' results of Condition 2 (Negative)[4]

Question	Intransitive verb (I)	Transitive verb (T)	Potential form of Intransitive verb (PI)	Potential form of Transitive verb (PT)	Passive form of Transitive verb (PaT)	No response (N)
5	9	0	7	12	6	6
8	6	8	8	13	2	3
12	13	4	5	3	9	6
Total	28	12	20	28	17	15
%	23.3	10.0	16.7	23.3	14.2	12.5

Table 9: Native Japanese speakers' results of Condition 2 (Negative)

Question	Intransitive verb (I)	Transitive verb (T)	Potential form of Intransitive verb (PI)	Potential form of Transitive verb (PT)	Passive form of Transitive verb (PaT)	No response (N)
5	40	0	0	0	0	0
8	37	1	0	2	0	0
12	38	1	0	1	0	0
Total	115	2	0	3	0	0
%	95.8	1.7	0.0	2.5	0.0	0.0

Note: 'I' – intransitive, 'T' – transitive, 'PI' – potential form of intransitive, 'PT' – potential form of transitive, 'PaT' – passive form of transitive, 'N' – no response

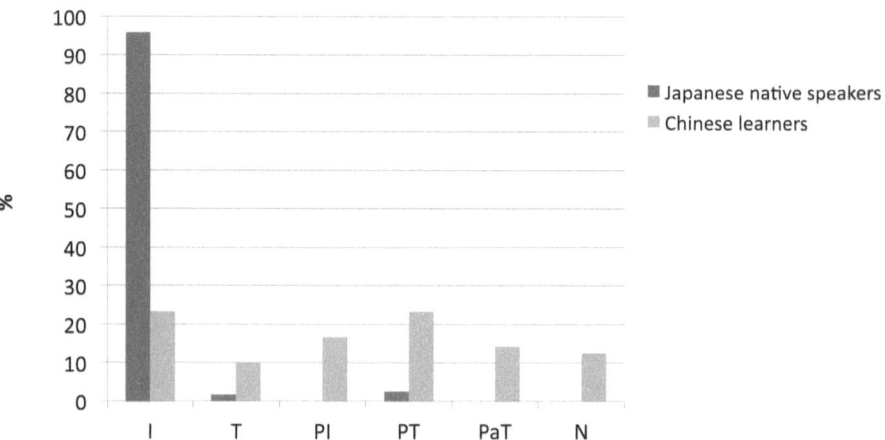

Figure 5: Percentages of verb forms chosen for the external causation condition (negative sentences)

---

4 As question 3 is problematic in a way that it leads to inconsistent result with Japanese native speakers, it is eliminated.

A multinomial logistic regression (nnet R package, Venables & Ripley, 2002) was used to estimate the effects of the predictors (i.e., participants' native language, condition, and affirmativity) and their interactions. It was found that there were main effects for all three predictors (for some of the constructions), and there was a significant three-way interaction of the predictors. Table 10 shows the coefficients of the logistic model. The three-way interaction suggests that native Japanese learners and Chinese-speaking learners of Japanese use different constructions depending on the condition (internally or externally caused) and affirmativity. In other words, knowing a participant's native language is crucial in predicting what construction he/she is likely to use in a given condition with a given affirmativity value.

Table 10: Coefficients of the multinomial logistic regression model

	T	PaT	PI	PT
Language Japanese	−54.944***	−3.672	−3.001	−91.763***
Condition 2	5.575***	5.285***	2.517*	2.491*
Affirmativity Negative	−0.649	−3.113**	1.576	2.491*
Language Japanese: Condition 2	48.87***	0.048	−1.102e+06***	−0.085
Language Japanese: Affirmativity Negative	52.87***	−0.024	−6.099e+05***	87.957***
Condition 2: Affirmativity Negative	−1.019	1.523	−0.034	1.347
Language Japanese: Condition 2: Affirmativity Negative	−30.606***	−3.911e+03***	5.806e+08***	−6.627***

* $p < 0.05$, ** $p < 0.01$, *** $p < 0.001$. The baseline of the model is Language Chinese, Condition 1, Affirmativity Affirmative, and Intransitive (I).

To summarize, the Chinese learners of Japanese preferred intransitive verbs under the internal causation condition, but preferred passive forms under the external causation condition for affirmative sentences, and the potential form under the external causation condition for negative sentences. This is in contrast to the native speakers, who showed a clear preference for intransitive verbs under all four conditions.

4 Discussion

4.1 Internal causation versus external causation

It was found that the Chinese learners were much more accurate (i.e., their performance was closer to that of native speakers) in using the intransitive forms where no agent was involved (internal causation) than where one was involved (external causation). Under the external causation condition, in which the event described by the sentence is believed to involve an agent, the Chinese learners tended to avoid the intransitive forms and select the passive form of the transitive verb when the sentence was affirmative and the potential form when the sentence was negative. The results support both our Hypotheses I and II.

These results resemble those of Ju (2000), who found that Chinese learners of English tend to overpassivize intransitive verbs when there is a conceptualizable agent. This suggests that Chinese learners are affected by the presence of external agents, tending to encode the agent in that case by using the transitive verb or other forms derived from the transitive – passive in the case of English, and transitive, passive, or potential in the case of Japanese.

4.2 Affirmative versus negative

It was also found that under the internal causation condition, the intransitive form remained the most preferred option for L2 learners regardless of affirmativity, whereas under the external causation condition their responses differed greatly depending on whether the sentence was affirmative or negative. In the affirmative external causation condition, passive forms were most preferred (about 32%), with only a few responses using potential forms (12.5%, when combining the potential forms of both intransitive and transitive verbs). However, under the negative external causation condition, the potential form of the transitive became the most preferred option (more than 20%), and responses using the passive form decreased to about 14%. These findings mirror those of Kobayashi (1996), who nevertheless does not discuss these discrepancies further.

Why is there such a difference between negative and affirmative under the external cause condition, but no such difference under the internal causation condition? When a change of state is perceived to be caused by an agent and the speaker wants to background the agent, s/he typically uses the passive form of the transitive verb. In contrast, when an event is perceived to be intended to be caused by an agent, but the event does not occur, the speaker still perceives the agent to be involved due to the presence of this intention. If the agent's intention is involved, but no change of state in another entity occurs, then it is natural to attribute this to the agent's inability to bring about the change, so that the agent is seen as responsible for the lack of change. It is reasonable to assume that the Chinese participants preferred the potential form as a way of expressing the agent's responsibility in this case. Consider the English sentences in (13):

(13) a. Mary cut her own steak. (affirmative with intention; change of state in the steak occurs)

b. Mary did not cut her own steak. (negative without intention implied; no change of state occurs)

c. Mary could not cut her own steak. (negative with intention; no change of state occurs)

In the affirmative transitive sentence in (13a), Mary is seen to have the intention of cutting the steak, and the change of state in question results. The negative sentence in (13b), on the other hand, implies no intention in Mary. The sentence in (13c), by contrast, involves a modal verb *can*, implying the existence of an intention in Mary to cause the steak to become cut, although she is unable to bring this change of state about.

Similarly in Japanese, rather than using a simple negative form of the transitive verb, which may imply a lack of intention, the use of the negative potential form (e.g., *irerarenai* 'cannot put in') allows the learners to express the presence of an intention in the agent and his/her inability to bring about the change. We propose that this is the reason why, under the negative sentence condition, the negative potential form of the transitive verb was preferred by the learners to the simple transitive verb + negative pattern, which usually denotes lack of intention, or the simple intransitive verb + negative pattern, which they likely associate with the non-occurrence of spontaneous events (e.g., *the bomb did not explode.*)

Following the transitive schema in Figure 1, adapted from Kobayashi (1996: 53)[5], the use of the potential form can be illustrated as in Figure 6, and the simple intransitive form as in Figure 7.

---

5 A similar schema is also proposed by other linguists (e.g., Langacker 1987).

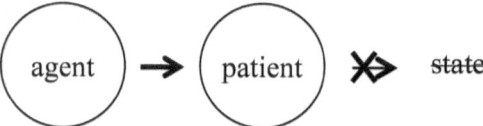

Figure 6: Scheme of conceptualization for an intended but non-occurring event

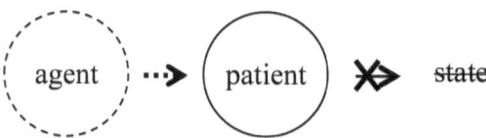

Figure 7: Scheme of conceptualization for a non-occurring spontaneous event

In Figure 7, the dotted line of the agent and of the arrow that indicates causation signifies a lack of attention by the speaker to the agent and causation. In our results under the negative external causation condition, the native Japanese speakers preferred intransitive verbs, seeming to pay no attention to the agent intending the event (as in Figure 7) and focusing instead only on the result (i.e., lack of change of state), whereas the Chinese learners preferred the potential construction, highlighting the agent's involvement (as in Figure 6).

Native Japanese speakers, on the other hand, are less likely to use the potential form, presumably because their conceptualization is shaped by the language with which they grow up. Growing up in a Japanese-speaking environment, they have been constantly exposed to use of intransitive verbs in situations where an intended action brings about no change of state in another entity. For example, a Japanese-speaking child is likely to encounter a situation in which his/her mother, trying to open a door but not succeeding, says *akanai* '(the door) doesn't open' rather than *akerarenai* '(I) can't open (the door)'. This creates a form-meaning mapping between change of state involving an agent and use of the intransitive verb, a mapping that is reinforced through many other similar experiences. Tsujimura (2006), for example, reports on a Japanese boy who used intransitive verbs more frequently than transitive verbs, suggesting that he was able to use intransitive verbs to focus on result as a consequence of the input to which he was exposed. Nomura & Shirai (1997) also report that intransitive verbs are used more often than transitive verbs by both Japanese-speaking children and adults. It may be that, as a result of childhood experience, the Japanese intransitive ends up mapping onto meanings different from the intransitive construction in other languages such as English, as discussed in Section 2.

4.3 Syntactic vs. semantic account of overpassivization

The results of the present study thus suggest that learners' errors correlate strongly with their conceptualization of events, and to the way they map this conceptualization onto different constructions such as the intransitive, transitive, passive, and potential. We claim that this is not a purely syntactic phenomenon, but requires instead a semantic account.

This claim is supported in two ways. First, as in the results of Ju (2000), the internal causation condition yielded different results from the external causation condition, where learners avoided the use of intransitive verbs. As Ju explains, this is because under the external causation condition, the learners understood an agent to be present, even though it is not linguistically expressed.

Second, the learners are sensitive to differences between the affirmative and negative forms of sentences only under the external causation condition. Under the syntactic account of overpassivization, based on English data (Zobl 1989; Balcom 1997), one would not predict there would be a difference in response between affirmative and negative forms, because the syntactic structure of an unaccusative verb is unchanged in either the affirmative or negative case. The affirmative form differs from the negative form only in terms of semantics, as suggested by Hopper & Thompson (1980: 252).

4.4 L1 transfer or universal?

The L2 learners of Japanese studied so far (including those in the present study) do not have native-like intuitions about the transitive-passive-intransitive continuum, as suggested by Kobayashi (1996) and Miyajima (1985). L2 learners of Japanese tend to choose to include agent in the scope of meaning and linguistically encode it when it is understood to be present, whereas native Japanese speakers are able to restrict the scope of meaning to the result, without mentioning agent. In Kageyama's (1996) terms, L2 learners tend to include the super-event (i.e., the causation part of the event) and the sub-event (i.e., the change-of-state part of the event), whereas native Japanese speakers tend to include only the sub-event under the kind of conditions described in our study.

There may be two reasons why L2 learners fail to adopt a native-like scope of meaning. The first is, of course, the influence of their L1. It may be that in Chinese, or indeed most languages except for Japanese and South Asian languages like Marathi (see Pardeshi 2008), when there is a perceivable agent, it must be encoded linguistically in some way.[6] This may cause L2 learners to choose the passive or other verb forms in L2, instead of the intransitive forms preferred by L1 speakers. This possibility would predict that speakers of a language such as Japanese and Marathi that prefer a 'sub-event scope' would be less likely to make overpassivization errors in learning a language such as English than, say, L1 Chinese learners. Accustomed as they are to taking a sub-event scope, Japanese speakers would be more 'willing' to use intransitive verbs than the passive form, as opposed to Chinese learners, who are accustomed to taking a super- plus sub-event scope and thus would be more likely to use the passive form. Considering example (8) above from Ju (2000), native Japanese speakers would likely be more willing to say *it broke gradually* after reading *Heavy trucks put more and more pressure on the bridge* than native Chinese speakers, given the frequency with which they use intransitive verbs to encode change of state even in the presence of an external cause. This hypothesis should be tested in future research.

The second possibility is that it is a cognitive universal that speakers prefer to linguistically encode agents when they are perceived to be involved in an event. The animacy hierarchy of Croft (1990) suggests that animate entities (especially humans) are more likely to be encoded as the subject of a sentence. Second language learners, regardless of their L1, may have the intuition that intransitive change of state verbs with an inanimate entity as subject (e.g., *The cup broke*) are marked or unnatural, as suggested by Kellerman (1979, 1983).

It might also be the case that even if it is a universal that speakers tend to express agents as subjects, this operates as a universal only in second language acquisition, not at the cognitive universal level. This may be related to the fact that, as reported in past studies, L2 learners lack confidence in their L2 proficiency and therefore tend to express the subject/agent, together with everything else they know about an event, to insure that their intended meaning is communicated (see studies on L2 acquisition of null-argument languages, where learners tend to produce more overt arguments than native speakers; e.g., Polio 1995 for Chinese, Phinney 1987 for Spanish).

5 Conclusion

In this chapter, we have considered how L1 Chinese learners of Japanese and native Japanese speakers differ in their use of transitive and intransitive verbs

---

6 It should be noted, however, that the speaker may intentionally hide the fact that there is an agent in cases where the speaker does not want to 'blame' anyone for the happening of an event for pragmatic reasons such as politeness.

in Japanese. In particular, we examined the influence that perception of a conceptualizable external agent has on their choice, extending Ju's (2000) account of overpassivization in L2 English by L1 Chinese learners. Our results showed that the Chinese participants preferred to use intransitive forms under the internal causation condition, as opposed to passive forms for the affirmative external condition, and potential forms under the negative external condition, contrasting with the tendency exhibited by native speakers to use intransitive verbs under all these conditions. These findings show that Chinese learners' use of transitive and intransitive verbs in Japanese is influenced by their perception of the presence (or absence) of an agent, echoing the findings of Ju's (2000) study of overpassivization by Chinese learners of English. We propose that the higher incidence of transitive-based forms, such as the passive or potential form of the transitive, in the Japanese produced by L1 Chinese speakers is a result of their attempt to encode the agent, even under conditions where native Japanese speakers use intransitive forms to focus solely on the result of the event. The use of the transitive potential form under negative conditions, in particular, is a result of their attempt to attribute responsibility for the absence of a change of state to an agent intending the event.

Future research should shed light on whether the often-observed tendency to include the agent for events with a conceptualizable agent is a true universal, and if so whether it is a cognitive universal or a universal operating solely at the level of second language acquisition. One way of doing so is to examine a given phenomenon in different L1/L2 combinations, such as overpassivization patterns by Japanese and Chinese learners of English. Ikegami (1981, 1991) claimed that Japanese is a BECOME-language, English a DO-language, and Chinese appears to be less of a BECOME-language than Japanese.[7] Therefore, if we find that Japanese learners make fewer overpassivization errors in English than Chinese speakers, this would be evidence that L1 influence plays a role in the overpassivization phenomenon. If there is no reliable difference in overpassivization patterns, that would be evidence that encoding of agent is at least a universal of SLA, although not necessarily a cognitive universal.

Abbreviations

intr intransitive; DAT dative case marker; NOM nominative case marker; TOP topic marker; tr transitive; Q question particle

---

[7] This claim is based on the observation that (1) Chinese, like English, gives prominence to the possessor (e.g., *wo you liang ge haizi* 'I have two children') (2) Chinese allows less *koto* expressions (e.g., *Mari no koto ga suki* 'I like Mary' cannot be translated into **wo xihuan Mali de shi* in Chinese) (Ikegami 1991).

Acknowledgement

The first author would like to thank Dr. Chiharu Ohga at Kyushu University, Japan, for her advice on the design of the questionnaire and assistance in the coordination of the experiment.

References

Alfonso, Anthony. 1966. *Japanese language patterns*. Tokyo: Sophia University L. L. Center of Applied Linguistics.
Balcom, Patricia. 1997. Why is this happened? Passive morphology and unaccusativity. *Second Language Research* 13 (1). 1–9.
Burzio, Luigi. 1986. *Italian syntax: A government-binding approach*. Dordrecht: D. Reidel Publishing.
Croft, William. 1990. *Typology and universals*. Cambridge: Cambridge University Press.
Guerssel, Mohamed, Kenneth Hale, Mary Laughren, Beth Levin & Josie White Eagle. 1985. A cross-linguistic study of transitivity alternations. In William H. Eilfort, Paul D. Kroeber & Karen L. Peterson (eds.), *Papers from the parasession in causatives and agentivity at the twenty-first regional meeting*, 48–63. Chicago, IL: Chicago Linguistic Society.
Hopper, Paul & Sandra A. Thomspon. 1980. Transitivity in grammar and discourse. *Language* 56 (2). 251–299.
Ikegami, Yoshihiko. 1981. *"Suru" to "naru" no gengogaku* [The Linguistics of "do" and "become"]. Tokyo: Taishukan.
Ikegami, Yoshihiko. 1991. 'DO-language' and 'BECOME-language': Two contrasting types of linguistic representation. In Yoshihiko Ikegami (ed.), *The empire of signs: Semiotic essays on Japanese culture*, 285–326. Amsterdam: John Benjamins.
Jacobsen, Wesley M. 1992. *The transitive structure of events in Japanese*. Tokyo: Kurosio Publishers.
Ju, Min Kyong. 2000. Overpassivization errors by second language learners: The effect of conceptualizable agents in discourse. *Studies in Second Language Acquisition* 22 (1). 85–111.
Juffs, Alan. 1998. Some effects of first language argument structure and morphosyntax on second language sentence processing. *Second Language Research* 14 (4). 406–424.
Kageyama, Taro. 1996. *Dōshi imiron: Gengo to ninchi no setten* [Verb semantics: The interface of language and cognition]. Tokyo: Kurosio Publishers.
Kamada, Osamu & Hiroyuki Yamauchi. 1999. KY corpus (Version 1.1)
Kellerman, Eric. 1979. Transfer and non-transfer: Where we are now. *Studies in Second Language Acquisition* 2 (1). 37–57.
Kellerman, Eric. 1983. U-shaped behavior in advanced Dutch EFL learners. In Susan Gass & Carolyn Madden (eds.) *Input in Second Language Acquisition*, 345–353. Rowley, MA: Newbury House.
Kobayashi, Noriko. 1996. Sōtaijidōshi ni yoru kekka/jōtai no hyōgen – nihongo gakushūsha no shūtoku jōkyō [The expression of resultative state with paired intransitive verbs – the state of acquisition of learners of Japanese]. *Bungen Gengo Kenkyū/Gengo Hen* 29. 41–59. University of Tsukuba.

Kobayashi, Noriko & Eriko Naoi. 1996. Sōtaiji/tadōshi no shūtoku wa kanō ka – supeingo washa no baai [Are Japanese transitive/intransitive verbs learnable? – the case of speakers of Spanish]. *Tsukuba Daigaku Ryūgaku Sentā Nihongo Kyōiku Ronshū* 11. 83–98. University of Tsukuba.
Langacker, Ronald W. 2008. *Cognitive grammar: A basic introduction*. New York: Oxford University Press.
Levin, Beth. 1993. *English verb classes and alternations: A preliminary investigation*. Chicago: University of Chicago Press.
Luk, Zoe Pei-sui. 2014. Investigating the transitive and intransitive constructions in English and Japanese: A quantitative study. *Studies in Language* 38 (4). 752–791.
Matsumoto, Yo. 2000. Causative alternation in English and Japanese: A closer look. *English Linguistics* 17. 160–192. The English Linguistic Society of Japan.
Miyajima, Tatsuo. 1985. *Doa wo aketa ga, akanakatta – dōshi no imi ni okeru kekkasei* [I opened the door but the door didn't open – resultativity in verb semantics]. *Keiryōkokugogaku* 14 (8). 335–353. The Mathematical Linguistic Society of Japan.
Montrul, Silvina. 2000. Transitivity alternations in L2 acquisition. *Studies in Second Language Acquisition* 22 (2). 229–273.
Nakaishi, Yuko. 2005. Nihongo gakushūsha ni yoru tui no aru jitadōshi no shiyō no fukinkōsei – OPI deeta no bunseki o tōshite [Imbalance in use of transitive-intransitive verb pairs by learners of Japanese through an analysis of OPI data]. *Nihongo kyōka kyōiku gakkaishi* 6 (1). 59–68. Japan Curriculum Research and Development Association
Nomura, Masami & Yasuhiro Shirai. 1997. Overextension of intransitive verbs in the acquisition of Japanese. In Eve V. Clark (ed.), *Proceedings of the Twenty-Eighth Annual Child Language Research Forum*, 233–242. Stanford, CA: CSLI Publications [Distributed by Cambridge University Press].
Pardeshi, Prashant. 2008. No smoke without fire: Invisible agent construction in South Asian languages. In Rajendra Singh (ed.), *Annual Review of South Asian Languages and Linguistics*, 63–82. Berlin & New York: Mouton de Gruyter.
Perlmutter, David. 1978. Impersonal passives and the unaccusative hypothesis. *Proceedings of the Fourth Annual Meeting of the Berkeley Linguistics Society* 4. 157–189.
Phinney, Marianne. 1987. The pro-drop parameter in second language acquisition. In Thomas Roeper & Edwin Williams (eds.), *Parameter setting*, 221–238. Dordrecht: D. Reidel.
Polio, Charlene. 1995. Acquiring nothing? The use of zero pronouns by nonnative speakers of Chinese and the implications for the acquisition of nominal reference. *Studies in Second Language Acquisition* 17 (3). 353–377.
Tomasello, Michael. 1992. *First verbs: A case study of early grammatical development*. New York: Cambridge University Press.
Tsujimura, Natsuko. 2006. Why not all verbs are learned equally? The intransitive verb bias in Japanese. In Natalia Gagarina & Insa Gülzow (eds.), *The acquisition of verbs and their grammar*, 105–122. Dordrecht: Springer.
Venables, William N. & Brian D. Ripley 2002. *Modern applied statistics with S*. 4th edn. New York: Springer.
Zobl, Helmut. 1989. Canonical typological structures and ergativity in English L2 acquisition. In Susan M. Gass & Jacquelyn Schachter (eds.), *Linguistic perspectives on second language acquisition*, 203–221. Cambridge: Cambridge University Press.
Zyzik, Eve. 2006. Transitivity alternations and sequence learning: Insights from L2 Spanish production data. *Studies in Second Language Acquisition* 28 (3). 449–485.

Appendix

Questionnaire

　日本語では、(1) 他動詞の可能形と受身形 (2) 他動詞と自動詞の可能形 (3) 自動詞と他動詞の可能形が同じ形になることがあります。同じ形があるものを選ぶ時は、どちらの意味で使っているかを選択してください。

　　例) イギリス人によってこの島 (が見つかった／を見つけた／が見つかれた／(が見つけられた)) [可能／(受身)]。

括弧の中からあなたがよく使う言い方を一つ選んでください。そして、右の空白に中国語に翻訳してください。

	中国語に翻訳
① 不景気で物価 (が下がった／を下げた／が下がれた／が下げられた [可能／受身])。	①
② 国会で新しい法律案 (が通った／を通した／が通れた／が通せた／が通された)。	②
③ 私の国は、車 (が止まらない／をとめない／が止まれない／が止められない [可能／受身])。	③
④ うっかりして前の車に (ぶつかって／ぶつけて／ぶつかれて／ぶつけられて [可能／受身]) しまった。	④
⑤ 「電気、(つかない／つけない [他動／自動可能]／つけられない [可能／受身]) の。壊れているかも。」	⑤
⑥ 冬 (は／を) 三月まで (続かない／続けない [他動／自動可能]／続けられない [可能／受身])。	⑥
⑦ 雨 (がやまない／をやめない [他動／自動可能]／がやめられない [可能／受身])。	⑦
⑧ この本は大きすぎて、バッグに (入らない／入れない／入れない／入れられない [可能／受身])。	⑧

　　　　　　　裏にもあります

⑨ ワインをこぼしてしまい、友達のシャツ(が汚れて／を汚して／が汚れられて／が汚せて／が汚されて)しまった。

⑩ 秋になると、葉の色(が変わる／を変える／が変われる／が変えられる[可能／受身])。

⑪ 新入学生徒は3クラスに(分かれて／分けて／分かれられて／分けられて[可能／受身])、オリエンテーションを受けた。

⑫ 不景気なので、もう二年も私の給料(が上がらない／を上げない／が上がれない／が上げられない[可能／受身])。

⑬ 常緑樹は、冬になっても葉(が落ちない／を落とさない／が落ちられない／が落とせない／が落とされない)。

⑭ 財布(が落ちた／を落とした／が落ちられた／が落とせた／が落とされた)。今日はお金がない。

⑮ 湿度が高いので、洗った服(は／を)なかなか(乾かない／乾かさない／乾けない／乾かせない／乾かれない)。

⑯ (焼けた[自動／他動可能]／焼いた／焼けられた／焼かれた)肉を食べていいよ。

⑰ お皿を洗っている時、うっかり茶碗(が割れて／を割って／が割れられて／が割れて／が割られて)しまった。

⑱ ドア(が／を)風で(閉まった／閉めた／閉まれた／閉められた[可能／受身])。

⑲ 出張する日(が決まった／を決めた／が決まれた／が決められた[可能／受身])。

⑳ 冬になって、木の葉(が落ちた／を落とした／が落ちられた／が落とせた／が落とされた)。

あなたの母語は何ですか？（北京語／広東語／日本語／その他：＿＿＿＿＿）

（日本語を母語とする人ではない場合）今まで日本語を約何時間勉強しましたか？
＿＿時間

ご協力ありがとうございました。

V **Beyond Japanese**

Andrej L. Malchukov
13 "Ambivalent voice": markedness effects in valency change

1 Voice ambivalence: preliminary illustrations

Since the 1960's there has been an upsurge of interest in typological aspects of voice and valency change, with important contributions made by Comrie, Siewierska and Shibatani, among others, as well as by members of the St. Petersburg Typology Group (e.g. Xolodovich [ed.] 1969; Comrie 1975, 1976; Shibatani [ed.] 1976; Dixon 2000; Shibatani & Pardeshi [eds.] 2002 on causatives; Xrakovskij 1974; Siewierska 1984; Shibatani 1985 on passives; Geniušiene 1987; Klaiman 1991; Kemmer 1993 on reflexives and middles; Peterson 2007 on applicatives; Nedjalkov [ed.] 2007 on reciprocals). This work has greatly contributed to recognizing the linguistic diversity of voice phenomena, as well as establishing the main parameters of cross-linguistic variation. One aspect of this topic that has not been sufficiently acknowledged so far is the pervasiveness of "ambivalence" of voice categories, the fact that a certain voice marker (or, more broadly, a valency-changing marker) performs different functions when applied to different valency classes of verbs (in the first place to intransitives and transitives). Admittedly, there have been occasional observations made about such polysemies in the literature on individual valency categories (cf. Shibatani 1985 on passives), but with a few exceptions (such as Kazenin 1994) no extensive typological studies have been undertaken, so a general picture is still lacking.

Before we proceed to discuss the phenomenon of voice ambivalence in more detail, a few illustrations are in order. Consider the case of resultatives, which has attracted much attention in the literature (Nedjalkov [ed.] 1988). As is well known (Nedjalkov and Jaxontov 1988), resultatives show an ergative behavior: the derived subject corresponds to S ((intransitive) subject) when a resultative form is derived from an intransitive verb, but to O ((direct) object), when derived from a transitive verb. The following familiar examples from English illustrate this:

(1) a. *It is broken.* (derived S = O)
     b. *It is gone.* (derived S = S).

Andrej L. Malchukov, Johannes Gutenberg University

Such cases raise several problems, as it turns out that in the former use the marker performs a valency changing function, and thus can qualify as a voice marker, while in the latter use it does not affect valency, and therefore can be treated rather as a marker of (stative) aspect. One solution would be to treat these two uses as two separate categories: stative passive in the former case, and stative aspect in the latter. Yet, as long as such polysemies are cross-linguistically recurrent, this approach, treating such cases as accidental homonymy, becomes less attractive.

My second example concerns antipassives, which are also known to have aspectual connotations. It has been repeatedly observed that the antipassive formation often has an iterative/habitual sense (Hopper and Thompson 1980; Tsunoda 1988; Cooreman 1994). Importantly in the present context, antipassives also often show an asymmetric behavior when applied to intransitive and transitive verbs. Consider the case of Bezhta (Daghestanian; Comrie, Khalilov and Khalilova 2015), which features a garden variety of antipassive, so it seems. While the basic construction in (2a) is transitive (with an ergative A and absolutive O), the antipassive construction in (2b) is rather intransitive: A is encoded (as S) by the absolutive case, while O is demoted to the instrumental oblique case. Note also the concomitant change in agreement: A, rather than P, controls the absolutive agreement prefix on the verb in the antipassive construction.

(2) Bezhta (Comrie et al. 2015)
    a. *Öždi   bäbä   m-üq-čä.*
       boy.OBL(ERG) bread(III) III-eat-PRS
       'The boy eats the bread.'

    b. *Öžö   bäbälä-d   Ø-ü^{n}q-dä̃-š.*
       boy(I) bread.OBL-INS I-eat-ANTIP-PRS
       'The boy is busy eating the bread.'

As is also evident from the translation of (2b), the antipassive form has an aspectual effect, characterizing an action as habitual or in progress. Now, the Bezhta antipassive, maybe somewhat surprisingly, can also apply to intransitive verbs (as in (3b)). In this case, it does not affect verbal valency, and its contribution is reduced to its aspectual value:

(3) Bezhta (Comrie et al. 2015)
    a. *Öžö   Ø-ogic'-iyo.*
       boy(I) I-jump-PST
       'The boy jumped once.'

b. *Öžö   Ø-ogiyac-ca.*
   boy(I)   I-jump.ANTIP-PRS
   'The boy jumps many times.'

Comrie, Khalilov & Khalilova (2015) comment on the meaning of the Bezhta antipassive as follows:

> "One might therefore argue that the construction overall should be called "iterative" rather than "antipassive". For historical-comparative purposes, we prefer to retain the term "antipassive", but note that with intransitive verbs this does not involve a valency alternation."

Thus, the problem raised by the antipassive example (in (2)) is similar to the one raised by resultative form (in (1)). If the antipassive in Bezhta is considered as a single "ambivalent" category (rather than two homonymous forms), what is an optimal way to characterize it? One solution indicated in the quote from Comrie et al. (2015)[1] is to rely on the general meaning of the form that is present in both uses. A potential disadvantage of this approach is that the valency-changing function can't be readily derived from its definition in aspectual terms ('iterative'). An alternative solution is to rely on the prototype definition of the antipassive that necessarily includes information about the diathetic shift incurred and treats its use in (2b) a 'vacuous application' of the antipassive rule. We will return to a discussion of the relative advantages of these two approaches in section 7. On any account, though, one should acknowledge that there is a markedness relation involved here: a category has a natural domain of application (say, transitive verbs), but can be extended to other domains as well. Such situations have been previously described in terms of local markedness (Tiersma 1982; Croft 2003) or in terms of felicitous vs. infelicitous combinations (Malchukov 2011).

In what follows, I will discuss similar cases of voice ambivalence across languages. In syntactic terms, these fall into different types:

a) some (morphological) categories are both valency-increasing and valency-decreasing;
b) some categories are both valency-increasing and valency-preserving;
c) some categories are both valency-decreasing and valency-preserving;
d) some categories are valency increasing, but yield different effects with different verb classes;
e) some categories are valency decreasing, but yield different effects with different verb classes.

---

[1] A similar proposal reducing the antipassive value to its aspectual core has been earlier advanced by Tchekhoff (1987).

Not all cases will be considered here, for space reasons, and also because some cases have been discussed in the prior literature more extensively than others. Thus, Kittilä (2009), building on Hopper & Thompson's (1980) work, discusses voice ambivalence of the (b) type, addressing cases where a causative marker performs an intensive function (as is the case in some stem alternations in Arabic), or indicates intentionality on the part of the A argument (as in Finnish):

(4) Finnish (Kittilä 2009)
    a. *Henkilö   laihtu-i   4.86   kilo-a.*
       person:NOM lose.weight-3SG: PAST 4.86 kilogram-PART
       'A person lost 4.86 kilograms of his/her weight
       (spontaneously, without conscious effort).'

    b. *Henkilö   laihdu-tt-i   4.86   kilo-a.*
       person:NOM lose.weight-CAUS-3SG:PAST 4.86 kilogram- PART
       'A person lost 4.86 kilograms of his/her weight (intentionally).'

Kittilä 2009 proceeds to explain this polysemy in terms of transitivity parameters along the lines of Hopper & Thompson (1980). Also, I will not address here cases of valency decrease of type (e) where the same voice can be used as anticausative with one subtype of transitive verbs, but has a reflexive or antipassive with another type of transitive verbs. Such cases have been extensively discussed in the literature on reflexive and middle markers (Geniušiene 1987; Kemmer 1993). Importantly in the present context, Kazenin (1994; cf. Dixon & Aikhenvald 2000: 20-21; Wunderlich 2006) highlighted a markedness pattern involved, showing that, other things being equal, agent-oriented verbs (corresponding to "unergatives" in the intransitive use) prefer an antipassive reading, while patient-oriented verbs (corresponding to "unaccusatives" in the intransitive use) prefer an anticausative or passive reading. This can be illustrated by familiar Russian examples involving the polysemous reflexive voice marker – *sja/s'* (note also their translational equivalents in English showing a similar pattern, albeit in the absence of voice morphology):

(5) Russian (cf. Kazenin 1994: 144)
    a. *Ja   sloma-l   palku.*
       I.NOM break-PAST.SG.MS stick.ACC
       'I broke the stick.'

    b. *Palka   sloma-la-sj.*
       stick.NOM break-PAST.SG.FM-REFL
       'The stick broke.' (anticausative)

(6) Russian
 a. *Sobaka   kusa-et   malčika.*
    dog.NOM   bite-PRES.3SG   boy.ACC
    'The dog bites a boy.'
 b. *Sobaka   kusa-et-sja.*
    dog.NOM   bite-PRES.3SG-REFL
    'The dog bites.' (antipassive)

I will largely leave such cases out of discussion, because much of the relevant literature centers on ambitransitive/labile verbs, where the markedness pattern involved is most clear.

In what follows I provide an overview of voice ambivalence, considering the following cases mentioned under (a), (c) and (d). Section 2 considers cases of passives of intransitives (showing type c-ambivalence), and section 3 considers causatives of transitives. Both sections are intended to highlight a markedness pattern involved, rather than focus on particular polysemy patterns, to be addressed in subsequent sections. I discuss passive-causative polysemy (type a-ambivalence) in section 4, causative-applicative polysemy (falling under the type d-polysemy) in section 5, and antipassive-applicative polysemy (of the type a) in section 6. In section 7 I return to the issue of the explanation of voice ambivalence. I propose a semantic map for major voice categories which is enriched in order to capture relationships of local markedness (felicity/infelicity of certain feature combinations).

Before we proceed, some qualifications are in order (partially prompted by a reviewer's comments). First, while speaking about valency and valency change I do not restrict myself to cases of change in numerical valency (increase or decrease in the number of syntactic arguments), as valency-rearrangement (alternative linking patterns, or 'alignment alternations', in terms of Shibatani this volume) is included in the purview as well. Second, while the main focus is on syntactic properties of the voice markers, this is not intended to downplay importance of other semantic and/or pragmatic aspects of voice categories, in particular, the connections between voice and aspect (see the connection between passives and stative aspect illustrated in (1) above, and antipassive with the incompletive/habitual aspect in (2)–(3)). The latter connections are well-known from the literature, and have been accounted for either in diachronic terms (as, e.g., in Haspelmath 1990), or in general functional terms (as in Hopper & Thompson 1980; Shibatani 2006). The point of this chapter is, however, to highlight dependency of the voice polysemy on the valency type of the verb (in particular, the verb's transitivity) to which voice morphology applies, and also to show that one can go a long way in explaining these polysemies in syntactic terms starting from commonly shared assumptions. As will be clear from the following discussion, many cross-linguistically recurrent polysemy patterns, involving some unexpected polysemies (such as causative-passive, or applicative-antipassive) can be straightforwardly explained in terms of shared syntactic properties (see the semantic map in section 7). Third, the advocated explanation of voice ambivalence as arising from an overextension of the voice morphology beyond its natural domain of application invites a diachronic interpretation. This interpretation is endorsed in the present study but not systematically pursued for two reasons. First, the diachronic scenarios behind voice polysemies are in many cases controversial (including many much discussed cases such as the question of the original meaning of the passive marker in Japanese). Further, while it is true that in many cases, one direction of an extension, which follows the well-known grammaticalization paths (say, from causative to passive) is much more plausible than a change in the opposite direction, it is far more challenging to disprove the possibility of both meanings developing from a third construction. Thus, the adopted perspective describing meaning extensions of a voice marker in terms of local markedness is more general, as it holds irrespective of particular diachronic scenarios. We will briefly return to these issues in the concluding section 7.

2 Passives of intransitives

It is well known from the work on passives (Xrakovskij 1974; Siewierska 1984; Shibatani 1985; Keenan 1985) that a passive if available applies primarily to transitives. In some languages it can be also extended to intransitives resulting in impersonal passives (like in German), but in other languages its application to intransitives is blocked. On the whole, the following implicational relation holds: if a passive can apply to intransitives it can apply to transitives as well, while the opposite needs not to be true (Keenan 1985: 249). One could interpret this generalization in terms of (local) markedness: the unmarked (more natural) combination would be passives applied to transitives, while application of passives to intransitives is more marked (less natural).[2] There could be different

---

[2] The term markedness is used here in a broad typological sense (as in Croft 2003) and relates to the cluster of properties comprising cross-linguistic frequencies of a particular construction, corpus frequencies in individual languages, formal complexity and semantic specificity. While, the correlation between different instantiations of the concept of markedness may not be perfect (see Haspelmath 2006 for a critical discussion), existence of such (statistical) correlation is widely assumed in the literature, even though a large-scale empirical verification of this assumption is still outstanding. Of particular importance in the present context is the concept of local markedness (Tiersma 1982; Croft 1990, 2003) pertaining to (un) markedness (naturalness) of certain combinations of grammatical and/or lexical categories (e.g., voice and transitivity).

interpretations of this relation depending on whether one assumes object promotion or subject demotion or both to be the characteristic feature of passives, but on the whole the conclusion that the application of passives to intransitives is a marked case is uncontroversial.

As in other cases of infelicitous category interaction (Malchukov 2011; cf. Moravcsik 2010), this infelicitous combination can be resolved in a different way: in some languages a passive can apply to intransitives, resulting in impersonal passives, but in other languages its application will be blocked (found only with transitives). Of most interest for us are situations where a passive, when applied to intransitives, shifts in meaning. This can be illustrated for Russian, where the reflexive passive when applied to intransitives is modalized (see Geniušiene 1987 for discussion of "modal-deagentive" constructions). A standard example of the "modal deagentive" construction from Russian involving the use of the reflexive-passive form is seen in (7):

(7) Russian
   Mne   ne   spit-sja.
   me.DAT not   sleep.PRES.SG-PASS
   'I cannot sleep.'

The modal use of impersonal passives of intransitives is widely attested in European languages and elsewhere (Geniušiene 1987). For example, in (Gulf) Arabic those intransitives that may be passivized usually carry modal meaning (Holes 1990). This phenomenon is widely attested in Altaic languages, including Turkic (Ščerbak 1981) and Tungusic (Nedjalkov 1992). In particular, in East Tungusic languages like Nanai the impersonal passive developed into a modal marker with the meaning of obligation (Avrorin 1962; Nedjalkov 1992). In Japanese passives of intransitives develop specific uses, such as potential and honorific, which are less characteristic of passives of transitives (Shibatani 1985: 822–823):

(8) Japanese (Shibatani 1985: 822–823)
   Boku wa   nemur-are-nakat-ta.
   I   TOP   sleep-PASS-NEG-PAST
   'I could not sleep.'

The Japanese example is different insofar as the passive form in (8) is not impersonal (i.e. lacking a referential subject). That is, unlike the Russian example in (7) or similar examples in other European languages, the Japanese passive is valency-preserving when applied to intransitives. In fact, this form is conventionally interpreted in Japanese studies as a distinct category of "potential" (largely) homophonous with the passive form.[3] Yet, importantly in the present context, when used with transitives, the potential may either preserve or change the valency. In the latter case it yields a structure similar to passive (with the base A in the dative, and the base O in the nominative) even though there remain some syntactic differences between the two constructions (Kishimoto et al. 2015). Example (9), built on an intransitive verb, shows that the potential does not affect valency with intransitive verbs: the subject remains nominative. Example (10), by contrast, illustrates that with transitives the potential form is either valency-preserving (as in (10a)), or valency-decreasing (as in (10b)):

(9) Japanese (Kishimoto et al. 2015)
   Kono uma-{ga/*ni} hasir-e-ru.
   this horse-{NOM/*DAT} run-POT-PRES
   'This horse can run.'

(10) Japanese (Kishimoto et al. 2015)
   a. *Ken-ga kotae-o kak-e-ru.*
      Ken-NOM answer-ACC write-POT-PRES
      'Ken can write the answer.'

   b. *Ken-{ni/ga} kotae-ga kak-e-ru.*
      Ken-{DAT/NOM} answer-NOM write-POT-PRES
      'Ken can write the answer.'

Shibatani (1976, and p.c.) attributes the fact that the potential is valency preserving with intransitives to the general 'obligatory nominative' requirement to the effect that there should be at least one *ga* marker in a clause. On my interpretation, this contrast shows that in Japanese as well, reanalysis of a passive marker into a modal (mood) marker is more strongly pronounced in the context of intransitives, while with transitives it may still qualify as a voice marker.

Thus, in both cases we have seen that in a marked context (that of intransitive verbs) the passive is interpreted as a modal marker. This seems to be also characteristic of other valency-reducing categories. For example, Seifert (2015) notes that in Bora (Amazonian), a marker with a basic reflexive function when used with intransitives performs a modal ("attempted action") function (which is a frequent concomitant of antipassive meaning, but which is not confined in Bora to transitive verbs).[4]

---

3 In contrast to the polysemous *–(ra)re-* allomorph (in (8)), the *-(r)e-* marker, as in (9) is exclusively associated with the potential uses (Wesley Jacobsen, p.c.).
4 It may also have a passive function with some (transitive) verbs.

(11) Bora (Amazonian; Seifert 2015)
   a. *Wajpi   tsájtyé-meí-hi.*
      man   carry-REFL-PRED
      'The man carried himself'

   b. *Wajpi   dsüné-meí-hi*
      man   run-REFL-PRED
      'The man tried to run.'

As a final illustration consider the case of Balkar (a Turkic language). In Balkar, application of the passive to intransitive may yield two distinct interpretations. First, it can result in an impersonal passive with modal function (of the type illustrated for Russian in (7) above):

(12) Balkar (Ljutikova & Bonch-Osmolovskaja 2006:400)
   Zas-ta   igi   cab-il-a-di.
   summer-LOC   good   run-PASS-PRS-3
   'In the summer, it is good to run.'

More interesting is another use of the passive of the intransitive, one that is dubbed "causal passive" by Ljutikova & Bonch-Osmolovskaja (2006):

(13) Balkar (Ljutikova & Bonch-Osmolovskaja 2006: 405)
   Alim   ü-de   qal-ın-dı.
   Alim   house-LOC   stay-PASS-PAST
   'Alim had to stay at home.'

Note that the latter construction is not impersonal; in fact, application of the passive here does not affect the verbal diathesis at all. Ljutikova and Bonch-Osmolovskaja qualify this function as a "causal passive", since it implies the presence of an external cause. Note that the presence of an external cause is inherent in the semantics of passives of transitives, which imply existence of an agent/causer at the semantic level (even if suppressed in the syntax), but is unexpected for the passive form of intransitives. I interpret the last example as an indication that the meaning of the verb has undergone a shift to a causative/transitive meaning in the presence of the passive morphology. Thus, (13) could be more adequately translated as 'Alim was made to stay at home', which is semantically equivalent to 'Alim had to stay at home'. On this interpretation, the base verb acquires a transitive/causative meaning in the context of passive, even though the verb cannot be used transitively outside of this construction (unlike the case of labile verbs such as English *walk*: *The dog was walked by its master* vis-à-vis nonpassive *The master walked the dog*.). Such a situation illustrates another scenario of resolution of this infelicitous combination (cf. Malchukov 2011 for discussion): either a passive shifts its meaning (to modal) in the context of intransitive verb, or an intransitive verb shifts to transitive in the context of passive. In terms of Xrakovskij (1996) and Malchukov (2011), in the first case the passive is a recessive category, in the second case it is a dominant category.

3 Causatives of transitives

It is well-known (at least since Nedjalkov & Sil'nitskij 1969) that some languages that allow causatives to apply to intransitives may not allow them to apply to transitives. The functional motivation behind this constraint may be less clear than in the case of passivization of intransitives, yet this combination may be seen as functionally infelicitous if we include the feature 'transitivization' into the causative prototype (cf. Dixon & Aikhenvald 2000:13). Since causatives are used for valency increase, they routinely apply to intransitives, yet at least in some languages their application to transitives is restricted. Admittedly, some languages do not show such restrictions: the causative of transitives is regularly used to derive ditransitives from transitives (in some languages all derived ditransitives are causatives). Other languages (such as Ket, or Yucatec Maya; see (16) below) do not allow causatives of transitives at all. Still other languages may use a causative marker, but the meaning is different (see my discussion of the causative-passive and causative-applicative polysemy below; cf. also example (4) from Finnish above). Arguably, the most interesting case of interaction is found in languages where a restriction on combining the causative with transitives leads to a situation where a transitive verb must first be detransitivized in order for a causative to be applied to it.[5] This can be exemplified for Mandinka (Creissels 2015). In Mandinka there are two causative markers: 'Causative 1' in *-ndi*, which applies to intransitive verbs, and 'Causative 2' in *-ri-ndi*, which applies to transitives. The second causative is illustrated below:

---

5 Song (1996: 179–181) cites a number of similar languages (Blackfoot, Halkomelem, Southern Tiwa, Bandjalang) and attributes the constraint against causativization of transitives to the (restricted) number of core object slots available in these languages.

(14) Mandinka (Creissels 2015)
 Kew-ó   ye   díndíŋ-o   dómó-rí-ndi   (mbuur-ôo la).
 man-DEF PF.POS child-DEF   eat-ANTIP-CAUS   bread.DEF OBL
 'The man made the child eat (bread).'

Note that Causative 2 differs from Causative 1 in having an additional marker –*ri*-. Remarkably, the same marker functions elsewhere as an antipassive:

(15) Mandinka (Creissels 2015)
 Mus-óo   ye   tábí-r-oo   ke.
 woman-DEF PF.POS cook-ANTIP-DEF   do
 'The woman did the cooking.'

In other words, in order to apply the causative to a transitive verb, this verb needs first to be antipassivized. This is somewhat similar to the situation in Balkar, where the use of the passive shifts an intransitive verb into a transitive one. One could also characterize this as a case of coercion: the application of the voice morphology conditions a category shift. The difference in the Mandinka pattern is that coercion in this case is overtly signaled (by the voice morphology) while in case of Balkar we are rather dealing with an implicit coercion.

A similar case of construction coercion is found in Yucatec Maya (Lehmann 2015). In this language as well there is a restriction to the effect that causatives can apply only to intransitives (but causativization is further restricted in that the intransitive verb must be stative, see below). Therefore in order to causativize a transitive verb, the verb must first be passivized. This option is available for some transitive verbs such as *ka'ns* 'teach,' whose stem is ultimately based on the transitive root *kan* 'learn'. This verb is first passivized, yielding *ka'n* 'be learnt', and in the second step it is causativized yielding *ka'ns* 'cause to be learnt'.

(16) Yucatec Maya (Lehmann 2015)
 T-in   ka'ns-ah   xokp'éelil-o'b   t-in   paal.
 PRFV-SBJ.1.SG teach-CMPL   number-PL   LOC-POSS.1.SG   child
 'I taught my child numbers.'

Yucatec Maya is also representative in another respect. It imposes a more strict restriction on the formation of causatives, which can apply only to stative intransitives, but neither to active intransitives or transitives. Shibatani 2002 reports further languages that show a similar restriction. Thus, the preferences of causatives and passives are actually converses of each other, and can be represented on the following (markedness) scale:

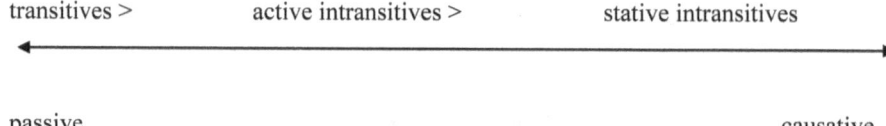

Figure 1: Markedness scale for causative and passive formation

Thus, the passive readily applies to transitives (highest on the hierarchy); it is less applicable to active intransitives, and is least applicable to inactive intransitives. In early work in Relational Grammar (Perlmutter 1978) it has been suggested that passives can't be applied to unaccusatives at all. Yet this generalization is better viewed as an implicational rather than an absolute universal: if a passive applies to unaccusatives (as, e.g., in Turkish) it would apply to higher categories as well. For causatives, the markedness relation is reversed: they are most felicitous with stative intransitives (unaccusatives), less so with active intransitives, and least felicitous with transitive verbs.

As noted by Shibatani (p.c.), these preferences have a functional explanation and can be derived from the functional characteristics of the passive vs. causative prototype. Thus, Shibatani (1985) attributes the preference of passives for transitive verbs to the function of agent-defocusing associated with the passive prototype; alternatively, one can assume with Haspelmath (1990) that passive does not apply to inactive intransitives since the very function of the passive morphology is 'inactivization' of the situation. The relation between causativization and stativity is more subtle, but Shibatani (1976 and p.c.) suggests that if causation means bringing about a change, where the change wouldn't happen otherwise, it is expected to apply more readily to time-stable, i.e. stative, situations.

4 Passive-causative polysemy

Typologists have been aware of the pervasiveness of passive-causative polysemy at least since Nedjalkov's (1964) seminal publication. One common pattern is that basically a causative marker is interpreted as a passive marker: an intermediate stage of reflexive causative is usually assumed here (Nedjalkov & Sil'nitskij 1969; Haspelmath 1990; I. Nedjalkov 1991; Li & Whaley 2012). Such extended use of causatives in a passive function is frequent in Altaic languages, and illustrated below for Khakas (a Siberian Turkic language):

(17) Khakas (Letuchiy 2006)
    Paba-m   xyr-tyr-š'a   parikmaxer-ya.
    father-1SG shave-CAUS-PRS   hairdresser-DAT
    'My father is shaved by the hairdresser.'

An opposite case where a marker with a basic passive function is used as a causative marker also exists, and is frequently characterized as an "adversative (passive)". This pattern is familiar from Japanese, where the adversative/passive marker is assumed to have derived from a 'spontaneous'/involitive marker (Shibatani 2006: 223). The effect of "indirect (adversative) passivization" in Japanese illustrated in (18) is characterized by Kishimoto et al. (2015) as follows:

> "By contrast, indirect passivization may apply to all kinds of (controllable) verbs, whether transitive or intransitive, and increases the verb's valency by adding a new subject called an 'affectee' or affected experiencer, with a concomitant change of the nominative marking on the original subject to the dative *-ni*."

The use of the adversative passive in a valency increasing function with intransitive (impersonal)) verbs is illustrated below:

(18) Japanese (Kishimoto et al. 2015)
    Ken-ga   ame-{ni/*ni-yotte}   hur-are-ta.
    Ken-NOM   rain-{DAT/*by}   fall-PASS-PAST
    'Ken got rained on.'

Of relevance here is the observation that the same marker can be used as a regular passive (a 'direct passive') when applied to transitives, but is used in a causative (more specifically, "involitive-permissive" function, in terms of V.P. Nedjalkov), when applied to intransitives. The same is true for Even (North-Tungusic), which also features adversative passives (Malchukov 1993). In Even as well, when a passive applies to a transitive verb, the usual outcome is a "direct passive", with O promoted to S and A demoted to a dative agentive phrase. Thus, it looks like a canonical passive, except for the fact that normally an adversative effect is implied. (For that reason the adversative passive is preferentially found with verbs of negative impact, or else induces adversative interpretation 'against one's will' when used with verbs with neutral semantics; Malchukov 1993).

(19) Even (Malchukov 1995)
    a. *Nugde   etike-m   maa-n.*
       bear.NOM   old man-ACC   kill-NONFUT:3SG
       'The bear killed the old man.'

    b. *Etiken   nugde-du   maa-w-ra-n.*
       old man.NOM   bear-DAT   kill-ADVPAS-NONFUT-3SG
       'The old man was killed by the bear.'

When applied to intransitive verbs the passive marker signals valency increase instead, in a way similar to the involitive-permissive causative in terms of Nedjalkov ('X lets V happen involuntarily'):

(20) Even (Malchukov 1995)
    a. *Huličan   böödele-n   ene-l-re-n.*
       fox(GEN)   feet.NOM-3SG   hurt-INCH-NONFUT-3SG
       'The fox's paws began to hurt.'

    b. *Huličan   böödel-i   ene-le-w-re-n.*
       fox.NOM   feet-REF POS SG   hurt-INCH-ADVPAS-NONFUT-3SG
       'The fox's paws began to hurt; it/the fox was negatively affected.'

Thus, also in the case of adversative passives, the regular passive structure is possible only when the verb is transitive. With intransitives and zero-valent (impersonal) verbs only the valency-increasing function obtains. This does not mean however, that the valency increasing function is impossible for transitive constructions as well: in fact, in Even, like in Japanese, an A-adding adversative derivation is also possible with transitives. Some other Tungusic languages may show more restrictions in this respect. Thus, according to Li & Whaley (2012), in Oroqen (a North-Tungusic variety spoken in China), the marker –*wu*- is used as a passive marker with transitives but as a causative marker with some (mostly stative) intransitives. The same is true of Manchu, at least as a statistical tendency (I. Nedjalkov 1991). Thus, the general markedness pattern is clear: the same marker is used with a valency-increasing function when applied to intransitives and valency decreasing function when applied to transitives. Some further examples have been discussed by I. Nedjalkov (1991) in terms of recessive-accessive polysemy.

5 Causative-applicative polysemy

A further case of polysemy involving causative markers relates to cases when the same marker has the causative meaning when applied to intransitives and an applicative meaning when applied to transitives (Shibatani & Pardeshi 2002; Peterson 2007). The use of the causative with intransitives is preferred, as expected (see above). The use of valency increasing applicatives with transitives may seem more dysfunctional, but makes sense provided that an applicative promotes the peripheral argument of an extended intransitive or extended transitive. Thus, in both cases the marker is used to increase valency, but adds either a new A (causer) or a new (applied) object.

This pattern can also be illustrated from Mapudungun. According to Golluscio (2010) and Zúñiga (2015), Mapudungun has a valency-increasing marker -*l* that functions as a causative (A-adding) marker with monovalent verbs, and as an applicative (O-adding) marker with both monovalent and bivalent verbs. The -*l*-causative is used to causativize intransitives with an animate subject, and is therefore, called a 'high-control causative' (in contrast to another 'low control causative' marker -*(i̵)m*- applying to inanimate subjects); cf.: *tranün* 'fall', and *tranelün* 'knock (smb.) down'. The applicative use (based on a ditransitive verb) is illustrated below:

(21) Mapudungun (Golluscio 2010: 737)
 Elu-l-fi-n   sañchu tañi   weṉüy   tañi   fotṳm.
 give-APPL1–3P-1SG.IND pig   1SG.PSR friend 1SG.PSR son.of.man
 'I gave my son's friend a pig.'

More examples of this sort of causative-applicative polysemy can be found in Shibatani & Pardeshi (2002) and in Peterson (2007). An example from Balinese (Austronesian; Shibatani & Artawa 2015; cf. Shibatani this volume) may serve as a further illustration. In Balinese, the same –*ang* marker has both causative and applicative uses. When applied to intransitives (inactive/stative predicates), its meaning is causative:

(22) Balinese (Shibatani & Artawa 2015)
 a. *Celeng=e   mati.*
    pig=DEF   PF.dead
    'The pig is dead.'

 b. *Anak=e   ento   nge-mati-ang   celeng=e.*
    person=DEF   that   AF-dead-CAUS   pig=DEF
    'The man killed the pig.'

When the -*ang* marker is applied to transitives the meaning is that of the instrumental applicative (with a theme/instrument promoted to the main object):

(23) Balinese (Shibatani & Artawa 2015)
    a. *Ia   nyikut   natah=e   aji   tungked.*
       s/he AF.measure yard=DEF with stick
       'S/he measured the yard with a stick.'

    b. *Ia   nyikut-ang   tungked ka natah=e.*
       s/he AF.measure-CAUS stick to yard=DEF
       'S/he used a stick to measure the yard.'

Expectedly, the causative meaning shows a preference for inactive intransitives, while the applicative meaning shows a preference for active intransitives or transitives (cf. Polinsky 2005). The preferences for a transitive or active intransitive verb may depend on the type of the applicative; thus a benefactive applicative preferentially applies to transitives, while some other applicative types (e.g., comitative) may preferentially apply to (active) intransitives (Shibatani 2002, and this volume).

This polysemy seems actually to be more wide-spread cross-linguistically than reported, as it may be masked by differences in terminology. Consider the case of Central Alaskan Yupik (Miyaoka 2015), which features a peculiar category of "adversative". When the adversative is used with intransitives, the (negatively) affected participant becomes an A:

(24) Central Alaskan Yupik (Miyaoka 2015)
    a. *Kicaq   kit'-uq.*
       anchor.ABS.SG sink-IND.3SG
       'The anchor sank.'

    b. *Kic-i-aqa   kicaq.*
       sink-ADV-IND.1SG.3SG anchor.ABS.SG
       'I had the anchor sunk (me negatively affected);'

In this function it comes close in meaning to permissive causatives or adversative passives, as illustrated above for Japanese and Even. However, when derived from transitives, the affected participant appears as an O (see the 1st person object agreement with the experiencer in (25b)):

(25) Central Alaskan Yupik (Miyaoka 2015)
a. *Neqe-m   neqcaq   ner-aa.*
   fish-REL.SG bait.ABS.SG   eat-IND.3SG.3SG
   'The fish ate the bait.'

b. *Ner-i-anga   neqe-m   neqca-mnek*
   eat-ADV-IND.3SG.1SG   fish-REL.SG   bait-ABM.1SG.SG
   'The fish ate my bait *(on me).*'

Thus, the adversative category has the function of the 'adversative causative' (or adversative passive) when derived from intransitives, but of 'adversative (malefactive) applicative' when derived from transitives.

More discussion of the causative-applicative polysemy is provided by Austin (1997), Shibatani ([ed.] 2002), and Peterson (2007). Peterson 2007 suggests that the causative meaning seems to be primary diachronically, and provides a scenario for the development of the applicative meaning on the basis of causative. This scenario is more straightforward for instrumental applicatives, which show a greater affinity to causatives (cf. (23b) from Balinese), and is less straightforward for benefactive applicatives ('do V for smb'); for the latter, sociative causatives ('help do V') may provide a link (Shibatani & Pardeshi 2002). See Shibatani (this volume) for further discussion of the causative-benefactive polysemy.

6 Applicative-antipassive polysemy

A somewhat different case of voice ambivalence is found in languages that use the same marker for two seemingly opposite functions: an applicative one, adding an object, and an antipassive one, demoting the object. Yet, this contradiction can be resolved taking into account that applicatives, when built on transitives, are often used for valency rearrangement. This has been reported for languages imposing restrictions on the number of core arguments, as discussed by Gerdts (1988) and Song (1996). For these languages, a promotion of a peripheral argument happens at the expense of the demoting an original patient. One such language that imposes strict restrictions on the number of core arguments is Halkomelem Salish, discussed by Gerdts (2010 *passim*). In Halkomelem, use of an applicative to introduce a main (absolutive) object is accompanied by a demotion of the O to the oblique:

(26) Halkomelem (Gerdts 2010)
   a. *Ni?*   *qʷəl-ət-əs*   *łə-nə*   *ten*   *kʷθə*   *səplil.*
      AUX   cook-TR-3ERG   DT-1S.POS   mother   DT   bread
      'My mother baked the bread.'

   b. *Ni?*   *qʷəl-əłc-t-əs*   *łə-nə*   *ten*   *łə*   *słeni?*
      AUX   cook-BEN-TR-3ERG   DT-1S.POS   mother   DT   woman
      ?ə   *kʷθə*   *səplil*
      OBL   DT   bread
      'My mother baked the bread for the woman.'

Admittedly, this construction can't be characterized as a canonical antipassive since patient-demotion is a mere side-effect of benefactive promotion. In some other languages, however, O-demotion can occur "spontaneously" without a concomitant promotion of an applied object. Again such languages seem to be similar to Halkomelem in having a restricted number of argument slots available. Consider again Central Alaskan Yupik (CAY), which has not been discussed in this context so far (my analysis is based on the comprehensive description in Miyaoka (2012, 2015), although my interpretation is somewhat different). Recall that CAY features a special adversative category which functions as a causative with intransitives and as a malefactive applicative with transitives. Now, the same marker can be also used as an antipassive elsewhere:

(27) Central Alaskan Yupik (Miyaoka 2015)
   a. *Angute-m*   *kuvya-ni*   *allg-aa.*
      man-REL.SG   net-ABS.3SG.SG   tear-IND.3SG.3SG
      'The man tears/tore his (own) net.'

   b. *Angun*   *kuvya-minek*   *allg-i-uq.*
      man.ABS.SG   net-ABM.3SG.SG   tear-APAS-IND.3SG
      'The man tore his (own) net.'

Note that (27b) is quite similar to (25b) above, which was analyzed above as an applicative: in both cases the original P argument is demoted to the oblique (instrumental/ablative) case. Yet, there is a crucial difference between the two constructions, which justifies their distinct treatment. Note that the verb in the applicative construction (25b) is transitive (as evident from the use of the transitive agreement), while in the antipassive use (27b) the verb is intransitive (as evident from the use of intransitive agreement).

Moreover, CAY also features a special applicative marker –*ut*- that can be used with both intransitives and transitives. When used with intransitives, it is as expected used to introduce a new object, but when built on transitives it may perform an antipassive function. Miyaoka (2015; cf. Miyaoka 2012) comments as follows:

> "It is noteworthy that the first and the second antipassive markers are identical with the adversative -*gi*- and applicative -*uc*- suggesting a parallel pattern between an antipassive and an applicative in this language."

On my view, a stronger claim can be made: in both cases we are dealing with applicative suffixes that have developed an antipassive function. Mithun (2000), likewise, in her in-depth study of valency change in CAY considers the antipassive use of these markers as extensions of the applicative use, but offers a somewhat different explanation. She writes (2000: 97):

> "It might be wondered how applicative morphemes like the benefactive and the malefactive, whose primary function is to increase the valency of the stem, could evolve into detransitivizers. The evolution is explicable in terms of the Yup'ik transitivity classes. The applicatives can derive agentive ambitransitives. When the agentive ambitransitives are inflected intransitively, they leave just an agent absolutive as the only core argument."

While this may be a plausible explanation for CAY, it is striking that antipassive-applicative polysemy is commonly attested elsewhere, in particular in languages that have a strict restriction on number of arguments. Moreover, even for Yupik, this analysis is not without problems since it seems to predict that antipassives should target (demote) the primary object (beneficiary), rather than the basic patient, as is actually observed in CAY. Instead, I suggest this case as another case of applicative-antipassive polysemy conditioned by restrictions on the number of argument slots (see Song 1996 for discussion of more languages). For CAY it has the effect of promoting a peripheral argument into the main (absolutive) argument, but given restrictions on the number of argument slots available, this promotion happens at the cost of the original patient. What is peculiar to CAY and other similar languages is that it has generalized the patient-demoting function beyond the context where promotion is involved. Thus, the antipassive use is better explained as analogical extension of the applicative pattern (note that the syntactic pattern is identical except for indexing on the verb in (25b) and (27b)).

A similar pattern is observed in Chukchi (Chukotka-Kamchatkan). Mel'čuk (2006), citing Polinsky & Nedjalkov (1987), discusses the applicative prefix *ine-/ena-* (called '2/3–permutative' by Mel'čuk) in Chukchi. Its use as the goal applicative is illustrated in (28), where it marks the 'promotion' of the erstwhile locative oblique in (28a) to a core (absolutive) object in (28b); note that the original theme is demoted to an instrumental oblique:

(28) Chukchi (Mel'čuk 2006: 224, citing Polinsky & Nedjalkov 1987)
    a. ətləy-e   təkəcʔ-ən   utkucʔ-ək pela-nen.
        father.SG.ERG bait.SG.ABS trap-LOC   leave.AOR.3SG → 3SG
        'Father left bait in the trap.'

    b. ətləy-e   təkəcʔ-a   utkucʔ- ən **ena**-pela-nen.
        father.SG.ERG bait.SG.INSTR trap-SG.NOM APPL-leave.AOR.3SG → 3SG
        'Father left/supplied the trap with bait.'

Elsewhere, Mel'čuk (2006: 233) notes that *ine-/ena-* is homophonous with the prefix of the "detransitivizer". The detransitivizing function is illustrated in (29); note that the object is demoted to the instrumental oblique in (29b), although nothing is promoted in this case:

(29) Chukchi (Mel'čuk 2006: 233–234, citing Polinsky & Nedjalkov 1987)
    a. yəm-nan   tə-ret-ərkən   kimitʔ-ən   (tomy-etə).
        I-ERG   1SG.A-transport-PRES.3SG.O load-SG.NOM friend-DAT
        'I transport a load (to a friend/friends).'

    b. yəm   t-**ine**-ret-ərkən   kimitʔ-e   (tomy-etə).
        I.ABS   1SG.S-ANTIP-transport-PRES load-SG.INSTR friend-DAT
        'I transport a load (to a friend/friends).'

Again, it may be argued that in (28b) and (29b) we are dealing with the same construction, yet, as in the case of (CAY) Eskimo examples (25) and (27) above, the agreement morphology distinguishes between the two constructions; the applicative construction in (28b) features a transitive verbs morphology, while the antipassive construction in (29b) features intransitive morphology. Also, I would rather speak of regular (applicative-antipassive) polysemy here, instead of mere homophony.

    A similar polysemy pattern has been observed for other languages as well. Thus, in Sliammon Salish (Watanabe 2015), the same suffix *-ʔəm* is used both as an 'indirective' marker and also as a suffix of the 'active-intransitive' forms:

(30) Sliammon Salish (Watanabe 2015)
 a. *Həy-ʔəm=č*   *ʔə=kʷ=kʷaxʷa.*
    make-A.INTR=1SG.INDC.SBJ   OBL=DET=box
    'I will make a box.' (active-intransitive)

 b. *Həy-ʔəm-θi=tθəm*   *ʔə=kʷ=kʷaxʷa.*
    make-IND-CTR+2SG.OBJ=1SG.INDC.SBJ+FUT OBL=DET=box
    'I will make a box for you.' (indirective)

Watanabe (2015) notes that the issue of whether to treat the two forms as distinct is unresolved. Given that 'indirective' is a variety of a benefactive applicative and 'active-intransitive' is a variety of (demoting) antipassives (with the notional patient introduced by the oblique preposition), I would assimilate this case as well to the cases of applicative-antipassive polysemy discussed earlier.

Thus, this case of voice ambivalence (O-promoting but also O-demoting behavior) can be attributed to the fact that this is basically an object rearranging operation. As suggested by Gerdts (1988) and Song (1996) this is ultimately due to the fact that some languages impose strict restrictions on the number of core arguments that can be accommodated by the verb. Yet only some of these languages extend applicatives to regular antipassives, through generalizing the 'demotional' part of the applicative rule (O → Oblique), which becomes 'decoupled' from the promotional part (Oblique → O), presumably by way of analogical extension. Interestingly, the same can be said of passives, which typically include both object-to-subject promotion and subject-to-oblique demotion. Therefore one could expect in analogy of the applicative pattern, that some languages may generalize the demotional part of the passive rule without having recourse to promotion: this is what happens in impersonal passives, which provide a parallel to the antipassive extension of the demotional use of the applicative.

7 Local markedness and semantic maps: Towards an explanation of voice ambivalence

As is clear from the previous discussion, ambivalency in valency markers is rampant cross-linguistically. One possible approach is to treat such categories as homonymous, but this analysis becomes less appealing if such polyfunctionality is cross-linguistically recurrent. Another option is to capture ambivalence in terms of general meaning (recall the quote from Comrie &

Khalilova (2015) commenting on the general meaning of the "antipassive" in Bezhta). As noted above, a potential disadvantage of this approach is that in many cases a general meaning (the shared component) may be not informative enough for our purposes. Thus, postulating a habitual meaning as a general meaning of the "antipassive form" in Bezhta does not readily explain the diathetic change involved. Still another possibility, which on balance seems preferable to me, is to treat such polyfunctionality as an extension of a basic meaning, supported by shared features (semantic, syntactic, and/or pragmatic). On the latter analysis, the basic meaning of antipassives ("the antipassive prototype") would include both voice related features (A promoted to S; O deleted/demoted), as well as aspect-related (conferring imperfective meaning on the verb) components. In the case of intransitives, only the aspectual function is available since the antipassive rule applies vacuously (the base verb is intransitive, so neither A or O need to be manipulated). This approach is consistent with a prototype approach to definitions of linguistic categories, as commonly practiced in the typological literature (cf. Shibatani's [1985] analysis of passives, and Dixon & Aikhenvald's [2000] description of other voice categories from a similar perspective). It is also compatible with the Construction Grammar approach insofar as it distinguishes between basic and extended meanings of particular constructions/markers. Furthermore, this approach is consistent with a diachronic interpretation of a polysemy chain as representing semantic evolution supported by shared semantic components. Perhaps most importantly in the present context, the latter approach, insofar as it relies on a basic meaning (*Hauptbedeutung*) rather than an abstract general meaning (*Gesamtbeduetung*), seems most amenable to a markedness explanation, where certain category combination are seen as unmarked (more natural) while the other are seen as marked (less natural, 'infelicitous combinations', in terms of Malchukov 2011). As is clear from the discussion above, the basic meaning is identified in unmarked contexts, while extended meanings arise in marked contexts. The only disadvantage of the prototype approach is that it is not explicit with respect to the unifying features of a polysemous form; here the general meaning approach clearly has an edge.

Ultimately, it seems that both analyses, one in terms of general meaning and the other employing the concept of prototype, can be reconciled within an approach positing 'family resemblances' between different senses of individual categories/constructions. This approach is different from the general meaning approach insofar as it does not presuppose the existence of certain meaning component shared by all uses of a polysemous marker. On the other hand, it is also less restrictive than the prototype approach insofar as it does not presuppose the existence of a single prototype either. Such approaches enjoy broad popularity in cognitive and typological studies. In Cognitive Grammar they are featured in the form of 'radial categories' (Langacker 1988), in Construction Grammar in the form of inheritance networks linking individual constructions (Goldberg 1995), and in functional-typological approaches in the form of semantic maps (Haspelmath 2003; Croft 2003; Cysouw, Haspelmath & Malchukov 2010). The semantic map approach is of particular interest, since a semantic map has not only a descriptive but also a predictive value, making certain predictions concerning possible vs. impossible polysemy patterns. Semantic map approaches are based on iconicity assumptions to the effect that cross-linguistically recurrent similarity in form reveals similarity in meaning (or, broader, a functional similarity). On this assumption, the configuration of a semantic map, once established, is assumed to be universal. It can be used to represent possible polysemy patterns through the extension of polyfunctional markers/constructions over contiguous regions of a semantic map, but at the same time excludes impossible patterns in the form of 'contiguity violations' on a semantic map (see Haspelmath 2003 for discussion of 'implicational maps'). Importantly, even though prototype approaches are sometimes viewed as an alternative to feature-based approaches, the latter approach is more compatible with the semantic map approach, insofar as similarity can be expressed in terms of shared features (Zwarts 2010; Malchukov 2010). The semantic map approach is also compatible with the diachronic approach insofar as grammaticalization chains can be viewed as 'dynamicization' of semantic maps (van der Auwera & Plungian 1998). In what follows, it will be shown how such an approach can explain voice ambivalence, taking conventional definitions of individual voice categories as a point of departure. In particular, it will be argued that polyfunctionality in this domain can be captured in terms of shared syntactic features.

Following on earlier theoretical[6] and typological approaches, I assume the following definitions of prototypes of the major voice categories (cf. the definitions of prototype for passive, antipassive, causative and applicative constructions in Dixon & Aikhenvald 2000; cf. Haspelmath &d Müller-Bardey 2004):

---

6 The following definitions of the valency changing categories as found in the typological literature are most compatible with multistratal theories in the tradition of Relational Grammar, but can be reconstructed in terms of 'linking theories' (such as Lexical Functional Grammar and Head-Driven Phrase Structure Grammar) which describe diathetic alternations in terms of mapping between semantic roles and grammatical functions. On the latter account, shared linking patterns will be held responsible for voice polyfunctionality. This analysis can be further reconstructed in the versions of Chomskyan generative approach (Principles and Parameters, Minimalism), which see polyfunctionality as a reflex of shared features (see, e.g., Embick 2004, where cross-linguistically frequent "syncretism" between passives, anticausatives and reflexives is attributed to the common feature 'lack of an external argument').

(31) Passive
 (Basic) A → (derived) Oblique or zero
 (Basic) O → (derived) S
 Verb: transitive → intransitive

(32) Antipassive
 (Basic) A → (derived) S
 (Basic) O → (derived) Oblique or zero[7]
 Verb: transitive → intransitive

(33) Causative (intransitive)
 Causer → (derived) A
 (Basic) S → (derived) O
 Verb: intransitive → transitive

(34) Applicative (intransitive)
 (Basic) S → (derived) A
 (Basic) Oblique → (derived) O
 Verb: intransitive → transitive

These definitions can readily account for causative-applicative polysemy (both categories share the feature of transitivization when applied to intransitives), as well as passive-antipassive-polysemy (both categories share the feature of detransitivization, when applied to transitives). Yet, given these definitions, the cases of voice ambivalence where the same category can be either valency-increasing or valency-reducing remain inexplicable. An explanation becomes possible, however, if we consider how causatives and applicatives apply beyond the intransitive domain:

(35) Causative (transitive)
 Causer → (derived) A
 (Basic) A → (derived) Oblique
 (Basic) O = O
 Verb: transitive

---

[7] As pointed out by a reviewer, there is a difference between passives and antipassives in the treatment of backgrounded arguments insofar as with antipassives a P argument is typically realized as oblique, while with passives it is often left unexpressed. This distinction is admittedly not captured in the present approach, yet it should be noted that "canonical passives" have been described as allowing for an expression of an oblique Agent, a feature which distinguishes them from anticausatives (Siewierska & Bakker 2012).

(36) Applicative (transitive)
   (Basic) A = (derived) A
   (Basic) O → (derived) Oblique
   (basic) Oblique → (derived) O
   Verb: transitive

There is more variation in the resulting pattern when the causative and applicative apply to transitives. Still, the dominant pattern for causatives involves demotion of the agent to an oblique (or indirect) object[8]; with applicatives the dominant pattern involves 'promotion' of an oblique to an object, with the base object demoted to an oblique (cf. Dixon & Aikhenvald 2000:14). This way of representation highlights selective similarities between passives and causatives of transitives (both involve A demotion), as well as similarities between applicatives based on transitives and antipassives (both demote a base O to an oblique). In both cases it is crucial that passives and antipassives are related to causatives of transitives and applicatives of transitives, respectively, but not to causatives of intransitives and applicatives of intransitives. Thus on a semantic map of voice categories presented below, causatives of transitives show connections with causatives of intransitives, on the one hand, and with passives, on the other hand. In a similar fashion, applicatives of transitives are related to applicatives of intransitives, on the one hand, and to antipassives, on the other hand. Thus a semantic map built around shared syntactic features would predict that if a certain "ambivalent" voice category such as adversative passive is found in the passive function, on the one hand, and as an adversative causative with intransitives, on the other hand, it will be found in the adversative function in the intermediate category of transitives as well. Similarly, recurrent similarities of other categories are explained in terms of shared syntactic components. To wit, causatives of transitives share certain features with causatives of intransitives (most notably, the feature causer-to-subject promotion), and applicatives

---

8 Demotion of an A to an oblique is clearly a preferred option for causatives of transitives in languages with dependent marking. This definition covers both cases when a causee is coded as an indirect object (conforming to Comrie's 1976 'Paradigm Case' of causative formation), but also to cases when a causee is introduced as an oblique (e.g., instrumental oblique; cf. Dixon 2000). It does not cover cases when a patient rather than the causee is demoted; the latter pattern has been reported for several languages (Dixon 2000:52–53), but still seems to be a minority pattern, at least for dependent marking languages. Neither does this definition cover cases, when a causee is marked as a primary object (by object agreement), as is common in head marking languages. The causative formation in such languages does not share any features (i.e. A-to-Oblique demotion) with passives, and in fact, I am not aware of cases of passive-causative polysemy reported for such languages.

of transitives and intransitives share the feature of (oblique-to-object promotion), which accounts for why the same marker can be used in both cases. And, as noted above, causatives and applicatives of intransitives share the feature of transitivization, while passives and antipassives share a feature of detransitivization. Recall that in cognitive-typological approaches it is assumed that it is the sharing of features that underlies cross-linguistically recurrent polysemies.

In this way we can arrive at the following map of voice categories capturing selective similarities between individual categories. This can be conceived as a kind of semantic map, with the qualification that the term "syntactic map" may be more appropriate to the extent that it captures connections in syntactic properties (indicated by connecting lines: see below on arrows).

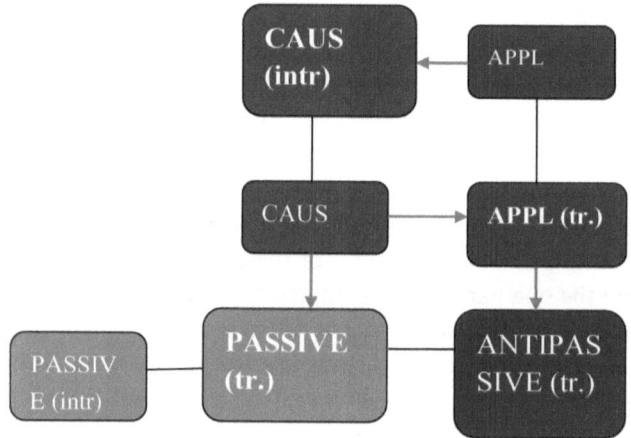

Figure 2: Semantic map for core voice categories

Of course, this map remains incomplete, as it only includes a subset of voice categories and furthermore ignores polyfunctionality patterns beyond voice categories (such as connections between antipassives and imperfectives, or passives and resultatives, as discussed in section 1). These connections between voice and aspect categories have been elucidated in terms of transitivity parameters (Hopper & Thompson 1980; cf. Tsunoda 1981; see also Shibatani 2006 for a somewhat different approach within the same tradition), or else in diachronic terms (Haspelmath 1990; Dixon 1994). Further it does not address certain other connections discussed in the literature such as those between reflexives, anticausatives, passives, and antipassives, which are known to be diachronically related (Haspelmath 2003). There are also other categories, such as the modal uses of passives, illustrated in section 2, that are not represented on the map, although the map can be naturally extended to these domains. In all cases it is assumed that cross-linguistically recurrent polysemies are supported by shared meaning components, even if such features lie beyond the voice domain. It is also possible to extend this discussion to subtypes of intransitive, transitive and ditransitive verbs. In this way one can account for the preference of patientive intransitives ("unaccusatives") to combine with causatives, and agentive intransitives ("unergatives") to combine with applicatives (cf. the scale in Figure 1). Extending this map to include further categories is a task for future research, but it is clear that an approach in terms of shared syntactic components can go a long way toward explaining and constraining voice ambivalence. Importantly, starting from commonly assumed definitions of voice categories, this approach can explain "unexpected" polysemies, where the same category is both valency-increasing and valency-decreasing. Yet it should be stressed that the sharing of syntactic features is understood to be a necessary rather than a sufficient condition for the development of certain polysemies. In many cases other (semantic) factors provide further enabling conditions. Thus, the availability of an adversative (or 'involitive-permissive') meaning for a causative might facilitate causative-to-passive reanalysis (cf. Malchukov 1993 on adversative as a missing link between causatives and passives), and assistive meaning on the part of the causative can facilitate causative-to-applicative reanalysis (see Shibatani & Pardeshi 2002).

More importantly, in the present context the map above is intended to capture relations of (local) markedness: the relative unmarkedness (naturalness) of combining a voice category and a valency class is iconically represented by the size of the cells on the map. In this way it is shown, for example, that causatives of intransitives represent the most natural (unmarked) combination (the causative prototype, in Dixon's approach), while causatives of transitives are a more marked category (a prototype extension). The unmarked combinations function as "attractors" in a dynamic system, conditioning a meaning shift on the part of the marked combinations, which, being less stable, will tend to be either absent or reinterpreted. The direction of reinterpretation is indicated by the arrows. These arrows also allow for a diachronic interpretation, even though evidence for certain transitions is stronger than for others. But the markedness account is more general than a diachronic account in that it also covers more complex scenarios, such as when categories develop from a third source (e.g., both passives and causatives developing from a source construction that specializes in the passive function in the context of transitives, and in the causative function in the context of intransitives). Moreover, while dynamicized semantic maps representing grammaticalization channels (as, e.g., in van der Auwera &

Plungian 1998) are "context-free", the transition network in Figure 2 is intended to capture relations of (local) markedness. Thus, methodologically, the most novel feature of the transition network above is that it tries to capture both iconicity of linguistic signs (underlying the representation of semantic maps) and (local) markedness. Iconicity restricts possible transitions in a network (through categories sharing certain features), while local markedness determines the direction of transition.

Finally, the present approach to voice ambivalence is in line with the research program of the St.-Petersburg typology group that investigates syntagmatic interaction between grammatical categories (e.g., Xrakovskij 1996; Malchukov 2011), a program that also relies on the notion of local markedness and functional usefulness. This approach is similar to the markedness approach, but capitalizes on meaning shifts in marked contexts in a more systematic way. This approach has been adopted in Malchukov (2011), who discusses the interaction of verbal categories from the perspective of local markedness, with a focus on the resolution of infelicitous combinations (such as the perfective present combination in the aspectual domain). As shown above, the same approach can be fruitfully applied to the domain of voice. Thus, passive markers preferentially apply to transitives and causatives to intransitives. If the same marker combines both functions, it will follow a markedness reversal pattern adopting the most "useful" (natural/frequent) interpretation. As we have seen, this may lead to the puzzling effect of the same marker performing two seemingly opposite functions (increasing or reducing valency). Again, as in other cases of category interaction, in principle, either category may shift its meaning in an infelicitous combination. This can be illustrated in the passive use of intransitives, even within a single language. Recall that in Balkar both scenarios are actually attested: either the passive shifts its meaning and becomes modalized (see the modalized impersonal passive in (12)), or else the passive causes the verb meaning to shift, coercing a transitive interpretation (see the causal passive in (13)). Thus, ways of conflict resolution in the domain of voice follow general scenarios attested elsewhere (Malchukov 2009, 2011; see also Moravcsik 2010 for a general discussion of conflict resolution in syntax). Either a voice category will occur only in a more natural (functionally felicitous) combination, and is blocked in a less natural (less felicitous) combination (e.g., a passive is blocked with intransitives), or it may be permitted but if so either undergoes a shift in its meaning (e.g., an antipassive marks iterative aspect with intransitives), or causes a shift in the interpretation of the verb type (the coercion scenario).

Abbreviations

A transitive subject; ABM ablative-modalis (case); ABS absolutive; ACC accusative; ADV adversative (voice); ADVPAS adversative passive; AF actor focus; ANTI(P), APAS antipassive; APPL applicative; CAUS causative; CL class/gender marker; CMPL completive; CTR control; DAT dative case; DEF definiteness marker; DT, DET determiner; ERG ergative case; F feminine (gender); INCH inchoative; IND indicative; INS instrumental case; INTR intransitive; LOC locative case; M masculine gender; N neutrum (gender); NFIN non-finite; NONFUT nonfuture; NOM nominative case; O (direct) object; OBJ object marker; OBL oblique object; PART partitive (case); PASS passive; PERF, PF perfect; PL plural; PFV perfective; POS possessive; POT potential; PRED predicative (marker); PRES, PRS present tense; PST, PAST past; REFL reflexive marker; REFPOS reflexive possessive; REL relative (case); S intransitive subject; SG singular; SUBJ subject; TOP topic; TR transitive marker; 1SG.3SG 1st p. A acting upon 3rd person O; 3 → 3 3rd p. A acting upon 3rd person O; I, II, III gender classes (also gender class prefixes).

Acknowledgements

The present work is an outgrowth from the DFG-funded project "Valency classes cross-linguistically" based at Max Planck Institute for Evolutionary Anthropology (Leipzig) and coordinated by Bernard Comrie, Martin Haspelmath, Iren Hartmann and me. The paper draws heavily on contributions to the "Valency classes in the world's languages" (Malchukov & Comrie 2015), whose authors are gratefully acknowledged. A version of this paper was presented at the NINJAL International Symposium on Valency Classes and Alternations in Japanese (August 2012), as well as at the SLE conference in Stockholm and at MPI EVA Leipzig (September 2012). I am grateful to the audiences, in particular, to Tasaku Tsunoda and John Whitman (NINJAL) for helpful discussion. I am also indebted to the editors of the volume, Wesley Jacobsen and Taro Kageyama, as well as to Masayoshi Shibatani for the useful feedback on the first draft. The usual disclaimers apply.

References

Austin, Peter. 1997. Causatives and applicatives in Australian Aboriginal languages. In Kazuto Matsumura & Toru Hayashi (eds.), *The dative and related phenomena*, 165–225. Tokyo: Hitsuzi Syobo.
Avrorin, Valentin A. 1962. *Grammatika nanajskogo jazyka [Nanai grammar]*. Leningrad: Nauka.
Comrie, Bernard. 1975. Causatives and Universal Grammar. *Transactions of the Philological Society* 1975. 1–32.
Comrie, Bernard. 1976. The syntax of causative constructions: Cross-language similarities and divergences. In Masayoshi Shibatani (ed.), *Syntax and semantics 6: The grammar of causative constructions*, 261–312. New York: Academic Press.
Bernard Comrie, Madzhid Khalilov & Zaira Khalilova. 2015. Valency classes in Bezhta. In Andrej Malchukov & Bernard Comrie (eds.). *Valency classes in the world's languages*, 541–571. Berlin & Boston: De Gruyter Mouton.
Cooreman, Ann. 1994. A functional typology of antipassives. In Barbara Fox & Paul Hopper (eds), *Voice: Form and Function* [Typological Studies in Language 27]. Amsterdam & Philadelphia: John Benjamins.
Creissels, Denis. 2015. Valency classes in Mandinka. In Andrej Malchukov & Bernard Comrie (eds.), *Valency classes in the world's languages*, 221–261. Berlin & Boston: De Gruyter Mouton.
Croft, William. 1990. *Typology and universals*. Cambridge: Cambridge University Press.
Croft, William. 2003. *Typology and universals*. Cambridge: Cambridge University Press.
Cysouw, Michael, Martin Haspelmath & Andrej Malchukov (eds.). 2010. Semantic maps: theory and applications. *Linguistic Discovery* 8 (1), 2010.
Dixon, R.M.W. 1994. *Ergativity*. Cambridge: Cambridge University Press.
Dixon, R. M. W. & Alexandra Y. Aikhenvald. 1997. A typology of argument-determined constructions. In Joan Bybee, John Haiman & Sandra A. Thompson (eds.), *Essays on language function and language type*, 71–113. Amsterdam & Philadelphia: John Benjamins.
Dixon, R. M. W. 2000. A typology of causatives: form, syntax and meaning. In R. M. W. Dixon & Alexandra Y. Aikhenvald, eds. *Changing valency. Case studies in transitivity*, 30–83. Cambridge: Cambridge University Press.
Dixon, R. M. W. & Alexandra Y. Aikhenvald (eds.). 2000. *Changing valency. Case studies in transitivity*. Cambridge: Cambridge University Press.
Embick, David. 2004. Unaccusative syntax and verbal alternations. In Artemis Alexiadou, Elena Anagnostopoulou & Martin Everaert (eds.), *The unaccusativity puzzle: Explorations of the syntax-lexicon interface*, 137–158. Oxford: Oxford University Press.
Geniušiene, Emma. 1987. *The typology of reflexives*. Berlin & New York: Mouton de Gruyter.
Gerdts, Donna B. 1988. *Object and absolutive in Halkomelem Salish*. New York: Garland Publishing.
Gerdts, Donna. 2010. Ditransitive constructions in Halkomelem Salish: a direct object/oblique object language. In Andrej L. Malchukov, Martin Haspelmath & Bernard Comrie (eds.), *Studies in ditransitive constructions: a comparative handbook*, 563–611. Berlin & New York: Mouton De Gruyter.
Goldberg, Adele E. 1995. *Constructions: A construction grammar approach to argument structure*. Chicago: The University of Chicago Press.

Golluscio, Lucia. 2010. Ditransitives in Mapudungun. In Andrej L. Malchukov, Martin Haspelmath & Bernard Comrie (eds.), *Studies in ditransitive constructions: A comparative handbook*, 710–757. Berlin & New York: Mouton De Gruyter.
Haiman, John. 1985. Iconic and economic motivation. *Language* 59. 781–819.
Haspelmath, Martin. 1990. The grammaticalization of passive morphology. *Studies in Language* 14. 25–72.
Haspelmath, Martin. 2003. The geometry of grammatical meaning: Semantic maps and cross-linguistic comparison. In Michael Tomasello (ed.), *The new psychology of language*, volume 2, 211–243. New York: Lawrence Erlbaum Associates Publishers.
Haspelmath, Martin & Thomas Müller-Bardey. 2004. Valency change. In Geert Booij, Christian Lehmann & Joachim Mugdan (eds.), *Morphology: A handbook on inflection and word formation*, volume 2, 1130–1145. Berlin & New York: de Gruyter.
Haspelmath, Martin. 2005. Argument marking in ditransitive alignment types. *Linguistic Discovery* 3 (1). 1–21.
Haspelmath, Martin. 2006. Against markedness (and what to replace it with). *Journal of Linguistics* 42 (1). 25–70.
Holes, Clive. 1990. *Gulf Arabic*. London: Routledge.
Hopper, Paul J. & Sandra A. Thompson. 1980. Transitivity in grammar and discourse. *Language* 56. 251–299.
Kazenin, Konstantin I. 1994. On the lexical distribution of agent-preserving and object-preserving transitivity alternations. *Nordic Journal of Linguistics* 17. 141–154.
Keenan, Edward L. 1985. Passive in the world's languages. In Timothy Shopen (ed.), *Language typology and syntactic description*, volume 1: *Clause structure*, 243–281. Cambridge: Cambridge University Press.
Kemmer, Suzanne. 1993. *The middle voice*. Amsterdam & Philadelphia: John Benjamins.
Kishimoto, Hideki, Taro Kageyama & Kan Sasaki. 2015. Valency classes in Japanese. In Andrej Malchukov & Bernard Comrie (eds.), *Valency classes in the world's languages*, 765–805. Berlin & Boston: De Gruyter Mouton.
Kittilä, Seppo. 2009. Causative morphemes as non-valency increasing devices. *Folia Linguistica* 43 (1). 67–94.
Klaiman, Mimi H. 1991. *Grammatical voice*. Cambridge: Cambridge University Press.
Langacker, Ronald W. 1988. A usage-based model. In Brygida Rudzka-Ostyn (ed.), *Topics in cognitive linguistics*, 127–161. Amsterdam & Philadelphia: John Benjamins.
Lehmann, Christian. 2015. Valency classes in Yucatec Maya. In Andrej Malchukov & Bernard Comrie (eds.), *Valency classes in the world's languages*, 1407–1461. Berlin & Boston: De Gruyter Mouton.
Letuchiy, Alexander. 2006. Case marking, possession and syntactic hierarchies in Khakas causative constructions in comparison with other Turkic languages. In Leonid Kulikov, Andrej Malchukov & Peter de Swart (eds.), *Case, valency, and transitivity*, 417–441. Amsterdam & Philadelphia: John Benjamins.
Li, Fengxiang & Lindsay Whaley. 2012. The grammaticalization cycle of causatives in Oroqen dialects. In Andrej Malchukov & Lindsay Whaley (eds.), *Advances in Tungusic linguistics*, 167–182. Wiesbaden: Harrasowitz.
Ljutikova, Ekaterina & Anastasija Bonch-Osmolovskaja. 2006. A very active passive: functional similarities between passive and causative in Balkar. In Leonid Kulikov, Andrej Malchukov, and Peter de Swart (eds.), *Case, valency, and transitivity*, 393–416. Amsterdam & Philadelphia: John Benjamins.

Malchukov, Andrej. 1993. The syntax and semantics of adversative constructions in Even. *Gengo Kenkyu* 103. 1–36.
Malchukov, Andrej L. 1995. *Even*. Munich: LINCOM.
Malchukov, Andrej. 2009. Incompatible categories: Resolving the "present perfective paradox". In Lotte Hogeweg, Helen de Hoop & Andrej Malchukov (eds.), *Cross-linguistic semantics of tense, aspect and modality*, 13–33. Amsterdam & Philadelphia: John Benjamins.
Malchukov, Andrej. 2010. Analyzing semantic maps: A Multifactorial Approach. In Michael Cysouw, Martin Haspelmath & Andrej Malchukov (eds.), *Semantic maps: theory and applications. Linguistic Discovery*, vol. 8, issue (1), 2010.
Malchukov, Andrej. 2011. Interaction of verbal categories: resolution of infelicitous grammeme combinations. *Linguistics* 49 (1). 229–282.
Mel'čuk, Igor. 2006. *Aspects of the theory of morphology*. Berlin & New York: Mouton de Gruyter.
Mithun, Marianne. 2000. Valency-changing derivation in Central Alaskan Yup'ik. In R. M. W. Dixon & A. Aikhenvald (eds.), *Changing valency: Case studies in transitivity*, 84–114. Cambridge: Cambridge University Press.
Miyaoka, Osahito. 2012. *A grammar of Central Alaskan Yupik (CAY)*. Berlin & Boston: De Gruyter Mouton.
Miyaoka, Osahito. 2015. Valency classes in Central Alaskan Yupik. In Andrej Malchukov & Bernard Comrie (eds.). *Valency classes in the world's languages*, 1145–1184. Berlin & Boston: De Gruyter Mouton.
Moravcsik, Edith. 2010. Conflict resolution in syntactic theory. *Studies in Language* 34 (3). 636–669
Nedjalkov, Igor V. 1991. Recessive-accessive polysemy of verbal suffixes. *Languages of the World* 1. 4–31.
Nedjalkov, Igor V. 1992. *Zalog, vid, vremja v tunguso-manjchzhurskix jazykax* [Voice, aspect, tense in Tungusic languages]. Habilschrift. St. Petersburg.
Nedjalkov, Vladimir P. 1964. O svjazi kauzativnosti i passivnosti. [On the relation between causatives and passives]. In J. M. Skrebnev (ed.), *Voprosy obščego i romano-germanskogo jazykoznanija* [Problems of Romace and Germanic linguistics], 301–310. Ufa: Baškirskoe knižnoe izdatel'stvo.
Nedjalkov, Vladimir P. & Georgij G. Sil'nitskij. 1969. Tipologija kauzativnyx konstrukcij [Typology of causative constructions]. In Alexandr A. Xolodovič (ed.), *Tipologija kauzativnyx konstrukcij. Morfologičeskij kauzativ*, 5–19. Leningrad: Nauka.
Nedjalkov, Vladimir P. (ed.). 1988. *Typology of resultative constructions*. Amsterdam & Philadelphia: John Benjamins.
Nedjalkov, Vladimir P. & Sergej Je. Jaxontov. 1988. The typology of resultative constructions. In Vladimir P. Nedjalkov (ed.), *The typology of resultative constructions*, 3–62. Amsterdam & Philadelphia: John Benjamins.
Nedjalkov, Vladimir P. (ed.). 2007. *Reciprocal constructions*, 5 vols. Amsterdam & Philadelphia: John Benjamins.
Perlmutter, David M. 1978. Impersonal passives and the unaccusative hypothesis. *Proceedings of the Fourth Annual Meeting of the Berkeley Linguistics Society*, 157–189.
Peterson, David. 2007. *Applicative constructions*. Oxford: Oxford University Press.
Polinsky, Maria. 2005/2011. Antipassive constructions. In Matthew Dryer & Martin Haspelmath (eds.), *The world atlas of language structures online*. Munich: Max Planck Digital Library, chapter 108. Available online at http://wals.info/chapter/109

Seifert, Frank. 2015. Valency classes in Bora. In Andrej Malchukov & Bernard Comrie (eds.), *Valency classes in the world's languages*, 1461–1495. Berlin & Boston: De Gruyter Mouton.
Shibatani, Masayoshi. 1976. The grammar of causative constructions: a conspectus. In Masayoshi Shibatani (ed.), *Syntax and semantics vokume 6: The grammar of causative constructions*, 1–40. New York: Academic Press.
Shibatani, Masayoshi. 1985. Passives and related constructions. *Language* 61. 821–848.
Shibatani, Masayoshi (ed.). 2002. *The crammar of causation and interpersonal manipulation*. Amsterdam & Philadelphia: John Benjamins.
Shibatani, Masayoshi. 2006. On the conceptual framework for voice phenomena. *Linguistics* 44 (2). 217–269.
Shibatani, Masayoshi. this volume. The role of morphology in valency alternation phenomena. In Taro Kageyama & Wesley M. Jacobsen (eds.), *Transitivity and valency alternations: Studies on Japanese and beyond*. Berlin & Boston: De Gruyter Mouton.
Shibatani, Masayoshi & Prashant Pardeshi. 2002. The causative continuum. In Masayoshi Shibatani (ed.), *The grammar of causation and interpersonal manipulation*, 85–126. Amsterdam & Philadelphia: John Benjamins.
Shibatani, Masayoshi & Ketut Artawa. 2015. Valency classes in Balinese. In Andrej Malchukov & Bernard Comrie (eds.). *Valency classes in the world's languages*, 857–920. Berlin & Boston: De Gruyter Mouton.
Siewierska, Anna. 1984. *The passive: A comparative linguistic analysis*. London: Routledge.
Siewierska, Anna & Dik Bakker. 2012. Passive agents: Prototypical vs. canonical passives. In Dunstan Brown, Marina Chumakina & Greville G. Corbett (eds.), Canonical morphology and syntax, 151–189. Oxford: Oxford University Press.
Song, Jae Jung. 1996. *Causatives and causation*. London/New York: Longman.
Ščerbak, A.M. 1981. *Očerki po sravnitel'noj grammatike tjurkskix jazykov. Glagol.* [Comparative grammar of Turkic languages: verbal categories]. Leningrad: Nauka.
Tchekhoff, Claude. 1987. „Antipassif": Aspect imperfectif et autonomie du sujet. *Bulletin de la Société de Linguistique de Paris* 82. 43–67.
Tiersma, Peter. 1982. Local and general markedness. *Language* 58. 832–849.
Tsunoda, Tasaku. 1981. Split case-marking in verb types and tense/aspect/mood. *Linguistics* 19. 389–438.
Tsunoda, Tasaku. 1988. Antipassives in Warrungu and other Australian languages. In Masayoshi Shibatani (ed.), *Passive and voice*, 595–649. Amsterdam & Philadelphia: John Benjamins.
Xolodovič, Alexander A. (ed.). 1969. *Tipologija kauzativnyx konstrukcij. Morfologičeskij kauzativ.* [Typology of causative constructions: Morphological causative]. Leningrad: Nauka.
Xrakovskij, Viktor S. 1974. Passivnye konstrukcii [Passive constructions]. In Viktor S. Xrakovskij (ed.), *Tipologija passivnyx konstrukcij* [Typology of passive constructions], 5–45. Leningrad: Nauka.
Xrakovskij, Viktor S. 1996. Grammatičeskie kategorii glagola: opyt teorii vzaimodejstvija [Grammatical categories of the verb: towards a theory of category interaction]. In Vladimir A. Bondarko (ed.), *Mežkategorial'nye svjazi v grammatike [Category Interaction in Grammar]*, 22–43. St. Petersburg: Nauka.
van der Auwera, Johan & Vladimir A. Plungian. 1998. Modality's semantic map. *Linguistic Typology* 2 (1). 125–139.
Watanabe, Honoré. 2015. Valency classes in Sliammon Salish. In Andrej Malchukov & Bernard Comrie (eds.), *Valency classes in the world's languages*, 1293–1338. Berlin & Boston: De Gruyter Mouton.

Wunderlich, Dieter. 2006. Towards a structural typology of verb classes. In Dieter Wunderlich (ed,), *Advances in the theory of the lexicon*, 57–166. Berlin & New York: Mouton de Gruyter.

Zúñiga, Fernando. 2015. Valency classes in Mapudungun. In Andrej Malchukov & Bernard Comrie (eds.), *Valency classes in the world's languages*, 1495–1525. Berlin & Boston: De Gruyter Mouton.

Zwarts, Joost. 2010. Semantic map geometry: Two approaches. In Michael Cysouw, Martin Haspelmath & Andrej Malchukov (eds.), *Semantic maps: Theory and applications. Linguistic Discovery* 8 (1).

Søren Wichmann
14 Quantitative tests of implicational verb hierarchies

1 Introduction

This chapter will begin by discussing the implicational verb hierarchy of Tsunoda (1985) as a convenient starting point for looking at what happens when a relatively large dataset and a principled, quantitative approach to their analysis are brought to bear on a linguistic typological hypothesis. After introducing new methods for assessing the validity of an implicational hierarchy, I go on to inquire into the presence of implicational hierarchies governing the distribution of 5 different alternation types across 87 verb meanings and 22 languages (Ainu, Balinese, Bezhta, Bora, Chintang, Eastern Armenian, Even, German, Hokkaido Japanese, Hoocąk, Icelandic, Italian, Ket, Mandarin Chinese [henceforth 'Mandarin'], Mandinka, Mapudungun, Mitsukaido Japanese, Modern Standard Arabic [henceforth 'Arabic'], Russian, Yaqui, Yucatec Maya, and Zenzontepec Chatino).[1]

The data used are from the database of the Leipzig Valency Classes Project (Hartmann et al. 2013) in the state it was in as of July 17, 2012, although the names used to designate different alternations have been updated. Contributors were asked to supply information about the presence or absence of different alternations for a fixed set of 87 verb meanings specified through a set of 'meaning labels', e.g. EAT, a 'role frame', e.g. 'A eats P', and 'typical contexts', e.g. 'the boy ate the fruit'. The alternations vary from highly language-specific ones, such as the '*be*-alternation' in German, to alternations that are more comparable across several languages, such as the 'passive' in Yaqui and Yucatec Maya, to

---

[1] An earlier analysis included 7 additional alternations (ambitransitive, anticausative, applicative, impersonal passive, locative, mediopassive, and resultative), but since comparable instances of all of these are represented by few languages (7 or less) and since, moreover, some of the results for these alternations were problematic in certain respects, possibly due to the scarcity of data, I chose to only include alternations for which 11 or more languages were attested. I would like to draw the reader's attention to Wichmann (2015), which is a sequel to the present paper, even though it was published earlier.

Søren Wichmann, Leiden University Centre for Linguistics and Kazan Federal University

which can be added alternations that are given language-specific designations by contributors but can still be considered instances of the general category of passive, such as the Mandarin 'BEI alternation', the Balinese 'passive -*a* alternation', the German 'passive with *werden*', the Russian 'participial passive', etc. (see Appendix 1 for a mapping between alternations as named in this study and designations in individual languages; readers are strongly encouraged to also consult the online database of Hartmann et al. 2013 for more information about individual alternations, should questions about these arise).

Christian Lehmann has expressed skepticism both about the viability of larger studies of implicational hierarchies among verbs and also about outcomes showing neat results:

> An empirically-based survey, no matter whether of predicate meanings or of situations functioning in linguistic structure, presupposes comprehensive research into the whole verbal and adjectival vocabulary. This has occasionally been tried for one language. It seems plainly impossible to do such research in depth on a cross-linguistic scale (...). Moreover, it should be clear from the outset that this kind of research cannot be expected to yield clear-cut cross-linguistic generalizations, to come up with regularities structuring the grammars of all languages.   (Lehmann 1991: 187)

One of the aims of the Leipzig Valency Classes Project is precisely to overcome the practical problem of labor-intensity by distributing work over many contributors. It has not aimed to achieve the kind of in-depth coverage of individual languages found in works such as Ballmer & Brennenstuhl (1986) on German or Levin (1993) on English, for instance, but the coverage within and across languages is good enough to enable a better assessment of the degree to which we can expect to find regularities and make generalizations.

The availability of relatively abundant and systematic data invites the application of quantitative methods. The methods will be introduced by way of studying a familiar example, the hierarchy of verb meanings of Tsunoda (1985), in the next section.

2 Tsunoda's hierarchy

In his well-known 1985 paper, following earlier work from 1981, Tasaku Tsunoda introduced the transitivity hierarchy of verb types displayed in (1).

(1) Direct Effect > Perception > Pursuit > Knowledge > Feeling > Relationship > Ability

Two-place predicates farther to the left in the hierarchy are more prone to take transitive case marking (ergative-absolutive or nominative-accusative, depending on the language type), and as one moves towards the right other types of case marking increasingly appear, with ergative-absolutive or nominative-accusative being completely absent for the Ability category. Moreover, Tsunoda (1985: 391) predicts that the following four types of construction, often regarded as morphosyntactic correlates of transitivity, will apply increasingly less often as one moves towards the right in the hierarchy: passive, antipassive, reflexive, reciprocal. This latter prediction is of special interest here since it can be tested through the data gathered under the auspices of the Leipzig Valency Classes Project. I wish to make clear from the outset that the evidence for Tsunoda's hierarchy which comes from case marking patterns is not addressed here, only the evidence that comes from alternations.

Not all verb meanings listed by Tsunoda are covered in the database, but the following representatives of the five leftmost types are available (unfortunately none are available for Relationship and Ability). Direct Effect: KILL, BREAK, HIT, EAT; Perception: SEE, HEAR, LOOK AT; Pursuit: SEARCH FOR; Knowledge: KNOW; Feeling: LIKE, WANT, FEAR. The dataset available for the behavior of alternation types across 12 verbs from 22 languages is provided in Appendix 2.

An example of the prediction of the transitivity hierarchy would be that if the reflexive applies to the Pursuit verb SEARCH FOR, then it should also apply to the various Perception and Direct Effect verbs. Moreover, the hierarchy predicts that a verb pertaining to a given type should have a behavior more similar to that of the other members of its type than to verbs pertaining to other types. I will test both predictions, starting with the latter.

NeighborNet (Huson & Bryant 2006) is useful for clustering[2] and also for showing how tree-like the data is. If verbs are ordered in an implicational scale the structure should be highly tree-like, ideally with the verbs ordered on a string, as in Figure 1.

---

[2] Clustering algorithms can either be character- or distance-based. Since we have characters at our disposal it may be argued that a character-based method is the best choice. However, since the distance-based NeighborNet algorithm is also useful for inspecting the tree-likeness of a dataset, I prefer to use it. From the characters the program computes Hamming distances and takes those as input to the algorithm. Since this potentially means a loss of information, I have also checked the results of a character-based method, as mentioned in note 4.

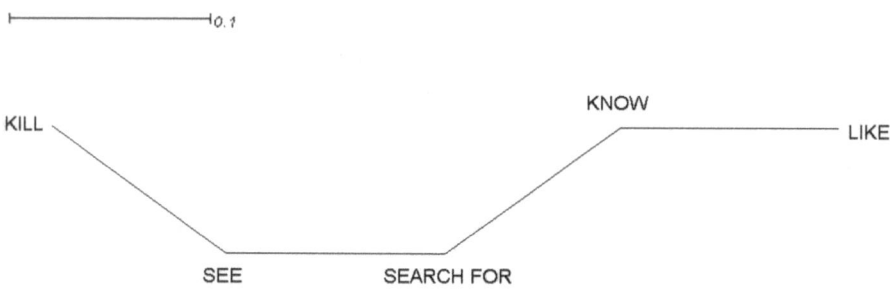

Figure 1: What a NeighborNet graph for five verbs showing perfect conformity with the Tsunoda hierarchy would look like.

Non-tree-like behavior is shown in NeighborNet by boxes. These boxes, along with deviation from the unidimensional case, where verbs are ordered in a single, particular direction, can provide visual clues as to how far from an implicational hierarchy a dataset strays. Moreover, the SplitsTree software has a function to calculate values of δ, which is a measure of the amount of reticulate behavior corresponding to the visual impression given by the boxes. δ takes values between 0 and 1 (see Holland et al. 2002 for the first description of this measure and Wichmann et al. 2011 for discussion and application to linguistic data). The results for the dataset pertaining to Tsunoda's hierarchy are shown in Figure 2.

Looking for clusters that confirm Tsunoda's types is disappointing. The Direct Effect type comprises KILL, BREAK, HIT, and EAT, but we find WANT interspersed among them in the lower part of the graph. SEE and LOOK AT are supposed to belong with HEAR in a Perception category, but the three verbs do not cluster, although they do appear in the same general region of the network.[3] In any case, they do not form a clean cluster, as is evident from the boxes connecting them, which indicate conflicts between different choices of how they could be clustered. LIKE and FEAR are supposed to group with WANT in a Verbs of Feeling category, but WANT strays far from the two others. Thus, there is not strong support to be found for the types proposed by Tsunoda, suggesting that typologists should be careful about making a priori assumptions about what constitutes a semantic class or 'type'.[4]

---

[3] With respect to the visual interpretation of the network it is important to realize that two taxa can be relatively closely grouped even if they appear on opposite sides of the network. That is, the distance between taxa is not determined by the length of the path on the periphery of the network, but by the shortest path between them. For instance, LOOK AT and SEE are not a lot closer to one another than either is to SEARCH FOR although LOOK AT and SEE are neighbors along the periphery, whereas SEARCH FOR is on the other side of the network.

[4] Using a character-based clustering algorithm such as Wagner Parsimony as implemented in the pars.exe program of Felsenstein (2009) does not improve these results.

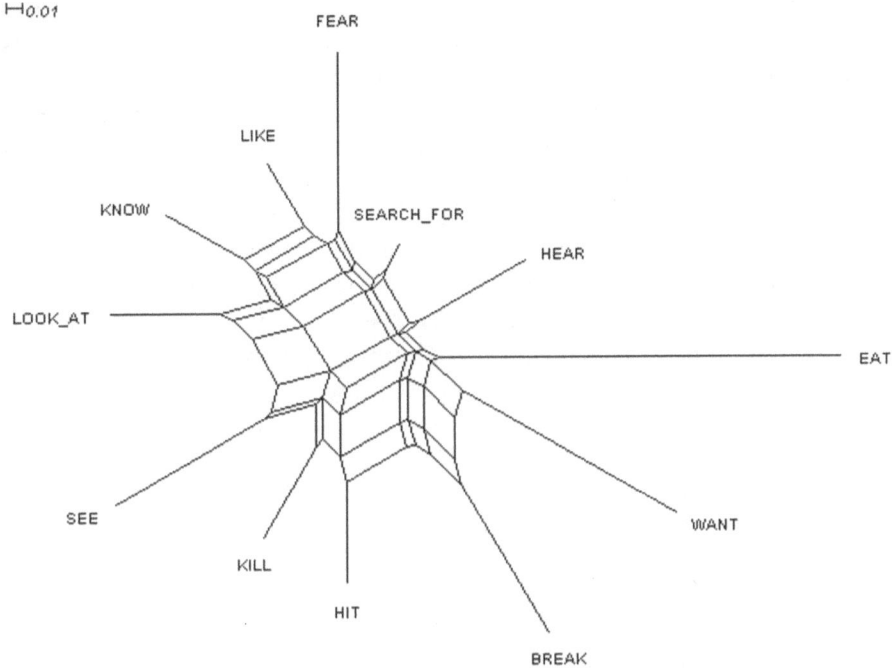

Figure 2: NeighborNet of 12 verbs argued by Tsunoda to form an implicational hierarchy

Having checked whether Tsunoda's types can be supported, we now go on to the perhaps more pressing issue of whether there is some support for an implicational hierarchy. The graph in Figure 2 can provide some visual leads in this regard, further enhanced by the δ-score. A δ-score around 0.5 or greater indicates strong non-tree-likeness. There is no cut-off point for what can be considered a tree and what not, but we know, for instance, that values in the vicinity of 0.3 are typical for lexically-based linguistic phylogenies (Wichmann et al. 2011). From the non-tree-like configuration and the δ-score, which is 0.45, we should not expect a perfect implicational hierarchy. On the other hand, there seems to be a tendency for the ordering of the verbs predicted by the Tsunoda hierarchy to recur in the structure of the graph. Thus, KILL, BREAK, HIT, and EAT do occur at one end of the graph, LOOK AT and SEARCH FOR and KNOW are in the middle region and LIKE, WANT, and FEAR are towards the other end. It is clearly worthwhile investigating how strong the evidence is for a hierarchy and what the best supported hierarchy would look like, so we need a method for this.

There is a method for measuring the one-dimensionality of a dataset – in other words, the degree to which it confirms to an implicational hierarchy –

which has been around for more than half a century although it has largely been ignored by language typologists,[5] namely the Guttman scale. The method is named after its inventor, who proposed it in Guttman (1944). In presenting it, I will follow the original model because of its conceptual simplicity, ignoring more recent derivatives which have been developed for the same purpose as the Guttman scale but are more complicated.

Following Guttman's method, the values (here: 'yes' or 'no') of an attribute (here: a certain alternation in a certain language) of a given individual (here: a certain verb) are first ordered in a 'scalogram', where individual and attributes are in rows and columns, and where these rows and columns are ordered such that the row with the most frequently occurring instance of a value is at one extreme of the scalogram, the next row following the first is the one with the next-most frequent instances of the value, and so forth. Consequently, the number of deviations from the pattern of a perfect scale can be counted. Let me first illustrate in (3) what a scalogram corresponding to the perfect implicational scale in Figure 1 would look like.

(3) LIKE   ynnnn
    KNOW   yynnn
    SEARCH_FOR   yyynn
    SEE   yyyyn
    KILL   yyyyy

Example (4) reproduces (3), but with the introduction of two changes, in the rows for LIKE and SEE.

(4) LIKE   ynnyn
    KNOW   yynnn
    SEARCH_FOR   yyynn
    SEE   ynyyn
    KILL   yyyyy

The changes I introduced in (4) illustrate two cases of deviation from perfect scalarity. The 'yes' value in the fourth column of LIKE is an error since it is found within a sequence of 'no's; the 'no' value in the second column of SEE is also an

---

5 Sasse (2001) is the only work which I am aware of that applies Guttman scaling to any larger extent, but it is limited to showing how a matrix structure can reveal an implicational scale and does not make use of the method's ability to numerically measure the deviation from scalarity. Croft & Poole (2008:7) mention Guttman scaling, but only in passing.

error since it is included among 'yes' values, where it does not belong. Errors involving a 'yes' value in the wrong place and a 'no' value in the wrong place count as having equal weight. In general, both for Guttman's method and for the construction of NeighborNets the availability of a construction carries the same weight as non-availability.

The Guttman Coefficient (GC) is a measure of scalarity. It is calculated in a simple manner, by subtracting the total number of errors from the total number of datapoints, T, then dividing by T, and finally expressing the result as a percentage. In (4), there are 2 errors among the 25 datapoints, so GC = (25 − 2)/25 = 92%. No statistical evidence has been brought to bear on the question of just how much deviation can be deemed acceptable, which is a weakness of the Guttman Coefficient; but Guttman found, based on practical experience, that "85 percent perfect scales or better have been used as efficient approximations to perfect scales" (Guttman 1944: 140). Thus, if we find that the Guttman Coefficient is 85% or greater we can probably regard this as good evidence for an implicational hierarchy. Nevertheless, in its application to linguistic data the Guttman scale needs to be tested more before we can place much confidence in such estimates. The following is therefore a somewhat tentative exploration of its application.

Having illustrated the Guttman scale by means of a toy example, we now go on to use it to test the Tsunoda hierarchy. To this end, the data in Appendix 2 are reordered such that the 'yes's are concentrated in the lower left corner and the 'no's in the upper right corner.[6] The arrangement producing the highest Guttman Coefficient implies the scale shown in (5). The subscript numbers indicate where the items fall in Tsunoda's hierarchy, a subscript 1 corresponding to the group of highest transitivity.

(5) Results of the test for Tsunoda's hierarchy
 $SEE_2 > KILL_1 > HIT_1 > LOOK\ AT_2 > KNOW_4 > EAT_1 > HEAR_2 > BREAK_1 > SEARCH\ FOR_3 > LIKE_5 > FEAR_5 > WANT_5$

In general, the way that a hierarchy such as the one in (5) is read is that a higher position on the scale indicates regular participation of a particular verb in alternations across languages, while a low position indicates that the verb participates in few or no alternations across languages.

---

[6] I am not aware of non-commercial software implementations of Guttman's method, but it can be carried out relatively simply by using sorting and counting functions in spreadsheet software. Here and elsewhere missing values are not counted as errors, but they are also not counted in the denominator of the Guttman Coefficient formula.

Unfortunately for Tsunoda's hypothesis, there are discrepancies between his hierarchy and the one in (5), with several displacements. Direct Effect and Perception type verbs are mixed among each other, and Knowledge is also displaced, whereas Pursuit and Feeling verbs behave as they should. The Guttman Coefficient is 85.6%, just enough to justify calling (5) an implicational hierarchy. This is not the place to inquire into possible explanations for the failure of the data to conform neatly to Tsunoda's hierarchy, and much less to propose or analyze alternatives.[7] The point of the exercise is to illustrate how quantitative methods such as graphic networks, δ scores, and Guttman scaling can be used to inquire into the existence of implicational hierarchies among verbs. This is meant to set the stage for the next section, where 5 different types of morphosyntactic alternation are investigated for the purpose of uncovering underlying hierarchies among the 87 verbs sampled in the Leipzig Valency Classes Project.

3 Implicational hierarchies among verbs across languages for different alternations

This section presents basic empirical findings on each of 5 different alternations. For each, the specific alternation is briefly introduced, and then a NeighborNet, a Guttman Coefficient, a δ score, and a hierarchy emerging from scalogram analysis (Guttman scaling) are provided. The hierarchies are produced by observing for each verb the length of the part of the row containing 'yes's. The procedure roughly amounts to counting the number of languages in which a given verb enters a given alternation, but since the scalogram analyses correct for missing values by treating them as being in conformity with the overall configuration, a simple count of languages per verb does not always yield the same results as the scalogram analyses. Very often several verbs have the same range of application in different languages for a given construction, in which case they are merged into clusters. The 'greater than' symbol (>) separates clusters, and within clusters verbs are listed in alphabetical order separated by commas.

NeighborNets, Guttman Coefficients, δ scores, and verb hierarchies are not further introduced in the subsections below, but at the end of each subsection a few brief comments on the findings are provided.

---

[7] Malchukov (2005) proposes a semantic map, i.e. a whole network of implicational relations, as an alternative to Tsunoda's hierarchy.

3.1 Antipassive

In the constructions gathered under the label of antipassive, objects are omitted or demoted. Complete omission is required in Ainu, Arabic, German, Italian, Ket, Mandarin, Zenzontepec Chatino, Even, and Russian, whereas Bezhta, Eastern Armenian, and Mandinka allow for the expression of the P (patient) marked as an oblique. In some languages the alternation incurs changes in the meaning of the predicate. Thus, in the Bezhta antipassive the predicate acquires a durative sense, in Eastern Armenian the focus shifts to the state or activity of the agent, in German the predicate acquires a more generic sense, etc.

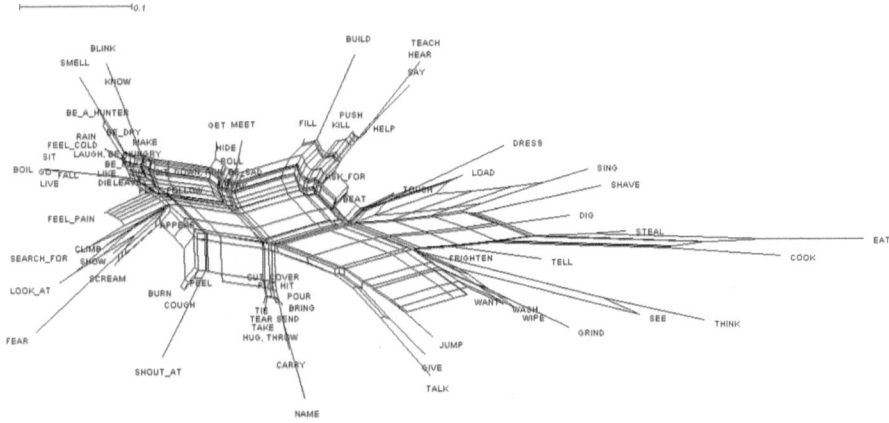

Figure 3: NeighborNet for the antipassive alternation
Guttman Coefficient: 86.0%
δ: 0.354

Hierarchy: EAT > SEE, SHAVE > COOK, GRIND, HEAR, SAY, SING, STEAL, TELL, THINK, WASH, WIPE > DRESS, NAME > DIG, FEAR, FRIGHTEN, GIVE, HELP, LOAD, TALK > ASK FOR, BUILD, TOUCH > BEAT, CARRY, COVER, CUT, FILL, HIT, HUG, JUMP, KILL, KNOW, LOOK AT, MEET, POUR, PUT, SEARCH FOR, SEND, SHOUT AT, SHOW, TAKE, TEACH, TEAR, THROW, TIE > BREAK, BRING, FOLLOW, GO, HIDE, PEEL, PUSH, ROLL, SMELL, WANT > BE A HUNTER, BLINK, BURN, CLIMB, COUGH, FEEL PAIN, LEAVE, LIVE, PLAY, SCREAM, SIT > APPEAR, BE DRY, BE HUNGRY, BE ILL, BE SAD, BOIL, CRY, DIE, FALL, FEEL COLD, GET, LAUGH, LIKE, MAKE, RAIN, RUN, SINK, SIT DOWN

Comments: The NeighborNet here suggests that one-dimensionality is not a very good approximate description for this alternation. On the other hand, it would probably take many dimensions to get a better fit. Increasing the parameter space drastically is not necessarily preferable, so one-dimensionality may still be a preferred description, and it finds mild support from the Guttman Coefficient, which is just above the conventional 85% cut-off point.

3.2 Causative

Most of the languages (Bora, Chintang, Eastern Armenian, Hokkaido Japanese, Ket, Mitsukaido Japanese, Yaqui, Yucatec Maya) add a suffixed element to the verb to derive a causative, whereas Arabic changes the stem shape from CaCaCa / CaCiCa / CaCuCa (stem I) to CaCCaCa (stem II) and Italian uses a periphrastic construction with either *fare* 'make' (factitive/coercive) or *lasciare* 'let' (permissive). The alternation introduces a causer and the S or A of the corresponding active construction becomes a P and is generally marked as

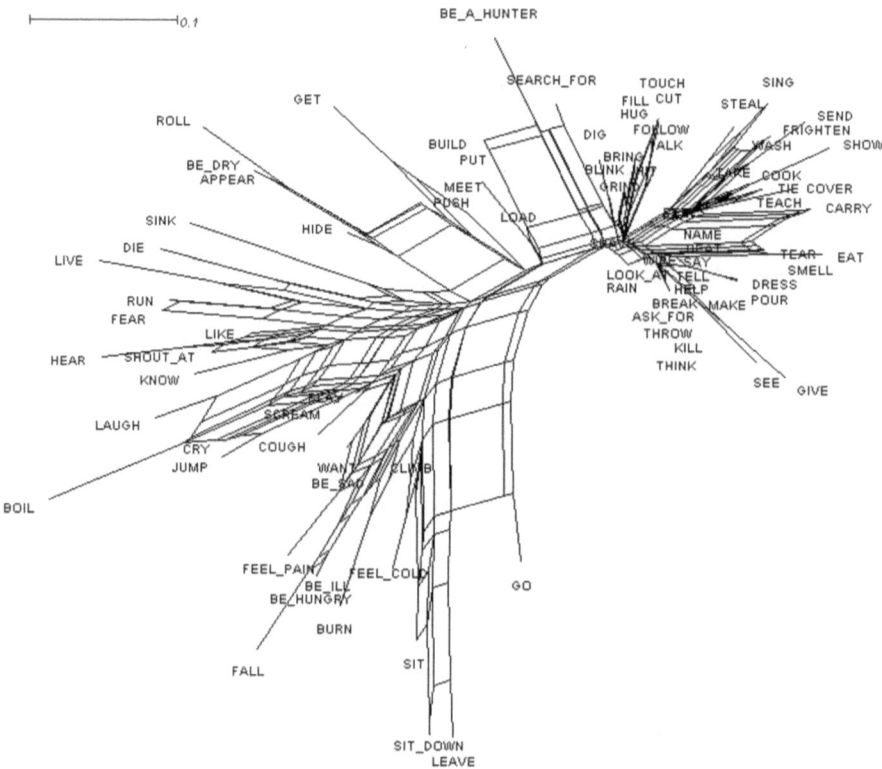

Figure 4: NeighborNet for the causative alternation

such in the languages in which grammatical relations are expressed morphologically through indexing (Chintang, Ket) or case (Bora, Hokkaido and Mitsukaido Japanese[8]). In some cases the causative introduces additional semantic effects. Thus, in Arabic there is sometimes an added intensive meaning, and in Ket typically an added inceptive meaning.

Guttman Coefficient: 85.4%
δ: 0.379

Hierarchy: FEAR, JUMP, LAUGH, RUN > CLIMB, COVER, FEEL COLD, LIVE, ROLL, SIT > BOIL > HIDE > PUT, SING > BE DRY, DIE, PLAY, SINK > CARRY, COUGH, CUT, EAT, FEEL PAIN, GO, KNOW, LEAVE, LOAD, MEET, SCREAM, SHOUT AT, SIT DOWN, TIE, TOUCH, WASH > APPEAR, ASK FOR, BE HUNGRY, BE SAD, BEAT, BLINK, BREAK, BUILD, BURN, CRY, DIG, DRESS, FILL, FOLLOW, FRIGHTEN, HEAR, HELP, HIT, HUG, KILL, LIKE, LOOK AT, NAME, PEEL, POUR, PUSH, RAIN, SAY, SEE, SEND, SHAVE, SMELL, STEAL, TAKE, TALK, TEACH, TEAR, TELL, THROW, WIPE > BRING, COOK, GRIND, SEARCH FOR, SHOW, THINK > BE ILL, FALL, GET, GIVE > BE A HUNTER, WANT > MAKE

Comments: The NeighborNet suggests a relatively sharp demarcation between clusters attracted by opposite poles at the left end of the network where verbs are typically semantically intransitive and the right end where they are typically semantically transitive.

3.3 Passive

Common to the alternations considered here is the promotion of the object in a transitive clause to subject in an intransitive clause. In several languages it is possible to optionally express the agent. In Balinese and German the agent is introduced in a prepositional phrase; in Yucatec by a preposition-like relational noun; in Hokkaido Japanese, Mitsukaido Japanese, and Russian it is marked by a non-core case. Mandinka does not allow for the expression of the agent. The Mandarin construction is accompanied by a sense of adversity, and appears to be the only one introducing a semantic affect. Some languages (Arabic, Icelandic, Russian) have more than one passive construction. In these cases the one that seems to be more frequent and/or general is selected here.

---

8 In Mitsukaido Japanese case-marking of the causee is dative when the corresponding non-causative sentence is transitive and accusative when the corresponding non-causative sentence is intransitive. This also seems to be the general pattern for Hokkaido Japanese.

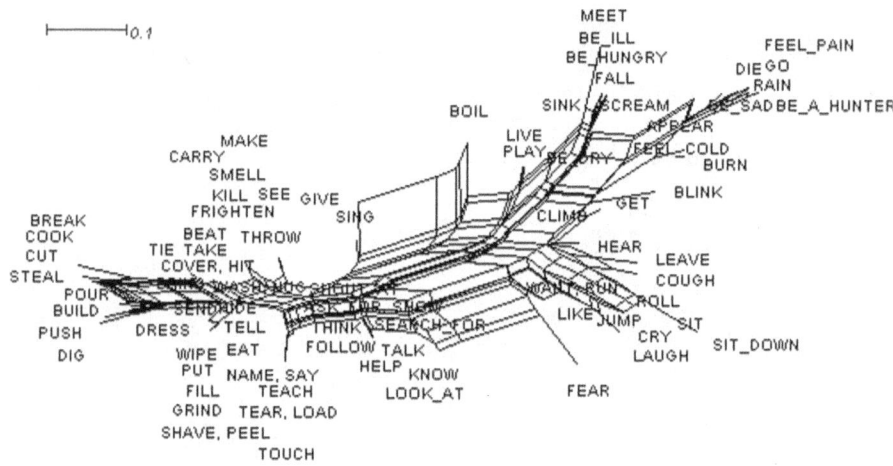

Figure 5: NeighborNet for the passive alternation

Guttman Coefficient: 86.6%
δ: 0.309

Hierarchy: BREAK, BEAT, BUILD, COVER, CUT > EAT, HIDE, HIT, KILL, CARRY, FRIGHTEN, HUG, PEEL, POUR, SEND, SHAVE, TEAR, TIE, TOUCH, WASH, ASK FOR, BRING, COOK, FILL, FOLLOW, LOAD, NAME, PUSH, PUT > SAY, SHOW, SMELL, STEAL, TAKE > TELL, THROW, DIG, DRESS, GRIND > KNOW, LOOK AT, SEARCH FOR, SEE, SING, THINK, WIPE, GIVE > HELP, TALK, TEACH, FEAR, HEAR, LIKE, SHOUT AT > BE DRY > BLINK, BURN, CLIMB > LAUGH, LEAVE, SINK, BE HUNGRY, BOIL, COUGH, GET, LIVE, MAKE, MEET, PLAY > ROLL > BE A HUNTER, BE ILL, BE SAD, DIE, FALL, FEEL COLD, RUN > SCREAM, SIT, APPEAR, CRY, FEEL PAIN, GO, JUMP, RAIN, SIT DOWN, WANT

Comments: Here is another case where unidimensionality is suggested both by the NeighborNet and the Guttman Coefficient, albeit weakly.

3.4 Reciprocal

In all the languages the reciprocal is typically used in a situation where two or more participants are at the same time agents and patients of the action.

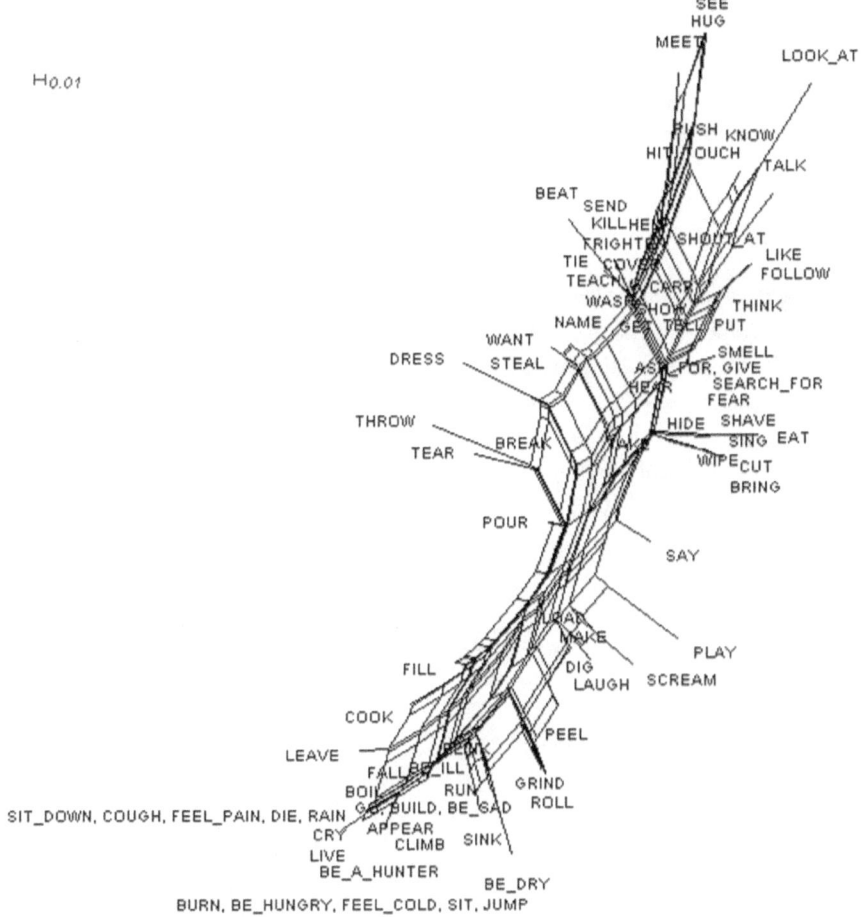

Figure 6: NeighborNet for the reciprocal alternation

Guttman Coefficient: 88.8%
δ: 0.285

Hierarchy: HUG, SEE > HIT, KNOW, LOOK AT > LIKE, MEET, TOUCH > HELP > BEAT, FRIGHTEN, WASH > ASK FOR, CARRY, COVER, DRESS, FEAR, FOLLOW, GIVE, KILL, NAME, PUSH, SEARCH FOR, SHAVE, SHOUT AT, SHOW, SMELL, TALK, TELL, TIE > BREAK, BRING, CUT, EAT, HEAR, HIDE, POUR, PUT, SAY, SEND, SING, STEAL, TAKE, TEACH, TEAR, THINK, THROW, WIPE > GET, PLAY, SCREAM > LAUGH, LOAD, WANT > BE DRY, BLINK, DIG, FILL, GRIND, MAKE, PEEL, ROLL > BE A

HUNTER, BE SAD, BUILD, CLIMB, GO, LEAVE, RUN, SINK > APPEAR, BE HUNGRY, BE ILL, BOIL, BURN, COOK, COUGH, CRY, DIE, FALL, FEEL COLD, FEEL PAIN, JUMP, LIVE, RAIN, SIT, SIT DOWN

Comments: Both the NeighborNet and the Guttman Coefficient suggest unidimensionality.

3.5 Reflexive

Across languages the reflexive is used to express a situation where the agent does something to him- or herself. For some languages (Ainu, Arabic, Hoocąk, Even) it is sometimes described as a valency-decreasing operation, whereas for some other languages, for which a reflexive pronoun is available (German, Yucatec Maya, Italian), it is explicitly or implicitly regarded as a subtype of a transitive construction. For some languages (German, Ket, Mapudungun) the construction overlaps with the reciprocal when there are multiple participants.

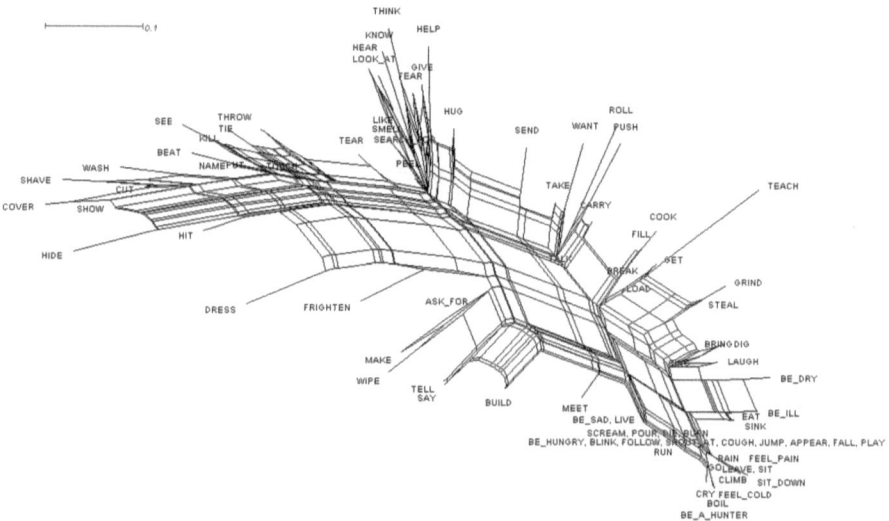

Figure 7: NeighborNet for the reflexive alternation

Guttman Coefficient: 84.7%
δ: 0.324

Hierarchy: COVER, SHAVE > HIDE, SEE, SHOW > CUT, WASH > BEAT, DRESS, FEAR, GIVE, HELP, HIT, KILL, KNOW, LOOK AT, NAME, PUT, THINK, THROW, TIE, TOUCH > HEAR, HUG, SMELL > ROLL, TEAR > TEACH, WIPE > FRIGHTEN > ASK FOR, BUILD, LIKE, PUSH, SAY, SEARCH FOR, SEND, TELL > BREAK, CARRY, FILL, LOAD, MAKE, MEET, PEEL, TAKE, TALK > BE DRY, COOK, GRIND, LAUGH, STEAL,

WANT > APPEAR, BE A HUNTER, BE HUNGRY, BE ILL, BE SAD, BLINK, BOIL, BRING, BURN, CLIMB, COUGH, CRY, DIE, DIG, EAT, FALL, FEEL COLD, FEEL PAIN, FOLLOW, GET, GO, JUMP, LEAVE, LIVE, PLAY, POUR, RAIN, RUN, SCREAM, SHOUT AT, SING, SINK, SIT, SIT DOWN

Comments: The Guttman Coefficient is just short of the threshold for unidimensionality, but the overall shape of the NeighborNet indicates that this is nevertheless a good approximate description.

3.6 Concluding comments on individual alternations

Overall the evidence presented shows that the assumption of single implicational hierarchies (unidimensionality) underlying the distribution of syntactic alternations across verbs and languages is supported in the majority, if not in all cases. We have observed relatively tree-like NeighborNets with relatively low δ-scores and acceptable Guttman coefficients. Interestingly, when we correlate the δ-scores and Guttman coefficients we find a high negative correlation of Pearson's $r = -0.707$ ($p = 0.182$, which is too high for significance, but p is not expected to reach significance with just five datapoints).[9] This justifies the use of NeighborNets as part of the toolkit for estimating unidimensionality.

The antipassive behaves somewhat multidimensionally but is just on the right side of Guttman's threshold for unidimensionality. Each alternation is worthy of more detailed study, leaving plenty of opportunities for future research. Here, however, we are interested in the larger picture. This has shown that effects of implicational hierarchies among verbs are ubiquitous. For all alternations there is some justification for assuming single underlying hierarchies, even if the justification is better in some cases than in others. This raises the issue of whether the hierarchies are the same or different across alternations. This is the topic of the next section.

4 Correlations among verb hierarchies

The previous section presented hierarchies among the verbs for each alternation. These were produced from scalogram analyses, which often yield a group-

---

9 Pearson's r can take values between 0 and 1, with higher values corresponding to better correlations. It can moreover be tested for significance, with the significance expressed as p-values, which get lower as significance increases, with the conventional thresholds of significance being <.05 or, more conservatively, <.01. The same goes for the Spearman Rank Correlation Coefficient, used in the next section.

ing of verbs at different steps of a hierarchy. To take the example of the reflexive (the last of the cases presented in the previous section), a hierarchy was found where COVER & SHAVE comprise a single group at the top of the hierarchy, and where the next group is HIDE, SEE & SHOW and the one following that CUT & WASH, and so on. For the purpose of investigating whether the hierarchies for different alternations are correlated, we can assign numbers to groups of verbs in each hierarchy according to their rank. In the case of the reflexive hierarchy we would assign a '1' to COVER and SHAVE, a '2' to HIDE, SEE, and SHOW, and so on. Given rank numbers for each verb in each alternation hierarchy, all the various hierarchies can be tested for intercorrelations by means of the Spearman Rank Correlation Coefficient. The significance test assumes independence of variables. This is a questionable assumption in this case because our sample includes related languages, even very closely related ones (different variants of Japanese). However, if a verb behaves identically in two languages, as will be the tendency if the languages are closely related, this does not affect the hierarchy, but simply adds redundant evidence. What matters is difference in behavior. So it does seem that we can rely on p-values in the present context. The results of testing for correlations among all pairs of verb hierarchies for the 5 alternations are given in Table 1.

The results in Table 1 are quite unambiguous. The hierarchy for the causative is not correlated with any of the other hierarchies. If this hierarchy is set apart, a very clear picture emerges according to which everything correlates with everything else! In other words, the distributions of the antipassive, passive, reciprocal, and reflexive across verbs and languages all appear to adhere to the same (loosely) implicational hierarchy. This finding supports the part of the claim of Tsunoda (1985) stating that these four alternations operate on the same hierarchy, even if we found above that this hierarchy is not quite the same as the one proposed by Tsunoda.

Table 1: Spearman's Rank Correlation Coefficient (lower left triangle) and p-values (upper right triangle) among all pairs of verb hierarchies for different alternations.

	apas	caus	pass	reci	refl
apas		0.124	<0.001	<0.001	<0.001
caus	−0.166		0.329	0.185	0.256
pass	0.608	−0.156		<0.001	<0.001
reci	0.590	−0.143	0.608		<0.001
refl	0.588	−0.123	0.621	0.745	

Correlations for which $p < 0.001$ are marked in grey.

This hierarchy can be extracted by adding up the numbers referring to positions in the individual hierarchies for each verb. When verbs are ranked by these sums a combined hierarchy emerges which is displayed in (6).

(6) A combined loosely implicational hierarchy partly governing the distribution of 4 alternations over 87 verbs in 22 languages

SEE, SHAVE > HUG, WASH > CUT > COVER > BEAT, HIT, TOUCH > KNOW > LOOK AT, NAME > DRESS, HIDE, KILL, TEAR, TIE > SHOW > FRIGHTEN, HELP, THINK > BREAK, EAT, GIVE, PUT, SMELL, THROW > BUILD, FEAR, HEAR > SAY, TELL, WIPE > ASK FOR, LOAD, SEND > CARRY, PUSH > COOK, POUR, STEAL > FILL, MEET, SEARCH FOR, SING, TAKE, TALK > FOLLOW, GRIND, LIKE, PEEL, ROLL > TEACH > BRING, DIG, SHOUT AT > BE DRY, PLAY > BLINK, BURN > CLIMB, LAUGH > LEAVE, RUN > COUGH, GET, LIVE, MAKE, SINK > WANT > BE HUNGRY, SCREAM > BE SAD, DIE, FEEL COLD, SIT > BE A HUNTER, BOIL, FEEL PAIN, GO, JUMP > RAIN, SIT DOWN > BE ILL, FALL > APPEAR, CRY

Verbs within one and the same group are not necessarily significantly more similar in their behavior than neighboring verbs, so the 'greater than' symbols do not represent sharp borders, but the existence of many groups nevertheless indicates that a high degree of granularity is necessary for capturing similarities and differences among verbs – in order words, one should avoid defining large groups such as 'effective action' or 'perception' a priori. Such groupings should clearly emerge from the data or else be discarded. If nothing else, the hierarchy in (6) can serve as a warning against relying on intuitions.

Calling (6) a 'transitivity hierarchy' would immediately invite questions like why, say, SEE is more 'transitive' than, say, KILL. It has become commonplace since Hopper & Thompson (1980) to view affectedness of the undergoer as part of the definition of transitivity. Nevertheless, the hierarchy is certainly relevant to the definition of transitivity since it underlies morphosyntactic transitivity-changing alternations. With the caveat in mind that the hierarchy might have deserved to be called 'the transitivity hierarchy' if the notion of transitivity was not already so loaded, I choose to not call it anything other than 'a combined loosely implicational hierarchy partly governing the distribution of 4 alternations over 87 verbs in 22 languages.'

5 Conclusions

This is a somewhat preliminary study of how the distribution of morphosyntactic alternations across languages is at least to some degree governed by implicational hierarchies among verbs. What I hope to have achieved is to demonstrate the following points:
- quantitative methods are available for detecting the existence of implicational hierarchies;
- deviation from the unidimensionality in implicational hierarchies can be measured;
- implicational hierarchies, although they are never completely perfect, are nevertheless ubiquitous with regard to the distribution of morphosyntactic alternations over verbs and languages;
- the causative responds to its own individual implicational hierarchy among verbs which is uncorrelated with other such hierarchies;
- in contrast, the antipassive, passive, reciprocal, and reflexive across verbs and languages all appear to adhere to the same or at least similar (loosely) implicational hierarchies.

Appendix 1: Mapping between general and language-specific alternation names

Name used here	Language	Name used in database
Antipassive	Ainu	Antipassive
	Bezhta	Antipassive 1
	Arabic, Eastern Armenian, German, Italian, Ket, Mandarin, Zenzontepec Chatino	Object omission
	Even, Russian	Object deletion
	Mandinka	Antipassive middle
Causative	Arabic	Stem II causative
	Balinese, Bora, Chintang, Eastern Armenian, Hokkaido Japanese, Italian, Ket, Mitsukaido Japanese, Yaqui, Yucatec Maya	Causative
	Hoocąk	Coercive/default causative (*hii*)
	Mandinka	Causative derivation 1
	Mapudungun	Causative 1
	Zenzontepec Chatino	Causative of active verb

Passive	Arabic	Stem VII passive
	Balinese	Passive -*a* alternation
	German	Passive with *werden*
	Hokkaido Japanese	DO passive
	Mandarin	BEI alternation
	Mitsukaido Japanese	Direct passive
	Yaqui, Yucatec Maya	Passive
	Icelandic	Nominative passive
	Mandinka	Active / passive alternation
	Russian	Participial passive
Reciprocal	Arabic	Stem VI reciprocal
	Bora	Reciprocal derivation
	Even	Direct reciprocal
	Ket	Reflexive/reciprocal alternation
	Chintang, Eastern Armenian, German, Icelandic	Reciprocal
	Hoocąk	Reciprocal (+*kiki*)
	Italian, Russian	Reciprocal reflexive
Reflexive	Ainu, Chintang, German, Ket, Mapudungun, Yucatec Maya	Reflexive
	Arabic	Stem V reflexive
	Bora	Reflexive derivation
	Even	Reflexive deleting alternation
	Hoocąk	Reflexive (+*kii*)
	Italian	Direct reflexive
	Russian	Semantic reflexive

Appendix 2: Data of relevance for the Tsunoda hierarchy

The numbers cross-reference the different columns. The capital letters in the second and third lines abbreviate languages, and should be read top down. The abbreviations are as follows. AR: Arabic; BA: Balinese; GE: German; HO: Hokkaido Japanese; IC: Icelandic; MA: Mandarin; MD: Mandinka; MI: Mitsukaido Japanese; RU: Russian; YA: Yaqui; YM: Yucatec Maya; AI: Ainu; BE: Bezhta; EA: Eastern Armenian; EV: Even; IT: Italian; KE: Ket; ZC: Zenzontepec Chatino; BO: Bora; CH: Chintang; HC: Hoocąk; MP: Mapudungun; YM: Yucatec Maya. Within the matrix, a y encodes presence of the availability of an alternation for a given verb (either marginally or regularly), an n the absence, and – indicates lack of data. Passives are in columns 1–11, antipassives in 12–23, reflexives in 24–35, and reciprocals in 36–47.

	1	2	3	4
	1234567890	1234567890	1234567890	1234567
	ABGHIMMMRY	YAABEEGIKM	MRZAABCEGH	IKMRYABCEEGHIIKRY
	RAEOCADIUAM	IREAVETEADUCI	ROHVECTEPUM	ROHAVEOCTEUM
EAT	nyyyyyyyyy	yyyyyyyyyy	ynyynnn-nn	nnnnnynn-nyyynnnny
LOOK AT	nyyyn-yyny	ynnnnnyn-nn	ynnyynyyyny	nyyyyynyyyynny
SEE	nyyyn-ynyy	yynnnnyyyyny	--yynyyyyyny	yyynyyyyyyy
FEAR	nynyn-nynyn	-ynnnnnynnyy	nynnnyynyny	nynnyyynynny
LIKE	nyyynyn-nyn	-nnnnnnn-nnn	-ny-nyynnyn	nyyyynyyynny
KNOW	nyyynyyyny-n	nnynnnynnn	nyn-nynynyn	yyyynyyyyynny
SEARCH FOR	nyyynyy-ny	yynnnnnyn-nnn	-ny-nnynny	nyny-nyyynynny
BREAK	yyyyyyyyyyy	-nnnnny-nnnn	ny-nnynynnnynny	nynyynn
KILL	nyyyyyyyyyy	-nnnnnyy-nn	-yny-nynyyy	nyny-nyynnyyny
HIT	nyyyyyyyyyy	-ynnnnny-nnn	-ny-nyynyy	yyyynyyyyyyny
HEAR	n-ynnyyny-y	ynnn-nyyyny	y-nyy-yynnyny	y-n-yynyny
WANT	n-y---n---n	-n-n-yy--n-n	-n---nyn-y-nn	--n-yy-y--n

Acknowledgments

Thanks go to Eric W. Holman for important input on this work and to Andrej Malchukov for many stimulating discussions and comments on a previous draft. My research was supported by an ERC Advanced Grant (MesAndLin(g)k, proj. no. 295918) and by a subsidy of the Russian Government to support the Program of Competitive Development of Kazan Federal University.

References

Ballmer, Thomas A. & Waltraud Brennenstuhl. 1986. *Deutsche Verben. Eine Sprachanalytische Untersuchung des deutschen Verbwortschatzes*. Tübingen: G. Narr.

Croft, William & Keith T. Poole. 2008. Inferring universals from grammatical variation: multidimensional scaling for typological analysis. *Theoretical linguistics* 34. 1–37.

Felsenstein, Joseph. 2009. PHYLIP. Phylogeny inference package. Version 3.69. http://en.biosoft.net/tree/Phylip.html.

Guttman, Louis. 1944. A basis for scaling qualitative data. *American sociological review* 9. 139–150.

Hartmann, Iren, Martin Haspelmath & Bradley Taylor (eds.). 2013. Valency Patterns Leipzig. Leipzig: Max Planck Institute for Evolutionary Anthropology. (Available online at http://valpal.info).

Holland, Barbara R., Katharina T. Huber, Andreas Dress & Vincent Moulton. 2002. δ plots: A tool for analyzing phylogenetic distance data. *Molecular biology and evolution* 19. 2051–2059.

Huson, Daniel & David Bryant. 2006. Application of phylogenetic networks in evolutionary studies. *Molecular biology and evolution* 23. 254–267.
Lehmann, Christian. 1991. Predicate classes and Participation. In Hansjakob Seiler & Waldfried Premper (eds.), *Partizipation. Das sprachliche Erfassen von Sachverhalten*, 183–239. Tübingen: G. Narr.
Levin, Beth. 1993. *English verb classes and alternations: A preliminary investigation*. Chicago: University of Chicago Press.
Malchukov, Andrej L. 2005. Case pattern splits, verb types and construction competition. In Mengistu Amberber & Helen de Hoop (eds.), *Competition and variation in natural languages*, 73–117. Amsterdam: Elsevier.
Sasse, Heinz-Jürgen. 2001. Scales between nouniness and verbiness. In Martin Haspelmath, Ekkehard König, Wulf Oesterreicher & Wolfgang Raible (eds.), *Language typology and universals. An international handbook*, 495–509. (Handbücher zur Sprach- und Kommunikationswissenschaft 20.1). Berlin & New York: Walter de Gruyter.
Tsunoda, Tasaku. 1981. Split case-marking patterns in verb-types and tense/aspect/mood. *Linguistics* 19. 389–438.
Tsunoda, Tasaku. 1985. Remarks on transitivity. *Journal of linguistics* 21. 385–396.
Wichmann, Søren. 2015. Statistical observations on implicational (verb) hierarchies. In Andrej Malchukov & Bernard Comrie (eds.), *Valency classes in the world's languages*, 155–181. Berlin & Boston: De Gruyter Mouton.
Wichmann, Søren, Eric W. Holman, Taraka Rama & Robert S. Walker. 2011. Correlates of reticulation in linguistic phylogenies. *Language dynamics and change* 1. 205–240.

Masayoshi Shibatani
15 The role of morphology in valency alternation phenomena

1 Introduction

Morphology plays an important role in linguistic analysis. In derivational morphology a morphological marking is taken as a sign flagging the secondary, derived status of the marked form in question vis-à-vis the unmarked counterpart. Morphological marking has also been considered integral to the definitions of syntactic constructions or the phenomena that those constructions represent. In the functional linguistic tradition efforts have been mounted in search of functional motivations for morphological complexity. But there remain general questions regarding the role of morphology such as what kind of morphology is functionally motivated and is meaningful in synchronic analysis.

This chapter examines the role of morphology in valency alternation phenomena specifically addressing the questions of (i) whether morphology properly delineates and identifies the constructions for a particular phenomenon and should be included in the definition of the constructions in question, and (ii) whether morphology is always reliable in determining directions of derivation and of the derived status of the alternating forms. These are important questions especially in view of recent trends in valency studies that tend to rely on morphological marking patterns, which are even considered as viable typological features for characterizing languages as either transitivizing or detransitivizing (Nichols et al. 2004). Prompted by the uncritical reliance on morphology in some of these studies (see sections 4 & 5 below), this chapter attempts to assess the role of morphology by examining two types of valency alternation phenomena, namely applicative and transitivity alternations.

Applicative and transitivity alternations, which overlap to some extent, provide good test cases because there is a wide array of morphological patterns associated with these phenomena, ranging from those involving highly productive morphology to no morphology at all, with many intermediate types involving morphology of various degrees of productivity. For example, while Balinese applicatives in general involve fairly productive morphology, the corresponding patterns found in English and Japanese lack morphology entirely. In German some applicative constructions require verbal morphological derivation while

Masayoshi Shibatani, Rice University

others do not. In Japanese, both the transitivizing causative process and the intransitivizing passive formation involve highly productive morphology, but there is also morphology of limited productivity involved in transitive-intransitive verb pairs, which contrast with the labile patterns in English and some other languages, where verb pairs may have no morphological indication of the transitivity status of the verb, e.g., Japanese *ak-u* (intr. *open*) vs. *ak-e-ru* (tr. *open*), Japanese *katam-ar-u* (intr. *harden*) vs. *katam-e-ru* (tr. *harden*).

The first half of this chapter is devoted to Balinese applicatives that challenge a number of assumptions made in the study of valency changing phenomena, including (a) that verbs have a basic valency value characterizing them as intransitive, transitive, or ditransitive in their basic form, (b) that valency alternation is to be characterized in terms of increase or decrease in valency, and (c) that productive valency alternations are syntactic processes, which, for example, turn an intransitive clause into a transitive one or a transitive clause to an intransitive one. We go on to compare Balinese and English in our discussion of the role of morphology in indicating directions of derivation of alternating applicative constructions. In the second half of the chapter our attention is turned to transitivity alternations, centering on Japanese transitive-intransitive pairs, many of which show different morphological marking patterns suggestive of directions of derivation. In the final section of the chapter we offer a principle, the Principle of Functional Transparency, that pays critical attention to the productivity of morphology and which captures a functional motivation for morphology.

2 Balinese applicatives

Applicative conversion is generally defined or characterized as a syntactic process that increases valency. In the introduction to the book *Changing Valency: Case Studies in Transitivity*, the editors R. M. W. Dixon and Alexandra Aikhenvald define applicatives, under the heading of valency increase, as shown in (1), where S, A and O stand for the sole argument of an intransitive clause, the agentive argument of a transitive clause, and the patientive argument of a transitive clause, respectively:

(1) (a) Applicative applies to an underlying intransitive clause and forms a derived transitive.

 (b) The argument in underlying S function goes into A function in the applicative.

(c) A peripheral argument ... is taken into the core, in O function.

(d) There is some explicit formal marking of an applicative construction, generally by an affix or some other morphological process applying to the verb.

OR

(a') Applicative applies to an underlying transitive clause and maintains transitivity, but with an argument in a different semantic role filling O function.

(b') The underlying A argument stays as is.

(c') A peripheral argument...is taken into the core, in O function.

(d') The argument which was in O function is moved out of the core in the periphery of the clause...

(e') There is some explicit formal marking of an applicative construction, generally by an affix or some other morphological process applying to the verb.

(Dixon & Aikhenvald 2000: 13–14).

The second type of applicative, characterized by (a')–(e') above, may also increase valency in that the derived applicative structure now requires both applied object in O function as well as the Patient argument, contrasting with the non-applicative counterpart, which has a Patient argument in O function with either an obligatory directional argument or an adjunct expressing an instrumental or other type of semantic role. Applicatives of this type may be ditransitive constructions with two obligatory Object arguments contrasting with non-applicative monotransitive counterparts.

Valency increase is widely assumed to be a hallmark property of applicatives as evidenced by the categorization of applicatives by Haspelmath & Müller-Bardey (2004: 1130–1135) as an object-adding process along with causativization, which is categorized as subject-adding. This and some other assumptions contained in the Dixon–Aikhenvald definitions of applicatives are challenged by Balinese, which points to an alternative characterization of applicatives with a central focus placed on the alignment patterns between O function and the role type, downplaying the importance of valency-increasing or object-adding effect as well as the role of morphological marking. In the new characterization of applicatives, valency increase is but a possible side effect of the alignment patterns imposed by applicativization rather than a defining property of the process. Before turning to these points, a brief description of Balinese clause structure and an introduction to its applicatives are in order.

As in most Western Malayo-Polynesian and Formosan languages, transitive verbs in Balinese allow two coding patterns. As illustrated below, one pattern has an A argument aligned with the sentence-initial Topic relation (Actor-focus or AF constructions) and the other has an O or P argument aligned with the Topic (Patient-focus or PF constructions).

(2) AF construction
    Tiang   nyepak   cicing=e.[1]
    I   AF.kick   dog=DEF
    'I kicked the dog.'

(3) PF construction
    Cicing=e   sepak   tiang.
    dog-DEF   PF.kick   I
    'I kicked the dog.'

Notice that the AF construction is marked by an initial nasal consonant in the verb, which reflects the proto-Austronesian AF marker *-um*, while the PF construction has an oral counterpart. In contrast to some other Western Malayo-Polynesian and Formosan languages, where the Object relation is not clearly delineated, the Object relation in AF constructions is a robust category in Balinese and can be borne by a definite Object. The Object nominal can also be made Subject/Topic of a passive construction. Indeed, it is the Object position that plays the central role in applicative phenomena in this language since the nature of the argument role aligned with this position determines the morphology of the two central applicative types of the language. Applicativization feeds the AF/PF alternation such that an applied Object may align with the Topic relation via P-focusing. In examples (4b) and (4c) below, the verbal suffix *-in* marks a locative applicative construction, which aligns a location nominal with the Object relation, as in (4b), which then alternates with a PF construction with the location nominal as the sentence topic, as in (4c).

(4) a. Intransitive (non-applicative)
       Ia   pules   telung   jam   (di   umah=ne   anyar).
       s/he   sleep   three   hour   (in   house=3SG.POSS   new)
       'S/he slept three hours (in his new house).'

---

[1] The Balinese examples used in this chapter are those of the middle register Ordinary/Medium Balinese. There are, in addition, Low and High Balinese.

b. Transitive AF construction (via applicativization)
 Ia   mules-**in**   umah=ne   anyar telung jam.
 s/he AF.sleep-**GR.APPL** house=3SG.POSS   new   three   hour
 'S/he slept three hours in his new house.'

c. Transitive PF construction (via applicativization)
 Umah=e   anyar pules-**in**   ia   telung jam.
 house=3SG.POSS   new   PF.sleep-**GR.APPL** s/he three hour
 'S/he slept in his new house for three hours.'

In the analysis of applicatives both within and across languages the Figure-Ground perceptual distinction posited in Gestalt psychology proves useful. In terms of thematic roles, the Theme corresponds to the Figure and represents an entity that is situated at a location or in a state or that moves from one location to another in physical space or from one state to another in the construal of a change-of-state as an abstract motion. The Ground is background against which a Figure is delineated and subsumes various locative expressions in language with respect to which a Figure expression is predicated as being located or moving. Locations can be both physical or human, and thus both so-called goal location (as in *John walked to **the station***) and human recipient (as in *John gave **Bill** the book*) count as instances of the Ground. Balinese applicative morphology reflects this Figure-Ground distinction dividing applicative constructions into two types. The verbal suffix -*in* marks the Ground=Object (GR=OBJ) applicative that aligns with Object a static location (corresponding to the prepositional expression *di* 'at, in, on' in non-applicative constructions), a goal location (*ka* 'to'), a recipient (*ka* 'to, for'), or a source location (*uli* 'from' or *sig* 'from'). The suffix -*ang*, on the other hand, yields the Figure=Object (FIG=OBJ) applicative, wherein an argument denoting an entity moving in physical or abstract space is aligned with Object. Figure subsumes theme, instrument in physical motion, and causee construed as an entity undergoing an abstract motion from one state to another. Compare GR=OBJ applicative (4b) above with FIG=OBJ applicatives (5b) and (6b) below:

(5) a. Basic intransitive construction
 lumur=e   ento   ulung.
 glass=DEF   that   PF.fall
 'The glass fell down.'

 b. FIG=OBJ applicative
 *Tiang ng-ulung-**ang**   lumur=e   ento.*
 I   AF-fall-**FIG.APPL** glass=DEF   that
 'I dropped the glass.'

(6) a. Basic GR=OBJ construction
Anak=e   ento   ng-lempag   lalipi=ne   (aji   tungked)
person=DEF that   AF-hit   snake=DEF (with   stick)
'The man hit the snake (with a stick).'

b. FIG=OBJ applicative
Anak=e   ento   ng-lempag-**ang**   tungked   ka   lalipi=ne.
person=DEF that   AF-hit-**FIG.APPL**   stick   to   snake=DEF
'The man hit the stick against the snake/Lit. The man caused the stick to hit (to) the snake.'

Notice that the above treatment of applicatives in terms of the alignment patterns holding between Figure/Ground and Object collapses traditional causativization and instrumental applicativization into a single construction of the FIG=OBJ applicative. The use of the same morphology for causativization and instrumental applicativization is seen not only in Balinese (the -*ang* suffix) but also in a fair number of other languages (e.g., Bantu and Australian aboriginal languages).[2]

The examples above illustrate the familiar types of applicatives that increase valency. However, there are two cases in Balinese that challenge the definition of applicativization as a valency-increasing process. The first case is where applicatives and the corresponding non-applicative constructions have the same number of arguments. Balinese has ditransitive verbs requiring two obligatory arguments. Like English, they allow two coding patterns. One, without applicative morphology, aligns a Figure (theme) argument with Object and codes a Ground (recipient/goal location) argument as a prepositional phrase. The other coding pattern yields the morphologically marked GR=OBJ applicative construction, in which a Ground argument is aligned with Object and a Figure argument coded as second Object. Compare (a) and (b) below:

---

[2] The suffix -*ang* also marks benefactive applicatives. The relationship between them and the FIG=OBJ applicative (or causatives) is not as straightforward as that between instrumental applicatives and causatives. Just as the situation type [X CAUSE Y (the child) to HAVE Z (a book)] under the direct causative construal lexicalizes as [X cause-HAVE Y Z] in a fair number of languages, [X CAUSE Y to BUY Z], for example, may give rise to a benefactive expression [X cause-BUY Y Z]. English lexicalization incorporates the causative meaning component into a hosting verb giving rise to expressions like "X *gives* Y (the child) Z (a book)" and "X *buys* Y (the child) Z (a book)", while many other languages realize the causative semantics as a causative or a Figure applicative affix, as in Ainu *kor-e* (have-CAUS) 'give' *nu-re* (hear-CAUS) 'inform' and in Balinese *tegul-ang* (tie-FIG.APPL), which permits either a causative reading (e.g., Lit. cause the horse to tie to the tree trunk > tie the horse to the tree trunk) or a benefactive construal (e.g., Lit. cause the man tie the horse to the tree trunk > tie the man the horse to the tree trunk/tie the horse to the tree trunk for the man).

(7) a. Basic FIG=OBJ construction
Tiang   maang   banyu   ka   celeng=e.
I   AF.give scrap   to   pig=DEF
'I gave food scrap to the pig.'

b. GR=OBJ applicative construction
Tiang   maang-in   celeng=e   banyu.
I   AF.give-GR.APPL   pig=DEF   scrap
'I gave the pig food scrap.'

(8) a. Basic FIG=OBJ construction
Anak=e   ento   ngirim   buku=ne   ka   sekolah.
person=DEF   that   AF.send   book=DEF   to   school
'The man sent the book to the school.'

b. GR=OBJ applicative construction
Anak=e   ento   ngirim-in   sekolah   buku=ne.
person=DEF   that   AF.send-GR.APPL   school   book=DEF
Lit. 'The man sent the school the book.'

The above case represents Dixon & Aikhenvald's second applicative pattern mentioned earlier. This pattern, which I believe is fairly widespread across different languages, is really argument-realigning rather than valency-increasing, since the number of arguments remains the same in the two alternating patterns. The structures between the two patterns, however, are not entirely identical. The GR=OBJ construction is a ditransitive construction with two Objects, while in the FIG=OBJ construction, there is a single Object. In the double object constructions, the status of the theme-bearing Object varies across different constructions and across different languages. Contrary to Dixon & Aikhenvald's description in (1d'), in some constructions/languages the double Objects are symmetrical in the sense that the two Objects both behave like the Object of a monotransitive sentence, e.g., both may become a Subject of a passive sentence, while in other constructions/languages, the theme-bearing Object is quite inert and much less like a direct Object as the Dixon-Aikhenvald definition has it.

There are also bivalent intransitive verbs in Balinese that obligatorily call for two nominal arguments. They are intransitive in that the second argument is coded as a prepositional phrase rather than as an Object. These verbs also permit a transitive coding pattern via applicativization.

(9) a. Bivalent intransitive construction
 Anak=e cenik ento menek ka gedebeg=e.
 person=DEF small that AF.climb to cart=DEF
 'The child climbed onto the cart.'

 b. FIG=OBJ applicative construction
 Ia menek-ang anak=e cenik ento ka gedebeg=e.
 s/he AF.climb-FIG.APPL person=DEF small that to cart=DEF
 Lit. 'S/he loaded the child onto the cart.'

(10) a. Bivalent intransitive construction
 Tiang sangsaya teken anak=e ento.
 I PF.distrust with person=DEF that
 'I distrust that man.'

 b. GR=OBJ applicative construction
 Tiang nyangsaya-in anak=e ento.
 I AF.distrust-GR.APPL person=DEF that
 'I distrust that man.'

While these applicatives are transitive, they do not increase valency in that they contain the same number of arguments as the non-applicative counterparts. But notice that both valency-increasing applicatives (see (4)–(6)) and non-increasing ones (see (7)–(10)) show exactly the same alignment patterns, where the suffix -*in* marks the GR=OBJ alignment and -*ang* the FIG=OBJ alignment, pointing to one of the central claims of this chapter, namely that applicatives should be defined in terms of the change in argument alignment patterns rather than in terms of increase in valency. The cases studied above can still be characterized in terms of increase in transitivity – from intransitive to transitive and from transitive to ditransitive. Such a characterization is insufficient to fully describe Balinese, however, because it also has a large number of verbs whose basic valency, and hence transitivity, is indeterminate.

One peculiar feature of the Balinese verbal lexicon, which is also seen in Bahasa Indonesia (Standard Indonesian) and perhaps other Indonesian languages of the Austronesian stock, is the existence of what Artawa (1994) and others call "precategorial" roots. While there are many verb roots that are associated with one (and rarely two) basic valency patterns without morphological marking, there are also a large number of roots that cannot be used as verbs without a derivational affix and, as such, whose valency value and alignment pattern remain undetermined until a derivational affix is selected.[3] Take the form *uruk* 'learn/teach'. In order for this form to function syntactically, it must take the middle prefix *m(a)-*, or the applicative suffix *-in* or *-ang*, as below, so that neither its intransitive use (11a) nor its transitive use in either the AF form (11b) or the PF (zero) form (11c) is possible without these affixes.

(11) Underived *uruk* 'learn/teach'
    a. **Tiang uruk (basa Inggeris).*
       I learn (language English)
       'I am studying (English).'

    b. **Tiang ng-uruk basa Inggeris (ka anak=e cenik ento).* (AF)
       I AF-learn language English to person=DEF small that
       'I am teaching English (to the child).'

    c. **basa Inggeris uruk tiang (ka anak=e cenik ento).* (PF)
       language English PF.learn I to person=DEF small that
       'I am teaching English (to the child).'

(12) *m(a)*-middle derived form
    *Tiang **m**-uruk (basa Inggeris).*
    I MID-learn (language English)
    'I am studying/learning (English).'

(13) *-in* derived GR=OBJ applicative
    a. *Tiang ng-uruk-in anak=e cenik ento (basa Inggeris).* (AF)
       I AF-learn-GR.APPL person=DEF small that (language English)
       'I am teaching the child (English).'

    b. *Anak=e cenik ento uruk-in tiang (basa Inggeris).* (PF)
       person small that PF.learn-GR.APPL I (language English)
       'I am teaching the child (English).'

(14) *-ang* derived FIG=OBJ applicative
    a. *Tiang ng-uruk-ang basa Inggeris (ka anak=e cenik ento).* (AF)
       I AF-lean-FIG.APPL language English (to person=DEF small that)
       'I am teaching English (to the child).'

---

[3] There are twenty seven precategorials in the seventy-some verbs in the list of the Leipzig valency project. See Shibatani & Artawa (2015).

b. *Basa   Inggeris uruk-ang   tiang (ka anak=e   cenik ento).* (PF)
   language English PF.learn-FIG.APPL I   (to person=DEF small that)
   'I am teaching English (to the child).'

Compare the above with the patterns shown by the non-precategorial verb *tulis* 'write' below, where the AF (15a) and the PF form (15b) without a derivational affix are both grammatical.

(15) Underived *tulis* 'write'
   a. *Tiang nulis   aksara   Bali   (di tembok=e) (aji pulpen).* (AF)
      I   AF.write characters Balinese on wall=DEF with pen
      'I wrote Balinese characters (on the wall) (with a pen).'

   b. *Aksara   Bali   tulis   tiang (di tembok=e) (aji pulpen).* (PF)
      characters Balinese PF.write I   (on wall=DEF) (with pen)
      'I wrote Balinese characters (on the wall) (with a pen).'

(16) *ma*-middle derived form
   Aksara   Bali   ma-tulis   (di tembok=e).
   characters Balinese MID-write (on wall=DEF)
   'Balinese characters are written (on the wall).'

(17) *-in* derived GR=OBJ applicative
   a. *Tiang nulis-in   tembok=e aksara   Bali   (aji pulpen).* (AF)
      I   AF.write-GR.APPL wall=DEF characters Balinese (with pen)
      Lit. 'I wrote the wall with Balinese characters (with a pen).'

   b. *Tembok=e tulis-in   tiang aksara   Bali   (aji pulpen).* (PF)
      wall=DEF PF.write-GR.APPL I   characters Balinese (with pen)
      Lit. 'I wrote the wall with Balinese characters (with a pen).'

(18) *-ang* derived FIG=OBJ applicative
   a. *Tiang nulis-ang   pulpen=e aksara   Bali   ka tembok=ne.* (AF)
      I   AF.write-FIG.APPL pen=DEF characters Balinese to wall=DEF
      Lit. 'I caused the pen to write Balinese characters to the wall.'

   b. *Pulpen=e tulis-ang   tiang aksara   Bali   ka tembok=e.* (PF)[4]
      pen=DEF PF.write-FIG.APPL I   characters Balienese to wall=DEF
      Lit. 'I caused the pen to write Balinese characters to the wall.'

---

4 Below, only AF versions of the relevant constructions will be given.

Besides the verb root *uruk* 'learn' above, precategorial roots include the following verbs: *edeng* 'show', *enjuh* 'give', *orah* 'say/tell', *selek* 'insert', *turuh* 'pour', *entung* 'throw', *engkeb* 'hide', and *payas* 'dress (someone)'. Many of these verbs are conceptually transitive, at least to speakers of languages like English, but in Balinese they lack basic valency and can function either as intransitive via *ma*-middle derivation or as transitive via either *-in* applicativization (GR=OBJ construction) or *-ang* applicativization (FIG=OBJ construction). There are also notionally monovalent precategorials such as *kokohan* 'cough' and *sumpah* 'swear' that must be *ma*-derived for an intransitive use and *-in* or *-ang* derived if the verb permits a transitive use as in (20).

(19) a. **Anak=e   cenik   ento   kokohan.*
       person=DEF   small   that   cough
       'The child coughed.'

   b. *Anak-e   cenik   ento   ma-kokohan.*
       person=DEF   small   that   MID-cough
       'The child coughed.'

(20) a. **Ia   nyumpah   unduk   Nyoman   ka   tiang.*
       s/he   AF.swear   about   Nyoman   to   I
       'S/he is swearing about Nyoman to me.'

   b. *Ia   ma-sumpah   unduk   Nyoman   ka   tiang*
       s/he   MID-swear   about   Nyoman   to   I
       'S/he is swearing to me about Nyoman.'

   c. *Ia   nyumpah-in   tiang.*
       s/he   AF.swear-GR.APPL   I
       'S/he is swearing to me.'

   d. *Ia   nyumpah-ang   Nyoman   teken   tiang.*
       s/he   AF.swear-FIG.APPL   Nyoman   with   I
       1. 'He swears about Nyoman to me.'
       2. 'He makes Nyoman swear to me.'

The crucial point raised by these precategorial roots is that, despite their precategorial status, applicativized transitive constructions pattern exactly like valency-increasing applicatives (see (4)–(6) above) and transitivity-increasing applicatives (see (7)–(10)), and yet they cannot be characterized either as a valency- or transitivity-increasing processes due to the lack of basic valency associated with these roots.

We have now seen three types of applicatives in Balinese: those that increase valency, those that increase transitivity without increasing the number of arguments, and those that cannot be characterized in terms of increase in valency or transitivity. Yet, they all involve suffixes -*in* or -*ang*, indicating that they are a unified phenomenon. Indeed, they constitute a unified phenomenon if we look at the alignment patterns of Ground and Figure expressions. The -*in* applicative aligns Ground with Object, while the -*ang* applicative aligns Figure with Object. These alignment alternations are the essence of applicativization and thus constitute central, defining properties of this process rather than increase in valency or transitivity (or morphological marking – see below). Increase in valency is simply a side effect under the proposed understanding of applicatives. If the thematic frame of the verb contains all the relevant arguments, as in the case of verbs like GIVE and SEND in many languages, no valency increase is observed. In such a case, only the alignment of O function is altered (with an attendant change in the syntactic status of the relevant arguments). If the basic thematic frame does not include a Ground or Figure argument to be aligned with Object, then it is newly introduced via applicativization with a valency-increasing effect. Balinese presents a somewhat unusual case with precategorial verb roots, whose valency and alignment patterns are determined only via middle or applicative derivation, defying the characterization of these derivation processes as either valency decreasing or increasing.[5]

Balinese applicatives also defy treatment as a syntactic process. As seen earlier, Dixon & Aikhenvald (2000) characterize applicatives as syntactic processes that apply to an intransitive or transitive underlying clause, but Balinese precategorial verb roots do not have a predetermined basic or underlying valence structure. In addition, there are two relevant phenomena that point to the lexical, as opposed to syntactic, derivation analysis of Balinese applicatives. The first of these is that both -*in* and -*ang* applicatives do not freely apply to syntactic structures that meet the structural descriptions of the applicative rules as posited by Dixon & Aikhenvald. As seen above, the *ma*-middle derivation yields an intransitive construction, but it cannot be an input to -*in* applicativization. Compare (21) and (22) below. (22a) has the same syntactic structure as a result of the *ma*-derivation as (21a), yet it cannot form an -*in* applicative construction.

(21) SIT (non-precategorial *tegak*)
    a. Ia   negak   di   kasur=e.   (underived intransitive)
       s/he AF.sit on   bed=DEF
       'S/he sat on the bed.'

---

[5] Precategorials may be widespread among Western Malayo-Polynesian and Formosan languages, in many of which nouns often function as verb roots.

    b. *Ia   negak-in   kasur=e.*   (*-in* derived FIG=OBJ construction)
       s/he   AF.sit-GR.APPL   bed=DEF
       'S/he sat on the bed.'

(22) SIT CROSS-LEGGED (precategorial *sila*)
    a. *Ia   ma-sila   di   kasur=e.*   (*ma*-derived intransitive)
       s/he   MID-sit.cross-legged   on   bed=DEF
       'S/he sat cross-legged on the bed.'

    b. **Ia   ma-sila-in   kasur=e.*
       s/he   MID-sit.cross-legged   bed=DEF
       'S/he sat cross-legged on the bed.'

The *-ang* applicative is also restricted so that it cannot apply to *-in* derived transitive structures. Compare (23a.b) and (23b.c) below:

(23) COVER (*rurub*)
    a. *Ia   ngerurub anak=e   cenik ento aji   saput.* (Underived transitive
       s/he AF.cover person=DEF small that with blanket GR=OBJ construction)
       'S/he covered the child with a blanket.'

    b. *Ia   ngerurub-ang   saput   ka anak=e   cenik ento.*
       s/he AF.cover-FIG.APPL blanket to person=DEF small that
       Lit. 'S/he covered the blanket to the child. (*-ang* derived FIG=OBJ construction)

(24) PUT (*ejang*)
    a. *Ia   ng-ejang   buku=ne   (di   meja=ne).* (Underived transitive
       s/he AF-put   book=DEF (on table=DEF) FIG=OBJ construction)
       'S/he put down the book (on the table).'

    b. *Ia   ng-ejang-in   meja=ne   aji   buku=ne.* (*-in* derived GR=OBJ
       s/he AF.put-GR.APPL table=DEF with book=DEF construction)
       Lit. 'S/he put the table with the book.'

    c. **Ia   ng-ejang-in-ang   buku=ne   ka/di meja=ne.*[6]
       s/he AF-put-GR.APPL-FIG.APPL book=DEF to   table=DEF
       'S/he put the book on the table/Lit. S/he caused the book to put to/on the table.'

---

6 The *-ang* applicativization here is functionally motivated, as it would have the effect of making an optional Ground argument obligatory. Compare (15a) and (18b).

Besides these apparently morphological restrictions on applicative derivations, the fact that certain applicative forms have idiomatic meanings different from the non-applicative counterparts indicates the lexical nature of applicative derivations. For example, the verb *tuut* means to copy someone's work, to imitate or to obey someone. The applicative form *tuut-in* means to obey or to emulate someone. *Pedih* means to be angry or to be angry at someone, while *pedih-in* means either to be angry at someone or to scold someone. *Gedeg* means to hate someone, but *gedeg-ang* means to be angry at someone. *Iget* means to remember someone, but *iget-in* means to recognize someone, to remind someone to do something, or to make someone remember something, whereas *iget-ang* means to make someone remember something or to remind someone to do something. Finally, *tegak di kursi* means 'to sit in a chair', but *tegak-in kursi*, in addition to the literal meaning of sitting in a chair, can mean to occupy a professional post.

The Balinese *-in/-ang* applicatives as lexical derivations yield a verb with specific argument alignment patterns. *Ang*-applicativization yields verbs with caused motion semantics that align a Figure argument with O function. It construes as caused motions both physical motions in space (see (5b), (6b), (9b) and others) and abstract motions of transfer as in (14), as well as metaphorical motions from one state to another, as in *putih-ang* 'whiten', *mati-ang* 'kill', etc., which are usually analyzed as change-of-state verbs. *In*-derivation, on the other hand, yields verbs that align Ground nominals with O function as may be used with surface-contact and fixing verbs.

3 The role of applicative morphology

The above treatment of Balinese applicatives as lexical derivation processes is in line with the recent trend in analyzing parallel constructions in English as lexical phenomena (Pinker 1989; Iwata 2006, 2008). Indeed, many Balinese applicative alternations find parallel counterparts in English, and also in Japanese to some extent, as the translations below show:

(25) a. *-ang* applicative FIG=OBJ construction
 Ia menek-ang somi=ne ka gedebeg=e.
 s/he AF.load-FIG.APPL hay=DEF to cart=DEF
 'S/he **loaded the hay** onto the cart.'

 b. *-in* applicative GR=OBJ constructions
 Ia menek-in gedebeg=e somi.
 s/he AF.load-GR.APPL cart=DEF hay
 'S/he **loaded the cart** with hay.'

(26) a. Underived FIG=OBJ construction
Guru=ne   ngirim   buku=ne ka anak=e   cenik.
teacher=DEF AF.send book=DEF to person=DEF small
'The teacher **sent the book** to the child.'

b. *-in* applicative GR=OBJ construction
Guru=ne   ngirim-in   anak=e   cenik buku=ne.
teacher=DEF AF.send-GR.APPL person=DEF small book=DEF
'The teacher **sent the child** the book.'

(27) a. Underived GR=OBJ construction
Ia   ng-lempag lalipi-ne   aji   tungked.
s/he AF-hit   snake=DEF with stick
'S/he **hit the snake** with a stick.'

b. *-ang* applicative FIG=OBJ construction
Ia   ng-lempag-ang   tungked ka lalipi=ne.
s/he AF-hit-FIG.APPL stick   to snake=DEF
'S/he **hit the stick** against the snake.'

(28) a. Underived GR=OBJ construction
Ia   ngecet   tembok=e aji   cat   pelung
s/he AF.paint wall=DEF with paint blue
'S/he **painted the wall** with blue paint.'

Kare wa **kabe o**   aoi   penki de   nutta.   (Japanese translation)
he   TOP wall ACC blue paint with painted

b. *-ang* applicative FIG=OBJ construction
Ia   ngecet-ang   cat   pelung ka tembok=e.
s/he AF.paint-FIG.APPL paint blue   to wall=DEF
'S/he **painted blue paint** on the wall.'

Kare wa aoi   **penki o**   kabe ni nutta.   (Japanese translation)
he   TOP blue paint ACC wall to painted

These parallel patterns between Balinese, on the one hand, and English and Japanese, on the other, raise an interesting but difficult question, detailed below, about applicative morphology. In fact, the same question can be asked within Balinese as well since the language has one or two verbs that do not require morphology in either the GR=OBJ or the FIG=OBJ pattern. There are two verbs meaning to 'give' in Balinese. One is *baang* 'give' and the other is precategorial *enjuh* 'give'. The former is interesting because it can be used in both FIG=

OBJ and GR=OBJ patterns without morphology when the recipient is human. But it requires -*in* for the GR=OBJ coding pattern when the recipient is non-human. In the case of precategorial *enjuh*, the -*in*/-*ang* morphology needs to be invoked in fixing the valency and the coding pattern.

(29) a. Underived FIG=OBJ construction
Guru=ne   (nge-)maang buku ka anak=e   cenik ento.
teacher=DEF (AF-)AF.give book to person=DEF small that
'The teacher gave the book to the child.'

b. Underived GR=OBJ construction
Guru=ne   (nge-)maang anak=e   cenik ento buku.
teacher=DEF (AF-)AF.give person=DEF small that book
'The teacher gave the child the book.'

(30) a. Underived FIG=OBJ construction
Tiang maang banyu ka celeng=e.
I   AF.give scrap to pig=DEF
'I gave the food scrap to the pig.'

b. -*in* applicative GR=OBJ construction
Tiang maang-in   celeng=e banyu.
I   AF.give-GR.APPL pig=DEF scrap
'I gave the pig food scrap.'

(31) a. *Guru=ne   ng-enjuh-ang   buku ka anak=e   cenik ento.*
teacher=DEF AF-give-FIG.APPL book to person=DEF small that
'The teacher gave the book to the child.'

b. *Guru=ne   ng-enjuh-in   anak=e   cenik ento buku.*
teacher=DEF AF=give=GR.APPL person=DEF small that book
'The teacher gave the child a book.'

The question is two-fold: (i) whether or not the morphologically unmarked patterns (e.g., (29a.b)) should be considered an applicative alternation, and (ii) whether or not morphology accurately indicates the direction of derivation and marks the derivational status of the forms in question, e.g., whether or not morphologically marked forms are in some sense cognitively complex compared to the unmarked counterparts. The same question in a cross-linguistic perspective is: (i) whether the English and Japanese constructions without derivational morphology, as seen in the translations for (25)–(28), should be considered instances of the applicative alternation, and (ii) whether or not one of the pair should be derived from the other member even in the absence of morphology. If the answer to (ii) is positive, then we need to ask how the direction of derivation is to be determined; e.g., following the morphological derivational patterns in Balinese or some other languages? A more general question here is the meaning or the role of morphology when parallel patterns may be achieved with or without morphology.

As for question (i), Dixon & Aikhenvald would answer that those without morphology should not be considered applicative because their definitions include a stipulation that there be "some explicit formal marking of an applicative construction" (see (1)). But considering Balinese forms (25a.b) as displaying an applicative alternation but not the parallel English forms, for example, would miss an obvious parallelism between the (a) versions and the (b) versions in the two languages. Indeed, not treating the English translation forms for the examples (25)–(31) as applicative alternations on the account that there is no morphology is like not treating the English verb *kill* as causative because there is no causative morphology involved in it. Just as valency- or transitivity-increase should not be part of the definitions of applicatives, morphology should not be stipulated in the definitions of applicatives.

As for question (ii), whether a form should be treated as derived even in the absence of morphology, there is a long tradition of permitting such interpretations under the term of "zero derivation", where English nouns such as a (*a*) *play* and (*the*) *walk*, for example, are said to be derived from verbs, as suggested by the term "deverbal nouns". Unfortunately current treatments of this kind of derivation do not generally make it explicit whether the derivation is meant to be a historical process or whether it is meant to capture a particular cognitive status of deverbal nouns.

As for the English applicatives paralleling the Balinese patterns, Pinker (1989) offers a zero-derivation analysis, under the term "locative alternation", deriving either a GR=OBJ or FIG=OBJ construction from the other alternate coding pattern via lexical derivation rules, as rendered diagrammatically below:

(32) a. "container-oriented" (GR=OBJ) verbs; *load, pack, cram, crowd*...

$$\begin{array}{ccc} \text{load}_1 & \rightarrow & \text{load}_2 \\ \text{(Balinese } \textit{benek-in}\text{)} & \text{lexical derivation rule} & \textit{(benek-ang)} \\ \downarrow & & \downarrow \\ \textit{He loaded the} & & \textit{He loaded the hay} \\ \textit{wagon with hay} & & \textit{onto the wagon.} \end{array}$$

b. "content-oriented" (FIG=OBJ) verbs: *spray, smear, pile, scatter...*

    spray$_1$ (*semprot-ang*)   →   spray$_2$ (*semprot(-in)*)
    ↓   ↓
    He sprayed the   *He sprayed the*
    paint on the wall.   *wall with paint.*

Pinker's zero-derivation analysis has been challenged recently by a number of practitioners of Construction Grammar, inter alia by Goldberg (1995) and Iwata (2006, 2008), who reject the account of the English applicative patterns in terms of lexical derivation rules and instead propose directly linking a single form of the relevant verb to the two constructions, as below:

(33) a.

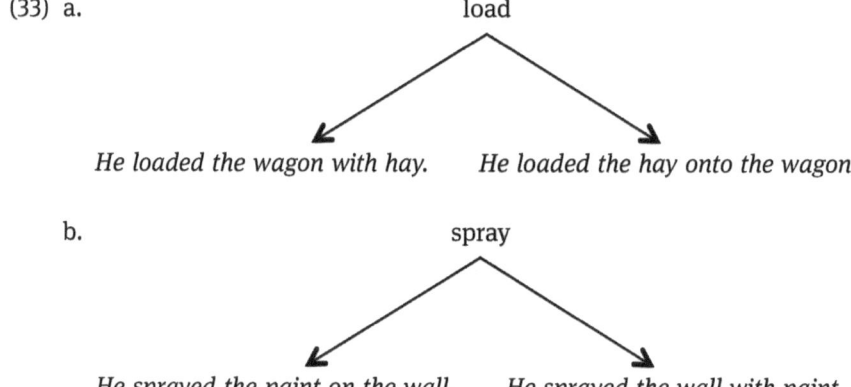

b.

He sprayed the paint on the wall.   *He sprayed the wall with paint.*

Concerning the criterion for derivation, Iwata (2006, 2008) is not explicit but appears to rely on morphology, so that he would analyze only morphologically marked forms as derived from the unmarked counterparts, but not forms lacking in any morphology indicating direction of derivation. This position can be surmised from his (2006) treatment of the German pair of FIG=OBJ and GR=OBJ construction with *spritzen* 'spray' and *bespritzen*, for which Iwata posits a derivation from the unmarked form to the marked counterpart.

(34) a. *Die Randalierer spritzen Farbe auf das Auto.* (FIG=OBJ)
        the vandals   spray   paint onto the car
        'The vandals spray paint onto the car.'

    b. *Die Randalierer be-spritzen das Auto mit Farbe.* (GR=OBJ)
        the vandals   spray   the car with paint

(35) [*spritzen*] → [*be-spritzen*]   (Iwata 2006: 109)

The following quote from Iwata (2008) on Japanese applicative patterns also suggests that he would recognize both derivational and non-derivational analyses of applicatives based on morphological marking:

(36) "the fact that some Japanese verbs enter into the alternation without any morphological changes, along with -*tsukusu* suffixation, means that both types of alternation [ones without derivation and ones with derivation] may co-exist in one and the same language, which in turn indicates that it is not necessary to collapse the two types of alternation into one type by brute force [as in Pinker's (1969) zero-derivation analysis]."

(Iwata 2008: 158)

It is rather surprising that linguists in general tacitly follow morphological indications without asking whether morphology is a reliable indicator for deriving one form from another and without seeking empirical support for a morphology-based analysis.[7] Those who allow zero derivation obviously consider the distinction between word derivation and morphology a relative one, but then the burden of proof on them is even greater – what evidence is there for the derived status of morphologically unmarked forms? In the balance of this chapter I would like to explore the role of morphology in valency alternations, seeking answers to some of the questions posed in the introduction, such as what kind of morphology is functionally motivated and what kind is less meaningful in synchronic analysis.

4 When does morphology count and when does it not?

My studies in this area have been informed by insights garnered in the long, if not always mainstream, functional linguistic tradition. Some notable quotes from this tradition are:

(37) "The more economical or more abundant use of linguistic means of expressing a thought is determined by need...
Everywhere we find modes of expression forced into existence which contain only just so much as is requisite to their being understood."

(Paul 1880)

---

[7] See various studies such as Nichols, et al. (2000) that talk about transitivizing/detransitivizing or causativizing/anticausativizing solely in terms of morphology, disregarding the question of whether or not they are really synchronic processes (see below).

(38) "the length of a word tends to bear an inverse relationship to its relative frequency" (38)
"The magnitude of complexity of speech-configuration...reflects also in an inverse way...the extent to which the category is familiar in common usage." (272)   (Zipf 1935)

While these and more recent functional grammarians and typologists (e.g., Haiman 1985; Dixon 2000) lay greater importance on the physical form of linguistic expressions, my approach to morphology has been more functional in that the notion of productivity and its cognitive import play a far more important role than formal difference in size and complexity. For example, recent studies of causative constructions reveal that morphology plays different roles along a continuum of direct- vs. indirect meaning depending on its productivity, going beyond traditional distinctions in terms of lexical, morphological, and syntactic/periphrastic form. Based on an assumed correlation between low frequency of occurrence of indirect causative situations due to their complexity (and difficulty in bringing them about) and a low degree of familiarity with less frequently occurring situations on the part of speaker, I once proposed the following principle to account for the correlation between the formal dimension (the lexical-morphological-periphrastic continuum) and the semantic dimension (the direct-sociative-indirect continuum) of causative constructions (see also Shibatani & Pardeshi 2002):

(39) **Principle of functional transparency**
Less familiar or unusual situations require functionally more transparent coding.
- Productive morphology, where the form-meaning relationship is easily discernible, is functionally more transparent than irregular morphology or no morphology.
- Periphrastic expression with a clearly distinguishable word form is functionally more transparent than morphological expression in terms of affixation or inflection.

This principle, which is in need of some refinement (see below), is consistent with the thinking in recent functionally-oriented studies of morphology. For example, Haspelmath & Müller-Bardey (2004) point out that "[f]rom this [functionalist] perspective, valence-changing morphemes serve to express an unusual or marked view (or construal) of the event expressed by the predication." These studies give an important empirical underpinning to the role of morphology in terms of usage pattern, for they predict that functionally transparent forms will have lower text frequency than functionally opaque forms. This can be easily demonstrated by checking the text frequency of lexical causatives and unproductive morphological causatives, on the one hand, and highly productive morphological causatives, on the other, as I tried once. My 2004 Google internet search yielded the following counts of Japanese causatives:

(40) a. Unproductive   Productive
        (functionally less transparent)   (functionally more transparent)
        koros-u   464,000   sin-**ase**-ru   3,960
        'kill'   'cause to die'
        tom-**e**-ru   624,000   tomar-**ase**-ru   832
        'stop'   'cause to stop'
        mi-**se**-ru   930,000   mi-**sase**-ru   3,860
        'show'   'cause to see'
        huku=o ki-**se**-ru 6,030   huku=o ki-**sase**-ru   424
        'put clothes on (someone)'   'make someone put on clothes'
        (-u/-ru are present-tense indicative suffixes)

The more controlled 65,479,503–word corpus (NINJAL-LWP corpus) of the National Institute for Japanese Language and Linguistics in Tokyo corroborates the above findings:

(40) b. Unproductive   Productive
        koros-u   5,881   sin-**ase**-ru   159
        'kill'   'cause to die'
        mi-**se**-ru 7,547   mi-**sase**-ru   84
        'show'   'cause to see'
        ki-**se**-ru 503   ki-**sase**-ru   12
        'dress (tr)'   'cause to wear (clothes)'

It is clear from the above that the productive, hence functionally transparent, suffix -(s)ase marks those indirect causative expressions that have low text frequency, whereas the direct causative forms marked by the unproductive, functionally less transparent, suffixes -se and -e occur as frequently as the lexical causative koros-u 'kill'.

In view of the systematic patterning between morphology and argument alignment in the Balinese -in/-ang alternations, it would be highly interesting to see whether the direction of derivation indicated by morphology in any way correlates with the usage patterns of these applicative forms. There are two considerations in pursuing this question. One is that while there is some degree of productivity, -ang/-in alternations are lexically governed and are not entirely productive, unlike the Japanese causative suffix -(s)ase seen above. The second, more practical problem is that there is no readily usable electronic corpus of spoken Balinese available at the moment. Instead, I searched Google for the corresponding applicative suffix forms in Bahasa Indonesia (Standard Indonesian) to see if there are lopsided frequency patterns in the use of the morphologically marked forms and their corresponding unmarked forms. The cursory search revealed the following patterns for these forms:

(41) Basic GR=OBJ form   -kan derived FIG=OBJ form
     mengikat   6,740,000   mengikat-kan   430,000
     'tie'
     menikam   1,040,000   menikam-kan   24,500
     'stab'
     memukal   3,940   memukal-kan   44
     'hit'
     (forms given in AF form)

(42) -i derived GR=OBJ form   Basic FIG=OBJ form
     mengirim-i   293,000   mengirim   35,000,000
     'send'
     melempar-i   536,000   melempar   3,820,000
     'throw'
     menanam-i   192,000   menanam   7,560,000
     'grow'

It is clear from the above counts that morphologically derived forms are far less frequently used than their corresponding basic verb forms, indicating that morphology here positively correlates with usage patterns. The situation, however, is less straightforward when both GR=OBJ and FIG=OBJ forms are morphologically marked.

(43) -i derived GR=OBJ form   -kan derived FIG=OBJ form
     memuat-i   60,000   memuat-kan   1,170,000
     'load'
     menawar-i 5,680,000   menawar-kan   75,800,000
     'offer'
     mengalir-i 274,000   mengalir-kan 2,740,000
     'flood'

If morphology accurately reflected usage patterns, we would expect these morphologically equipollent pairs to show either random or balanced frequency patterns. If the pattern in (43) represents the general picture for equipollent pairs, then we might be seeing a situation where morphology does not correlate with usage patterns. That is, for those verb roots whose role alignment is basically oriented either to GR=OBJ or to FIG=OBJ, the morphologically unmarked-marked contrast accurately reflects the basic/derived distinction, but with many other verb roots, morphological marking simply does not reflect the basic vs. derived distinction, due to morphological constraints. In the case of Balinese and Indonesian, precategorial verb roots impose a requirement that both alternant alignment patterns be morphologically marked, yielding patterns like (43), which might obscure the actual basic/derived contrast. In English there is no morphology associated with applicative alternations, again hiding a possible basic/derived contrast.

To summarize our findings from the admittedly very crude preliminary survey above, we note first that for pairs of unmarked and marked forms, morphology indicates a direction of derivation such that the unmarked forms represent the normal pattern of event construal, while the marked counterparts represent the alternate, unconventional construal. Verbs are divided into two basic groups based on their semantics. Verbs of surface-contact (*lempag* 'hit', *tundik* 'touch', etc.) are Ground-oriented in that they construe Ground as representing an element of greater cognitive saliency than Figure, aligning the former with Object. The Balinese suffix *-ang* and the Indonesian *-kan* suffix mark an alternate unconventional construal that accords greater cognitive saliency to Figure than to Ground. For caused-motion verbs such as *kirim* 'send' and *maling* 'steal', as well as verbs of fixing (*tegul* 'tie', *pacek* 'nail', *elim* 'glue', etc.), the above construal pattern is reversed in that the normal construal takes Figure as cognitively more salient than Ground, aligning the former with Object so that the FIG=OBJ construction is basic. These verbs allow an alternate event construal, where Ground is accorded higher cognitive saliency than Figure, resulting in a GR=OBJ alignment, but at the cost of morphological complexity in the form of *-in* (Balinese) or *-i* (Indonesian) suffixation.

From a morphological point of view, the most interesting case is the equipollent pattern seen in (43) above. Morphology here plays the important grammatical role of marking the alignment patterns, *-i* (or Balinese *-in*) highlighting the GR=OBJ alignment and *-kan* (Balinese *-ang*) the FIG=OBJ alignment. However, morphology does not here mark a difference in derivational status, since both forms are marked. Yet the frequency patterns are in fact skewed in a way highly similar to other morphologically distinguished patterns, as seen in (41) and (42). Indeed, (42) and (43) show a high degree of parallelism, with the forms for FIG=OBJ alignment in the right column far outnumbering the corresponding GR=OBJ forms in the left. If this limited data means anything, the *-kan* marked forms in (43) represent the basic alignment pattern, as do the unmarked forms in (42); both groups of verbs take the FIG=OBJ alignment to be basic, despite the difference in morphological marking patterns. This is an interesting case, if true. In one situation, where verb pairs show a marked/unmarked marking contrast, morphology correlates with the usage pattern, while in another situation, where there is no marking contrast, morphology is less reliable in assessing the cognitive status of alternate syntactic patterns.

Turning now to the controversy over English applicative alternations, here also there is no morphological contrast between GR=OBJ and FIG=OBJ alignment patterns. Interestingly enough, Iwata (2008)'s manual survey of usage patterns reveals a skewing similar to (43), but this time in both directions – the number in the square brackets indicates the number of additional occurrences without a direct object. "82[+29] (with)" for *spray* means that there were 82 instances of the *spray NP with NP* pattern and additional 29 instances of the *spray with NP* pattern.

(44)   GR=OBJ   FIG=OBJ
    spray   82[+29] (with) 6[+1] (onto)
                             1[+1] (onto)
                             14[+6] (on)
                             9 (into)
                             25[+3] (over)
    smear   73 (with)   33[+3] (on)
                             3 (onto)
    pile   121 (with)   60[+1] (on)
                             6[+3] (onto)
    scatter 65 (with)   **167**[+8] (over)
                             60 (around)
                             30 (about)
    spread   124 (with)   **204** (on)
                             91(over)

(Iwata 2008: 15–16)

Iwata's findings above are extremely interesting in that they suggest (i) that these verbs may be associated with a basic orientation, justifying a derivational analysis that would reflect usage patterns, despite lack of morphology, and (ii) that Pinker (1989)'s derivational analysis, however, might be incorrect in that the directions of derivation contradict the usage patterns in many cases. For example, Pinker analyzes *spray, smear,* and *pile* as having the FIG=OBJ alignment as basic and deriving the GR=OBJ alignment pattern (see (32b) above), whereas the usage patterns of these verbs seen in (44) above suggest the opposite. A major problem with Iwata's survey is that he did not count the frequency of the V NP=FIG and the V NP=GR pattern without a prepositional expression (e.g. *He sprayed water* vs. *He sprayed the flowers; He piled the books* vs. **He piled the floor; *He decorated the flowers* vs. *He decorated the room.*). From my perspective (and perhaps for Pinker as well), the frequency of these patterns is very crucial since the essential property of this type of applicative alternation is whether a Figure or a Ground is aligned with Object. This alternation also yields a transitive/intransitive pattern, where a transitive sentence without a prepositional phrase (e.g. an equivalent of *He arrived-APPL Bali*) alternates with an intransitive sentence (*He arrived in Bali*). Obviously, more research is needed to settle the controversy between the derivational (e.g., Pinker 1989) and the non-derivational analysis (e.g. Iwata 2006, 2008) of English applicative alternations.

5 Transitive-intransitive pairs

Languages display various patterns of morphological marking for verbs entering into transitive-intransitive valency alternations. Particularly interesting here are situations where two languages show opposite marking patterns. For example, according to Matsuse & Kiryu (2010: 38), the direction of morphological derivation for certain transitive-intransitive verb pairs is opposite in the Tibeto-Burman language Newar and Japanese, as illustrated below:

(45) Newar   Japanese
    a. **ph**yene   ← **b**yene   hodok-u   → hodok-**e**-ru
       'untie (tr)'   'untie (intr)'   'untie (tr)'   'untie (intr)'
       ta:**chy**āye ← ta:**j**yāye   war-u   → war-**e**-ru
       'break (tr)'   'break (intr)'   'break(tr)'   'break(intr)'
       khuye   ← **g**uye   sak-u   → sak-**e**-ru
       'tear (tr)'   'tear (intr)'   'tear(tr)'   'tear (intr)'
    b. chuw**ae**ke ← chw**ay**   yak-u   → yak-**e**-ru
       'burn (tr)'   'burn (intr)'   'burn (tr)'   'burn (intr)'
       jw**ak**e   ← jw**ay**e   tog-u   → tog-**ar**-u
       'sharpen (tr)' 'sharpen (intr)'   'sharpen (tr)' 'become pointed'

Here again, the co-authors judge the direction of derivation solely on the basis of morphology. They believe that the Newar transitive forms in (45a) are derived from the intransitive because they are traceable to causative formation involving the proto-TB causative prefix *s-, whose reflex is seen as an aspiration in modern Newar forms. The transitive forms in (45b) contain a clearer causativizing -k suffix, which is a productive causative morpheme in the contemporary language. On the other hand, in the Japanese counterpart pairs, the intransitive verbs invariably have an extra marker not seen in their transitive versions. The obvious question we wish answered in the context of this chapter is whether the morphology in (45) really means anything or what the real meaning of the posited directions of derivation is.

Along with Vladimir Nedjalkov's works dating back to the 1960's (e.g., Nedjalkov & Sil'nickij 1969/1973), Jacobsen (1982/1992) is a seminal work that examines the extra-grammatical meaning of morphological marking in transitive-intransitive verb pairs. Dealing with pairs of morphologically related transitive and intransitive verbs in Japanese, he tells us that "[c]ertain types of change are perceived as normally occurring of their own accord or as being brought about by an entity in itself, while others are perceived as normally being brought about under the influence of some outside entity" and gives two tables of transitive-intransitive verb pairs, one table listing pairs of verbs whose intransitive forms contain the extra -e formative and the other listing pairs with the opposite marking pattern between transitive and intransitive members (Jacobsen 1992: 11, 76–77). Jacobsen's point is that unmarked transitives denote changes "perceived as normally being brought about under the influence of some outside entity" (see (46) below) and the unmarked intransitives represent "types of change... perceived as normally occurring of their own accord" (see (47) below), suggesting that the -e formative marks the types of changes opposite to these normal perceptions of events.

If morphology and our world view, as described by Jacobsen, were connected in a straightforward manner, the opposite patterns of morphological marking between Newar and Japanese shown in (45) would have an interesting implication for human cognition. Jacobsen, of course, is fully aware that morphology and our world view are not connected straightforwardly, noting the possibility that historical changes may obscure the connection (see Jacobsen's paper in this volume on this and related issues). What is lacking in Jacobsen's work, however, is a discussion of when morphology counts and when it does not and empirical support for his claims. That is, a general question remains as to whether the morphological patterns between transitive and intransitive verbs in modern Japanese (and also in other languages) have synchronic relevance. I, therefore, conducted a Google internet search to see whether the transitive-intransitive marking patterns in Japanese correlate with usage patterns as in the case of the productive causative morpheme seen above. Table (46) below lists Jacobsen's verbs, where the transitive forms are unmarked and the intransitive counterparts marked by -e. Since those events "perceived as normally being brought about under the influence of some outside entity" are likely to occur as causative/transitive events more frequently and are likely to be talked about more often in such terms, we would expect the unmarked transitive forms denoting them to be used more frequently than the corresponding morphologically marked intransitives representing the less expected non-causative, spontaneous framing of the relevant events.

(46) -Ø (Transitive)   -e (Intransitive)
  a. kir-u   'cut'   46,000,000   kir-e-ru   25,200,000
     yak-u   'burn'   23,200,000   yak-e-ru   5,640,000
     hag-u   'peel off'   22,100,000   hag-e-ru   603,000
     yabur-u   'tear off'   7,070,000   yabur-e-ru   2,500,000
     war-u   'break'   7,940,000   war-e-ru   6,390,000

  b. nuk-u   'pull out'   25,500,000   nuk-e-ru   **30,400,000**
     or-u   'break off'   4,300,000   or-e-ru   **6,160,000**
     tur-u   'fish'   7,880,000   tur-e-ru   **9,470,000**
     sak-u   'split'   980,000   sak-e-ru   **1,090,000**

Contrary to our expectation, just about a half of Jacobsen's verb pairs show that the marked intransitive forms occur more frequently than the unmarked transitive forms. Jacobsen's second list fares better, where the unmarked forms are intransitive and the -e marked forms transitive; yet there are enough verb pairs of the same type outside Jacobsen's list whose frequency patterns are counter to our expectation (see (47b)).

(47) -Ø (Intransitive)   -e (Transitive)
  a. ak-u   'open'   373,000,000   ak-e-ru   32,200,000
     ukabu   'float'   22,000,000   ukab-e-ru   3,300,000
     sizum-u   'sink'   10,100,000   sizum-e-ru   1,750,000
     tizim-u   'shrink'   2,870,000   tizim-e-ru   1,350,000
     muk-u   'face'   17,900,000   muk-e-ru   11,900,000
     tat-u   'stand up'   49,500,000   tat-e-ru   34,500,000
     narab-u   'line up'   32,400,000   narab-e-ru   12,100,000
     susum-u   'advance'   26,800,000   susum-e-ru   9,730,000
     sirizok-u 'retreat'   2,300,000   sirizok-e-ru   793,000
     kurusim-u 'agonize'   12,600,000   kurusim-e-ru 2,210,000
     itam-u   'hurt'   7,590,000   itam-e-ru   645,000

b. *tuk-u* 'attach' 43,900,000 *tuk-e-ru* **75,000,000**
　sodat-u 'grow' 15,300,000 *sodat-e-ru* **32,400,000**
　kagam-u 'bend down' 162,000 *kagam-e-ru* **309,000**
　yawarag-u 'soften' 1,400,000 *yawarag-e-ru* **2,870,000**
　tat-u 'build up' 8,100,000 *tat-e-ru* **18,700,000**

The above pattern is perhaps less surprising in view of the fact that the *-e* marking is seen in both intransitive and transitive verbs, and therefore the marking itself is not functionally transparent. A comparison of *tat-u/tat-e-ru* 'stand up' in the middle of (47a) and the homophonous, and no doubt etymologically related, *tat-u/tat-e-ru* 'build up' at the bottom of (47b), reveals both (i) that the -Ø intransitive/-*e* transitive pairs may have had a better correlation in the past with the normal/unexpected situation types, and (ii) that there are cases where the verbal meaning dictates usage patterns, rendering the morphological marking irrelevant to text frequency.[8]

The intransitive verb *tat-u* 'build up' is one of those intransitive verbs that Kindaichi (1957) characterizes as expressing changes-of-state resulting from anterior actions or processes. As such, the intransitive events expressed by these verbs, dubbed "middle verbs" by these authors, presuppose the corresponding transitive events. The result is that the transitive use of the verb outranks the intransitive use:

(48) a. -Ø (Intransitive)   -*e* (Transitive)
　　　tenazuk-u ' become tamed' 997 *tenazuk-e-ru* **155,000**
　　　totono-u 'become orderly' 1,110,000 *totono-e-ru* **7,400,000**

　　b. -*e* (Intransitive)   -Ø (Transitive)
　　　ni-e-ru 'become cooked' 241,000 *ni-ru* **5,150,000**
　　　tak-e-ru '(rice) gets cooked' 1,100,000 *tak-u* **4,290,000**

　　c. -*ar* (Intransitive)   -*e* (Transitive)
　　　uw-ar-u 'get planted' 155,000 *u(w)-e-ru* **4,490,000**
　　　kim-ar-u 'get decided' 28,500,000 *kim-e-ru* **53,000,000**

We see above three different morphological marking patterns, but, regardless of the morphology, the transitive versions are far more frequently used.

---

8 See Narrog (2007) on the correlations between morphological marking and frequency patterns in Old Japanese. He sees better correlations following the marking patterns in the OJ data he examined, pointing to the importance of taking a historical perspective into consideration in this type of research.

This is a clear case where morphology does not correlate with usage patterns; thus, there is little motivation for synchronically deriving transitive and intransitive forms following the morphological marking patterns.

In addition to these cases, where morphology does not correlate straightforwardly with usage patterns, there are situations where morphology counts more. These are cases where the transitivizing formatives are functionally more transparent due to their resemblance to the modern productive causative suffix *-(s)ase*. Irrespective of the morphological relationship to the intransitive/transitive counterparts, the transitive/ditransitive versions occur less frequently than the corresponding intransitive versions, though there are some exceptions to this tendency.

(49) a. -Ø (Intransitive/Transitive)   *-as* (Transitive/Ditansitive)
      kawak-u 'dry' **5,320,000**   *kawak-as-u* 2,860,000
      tir-u 'fall/scatter' **11,300,000**   *tir-as-u* 5,730,000
      hukuram-u 'inflate' **5,290,000**   *hukuram-as-u* 739,000
      haram-u 'become pregnant' **618,000**   *haram-as-u* 66,400

    b. *-e* (Intransitive)   *-as* (Transitive)
      kar-e-ru 'wither' **2,930,000**   *kar-as-u* 537,000
      tok-eru 'melt' **7,130,000**   *tok-as-u* 2,860,000
      sam-e-ru 'awaken' **6,580,000**   *sam-as-u* 3,470,000

    c. (-Ø/)-e (Intransitive)   *-as* (Transitive)
      mor-e-ru 'burn' **5,490,000**   *mor-as-u* 4,680,00

    d. *-r* (Intransitive)   *-s* (Transitive)
      noko-r-u 'be left over' **73,600,000**   *noko-s-u* 46,800,000
      mawa-r-u 'turn around' **30,500,000**   *mawa-s-u* 21,900,000
      wata-r-u 'cross' **22,600,000**   *wata-s-u* 20,600,000

    e. -Ø (Intransitive/Transitive)   *-(ka)se* (Transitive/Ditransitive)
      mi-ru 'see' **3,030,000,000**   *mi-se-ru* 'show' 58,400,000
      ki-ru 'wear' **28,900,000**   *ki-se-ru* 'put clothes on someone' 2,710,000
      ne-ru 'sleep' **85,400,000**   *ne-kase-ru* 'put to sleep' 1,700,000

Functional transparency in morphological marking is likely correlated with the historical depth of the markers; the older the marker is, the less functionally transparent it is due to possible layering of morphological processes and loss of productivity. Indeed, the least transparent morphological patterns involving the -*e* formative (see (46)–(47)) are generally believed to be the oldest transitivity alternation patterns by specialists of Japanese, some of whom further believe the functionally most transparent -*as* formative discussed above to be the most recently developed transitive marker, with a less restricted occurrence morphophonologically compared to other functionally similar formatives such as -*r*, -*s*, and -*e* (Kuginuki 1996; Mabuchi 1999).[9] This and other formatives discussed in this section are unproductive, hence lexicalized, in modern Japanese, and are generally considered to be part of their verb roots, despite morphological – not functional – transparency (cf.*war-u* 'break (tr)' vis-à-vis *war-e-ru* 'break (intr)', *tat-u* 'stand (intr)' vis-à-vis *tat-e-ru* 'stand (tr)', *mi-ru* 'see (tr)' vis-à-vis *mi-se-ru* 'show', etc.). Again, the difference in functional transparency due to a difference in productivity accounts for the low frequency of causatives involving the productive suffix -*(s)ase* compared to unproductive causative forms. Compare the following with the transitive/ditransitive causatives in the right-hand column in (49), especially the parallel forms in (49e).

(50) Causatives with productive suffix -*(s)ase*
  mi-sase-ru   'make see'   295,000
  ki-sase-ru   'make wear clothes'   269,000
  ne-sase-ru   'make sleep'   63,300

This brings us back to the Newari case briefly discussed at the beginning of this section. Contrary to the directions of derivation marked the same way by Matsuse & Kiryu (2010), the derivation of the transitive forms in (45a) is only valid as a historical account, whereas the derivation of transitive forms in (45b) by the productive causative suffix -*k* is likely meaningful as a synchronic description; the two must be kept apart. In a similar vein, the function of the productive Newari causative -*k*, which freely attaches to various transitive verbs as well, is not comparable to the restricted function of the Japanese -*e* and -*ar* formatives in the right-hand column of (45b).

6 The Principle of Functional Transparency again

Before concluding this chapter, let us return to the Principle of Functional Transparency discussed earlier. The principle, as phrased in (39), needs refinement in view of some of the applicative patterns examined earlier and the morphological

---

[9] As for intransitivizing formatives, we expect the formative -*ar*, which resembles the passive morpheme -*(r)are* (-*(r)ar* in Old Japanese) to be more functionally transparent than other intransitivizing formatives.

patterns seen in transitivity alternations discussed above. With regard to applicative alternations, we have seen two cases where morphological marking patterns do not reflect possible basic/derived distinctions. One is where both GR=OBJ and FIG=OBJ alignment patterns are morphologically marked (see (43)), and the other is the English case where both patterns are unmarked. Transitivity alternations also exhibit situations where the functional difference is not indicated by morphological marking, either where both transitive and intransitive members of a pair are marked (see (49b–d) above), or unmarked, as in the case of English labile verbs. That morphological markedness and conceptual complexity are not entirely isomorphic has been widely observed (Croft 1990/2003). Morphological markedness theory demands only that a commonplace, familiar concept not be formally more marked than the complex counterpart category. In other words, a familiar concept can be morphologically as marked or unmarked as the complex counterpart concept, but if there is a difference in morphological complexity, it is the complex concept that is associated with the marked morphological category. Taking this general situation into account, I propose to revise the Principle of Functional Transparency as follows:

(51) Principle of Functional Transparency (revised)
A less familiar concept/experience/situation requires formal coding that is equal to or greater in functional transparency than that expressing a familiar concept/experience/situation in the relevant functional domain.
 – Productive morphology, where the form-meaning relationship is easily discernible, is functionally more transparent than irregular morphology or no morphology.
 – Periphrastic expression with a clearly distinguishable word form is functionally more transparent than morphological expression in terms of affixation or inflection.

To summarize the correlations, productivity is defined in terms of type frequency, where a construction type more widely instantiated (e.g., the English -ed past forms (*walked, killed,* etc.)) is more productive than the one instantiated by fewer forms (e.g., the English -ew past forms (*flew, threw,* etc.)). Familiarity of a concept/experience/situation is correlated with token frequency. We tend to talk more about familiar experiences than unfamiliar ones. Accordingly, words denoting a familiar concept/experience/situation are heard and used more frequently than those representing an unusual concept/experience/situation. The Principle of Functional Transparency demands functionally transparent coding for unusual experiences as a way to compensate for their unpredictability. If unusual, less familiar experiences add to conceptual complexity, then the

Principle captures the relationship between grammatical coding and conceptual complexity. The key point here is the notion of "functionally transparent coding" rather than any kind of morphological or structural complexity. This point has not been made sufficiently clear in past studies on the correlation between formal complexity and conceptual complexity.

7 Conclusion

Discussion and analysis of valency alternation phenomena, including applicative and transitive-intransitive alternations, have tended to be based on morphology. The importance attached to morphology is seen in both definitions of the relevant phenomena/constructions and analyses of the phenomena. This chapter has called into question the wisdom of an uncritical reliance on morphology in both of these areas and has attempted to show that there are both meaningful and less dependable morphological patterns. Similar to the Dixon–Aikhenvald definitions of applicatives, the Leningrad/St. Petersburg typologists define voice as follows: "[Voice] is **a regular marking in the verb** of the correspondences between units at the syntactic level and units at the semantic level. In short, voice is a diathesis grammatically marked in the verb." (Xolodovič 1970 as quoted in Geniušienė 1987: 42–53; emphasis added) These definitions are unnecessarily restrictive, resulting in the exclusion of those morphologically unmarked instances that share the essential syntactic and functional features of the relevant phenomena such as the English applicative alternations and various voice phenomena in isolating languages, where there is no grammatical marking in the verb.

Purely morphological analysis yields various types of word formatives, but not all of them have the same grammatical status. Some are historical relics, while others are productive and active in synchronic word formation processes. Talking about derivations purely based on morphology, as is often done in discussions of transitive-intransitive verb pairs, without ascertaining the productivity of the relevant formatives, risks lacking any synchronic relevance. This chapter has attempted to illustrate these points by examining the correlation between morphological marking and usage patterns, which is one method of making morphological studies empirical. Admittedly, Google search results are not an entirely reliable indicator of usage patterns. But as Tables (40a) and (40b) show, Google search results do not seem to be off the mark entirely. If the present work prompts further empirical research in this vein based on a better controlled and more reliable database, its purpose is fulfilled.

Abbreviations

AF actor focus; DEF definite; PF patient focus; GR ground; APPL applicative; POSS possessive; FIG figure; MID middle voice

Acknowledgments

I am indebted to Wesley Jacobsen and Heiko Narrog as well as an anonymous reviewer for their useful comments in improving the content and the readability of this paper. This work was supported in part by National Science Foundation grant BCS-0617198.

References

Artawa, Ketut. 1994. *Ergativity and Balinese syntax*. Melbourne: La Trobe University dissertation.
Croft, Wiliiam. 1990/2003. *Typology and universals*. Cambridge: Cambridge University Press.
Dixon, R. M. W. 2000. A typology of causatives: form, syntax and meaning. In R. M. W. Dixon & Alexandra Y. Aikhenvald (eds.), *Changing valency: Case studies in transitivity*, 30–83. Cambridge: Cambridge University Press.
Dixon, R. M. W. & Alexandra Y. Aikhenvald. 2000. Introduction. In R. M. W. Dixon & Alexandra Y. Aikhenvald (eds.), *Changing valency: Case studies in transitivity*, 1–29. Cambridge: Cambridge University Press.
Geniušienė, Emma. 1987. *The typology of reflexives*. Berlin & New York: Mouton de Gruyter.
Goldberg, Adele. 1985. *Constructions: A construction grammar approach to argument structure*. Chicago: University of Chicago Press.
Haiman, John. 1983. Iconic and economic motivation. *Language* 59. 781–819.
Haspelmath, Martin & Thomas Müller-Bardey. 2004. Valency change. In Geert Booij, Christian Lehmann & Joachim Mugdan (eds.) *Morphology: A handbook on inflection and word formation*, vol. 2. (Handbücher zur Sprach-und Kommunikationswissenschaft), 1130–1145. Berlin & New York: de Gruyter.
Iwata, Seizi. 2006. *A lexical constructional approach to the locative alternation: with special reference to English and Japanese*. Research report for a Ministry of Education grant-in-aid for the years 2003–2005.
Iwata, Seizi. 2008. *Locative alternation: A lexical-constructional approach*. Amsterdam & Philadelphia: John Benjamins.
Jacobsen, Wesley. 1982. *Transitivity in the Japanese verbal system*. Chicago: University of Chicago dissertation.
Jacobsen, Wesley. 1992. *The transitive structure of events in Japanese*. Tokyo: Kurosio Publishers.
Jacobsen, Wesley M. this volume. The semantic basis of Japanese transitive-intransitive derivational patterns. In Taro Kageyama & Wesley M. Jacobsen (eds.), *Transitivity and valency alternations: Studies on Japanese and beyond*. Berlin & Boston: De Gruyter Mouton.

Kindaichi, Haruhiko 1957. Toki, tai, sō oyobi hō [Time, voice, aspect and mood]. *Nihon bunpō kōza*, 223–245. Tokyo: Meiji Shoin.
Kuginuki, Toru. 1996. *Kodai Nihongo no keitaihenka* [Morphological changes in Old Japanese]. Osaka: Izumi Shoin.
Mabuchi, Kazuo. 1999. *Kodai Nihongo no sugata* [The form of Old Japanese]. Tokyo: Musashino Shoin.
Matsuse, Ikuko & Kazuyuki Kiryu. 2010. Newāru-go ni okeru jidōshi to tadōshi no taiō [Intransitive-transitive correspondences in Newar]. In Yoshihiro Nishimitsu & Prashant Pardeshi (eds.), *Jidōshi tadōshi no taishō* [Comparison of transitive and intransitive verbs], 33–68. Tokyo: Kurosio Publishers.
Narrog, Heiko. 2007. Nihongo jita dōshi-tsui no yūhyōseisa no dōkizuke [Motivating the markedness differences in the intransitive-transitive verb pairs in Japanese]. In Mie Tsunoda, Kan Sasaki & Tōru Shionoya (eds.) *Tadōsei no tsūgengo-teki kenkyū* [Crosslinguistic studies in transitivity], 295–306. Tokyo: Kurosio Publishers.
Nedjalkov, Vladimir P. & Georgij G. Sil'nickij. 1969. Tipologija morfologičeskogo i leksičeskogo kauzativov [Typology of morphological and lexical causatives]. In A. A. Xolodovič (ed.), *Tipologija kauzativnyx konstrukcij*, 20–60. Leningrad: Nauka.
Nedyalkov, Vladimir P. & Georgij G. Sil'nitsky. 1973. The typology of morphological and lexical causatives. In Ferenc Kiefer (ed.), *Trends in Soviet theoretical linguistics*, 1–32. Dordrecht: Reidel.
Nichols, Johanna, David A. Peterson & Jonathan Barnes. 2004. Transitivizing and detransitivizing languages. *Linguistic Typology* 8 (2). 149–211.
Paul, Hermann.1880. *Prinzipien der Sprachgeschichte*. Transl. into English by H.A. Strong as *Principles of the History of Language*, 1889; reprint of 8th edition 1970.
Pinker, Steven. 1989. *Learnability and cognition: The acquisition of argument structure*. Cambridge, MA: MIT Press
Shibatani, Masayoshi. 2002. A colloquium talk on the form of causative constructions. Department of Linguistics, Rice University.
Shibatani, Masayoshi & Prashant Pardeshi. 2002. The causative continuum. In Masayoshi Shibatani (ed.), *The grammar of causation and interpersonal manipulation*, 85–126. Amsterdam & Philadelphia: John Benjamins.
Shibatani, Masayoshi & Ketut Artawa. 2015. Balinese valency classes. In Andrej Malchukov & Bernard Comrie (eds.), *Valency classes in the world's languages*, 857–920. Berlin & Boston: De Gruyter Mouton.
Zipf, George Kingsley. 1935. *The psycho-biology of language: An introduction to dynamic philology*. Boston: Houghton Mifflin.

Appendix A: List of core causativity pairs in Japanese (by Yo Matsumoto, a revision of Jacobsen (1992))

#	marked-ness type	affix & stem-final sound	Noncausative V		Causative V		base stem-final sound	Under-goer	Causal nature	broad semantic class	narrow semantic class	notes on listing	semantic notes
1	1	0 / -e	ak-u	open (vi)	ak-e-ru	open (vt)	k	I/N	F	ObjCh	sp-rel		
2	1	0 / -e	akaram-u	redden (vi)	akaram-e-ru	let redden	m	H/A		AniCh	outer	not in J	c-int
3	1	0 / -e	dok-u	get out of the way	dok-e-ru	put out of the way	k	H/A		AniMo	loc+state	cf. A39	tr/dtr
4	1	0 / -e	hisom-u	lurk	hisom-e-ru	hide (self)	m	I/N		AniCh	outer		
5	1	0 / -e	hukum-u	include (in self)	hukum-e-ru	include (in another)	m	I/N		ObjCh	sp-rel		
6	1	0 / -e	hus-u	lie down	hus-e-ru	lay down	s	H/A		AniCh	outer		
7	1	0 / -e	itam-u	hurt	itam-e-ru	injure	m	H/A	F	AniCh	outer		
8	1	0 / -e	kagam-u	stoop, get bent	kagam-e-ru	bend (one's body)	m	H/A		AniCh	outer	cf. A210	c-int
9	1	0 / -e	kanasim-u	grieve	kanasim-e-ru	make grieve	m	H/A		AniCh	psych	not in J	
10	1	0 / -e	kanaw-u	come true	kanaw-e-ru	make come true	w	I/N	S	ObjCh	abst	not in J	
11	1	0 / -e	karam-u	twine around	karam-e-ru	entwine	m	I/N	H(eff)	ObjCh	sp-rel	cf. A212	
12	1	0 / -e	kasig-u	lean (vi)	kasig-e-ru	lean (one's head)	g	H/A		AniCh	outer	not in J	c-int
13	1	0 / -e	kubom-u	become hollow	kubom-e-ru	make hollow	m	I/N	F	ObjCh	shape	not in J	
14	1	0 / -e	kurusim-u	suffer	kurusim-e-ru	torment	m	H/A	S	AniCh	psych		
15	1	0 / -e	muk-u	face toward	muk-e-ru	turn ... toward	k	I/N		ObjCh	sp-rel		
16	1	0 / -e	narab-u	line up (vi)	narab-e-ru	line up (vt)	b	I/N		AniMo	loc+state		
17	1	0 / -e	nok-u	get out of the way	nok-e-ru	remove	k	I/N		AniMo	loc+state	not in J	
18	1	0 / -e	sirizok-u	retreat	sirizok-e-ru	drive away	k	H/A		AniMo	path		
19	1	0 / -e	sitagaw-u	obey, follow	sitagaw-e-ru	make ... follow obediently	w	I/N	H(soc)	NeutMo	path		spec-m
20	1	0 / -e	sizum-u	sink (vi)	sizum-e-ru	sink (vt)	m	I/N	N	NeuMo	loc+state		
21	1	0 / -e	sodat-u	grow up	sodat-e-ru	bring up, raise	t	H/A	N	AniCh	bio		
22	1	0 / -e	sorow-u	become complete (as a set)	sorow-e-ru	collect completely (as a set)	w	I/N	H(eff)	ObjCh	semi-abst		
23	1	0 / -e	subom-u	become thinner/shrunk	subom-e-ru	make thinner, shrink	m	I/N		ObjCh	shape	cf. A238	
24	1	0 / -e	sukum-u	cower	sukum-e-ru	shrug, duck (one's head)	m	I/N		AniCh	outer		c-int
25	1	0 / -e	susum-u	advance (vi)	susum-e-ru	advance (vt)	m	I/N		NeuMo	path		
26	1	0 / -e	tat-u	stand (vi)	tat-e-ru	stand (vt)	t	H/A		AniCh	outer		
27	1	0 / -e	tawam-u	bend, curve (vi)	tawam-e-ru	bend, curve (vt)	m	I/N	F	ObjCh	shape		

#	marked-ness type	affix & stem-final sound	Noncausative V		Causative V		base stem-final sound	Under-goer	Causal nature	broad semantic class	narrow semantic class	notes on listing	semantic notes
28	I	0 / -e	tizim-u	shrink (vi)	tizim-e-ru	shrink (vt)	m	I/N		DegCh	loc+state	cf. A241	
29	I	0 / -e	todok-u	be delivered, reach	todok-u	deliver	k	I/N	H(soc)	NeuMo	semi-abst		spec-m
30	I	0 / -e	totonow-u	become ready	totonow-e-ru	make ready	w	I/N	H(care)	ObjCh	sp-rel	not in J	
31	I	0 / -e	tuk-u	adhere to	tuk-e-ru	attach	k	I/N		ObjCh	aspect		
32	I	0 / -e	tuzuk-u	continue (vi)	tuzuk-e-ru	continue (vt)	k	I/N		ObjCh	loc+state		
33	I	0 / -e	ukab-u	float (vi)	ukab-e-ru	float (vt)	b	I/N	N	NeuMo	aspect		ext-m
34	I	0 / -e	yam-u	cease	yam-e-ru	stop (one's action)	m	I/N		ObjCh	inner		c-int
35	I	0 / -e	yasum-u	take a rest	yasum-e-ru	put (one's body) to rest	m	H/A		AniCh	inner	cf. A253	
36	I	0 / -e	yawarag-u	become soft/mild	yawarag-e-ru	soften, mitigate	g	I/N		ObjCh	semi-abst		
37	I	0 / -e	yugam-u	be warped/distorted	yugam-e-ru	warp (vt), distort	m	I/N	F	ObjCh	shape	cf. B80	
38	I	0 / -e	yurum-u	become loose	yurum-e-ru	loosen	m	I/N		ObjCh	physical		
39	I	0 / -as	dok-u	get out of the way	dok-as-u	remove	k	I/N		AniMo	loc+state	not in J; cf. A3	
40	I	0 / -as	hekom-u	become dented	hekom-as-u	dent	m	I/N	F	ObjCh	shape		
41	I	0 / -as	her-u	decrease (vi)	her-as-u	decrease (vt)	r	I/N		DegCh			
42	I	0 / -as	hur-u	rain, fall	hur-as-u	make (rain) fall	r	I/N	N	NeuMo	path		tr/dtr
43	I	0 / -as	kam-u	bite, chew	kam-as-u	put between teeth	m	H/A	N	AniCh	other	not in J	
44	I	0 / -as	kawak-u	dry (vi)	kawak-as-u	dry (vt)	k	I/N	N	ObjCh	physical		
45	I	0 / -as	koor-u	freeze (vi)	koor-as-u	freeze (vt)	r	I/N		ObjCh	physical		
46	I	0 / -as	kik-u	take effect	kik-as-u	use, exercise	k	I/N		AniCh	abst		spec-m
47	I	0 / -as	korob-u	tumble, fall	korob-as-u	trip (vt)	b	H/A		AniCh	outer	not in J	
48	I	0 / -as	kuram-u	become dizzy	kuram-as-u	make dizzy	m	I/N	S	AniCh	inner	not in J	
49	I	0 / -as	kuw-u	eat	kuw-as-u	feed	w	H/A		AniCh	other	not in J	
50	I	0 / -as	madow-u	get perplexed	madow-as-u	perplex	w	I/N	S	AniCh	psych		
51	I	0 / -as	mayow-u	become bewildered	mayow-as-u	bewilder	w	I/N	S	AniCh	psych		
52	I	0 / -as	megur-u	go around	megur-as-u	make go around	r	I/N		NeuMo	path	cf. A103	tr/dtr
53	I	0 / -as	mor-u	leak (vi)	mor-as-u	leak (vt)	r	I/N		NeuMo	other		
54	I	0 / -as	nar-u	ring (vi)	nar-as-u	ring (vt)	r	I/N		ObjCh	other		
55	I	0 / -as	naraw-u	learn	naraw-as-u	make learn, accustom	w	H/A	H(soc)	AniCh	pos	not in J	ext-m
56	I	0 / -as	nayam-u	be troubled	nayam-as-u	trouble	m	H/A	S	AniCh	psych		
57	I	0 / -as	odorok-u	get surprised	odorok-as-u	surprise	k	H/A	S	AniCh	psych		
58	I	0 / -as	sek-u	hurry (vi)	sek-as-u	hurry (vt)	k	H/A		AniMo	manner	not in J	
59	I	0 / -as	sor-u	get warped	sor-as-u	warp	r	I/N		ObjCh	shape	cf. A113	

Appendix A — 481

#	marked-ness type	affix & stem-final sound	Noncausative V		Causative V		base stem-final sound	Under-goer	Causal nature	broad semantic class	narrow semantic class	notes on listing	semantic notes
60	I	0 / -as	suk-u	get hungry/sparse	suk-as-u	make hungry	k	H/A	N	AniCh	inner	cf. A114	
61	I	0 / -as	sum-u	end (vi)	sum-as-u	finish	m	I/N		ObjCh	aspect		
62	I	0 / -as	tir-u	scatter (vi), fall	tir-as-u	scatter (vt)	r	I/N	N	NeuMo	loc+state		
63	I	0 / -as	tob-u	fly (vi)	tob-as-u	fly (vt)	b	H/A		AniMo	manner	not in J	
64	I	0 / -as	tokimek-u	be thrilled	tokimek-as-u	thrill	k	H/A	S	AniCh	psych		
65	I	0 / -as	tom-u	be rich	tom-as-u	make rich	m	H/A		AniCh	pos		
66	I	0 / -as	ugok-u	move (vi)	ugok-as-u	move (vt)	k	I/N		NeuMo	other		
67	I	0 / -as	ugomek-u	wriggle	ugomek-as-u	wriggle (one's body)	k	I/N	N	NeuMo	other	not in J	
68	I	0 / -as	uk-u	float (vi)	uk-as-u	float (vt)	k	I/N		NeuMo	manner	not in J	
69	I	0 / -as	wak-u	boil (vi)	wak-as-u	boil (vt)	k	I/N	H(tool)	ObjCh	physical		
70	I	0 / -as	yurug-u	get shaken	yurug-as-u	shake the foundation of	g	I/N	F	ObjCh	abst	not in J	
71	I	0 / -ase	aw-u	meet, match	aw-ase-u	put together	w	I/N		ObjCh	sp-rel		spec-m
72	I	0 / -ase	nozok-u	peep out	nozok-ase-u	let … peep out	k	I/N		ObjCh	semi-abst	not in J	spec-m
73	I	0 / -ase	sinob-u	endure, hide self from	sinob-ase-u	conceal	b	H/A		AniCh	abst	not in J	
74	I	0 / -os	horob-u	meet with ruin	horob-os-u	ruin	b	H/A	F	AniCh	exist	not in J; cf. A138	
75	I	0 / -os	oyob-u	reach	oyob-os-u	extend (influence) to	b	I/N		NeuMo	path		
76	I	0 / -se	abi-ru	have … poured over oneself	abi-se-ru	pour … over	i	I/N		NeuMo	loc+state		tr/dtr
77	I	0 / -se	ki-ru	get dressed, put on	ki-se-ru	dress, put on (other's body)	i	H/A		AniCh	pos		tr/dtr
78	I	0 / -se	mi-ru	see	mi-se-ru	show	i	H/A		AniCh	inner		tr/dtr
79	I	0 / -se	ne-ru	go to sleep	ne-se-ru	put to sleep	e	I/N	N	ObjCh	inner	not in J; cf. A81	
80	I	0 / -se	ni-ru	resemble	ni-se-ru	model after	i	I/N		ObjCh	semi-abst		
81	I	0 / -kase	ne-ru	go to sleep	ne-kase-ru	put to sleep	e	H/A	N	AniCh	inner	cf. A79	
82	I	(e) / -as	ake-ru	dawn	ak-as-u	pass (the night)	ke	I/N	N	ObjCh	semi-abst		ext-m
83	I	(e) / -as	are-ru	get rough	ar-as-u	ravage	re	I/N	F	ObjCh	semi-abst		
84	I	(e) / -as	bake-ru	turn into	bak-as-u	bewitch	ke	I/N	H(soc)	ObjCh	abst		
85	I	(e) / -as	bare-ru	come to light	bar-as-u	expose	re	I/N		ObjCh	abst		
86	I	(e) / -as	boke-ru	become blurred	bok-as-u	make blurred	ke	I/N		ObjCh	physical		
87	I	(e) / -as	de-ru	go out	d-as-u	take out	de	I/N		NeuMo	path		
88	I	(e) / -as	hage-ru	peel off (vi)	hag-as-u	peel off (vt)	ge	I/N	N	ObjCh	disinteg	cf. A147, A286	
89	I	(e) / -as	hare-ru	swell	har-as-u	make swell	re	I/N	F	AniCh	outer	not in J	
90	I	(e) / -as	hare-ru	clear up (vi)	har-as-u	clear (one's feelings)	re	H/A		AniCh	psych		spec-m

482 — Appendix A

#	marked-ness type	affix & stem-final sound	Noncausative V	Causative V	base stem-final sound	Under-goer	Causal nature	broad semantic class	narrow semantic class	notes on listing	semantic notes
91	I	(e) / -as	haye-ru	grow out of ground	hay-as-u	let grow	ye	H/A	N	AniCh	bio		
92	I	(e) / -as	hiye-ru	become colder	hiy-as-u	make colder	ye	I/N		DegCh			
93	I	(e) / -as	huyake-ru	become soaked	huyak-as-u	soak	ke	I/N		ObjCh	physical		
94	I	(e) / -as	huye-ru	increase (vi)	huy-as-u	increase (vt)	ye	I/N		DegCh			
95	I	(e) / -as	iye-ru	heal (vi)	iy-as-u	heal (vt)	ye	H/A	N	AniCh	inner		
96	I	(e) / -as	kake-ru	become lacking	kak-as-u	miss (doing...)	ke	I/N		ObjCh	abst		ext-m
97	I	(e) / -as	kare-ru	wither; dry out	kar-as-u	let wither; dry out	re	I/N		ObjCh	physical		
98	I	(e) / -as	kire-ru	become cut, run out	kir-as-u	run out of	re	I/N		ObjCh	exist	cf. A154	spec-m
99	I	(e) / -as	koge-ru	get scorched	kog-as-u	scorch	ge	I/N		ObjCh	physical		
100	I	(e) / -as	koye-ru	become fat, fertile	koy-as-u	fatten, fertilize	ye	H/A		AniCh	outer		
101	I	(e) / -as	magire-ru	get distracted	magir-as-u	distract	re	I/N		AniCh	psych		
102	I	(e) / -as	make-ru	be defeated	mak-as-u	defeat	ke	H/A	H(soc)	AniCh	abst		
103	I	(e) / -as	more-ru	leak (vi)	mor-as-u	leak (vt)	re	I/N		NeuMo	manner	cf. A53	
104	I	(e) / -as	moye-ru	burn (vi)	moy-as-u	burn (vt)	ye	I/N	H(tool)	ObjCh	disinteg		
105	I	(e) / -as	mure-ru	get steamed/musty	mur-as-u	steam soft	re	I/N	H(tool)	ObjCh	physical	cf. B132	spec-m
106	I	(e) / -as	nare-ru	get accustomed to	nar-as-u	accustom, tame	re	H/A		AniCh	inner		
107	I	(e) / -as	nige-ru	escape	nig-as-u	let escape	ge	H/A		AniMo	loc+state		
108	I	(e) / -as	nuke-ru	come off/out	nuk-as-u	leave out	ke	I/N		NeuMo	path	cf. A166	
109	I	(e) / -as	nure-ru	become wet	nur-as-u	make wet	re	I/N		ObjCh	physical		
110	I	(e) / -as	okure-ru	become delayed	okur-as-u	delay	re	I/N		DegCh			
111	I	(e) / -as	same-ru	wake up (vi)	sam-as-u	wake up (vt)	me	H/A	N	AniCh	inner		
112	I	(e) / -as	same-ru	become cooler	sam-as-u	cool	me	I/N	N	DegCh			
113	I	(e) / -as	sore-ru	veer away	sor-as-u	divert	re	I/N		NeuMo	path	cf. A59	
114	I	(e) / -as	suke-ru	become transparent	suk-as-u	make sparse, see through	ke	I/N		ObjCh	physical	not in I; cf. A60	ext-m
115	I	(e) / -as	tare-ru	drip, hang (vi)	tar-as-u	let drip, let hang	re	I/N		NeuMo	manner		
116	I	(e) / -as	taye-ru	die out	tay-as-u	let die out	ye	H/A	H(plan)	AniCh	exist		
117	I	(e) / -as	tizire-ru	become curly	tizir-as-u	curl	re	I/N	N	ObjCh	shape		
118	I	(e) / -as	toke-ru	melt (vi)	tok-as-u	melt (vt)	ke	I/N	N	ObjCh	physical		
119	I	(e) / -as	toroke-ru	melt, be bewitched	torok-as-u	melt, bewitch	ke	I/N	H(tool)	ObjCh	physical	cf. A175	spec-m
120	I	(e) / -as	tuiye-ru	come to nonexistence/an end	tuiy-as-u	spend, consume	ye	I/N		ObjCh	exist		ext-m

Appendix A — 483

#	markedness type	affix & stem-final sound	Noncausative V		Causative V		base stem-final sound	Under-goer	Causal nature	broad semantic class	narrow semantic class	notes on listing	semantic notes
121	I	(e) / -as	yure-ru	sway (vi)	yur-as-u	sway (vt)	re	I/N		NeuMo	other	not in J	
122	I	(e) / -as	zire-ru	become impatient	zir-as-u	irritate	re	H/A	S	AniCh	psych		
123	I	(e) / -as	zure-ru	get out of position	zur-as-u	shift out of position	re	I/N	H(care)	NeuMo	loc+state		
124	I	(e) / -as	zyare-ru	be playful	zyar-as-u	play with	re	H/A		AniCh	other		
125	I	(e) / -ase	huruwe-ru	tremble	huruw-ase-ru	make tremble	we	I/N		NeuMo	other	not in J	
126	I	(e) / -ase	kozire-ru	get complicated	kozir-ase-ru	complicate	re	I/N		ObjCh	abst		
127	I	(e) / -akas	amaye-ru	act dependent (on)	amay-akas-u	spoil (a person)	ye	H/A		AniCh	psych		
128	I	(e) / -akas	obiye-ru	be frightened	obiy-akas-u	frighten, threaten	ye	H/A	S	AniCh	psych		
129	I	(e) / -akas	sobiye-ru	rise high	sobiy-akas-u	hold (shoulders) high	ye	H/A		AniCh	outer		spec-m, c-int
130	I	(e) / -as; irreg	kie-ru	disappear	kes-u	extinguish	(ye)	I/N		ObjCh	exist	c < kiy-as-u	
131	I	(e) / (aw)-as	magire-ru	get diverted	magiraw-as-u	divert (one's mind)	re	H/A		AniCh	psych	not in J	
132	I	(i) / -as	deki-ru	come into existence	dek-as-u	bring about	ki	I/N	H(plan)	ObjCh	exist		ext-m
133	I	(i) / -as	iki-ru	live	ik-as-u	let live, bring to life	ki	H/A		AniCh	bio		
134	I	(i) / -as	miti-ru	get filled	mit-as-u	fill	ti	I/N		NeuMo	loc+state		
135	I	(i) / -as	nobi-ru	become extended	nob-as-u	extend	bi	I/N		DegCh	sp-rel		
136	I	(i) / -as	tozi-ru	shut, close (vi)	toz-as-u	shut (vt)	zi	I/N	H(plan)	ObjCh	exist		spec-m
137	I	(i) / -as	tuki-ru	run out	tuk-as-u	use up	ki	I/N		ObjCh	exist	not in J; cf. A143	spec-m
138	I	(i) / -os	horobi-ru	meet with ruin	horob-os-u	ruin	bi	H/A	F	AniCh	exist	cf. A74	
139	I	(i) / -os	oki-ru	get up, wake up (vt)	ok-os-u	get up, wake up (vt)	ki	H/A		AniCh	outer	cf. A277	
140	I	(i) / -os	ori-ru	go down, get off	or-os-u	bring down, let off	ri	I/N		NeuMo	path		
141	I	(i) / -os	oti-ru	fall	ot-os-u	drop (vt), let fall	ti	I/N	N	NeuMo	path		
142	I	(i) / -os	sugi-ru	go past	sug-os-u	let go past, (live a life)	gi	I/N		NeuMo	path		ext-m
143	I	(i) / -us	tuki-ru	run out	tuk-us-u	use up	ki	I/N		ObjCh	exist	cf. A137	spec-m
144	I	(ow) / -os	uruwow-u	become moist	uruw-os-u	moisten	w	I/N		ObjCh	physical		
145	I	(aw) / -as	nigiwaw-u	be alive with	nigiw-as-u	enliven	w	H/A		AniCh	abst		

484 — Appendix A

#	marked-ness type	affix & stem-final sound	Noncausative V	Causative V		base stem-final sound	Under-goer	Causal nature	broad semantic class	narrow semantic class	notes on listing	semantic notes
146	II	-e / 0	egur-e-ru	egur-u	scoop out	r	I/N	F	ObjCh	disinteg	not in J	
147	II	-e / 0	hag-e-ru	hag-u	tear off (vt)	g	I/N	F	ObjCh	disinteg	cf. A88, A286	
148	II	-e / 0	hirak-e-ru	hirak-u	open (vt)	k	I/N		ObjCh	sp-rel		spec-m
149	II	-e / 0	hodok-e-ru	hodok-u	untie	k	I/N		ObjCh	sp-rel		
150	II	-e / 0	hur-e-ru	hur-u	shake (vt)	r	I/N		NeuMo	means		
151	II	-e / 0	kak-e-ru	kak-u	lack (vt)	k	I/N		ObjCh	semi-abst		
152	II	-e / 0	kasur-e-ru	kasur-u	graze, brush	r	I/N	F	ObjCh	impact	not in J	
153	II	-e / 0	kezur-e-ru	kezur-u	shave, plane	r	I/N	F	ObjCh	disinteg	not in J	
154	II	-e / 0	kir-e-ru	kir-u	cut, sever	r	I/N	F	ObjCh	disinteg	cf. A98	
155	II	-e / 0	kosur-e-ru	kosur-u	rub, scrape	r	I/N	F	ObjCh	impact		
156	II	-e / 0	kudak-e-ru	kudak-u	smash	k	I/N	F	ObjCh	disinteg		
157	II	-e / 0	kuzik-e-ru	kuzik-u	sprain, discourage	k	H/A	F	AniCh	psych		
158	II	-e / 0	makur-e-ru	makur-u	tuck up	r	I/N	H(care)	NeuMo	loc+state		
159	II	-e / 0	mekur-e-ru	mekur-u	turn up/over	r	I/N	H(care)	NeuMo	loc+state	not in J	
160	II	-e / 0	mi-ru	mi-ru	see	i	I/N	H(cog)		semi-abst		
161	II	-e / 0	mog-e-ru	mog-u	pluck off	g	I/N	F	ObjCh	disinteg		
162	II	-e / 0	muk-e-ru	muk-u	peel (vt)	k	I/N	F	ObjCh	disinteg		
163	II	-e / 0	nezir-e-ru	nezir-u	twist	r	I/N		ObjCh	shape		
164	II	-e / 0	ni-ru	ni-ru	boil (vt)	i	I/N	H(tool)	ObjCh	physical	cf. B121	
165	II	-e / 0	nug-e-ru	nug-u	take off (lower body)	g	I/N	H(body)	ObjCh	sp-rel		
166	II	-e / 0	nuk-e-ru	nuk-u	pull out	k	I/N	H(care)	NeuMo	path	cf. A108	
167	II	-e / 0	or-e-ru	or-u	break off (vt)	r	I/N	F	ObjCh	disinteg		
168	II	-e / 0	sabak-e-ru	sabak-u	judge, sell (out)	k	I/N	H(soc)	ObjCh	abst		spec-m
169	II	-e / 0	sak-e-ru	sak-u	tear	k	I/N	F	ObjCh	disinteg		
170	II	-e / 0	sir-e-ru	sir-u	come to know	r	I/N	H(cog)	ObjCh	abst		
171	II	-e / 0	sog-e-ru	sog-u	chip off	g	I/N	F	ObjCh	disinteg		
172	II	-e / 0	sur-e-ru	sur-u	rub	r	I/N	H(tool)	ObjCh	impact	not in J	
173	II	-e / 0	tak-e-ru	tak-u	cook (rice)	k	I/N	F	ObjCh	physical		
174	II	-e / 0	tigir-e-ru	tigir-u	tear off	r	I/N	F	ObjCh	disinteg	cf. A118	
175	II	-e / 0	tok-e-ru	tok-u	solve	k	I/N	H(cog)	ObjCh	abst		spec-m
176	II	-e / 0	tor-e-ru	tor-u	take	r	I/N	H(tool)	NeuMo	loc+state		spec-m
177	II	-e / 0	tur-e-ru	tur-u	catch (fish)	r	I/N	H(tool)	NeuMo	means		

Appendix A — 485

#	marked-ness type	affix & stem-final sound	Noncausative V		Causative V		base stem-final sound	Under-goer	Causal nature	broad semantic class	narrow semantic class	notes on listing	semantic notes
178	II	-e / 0	ur-e-ru	be sold	ur-u	sell	r	I/N	H(soc)	ObjCh	abst		
179	II	-e / 0	war-e-ru	break (vi)	war-u	break (vt)	r	I/N	F	ObjCh	disinteg		
180	II	-e / 0	yabuk-e-ru	get torn	yabuk-u	tear	k	I/N	F	ObjCh	disinteg	not in J	
181	II	-e / 0	yabur-e-ru	get torn	yabur-u	tear	r	I/N	F	ObjCh	disinteg		
182	II	-e / 0	yak-e-ru	burn (vi)	yak-u	burn (vt)	k	I/N	H(tool)	ObjCh	physical		
183	II	-e / 0	yozir-e-ru	get twisted	yozir-u	twist	r	I/N	F	ObjCh	shape		
184	II	-ar / 0	hasam-ar-u	get caught between	hasam-u	put between	m	I/N	H(tool)	ObjCh	sp-rel	cf. A204	
185	II	-ar / 0	husag-ar-u	get obstructed	husag-u	obstruct	g	I/N	H(tool)	ObjCh	sp-rel		
186	II	-ar / 0	kurum-ar-u	get wrapped up in	kurum-u	wrap up in	m	I/N	H(tool)	ObjCh	sp-rel	cf. A217	
187	II	-ar / 0	sas-ar-u	get stuck	sas-u	stick, thrust into	s	I/N	H(tool)	ObjCh	disinteg		tr/dtr
188	II	-ar / 0	tamaw-ar-u	be granted	tamaẹ-u	grant	w	H/A	H(soc)	AniCh	pos		ext-m
189	II	-ar / 0	tog-ar-u	become pointed	tog-u	sharpen	g	I/N	H(tool)	ObjCh	shape		ext-m
190	II	-ar / 0	tukam-ar-u	get captured	tukam-u	grab, catch	m	H/A	H(body)	AniCh	abst		
191	II	-ar / 0	tunag-ar-u	get connected	tunag-u	connect	g	I/N	H(tool)	ObjCh	sp-rel	cf. A246	
192	II	-are / 0	um-are-ru	be born	um-u	give birth to	m	H/A	H(body)	AniCh	bio		
193	II	-are / 0	wakat-are-ru	become divided	wakat-u	divide	t	I/N	F	ObjCh	disinteg	not in J	
194	II	-or / 0	tum-or-u	pile up (vi)	tum-u	load	m	I/N		NeuMo	loc+state		spec-m
195	II	-oe / 0	kik-oe-ru	become audible	kik-u	hear	k	I/N	H(cog)	ObjCh	semi-abst		
196	II	-ar / (e)	ag-ar-u	rise	age-ru	raise	ge	I/N		NeuMo	path		
197	II	-ar / (e)	aratam-ar-u	get renewed	aratame-ru	renew	me	I/N	H(eff)	ObjCh	abst		
198	II	-ar / (e)	at-ar-u	hit against	ate-ru	hit ... against	te	I/N	F	DegCh	impact		
199	II	-ar / (e)	atatam-ar-u	get warmed up	atatame-ru	warm up	me	I/N	H(care)	NeuMo	loc+state		
200	II	-ar / (e)	atum-ar-u	gather (vi)	atume-ru	gather (vt)	me	I/N	H(soc)	ObjCh	pos		
201	II	-ar / (e)	azuk-ar-u	be entrusted with	azuke-ru	entrust to	ke	H/A	H(soc)	AniCh	impact		tr/dtr
202	II	-ar / (e)	butuk-ar-u	bump into	butuke-ru	strike against	ke	I/N	F	ObjCh	loc+state		
203	II	-ar / (e)	ham-ar-u	fit in	hame-ru	fit ... in	me	I/N	H(care)	NeuMo	loc+state		
204	II	-ar / (e)	hasam-ar-u	be put between	hasame-ru	put between	me	I/N	H(care)	ObjCh	sp-rel	not in J; cf. A184	
205	II	-ar / (e)	hazim-ar-u	begin (vi)	hazime-ru	begin (vt)	me	I/N	H(tool)	ObjCh	aspect		
206	II	-ar / (e)	hedat-ar-u	get separated	hedate-ru	separate	te	I/N	F	NeuMo	loc+state		
207	II	-ar / (e)	hirog-ar-u	spread out (vi)	hiroge-ru	spread out (vt)	ge	I/N		DegCh			

Appendix A

#	marked-ness type	affix & stem-final sound	Noncausative V	Causative V	base stem-final sound	Under-goer	Causal nature	broad semantic class	narrow semantic class	notes on listing	semantic notes
208	II	-ar / (e)	itam-ar-u	itame-ru	be fried/sautéed	fry, sauté	me	I/N	H(tool)	ObjCh	physical	not in J	
209	II	-ar / (e)	kabus-ar-u	kabuse-ru	cover, lie over	cause ... to cover	se	I/N	H(plan)	NeuMo	loc+state	cf. A302	
210	II	-ar / (e)	kagam-ar-u	kagame-ru	become bent	bend (knees)	me	H/A	H(body)	AniCh	outer	not in J; cf. A8	
211	II	-ar / (e)	kak-ar-u	kake-ru	hang, come in contact	hang, put in contact	ke	I/N	H(care)	NeuMo	path		
212	II	-ar / (e)	karam-ar-u	karame-ru	get entwined	entwine (vt)	me	I/N	H(care)	ObjCh	sp-rel	cf. A11	
213	II	-ar / (e)	kasan-ar-u	kasane-ru	lie on top of	lay on top of	ne	I/N	H(care)	NeuMo	loc+state		
214	II	-ar / (e)	kaw-ar-u	kawe-ru	change (vi)	change (vt)	we	I/N		ObjCh	semi-abst		
215	II	-ar / (e)	kim-ar-u	kime-ru	be decided	decide	me	I/N	H(cog)	ObjCh	abst		
216	II	-ar / (e)	kiwam-ar-u	kiwame-ru	reach an extreme	carry to an extreme	me	I/N	H(eff)	ObjCh	abst	cf. A186	ext-m
217	II	-ar / (e)	kurum-ar-u	kurume-ru	get wrapped up in	lump together with	me	I/N	H(tool)	ObjCh	sp-rel		
218	II	-ar / (e)	kuwaw-ar-u	kuwawe-ru	join, be added	add	we	I/N	H(care)	DegCh	abst		
219	II	-ar / (e)	mag-ar-u	mage-ru	bend (vi)	bend (vt)	ge	I/N	F	ObjCh	shape		
220	II	-ar / (e)	mak-ar-u	make-ru	get discounted	discount	me	I/N	H(soc)	ObjCh	abst	not in J	
221	II	-ar / (e)	matom-ar-u	matome-ru	become united into a whole	put together into a whole	me	I/N	H(eff)	ObjCh	abst	cf. A260	
222	II	-ar / (e)	maz-ar-u	maze-ru	get mixed	mix	ze	I/N		ObjCh	sp-rel		
223	II	-ar / (e)	maziw-ar-u	maziwe-ru	mingle with	mix with	we	I/N		ObjCh	sp-rel		
224	II	-ar / (e)	mook-ar-u	mooke-ru	be earned	earn	ke	I/N	H(soc)	ObjCh	abst		
225	II	-ar / (e)	motom-ar-u	motome-ru	be sought and found	seek after	me	I/N	H(cog)	ObjCh	psych	not in J; cf. B82	
226	II	-ar / (e)	nagusam-ar-u	nagusame-ru	get consoled	console	me	H/A	S	AniCh	path	not in J	
227	II	-ar / (e)	nokk-ar-u	nokke-ru	be placed on	place on	ke	I/N	H(care)	NeuMo	loc+state	not in J	
228	II	-ar / (e)	osam-ar-u	osame-ru	get put in place, subside	put in place, govern	me	I/N	H(care)	NeuMo	inner		tr/dtr
229	II	-ar / (e)	osiw-ar-u	osiwe-ru	learn	teach	we	H/A	H(soc)	AniCh	aspect		
230	II	-ar / (e)	ow-ar-u	owe-ru	end (vi)	end (vt)	we	I/N		ObjCh	abst		
231	II	-ar / (e)	sadam-ar-u	sadame-ru	become determined	determine	me	I/N	H(cog)	ObjCh	path		
232	II	-ar / (e)	sag-ar-u	sage-ru	become lower	lower	ge	I/N		NeuMo	path		tr/dtr
233	II	-ar / (e)	sazuk-ar-u	sazuke-ru	be granted with	grant	ke	H/A	H(soc)	AniCh	pos		
234	II	-ar / (e)	sim-ar-u	sime-ru	close (vi), get tight	close (vt), tighten	me	I/N		ObjCh	sp-rel		
235	II	-ar / (e)	sizum-ar-u	sizume-ru	beome quiet	make quiet	me	I/N		ObjCh	physical		
236	II	-ar / (e)	som-ar-u	some-ru	get dyed/colored	dye, color	me	I/N		ObjCh	semi-abst		
237	II	-ar / (e)	sonaw-ar-u	sonawe-ru	be provided	provide with	we	I/N	H(care)	ObjCh	shape	cf. A23	
238	II	-ar / (e)	subom-ar-u	subome-ru	become thinner	make thinner	me	I/N		NeuMo	loc+state		
239	II	-ar / (e)	tam-ar-u	tame-ru	be collected, saved	collect, save	me	I/N	H(eff)	AniCh	abst	cf. A28	
240	II	-ar / (e)	tasuk-ar-u	tasuke-ru	be saved, helped	help, save	ke	H/A					
241	II	-ar / (e)	tizim-ar-u	tizime-ru	shrink (vi)	shrink (vt)	me	I/N					
242	II	-ar / (e)	todom-ar-u	todome-ru	remain	prevent from going	me	I/N	H(care)	DegCh	cesation		
243	II	-ar / (e)	tom-ar-u	tome-ru	stop (vi)	stop (vt)	me	I/N		NeuMo	cesation		
244	II	-ar / (e)	tuk-ar-u	tuke-ru	soak in (vi)	soak in (vt)	ke	I/N		NeuMo	loc+state		
245	II	-ar / (e)	tum-ar-u	tume-ru	get plugged	pack, plug	me	I/N		NeuMo	loc+state		
246	II	-ar / (e)	tunag-ar-u	tunage-ru	get connected	connect	ge	I/N	H(tool)	ObjCh	sp-rel	not in J; cf. A191	

Appendix A — 487

#	markedness type	affix & stem-final sound	Noncausative V	Causative V	meaning	base stem-final sound	Undergoer	Causal nature	broad semantic class	narrow semantic class	notes on listing	semantic notes
247	II	-ar / (e)	turan-ar-u	turane-ru	line up (vt)	ne	I/N	H(care)	NeuMo	loc+state		
248	II	-ar / (e)	tutaw-ar-u	tutawe-ru	transmit, inform	we	I/N	H(soc)	ObjCh	semi-abst	cf. B119	
249	II	-ar / (e)	tutom-ar-u	tutome-ru	undertake the duty of	me	I/N	H(eff)	ObjCh	abst	cf. A258	
250	II	-ar / (e)	um-ar-u	ume-ru	bury, fill in	me	I/N		NeuMo	loc+state	not in J	
251	II	-ar / (e)	uzum-ar-u	uzume-ru	bury, cover up	me	I/N		NeuMo	loc+state		
252	II	-ar / (e)	uw-ar-u	uwe-ru	plant	we	I/N		ObjCh	sp-rel	cf. A35	
253	II	-ar / (e)	yasum-ar-u	yasume-ru	put (one's body) to rest	me	H/A		AniCh	inner		c-int
254	II	-ar / (e)	yud-ar-u	yude-ru	boil	de	I/N		ObjCh	physical		
255	II	-are / (e)	toraw-are-ru	torawe-ru	seize, catch	we	H/A	H(eff)	AniCh	abst		ext-m
256	II	-are / (e)	wak-are-ru	wake-ru	divide	ke	I/N		ObjCh	disinteg		
257	II	-or / (e)	kom-or-u	kome-ru	stay within, occupy fully	me	I/N	H(eff)	NeuMo	loc+state		spec-m
258	II	-or / (e)	nukum-or-u	nukume-ru	put into, fill up with warm up	me	I/N		DegCh	path	cf. B78	
259	II	-ore / (e)	um-ore-ru	ume-ru	bury, fill in	me	I/N		NeuMo	loc+state	not in J; cf. A249	
260	II	-ore / (e)	uzum-ore-ru	uzume-ru	bury, cover	me	I/N		NeuMo	loc+state		
261	II	-ir / (e)	maz-ir-u	maze-ru	mix with	ze	I/N		ObjCh	sp-rel	cf. A222	
262	II	-ar / (awe)	tukam-ar-u	tukamawe-ru	capture		H/A	H(eff)	AniCh	abst		
263	III	r / s	amar-u	amas-u	leave over		I/N		ObjCh	semi-abst		
264	III	r / s	hitar-u	hitas-u	soak in (vi) / soak in (vt)		I/N		NeuMo	loc+state		
265	III	r / s	ibur-u	ibus-u	smoke / fumigate		I/N		ObjCh	physical		
266	III	r / s	kaer-u	kaes-u	return (vi) / return (vt)		I/N	H(tool)	NeuMo	path		
267	III	r / s	kaer-u	kaes-u	hatch (vi) / hatch (vt)		H/A	N	AniCh	bio		
268	III	r / s	kitar-u	kitas-u	come / bring about		I/N		NeuMo	path	listed in J	
269	III	r / s	korogar-u	korogas-u	roll (vi) / roll (vt)		I/N		NeuMo	manner		
270	III	r / s	kudar-u	kudas-u	go down / lower		I/N		NeuMo	path		
271	III	r / s	mawar-u	mawas-u	go around / turn ... around		I/N		NeuMo	path		
272	III	r / s	modor-u	modos-u	return (vi) / return (vt)		I/N		NeuMo	path		
273	III	r / s	naor-u	naos-u	get healed/fixed / heal/fix		H/A		ObjCh	semi-abst		
274	III	r / s	nar-u	nas-u	become / do		I/N		ObjCh	other		
275	III	r / s	nigor-u	nigos-u	get muddy / make muddy/vague		I/N		ObjCh	physical		spec-m
276	III	r / s	nokor-u	nokos-u	remain / leave behind		I/N		NeuMo	cesation		
277	III	r / s	okor-u	okos-u	happen / bring about		I/N		ObjCh	exist	cf. A139	
278	III	r / s	sator-u	satos-u	realize / make realize		H/A		AniCh	inner		tr/dtr
279	III	r / s	tirakar-u	tirakas-u	get scattered / scatter		I/N	H(tool)	NeuMo	loc+state		
280	III	r / s	tomor-u	tomos-u	become lit / light		I/N		ObjCh	physical		
281	III	r / s	toor-u	toos-u	pass through / let pass through		I/N		NeuMo	path		
282	III	r / s	utur-u	utus-u	move (vi), be transferred / move (vt), transfer		I/N		NeuMo	path		

468 —— Appendix A

#	marked-ness type	affix & stem-final sound	Noncausative V	Causative V	base stem-final sound	Under-goer	Causal nature	broad semantic class	narrow semantic class	notes on listing	semantic notes
283	III	r/s	watar-u	watas-u	cross over	hand over, let...cross			NeuMo	path		spec-m
284	III	r/s	yador-u	yados-u	lodge at	have (a baby) in one's body		H(body)	AniCh	abst		spec-m
285	III	re/s	araware-ru	arawas-u	appear	show, express	I/N		NeuMo	exist		
286	III	re/s	hagare-ru	hagas-u	peel off (vi)	peel off (vt)	I/N		ObjCh	disinteg	cf. A88, A147	
287	III	re/s	hanare-ru	hanas-u	move away	separate (vt)	I/N		NeuMo	loc+state		
288	III	re/s	hazure-ru	hazus-u	get dislocated	take off, dislocate	I/N		NeuMo	loc+state		
289	III	re/s	hogure-ru	hogus-u	become disentangled	disentangle	I/N		ObjCh	sp-rel		
290	III	re/s	kakure-ru	kakus-u	become hidden	hide	I/N		NeuMo	loc+state		
291	III	re/s	kegare-ru	kegas-u	become unclean	make unclean	I/N	H(soc)	ObjCh	abst		
292	III	re/s	kobore-ru	kobos-u	spill (vi)	spill (vt)	I/N		NeuMo	manner		
293	III	re/s	konare-ru	konas-u	be handled nicely	cope with	I/N	H(eff)	ObjCh	abst		spec-m
294	III	re/s	koware-ru	kowas-u	break (vi)	break (vt)	I/N	F	ObjCh	disinteg		
295	III	re/s	kuzure-ru	kuzus-u	collapse, fall apart	make collapse, break apart	I/N		ObjCh	disinteg		
296	III	re/s	midare-ru	midas-u	become disordered	put into disorder	I/N		ObjCh	semi-abst		
297	III	re/s	nagare-ru	nagas-u	flow	let flow away	I/N	N	NeuMo	manner		
298	III	re/s	nogare-ru	nogas-u	escape	let escape	H/A		AniMo	manner		
299	III	re/s	taore-ru	taos-u	fall over	topple	I/N	F	ObjCh	sp-rel		
300	III	re/s	tubure-ru	tubus-u	be crushed	crush	I/N	F	ObjCh	disinteg		
301	III	re/s	yature-ru	yatus-u	become worn out	make (self) look worn out	H/A		AniCh	outer	not in J	
302	III	re/s	yogore-ru	yogos-u	become dirty	make dirty	I/N		ObjCh	physical		
303	III	r/se	kabur-u	kabuse-ru	put on (own) head	cause...to cover; put on other's head	H/A		AniCh	pos	cf. A209	tr/dtr
304	III	r/se	nor-u	nose-ru	get on, ride	put...on, give a ride to	H/A		AniMo	path		
305	III	r/se	yor-u	yose-ru	approach	let...draw near	I/N		NeuMo	path		
306	III	ri/s	kari-ru	kas-u	borrow	lend (=make borrow)	H/A	H(soc)	AniCh	pos		tr/dtr

Undergoer types: H/A = Human/Animate, I/N = Inanimate/Neutral
Causal nature: N = Naturally occurring, F = External force, S = External stimulus, H(tool) = Humanly induced with use of tool, H(body) = Humanly induced with use of own body part, H(care) = Humanly induced with care in execution, H(eff) = Humanly induced with effort, H(cog) = Humanly induced through perception or cognition, H(soc) = Humanly induced by means of social convention.
Broad semantic classes: AniMo = Animate motion, AniCh = Animate change, NeuMo = Neutral or Inanimate motion, ObjCh = Object change.
Narrow semantic classes: manner = manner of motion, path = path of motion, loc+state = change in location accompanied by change in state, inner = change in human inner condition, outer = change in human outer physical condition, psych = psychological change, bio = biological change, pos = possessional change, abst = change in abstract property or status, disinteg = disintegration, shape = change in shape, physical = physical change (other than disintegration and change in shape), sp-rel = spatio-relational change, exist = change in existential status, semi-abst = change in semi-abstract state.
Notes on listing: Not in J = Not found in Jacobsen's (1992) list.
Semantic notes: c-int = causer-internal causation, tr/dtr = transitive/ditransitive pairs, ext-m = derived verb having an extended meaning, spec-m = derived verb having a meaning based on a specific meaning of the base verb.

Appendix B: List of additional causativity pairs in Japanese (by Yo Matsumoto, a revision of Jacobsen (1992))

	types	markedness type	affix & stem-final sounds	noncausative V		causative V		base stem-final snds	notes on listing	notes on form
1	compound verbs	I	0 / -as	hik-kom-u	draw back	hik-kom-as-u	pull back	m	cf. B23	(V)-V
2		I	0 / -e	tika-duk-u	approach	tika-duk-e-ru	make ... closer to	k		A-V
3		I	0 / -e	ara-dat-u	become rough	ara-dat-e-ru	make rough	t		A-V
4		I	0 / -e	ira-dat-u	become irritated	ira-dat-e-ru	irritate	t		Adv-V
5		I	0 / -e	saka-dat-u	stand on end	saka-dat-e-ru	ruffle up	t		Adv-V
6		I	0 / -e	kata-muk-u	lean (vi)	kata-muk-e-ru	lean (vt)	k		N-V
7		I	0 / -e	kata-duk-u	become tidy	kata-duk-e-ru	tidy up	k		N-V
8		I	0 / -e	kizu-tuk-u	get hurt	kizu-tuk-e-ru	hurt	k		N-V
9		I	0 / -e	genki-duk-u	cheer up (vi)	genki-duk-e-ru	cheer up (vt)	k		N-V
10		I	0 / -e	so-muk-u	turn (one's back) on	so-muk-e-ru	turn away	k		N-V
11		I	0 / -e	utu-muk-u	look down	utu-muk-e-ru	cause to face down	k		N-V
12		I	0 / -e	yaku-dat-u	be useful	yaku-dat-e-ru	make available for use	t		N-V
13		I	0 / -e	awa-dat-u	lather up (vi)	awa-dat-e-ru	lather up (vt)	t		N-V
14		I	0 / -e	zyunzyo-dat-u	be orderly	zyunzyo-dat-e-ru	make orderly	t		N-V
15		I	0 / -e	omoi-ukab-u	come to mind	omoi-ukab-e-ru	imagine	b		V-V
16		I	0 / -e	musubi-tuk-u	get connected	musubi-tuk-e-ru	connect	k		V-V
17		I	0 / -e	hari-tuk-u	get attached firmly	harituk-e-ru	attach firmly	k		V-V
18		I	0 / -e	karami-tuk-u	get entangled	karami-tuk-e-ru	entangle	k		V-V
19		I	0 / -e	maki-tuk-u	get wrapped onto	maki-tuk-e-ru	wrap onto	k		V-V
20		I	0 / -e	sui-tuk-u	get sucked onto	sui-tuk-e-ru	suck onto	k		V-V
21		I	0 / -e	yaki-tuk-u	get burned onto	yaki-tuk-e-ru	burn onto	k		V-V
22		I	0 / -e	hiki-tat-u	stand out	hiki-tat-e-ru	make stand out	t		V-V
23		I	0 / -e	hik-kom-u	draw back	hik-kom-e-ru	pull back	m	cf. B1	(V)-V
24		II	(i) / -os	suberi-oti-ru	slide down	suberi-ot-os-u	let slide down	ti		V-V
25		II	-ar / 0	tuki-sas-ar-u	get punctured	tuki-sas-u	puncture	s		V-V
26		II	-ar / (e)	buk-kak-ar-u	splash (vi)	buk-kake-ru	splash (water) on	ke		(V)-V
27		II	-ar / (e)	huk-kak-ar-u	get blown on	huk-kake-ru	blow (breath) on	ke		(V)-V
28		II	-ar / (e)	hik-kak-ar-u	get caught	hik-kake-ru	hook on	ke		(V)-V
29		II	-ar / (e)	too-zak-ar-u	move further away	too-zake-ru	keep at a distance	ke		A-V
30		II	-ar / (e)	bura-sag-ar-u	hang down(vi)	bura-sage-ru	hang down(vt)	ge		Adv-V
31		II	-ar / (e)	koto-duk-ar-u	be entrusted with	koto-duk-e-ru	entrust	ke		N-V

490 — Appendix B

types	markedness type	affix & stem-final sounds	noncausative V		causative V		notes on listing	base stem-final snds	notes on form
compound verbs									
32	II	-ar / (e)	yoko-taw-ar-u	lie down	yoko-tawe-ru	lay down		we	N-V
33	II	-ar / (e)	kaki-ag-ar-u	get written up	kaki-age-ru	write up		ge	V-V
34	II	-ar / (e)	mori-ag-ar-u	get mounded up	mori-age-ru	mound up		ge	V-V
35	II	-ar / (e)	hane-ag-ar-u	get splashed up	hane-age-ru	splash up		ge	V-V
36	II	-ar / (e)	huki-ag-ar-u	get blown up	huki-age-ru	blow up		ge	V-V
37	II	-ar / (e)	moti-ag-ar-u	get lifted	moti-age-ru	lift		ge	V-V
38	II	-ar / (e)	sui-ag-ar-u	get sucked up	sui-age-ru	suck up		ge	V-V
39	II	-ar / (e)	turi-ag-ar-u	get hauled up	turi-age-ru	haul up		ge	V-V
40	II	-ar / (e)	tumi-ag-ar-u	get piled up	tumi-age-ru	pile up		ge	V-V
41	II	-ar / (e)	kiri-ag-ar-u	get rounded up	kiri-age-ru	cut short, round up		ge	V-V
42	II	-ar / (e)	kuri-ag-ar-u	get moved up	kuri-age-ru	move up		ge	V-V
43	II	-ar / (e)	some-ag-ar-u	get completely dyed	some-age-ru	dye completely		ge	V-V
44	II	-ar / (e)	ni-ag-ar-u	get completely boiled	ni-age-ru	boil completely		ge	V-V
45	II	-ar / (e)	taki-ag-ar-u	get completely steamed	taki-age-ru	steam completely		ge	V-V
46	II	-ar / (e)	yaki-ag-ar-u	get burned up	yaki-age-ru	burn up		ge	V-V
47	II	-ar / (e)	tukuri-ag-ar-u	get completely made/done	tukuri-age-ru	finish making/doing		ge	V-V
48	II	-ar / (e)	maki-ag-ar-u	get rolled up	maki-age-ru	roll up		ge	V-V
49	II	-ar / (e)	tuki-ag-ar-u	get thrust up	tuki-age-ru	thrust up		ge	V-V
50	II	-ar / (e)	hori-ag-ar-u	get carved up	hori-age-ru	carve up		ge	V-V
51	II	-ar / (e)	nui-ag-ar-u	get sewn up	nui-age-ru	sew up		ge	V-V
52	II	-ar / (e)	yude-ag-ar-u	get completely boiled	yude-age-ru	boil completely		ge	V-V
53	II	-ar / (e)	mai-ag-ar-u	soar up (vi)	mai-age-ru	soar up (vt)		ge	V-V
54	II	-ar / (e)	uti-ag-ar-u	get shot high up	uti-age-ru	shoot high up		ge	V-V
55	II	-ar / (e)	mi-tuk-ar-u	be found	mi-tuk-e-ru	find		ke	V-V
56	II	-ar / (e)	ii-tuk-ar-u	receive an order	ii-tuk-e-ru	give an order		ke	V-V
57	II	-ar / (e)	moosi-tuk-ar-u	receive an order	moosi-tuk-e-ru	give an order		ke	V-V
58	II	-ar / (e)	huri-kak-ar-u	get sprinkled	huri-kake-ru	sprinkle		ke	V-V
59	II	-ar / (e)	ate-ham-ar-u	be applicable	ate-hame-ru	apply		me	V-V
60	II	-ar / (e)	ni-tum-ar-u	get boiled down thick	ni-tume-ru	boil down thick		me	V-V
61	II	-ar / (e)	tumi-kasan-ar-u	pile up (vi)	tumi-kasane-ru	pile up (vt)		ne	V-V
62	II	-ar / (e)	ori-kasan-ar-u	get folded into layers	ori-kasane-ru	fold into layers		ne	V-V
63	III	r / s	hiru-gaer-u	flutter in wind	hiru-gaes-u	turn over			?-V
64	III	r / s	kutu-gaer-u	get overturned	kutu-gaes-u	overturn			?-V

Appendix B — 491

	types	markedness type	affix & stem-final sounds	noncausative V		causative V		base stem-final snds	notes on listing	notes on form
65	deadjectival	II	-ar / (e)	aka-m-ar-u	become reddish	aka-me-ru	make reddish	me		
66	Vs with -m(-)ar/-me	II	-ar / (e)	haya-m-ar-u	become early/hasty	haya-me-ru	hasten	me		
67		II	-ar / (e)	hiku-m-ar-u	become lower	hiku-me-ru	lower	me		
68		II	-ar / (e)	hiro-m-ar-u	become wide-spread	hiro-me-ru	make wide-spread	me		
69		II	-ar / (e)	huka-m-ar-u	deepen (vi)	huka-me-ru	deepen (vt)	me		
70		II	-ar / (e)	kata-m-ar-u	harden (vi)	kata-me-ru	harden (vt)	me		
71		II	-ar / (e)	kiyo-m-ar-u	become pure	kiyo-me-ru	purify	me		
72		II	-ar / (e)	maru-m-ar-u	become round	maru-me-ru	make round	me		
73		II	-ar / (e)	nuku-m-ar-u	become warmer	nuku-me-ru	warm up	me	cf. A258	
74		II	-ar / (e)	nuru-m-ar-u	become warmer	nuru-me-ru	warm up	me	cf. B83	
75		II	-ar / (e)	seba-m-ar-u	become narrower	seba-me-ru	make narrower	me		
76		II	-ar / (e)	taka-m-ar-u	rise	taka-me-ru	heighten	me		
77		II	-ar / (e)	tuyo-m-ar-u	become strong	tuyo-me-ru	strengthen	me		
78		II	-ar / (e)	usu-m-ar-u	become thinner	usu-me-ru	make thinner	me		
79		II	-ar / (e)	yowa-m-ar-u	weaken	yowa-me-ru	weaken	me		
80		II	-ar / (e)	yuru-m-ar-u	loosen (vi)	yuru-me-ru	loosen (vt)	me	cf. A38	
81		I	0 / -as	kaw-u	go past each other	kaw-as-u	exchange with each other	w		
82	non-causative member obsolete or rare	II	0 / -e	nagusam-u	become consoled	nagusam-e-ru	console	m	cf. A226	
83		II	0 / -e	nurum-u	become lukewarm	nurum-e-ru	make lukewarm	m	cf. B74	
84		II	0 / -e	tagaw-u	differ	tagaw-e-ru	break (one's word)	w		
85		II	0 / -e	tugaw-u	mate with	tugaw-e-ru	put (arrows) to a bow	w		
86		II	0 / -e	kasig-u	lean (vi)	kasig-e-ru	lean (one's head)	g		
87		II	0 / -e	tum-u	become packed	tum-e-ru	pack	m		
88		II	(e) / -as	koroge-ru	roll(vi)	korog-as-u	roll(vt)	ge		
89		II	(i) / -os	hi-ru	become dry	h-os-u	dry	hi		
90		III	re / s	mabure-ru	become smeared	mabus-u	smear			

Appendix B

	types	markedness type	affix & stem-final sounds	noncausative V		causative V		base stem-final snds	notes on listing	notes on form
91	causative member obsolete or rare	I	0 / -akas	kusar-u	go bad, rotten	kusar-akas-u	let ... go bad, rotten	r		
92		I	(e) / -ase	hukure-ru	swell	hukur-ase-ru	swell (vt)	re		
93		I	(e) / -as	tukare-ru	get tired	tukar-as-u	make tired	re		
94		I	(e) / -as	huke-ru	grow late	huk-as-u	stay up late at (night)	ke		
95		I	(i) / -as	aki-ru	get bored of	ak-as-u	make ... bored of	ki		
96		I	(i) / -as	kori-ru	learn (from experience)	kor-as-u	give ... a lesson	ri		
97		I	0 / -e	natuk-u	become attached to	natuk-e-ru	win over	k		
98		I	0 / -e	tarum-u	slacken (vi)	tarum-e-ru	slacken (vt)	m		
99		I	0 / -e	tigaw-u	differ	tigaw-e-ru	mistake	w		
100		I	(i) / -e	nobi-ru	become extended	nob-e-ru	extend(vt)	bi		
101		II	-e / 0	yur-e-ru	shake(vi)	yur-u	shake(vt)	r		
102		II	-ur / (e)	kusub-ur-u	smoke	kusube-ru	fumigate	be		
103		III	r / s	nakunar-u	become lost, die	nakunas-u	lose			
104		III	r / s	nobor-u	rise	nobos-u	bring up, serve			
105		III	r / s	her-u	decrease(vi)	hes-u	decrease(vt)			
106		III	r / s	simer-u	become wet	simes-u	wet			
107	both members rare	I	0 / -as	kuyur-u	smolder	kuyur-as-u	smoke	r		
108		I	0 / -e	kogom-u	stoop (vi)	kogom-e-ru	stoop (vt)	m		
109		II	-ar / (e)	tudum-ar-u	shrink (vi)	tudume-ru	reduce	me		

Appendix B — 493

	types	markedness type	affix & stem-final sounds	noncausative V		causative V		base stem-final snds	notes on listing	notes on form
110	semantic relationship indirect	I	0 / -as	hagem-u	work hard at	hagem-as-u	encourage	m		
111		I	0 / -as	huk-u	blow	huk-as-u	puff, smoke	k		
112		I	0 / -as	kor-u	become absorbed in	kor-as-u	concentrate (eyes) on	r		
113		I	0 / -as	wazuraw-u	be sick with	wazuraw-as-u	trouble	w		
114		I	0 / -e	kamaw-u	bother oneself about	kamaw-e-ru	get set (to do)	w		
115		I	0 / -e	komu	get crowded	kom-e-ru	load, fill	m		
116		I	0 / -e	mukaw-u	head for	mukaw-e-ru	meet, welcome	w		
117		I	0 / -e	sow-u	go along with	sow-e-ru	put ... beside	w		
118		I	0 / -e	tutaw-u	go along	tutaw-e-ru	inform	w	cf. A248	
119		I	(e) / akas	hagure-ru	stray from	hagur-akas-u	put off, evade	re		
120		I	(e) / -as	hate-ru	come to an end	hat-as-u	carry out	t		
121		I	(e) / -as	niye-ru	boil (vi)	niy-as-u	let oneself boil over	ye	cf. A164	
122		I	(e) / -as	kure-ru	(day) come an end	kur-as-u	pass (time)	re		
123		I	(i) / -e	iki-ru	live	ik-e-ru	arrange (flower)	ki		
124		II	-ar / (e)	suw-ar-u	sit	suwe-ru	set	we		
125		II	-ar / (e)	tazusaw-ar-u	participate in	tazusawe-ru	carry on oneself	we		
126		II	-are / (e)	sut-are-ru	fall into disuse	sute-ru	throw away	te		
127		II	-e / 0	hinekur-e-ru	get twisted in personality	hinekur-u	twist	r		
128		II	-e / 0	mom-e-ru	have a dispute	mom-u	crumple	m		
129		III	r / s	damar-u	become silent	damas-u	deceive			
130		III	r / s	tar-u	suffice	tas-u	add, supplement		cf. B133	
131		III	re / s	kogare-ru	burn with passion for	kogas-u	scorch			
132		III	re / s	mure-ru	get steamed/musty	mus-u	heat with steam		cf. A105	
133		III	ri / s	tari-ru	suffice	tas-u	add		cf. B130	

	types	markedness type	affix & stem-final sounds	noncausative V		causative V		base stem-final snds	notes on listing	notes on form
134	morphological relationship indirect			hair-u	go in	ir-e-ru	put in			
135				hosor-u	become thin	hosome-ru	make narrow			
136				hukure-ru	swell	hukuram-as-u	cause to swell			
137				kake-ru	run	kar-u	drive, spur			
138				kasure-ru	become hoarse	karas-u	make hoarse			
139				kudar-u	go down	kudasar-u	bestow			
140				naku-nar-u	become lost, die	naku-s-u	lose			
141				obusar-u	get on (someone's back)	obuw-u	carry on (one's back)			
142				use-ru	disappear	usinaw-u	lose			
143	no contrast in causativity	I	0 / -e	matigaw-u	mistake	matigaw-e-ru	mistake	w		
144		I	0 / -e	hasam-u	catch between	hasam-e-ru	catch between	m		
145		I	0 / -e	kurum-u	wrap	kurum-e-ru	wrap	m		
146		I	0 / -e	tunag-u	connect	tunag-e-ru	connect	g		
147		I	0 / -as	ter-u	shine	ter-as-u	illuminate	r		
148		II	-e / 0	mor-e-ru	leak (vi)	mor-u	leak (vi)	r		
149		II	-e / 0	suk-e-ru	become transparent	suk-u	get hungry/sparse	k		
150		II	-e / 0	sor-e-ru	veer away	sor-u	bend (vi)	r		
151		II	-e / 0	ter-e-ru	show signs of shyness	ter-u	shine	r		
152		II	-ar / 0	matag-ar-u	sit astride	matag-u	straddle	g		
153		II	-ar / e	uk-ar-u	pass (an exam)	uke-ru	receive, take (an exam)	ke		
154		II	-ar / e	koe-ru	go over	kos-u	go over			

Appendix B — 495

	types	marked-ness type	affix & stem-final sounds	noncausative V		causative V		base stem-final snds	notes on listing	notes on form
155	causatives possible	I	0 / -as	hukuram-u	swell	hukuram-as-u	cause to swell	m		
156	variants of -sase form	I	0 / -as	kagayak-u	shine	kagayak-as-u	cause to shine	k		
157		I	0 / -as	kusar-u	go bad	kusar-as-u	let go bad	r		
158		I	0 / -as	nak-u	cry	nak-as-u	cause to cry	k		
159		I	0 / -as	sawag-u	become excited	sawag-as-u	cause excitement	g		
160		I	0 / -as	suber-u	slip	suber-as-u	let slip	r		
161		I	0 / -as	sum-u	become clear	sum-as-u	make transparent	m		
162		I	0 / -as	togar-u	become sharp	togar-as-u	sharpen	r		
163		I	0 / -as	yorokob-u	be happy	yorokob-as-u	please	b		
164	lexical -sase causatives	I	0 / -(s)ase	hak-u	put … on own lower body	hak-ase-ru	put … on other's lower body			
165		I	0 / -(s)ase	kik-u	hear	kik-ase-ru	tell, let … hear			
166		I	0 / -(s)ase	mot-u	come to have	mot-ase-ru	put in the hand of			
167		I	0 / -(s)ase	nom-u	drink	nom-ase-ru	feed, make … drink			
168		I	0 / -(s)ase	shir-u	come to know	shir-ase-ru	inform, let … know			
169		I	0 / -(s)ase	tabe-ru	eat	tabe-sase-ru	feed, make … eat			

"Compound verbs" are pairs where both members are transparently compounds.
"Deajectival verbs with -mar/-me" are those often regarded as involving -ar suffixation to deadjectival causative verbs suffixed with -me. However, there is an alternative possibility that -mar is a suffix attached to an adjectival root. See Sugioka 2002.
Pairs in the "semantic relationship indirect" category are mostly from Jacobsen's list, but the semantic relationship between the two member verbs is remote and they cannot be regarded as normal noncausative-causative verb pairs.
Pairs in the "morphological relationship indirect" category are also taken from Jacobsen's list, but their formal noncorrespondence makes them difficult to regard as normal noncausative-causative pairs.
Those pairs with "no contrast in causativity" have member verbs that appear to have the same morphological contrast as noncausative-causative pairs but do not in fact exhibit a contrast in causativity between the two members.
Pairs with "causatives possible variants of -sase form" are those found in Jacobsen's list but where the causative member with -as occurs with low frequency in comparison to the -sase form, and may therefore be no more than a phonological variant of the -sase morphological form preferred by certain speakers. By contrast -as verbs in the Core List occur with high frequency relative to their -sase counterparts and so it is clear that they are not mere phonological variants of the latter.
Pairs with "lexical -sase causatives" are those whose causative members have the form of -sase morphological causatives but whose syntactic and semantic behavior suggests that they are in fact lexical. See Matsumoto (2000a,c, 2003).

Subject index

accomplishment 113, 118, 139, 163, 185–186, 189, 196–198, 204–208, 218, 290
achievement 113–114, 163, 177
acquisition 33, 47, 314, 318, 327, 335, 341–344, 357, 360, 366, 380
activity 41, 44, 113, 116, 120, 139, 163, 185, 189, 196, 197, 204, 209, 218, 249, 300
Actor-focus 448
act-out paradigm 353
affected 237, 240, 404, 439
affix choice 53, 70
agent 35, 40–42, 60, 75, 89–92, 96, 99–105, 108–110, 117, 121, 135–137, 140, 148, 156–157, 160, 163–164, 188–191, 194, 198, 200, 203, 206, 210, 237, 298, 320, 330–331, 334, 344, 353, 357–366, 376, 378–380, 397, 413, 431, 433, 436
alternation
– causative 27, 53, 56, 60, 200, 250, 252
– dative-nominative 127, 133, 135
– nominative-accusative 127, 133
– plural-agent 140, 143, 146
– source-argument 135, 138
– transitive-intransitive 32, 198, 200, 313, 318
– transitivity 21, 89, 91–93, 108, 120, 139, 203, 236, 275, 289, 291, 294–296, 306, 360, 474
– verb 36, 55, 84, 91, 121
anticausative 22–28, 89–91, 97, 100–109, 184–197, 199–202, 252, 258, 392, 414
anticausativization 23, 90, 93, 95, 107, 183–191, 199–202, 208–210
antipassive 390–394, 399, 405–407, 410, 412–414, 425, 431, 437
applicative 393, 398, 403–409, 412, 445–453, 458–462, 475
argument-realigning 451

backformation 253, 256, 281–282
Balinese 403, 446ff.
benefactive 404, 406–407, 450
bootstrapping 341, 343–344, 347–351

case feature 125, 141–142, 147, 151
case marker 35, 136, 142, 147, 216, 220, 236, 345, 347, 349–352
causation 36, 42, 47, 55, 65, 74–77, 83, 104, 185, 255, 345, 367–378, 400
– internal 42, 74, 367–368, 372, 376, 379
– external 36–37, 42, 367–368, 376, 378–379
causative 40, 52, 55–56, 59, 70, 72, 80, 90, 93, 100, 104, 143, 252, 254, 262, 278, 296, 299, 305–308, 317–318, 327–336, 342, 344, 350, 392, 398–405, 412, 414, 432, 440, 461, 464–466, 471, 474
– lexical 53, 59, 185, 318, 327, 332, 334–336, 465
causativization 52, 60, 66, 70, 74, 77, 183, 400, 447, 450
Chinese 250, 342, 344, 357, 360, 362, 364–367, 376, 380
co-composition 115
complex predicate 314
compound verb
– aspectual 93–95, 108
– thematic 94–96
Construction Morphology 53, 78

decausative 90–91, 110, 115, 121
decausativization 52, 59–60, 70–71, 77, 90, 108, 119, 185, 200, 358
detransitivization 191, 250, 252, 268, 282, 364, 412
direction of derivation 37, 256, 460, 465, 469
ditransitive verb 138, 253, 322, 326, 403, 415, 450
double object construction 451

English 31, 36, 38, 54, 90, 100, 103–104, 114, 137, 170, 184, 209, 284, 299, 307, 317, 320, 328, 342–348, 351, 358–368, 378, 380, 450, 458, 461
equipollent 22–23, 27, 38, 52, 58, 117, 250–253, 261, 271, 274, 280–283, 462, 468, 475

event conceptualization 357
event type 34, 43–44
existential binding 90, 185, 209–210
external causation hypothesis 36–37

Figure-Ground 449, 450, 456, 467
functional transparency 464, 473–475

German 219, 307, 423, 462
grammaticalization 31, 97, 290, 394, 411
Guttman scale 428, 429

Hokkaidō dialect 183, 186, 190, 195, 199, 201, 204, 208

imperfective aspect 216, 224, 229–231, 236, 238, 241
implicational hierarchy 426–427, 430, 438
inchoative 55, 90, 200, 249, 256, 308, 357–358
indeterminate 23, 250, 252, 274, 281
intentional action 40, 172, 362
intermodal preferential looking paradigm 343, 350
intransitive verb 22, 38, 42, 45, 92, 99, 103, 158, 160, 168–175, 250, 253, 316, 332, 345–349, 358–360, 363, 366, 375, 378, 380, 390, 396, 398, 402, 451, 470, 472
intransitivization 55, 89–92, 99, 116, 188, 209, 252

Korean 341, 360, 362

labile 97, 250, 252, 259, 273, 278–282, 393, 446
language change 174–175
lexical aspect 94, 113, 161, 185
lexical semantics 178, 260
lexicalization 251, 358
linguistic variation 168
local markedness 391

markedness 22–29, 31–33, 48, 56, 59–66, 80, 84, 98, 253, 261, 282, 389, 391–394, 400, 402, 409–410, 415–416, 475

NeighborNet 425, 426, 429, 430, 437
nominative-case constraint 126–127, 135, 140–147
non-standard variant 167, 171
noncausative-causative verb pair 51, 53–54, 57, 65, 72–73, 85, 495
number of NPs 227, 346, 348

oblique-case replacement 135, 144
Old Japanese 70, 185–186, 254, 257, 261, 289–291, 294
overgeneration 332–333
overpassivization 363–366, 379–381

partitive 215–221, 226–232, 234–242
passive 38, 40, 90, 93, 121, 131, 139, 147, 157, 162, 172, 184, 191–192, 195–197, 254, 278, 296, 308, 358–359, 365–366, 370, 376, 394–398, 400–402, 413–414, 424, 433, 448, 441
– lexical 90, 117
Patient-focus 448
possessor raising 128–130, 135
potential 40, 126, 143, 190, 281, 298, 306, 360, 366–368, 376–379, 395–396
precategorial roots 452, 455
pro-drop language 342, 344, 348, 441
prototype 33–36, 44–45, 66, 161, 398, 400, 410, 415

reciprocal 207, 434, 438,
reflexive 41–42, 75, 129–130, 137, 185, 202–204, 329, 392, 395, 414, 436, 438
reflexive binding 129
reflexivization 90, 132, 185, 202
resultative construction 104, 107, 155, 157, 160–166, 170–174, 178, 194–195
Russian 24, 240, 250, 392, 395, 424
Ryukyuan 211, 201, 220, 227, 236, 243, 290, 304, 305

scalogram 428, 430
schema 41, 53, 79–85, 114, 116, 361
semantic drift 33
semantic map 77, 393, 411, 413, 414
semantic reanalysis 91, 99, 108
Sino-Japanese verbal noun 278–281

spontaneous 44–47, 96, 102, 104, 186–190, 198, 200, 208–210, 377, 401
stative 127, 129, 131–135, 185, 189, 196, 226, 229, 249, 256, 290, 297, 301, 308, 364, 390, 393, 399, 402
syntactic bootstrapping hypothesis 341, 343, 346

-*te aru* construction 117, 156, 158–161, 163–164, 168–177
-*te iru* construction 156, 174, 177
tense 123, 135, 145, 198, 222
text frequency 465, 472
transitive verb 22, 92–93, 100, 111, 115, 157, 163, 168, 171–172, 189, 201, 250, 302, 316, 318, 333, 335, 345, 347, 358, 365, 373, 376, 392, 398, 400, 448, 472
Transitivity Harmony Principle 91–92, 94, 107
Transitivity Hypothesis 236
transitivity pair 23, 249, 251, 254, 259, 261, 275, 278, 281, 479, 489

transitivization 55, 250–253, 263, 276, 280–282, 302, 398, 412
Turkish 344–348

unaccusative 92, 98, 100, 322, 363, 366
unergative 92, 363, 392, 415

valency 93, 107, 119, 125, 127, 135, 147, 156, 160, 191, 254, 296, 306, 389–393, 396, 398, 402, 407, 336, 445–447, 452, 456
valency-increasing 391, 402–403, 447, 450, 452, 456
valency-reducing 157, 168, 396, 412
verb acquisition 342, 349, 353
voice 187, 389–394, 409–416
voice ambivalence 389, 391–394, 405, 409, 412
voice polysemy 393
VP-shell hypothesis 314, 337

word order 343–347, 353

zero-derivation 461–463

www.ingramcontent.com/pod-product-compliance
Lightning Source LLC
Chambersburg PA
CBHW051200300426
44116CB00006B/390